Revision Checklist

ORGANIZATION

1 Is the thesis statement clear?

2 Is the main idea evident throughout the paper?

3 Is the order of the ideas the most effective for your purpose?

4 Is your conclusion logically consistent with the rest of the paper?

SENTENCES

1 Is there variation in sentence length and structure?

2 Are there any sentences that are unclear or that could be misconstrued?

3 Is each sentence connected to the previous one?

4 Is there parallel structure in lengthy sentences?

PARAGRAPHS

1 Does each paragraph contain a clearly stated topic sentence?

2 Is each paragraph well developed with reasons, examples, statistics, or other details?

3 Is there effective transition between paragraphs?

4 Does the introductory paragraph attract and inform readers?

5 Does the concluding paragraph effectively end your discussion?

WORDS

1 Does each word convey a precise, specific meaning?

2 Are there unnecessary or "lazy" words?

3 Have you selected words that can delight, as well as inform, readers?

VOICE

1 Is the voice appropriate to the audience and for the writing purpose?

2 Does your language usage convey the kind of voice you wish to project?

The Writing Commitment

The Writing Commitment

Michael E. Adelstein

UNIVERSITY OF KENTUCKY

Jean G. Pival

UNIVERSITY OF KENTUCKY

HARCOURT BRACE JOVANOVICH, INC.

NEW YORK   CHICAGO   SAN FRANCISCO   ATLANTA

ISBN: 0-15-597855-1

Library of Congress Catalog Card Number: 76-558

Printed in the United States of America

Preface

We came to the writing of this textbook after ten years of wrestling with the problems and frustrations inherent in directing freshman composition at a large state university with open enrollment. During this decade, we have administered a widely diversified program to more than 3,000 students annually and developed teaching and teacher-training materials for a staff composed mainly of graduate assistants. In addition to the usual headaches attendant on such a local situation, we have been aware of the constantly shifting philosophical foundations of composition pedagogy: nationally, programs have ranged from emphasis on traditional methods to formulaic, Skinnerian approaches, to the use of loosely structured, free-writing techniques. We have tried to keep abreast of the new approaches and theories while retaining balance and continuity in our own program. Thus, operating largely from a traditional base, we have experimented with personal writing, films, language approaches, and other innovations. Our studies of these experiments have indicated that students who are trained to write only from personal experience or who are accustomed to responding subjectively to films, literature, and other art forms have difficulty adjusting to rhetorically oriented, logically organized expository writing. Yet our students did gain important skills in these personal writing programs—a zest for writing and a freedom of expression not often stimulated in a traditional expository course. We realized that what students need is an approach designed to guide them from highly private, personal writing, with its time-space organization and informal language usage, to the logically organized, public, exposi-

v

tory writing addressed in more formal language to a distant audience. We also realized that students need a textbook that integrates the workable aspects of the "new rhetoric" with the best of the traditional.

Therefore, in *The Writing Commitment,* we have launched a rhetorical approach that starts from the writer-oriented personal journal and autobiographical narrative and proceeds to audience-oriented exposition and argument. Our book moves on a pedagogical continuum from the relative freedom of writing for an intimate, friendly audience to the tighter restraints of form, language usage, and sentence structure required in writing for a distant, critical audience. Thus, instead of the usual organization of one chapter on the sentence, one on the paragraph, one on words, and so forth, our book is integrated to produce a spiral arrangement. That is, the new material presented in the later sections of the book circles back to pick up on and assimilate skills taught earlier. Convinced that each kind of writing demands different rhetorical strategies, we emphasize within each part the considerations of diction, sentences, paragraphs, and form that are most useful in—though not exclusive to—the type of writing being discussed. Committed to a philosophy that no language usage is "wrong" in itself, but undesirable only when inappropriate, we emphasize the function of language usage in relation to the writing purpose rather than to some abstract standard of "correctness." Convinced also that individual writing style arises mainly from sentence structure and language choice, we strongly emphasize these basics along with paragraph form, paragraph development, and organizational techniques—all in reference to the demands of each form of writing: for example, narrative paragraphs for personal writing, sentence expansion for description, cause-and-effect organization for argument. In our discussions, we integrate new approaches with older, tried-and-true methods, avoiding technical terminology wherever possible. Throughout we emphasize that different purposes, contexts, and audiences influence writing technique and commit the writer to different organizational schemes, sentence and paragraph structures, and language usage.

Because we have found that most students—and instructors—pay little attention to material in a glossary at the back of a book, we have incorporated information on matters of mechanics and usage throughout the book at relevant points. For instance, following a separate introductory chapter on punctuation (Chapter 6), punctuation conventions are discussed within later chapters when pertinent: punctuation of subordinate sentences after an analysis of these structures; punctuation of quoted materials with critical and documented writing; and so forth. Usage variants for comparisons such as *like, as,* and *as . . . as* are presented in a glossary of usages in Part 2, on descriptive writing, where such rhetorical devices are frequently used. This integrated, spiral approach is appealing because it treats conventions when students need to use and master them—and are interested in them. In addition, the integration of all these aspects of writing helps students perceive the relationship between writing as form and writing as process. Though these materials are scattered throughout the book, students can be directed to the Reference Chart and aids for revision on the endpapers or to the Index for quick reference to solve a specific writing problem.

Instead of being considered in a separate chapter on prewriting, the skills of invention are treated in the discussions of strategy for each form of writing—the steps in planning a personal narrative, the preliminaries to organizing an expository theme, the methods for preparing to write a documented paper. Prewriting, therefore, is not discussed in an introductory chapter and never mentioned again, but is referred to numerous times, each time with specific references to the problems inherent in the kind of writing under consideration.

Another valuable feature is the stress we place on revision. Most professional writers testify emphatically to the importance of revision in their own writing; most students, however, not only fail to revise but do not know how to go about it. Consequently, we have taken pains to emphasize how vital revision is and to show at the end of each part how students might approach the revision of their papers.

Our focus throughout has been on trying to help students. The book is addressed to them, specifically to first-year students required to take freshman English. Thus we have braved the hazards of oversimplification and of using an informal, conversational tone. And because our experience has taught us that freshman students usually respond better to examples written by their peers, we have quoted from many freshman papers as well as from essays by professional writers.

Finally, for those instructors who want to spend considerable time on one aspect of writing, such as sentence or paragraph structure, we provide alternate sequences in the accompanying Instructor's Manual: thus, instructors who wish to stress personal writing have ample material in the first two parts of the book; those who prefer to emphasize expository writing can start with Part 2, dipping into Part 1 only for chapters needed for background; and those who favor a handbook as a reference for students with particular problems can direct them to our extensive discussions of usage, mechanics, sentence structure, and so on.

Our aim throughout the book reflects our own philosophy of teaching: that a course in composition should open up the language horizons of the students; that it should introduce them to the many and various voices available in written English; and that it should make them aware of their commitment to themselves and to their readers.

We would like to acknowledge with sincere gratitude the tremendous help we have received from more people than we can possibly name in the short space appropriate for expressions of appreciation. Eben Ludlow, our editor at Harcourt Brace Jovanovich, the godfather of this book, has been most urbane, considerate, and kind in working with us. Our manuscript editor, Cecilia Gardner, was superb in her delivery of it, performing her arduous task with magnificent skill, patience, and humor. We cannot speak too highly of her. We also appreciate the grueling hours our copy editor, Lee Shenkman, spent in assisting in the delivery. Then there are our colleagues at other colleges who examined our manuscript and made many valuable suggestions: Julie Carson, University of Minnesota; Boyd H. Davis, University of North Carolina, Charlotte; James E. Duckworth, University of Richmond; Connie C. Eble, University of North Carolina, Chapel Hill; Louis C. Eisenhauer, Catonsville Community College; Gertrude L. Golladay, University of Texas at Arlington; Robert M. Gorrell, University of Nevada; Gerald Levin, University of Akron; and our colleagues here — both regular staff members and graduate assistants — who contributed so much directly or indirectly: Fred Cornelius, Alfred L. Crabb, Jr., L. Larry Greenwood, Thomas Olshewsky, and Eileen B. Skaggs. A special word of praise and gratitude goes to our typist-editor, Colleen Herrmann, who efficiently ministered the manuscript through many deadline periods.

Finally, we are indebted to our patient, understanding, and sadly neglected spouses, Carol and Joe, who will be delighted that this book is completed and that we can now return to our families, leaving this brain child to make its own way in the world.

MICHAEL E. ADELSTEIN
JEAN G. PIVAL

Contents

PART TWO   The Informative Voice: Descriptive Writing

8 Introduction to Descriptive Writing   129

9 Writing Descriptions   138

10 Language in Descriptive Writing   163

Introduction:
In Praise of
Writing Well

Before you begin to read this book, you deserve answers to certain questions — the ones that our students usually ask:

Why learn to write?
Can I learn to write? How?
What is good writing?

As a reader of this textbook, you are entitled to the answers to other questions as well:

What's this book about?
How can I best use this book?
What does the title mean?

First questions first.

WHY LEARN TO WRITE?

Some teachers of composition may assume that students are naturally eager to learn how to write. We don't. We are aware that writing can be one of the most upsetting, frustrating, and exasperating of all human activities. Seldom do the words pour out; seldom do they sound or look the way we want them to. And seldom do we or our students — or most people, for that matter — want to write. Then why learn to do so?

True, some people do find writing a release, an act of creation, a means of self-expression comparable to painting, sculpting, or composing. For other people, writing can provide emotional relief or ego satisfaction by allowing them to sound off, to state their ideas in articles and books or their gripes in letters to college or community newspapers. But you may have neither artistic urges to satisfy nor strong opinions to air. If so, what's the point of learning to write?

The honest answer is that occasionally you will *have* to write even though you won't be eager to do so — just as you have to write in freshman English. What's more, the subjects may be even less appealing. Look, for example, at the writing you've done in the past. Let's start with that thank-you letter you struggled over to an aunt, uncle, or other relative for a graduation or birthday gift. If you're like most people, you probably put it off as long as possible, always finding something else that had to be done, telling yourself that you would get to it ... soon. Finally, nagged by your parents or tormented by your conscience, you dragged yourself to face the torture of scratching out a few sentences of gratitude. Because you wanted to? Or because — for social or other reasons — you were compelled to?

Then there was that application letter for a summer job. Or the biographical sketch for a high school or college form. Or your letter of inquiry about a scholarship, loan, or dorm room, or about camping facilities, group travel rates, baseball tickets. Or the speech you prepared for a contest, debate, class election, graduation. Weren't you required to write in these situations?

And what of the road ahead? Largely on the basis of your writing skills, you will be evaluated by college professors who will determine what you have learned and understood in their courses from written examinations and papers. As you progress from introductory courses to more advanced ones, more writing will be required. And then there are various organizations, scholarships, or honors competitions that require you to furnish written information: applications, biographical material, project plans.

And after the undergraduate years? Admission to graduate, law, medical, and other professional schools often hinges on written applications and the verbal ability you can demonstrate in entrance examinations. Graduate and professional schools require research papers, comprehensive examinations, master's and doctor's theses. And your career may be chock-full of writing assignments. If you plan to enter business, government, or one of the professions, you should heed the words of Peter Drucker, a nationally recognized management consultant: "As soon as you move one step up from the bottom, your effectiveness depends on your ability to reach others through the spoken or written word."

Which brings us back to where you are: at the bottom, in a sense — looking ahead to two or four years of college, perhaps graduate school, and a career. For many important purposes in that future, you will be represented by your writing. You will be known, evaluated, admitted, given a job, promoted — achieve success or not — on the basis of your writing.

Professors, registrars, deans, award and admissions committees, personnel managers, executives, and others ordinarily cannot take the time to listen to you at length. You must state your case in effective writing. Your message is you.

There is another reason for learning to write — less practical, perhaps, but more meaningful. Writing is a form of discovery about who you are and what you think. Learning about yourself may not guarantee that you will attain better grades in college or a rewarding job later on, but it can help lead you to self-realization. Writing, then, can be a process of self-discovery. How?

Usually you don't know exactly what you think until you've expressed it in either speech or writing. In speech, you talk with an instantaneous rush of words, taking little time for deliberation or reflection, organization or arrangement, refinement or revision. Also, in speech you can generally get by with flip remarks; in writing, you are forced to express your ideas more carefully. Suppose you were asked what you think happiness is, or whether women are completely equal to men, or what true friendship consists of, or if war is inevitable. In conversation, an off-the-cuff response would probably not be subjected to penetrating scrutiny by others. But in writing, you would surely treat the subject more cautiously and comprehensively; and because you would not be entirely sure who would be reading what you wrote, you would take the time to reflect on your ideas, deliberate about particular words, consider the implications of some sentences, change, shift, eliminate, revise, edit. Speaking is easier, less demanding, but writing is more likely to bring out the best in us, producing our clearest and most comprehensive statement on any subject. In the process of writing, we give shape to our thoughts, our feelings, even our values. Thus, the writing process is discovery of self.

Finally, although writing is hard work, we believe it brings its own rewards. There is something very satisfying and fulfilling about completing a paper that expresses your feelings or opinions about a subject. It may be compared to other creative acts: cooking a gourmet meal, taking photographs, designing a house, making pottery — all contain your flavor, your signature, your touch.

Even if you concede that practicality, self-discovery, and creative fulfillment are admirable reasons for learning to write, the second question may still plague you: Can I learn to write?

CAN I LEARN TO WRITE? HOW?

Of course you can. Every college freshman can learn to write. But we are not talking about writing stories, poems, or plays. Imaginative literature requires creative gifts — unusual powers of imagination, perception, sensitivity, and intelligence. Not every college student can write literature or probably even learn to write gracefully and fluently. But every college student can learn to write the clear, concise, appropriate prose required in college and the working world. Writing may come more slowly to some than to others, but come it will.

Learning to write, like learning practically any other skill, involves three components: instruction, practice, and criticism. Let's apply them to learning how to play a sport—say, tennis. Instruction is provided by a book or a coach, telling and showing you how to hold a racquet, how to stand, how to swing, and the like. Then come hours of practice, hitting a ball against a backboard, volleying with friends, entering tournaments. And during this time, your coach or a relative or friend often provides criticism, pointing out that you're not throwing the ball up properly on your serve or not getting your racquet back far enough on your backhand. So you practice throwing the ball up properly or getting your racquet back. Instruction, practice, criticism. That's also how you learned to swim, read, or fish; or play the piano, chess, or hearts; or drive a car, truck, or tractor.

How will you learn to write? You guessed it. This textbook and your professor will provide the instruction. And you will write papers—to some extent, the more the better. You can learn to write and improve your writing only by writing. There is no other way. And just as college football players spend hundreds of hours in practice—blocking, running, tackling, passing, catching, punting—so you will spend many hours in practice—considering subjects, organizing, writing, revising, and proofreading papers. It would be delightful if you could merely read this book or listen to your instructor or pop answers into workbook exercise slots, but unfortunately none of these can replace practice in writing. And your instructor will criticize your efforts, acting like a coach to praise what you are doing well, point out what you are doing poorly, and show you how to improve.

That's how the semester will pass—instruction, practice, criticism—and that's how you will learn to write.

We assume, of course, that you are willing to learn to write and to work hard at it. It will not come easily or quickly; nothing complex and demanding and significant ever does. At times you may doubt that you are making progress, but we assure you that at the end of the term, by comparing your first papers with your later ones, you will be able to see that your writing has improved a great deal.

WHAT IS GOOD WRITING?

Since "good writing" is one of those ideal abstractions that are seldom pinned down—held in high esteem, but rarely defined—let's list some of its characteristics.

- Good writing reflects the writer's ability to use the appropriate voice. Even though all good writing conveys the sound of someone talking to someone else, the voice heard through the writing must also suit the purpose and audience of the writing occasion. Just as you change speaking styles when moving from highly informal to formal situations, so too your writing voice should vary to create your desired relationship with your readers. A good writer is adaptable: capable of shaping language usage, writing form, and methods of handling the material to the purpose of the writing and to the needs of the intended readers.
- Good writing reflects the writer's ability to organize the material into a coherent whole so that it moves logically from a central, dominant idea to the supporting points and finally to a consistent ending, conveying to the reader a sense of a well-thought-out plan.
- Good writing reflects the writer's ability to write clearly and unambiguously—to utilize sentence structure, language, and examples so that the only possible meaning is the writer's intended one. Readers should not have to strain or struggle to understand what is written.
- Good writing reflects the writer's ability to write convincingly—to interest readers in the subject and to demonstrate a thorough and sound understanding of it. Important, too, in developing a tone of conviction is economy: all unnecessary words and repetitive phrases are eliminated, and every word contributes to meaning.
- Good writing reflects the writer's ability to criticize the first draft and revise it. All the previously discussed characteristics are rarely achieved at a first writing. You must learn early that thorough revision—painful though it can be—is the key to effective writing.
- Good writing reflects the writer's pride in the manuscript—the willingness to spell and punctuate accurately, to check word meanings and grammatical relationships within the sentences before submitting the finished product to the scrutiny of an audience. A good writer realizes that such surface defects can ruin the overall effect of the written material.

We assure you that none of these characteristics is beyond your capacity to master. As you work your way through the textbook and the course, you will be given instruction, practice, and criticism at each step. If you are willing to experiment, start over, and revise until you achieve the effect you want, then you will be on your way to writing well. Remember, writing is a complicated, ongoing skill: you cannot hope to master it in a one- or two-semester course. We can point you down the right road, but you must do the traveling toward good writing yourself. We hope that you find this book a useful road map.

WHAT'S THIS BOOK ABOUT?

The Writing Commitment uses a rhetorical approach, which means that it provides instruction in the art of discovering the most effective way to express ideas. Rhetoric is practical, involving a search for the form of writing that will succeed in achieving a particular purpose with a particular audience in a particular context. Thus rhetoric is primarily concerned with effectiveness, with what works best.

Underlying a rhetorical approach such as this is a key concept: all writing is not the same. Everything you write — a letter home for money, a newsy note to a friend, an application for a work-study grant — is written for a particular purpose to a particular audience in a particular context. The purpose of the letter home is to persuade, the audience is friendly, the context is serious. The newsy note aims to inform and entertain, its audience is friendly, its context is informal. The application tries to persuade, the audience is unknown, the context is formal.

The rhetorical approach to writing can help in these and all other writing situations by preparing you for the different problems in each and making you aware of the different ways to cope with them. In a manner of speaking, rhetoric provides you with numerous game plans to use in various circumstances instead of giving you one set pattern to use in all situations. Consequently, mastering rhetorical principles requires reason rather than memory and necessitates an analysis of purpose, audience, and context. These principles, indeed, are more difficult to learn than a set of rules. But they are more interesting, practical, and valuable because they prepare you for the various writing assignments you will receive in your college and career.

HOW CAN I BEST USE THIS BOOK?

To make this book more useful to you, we have organized it according to types of writing, moving from what is usually the simplest form — personal narrative — to the most difficult — the formal research paper.

In personal narrative you write about a subject you know well — yourself and your experiences — to an intimate audience — yourself, friends, and members of your family. The familiar subject and sympathetic readers in this kind of writing place few restraints on you. Next we move to descriptive writing, in which the subject — an object, scene, or person — is familiar but the audience is often unknown to you and likely to expect more careful observance of writing conventions. Then on to expository writing: papers of classification, definition, analysis, and opinion. These kinds of subjects generally are more difficult to select and organize than are those in personal narrative and descriptive writing. Also, there may be special problems with readers because they are likely to be larger in number and more diverse in background. In the fourth kind of writing we discuss, persuasion and argumentation, the subject must be thoroughly understood, its logical structure analyzed, its surface and underlying assumptions tested. And the material must be shaped according to the backgrounds and attitudes of readers, who may favor, oppose, or be neutral toward the subject.

Finally, we discuss two special writing assignments: literary and research papers. Writing critical papers about literature requires some understanding of character, plot, setting, time, theme, and technique. And writing research papers demands a knowledge of the library, research techniques, and such formal conventions as footnotes and bibliography.

Within each unit of this six-part sequence about various kinds of writing is a consideration of certain rhetorical principles. Instead of going along with the traditional textbook treatment of these matters by providing separate chapters on sentences, language, paragraphs, organization, and the like, we discuss each of them as it pertains to a particular writing problem. The result is an integrated, spiral structure in which we take up each major rhetorical principle in relation to each kind of writing. Language use, for example, is considered in relation to its desired effect: in narrative and descriptive writing, language is selected for its richness of meaning; in expository writing, for its clarity; in persuasion, for its logical impact. Similarly, organization is not treated in one chapter but in several. In the discussion of personal writing, the emphasis is on chronological organization; in descriptive writing, on spatial arrangement; in expository writing, on logical, cause-and-effect patterns. To offer you a single chapter that advocates one organizational plan for all kinds of writing would be to create a rhetorical torture rack, one that would force you to stretch all writing problems onto a single monstrous form.

We believe that our approach is not only more functional, presenting material when you need it most, but also more realistic. Instead of seeing a paper as a composite of separate parts gleaned from individual chapters on language, sentence structure, the paragraph, and so forth, you can see in this book how each of these aspects contributes to a particular writing assignment to make your paper an organic whole.

Because no aspect of the writing process is exclusively the property of any one kind of writing, we must circle back now and then to refer to what we discussed previously. For example, in a consideration of descriptive writing, we discuss sentence expansion by insertion because this technique is particularly helpful in papers of description. But because this technique may also be valuable in other kinds of papers, we remind you of it later. To give you easier access to all the references in the various parts of the book to sentences, punctuation, usage, and other writing concerns, we have provided a Reference Chart and aids for revision on the inside covers. The Index will also help you to locate quickly all the references in the book to a particular aspect of writing.

WHAT DOES THE TITLE MEAN?

We selected *The Writing Commitment* as our title to impress upon you the fact that every time you write, you commit some portion of yourself to paper, and you also enter into a commitment with readers. When you turn in a well-organized, logically reasoned, adequately developed, and carefully written paper, it reflects advantageously on you as an individual, conveying a high estimation of you to someone else. Thus you have a commitment to yourself: to work hard, to do your best, to set high standards for yourself. Remember, your message is you—you are what you write.

Then there is your commitment to your readers. This is a moral commitment, derived from the Golden Rule: do unto your readers as you would have them do unto you. As a reader, what do you look for in a paper? Surely, that it be interesting. And so clear that you need not reread any of it. And concise—not padded with unnecessary words. And written in appropriate language with competent handling of the conventions of spelling, punctuation, and the like. And lively, pleasant, friendly. If you expect these qualities when you read, you should provide them when you write.

Thus you have a commitment to others and to yourself—that is your writing commitment.

The Writing Commitment

The Intimate Voice: Personal Writing

1

Introduction to Personal Writing

In the Introduction we pointed out that self-discovery is one of the benefits of writing. This is especially true in personal writing, a form that provides the most delight in the exploration of self.

THE ADVANTAGES OF PERSONAL WRITING

Reading what you have written about a past experience is much like looking at snapshots of the event. A photograph may stir memories by reminding you of how everything and everyone *looked,* but your memory of the occasion may be dulled by time or sweetened by nostalgia. Only a written personal account can recapture exactly how you *felt.* For example, you may have memories of your high school graduation, your first day on a job, a musical recital, a friend's wedding, a thrilling basketball game, or an automobile accident, but unless you have written about the experience, you will not be able to retain a permanent, vivid, complete, and accurate memory of it.

Apart from this usefulness of a written account, the very act of writing is itself valuable. Anne Morrow Lindbergh discloses the reason when she explains why she wrote such voluminous letters and diaries:

I must write it all out, at any cost. Writing is thinking. It is more than living, for it is being conscious of living.

— *Locked Rooms and Open Doors*

Writing is being conscious of living, because when we put our thoughts about life into words, we become more aware of life itself. In your first days of college, for instance, you encounter many new experiences; writing letters about these experiences to your family or friends causes you to become more fully conscious of them by making you recall and reflect upon their nature and significance.

Personal writing may also be therapeutic, a means for self-analysis that allows you to understand yourself better. Eldridge Cleaver was referring to this benefit when he stated that he started to write in prison "to save myself." He explained:

I realized that no one could save me but myself. The prison authorities were both uninterested and unable to help me. I had to seek out the truth and unravel the snarled web of my motivations. I had to find out who I am and what I want to be, what type of man I should be, and what I could do to become the best of which I was capable.

Writing forced Cleaver to evaluate himself and to realize that he had gone astray, "astray not so much from the white man's law as from being human, civilized." The result of Cleaver's self-analysis was *Soul on Ice*, a brilliant account of his growth and development, and a penetrating criticism of American culture during the 1960s.

Personal writing also prepares you for more difficult writing assignments by enabling you to practice with a subject that you know well—yourself—and can easily organize in a simple time sequence. And the subject has great appeal to readers. Although most of us feel that our lives are dull and routine, each of us is interesting to other people. Everyone is curious about what others say and do, fascinated by motives, amused at eccentricities, absorbed by problems and predicaments. Personal writing provides you with an appealing, built-in subject.

Finally, personal writing is more fun than most other kinds of writing. Because you are naturally concerned with yourself, you should enjoy reflecting and reminiscing. And because personal writing gives you an opportunity to learn about yourself—to sharpen your perceptions of yourself and to discover more about yourself—you should find pleasure and fulfillment in it.

THE CHARACTERISTICS OF PERSONAL WRITING

Exactly what is personal writing and what is it like?

Personal writing is a statement of your ideas and feelings about your own experiences written either for your own pleasure or for the interest and enjoyment of family or friends. It may take the form of a diary, journal, informal narrative, letter, or poem. It is characterized by natural, unpretentious language and the normal, everyday syntactical conventions of speech. Freed from most formal restrictions, personal writing should be vivid, lively, interesting, and refreshing. It can be chatty, colorful, gay, and full of the liveliness of conversation — but without the many repetitions, digressions, and "uhs" and "y'knows."

Naturalness

Whatever the subject of personal writings may be, it always focuses on the thoughts and feelings of the writer, not of other people. So the writing should be natural, in order to reveal the nature of the writer. This means that you must cast off all affectations and pretenses and let yourself go, turning away from any previous restraints developed from misconceptions about good writing.

You probably view good writing as consisting of long, obscure words inserted in complicated sentence structures to sound formal and impressive. As a result, you feel inhibited when you write and you worry constantly about such matters as misplacing a modifier, misusing a pronoun, or mistaking one word for another. In the process, you may have become almost schizophrenic: delightfully interesting, natural, and vibrant in person, but dull and dreary on paper. Here's an example of this personality transformation in a high school senior writing to a college admissions official:

Dear Mr. Evans:

Being a senior in high school this fall, I feel that it would be beneficial for me to acquaint myself with colleges and their environs. As a consequence, it is my plan to travel to various institutions of higher learning to engage in discussions about various and sundry matters.

According to my itinerary, your university is scheduled for a visit by my family and I on November 5. We would be most grateful if you would make the necessary arrangements so that I might have the privilege of an interview on that occasion.

Respectfully,

Frank Newman

This is not the real Frank writing, but a plastic Frank, using a formal, pretentious language and sentence structure that is anything but natural. Admissions officials would certainly not look forward to meeting Frank — although we suspect they receive so much of this artificial prose that they know it does not truly represent the writer.

Please do not misunderstand. We are not suggesting that you go to the other extreme by switching to the locker-room voice of the following letter, which we hope no one would write:

Dear Mr. Evans:

My family and me thought we'd buzz down on Wednesday, November 5, to cruise around the school. The way I figure it, I ought to give the place the once-over to see if I really dig it, know what I mean?

I'd like to rap with you about drinking, driving cars, drugs, and bringing girls to my dorm room. Let me know if you can make the scene.

Your buddy,

Peter Arnold

This could be Peter's natural voice, but it's as out of place here as a bikini in a chemistry lab. Later we'll discuss in detail the subject of rhetorical role — the appropriate voice for the writer in relation to the purpose, audience, and occasion. For now, bear in mind that just as you change your clothes for a particular event such as a wedding, picnic, or tennis match, so you must change your writing to fit the circumstances. But just as certain everyday clothes are acceptable in a variety of places, so too is a natural, normal voice and style. Here's what we mean:

Dear Mr. Evans:

I am a high school senior interested in visiting your campus to learn about the University.

My family and I plan to arrive Wednesday morning, November 5. May I have an interview with you then?

Sincerely,

Jane Allen

You may be tempted to disparage Jane's letter for being short and simple. If so, you fail to realize that a brief letter like Jane's, direct and to the point, is precisely what the admissions official wants. Effective writing satisfies readers, providing them with the pertinent information clearly and concisely.

Many people fail to write like Jane because they wish to impress readers, a habit probably developed from a false notion of what will please teachers. But this leads to the stilted, pretentious, lifeless language of Frank's letter and of too many student papers, business letters and reports, government documents, political pronouncements, textbooks, and scholarly articles. This stuffy prose style results from the desire to impress others. Many people believe that the more formal their writing sounds — like that in a legal contract, for example — the more respect readers will have for it. And how do they imitate a lawyer? By writing at length, by using long words, and by selecting words that sound important.

How to convince these writers to base their approach on common sense and concern for readers? How to get them to return to what is natural, to a mature version of the clarity and purity of a child's letter to Santa Claus? How to help writers sound like themselves and be themselves?

Perhaps natural writing cannot be achieved in a single draft. Perhaps you must resign yourself to a heavy, formal first draft that you will lighten in rewriting. This is the system used by John Galbraith, economist, statesman, and author, who counts on writing five drafts of important material, the last one devoted to achieving "that tone of spontaneity" that makes his writing so easy and natural.

Naturalness, therefore, may not come naturally. But come it must if you wish to write effectively, and come it should in writing about yourself. That is why we begin with personal writing: it will give you an opportunity to deal with a subject that should interest you and that you are best qualified to write about. It will also give you a chance to learn a great deal about yourself as you probe into matters you may not have considered thoroughly before. But you must be honest.

Honesty

Being honest requires stripping off all the layers of pretext and pretense to find the authentic you. It involves writing what you really feel and believe and think, not what others expect. It means letting yourself go, talking as you would to a close friend, saying things that you might not have said to others before. It requires getting your unique voice down in writing, your choice of words, your flow of phrases, and your sweep of sentences. It demands that you stop worrying about whether people will approve, or be shocked, or feel sorry for you, or laugh at you. Honesty takes courage and work and confidence and the desire to be true to yourself. It is the most vital quality of personal writing.

Listen to the clear, honest ring of Patricia Breen-Bond's introduction to her article in *Ms.* magazine, "Running in the Rain":

Just as I'm putting on my sneakers and adjusting my headband, my stomach begins revolting. You'd think after nearly two years of running I'd be used to it now. I never quite get my breath until I'm a full mile into the run. Then, I guess, my body consents because there's no turning back.

Most people like to jog. Not me. Jogging's too slow and ponderous. I run. I run until I feel the tourniquet in my gut, until my heart begins to twist, until I can see the muscles jutting in my legs like a medical drawing. I run six miles.

Here's another honest voice, John Steinbeck's:

When I was very young and the urge to be someplace else was on me, I was assured by mature people that maturity would cure this itch. When years described me as mature, the remedy prescribed was middle age. In middle age I was assured that greater age would calm my fever and now that I am fifty-eight perhaps senility will do the job. Nothing has worked. Four hoarse blasts of a ship's whistle still raise the hair on my neck and set my feet to tapping. The sound of a jet, an engine warming up, even the clopping of shod hooves on pavement brings on the ancient shudder, the dry mouth and vacant eye, the hot palm and the churn of stomach high up under the rib cage. In other words, I don't improve; in further words, once a bum always a bum. I fear the disease is incurable. I set this matter down not to instruct others but to inform myself.

— Travels with Charley

"To inform myself." Writing it down has brought Steinbeck to the self-discovery that "once a bum always a bum." And it has brought us to the discovery that the great American writer John Steinbeck is a true human being, the real thing. After reading these two passages, we'd like to meet Patricia and John, have dinner or a few beers with them, talk into the night. What about Jane and Anne, the two students who wrote the following papers? How do they strike you?

YOUTH VERSUS AGE

I shall never forget that period in my lifetime when the whole world seemed to be my enemy! I was in my fifteenth year. Oh, how anxious I was to be an adult, and so impatient! To be admitted into the grown-up world, however, demanded maturity and a sense of responsibility. I was sure that I had developed this, and I believed myself to be capable of and competent in making sensible decisions. Unfortunately, my parents were not in agreement with me. Like most protective parents, they wanted their Jane to be home at a respectable hour, and wanted to know about my destinations or my companions. When they were not to the liking of my parents, I was forced to remain at home. On other occasions, the curfew hour that they established was far too early for me. The embarrassment that I felt when I was the first of a group to have to return home developed within me a feeling of resentment.

I hated to have those restrictions put upon me. They were so completely unnecessary. A girl of fifteen is certainly old enough to decide for herself when to return home, or so I thought. And to have to be the first one to leave!

I recall well one night when, due to my own stubbornness and ignorance, I came prancing home, an hour late. Naturally, my parents were awake and waiting anxiously for my return. I interpreted their anger as distrust of me. A young person does not always comprehend how parental love is shown. I grew bitter that they would be so protective of me. My bold attitude as I answered their queries stirred greater anger with them. The gap of misunderstanding spread wider and we were soon unable to communicate with each other. I felt unfairly treated because they weren't giving me a chance to exert my independence. My attitude towards my parents at this time was hostile.

My parents were at a loss as to what should be done about this situation, which was progressively growing worse. A total lack of understanding existed between us. I felt completely alienated from my parents and tears of frustration overwhelmed me. Well-intentioned discussions resulted in further upsets. There seemed to be no reasonable solution to calm the fires that flared between my parents and me. The tension was not resolved overnight. Only time dissipated the turmoil.

Now as I reflect, I am able to view the situation that existed from a more objective point of view. It seems that it resulted from the opposition of two forces: maturity and immaturity. Perhaps only the time necessary for development and growth has allowed me to reach an understanding of my parents' position.

BEING AN ISLAND

When people want to criticize my habit of being alone, they ask, "Were you always that way, Anne?" I've learned that the best answer is a simple "yes." A loner should be proud of her state of mind. So I boldly reply, nod my head, hint at a smile, and walk off into the sunset—for effect.

There was that party for me when I was seven. (I have no recollection what the big deal was, probably a birthday.) All I remember of the trial was a super desire to barricade myself in my room. So I did. Mom was upset later that evening when one of her friends remarked that I was a loner. It was true. But for a seven-year-old, it appeared to be a crime.

Later I developed an even stronger need to dart from the throng. During high school I slowly dropped out of attending parties and dances. Whether in a bustling pep rally or a tightly packed school assembly, I felt strangled. Finally, it came to the point where only a long walk alone out of the sight of the school could enable me to face another busy event. I recall always being the first to my locker in the morning and then up to homeroom so that I could avoid the clamor.

I am an only child. This seems sufficient reason for my so-called wayward behavior. However, I have not been tempted to change myself. If being an individual with independent thoughts and actions is wayward, then let me state a fact—I am wayward.

I refuse to accept the "get into it" way of life. Anyone not involved today is a social outcast. For people like me, the situation is quite opposite. We have cast ourselves out. I have taken a long hard look at where the crowds are going and want no part of it. Joiners are fine. Social beings with concern for the masses are needed in society. Civilization moves by the masses but is cultivated by the obscure. Perhaps I have set myself too difficult a role. All I know is that I enjoy constantly breaking away.

In college, parties are the weekend wonders. College life wouldn't be much without all the crowd and all that is loud. The other night I was invited to one of those events. I went out for a walk alone instead. No one gets to a loner because no one can catch her.

Both these papers are written by intelligent students, both are unified around a central idea or experience, both deal with interesting personal material, both provide details or examples to illustrate their points, both are free of serious mechanical or grammatical errors, and both appeal to readers. Yet we'd probably prefer to meet Anne; her paper succeeds. Jane's misses. Why?

Jane's paper just does not ring true. Nagging questions remain. Most people who suffered the embarrassment of having to be the first one to leave a party would still recall the experience with resentment and irritation. Why not Jane? Why does she now view the situation from "a more objective point of view"? What is that point of view? If Jane were to have a daughter, would she insist that her fifteen-year-old come home before the others? Also, why is the issue that of maturity versus immaturity? Couldn't it be viewed as a conflict between Jane's desire to assert her independence and her parents' wish to keep her their little girl? More important: is Jane reluctant to blame her parents for fear of not being a loving daughter? Is she truthfully describing how she feels about the incident, or is she adopting the pose of the repentant girl, now mature, who realizes how wise and intelligent her parents were?

We wonder. And our suspicions are increased by the false sounds. Occasionally we hear Jane's real voice: the opening exaggeration ("When the whole world seemed to be my enemy"), the exclamatory third sentence ("Oh, how anxious I was"), the delightful verbal phrase ("I came prancing home"). These and a few other touches seem authentic. But those notes are drowned out by the discords of artificial prose: "to calm the fires that flared between my parents and me," "only time dissipated the turmoil," and "stirred greater anger in them." These are only a few examples of the affected voice of the writer instead of her true one. Jane is trying to impress others, attempting to be a Great Author instead of herself. As a result, the language is distracting and the paper is disconcerting. We are uncertain about Jane.

But not about Anne. As we follow her from her seventh birthday party to high school pep rallies, assemblies, and early-morning "clamor" (a wonderful word choice here), and then on to college parties, we feel her sincerity and conviction (except for one stilted sentence near the end, "Civilization moves by the masses . . ."). Her sound rings true: "the big deal," "So I did," "It was true," "I felt strangled," "Joiners are fine." This is an authentic voice. There is no reason to doubt or suspect Anne. We feel that she could be sitting in a room with us, sprawled in a cushion on the floor, looking us in the eye as she chats about herself in relaxed and easy tones. Her voice is informal, natural, lively — and honest to the bone.

Simple to achieve? Not in the least. But if you are to show your self in personal writing, then you must tell it like it is — naturally and honestly.

ASSIGNMENTS

For Discussion

1   What is the advantage of writing about some incident instead of trusting to memory? Can you provide an example from your own life of the distortion of memory?
2   Do you agree with Anne Morrow Lindbergh's statement that writing "is being conscious of living"? Provide an example.
3   Why is personal writing likely to be easier and more pleasant than other forms of writing?
4   Define personal writing and explain how a personal account of a wedding, accident, or death would differ from a fictional narrative account.
5   Why is it so important that personal writing be natural and honest?
6   What is your reaction to the following thank-you letter written by a college freshman to his aunt?

> Dear Aunt Gert,
>
> It is with utmost gratitude that I wish to express my appreciation to you for the splendid dictionary that you gave me. I shall cherish this gift of great utility during my college career and afterwards. I truly hope that this epistle finds you in excellent health and in full and complete enjoyment of life.
>
> > Sincerely,
> >
> > Albert

How would you reword this letter?

7   What will you have to unlearn about writing in order to write about

yourself effectively? Specifically, did you believe that all written English should be formal? What created that impression? How informal should personal writing be?

For Writing

1　Write about some event that time or your memory has probably distorted. Then it may have caused you embarrassment, anguish, despair, or fear, but now you can laugh about it. Or you may have thought highly of yourself on some past occasion but now can view your achievement in proper perspective.

2　Reminisce about some fascinating, unusual, significant, or memorable incident in your life. You might begin with the sentence, "It all comes back to me now."

3　Write about the tension between you and your parents that was caused by an episode involving your attempt to assert your independence.

4　In Anne's paper (see p. 9), she typified herself as a loner. Write a paper stating how you view yourself.

5　Describe a recent college experience in order to preserve your feelings and sensations so that you can relive it months or years from now.

6　Write a "now-it-can-be-told" letter to one or both of your parents, explaining how embarrassed, proud, hurt, grateful, annoyed, or happy you felt on some occasion involving them. Of course, you need not mail the letter.

The Forms of Personal Writing

THE JOURNAL

Perhaps you can best find your natural, honest voice in a diary. But because of their intimate nature, diaries are usually locked away from the eyes of others. Keeping a diary, then, might be an excellent way for you to practice writing in a free, sincere voice, but you would probably be reluctant to show these personal thoughts to others, such as a classmate or teacher, for advice about writing. Keeping a journal, however, is an excellent alternative that provides the same advantages.

In a diary, *you* are the subject matter; in a journal, *you* are the subject matter. In a diary, *you* are your own audience; in a journal, *you* are your own audience—but with a difference. Even though you write in your journal to and about yourself, you are usually prepared for someone else to read it. Therefore, you write with the awareness that another reader will share your experiences, and in the process will learn something about you as a person. Thus you write about yourself not only to yourself but also to someone else. This dual role of the journal has made it an effective tool in the teaching of writing. It has also made the journal a highly satisfying, self-motivated writing experience for many people.

Why Keep a Journal?

Unless required to do so in school, why would anyone want to keep a journal, whose contents might become available to other people? Some novelists, poets, and journalists keep journals to improve their writing and to preserve their experiences and impressions. Sometimes their entries serve as the basis for books or articles. Sometimes the journal itself appears in print. For example, the journals of Albert Camus, F. Scott Fitzgerald, Gustave Flaubert, and Henry James are fascinating to read and have helped scholars to gain insight into the literary works of these authors. One of the most prolific journal keepers of all time, James Boswell, the biographer of Samuel Johnson, vividly portrayed eighteenth-century London and gave readers an acquaintance with great historical figures that more objective reports could not provide. Many writers, following Boswell's example, have used journals to record their experiences with famous people or their close contact with great historical events. Others have kept a journal to preserve the memory of a journey or a cherished vacation.

Journals have also been written for different purposes. Leonardo da Vinci's journal entries about his observations of birds and his theories of flight dynamics contributed greatly to modern aviation. Lewis and Clark's journals of their long journey in search of a northwest passage by water to the Pacific not only record detailed information about indigenous plants and animals, the customs and territory of Indian tribes, and many previously unknown geographical features of the Pacific Northwest, but also narrate one of the most exciting episodes in American history. Anne Frank, a Jewish teenager hiding out from the Nazis in the Second World War, wrote a diary-journal to "support and comfort" her through a frightening, dehumanizing experience. Anne Morrow Lindbergh kept a diary-journal "not to preserve the experience but to savor it, to make it more real, more visible and palpable, than in actual life."

Keeping a journal, then, can be more than an assignment in a composition class to give you writing practice. You may be inspired to keep a journal for the rest of your life, thus acquiring an extremely valuable instrument that will help you record, assimilate, and enrich your experience in a way that photographs, tape recordings, films, and souvenirs cannot.

In fact, good journal writing should combine all the possibilities of these three devices for recording experience: a journal entry can create as graphically descriptive a picture as a photograph; it can capture the essence of a moment as effectively as a tape recording; and it has the ability of a souvenir to trigger a remembrance. But the journal entry can do even more. First, it can capture you, your personality, and your thoughts, rather than just your image, as in a photograph. Second, it can provide detailed information of a kind that evades a camera, tape recorder, or souvenir.

The Characteristics of Journal Writing

This passage from the notebooks of Albert Camus illustrates how the journal writer can capture a photographic image in words and at the same time embellish it with information that a picture cannot provide.

Trouville, a plateau, covered with asphodels, facing the sea. Little villas with green or white gates, some buried under tamarisks, a few others bare and surrounded by stones. A slight complaint rises from the sea. But everything, the sun, the slight breeze, the whiteness of the asphodels, the already hard blue of the sky, brings to mind the summer, the gilded youth of its daughters, and sunburned sons, passions coming to life, long hours in the sun, and the sudden softness of the evenings. What other meanings can we find to our days but this, and the lesson we draw from this plateau: a birth, a death, and between the two, beauty and melancholy?

—Notebooks: 1939–1942

Note how the following journal entry shows one freshman writer's ability to approximate Camus' picture painting, in this case making a social rather than a metaphysical statement.

To walk up Park Avenue in New York City is a delightful experience. Downtown the fashionable little shops and the department stores, ornate hotels and glittering limousines serving their occupants. As one moves on uptown the sidewalks are full of doormen walking diamond-stud-collared poodles and other breeds, all as elegantly groomed as their owners always are. But on arrival at Park and 105th Street, there is a sudden departure from the extravagant to the deprived. No doormen—instead, garbage cans with rats and flies, children playing hopscotch on the sidewalks, ill-kept and ragged. Alley cats and mongrels scrounging and pulling over garbage cans. Smothering odors of garlic cooking from rooms occupied by ten or twelve people. In summer, recreation consists of children turning on a fire hydrant for thirty minutes or so—a kind policeman, black or white, turns his back and lets them flood the street. Then with all the "authority vested in me" he indignantly makes an appearance, when the basements look ready to flood. The children scatter. He turns it off. The children, wet and sticky, sit on their stoops with the flies and the rats and the cats and the dogs. Sing, clap hands, and think up some other scheme.

Like Camus, the freshman writer captures an impression of a place and instills a touch of personal philosophy. Note that the student writer does not sermonize on the contrast between wealth and poverty, but uses words and details to accent the difference. Neither example forces the writer's reaction upon the reader. Instead, readers are involved in the experience but can reject the inherent philosophy, substituting their own interpretations or reactions. We might call this kind of shared communication "involvement writing."

A good example of how involvement writing can re-create a situation is illustrated in this excerpt from thirteen-year-old Anne Frank's diary. Note that she not only re-creates the experience for herself but permits other readers to share in it as if they were there—as if they, too, were living in constant fear of detection.

Continuation of the "Secret Annexe" daily timetable. As the clock strikes half past eight in the morning, Margot and Mummy are jittery: "Ssh . . . Daddy, quiet, Otto, ssh . . . Pim." "It is half past eight, come back here, you can't run any more water; walk quietly!" These are the various cries to Daddy in the bathroom. As the clock strikes half past eight, he has to be in the living room. Not a drop of water, no lavatory, no walking about, everything is quiet. As long as none of the office staff are there, everything can be heard in the warehouse. The door is opened upstairs at twenty minutes past eight and shortly after there are three taps on the floor! Anne's porridge. I climb upstairs and fetch my "puppy-dog" plate. Down in my room again, everything goes at terrific speed; do my hair, put away my noisy tin pottie, bed in place. Hush, the clock strikes! Upstairs Mrs. Van Daan has changed her shoes and is shuffling about in bedroom slippers, Mr. Van Daan, too; all is quiet.

—Anne Frank, *Diary of a Young Girl*

Re-creating an experience requires putting down on paper its specific details. When this is done effectively, the writing becomes vivid, alive, colorful, and pungent, even if the mechanics are shaky. The following excerpt from one of William Clark's entries in *The Journals of Lewis and Clark* is effective despite Clark's obvious difficulties with the conventions of written English.

. . . one of those mat lodges I entered found it crouded with men women and children and near the enterance of those house I saw maney spears engaged [in] splitting and drying Salmon. I was furnished with a mat to set on, and one man set about preparing me something to eate, first he brought in a piece of a Drift log of pine and with a wedge of elks horn, and a malet of Stone curioesly carved he Split the log into Small pieces and lay'd it open on the fire on which he put round Stones, a woman handed him a basket of water and a large Salmon about half Dried, when the Stones were hot he put them into a basket of water with the fish which was soon sufficiently boiled for use it was then taken out put on a platter neetly made, and set before me. . . . after eateing the boiled fish which was delicious, I set out and halted or come too on the Island at the two Ledges, Several fish was given to me, in return for which I gave small pieces of ribbond.

Note how the details add life and authenticity to the experience. Clark's readers could boil a fish by following his description. Clark and his fellow explorer Meriwether Lewis did not merely record dry, scientific data to take back to President Jefferson. Each of them left a living record of himself as a distinct human being with his own natural, authentic voice.

In your own journal writing, try to find your true voice. Then try to re-create each experience in detail. Your entry should have the quality of an "instant replay" rather than a later news analysis. Suppose Clark had described his meal like this:

I visited some Indians at their camp and they fed me fish cooked in an unusual way. It was delicious.

Or that Anne Frank had written:

We were always anxious about the time and whether our daily activities would be detected.

Obviously, without specific details most of the essence of their experiences would be lost.

Hints for Writing a Journal

In keeping your journal, try to follow these suggestions:

1. Write something every day, even if only a few sentences. The entries can be about any subject: something you experienced that day or some memory triggered by an experience. It helps to carry your journal with you so that you can make an entry when you have a free moment and while the incident is fresh.
2. Restrict each journal entry to an account of only one major or unusual subject. A running discussion of the day's activities will have no more interest or vividness than a bus schedule.
3. Be more concerned with capturing every significant detail of the experience than with the mechanics of writing. Keep the words flowing; write on and on and on, not stopping to look up words or revise.
4. Tell it in your own language. Slang and idiomatic expressions are discouraged in most other forms of writing because they may be too informal for the situation and may not be understood by readers; but they are appropriate in journal writing because they reflect the times and the personalities of real people.
5. Occasionally read your entries a day or two later. Check the ones you think were most successful in re-creating the experience. Try to discover why these entries succeeded.

THE AUTOBIOGRAPHICAL NARRATIVE

The Characteristics of Autobiographical Narrative

In an autobiographical narrative, you write about yourself and your experiences. In that sense it is like journal writing. But whereas journal writing requires little attention to form and you can try your hand at many kinds of writing, autobiographical narrative is similar to other types of narrative writing, both biographical and fictional, and form is important in all of them. The autobiographical narrative, like the others, needs a plot, or unifying action; a time framework; a narrator who tells the story; development of characters; and a setting, the place where the story happens.

UNIFYING ACTION

Ideally, a narrative should be limited either to a single, unifying action or to a single perspective or theme. *Action* is used here both in the strict traditional sense of a single incident that takes place within a brief, circumscribed period of time and in the sense of a situation that extends over a long period of time and involves a closely related chain of events. James Thurber's short autobiographical narratives, such as "The Night the Bed Fell on Father," are limited to a single episode. Henry David Thoreau's *Walden,* on the other hand, is a long autobiographical narrative about a series of incidents all closely related to his year of experimenting with a simple, self-reliant life at Walden Pond.

However, since autobiographical narratives that cover a long period of time usually cannot be limited to a single action or to simple chronological narration, writers may rely instead upon a unifying perspective or theme. They may select only the events that somehow influenced their philosophic view or had an effect in shaping their character. Or they may search for a thread of meaning (a theme) in a series of personal experiences in order to resolve a problem that they have been struggling with for a long time—perhaps a whole lifetime. Vladimir Nabokov's autobiographical narrative *Speak, Memory,* for instance, relates the episodes that shaped his philosophy of life and art. Many black writers have written about their personal experiences from the perspective of their search for identity or their attempt to find in the story of their lives an understanding of the complex black-white relationships in our country. James Baldwin's *Notes of a Native Son* and Eldridge Cleaver's *Soul on Ice* are good examples of thematically controlled personal narratives. But in a composition class, you will not be asked to embark on such ambitious projects. Rather, your personal narrative should be limited to a single incident or several related events. This restriction permits you to describe and explore your characters in depth and encourages you to use vivid and appropriate details in picturing the scene and the action. In addition, limiting yourself to a single situation simplifies the writing task: it almost automatically creates a sense of unity and coherence. Remember that everything in the narrative should be closely related and should move the story along. A good rule of thumb is to permit no digression, to include nothing that could be excluded without seriously damaging the narrative.

TIME FRAMEWORK

Narratives move in time; events are chronological. But in your writing you are not restricted to the natural linear passing of time, though most writers prefer to emulate time as it passes in real life—that is, to begin the action at some moment and move it forward to a subsequent time. The following student narrative demonstrates this chronological treatment.

I was spending the weekend at grandma's, as I had done many, many times before. I woke up early in the morning, about five o'clock. All the lights were on and grandpa was sitting in his big chair across the room waiting for grandma to cook breakfast. I rolled off the sofa where I had spent the night. I picked my pillow off the floor and walked into the smell of bacon and eggs. In the kitchen grandma turned and smiled a wide wrinkled smile, her shaggy gray hair in tufts like chicken down. "What do you want for breakfast, Michael?" "Bacon and eggs and coffee," I said, running back into the living room to tell grandpa his breakfast was ready. He was asleep in the big chair. Then I shook him. Startled, he snorted, "Hey there, big boy." As I followed him into the kitchen, he shouted back over his shoulder, "Let's go eat some breakfast." Grandma laughed as she told grandpa, "He says he wants coffee for breakfast."

Grandpa chuckled. "He's gettin' to be a big boy now, mom, I think he can handle it."

I sat up straight in my chair and stretched my neck to make myself tall. Grandma brought me a big white glass coffee mug—just like grandpa's. She set the steaming bacon and eggs down in front of me, but I didn't immediately dig in. With both hands, I eagerly extended the cup. Grandma poured.

Actually, this incident occurred in the narrator's past. The college student is reminiscing about a completed experience that was important in his growing up. But the narrative time is not static; it moves chronologically from five o'clock in the morning to breakfast.

Another way to handle time in an autobiographical narrative is to start from a certain point and move backward. This flashback technique is, of course, a psychological manipulation of time; it occurs only in the narrator's mind. But it permits the writer to take a journey backward in time, a feat not possible in the physical world. In the following excerpt from *I Remember Papa,* Harry Dolan, visiting his father in prison, flashes back to a day he, his mother, and his sister took a picnic lunch to the rock quarry where his father worked.

And then I saw my father. He sat among fifty other black men, all surrounded by great boulders marked with red paint. They all held steel chisels with which they cut along the marked lines. They would strike a certain point and the boulder would split into smaller pieces and as we approached there was a silence around them except for the pinging of the hammer against the chisel.

In all the noise it was a lonely sound, futile, lost, oppressive. My father seemed to be concentrating, his tremendous arm whipping the air. He was stripped to the waist, black muscles popping sweat, goggled eyes for metal and stone only. We stood there, the three of us, my mother, my sister, and I, and watched my father work for us, and as he conquered the huge boulder my chest filled with pride. Each stroke shouted for all the world to hear: "This is my family and I love them!" No one can tell me this was the act of a lazy man.

At this point, Dolan's narrative returns to a normal chronological sequence. The flashback interrupts the main narrative only momentarily, serving to provide a sympathetic presentation of character. In autobiographical narrative, flashback is usually handled as Dolan has done it, as a reminiscence by the narrator.

Closely related to flashback and perhaps more common to fiction than to autobiographical narrative is a third method of handling time: beginning the action in the middle and moving both backward and forward in time. This device will be discussed in greater detail in Chapter 29.

Each of these devices has its advantages. Normal chronological sequence permits you to create urgency and tension, and move the narrative along at a pace not possible with the others. The flashback permits you to illustrate immediately the relationship between the past and the event that triggered the flashback. The action in the latter, however, is slower-moving than in the normal time sequence, and in using it you must be aware that you are sacrificing a certain amount of momentum. In fact, without special care, the story can become ponderously slow. Your first attempts at narrative, then, are more likely to succeed if you use a normal time sequence.

NARRATOR

Before beginning a fictional narrative, you must select a narrator, the person who tells the story. One technique is to place yourself outside the action, using an anonymous voice to tell the story in the third person (*he, she, they*). Or you may create a character who tells the story from his or her own point of view, using the first person (*I, we*). But if an auto-biographical narrative is to be authentically and unabashedly personal, the narrator virtually must be the writer. The writer then uses the first-person voice; otherwise the work may be regarded as a fictionalized autobiography, as is James Joyce's *A Portrait of the Artist as a Young Man*.

We will discuss the role of the narrator in more detail in Chapter 28.

DEVELOPMENT OF CHARACTERS

Characterization, or development of characters, is another concern of narrative writing. In a very short narrative or anecdote the emphasis may be on the action: the brevity of the story does not permit extensive char-acterization. In longer narratives, however, character development is often more important than the action or plot. But writers may use the plot and the interaction of the characters to develop them. In any case, they do not write expository explanations of the characters such as a psychologist might in writing a case study.

In the student example above, brief as it is, the characterization is as important as the action. The personalities of the grandparents interact-ing with that of the child account for the action. Despite the narrative's brevity, the geniality and love of the grandparents toward each other and toward the child become evident through the dialogue. Harry Dolan's flashback to an episode showing his father's pride in supporting his family enables Dolan to show the personality change in his father by con-trasting his prison personality with an earlier picture of him as a proud, productive man. Character development, then, can result from such plot devices or from what the people say and do or how they respond to each other.

It is the emphasis on characterization that differentiates autobio-graphical narrative from diary entries and anecdotes, in which the emphasis may instead be on the action; in autobiographical narrative, the action may simply be a vehicle to portray some change in the charac-ters, particularly the narrator.

SETTING

In fictional narrative, descriptions of the setting can establish a cer-tain mood or become an essential ingredient of the action or contribute to the development of character. These possibilities will be discussed in Chapter 29. In autobiographical narrative, however, setting is usually treated realistically and factually. Only those descriptive details neces-sary to establish the place of the action or to indicate the setting's re-lationship to the events in the narrative are needed. For example, in relating an embarrassing event that happened in a high school classroom, you do not need to provide a detailed description of the room—only enough to give your readers a sense of the place. However, if the location of the teacher's desk or the door contributed to the situation, then obviously you would need to discuss the spatial arrangement of the room at greater length. But remember, unnecessary details only slow down the action, so you should be especially selective in providing information about the setting.

Techniques of Autobiographical Narration

DRAMATIC AND DESCRIPTIVE APPROACHES

Our two examples also illustrate the two major ways in which narrative writers can approach their subjects: a dramatic approach, relying heavily on dialogue, and a descriptive approach, relying primarily on description of the action and conversation. In the dramatic approach, the action moves forward and characters are developed through direct discourse. The characters are made to speak as they would in a real conversation. The student paper makes some use of this approach. The Dolan example, however, relies heavily on simply telling the story. The writer describes the action and the characters while reporting conversation primarily through indirect discourse. Examples of direct and indirect discourse will help to clarify the difference between them:

> Dramatic Approach—Direct Discourse:
> "I intend to get to the bottom of this crime if it takes the rest of my life!" snarled the detective.

> Descriptive Approach—Indirect Discourse:
> The detective jumped to his feet and began shouting to the people assembled in the room. Purple with rage, he made it clear that he would solve the crime if it took the rest of his life.

Each approach has its advantages, of course, and a combination of the two is often used in narrative writing.

In the following student paper, the writer relies heavily on the dramatic approach.

WAR GAMES

"Hey! Hey, boy! Get the hell out of that bed. You hear me, boy? Get the hell out of that bed."

This was unmistakably the tired, southern drawl of my short, crewcut, red-necked platoon sergeant. We had a run-in before about his language when he was talking to me. Not that I'm better than anyone else, it's only that I expect others to do unto me as I do unto them, and because I was a black wearing the stripe of a specialist E-4. He was a white sergeant E-6 and he couldn't go against the KKK rules about how to treat a nigger, and give one of *them* any type of respect.

Without moving, I answered in a cold even voice. "Look man, haven't I told you about talking to me like that."

"Number one, boy, you don't tell me anything. Number two, boy, I'll talk to you any way I want to!"

Before I could respond, the C.O. was standing in the door, all starched and shining. In a calm, pleasant tone of voice he told me to be in his office in ten minutes, and left. He was the only officer, or NCO for that matter, in the company that I couldn't figure out. He had a strange gleam in his eyes, something like the gleam of a vampire, if such things exist. You could never picture him without that gleam and the smile of your family doctor.

Thinking about my defense I dressed as fast as I could, putting on my best pair of starched fatigues, and inspection display boots, shined to perfection. Without making my bunk, or straightening my area, I started toward the C.O.'s office at the other end of the hall. The hall was completely empty, everyone else having stood reveille and work call and gone to their section. I arrived at his door and stopped. It being closed, I leaned against the wall to wait. When the first shirt came out of his office next to the C.O.'s I immediately snapped to attention, and gave him my best rat-eating-cheese smile, which was returned by a look of pure contempt.

The first shirt went into the C.O.'s office only to come back out before the door shut. Without saying anything he motioned me in like a hitchhiker.

I walked in briskly, closed the door quietly, walked within two paces of the C.O.'s desk, loudly snapped to attention, saluted with the speed of a karate chop, and in my best military voice shouted, "Sir, Specialist 4th Class Haskins reporting as ordered, sir." He saluted, and I dropped my arm. He just sat there with his hands together as if he was in prayer. Finally he spoke.

"Haskins, why did you miss the formations this morning?"

"I didn't wake up, sir."

"That's evident, Haskins. I want an explanation."

"It was the pills, sir."

"How many times have you used that excuse, Haskins?"

"I can't remember, sir."

"The same type of headache again?"

"Yes, sir."

"What brought this one on?"

"Well, you see, sir, I was reading about the riots in Watts, and I started worrying about my mother and my little sister."

The C.O. had sent me to the dispensary a month ago to be examined by the doctors and the psychiatrist. They probed and searched in vain for the cause of my trouble. Nothing was found, to everyone's dismay but mine. Continuing with my explanation, I played the frustration overture.

"What if our apartment was one of those burned? Who would look after them, see that they had food and a place to stay? And what if they were hurt? I went to the Red Cross last night but they were closed. I didn't know what to do. I was worried and scared and nervous and . . ."

At this point he held up his hand for me to stop, concern showing on his face. He thought for a minute or two, while I choked back my hysteria. Man! I could hang it up if I lost control now.

I knew what was coming next, and it did. He told me to go to my section, and he would investigate for me, and let me know as soon as possible. I thanked him, saluted, and left. Once in the hallway I looked around as cautiously as if I were being hunted. I started for my section, which was Supply. Being a desk jockey I didn't mind going to work. There were five of us, two black and three white—token integration.

About halfway there I started running as fast as I could. Tech. Supply was housed in what was formerly a German motor pool, now turned into a warehouse, with our office occupying a portion of one end, and the trucks and stock the rest. About thirty yards from the office door stood two second lieutenants talking. I deliberately ran past them, knowing I'd be called back, but trusting my luck. The shortest one called, "Hey, boy, don't you know to salute officers?" I came back, and still panting said, "Sor-sor-sorry, sir, but I just got the news that my wife had a baby boy." At this a wide smile spread across their faces. I gave them both a Winston, explaining that I hadn't bought any cigars yet, but when I did, they would be among the first to get one. They told me to carry on and I turned and walked away, still without saluting.

I went into the office and sat down unsmiling. Not trying to fool my buddies because they saw I still had my stripe, and knew that I had won. My black brother was the only one to speak, "You bastard," he said, with awe and admiration, "you did it again." We both laughed, broke out the wine, and chanted together, "Black Power, Black Power, Black Power." All the time I was thinking about home—in Kentucky.

The student writer wisely chose the dramatic approach. It allows him through dialogue to illustrate vividly the complexity of black-white relationships in the United States and to avoid the tone of self-pity or personal hostility that a descriptive approach might have created. Instead, the action reveals the writer as a self-sufficient young black man perfectly capable of survival in a hostile world, while the dialogue creates a tone of sardonic humor. The use of direct discourse also reveals the narrator to be a master of black street culture, disclosing a series of linguistic maneuvers in which he plays upon his officers' attitudes, stereotypes, and guilt by his mocking deceit. Direct discourse is vital for this effect; indirect discourse could not have provided the necessary verbal arena. Indeed, the writer, in using this approach, permits the reader to participate in much the same way bystanders "participate" in a verbal-insult street game.

The next student example, however, benefits from the use of indirect discourse and the heavy emphasis on description and word choice in the opening and closing paragraphs.

THE CARNIVAL

It was unusually cold for an autumn night. A delicate blanket of frost had silently formed on the tent tops. But the gay calliope music from the merry-go-round and the whirling masses of multicolored lights and the laughter of happy people and the tempting smell of hot dogs, cotton candy, and popcorn made me feel warm inside. I didn't even notice the cold. I stuffed my hands in my coat pockets and casually made my way through the milling crowd. Overhead, the Ferris Wheel was revolving like a giant neon top in an ocean of black. To my right I noticed a pack of people, thick, like a swarm of bees. The center of interest was a shriveled old man with a thin moustache. "Step right up folks. See the headless woman. Eighth wonder of the world!" As I silently chuckled at the old man, I blindly collided into a squat, roly-poly lady. She was violently attacking a huge mound of cotton candy and the sudden jolt set her plump face squarely into the sticky mass. I mumbled a sick "Excuse me" and promptly disappeared into the crowd.

As I rounded the Bingo stand, I noticed a small tent by the penny arcade, one I had not seen before. I sauntered over to where several men were engrossed in a boisterous game of chance. Behind the counter was a tawdry, gypsy-looking woman arrayed in layers of cheap costume jewelry. As I turned to leave, my eye caught an unobtrusive, sandy-haired little girl of about eight or nine. She was clad in a scanty cotton dress and her frail body trembled like a tiny leaf in a windstorm. She stood in her bare feet beside one of the burly men. Her dirty face looked up at me and her sad, pale blue eyes met mine.

Presently the little girl gave a tug at the man's weatherworn coat. "Daddy, Daddy, I'm cold," she whispered. As she spoke, gray puffs of steam rose into the crisp night air and then melted. With a curse her father brusquely pushed her aside and resumed his game. The gypsy lady gave a sensuous shriek of laughter as she raked a pile of money into her apron.

Disgusted, I turned and walked away. The tin-like calliope music droned monotonously above the harsh sounds of moving machinery. My nostrils were filled with the pungent odor of stale food. An icy draft of wind swept down my collar and I sank deeper into my coat. I leaned against a huge post and closed my eyes. The swirling masses of bright lights made me ill. "Step right up folks. See the headless lady. Eighth wonder of the world!"

As you can see, the descriptive approach was an effective vehicle for the author of "The Carnival" to paint two different versions of the same scene. The setting is the same, but the words to describe it reveal the writer's mood and his impressionistic reaction to the scene—not easily achieved with exclusive use of the dramatic approach.

NARRATIVE TENSION

These two student papers, particularly "War Games," illustrate another aspect of narrative writing. Frequently, narrative builds tension or suspense by setting up a conflict or obstacle to be overcome. In "War Games," the immediate conflict is between the black soldier and his white officer over missing the morning formation. But implicit in the story is the sense that this confrontation is only a symbol of the never-ending conflict the soldier faces in white America. He wins this particular battle, leaving readers with the knowledge that he has the will for combat in future ones. In "The Carnival," however, the writer internalizes the conflict. He is angered and disgusted, unable to resolve the problem, but it temporarily colors his outlook on the world. Because the conflict and reaction in both stories are common to us all, we are able to identify with the situation; thus the writer, through the narration of one personal experience, can make a subtle comment on a larger problem.

CONSISTENCY

Both student narratives maintain a consistency of character, particularly in the portrayal of the narrator. Each narrator's reaction at the end is "true to character"—that is, it is consistent with the character's personality and development up to that point. For instance, the "Black Power" toast Haskins makes at the end indicates that he views the psychological victory over his officers as vindication for the many wrongs that have shaped his hostility toward whites.

The resolution of the action must also be consistent. When Yossarian goes wildly AWOL at the end of *Catch-22*, the reader has been prepared for it by all his previous attempts to escape his never-ending tour of duty. His final action is credible because it fits his earlier character development. If a writer does not fulfill the expectations previously established, readers feel betrayed and angry. Even surprise endings should permit your readers to recall hints and clues, however subtle, that in some way foreshadow what happens.

The setting, too, should be consistent: historically accurate and suitable to the purpose. For instance, if you write about an experience you had in 1965, your narrative would be inconsistent if the setting was the Spokane World's Exposition of 1974. Your characters of the 60s might be listening to pop records by the Beatles, but not by John Denver or Alice Cooper.

Finally, the language you use should be consistent with the time at which your narrative takes place. Avoid using current slang if your autobiographical narrative is set in your early childhood.

Hints for Writing an Autobiographical Narrative

Many of these techniques will evolve naturally as you write about personal experiences. But if you want to learn to write effective autobiographical narrative, you might keep the following in mind as you write or as you map out your prewriting strategy.

1. Try to limit your paper to a single action—that is, to one incident or situation that includes several closely related events. Try to use the action to develop your characters.
2. Decide upon the most effective way to handle time and follow it throughout the paper.
3. Before you start to write, choose whatever narrative technique will best suit your purposes: the dramatic approach of "War Games," the descriptive approach of "The Carnival," or a combination of the two.
4. Keep characters, setting, and action consistent throughout the narrative. If there are to be surprises, make certain that they are not only possible but probable and foreshadowed.
5. Choose details and events carefully. Use only those that will contribute to the characterization, the setting, or the action. Whenever you write about your own experiences, there will be a strong temptation to include everything, down to the smallest and least relevant details. A good way to avoid this is to call to mind the most tedious storyteller you know and analyze why that person bores you. Chances are it is because he or she includes meaningless details and meanders off on long digressions. Avoid these pitfalls by sticking to the main story line, being selective, and striving always to be interesting.
6. Try to add interest and suspense by including some kind of conflict in your narrative: a struggle between yourself and another person or other people; between yourself and some force, psychological or otherwise.

THE AUTOBIOGRAPHICAL ANECDOTE

All of us tell autobiographical anecdotes in the course of our conversations to amuse our friends or to interest them in the incident itself. Or we may include one in a letter home to share with the family a funny or frightening experience. But in writing, personal or otherwise, an autobiographical anecdote is often incorporated into a longer paper as an introduction, conclusion, or illustrative example.

The purpose of using an anecdote as an introduction is to "hook" the reader's interest in the subject. The following attention-getting anecdote introduces an article about the history and advantages of the banana.

My grandfather was a country doctor, and in his last years, when I knew him, he liked to talk about his experiences in practice. One story that I remember had to do with a call to a backwoods farmhouse to deliver a baby. It was late afternoon when he got there, and by the time the baby had been born and bathed and swaddled it was night, and the farmer offered to fix him some supper. My grandfather said he thanked him but declined.

"That's right," he told me. "But there were some bananas in a bowl on the kitchen table, and I said if he didn't mind I'd just have one of them."

"A banana!" I said. I was eight or nine years old, and always ready to eat. "That's all you wanted for supper, Grandpa—just an old banana?"

"No, sir," he said. "It wasn't that. I was good and hungry. But I was afraid to eat in that house. I was sure it was crawling with germs. It was filthy. It was the dirtiest house I've ever had to set foot in. Those people were worse than hogs. But now I'll tell you a secret. Bananas are a remarkable fruit. I mean, they are a whole lot more than just good eating. And one of the remarkable things about them is this: They're *safe*—there isn't anything cleaner than a banana sealed inside its skin. Just be sure that you peel it yourself."

— Berton Roueche, "The Humblest Fruit," *The New Yorker*

An anecdote may be effectively used within a paper at any place to illustrate or develop a point.

Occasionally, a writer wishes to end a paper with an autobiographical anecdote, achieving a special effect not possible with a less dramatic final statement. The following anecdote concluding an article about the dangers encountered on a boat exploration of the Colorado River demonstrates how effective an anecdotal ending can be. The writer had been advised to walk around Lava Falls rather than go over them in a wooden boat, but he chose to go by boat.

We went into Lava Falls at what seemed the perfect place and angle, but suddenly the boat plunged down into a hole and then pitched almost straight upward, standing on its stern. As the water broke over my head I saw Litton still rowing, his oars sawing the air. My next vision was of a wave engulfing us from the right, and when my eyes cleared and I could breathe again I saw that he had been swept overboard.

The oars were still in the rowlocks. I moved into his place and took them, glancing hopefully right and left in the foam in search of him. Soon he bobbed to the surface, seized an oar that I held out to him, and pulled himself up to the gunwale. But his bulky life-jacket prevented him from climbing back into the boat, even though it was swamped and riding very low. After a few moments he told me to try to beach the boat on the right bank; he would float along and make his way to shore by himself.

Empty, the boat weighed 50 pounds. Full of water, I could barely move it across the current and several times it bounced off rocks that a more competent boatman would have avoided. But at last I beached it, tied it to the roots of a tamarisk tree and sat on the bow, panting. Nearly ten minutes later Litton, who had been swept far downstream, came sauntering up the riverbank toward me. He grinned broadly. "Pleasant day," he said.

That was in 1971. Last year I found myself once more at Lava Falls, standing above it, while a boatman offered advice: "I wouldn't ride through there if I were you." And I didn't. I walked.

> —Robert Wallace, "Wooden Boats Plus Colorado Rapids
> Equals Adventure," *Smithsonian*

Because of their brevity, anecdotes usually emphasize an action rather than character development. And, although the action may briefly illuminate a character's personality or life view, characterization in an anecdote is often achieved by the use of stock situations and stock characters, or stereotypes.

THE PERSONAL ESSAY

"Don't you remember me?" I always hear the question with an uncontrollable sinking of heart. I cannot put aside the feeling of panic. I do not remember the person and the person knows perfectly well that I do not. I am desperately trying to find some adequate answer, although I know there is none, and the person is trying, with more or less success, usually less, not to show his pique.

One of my latest experiences was in Asbury Park. I was lecturing on a warm night. There was a large audience in a low-ceilinged room—a kind audience who listened a long time, not simply to what I said, but to what many others said. It was late before I was released, and I was tired. I came out on the darkened street. A man was standing in the shadow. I saw his bulk but I had not yet seen his face clearly. He was very dark and reticent.

"Don't you remember me?" he said. I wanted to say, "I have not seen your face yet," but I tried to be pleasant. "I am afraid—" I began gropingly.

> —W. E. B. DuBois, "Don't You Remember Me?" *W. E. B. DuBois: A Reader*

In these opening paragraphs, the writer sketches an encounter that could have been related as a full-blown anecdote or narrative. Instead, he sees this particular incident as only one of many similar ones that have formed a recurring pattern in his life. Each has been as frustrating as the ones before it, and the writer is concerned with the frustration triggered by such events, not with a single incident as such. His aim in the essay is not to reproduce the happening in vivid, narrative action, but to talk about it in relation to others and to the thread or theme that ties them together. Like autobiographical narrative, the subject matter of the personal essay is personal experience, but the purpose is different: you "talk about" rather than simply "tell."

All of us have had recurrent experiences such as the one in the example. They can involve our relationships with other people or everyday misadventures with the products of our machine age — encountering vending machines, starting the car on cold mornings, catching the bus or commuter train daily, fighting the red tape of computer mailing or billing systems. Out of these recurring events, we begin to formulate attitudes, to draw inferences about them, as DuBois does: "I always hear the question with an uncontrollable sinking of heart." A series of such personal experiences might be prefaced by an opening statement like, "There's a little gremlin who sits on my choke every morning"; "That vending machine in the lobby is a con artist"; or "Why is it that the bus on my line is the only one that doesn't run on schedule?" Two ingredients, then, provide the raw materials for a personal essay: an opening generalization arising from recurring experiences and a representative selection of those incidents to illustrate the generalization.

The personal essay is only one of the varieties generally classified as *essays,* which are usually of two major types: formal and informal. Formal essays deal seriously with significant subject matter and are characterized by fairly tight structural restrictions; they are usually written to inform the reader. Informal essays, on the other hand, are mainly written to amuse and entertain. Casual in tone, they tend to be freer and more individual in structure than formal essays. The personal essay (or familiar essay, as it is sometimes called) is one of the subclasses of the informal essay.

Although the personal essay has been a literary form for centuries, the chatty, informal essay of today has become a perfect vehicle for contemporary essayists to communicate their whimsical views on almost any subject — often amusing and delighting their readers as they comment on universal, mundane matters. Writers as diverse as Will Rogers, Art Buchwald, and Erma Bombeck have found that their satiric, impressionistic essays have been well received. With homespun humor, Will Rogers commented on the absurdities of bureaucratic government. Art Buchwald writes of the incongruities in a wide range of contemporary subjects, from his daughter's Barbie dolls to the foibles of American politicians. Erma Bombeck's essays deal with the frustrations inherent in family life. In short, personal essays can range across the whole spectrum of human experience, but they dwell especially on the ordinary, on the daily situations that are common to us all and that take up so much of our time and thought.

Although the subject matter of personal essays is almost unrestricted, modern ones often display similar characteristics of form and style. Their tone is usually relaxed, genial, somewhat amused, conversational. Also, because the personal essay reveals the writer's attitude or impressions about a topic, it is generally written in the first person. The writer's point of view is central, though his or her outlook often strikes a universal chord. Another characteristic of many personal essays is that they are mildly satirical, poking gentle fun at their subjects.

Despite its looseness of form, the personal essay demands more structure than the autobiographical narrative. First, personal essays open with a focusing statement, usually in the first or second sentence of the paper. This beginning not only introduces the subject but also reflects the writer's approach to it, and at the same time establishes the tone of the essay. Note how the following opening statements achieve these ends.

Surely nothing in the astonishing scheme of life can have nonplussed Nature so much as the fact that none of the females of any of the species she created really cared very much for the male as such.
                    — James Thurber, "Courtship Through the Ages"

In this beginning statement, Thurber introduces his subject, the universal indifference of females toward males. In addition, this sentence establishes the tongue-in-cheek tone that is sustained throughout the essay. The words "astonishing" and "nonplussed" contribute to this end, as does the ironic suggestion that this indifference is not what Nature intended.

There is a book out called *Dog Training Made Easy* and it was sent to me the other day by the publisher, who rightly guessed that it would catch my eye. I like to read books on dog training.
                    — E. B. White, "Dog Training"

Here again, in his opening statement the writer introduces his subject and establishes his sympathetic point of view toward it. Note, too, how the first-person pronouns and the commonplace vocabulary help to establish a conversational, familiar tone.

I'm wild about walking . . . .
                    — Leo Rosten

In this succinct statement, Rosten introduces his subject, walking, and establishes his enthusiasm for it by using the word *wild*. To make yourself aware of how one word can make a difference in tone and point of view, try substituting different adjectives for *wild*. "I'm *fond* of walking," for instance, has a markedly different tone.

From these examples, we can see that the opening statement acts as a direction pointer and a barometer: it sets the personal essay off in a particular direction and indicates its climate or the writer's attitude toward the subject—sympathetic, sardonic, hostile, or amused. Sustained throughout the paper, this attitude supplies the second characteristic necessary to the personal essay: focus, or unity. In the following personal essay, the opening statement focuses the subject—living with a husband obsessed with his lawn—and the essay retains its coherence or unity, its sense of direction, from the writer's amused attitude toward the situation.

THERE'S NO PLEASING A LAWN FREAK[1]

Erma Bombeck

I just figured out if my husband paid just half the attention to me as he does the lawn, my 70-year-old mailman would never have started to look like Robert Redford.

If ever there were a valid suit for alienation of affection, it's that lousy lawn.

There is something about the ability of a man to grow a few blades of grass that contributes to his masculinity. He is either a grass grower or he is not a grass grower. I have seen virile men move into the neighborhood with tattoos on their lips, but if they have fungus on their dwarf tiff, forget it. They're just not one of the boys.

A lawn enthusiast has two moods: irritable and irritable. These are interchangeable depending on whether the grass is growing or whether the grass is not growing.

When the grass is not growing, my husband goes to the library to see what could be missing, has his soil analyzed, waters, soaks, fertilizes, and has the nurseryman who sold him the seed make a house call.

When the grass is growing, he runs the mower back to the store to make sure the blade is cutting, trims, rakes, rolls and makes an obscene phone call to the dog next door who over-fertilized it in the first place.

There is no pleasing a lawn freak.

Some say it is normal for a man to want a pretty lawn. I don't know what is normal anymore. I sent the kids to Mother's, blew an entire food budget on steaks and wine, put a dab of garlic on the lightbulb and slipped into some-

[1] Erma Bombeck, "There's No Pleasing a Lawn Freak," from her column "At Wit's End." Courtesy of Field Newspaper Syndicate.

thing that had not been paid for. "What are you thinking?" I teased, turning off the TV set.

"Did you turn the hose off?" he asked.

Is it normal for a man to call the police and report a flock of birds that are eating our grass seed? Is it normal for a grown man to mourn a brown spot for three years?

I was all set to tell the mailman about my infatuation with him when he said, "I see your husband uses a chemical fertilizer of nitrogen, phosphorus, and potash. Tell him if he invested in a little sheep dip, he'd do away with that crabgrass. Is there something you wanted?"

"I thought you looked like someone I knew," I said. "But I was mistaken. You all look alike."

Bombeck sustains the breezy, humorous tone established in her first sentence by using several rhetorical devices: hyperbole, rhetorical question (one that requires no answer), and direct discourse. Hyperbole, or exaggeration for effect, is a primary ingredient of Bombeck's style. For example, she writes that her mailman is seventy years old (well past the normal retirement age); men whose grass is invaded by a fungus cannot be virile; her husband's mood depends entirely on whether the grass is growing, and when it is, he makes obscene phone calls to the dog next door. Even her rhetorical questions employ hyperbole: "Is it normal for a grown man to mourn a brown spot for three years?" The use of direct discourse for the crucial conversations heightens the breeziness of tone and continues the fast pace sustained throughout. Note that she ends the essay with a surprise twist, a technique common in the humorous personal essay. This contributes to the final focusing on the subject: it closes the circle, ties the knot, leaves the reader satisfied.

Not all personal essays are as openly humorous as Bombeck's, but they are light in tone and subject matter. They deal with the minor, petty joys and discomforts of human existence; weighty problems deserve a more formal and serious treatment. Writing a personal essay should be fun; you should not worry about explaining difficult concepts or relationships.

Hints for Writing a Personal Essay

The personal essay, although widely varied in subject matter and loose in form, demands more attention to structure than journal entries and autobiographical narratives.

1. The opening statement or paragraph should introduce the subject and reveal the writer's attitude or point of view toward the subject.
2. The writer's point of view provides the paper's focus, or unity.

3. The personal essay often ends with a humorous twist or sardonic observation that reinforces the content and tone of the opening statement.

ASSIGNMENTS

For Discussion

1 Examine the language in "War Games" and "The Carnival." List five to ten words in each that contribute to the effectiveness of the narratives.

2 In movies, plays, or TV drama, what are some of the techniques used in flashbacks? What are some ways that a writer of personal narrative might handle the transition from the present to the past? For example, Harry Dolan prefaced the flashback used as an example in this chapter with: "I remember an earlier time, an earlier chapter of my growing up."

3 Make a chronological list of all the incidents you can remember that occurred on your pre-registration day at college. If you were asked to write a narrative depicting the frustration you felt on that day, which incidents would you delete?

4 Read this personal essay and consider the questions that follow.

IF I COULD CHANGE MY NAME

We are living in an age when a person must be able to prove at any time that a particular name belongs to him or her. Nearly everyone carries some kind of identification. Driver's licenses, Social Security cards, and military registration cards are samples of acceptable proof that your name is what you say it is.

Most people are happy with their name and love the sound and sight of it. However, I am not a member of this fortunate group. Since my sister, in a word study class, traced the origin of our last name and found it was derived from a word meaning ignorant, I have been a little dissatisfied. But as I have hope of changing it in the future, this is a minor problem.

Mary Jo, on the other hand, I seem to be stuck with. Mary, pronounced from Murry to Merry, is a nice, conventional, feminine name, but I think my mother was a little confused when she added the Jo. Relatives who don't visit us very often are usually surprised that I am a girl because mother always refers to me as "Jo."

When I answer the phone with "Jo Ingram speaking," the person on the other end of the phone quite often calls me son or Mr. Ingram. I do believe if I could change my name to some nice, definitely feminine name, it would clear up the confusion of my identity.

However, when I think of the fact that all of my brothers were named after some "beloved" relatives, I review the list of family names mine could have been chosen from. Juletia, Axie, Mahalia, Hannah, Biddy, Obedience, Polly, and Willy are some of the possibilities. Maybe Mary Jo isn't so bad, after all.

a Does this personal essay have a focusing statement? What is it?
b Does the first paragraph catch the reader's interest? Could it be better related to the second paragraph?
c Does the opening paragraph or the focusing statement adequately establish the tone of the essay?
d What improvements would you suggest to the writer?

5 The following are opening statements from student papers. Discuss whether each is effective in identifying the subject and establishing the paper's tone and purpose. Suggest some types of anecdotes that might be used in a paper written on each subject.

a Mother's school days were not *my* school days.
b Let's face it. I'm a hypochondriac. I know because I immediately develop the symptoms of any new disease that I hear about.
c Why am I the only one who doesn't understand football?
d Hiking in the woods is a healthy activity?
e It isn't only the three-year-olds who can't open the child-proof packages.
f After a day of shopping, I look in the mirror to see if I'm really there. The clerks obviously think of me as the Invisible Man.

For Writing

1 Write an action-focused narrative about some personal experience that had a lasting significance to you:

a An episode that contributed to better understanding of someone in your family.
b An incident or series of related incidents that changed your outlook on human nature, your school, parental authority, or whatever.
c An incident that helped you decide on a different course of action —for example, a change in career plans, college or summer plans, marriage plans.

2 Both "War Games" and "The Carnival" have several levels of meaning. Both depict a personal experience and at the same time make a social comment on an aspect of our society. Write a narrative about a personal experience you have had that implicitly contained a universal situation. Be careful to avoid moralizing. Permit the action, the dialogue, and the expository description to convey the "message" to your readers.

3   Write a narrative including several related events that rely on a unifying perspective. The central theme could be your developing a tolerance for someone different from you in race, religion, or age; or it could be a series of events that contributed to your perfecting a skill, developing an awareness and appreciation of the opposite sex, or learning the give and take of dormitory life.

4   Write one brief account of an episode using the descriptive approach and indirect discourse. Write a second version using the dramatic approach, making extensive use of direct discourse.

5   Write an anecdote about a personal experience using the approach and language you would use in telling it to your best friend. Then write another version for your grandparents.

6   Write a short narrative from your own experiences that might be used in the introduction to a paper on one of these subjects:

Fly-fishing	Band or orchestra experience
Drag racing	Birthday parties
Christmas shopping	Dating practices
Acting	Registering for classes
Camping	Overcoming shyness

7   Write a personal anecdote on any subject you wish. In a separate paragraph, explain how the anecdote might be incorporated into an essay —as an introduction, as an illustration, or as a dramatic ending.

8   Write a personal essay on coping with some fairly insignificant, everyday, recurrent activity that has an absurd aspect. The following suggestions may be helpful:

Dialing wrong numbers
Commuting
Church experiences
Trying to make a good impression
Applying for a job
Finding a campsite or motel
Getting the family car
College meals
Opening plastic and cardboard packages
Receiving junk mail
Finding a parking space

3

Language in Personal Writing

"Watch your language!"

You may have heard this warning from your parents when you were a child. Here it is again, this time referring not only to rude, vulgar, or offensive language but also to the importance of selecting all words thoughtfully and carefully. In a sense, writing involves three components: the writer, the subject, and the reader. The subject of personal writing is the writer. Therefore, writers are revealed not only in what they tell about themselves in an anecdote, autobiographical narrative, or personal essay, but in what they show of themselves by their choice of words. For example, you reveal your attitude toward eighteen-year-olds by the term you use to refer to them: *kids, teenagers, adolescents, juveniles, youngsters, young men and women.*

You must also watch your language to determine whether it is communicating the experience clearly and accurately to readers. If they cannot easily read what you have written, they may not finish it, or if they do, they may not understand it. And if you fail to convey it accurately, they may not grasp exactly what you are saying.

Finally, you must watch your language to see that it interests and appeals to readers. Because it is easier to put down a book or paper than to click off a television set, walk out of a film, or leave a lecture, writers must always be particularly concerned about attracting and holding their audience.

Language is like furniture in a home: revealing much about the person selecting it, performing certain necessary functions, and establishing a particular atmosphere. In view of its importance, let us consider how language can be used effectively in personal writing.

NATURAL LANGUAGE

In Chapter 1 we tried to dispel the notion that language in personal writing must be formal and flowery. Although we talked about natural-ness, we did not specify how to attain it; instead, we tried to show you that the goal in personal writing is to achieve the free and easy style of relaxed, friendly conversation, sharpened and polished, but flowing along, casual and intimate. What should come through to readers is your voice as it would sound if you were sitting in a room talking with them. But being natural in writing is about as difficult as relaxing in a dentist's chair. As a first step in helping you achieve naturalness, we offer two suggestions:

1. Rely on short, simple words.
2. Listen to every sentence to determine whether it sounds like you.

Let's apply these suggestions to this sentence from a student paper:

It was on the day following high school graduation that I com-menced the task of locating employment.

First we'll replace long, formal words with short, simple ones and see how much better the sentence sounds:

It was on the day following high school graduation that I *started* the task of *looking for work.*

Then we might decide that "It was on the day following" sounds stilted and change it to "The day after." And we might think that "the task of" is unnecessary. These changes would result in the simple statement:

The day after high school graduation I started looking for work.

Applying the same two suggestions to the student's next sentence, we might change it as follows:

Original: In view of the scarce number of vocational opportunities that appear to be available to members of the feminine sex in the community where I reside, my expectations of suc-cess were at a minimum.

Revision: Because few jobs seem to be open to women in my home town, I expected little success.

If you are afraid that short, simple words will make your personal writing sound childish, remember that such words have been used in many of the most memorable statements in our language:

Ask not what your country can do for you—ask what you can do for your country.   —John F. Kennedy

Government of the people, by the people, for the people shall not perish from this earth.   —Abraham Lincoln

I have nothing to offer but blood, toil, tears, and sweat.
                                                                                          —Winston Churchill

We have nothing to fear but fear itself.   —Franklin D. Roosevelt

That's one small step for a man, one giant leap for mankind.
                                                                                          —Neil Armstrong

Unfortunately, some student writers show off by reaching for the long, pretentious word instead of the short, simple one. They believe that *find* is too common so they switch to *ascertain; agree* too unsophisticated so they substitute *concur;* and *put off* too childish so they use *procrastinate.* In some contexts, formal language may work well. But in personal writing, where the written language should closely resemble the spoken one in order to achieve the desired friendly voice, shorter words are generally more appropriate and effective.

CLEAR LANGUAGE

All writing, including personal writing, should be thought of as communication. The purpose of placing words on paper instead of retaining them in your head is to convey ideas and feelings to someone else, whether to a friend, to a stranger, or even to yourself, who, in a sense, will be a different person in six months or six years. Consequently, to communicate effectively, you must describe the subject clearly, selecting words that cannot be misunderstood and that will transmit your ideas from your mind to the reader's with as little distortion or difficulty as possible.

In personal writing you probably have few problems selecting words recognizable to readers. Unless you are writing about complex scientific experiments, unusual hobbies, foreign customs, or other specialized matters, your language will be generally familiar to your readers. But you must always be alert to explain any slang or technical terms that might be puzzling, as in this example:

The teachings of Mr. Muhammad stressed how history had been "whitened" —when white men had written history books, the black men simply had been left out.

                                                              —*The Autobiography of Malcolm X*

Here a short explanation has sufficed; elsewhere, a synonym may do. Treating the problem is not difficult, but being aware of it is; so you must worry constantly about your readers, just as considerate hosts are always concerned about their guests. By always thinking of how readers will respond to your language, you can anticipate problems and adjust for them.

Conveying an experience clearly is far more complex. It hinges mainly upon your ability to describe what has happened in specific words. What are specific words? They are usually concrete words, ones that refer to anything you can see, hear, touch, taste, or smell. Obviously, *camping* does not fit in this category; *tent* does. But though the word *tent* is concrete, it is specific only in a relative sense. It is general when compared with *pup tent* or *umbrella tent*. So words may be concrete but still not as specific as they could be. Effective writing usually requires the writer to be highly specific, getting down to earth instead of floating around in vague generalities. Note how this works in the following example:

General:	I was feeding my *pet*.
Less general:	I was feeding my *dog*.
Even less general:	I was feeding my *small dog*.
Specific:	I was feeding my *poodle*.
More specific:	I was feeding my *white toy poodle*.

The more specific you are, the more information you convey, and the more clearly readers perceive what you are writing about.

Two language authorities, Bergan and Cordelia Evans, consider the use of general instead of specific words to be the most obvious characteristic of ineffective writing. They advise aspiring writers to ask themselves constantly, "Does what I have written cover more ground than I meant to cover?" These authorities contend that remembering this question while writing "will do more to develop a respectable style than all the grammar books and vocabulary builders in the world."[1]

"Covering more ground than I meant to cover" may result not only from using a general word for a specific one (*transportation* for *subway*) but from omitting details. To re-create an experience for yourself or your readers, you must recount all the significant particulars, as if placing everything under a microscope for others to view. Let us illustrate this point by comparing how a student might write about a personal scene with the way that Alfred Kazin treated it at the close of his "Brownsville" chapter in *On Native Grounds*. First, the student's version:

I can remember Mother always working from early morning until late evening.

---

[1] *A Dictionary of Contemporary English Usage* (New York: Random House, 1957), p. 6.

She was always busy, shopping, cooking, or sewing despite her hand that had been pierced and crudely patched together when she was a girl.

Now Kazin's account:

I can never remember a time when she was not working. . . . When I awoke in the morning she was already at her machine, or in the great morning crowd of housewives at the grocery getting fresh rolls for breakfast. When I returned from school she was at her machine, or conferring over *McCall's* with some neighborhood woman who had come in pointing hopefully to an illustration —"Mrs. Kazin! Mrs. Kazin! Make me a dress like it shows here in the picture!" When my father came home from work she had somehow mysteriously interrupted herself to make supper for us, and the dishes cleared and washed, was back at her machine. When I went to bed at night, often she was still there, pounding away at the treadle, hunched over the wheel, her hands steering a piece of gauze under the needle with a finesse that always contrasted sharply with her swollen hands and broken nails. Her left hand had been pierced through when as a girl she had worked in the infamous Triangle Shirtwaist Factory on the East Side. A needle had gone straight through the palm, severing a large vein. They had sewn it up for her so clumsily that a tuft of flesh always lay folded over the palm.

Note how the details vividly and convincingly describe the endless activity of the writer's mother. We derive a clearer picture of Mrs. Kazin because of the information about her getting breakfast rolls, conferring over *McCall's* (not just *a magazine*) with the neighborhood women, making supper, washing dishes, and so on. Also, observe how the details about her hand create a more graphic and moving account than the stuent's version did. Throughout, Kazin's specific language enables readers to visualize his mother's ceaseless work.

Without such descriptive details most writing is flat and colorless. Note how the absence of details makes the following student paper seem drab and lifeless.

As we were trotting along, an unsuspecting cottontail crossed our path, startling Betty's horse. The frightened animal dashed off with Betty trying to stop it. Following behind them, I could see that she was getting tired from the way she was riding.

Suddenly, she fell, hitting her head on the broken limb of a tree. I stopped, got off, and raced over to her, wondering what to do. I decided to pick her up and carry her to my car, which fortunately was parked nearby.

She was still unconscious when we got to the hospital. I carried her to the emergency room and waited there for the doctor to examine her.

This incident is related in such general terms that few pictures flash in our mind's eye. We do not see how Betty was riding, what she looked like lying by the tree, where she was placed in the car, what occurred during the drive to the hospital, and how she was admitted there.

A writer should savor an experience like a gourmet does a fine wine. It should not be gulped hastily, but should be sipped slowly to be fully enjoyed and remembered. Of course, you must consider your purpose in writing. For example, if the writer of the preceding paper had wished to reveal the haphazard emergency care in a hospital, then he might have treated the preliminaries generally or even omitted them by beginning the paper at the hospital instead of at the accident. Some introductory and concluding generalizations may be necessary in a paper, but otherwise you should pour on the particulars. A person reading only generalities is like a viewer watching a poorly tuned television set with blurred and fuzzy images. Neither has a clear picture of what is happening.

This emphasis on clarity adds up to the importance of finding words to convey your exact meaning to readers in order to let them see and experience what you did.

LIVELY LANGUAGE: THREE PITFALLS

At the risk of annoying you, we shall keep repeating throughout this book the importance of trying to interest readers, whether they be family, friends, teachers, classmates, or even yourself. Some students seem to forget that writing should be lively and engaging, not drab and dull. In talking, you can tell whether or not you are boring people from their expressions, the direction of their eyes, and even the position of their bodies. If you are, you can change your subject or your manner of speaking, or you can just stop talking. No such feedback is available in writing. But even though you cannot see the yawns, the glances at the watch, the day-dreaming stares, you can learn to sense them. One way to pep up your prose and make it livelier is to avoid lifeless words. What are they? They consist mainly of overworked verbs, worn-out nouns, and petrified phrases.

Overworked Verbs

The life of a sentence depends to a great extent on its verb, the word that directs the action. The flow and movement of ideas revolve around the verb, which functions like a quarterback directing the offense. In the following sentences, note how the substitution of lively, specific verbs for the general, lifeless *looked* communicates the writer's meaning more accurately and engages the reader's interest more fully!

The professor *looked* at the student.
The professor *gazed* at the student.
The professor *glanced* at the student.
The professor *peered* at the student.
The professor *stared* at the student.

Looked is the most general word in the list, suffering therefore from the weakness of all generalizations. *Looked* has the added disadvantage of being used so frequently and in so many different senses that it no longer arouses interest. The other verbs, being more unusual, command more attention and convey more information. *Stared* suggests a lengthy look, perhaps at some wrongdoing; *gazed* a steady look, maybe of admiration or appreciation; *glanced* a quick look, probably as a check; and *peered,* a searching look, probably through glasses or with squinting eyes.

Looking away from *look,* we find the most deadly of all the overworked verbs: the members of the *be* family. Like termites, they swarm everywhere, gnawing away at the foundations of sentences. Here they are:

am	be
is	being
are	been
was	were

Here's how these termites work and how they can be exterminated:

Before	*After*
Our response was in the negative.	We responded negatively. (*Or:* We declined, refused, and so on.)
He is a player for the Cincinnati Reds.	He plays for the Cincinnati Reds.
I am a worker on the assembly line.	I work on the assembly line.

In each of these simple examples, the overworked, worn-out form of *be* has been replaced with a livelier verb (*responded, plays, work*), thus tightening the sentences and transferring the action where it belongs—to the verb. By scouring the forms of *be* out of your sentences whenever possible, you will make them sparkle and shine with interest and appeal for your readers.

Please note the phrase "whenever possible." Remember that *be* functions not only as a main verb but also as a helping verb. When used alone, it may be avoided; when used as an auxiliary, it may not. For example:

The dual function of the verb *be* IS (main verb) an excellent example of what many students ARE (helping verb) surprised to discover about their language.

The first use of *be* (IS) may be avoided by changing the sentence to read: "The dual function of the verb *be* illustrates . . . ." The second use of *be* (ARE) may not be avoided because it functions here as an auxiliary, necessary for *surprised*. As you can see, there are good *be*'s and bad *be*'s: auxiliaries that help your sentences, and main verbs that hinder them. Keep the difference in mind, and look out for unnecessary *be*'s.

Other worn-out verbs can weaken sentences. A few of the more common feeble verbs are listed here:

do	hold
give	make
got	put
have	take

Here they are in action, or more appropriately, inaction, along with *be:*

My professor *is* in the habit of *being* late, but on Thursday he *got* to our class on time, *giving* as an excuse for his promptness the need to consider the assigned subject carefully. After *making* a simple diagram of the object on the board, he requested those who *had* some recognition of it to *do* a rough sketch in their notebooks, *putting* the proper label by each part. After a while, I saw him *take* a glance out the window, *give* a look at his watch, *hold* a brief discussion with the graduate assistant, and *take* his leave of the astonished class. I *made* a decision then to *have* a talk with the chairman.

Without the overworked verbs, the paragraph gains vitality:

The professor habitually arrives late, but on Thursday he appeared in our class on time, excusing his promptness by pointing out the need to consider the assigned subject fully. After diagramming the object on the board, he requested those who recognized it to sketch it roughly in their notebooks, labeling each part properly. After a while, I saw him glance out the window, look at his watch, briefly discuss something with the graduate assistant, and leave the astonished class. I decided then to talk to the chairman.

Worn-Out Nouns

Let's admit it, most of us are basically lazy! If avoiding work is not too difficult or painful or costly or embarrassing, we'll do so. For example, in selecting nouns, we often rely on the same worn-out few, instead of struggling to find the precise one to explain exactly what we mean. Sometimes we sound like this:

I took this thing to the store because I needed a new thing to make it work. If they didn't have the right thing, maybe they could find some other thing to put in its place. But the man told me that they didn't have the thing and there wasn't anything else that would do the job. I don't think he cared a thing about helping me. So I told him a thing or two.

Here are some other catchall words you should try to avoid:

area	fashion	nature
aspect	field	process
case	kind	situation
factor	manner	type

Please don't misunderstand: you cannot always avoid these worn-out nouns. They are particularly necessary when referring to concrete objects, people, or qualities (a *case* of bourbon, the latest *fashion,* the *type* for the newspaper). But often you can eliminate them:

Before: In many *cases,* students fail to learn about career opportunities.

After: Many students fail to learn about career opportunities.

Before: The *nature* of this emergency *situation* called for drastic action.

After: This emergency called for drastic action.

Before: In the *field* of veterinary science, demand exceeds supply.

After: In veterinary science, demand exceeds supply.

Watch for these worn-out nouns and strike them out whenever possible.

Petrified Phrases

Often student writers turn to trite but true phrases that once may have been as pretty as a picture but now are as old as the hills. These students may think they are being as sharp as a tack, but the expressions, to make a long story short, are as dead as a doornail and as ugly as sin, being much the worse for wear. It goes without saying that it is penny wise but pound foolish to let them rear their ugly heads in your writing. If you do, you may even bore your own family although blood is thicker than water. Truer words were never spoken!

Hackneyed phrases, or clichés, such as these, once fresh and striking, have lost all their sparkle. They pop into our mouths when we talk, and in our haste to express ideas, we find them handy. But in writing we have an advantage: the time to search for other words in the first draft or a later one. Of course, sometimes the clichés cannot be avoided. In a particular context, you may find no effective substitute for "Variety is the spice of life." Use it, but realize that you are not being clever: give it as little emphasis as possible.

If you must use petrified phrases, try to limit yourself to those that are apt. The following, for example, may confuse rather than clarify:

brown as a berry
cool as a cucumber
fit as a fiddle
drunk as a lord
poor as a churchmouse
sick as a dog

Whenever you can, devise your own figurative language — similes, metaphors, or personifications. Here are some examples of these figures of speech:

Simile:	He looked as innocent as a first grader.
Metaphor:	Excessive team loyalty can be a disease that eats away good sportsmanship.
Personification:	Rumor scurried up and down the halls the day before busing began.

All three suggest a comparison. A simile does it explicitly or openly, signaling with the words *as* or *like* ("as a first grader"), a metaphor does it implicitly, not directly expressing the comparison ("can be a disease" = can be like a disease), and personification also works implicitly but by assigning human attributes to an inanimate object or abstraction ("Rumor scurried up and down" = Rumor was like a human being running around).

Of the three figures of speech, personification occurs least often in personal writing because it seems strained and artificial, especially when invoking such loftly abstractions as Life, Time, Nature, and Death. Metaphor is more common, often slipping unnoticed into our daily speech *(the light at the end of the tunnel, a foot in the door, break the ice)*. The test of a metaphor is to determine whether the comparison is literally possible. For example:

He is the captain.

Captain is not a metaphor because its literal meaning is not violated.

He is a rock in times of trouble.

Rock is a metaphor because a human being cannot literally be one.

Metaphors may be as simple as this example or they may be extended to great complexity, like this famous one by John Donne, presented in its original form:

No man is an *Iland,* intire of it selfe; every man is a peece of the *Continent,* a part of the *maine;* if a *Clod* bee washed away by the *Sea, Europe* is the lesse, as well as if a *Promontorie* were, as well as if a *Mannor* of thy *friends* or *thine* owne were; any mans *death* diminishes *me,* because I am involved in *Mankinde;* And therefore never send to know for whome the *bell* tolls; It tolls for *thee.*

— *Meditation XVII*

Here an abstract concept, the human community, is explained in two related parts of a geographical metaphor: we are not islands; we are parts of a continent.

Metaphor allows a writer to inform readers about something unknown or unfamiliar in terms that are easy to grasp and enjoyable to consider because of their imaginativeness and originality. Unfortunately, in straining for metaphors, writers sometimes produce artificial or mixed ones:

> He thought he had a key to the problem, but he found he did not get to the heart of it.

In the first clause, the problem is treated like a lock; in the second, like a human being. The resulting mixed metaphor is disconcerting and confusing.

Similar to metaphors are similes, explicit comparisons signaled by *as* or *like.* The metaphor "He is a rock" becomes a simile when the form is changed to "He is like a rock." Perhaps because they are more obvious and less compressed than metaphors, similes are easier to write, and thus more common, just as cars with automatic transmissions are easier to drive and thus more common.

ASSIGNMENTS

For Discussion

1 The first two sentences from a student's paper were discussed and revised in the opening pages of this chapter. Here are some of the following sentences from that paper. Replace the long, formal words with short, simple ones and change any other words or phrases that do not sound natural.

Therefore, I was restricted in the amount of places at which I could make application. However, after pursuing my objective for two days, I was given employment and informed that I was to commence my new occupation the following day. It was with great joy and excitement that I informed my parents that I had secured the position of manager of the sporting equipment shop at the state park, which was located in the immediate vicinity of our residence.

2 As was done on page 40, use each of the following very general words as the basis for a graduated list of increasingly specific words.

a game
b horse
c lamp
d collateral
e publication
f woman

3 In the following passages, the writers have substituted colorful verbs for prosaic ones. Identify them and discuss their effect. What figures of speech do you recognize?

a You would play upon me, you would seem to know my stops, you would pluck out the heart of my mystery, you would sound me from my lowest note to the top of my compass; and there is much music, excellent voice, in this little organ, yet cannot you make it speak. 'Sblood, do you think that I am easier to be played on than a pipe? Call me what instrument you will, though you can fret me, you cannot play upon me.

—William Shakespeare, *Hamlet*

b But even now, when there are flash floods on the high plateau, cocoa-colored gully washers come roaring and rejoicing down the side canyons.

—Robert Wallace, "Wooden Boats Plus Colorado Rapids Equals Adventure"

c Her hands trembled among the hooks and eyes, and her eyes had a feverish look, and her hair swirled crisp and crackling under the comb.

—William Faulkner, "Dry September"

d The rangy dog darted from between the wheels and ran ahead. Instantly two ranch shepherds flew out at him. Then all three stopped and with stiff and quivering tails, with taut straight legs, with ambassadorial dignity, they slowly circled, sniffing daintily.

—John Steinbeck, "The Chrysanthemums"

4 Analyze the language in the following letter from President Abraham Lincoln to General Ulysses S. Grant. Is the language natural, simple, concrete, and concise? How appropriate, sincere, and effective is the letter?

My Dear General:

I do not remember that you and I ever met personally. I write this now as a grateful acknowledgment for the almost inestimable service you have done the country. I wish to say a word further. When you first reached the vicinity of Vicksburg, I thought you should do what you finally did—march the troops across the neck, run the batteries with the transports, and thus go below; and I never had any faith, except a general hope that you knew better than I, that the Yazoo Pass expedition and the like could succeed. When you got below and took Port Gibson, Grand Gulf and vicinity, I thought you should go down the river and join General Banks; and when you turned northward, east of the Big Black, I thought it was a mistake. I now wish to make the personal acknowledgment that you were right and I was wrong.

Yours very truly,

For Writing

1 Rewrite the following student anecdote, adding specific details and verbs that contribute to the action.

After a collision, when we finally stopped moving, I opened my eyes. I was alive and so was my mother. I tried to get out of the car but my door was jammed. So I had to crawl out the back window. My mom got out finally when someone got her door open, but she couldn't really do anything for herself. The condition of the cars after impact made me feel small and powerless. Our car was not badly damaged, because we had a much heavier car; still the front, left side was completely crushed. There was broken glass everywhere, but when I looked at the other car I was completely horrified. It was about half the weight and size of our car. The remains of the vehicle looked like someone had taken parts of it and crumbled, crushed, and thrown these parts into the air to land wherever they pleased. The battery was on one side of the road and the radiator on the other.

2 Write three paragraphs relating the same event, but design each to appeal to a different sense. In the first, use concrete words that appeal to the sense of smell; in the second, the sense of sight; and in the third, the sense of hearing.

3 Write a brief narrative involving some incident you witnessed or experienced today that involved considerable activity—a game on campus, a traffic snarl, a last-minute scurry to class. Make sure that your choice of verbs contributes to the action.

Grammar, Usage, and the Many Voices of Language

Which of the following sentences would you consider grammatical?

1. a. Who did you go to the movies with?
   b. Whom did you go to the movies with?
   c. With whom did you go to the movies?
2. Are you gonna go with us or not?
3. Youse guys ain't got no natural smarts.
4. The argsters had flinly tooglized the stidments.
5. No dog the bones closet skeletal eats the in.
6. Every day he is asking me the same thing.

If you selected only the three versions in sentence 1, then you would agree with most people. Trained to equate the term *grammatical* with correctness, most people would probably consider sentence 2 sloppy, and would unhesitatingly classify 3 as "incorrect" or "bad" grammar. They would probably find 4, 5, and 6 perplexing and would probably feel uneasy about considering them as examples of English, much less of "good" or "correct" English.

But modern language researchers would find all the choices except 5 and 6 grammatical. Why the difference? Obviously, it is a matter of both definition and attitude: whether you consider "grammar" in terms of the whole language or only bits and pieces of it and whether you feel that language must be "correct" to be acceptable. It would be ideal if everyone would apply the same attitudes toward language use that they have about other social conventions, such as styles of clothing. They could then find that some uses are more appropriate in some situations than in others and some are not acceptable at all, not because they are "incorrect" but simply because they don't communicate. Then the choices in example 1 would be analogous to the clothing you choose for public occasions: 1a for everyday, "school" clothing; 1b and 1c for formal affairs when you need a tuxedo or a formal gown. The language used in examples 2 and 3 would compare to wearing blue jeans or cut-offs; that in number 4 to donning a barrel or a large paper bag that others recognize as body covering, but not as clothing. Sentence 5 seems as odd as clothing worn in the wrong places — socks on the hands, a mitten on the ear, a hat on the foot. Example 6 seems to be a foreigner, wearing clothing a little different from our styles. But most of us are unable to have this kind of relaxed attitude about the way we use language.

One reason for this perhaps is the grammar traditionally taught in our schools. For the most part, textbooks have been primarily concerned with prescribing acceptable choices among several possible ways of saying the same thing: recommending the "correct" choice between items such as *is/are; who/whom; I/me;* and *like/as.* Thus, grammar textbooks have dealt mainly with isolated language structures and their use, rather than with the total system of the language. For generations, they have instructed American students about whether it is more "correct" for plural subjects to take a singular or plural verb form, as in "Ham and eggs *is/are* good"; or whether pronouns like *somebody* should take singular or plural pronoun referents, as in "Somebody left *his/their* umbrella." Conversely, contemporary language scholars prefer not to classify these concerns about isolated usages as *grammar* but to define the term more carefully than is done in the traditional texts.

GRAMMAR

In current terminology, then, *grammar* has two meanings: it can refer either to the total underlying system or structure of a language (in our case, English), or to a description of that basic system. In the first sense, each language has only one grammar or underlying system, but in the second, a language may have many grammars, or ways of describing its system. In either of these current uses of the word, *grammar* involves the whole system, or all the available options of a language. Thus, any sentence or utterance within the structural limits of English is considered *grammatical.*

By *structural limits* we refer to any utterance of a native speaker that is recognized as a possibility of the language by other such speakers. For our purposes, native speakers of English are those beyond the age of six who have learned English as their first language, assuming, of course, that they have had general exposure to it.

With this understanding that any language structure possibly used by native speakers is grammatical, let's take another look at each of the examples that opened this chapter.

1. a. Who did you go to the movies with?
   b. Whom did you go to the movies with?
   c. With whom did you go to the movies?

Obviously, all three versions are grammatical because they could be used by any English speaker. Choice among them is based not on "correctness" but on a scale of formality. Sentence 1a would generally be considered less formal than the others and would be mainly acceptable in relaxed, casual situations. Traditional English might demand *whom* in place of *who*, despite the strong influence of the initial subject position that encourages the use of *who*. The last two examples illustrate more formal language influences, using *whom* as the object of the preposition *(with)*. These two would certainly be more suitable in situations requiring careful usage, with 1c being probably the most formal of the three.

2. Are you gonna go with us or not?

This example represents one possible spoken version of "Are you going to go with us or not?" and is certainly grammatical, being used by most native speakers. But on a formality scale it would be classed as highly informal, most appropriate to casual, spoken English.

3. Youse guys ain't got no natural smarts.

This sentence is also a grammatical possibility: nothing in it violates English structure; every element is recognizable to native speakers. However, because of the substitution of *youse* for the plural *you*, the occurrence of *ain't*, the double negative *ain't got no*, and the slang word *smarts*, the sentence would be rated very low on a formality scale; in fact, many people would consider it questionably acceptable and limited only to a small range of language situations.

4. The argsters had flinly tooglized the stidments.

In terms of the vocabulary and its meaning, this sentence is definitely not English; *the* and *had* are the only two recognizable words. But in terms of structure, it is grammatical; both the word order and the word forms are English. The suffixes *-ster*, *-ly*, and *-ize* belong to a group of commonly used derivational affixes in English that combine with meaning-carrying bases to form words traditionally called parts of speech: *young* + *-ster* produces the noun *youngster*; *happy* + *-ly* becomes the adverb *happily*; and *sterile* + *-ize* results in the verb *sterilize*. In addition to these derivational suffixes, another class of inflections such as the plural *-s* on *argsters* and *stidments* signals English structure. Elements such as these bases and suffixes are parts of English grammar that can be combined in many ways to form new words, as in example 4.

The "Englishness" of the sentence is also apparent in its word order, which is completely consistent with English grammar. "The argsters" and "the stidments" exhibit the structure of English noun phrases (Article [*the*] + Noun) in two normal English sentence positions: preceding and following a verb, as in

> The pirates   found   the treasure.
>   Subject   + Verb +   Object
> Noun phrase   Noun phrase

Also, the positions of "structure" words such as *the* (marking a noun phrase) and *had* (heading a verb phrase) signal particular grammatical structures in English. Thus, despite its non-sense, the sentence is structurally grammatical.

5. No dog the bones closet skeletal eats the in.

Despite its English vocabulary, this sentence is ungrammatical because the word order is random and violates those aspects of English word order described in example 3. By rearranging the sentence into normal order, you will discover that you innately know the necessary rules for reordering the words. What's more, you will be following patterns you apply every time you create a new sentence. You should realize, too, that any attempt at reordering will permit only limited possibilities: the most meaningful and least ambiguous rearrangement possible is "No dog eats the skeletal bones in the closet." This revised version fits English structure; it is grammatical. But the original does not, and is ungrammatical: no native speaker would utter it in serious communication.

6. Every day he is asking me the same thing.

This sentence is foreign to English. Native speakers could use either *has asked* or *asks,* but not *is asking* in this context; it is ungrammatical, violating modern English structure.

In this discussion we have indicated that, as native speakers, we often have a variety of choices, as in the three versions of example 1. We have also hinted that factors other than mere concern for grammatical structure are involved in our use of language. Our grammar, with its rich variety of structure, permits choice, but what influences that choice?

USAGE AND SOCIAL VALUES

One major influence on language choice is *custom.* For everyday purposes, we tend to use the language structures that we encounter most frequently at home, work, and play—the ones that seem most natural or comfortable. A second influence is the *situation* in which we use language. Language, after all, is a form of social behavior used mainly to communicate with other people who share the same language. As social behavior, language usage is tempered by the societal forces influencing other kinds of human interaction: the seriousness of the situation, the demands of established etiquette, and the ritualistic character of the event, to cite only a few. Our society demands a more subdued pattern of behavior at a funeral, for instance, than at a Saturday night dance. If we switched these behavioral modes, our social audience would be uncomfortable.

In language usage, another major influence is the *audience*. When you visit your grandparents, you probably leave your comfortable, faded jeans and sagging T-shirts in the closet and wear clothes more to their liking than yours, clothes that look more formal and that pinch here and there. Perhaps, without realizing it, you also tuck away your wardrobe of comfortable language usage and don a more respectable garb of words and sentences. For the easy, loose, slang vocabulary of your peers, you substitute more generally used words or even switch to the special vocabulary of your grandparents' generation. You may shift from a looser, more relaxed sentence form to a tighter, more concise wardrobe of sentences, substituting complete structures for the short idiomatic phrases and sentence fragments used in conversation with your friends. You consciously avoid usages that your elders would find crude or unacceptable, just as you avoid dressing in a way that might be offensive to them.

But whether you are with your closest buddies or your grandparents, whether you are in an intimate, relaxed situation or a formal one, you speak in the English *language;* you utilize structures of English *grammar;* but the choices you make in any social situation are in the province of *usage.* Let us now consider in more detail the various social influences on language usage. Most of this discussion of usage has centered—and will center—on spoken varieties of English and very little has been said about the written forms. But since you learn the spoken form first and use it more frequently, it is the primary form that influences the written language in many, sometimes very subtle ways. It is important, therefore, that as a writer of English, you know and understand some of these influences on your writing habits.

Robert C. Pooley, in *The Teaching of English Usage,* wrote that good usage lies in making choices in spoken or written English that are "appropriate to the purpose of the speaker, true to the language as it is, and comfortable to speaker and listener."[1] As a speaker of English, you should

---

[1] Robert C. Pooley, *The Teaching of English Usage* (Urbana, Ill.: National Council of Teachers of English, 1974), p. 12.

be able to write in your language in such a way that you are not cramped by the discipline of its structure, but at the same time you must accept its discipline and restraints if you wish to communicate effectively to your listeners.

Students sometimes fail to be concerned about audience reaction to their language usage. Instead, they often view their particular way of speaking as something not to be questioned or tampered with. But as a student of composition, you need to realize that language communication is a two-way process. Language communication is social behavior, and as such, its use involves a complex set of behavioral patterns. On the one hand, it is highly personal and individualized: each of us has a distinctive way of speaking and writing, just as each of us has a unique set of fingerprints or our own special ways of forming letters in our handwriting. And perhaps because language is learned in the context of early child-parent relationships and situations, its use becomes involved with all kinds of emotional attitudes. In a very real sense, it can be said that your language is *you*—an integral part of your personality and personal identity.

On the other hand, language is not used simply for self-gratification. As the most complex form of all human communication, it must operate with conventional structures and with usages shared by all members of the language community. You might, for instance, find fun in greeting your friends with "Dirky ratafratch" or "Morning to good you," but in doing so you would not provide them with much information. To communicate effectively you can't make up your own rules, but must respect the restraints the language community imposes, not only on grammatical possibilities but on word meanings as well. "The argsters had flinly tooglized the stidments" does not communicate, even though it satisfies the grammatical requirements of English. But a sentence that uses the same grammatical structure and at the same time adheres to the limitations of English meaning does achieve communication: "The youngsters had quickly summarized the arguments."

However, the demands of communication are not the only societal forces that influence language use. Certain language options may be given greater social value than others, even though the preferences may be completely arbitrary and may shift from one generation to another. Language uses, like clothing and hair styles, can lose or win public favor. An example of this is the double negative used for emphasis. The modern English community frowns upon usages like "I ain't got no money" or "I won't go noplace with you," but there was a time when this form was perfectly respectable. In Anglo-Saxon texts written a thousand years ago, the emphatic double negative occurs frequently. As recently as the early seventeenth century, it was permissible for Shakespeare to allow the most aristocratic of his characters to use it. For instance, in *Romeo and*

Juliet, Mercutio emphatically states, "I will not budge for no man's pleasure." If a modern Mercutio were to utter this challenge, a present-day, aristocratic Romeo would view him as a low-class hothead, rather than the high-class hothead he really was.

Usage changes, and so eventually does the grammar of a language. Major structural changes in language, such as many of those from Old English to Modern English, take place over centuries and not within the lifetime of any one individual; but because usages may become fashionable or taboo within a few years, speakers of a language must be prepared to adjust to the new values. The English you will speak when you are older will probably be grammatically the same as that you speak now. But it will be characterized by the loss of some present usages and the additions of others. These individual changes will be strongly influenced by your profession, your geographical location, your educational background, and your social group.

In summary, your language communication is shaped by two major forces, sometimes without your awareness: (1) your subconscious, built-in knowledge of the restraints and demands of English *grammar,* and (2) the *usage* dictates of social behavior. If you wish to communicate effectively, you must not only restrict your language to the possibilities of English structure, but you must also make it acceptable to your social community. As a college student, your social community is the college or university you attend. It will place its own special demands upon your English usage—demands that you may find distasteful at times. But as you become a successful participant in this new language community, you will fashion yet another garment to hang in your usage closet and will don it comfortably and easily when the social occasion demands it.

VARIETIES OF SPOKEN ENGLISH: DIALECTS

As we have indicated, although the grammar of a language is fairly static, usage is flexible. We all speak our own brand of English, and this is as it should be. But in writing to a general audience, we must continually decide which of our particular usages will aid communication and which will interfere with it. A knowledge of the forces shaping our language patterns and of the usages peculiar to the different varieties of American English can help us make those choices. In this discussion, we will briefly examine the geographical and social varieties of spoken English that skillful users of the language must be able to recognize.

Since we will use terms like *language* and *dialect* in a more specialized sense than you have perhaps encountered, we need to define and differentiate them. Previously, we referred to English as a "language," meaning that it is a systematic set of symbols used for communication, symbols both peculiar to and shared by a certain language community. English as a language is distinguished from others by the nature of its sound system, its grammar, and vocabulary. The differences in these three areas are so great from one language to another that two languages are never mutually intelligible. A speaker of German, for instance, cannot understand English without learning it as a second language, even though German and English are historically related languages. Despite some shared similarities of structure and vocabulary, German and English are different in more ways than they are alike.

But even within the confines of a given language, such as English, there is much variety. All people who speak English do not talk exactly alike. However, after perhaps some minor initial difficulties, we can understand one another with comparative ease because the varieties of English are more similar to one another than dissimilar. Such varieties sharing the same basic language patterns are called dialects. For our purposes, *dialect* refers to a variety of language containing most of the basic structures of English, but differing from other varieties in specific, habitual, patterned features of pronunciation, syntax, and vocabulary. In addition, to qualify as a dialect, a variety must be sustained over several generations.

Factors in the Creation of Dialects

Geographical limitations, social or ethnic influences, and infiltration of specialized jargon or vocabulary — all influence the language usages of a particular group.

First, geographical isolation has been responsible for varieties called geographical or regional dialects. Second, because of differences in educational background and economic advantages, some people speak a variety considered more or less prestigious than others, thus giving rise to social dialects. Third, variety can result when non-English-speaking people immigrate to this country and aspects of their native tongue are borrowed into English. The dialect known as Pennsylvania Dutch is an example of this. It retains some vocabulary and grammatical features of the German spoken by the settlers of that region of Pennsylvania. One well-known example has come into general English as a slogan: "We grow too soon old and too late smart." Finally, other varieties come from specialized occupational jargon, usually called *argot:* jazz musicians, coal miners, gangsters, and horse breeders are some groups that have such a specialized jargon. Words like *con, sting,* and *hook* have special meanings in the underworld argot.

Each of us is influenced by all these sources of variety. Our speech bears the stamp not only of our home geographical region but also of our social or ethnic backgrounds, and it includes elements of a specialized jargon. Your own jargon probably derives from the slang usage of your particular high school friends.

Geographical and social dialects usually meet all the qualifications of a true dialect, but occupational and ethnic varieties rarely encompass enough distinctive features or last long enough to be classified as a true dialect. For instance, occupational varieties usually differ from their geographical-social base only in vocabulary; that is why they are classed as argots rather than true dialects. Occasionally an argot does manifest pronunciation peculiarities, such as the horse industry's *hoss* for *horse,* but this is not a systematic feature; that is, it does not extend to other words rhyming with *horse,* such as *course, coarse,* and *force.* Ethnic varieties, such as the Irish-English spoken in Boston at the turn of the century, may last only through two generations, until the descendants of the original immigrant group are assimilated into the general language community, and therefore do not fit our definition of dialect.

Geographical Dialects: Three Main Regions

The English language is rich in regional dialects because of the massive migration of its speakers to many parts of the world. Today, because of separation from the English spoken in homeland Britain and the influence of local languages, many varieties of English exist throughout the world. In the United States, where English became the dominant language despite the many early French and Spanish settlers, three main geographical or regional dialects have evolved. Their distribution and peculiar characteristics are closely tied to the history of the British settlement of the New World and the geographical barriers the settlers encountered. The settlers of New England and the central Atlantic coastal states came largely from the eastern and southern parts of England, while later immigrants to the Piedmont areas came from north and northwest of London. The differences in their original dialects account for many of the present speech variations we encounter in these regions.

As the years passed, not only did the speech of these immigrants change from their parent dialects, but because of the mountain barriers, such as the Appalachians, and the lack of easy transportation and communication, each region acquired its own peculiar characteristics. Within a few generations, before the westward movement had gained great impetus, the coastal region had already developed many dialect characteristics that are still evident.

In the dialect studies initiated in the 1930s, Hans Kurath and his fellow researchers discovered that three distinct dialect regions exist along the east coast of the United States and that emigrants from these areas carried their speech characteristics with them as they moved across the continent to the west coast. The dialects—Northern, Midland, and Southern—share more language similarities than differences, of course, since all American dialects are mutually intelligible. However, each also demonstrates peculiar characteristics of pronunciation, grammatical structures, and vocabulary. But let's look first at their geographical distribution. The accompanying map shows a rough approximation of the main contemporary dialect areas of the United States.

—Adapted from Roger Shuy, *Discovering American Dialects*

NORTHERN DIALECT REGIONS

Northern dialect includes both Northeastern Northern (spoken in the New England area north of New York City) and Great Lakes Northern (spoken in the area surrounding the Great Lakes and extending north and west to the Rocky Mountains). The division of Northern into two subclasses results from the difference in the pronunciation of *r*. Northeastern Northern speakers pronounce a word like *mother* as *mothah*, whereas those in the Great Lakes region say *mother*, pronouncing the *r* sound after the vowel. Some Northeastern speakers also have an intrusive *r*; that is, they include an *r* sound between two vowels, as in John F. Kennedy's highly publicized pronunciation of *Cuber* for *Cuba* in such contexts as "*Cuba*(r) *and* the United States," in which *Cuba* ends with a vowel sound and *and* begins with one.

MIDLAND DIALECT REGIONS

Like the Northern, the Midland region is subdivided into two dialect areas, North and South Midland. As the map shows, the Midland region extends from the east coast across the central part of the United States, including the Appalachian region, the Midwest corn belt, and the states on the west coast. The dividing line between North and South Midland is roughly along Route 40, formerly the National Highway and now approximate to Interstate 70. The Midland area has been subclassified into North and South Midland mainly because of variant pronunciations in words like *greasy* (North Midland: greasy; South Midland: greazy) and in whether there is a *pin/pen* distinction. South Midlanders tend to pronounce the latter two words exactly alike, so that they often must be asked whether they mean "stickin' pins" or "writin' pins."

SOUTHERN DIALECT REGION

The Southern dialect area not only manifests the most variation within a speech region in the United States, but is also the smallest geographical area. During the nineteenth-century westward migration, Southern settlers were more limited by the laws prohibiting slavery in the new territories than by geographical barriers. If Southern families wished to move west, taking their slaves with them, they were confined to those areas where slavery was legal. The Southern dialect shares the pronunciation of *greasy* as greazy, the lack of *pin/pen* distinction, and similar vowel sounds with South Midland dialect, but lacks the *r* sound after vowels characteristic of Midland varieties.

DIFFERENCES IN PRONUNCIATION, VOCABULARY, AND GRAMMATICAL STRUCTURES

Whether or not the speakers of a region make a *pin/pen* distinction is only one of the specific ways in which dialects vary. Following is a chart listing a small but significant sampling of dialect differences:

	NORTHERN	MIDLAND	SOUTHERN
PRONUNCIATION FEATURES			
r after vowels	deleted in N.E. present in G.L.	present in all varieties in words like *wash* (warsh)	deleted
intrusive *r*	between vowels in some N.E. varieties	absent	absent

	NORTHERN	MIDLAND	SOUTHERN
PRONUNCIATION FEATURES			
pin/pen distinction	clear distinction	N.—clear distinction S.—no distinction	no distinction
pronunciation of *greasy*	greasy	N.—greasy S.—greazy	greazy
vowel contrast in *on/not*	no contrast (both rhyme with *hot*)	*on* pronounced as in *pond; not* rhymes with *hot*	same as Midland
VOCABULARY ITEMS			
animal with strong scent	skunk	skunk	polecat
small ground animal	chipmunk	ground squirrel	ground squirrel
nocturnal insect	firefly (urban) lightning bug (rural)	lightning bug fire bug	lightning bug
wild plants used for salad	———	greens salat (S. Midland)	greens, salad, salat
large sandwich	hoagie	submarine poor boy (S. Midland)	poor boy
GRAMMATICAL STRUCTURES			
nauseated	sick *to* my stomach	sick *on/in* my stomach	sick *at* my stomach
plural of *pair*	two *pair* of	two *pairs* of	two *pair* of
fifteen minutes before the hour	quarter *to,* quarter *of*	quarter *till*	quarter *till*

SIGNIFICANCE OF REGIONAL DIFFERENCES

Obviously, this discussion of American dialects has touched on only a few of the pronunciation, syntactical, and vocabulary differences in regional speech, but even from this small sample of socially acceptable features, it is clear that in the United States there is no one "correct" way of speaking. Instead, each geographical dialect has its own norm; each has its own cluster of pronunciations, its own grammatical and word usages that the majority of that region's people, including the most educated and influential, look upon as respectable English. In their spoken language, Americans do not impose a single "standard" dialect upon their speakers as people in other countries, such as France and England, have attempted to do. True, some Americans training for the stage or national broadcasting may adopt a leveled-off form of American English, sometimes referred to as "CBS" or "network" English, which avoids regional characteristics. But most cultured Americans talk in the voice of their home region, thus helping to preserve the flexibility of speech and the individuality that are so highly valued in our country.

Social Dialects

However strong a factor in language variety it is, geographical variety can account only in part for the complexity of speech patterns in the United States. A second influence, on both spoken and written English, comes from the many social dialects: clusters of language usages that become associated with social prestige and approval. In the preceding discussion of language, we emphasized that speakers place social values on certain usages: some are greatly respected and looked upon as standard; others, less respected, are therefore viewed as nonstandard. This value system seldom has a linguistic basis; it has to do with social snobbery rather than linguistic effectiveness. "Ain't nobody see nothin' " communicates to speakers of English just as effectively as the socially valued "Nobody has seen anything," and both are certainly grammatical possibilities of English. In fact, the former structure undoubtedly carries more emphasis than the latter, particularly when the accompanying intonation features of speech are added. But rightly or wrongly, the people who create the standards of speech in a language—a group made up of the majority of speakers, including the most educated and socially prestigious—would not generally accept as respectable the usage of "Ain't nobody see nothin'." Ironically, included in that majority are those who might themselves use the double negative, drop the verb inflection (*see* for *seen*), and include *ain't* as a regular dialect feature, but who consider such usages, even in their own speech, as "bad grammar."

To summarize, each geographical dialect region has a distinctive cluster of features that make up the norm or standard variety of the dialect —the prestigious social dialect. Other varieties within the regional dialect containing a pattern of usages considered socially unacceptable are looked upon as nonstandard. Thus, each regional dialect includes several social dialects: the standard form and a number of variants considered by the "standard" speakers to be "nonstandard." Many critics of this nonegalitarian classification refer to standard dialects as "Establishment English," that spoken by the educated and socially influential people in the community. Nonstandard varieties, on the other hand, are usually spoken by people less educated, less affluent, and generally less influential in the "power structure" of the community. Language use, then, whether we approve of the practice or not, becomes a tool of social prestige. The standard dialects, like a Cadillac or Rolls-Royce, indicate a more respected social position. The fact that the nonstandard forms, like a Volkswagen or Pinto, are just as functional as the standard forms is often obscured by highly emotional factors.

But the speech of a person who only occasionally uses an isolated nonstandard usage cannot be classified as a separate social dialect. To be thus classified, the speaker's language must be characterized by a set of patterned, distinctive features of pronunciation, vocabulary, and grammatical structures. If these features include a large number held in low esteem by other people in the society, then the dialect is considered a nonstandard social variety. Since "nonstandard" carries such snobbish connotations, we prefer to call them *community dialects* — subdialects within a regional variety that are limited to tightly integrated, close-knit social groups. The community dialects most thoroughly studied to date are those in the large urban centers settled largely by southern black people who migrated north for economic reasons. Because of their social isolation in the northern city ghetto, they have retained most of the features, both standard and nonstandard, of their Southern and South Midland origins.

The findings of these studies should help dispel some misconceptions about community dialects: (1) that there is only one standard dialect of spoken English and all else is nonstandard; (2) that nonstandard dialects are inferior to the standard in communication and reasoning power; and (3) that nonstandard variants are drastically different from standard dialects. Contrary to these misconceptions, current study has found that like regional varieties, social dialects are alike in more ways than they are different. Also, researchers like William Labov contend that "nonstandard" community dialects are far from being verbally deficient; he offers convincing evidence that they have the same abilities to express logical relationships and to communicate as effectively as do more socially acceptable dialects. In fact, Labov and others claim that some community dialect usages may be superior to standard ones. For instance, a person who creates sentences like "She working" and "She be working" can use them to make distinctions between present action and continuous action that standard speakers cannot make without the addition of adverbial modifiers—"She is working *now*" and "She works *every day*."[2]

Community dialects are usually more closely related to the regional dialect of their origin than to other community dialects; the ghetto English of Detroit, for instance, is more closely related in many ways to the Southern and South Midland regions where its speakers originated than to the nonstandard varieties of native Detroiters. However, many community dialects share some features considered nonstandard. For example, many widely separated community dialects omit third person singular, subject-verb agreement: "He *do* like it" for the more socially acceptable, "He *does* like it." Or they may share the same pattern of omitting verb auxiliaries and endings in verb phrases: "He been here" for "He's/has been here."

The speakers of any community dialect, whatever its characteristics might be, communicate fully with one another. It is only when a community dialect is used outside the group that certain usages might interfere. Just as some regional forms can temporarily impede communication and social interaction, so too can specialized community usages. The broader our personal social base becomes, the more "voices" we need. When we attempt to inform or persuade a widely divergent audience, then we should strive for a voice free of usages that would confuse or irritate some of those people. We should particularly avoid the following usages, claimed by Raven I. McDavid, Jr., to be those universally considered nonstandard throughout the United States.[3]

1. Very few pronunciation features would be considered unacceptable, except perhaps to the most hypercorrect listener. Probably the most universally questioned are the pronunciation of *thing/then* as *ting/den* and of the italicized sounds in *th*ree/bro*th*er as *f*ree/bru*vv*er.
2. The omission of inflections indicating noun plurals and possessives, as in "Those two boy ran away" and "We found Mr. Smith hat." These would be frowned upon in all regional dialect areas. So too would the deletion of the third person singular -*s* and of other verb inflections:

   He really bug me. (Omission of third person singular -*s*.)
   He scold me yesterday. (Omission of past tense inflected -*ed*.)
   He'd finish it at home. (Omission of past participle inflection: He'd [He had] finish*ed* it at home.)

3. The consistent omission of any element in a verb phrase, as in:

---

[2] William Labov, *The Logic of Nonstandard English,* Monograph Series on Language and Linguistics, No. 22 (Washington, D.C.: Georgetown University Press, 1969).
[3] Raven I. McDavid, Jr., "A Checklist of Significant Features for Discriminating Social Dialects," *Dimensions of Dialect,* ed. Eldonna Everts (Urbana, Ill.: National Council of Teachers of English, 1967), pp. 7–10.

He a good boy *for* He *is* a good boy.
He been drinking *for* He *has* been drinking.
I going home *for* I *am* going home.

4. Deviant case inventions:

Those are our'*n for* Those are ours.
He told me his*self for* He told me hi*m*self.
Them hot dogs were good *for Those* hot dogs were good.

Although the list is surprisingly short, it is highly significant because it provides the usages that should be avoided by all speakers and writers trying to communicate with a general audience. But, as a student writer, you cannot assume that these are the only items that might be unacceptable to members of your audience, many of whom will have regional preferences, hypercorrect biases, or just plain distaste for certain usages. But if one of these critics, even a teacher, questions a word or its pronunciation, or your use of a grammatical structure, you can expect the objection to be justified on grounds other than that it is nonstandard. For instance, a usage can legitimately be questioned if it does not seem appropriate to your social situation or to your audience, or if it violates the effect you are trying to achieve. Language usage appropriate to one writing assignment could be unacceptable for another: vocabulary perfectly acceptable to your peers, such as in the statement "Seeing that movie is a *must,*" may fall offensively on the ear of a middle-aged English teacher. Or the use of colloquially acceptable idiomatic structures may mar the tone of a paper written to persuade a well-educated audience of doctors or lawyers.

When you write, you should remember that all usages—even those in our nonstandard listing—are relative to the language situation. Just as some standard speakers might be offended by usages they consider nonstandard, so might speakers of community dialects, having many of our listed items as regular dialect features, find "correct" forms offensive. In highly personal interrelationships, we must tailor our language usages to the situation and the moment. But in communicating with a general audience, you as a person committed to effective communication should attempt to avoid generally unacceptable usages and the special vocabulary of community dialects, just as a network TV announcer omits features of specific geographical dialects.

FROM SPOKEN DIALECTS TO WRITTEN ENGLISH

In talking, we speak mainly to other people from our dialect region or to people who accept our speech patterns. As long as we write to that same audience, particularly if it is on a personal, informal basis—letters, diary entries, narratives, or even local editorials—we can operate almost as freely in the written language as in the spoken, following only the restrictions of purpose, audience, or occasion discussed earlier in this chapter. But when we write to a large, general audience with a wide variety of language patterns, we face the same problems as the national broadcasters. Like Walter Cronkite and John Chancellor, to ensure maximum communication we strive for a variety of English that contains grammatical and word usages common to all the regional dialects and acceptable to all social dialects. We avoid regionalisms such as the word *cooter* because that would communicate only to people from the deep South, who would recognize it as a synonym for *turtle.* If syntactical constructions such as in "I *might could* go" or "I *feel like that* it might be worthwhile" exist as acceptable usages in our own regional area, we are expected to avoid them in writing, not because they are "incorrect," but because all those in the reading audience who speak another dialect would find these usages confusing or jarring. Similarly, we adopt the usages of a generalized, standard English to ensure maximum communication. Of course, in free, personal writing and in narrative attempting to be realistically accurate, written English, particularly dialogue, is enhanced by regional and social usages. But in writing designed to inform or persuade a wide, divergent audience, the writers adopt a new dialect —one that has universal features, rather than regional ones or those of a particular social group. Writers do this even if it means sacrificing some of their individuality and the regional flavor characteristic of their spoken English.

GLOSSARY OF USAGES FOR REFERENCE IN PERSONAL WRITING

Personal writing permits the widest range of language usage, particularly when you are striving to create your most natural, intimate, and honest voice. This is best achieved when you stay as close as possible to your normal spoken language style, particularly in writing a journal, autobiographical narrative, or dialogue. The intimate nature of writing from personal experience demands little restraint in using slang, colloquial idioms, or usages that might be considered inappropriate or unacceptable for other writing purposes.

Even personal writing is characterized by more than one level of conversational English. For your nondialogue passages—descriptive and explanatory sections—you should select usages that are generally acceptable to most informal, colloquial situations. Dialogue, however, permits a wider range of possibilities—even the slang vocabulary and nonstandard usages of a community dialect when appropriate.

All the same, you need to follow a few guidelines and exercise some discretion. You should be aware that many readers — even in an audience close to your age and interests — may be offended by an overdose of profanity or confused by highly specialized jargon, such as street slang, the argot of jazz, or the in-language of drag racing. If you are constantly sensitive to your audience and are judicious about the words you put into your characters' mouths, most readers will tolerate usages they might otherwise find offensive.

Making usage choices can often be confusing even to experienced writers. To help you develop your own guidelines for personal writing, we offer the following suggestions about some troublesome items. Remember, all are appropriate for dialogue.

adjective comparison

Traditionally, adjectives of one or two syllables add the comparative suffix *-er* for comparing two items and the superlative *-est* for comparing more than two. Multisyllabic adjectives substitute the intensifiers *more* and *most* for *-er* and *-est*. Many reputable speakers use the superlative *-est* when comparing only two items, particularly when special emphasis is desired or when the number being compared is unclear.

He is the *most* erudite of the two.
May the *best* man win.

Both are acceptable for most uses in written English except in formal writing.

Except in dialogue, double comparisons, formed by using both the intensifier and the suffix, are viewed with disfavor in written English:

She is *more* smart*er* than her sister.
She is the *most* happi*est* person I know.

adverbs (-*ly*)

Although most adverbs in modern usage end in *-ly*, there are a number of instances when an adverb has the same form as an adjective or has two adverb forms, and it is in these instances that usage choice becomes a problem.

That is a *fast* car. (adjective acceptable)
He runs *fast*. (adverb acceptable)

He is a *good* runner. (adjective acceptable)
He runs *good*. (adverb unacceptable)
He runs *well*. (adverb acceptable)

Some adverbs, like *slow,* present an even greater usage problem because they not only resemble an adjective in form, but have two acceptable adverb possibilities, as an uninflected form and with the *-ly* suffix.

He threw a *slow* ball. (adjective acceptable)
Drive *slow*. (adverb acceptable)
He *slowly* chewed the candy. (adverb acceptable)

Although the *-ly* forms are generally preferred in most writing, make sure that you do not add them to adverbs that are normally uninflected; otherwise you will create hypercorrect monstrosities such as:

Thusly, the war came to an end. (unacceptable)
Funnily enough, he couldn't find his own house. (unacceptable)

almost/most as adverbs

In spoken English, there is very little resistance to the use of *most* in situations that would traditionally require *almost*. However, written English does have restrictions.

Most everyone arrived late. (acceptable in spoken English)
Almost everyone arrived late. (preferred usage in written English)
He is *most* the kindest person I know. (unacceptable in written English; *almost* is obligatory here)

between/among

Traditionally, *between* is preferred when referring to two items, *among* when more than two. This distinction is still observed in formal writing. In modern usage, however, *between* is acceptable in almost all instances involving more than two, unless the context obviously refers to a group engaged in collective action.

The four men divided the skimpy lunch *between* themselves. (individuals dividing one with another)
The four men agreed *among* themselves on a course of action. (group deciding on a collective action)

A rather common usage, questionable even in personal writing, is that of following *between* with a subject-form pronoun.

Between John and *I*/Between *he* and *I*, we ate the whole thing. (unacceptable subject-form pronouns)
Between John and *me*/Between *him* and *me*, we ate the whole thing. (acceptable object-form pronouns)

negatives, multiple

Multiple negatives are generally unacceptable in all forms of written English except dialogue. Acceptable negatives in English are formed by negating only one element of the sentence—subject, verb, or object. One negative rules out the need for any others, as these examples show:

No crisis was ever quite like it.

Nobody knows anything about it.
(one negative element attached to the subject—makes the whole statement negative)

Harry *did not/didn't* understand the question. (one negative element attached to auxiliary verb)

He had heard *no* sound in the house. (one negative element preceding the object noun)

The following examples of multiple negatives are considered unacceptable in written English except in realistic dialogue.

Ain't nobody seen *nothin'*.
Nobody ain't seen *nothin'*.
(negative added to subject, verb, and noun following the verb)

He *don't* know *nothin'*. (negative added to auxiliary verb and to object of verb)

However, several kinds of double negatives are acceptable, but have rather restricted use, even in spoken English. Since these negatives can be vague or confusing to readers, they should be avoided even in personal writing.

The meaning is *not* altogether *unclear*. (*not* plus the *un-* negative)
He *couldn't* very well *not* have seen it. (rare, used only for special emphasis)
Everybody *doesn't* like something, but *nobody doesn't* like Sara Lee. (one of the rare times when two negatives do in fact make a positive)

nouns

Another usage puzzle involves the different kinds of nouns in English and how they operate in the grammar. Although these present no real problems in dialogue, there are usage preferences for all other writing situations. Most usage problems involving nouns derive from two sources: subject-verb agreement and the kinds of determiners that precede a noun. Choice depends largely upon how the noun is classified. Here are some examples:

1. Count nouns—two-form nouns that can show plurality in some way and that can be preceded by numbers (for example, one bird; two books; three teeth; four deer).

   Singular count nouns take a singular verb:

   One girl *is*   One goose *is*   One deer *is*

   Plural count nouns take a plural verb:

   Two girls *are*   Two geese *are*   Two deer *are*

Articles with count nouns: The articles *a/an* can be used only with singular count nouns and carry the connotation of indefinite quality.

A book is on the table. (Meaning any single book)

The before a singular count noun makes it more definite:

The book is on the table. (refers to a particular book)

2. Mass nouns—one-form nouns that refer to qualities, substances, or masses.
    In American English, most mass nouns take a singular verb.

    Glass *has* been used for windows for many years.
    Wheat *has* become a political issue.
    The government *needs* dedicated leaders.

    Article use:

    Milk is a good food for babies. (absence of determiner makes the mass noun *milk* indefinite)
    The bread is on the table. (*the* makes the noun more definite)

3. Defective plural nouns—nouns with only one form: *pliers, cattle, pants, trousers, scissors.* Generally, plural verbs are used with such items. To make them singular, a "count" phrase such as *a pair of, a head of, a lot of* is usually added:

    The pliers *are* on the table. (defective plural noun with plural verb)
    A pair of pliers *is* on the table. (singular verb agrees with singular *pair*)

    Some mass nouns, such as *couple,* can also behave like defective plural nouns. With such nouns the choice of a singular or plural verb varies from writer to writer. Some people feel comfortable with "The couple *are* going to spend their honeymoon in Jamaica," while others feel constrained to use the singular *is.*

possessives

Writing problems stemming from possessive usage are of several kinds. One arises from the tendency of some social dialects to omit the noun possessive -'s altogether, as in "John old lady house on fire." Acceptable in journal writing or in dialogue, this usage is considered unacceptable elsewhere.

A second usage problem involves punctuation. Many students omit the apostrophe or confuse the possessive form with plurals or third person singular verbs because all three forms add -*s.*

Unacceptable	Acceptable
Johns house is on fire.	John's [singular possessive] house is on fire.
The sisters parents' died in their early thirties.	The sisters' [plural possessive] parents [plural] died in their early thirties.
He strongly regret's his past action.	He strongly regrets [third person singular verb] his past action.

Pronoun and demonstrative possessives also create choice problems. Students sometimes mistakenly substitute noun possessive punctuation for pronoun possessives, particularly with *its* and *theirs:* "Don't fire until you feel *it's* breath on your face" should be "Don't fire until you feel *its* breath on your face." *It's* is the contracted form of *it is,* not a possessive pronoun. Another problem involves substitution of the object form *them* or *him* respectively for *those* or *his.* This usage is considered unacceptable for most writing purposes.

Those apples don't look as ripe as the others. (acceptable)
Them apples don't look as ripe as the others. (unacceptable)

That's John's and *his* baseball. (acceptable)
That's John and *him* baseball. (unacceptable)

verb usage

Most verbs in English are regular; that is, the spelling *-d* or *-ed* is added to form both the past tense and the past participle form:

Present	Past	Past Participle
kick	kicked	kicked

But because many verbs in English are irregular, they create usage headaches. These problems are intensified by two factors: (1) many irregular verbs are used frequently; and (2) many have more than one acceptable past or past participle form. Even though this makes irregular verbs seem chaotic, they do fall into certain patterns. Being aware of these patterns may help you make appropriate choices.

1. Irregular verbs whose past and past participle forms are identical but differ from the present tense.
   a. *-d* in the spelling of the present tense form changes to *-t:*

Present	Past	Past Participle
lend	lent	lent
send	sent	sent
spend	spent	spent

b. *-ee-* and *-ea-* spellings change to *-e-;* present tense vowel sound rhymes with *beet;* past and past participle vowel sound rhymes with *bet:*

Present	Past	Past Participle
breed	bred	bred
bleed	bled	bled
feed	fed	fed
flee	fled	fled
lead	led	led
leave	left	left

Some irregular verbs following this pattern also add *-t* to the past and past participle forms:

Present	Past	Past Participle
creep	crept	crept
feel	felt	felt
weep	wept	wept

c. *-ou-* spelling in past and past participle (pronunciation varies):

Present	Past	Past Participle
bring	brought	brought
bind	bound	bound
grind	ground	ground
seek	sought	sought
think	thought	thought
wind	wound	wound

d. Past and past participle vowel spelling changes to *-u-:*

Present	Past	Past Participle
dig	dug	dug
fling	flung	flung
sting	stung	stung
swing	swung	swung
slink	slunk	slunk

e. Miscellaneous:

Present	Past	Past Participle
make	made	made
mean	meant	meant
win	won	won

2. A second class of irregular verbs consists of those with three differ-

ent forms, the past participle adding the suffix *-n* or *-en*:

Present	*Past*	*Past Participle*
blow	blew	blown
break	broke	broken
freeze	froze	frozen
give	gave	given
go	went	gone
grow	grew	grown
ride	rode	ridden
throw	threw	thrown
write	wrote	written

3. A third set of irregular verbs shows a vowel change (in both spelling and pronunciation) in the past and past participle forms:

Present	*Past*	*Past Participle*
begin	began	begun
ring	rang	rung
fly	flew	flown
see	saw	seen

4. Many verbs in modern English have more than one acceptable form. Some of the more commonly used of these verbs are:

Present	*Past*	*Past Participle*
beat	beat	beaten, beat
broadcast	broadcasted, broadcast	broadcasted, broadcast
dive	dived, dove	dived
forget	forgot	forgotten, forgot
get	got	got, gotten
hide	hid	hidden, hid
kneel	knelt, kneeled	knelt, kneeled
light	lighted, lit	lighted, lit
prove	proved	proven, proved
show	showed	shown, showed
wake	waked, woke	waked, woke, woken

In addition to the usage problems involving the choice of form, there are all kinds of sticky decisions involving verb phrases. We shall deal with only a few of the most acute here.

1. *Be.*

Many American dialects omit the verb *be* as either a main verb or an auxiliary. Except in dialogue writing, these omissions are universally considered unacceptable.

Unacceptable	*Acceptable*
Jack a good teacher.	Jack is a good teacher.
They going home.	They are going home.

Some social dialects have two peculiar usages involving *be* to express variant degrees of continuing time. Both are unacceptable in writing, except in a journal or dialogue.

Unacceptable	*Acceptable*
His mother working.	His mother is working [now].
His mother be working.	His mother works *or* His mother works all the time.

2. *Have* as an auxiliary verb.

   In both spoken English and in personal writing, we usually contract the forms of *have* (have, has, had) in verb phrases such as "I've never noticed that." This practice leads to two writing usage problems, both inappropriate except for dialogue:
   a. Deletion of *have* altogether:

   I been there.

   b. Substitution of *of* for *-'ve:*

   I should *of* known it *for* I should*'ve* known it.

3. Passive forms.

   Modern English has two ways to show passive:
   a. The auxiliary *be* plus the past participle form of the verb:

   She *was* see*n* by many people.

   (For further discussion, see Chapter 27.)
   b. The auxiliary *get* plus the past participle:

   They *got* disgust*ed* and left.

   This is widely used in informal, spoken English. It is acceptable in all personal writing situations, but it should be avoided in more formal writing.

verb phrases, contracted

In personal writing, a simple, yet highly effective device for achieving a natural voice is to use the verb contractions so common to spoken English. We*'re* going; We*'ve* seen her; He*'s* a good friend; I*'m* not sure—all are highly appropriate for all personal writing purposes from journal entries to personal essays. Just remember that they require the apostrophe to indicate the omissions (we + are = we're; "a" is omitted and replaced by an apostrophe).

you (indefinite pronoun)

You meaning "you, the reader," is now widely used except in formal English.

Future shock occurs when you are confronted by the fact that the world you were educated to believe in doesn't exist.

—Postman and Weingartner, "Crap Detecting"

You meaning "anyone in general and no one in particular," though commonly used in spoken English, should be avoided in all written English, if for no other reason than that it often results in a poor writing style.

The first thing you see is a table of steaming crabs. (questionable usage in a student paper)

(For more discussion of indefinite pronouns, see Chapter 20.)

ASSIGNMENTS

For Discussion

1 What distinctions are made between grammar and usage?
2 According to the definition of *grammatical* developed in this chapter, which of the following examples are grammatical? Discuss the social acceptability and communicative effectiveness of each example. (Read them aloud before deciding.)

   a Ja eat yet?
   b Where's he at?
   c Ask him where is he.
   d Ain't nobody seen nothin' around here.
   e "Twas brillig, and the slithy toves
      Did gyre and gimble in the wabe."
         —Lewis Carroll, "Jabberwocky"
   f The question is, who's fooling who?
   g At what are you looking?
   h What are you looking at?
   i He's never at home when I call.

3 Analyze the following three passages. What does the usage in each reveal about the situational context? How do vocabulary and structure indicate situation and audience?

   a Well, it's been over an hour. Things are getting dull. Walking block after block. Where are we, 5th? Who cares? The walk will do you good. But the County building's just up ahead; things will liven up then.

City Hall. The pigs are there, all lined in their sty. Get them with bottles? What are they anyhow?

They're running with dogs, all they do is oppress us — the people. We should destroy the animals.

Fall back, they're charging, don't trip, someone did. Better get up, did they beat him? Probably. Don't run, walk. Remember Washington! Remember Chicago! We must walk, not run — that's the favorite riot shout.

— Rich Perloff, "Caught in the Dreams of Revolution"

b The ketch *Palawan* is built of aluminum, with one-quarter-inch maximum thickness, so we were very cautious about our predicament. Visions of various Arctic explorers frozen in over a winter; visions of how we would explain to our friends what had happened to our vessel; visions of how a helicopter would have to come from Thule to rescue us; visions of dealing at close quarters with water temperatures of 33 degrees F. — all sorts of unpleasant visions of being considered not intrepid explorers but amateur troublemakers — crossed our minds. We cautiously backed the boat into an open lead, and after three hours of work, were able to get her turned around and headed to the open sea.

— Thomas J. Watson, Jr., "Sailing in the Arctic Is a New
Challenge for a Yachtsman," *Smithsonian*

c And so, my fellow Americans: ask not what your country can do for you — ask what you can do for your country.

My fellow citizens of the world: ask not what America will do for you, but what together we can do for the freedom of man.

Finally, whether you are citizens of America or citizens of the world, ask of us here the same high standards of strength and sacrifice which we ask of you. With a good conscience our only sure reward, with history the final judge of our deeds, let us go forth to lead the land we love, asking His blessing and His help, but knowing that here on earth God's work must truly be our own.

— John F. Kennedy, "Inaugural Address"

4 Discuss the differences between a language and a dialect as defined in this chapter.
5 Chinese has many varieties, which are often referred to as dialects. However, a number of them, such as Mandarin and Cantonese, are mutually unintelligible. According to our definitions, how would they be classified?
6 Have you ever had difficulty communicating with a person from a dialect region different from yours? Or have you ever been confused by regional names when traveling outside your geographical area? Discuss.

7   Underline or write in the blanks the word you use for the following
    items. If there is a wide diversity of answers in the class, try to
    establish the regional source of each word.[4]

    a   Halloween greeting: trick or treat, tricks or treats, beggar's night,
        help the poor, Halloween!, give or receive, _____

    b   Landing on stomach when diving: belly-flop, belly-flopper,
        belly-bust, belly-buster, _____

    c   Be truant from school: bag school, bolt, lay out, play hookey, play
        truant, ditch, flick, flake school, blow school, _____

    d   Drinking fountain: cooler, water cooler, bubbler, fountain, drink-
        ing fountain, _____

    e   Knee-length pants worn by men: shorts, bermuda shorts, ber-
        mudas, walking shorts, knee pants, knee knockers, pants,
        _____

    f   Knee-length pants worn by women: shorts, bermudas, walking
        shorts, pants, _____

    g   Location of instruments in automobile: dash, dashboard, instru-
        ment panel, panel, crash panel, _____

    h   Device for accelerating an automobile: accelerator, gas, gas pedal,
        pedal, throttle, _____

    i   The car needs _____: a grease job, lubrication, a lube job, to be
        greased, to be lubed, servicing, to be serviced, _____

    j   New limited access road: turnpike, toll road, freeway, parkway,
        post road, tollway, thruway, expressway, _____

    k   Place where an audience watches movies in their cars: drive-in,
        drive-in movie, outdoor movie, outdoor theater, open-air movie,
        passion pit, _____

8   Compare slang terms for the following items with other members of
    your class or friends in the dormitory:

    a   an automobile   h   an unpleasant person
    b   a policeman   i   money
    c   a party   j   a homosexual (male and female)
    d   an attractive male   k   marijuana
    e   an attractive female   l   being drunk or high
    f   an unattractive male   m   a conceited male
    g   an unattractive female   n   a conceited female

9   What is meant by the terms *standard* and *nonstandard* dialects? Who
    sets language standards and how?

---

[4] Examples taken from Roger Shuy, *Discovering American Dialects* (Urbana, Ill.: National Council of Teachers of English, 1967).

10 Why is it difficult to find a social dialect (standard or nonstandard) that would be consistent throughout the United States in vocabulary, syntax, and pronunciation? What are some of the characteristics shared by nonstandard community dialects of American English?

11 Look up the listed items in any two of these three books (available in the reference room of the library). Do they agree? Discuss.

Bryant, Margaret M. *Current American Usage* (1962).

Evans, Bergen and Cornelia. *A Dictionary of Contemporary American Usage* (1957).

Follett, Wilson. *Modern American Usage* (1966).

a	*the reason is because*	**e**	*can* and *may*
b	*ensure/insure*	**f**	*lie/lay*
c	*hangs, hung/hanged*	**g**	*sit/set*
d	*dive, dove/dived*		

12 Currently, *plus* is increasingly used as a conjunction to substitute for *and* and *in addition to,* as in: "She expected her tour of France to be very educational. *Plus* she planned to buy a lot of new clothes." Check several recent dictionaries to see if this usage is noted. Note all the occurrences of the usage that you encounter over a two- or three-week period. Jot them down on 3 x 5 cards, indicating the age and educational background of the user. Compare your findings with those collected by the other members of your class. Decide on the appropriateness of the usage.

For Writing

1 In the following selections are usages generally considered unacceptable for many writing purposes. Replace the questionable ones with standard forms. Then write a letter to the local school board justifying the original usages.

a The father grunted. "I'll be bound. If there was trouble there, I'll be bound he was in it. You tell him," he said violently, "if he lets them yellow-bellied priests bamboozle him, I'll shoot him myself quick as I would a reb."

—William Faulkner, *Light in August*

b David sat down. Fascinated, he stared at the shining cogs that moved without moving their hearts of light. "So wot makes id?" he asked. In the street David spoke English.

"Kentcha see. Id's coz id's a machine."

"Oh!"

"It wakes up mine fodder in de mawning."

"It tells yuh w'en yuh sh'd eat an' w'en yuh have tuh go tuh sleep. It shows yuh w'ea, but I tooked it off."

"I god a calenduh opstair's," David informed him.

"Puh! Who ain' god a calenduh?"

"I save mine. I godda big book outa dem, wit numbuhs on id."

"Who can't do dat?"

"But mine fodder made it," David drove home the one unique point about it all.

—Henry Roth, *Call It Sleep*

c   "There was her hens," suggested Mrs. Fosdick, after reviewing the melancholy situation. "She never wanted the sheep after that first season. There wa'n't no proper pasture for sheep after the June grass was past, and she ascertained the fact and couldn't bear to see them suffer; but the chickens done well. I remember sailin' by one spring afternoon, an' seein' the coops out front o' the house in the sun. How long was it before you went out with the minister? You were the first ones that ever really got ashore to see Joanna."

—Sarah Orne Jewett, *The Country of the Pointed Firs*

2   Write a paragraph describing the dating activities of your high school crowd, using the group's vocabulary.

3   Write a second paragraph describing the same activities but addressing yourself to a general audience.

4   Describe an event typical of your home region that attracts many kinds of people, such as an arts and crafts fair; a drag race; a state or county fair; a street fair or festival. Use words and expressions you hear at home but not in other places.

Special Assignment

The following student sentences contain items that would be unacceptable for most writing purposes other than dialogue. Rewrite them so that they are more acceptable to a general audience.

1   *Boomsville* warns that unless we change ourselves we will continue to make our grandparents mistakes.

2   I never tried to beat nobody out of nothing since I been in this world.

3   The easy turn consist of staying directly behind the boat all through the turn.

4   The only reasons I can think for closing on Sunday is religious beliefs, to give one day free of commercialism or because of custom.

5   Its their business and they should be allowed to stay open by choice.

6   The television series *All in the Family* with Archie Bunker as it's star can be a hilariously funny, but at the same time, anger provoking program.

7   We parked the motorcycle on the side of the hill and climbing up.
8   The clothes were all hung neatly in the closet like tuxedo on a rack in a formal dress shops.
9   The inspector opened the door only to found himself coughing and gasping for air.
10 The city must also possessed a bakery because loaves of bread have been found with a baker's stamp.
11 In my Junior year, I drop math altogether.
12 To have a best friend—a confidant with whom you can share innermost thoughts—is something of great value to me.
13 They was from a different school and really thought I was somebody.
14 Our new three-way situation began the stress between us all.
15 The seat cover and the carpet on the driver's side is thread-bare.
16 It would be impossible for me to think of life in this way, but I have come awful close.
17 On the other three day I most had a fight with my sisters.
18 When we came back, me and Russell played baseball.
19 What's you going to do?
20 The bed were made so careful that not even a single wrinkle was visible.
21 By the middle of the year my talent growed even more.
22 An infinite number of pants, shirts, socks, and shoes, along with the blankets from unmaded beds scattered about the floor made the room look as though a tornado had pass through it.
23 It would maked a stockyard smell like a bakery.
24 It would be impossible for one college freshman with an hangover to clean up a room that looked and smelled like a garbage dump.
25 After a hour of cleaning, the room was presentable again.
26 We sawed the monster movie at the drive-in.
27 He ain't gone nowheres.
28 We be using a new set of books in my high school.
29 They no be home; they be work.
30 I brung everything she told me to.

Sentence Strategies in Personal Writing

SIMPLE SENTENCES

The police did not come. In my agitation I found myself beside Ruth First whose article I had not written. She didn't seem to mind at all. Time passed and the knots began to shred away slowly. I joined the head-shaking people making their way to the Anglican Mission in Proes Street, shaking my head as I went. I looked back. There was no one on the pavement outside the old synagogue. The police had also left.

— Alfred Hutchinson, *Road to Ghana*

This passage is taken from an autobiographical narrative describing the release of a number of black political hostages after two years in prison. If you read it aloud, you will find that the short sentences encourage fast reading, thus heightening the sense of action and urgency in the situation. With the exception of a few sentences in the passage, most are what we traditionally call simple sentences. Actually, the term *simple* is a little misleading because it connotes short, simple-minded sentences, and simple sentences need not be all that simple. In the above paragraph, there are some short examples: "I looked back," "The police did not come," and "The police had also left." But what of "I joined the head-shaking people making their way to the Anglican Mission in Proes Street, shaking my head as I went"? Although not short, it too fits the traditional definition of a simple sentence as one that consists of only one independent clause.

And what is an *independent clause*? First, a look at what a clause is.

This term refers to a grammatical structure made up of a subject, a verb, and usually a complement following the verb. An independent clause is one that can stand by itself as a complete sentence. The subject-verb-complement structure of such a single-clause sentence is easily identified in "I looked back": *I* is the subject; *looked* is the verb; the complement in this case is *back,* an adverb. Other SVC structures can have other kinds of complements, as we will see later. Sentences that are stripped down to this underlying SVC clause structure are the basic sentence patterns in English—the raw materials from which we build all sentences, from the most simple to the most complex. We can add to one of the basic patterns; reorder the elements; join several together in various ways; omit parts to produce sentence fragments, as we often do in conversation ("Where's the milk?" *"In the refrigerator."*).

The basic sentence patterns in English that share the SVC structure are limited in number (no more than eleven or twelve), but they can be used to produce an almost infinite variety of sentences. And although all have a subject, a verb, and a complement, each is characterized by a particular kind of verb and complement. Here's how the most commonly used basic patterns look in reference to the SVC scheme. (Reminder: *transitive* verbs are those that take objects; *intransitives* do not; and *linking* verbs simply establish a direct link of meaning between the subject and the complement, as in "Mary seems intelligent.")

S (*Subject*)	V (*Verb*)	C (*Complement*)	
The professor	was jogging. (intransitive verb)		
The professor	was jogging (intransitive verb)	tirelessly. (adverb)	
The student	saw (transitive verb)	the professor. (direct object)	
The student	gave (transitive verb)	the professor (indirect object)	a note. (direct object)
The professor	seemed (linking verb)	happy. (adjective)	
The student	is (linking verb *be*)	his friend. (predicate noun)	
The students	made (transitive verb)	Henry (direct object)	the student representative. (object complement)

In personal writing you should feel free to use many short, simple sentences because they suggest casual conversation, though the practice may be discouraged in other college writing. Even in personal narrative, if overused they sound like a "Dick and Jane and Spot" primer. However, for some purposes, as in the opening example, piling up a series of simple sentences that closely follow the basic sentence patterns can be very effective: to describe a fast-moving, violent, exciting, or suspenseful action and to establish a breathless, dramatic quality. Here's an effective student example using such sentences:

Suddenly we heard a scream. Ahead a man was pulling a young child into a car. We started to run towards it. He slammed the door and started the car. The child continued to cry. We reached the car and banged on the window. Then the car moved away. I saw the license plate: Michigan WN 69837. I kept repeating it aloud: Michigan WN 69837. Michigan WN 69837. Then I dashed to a nearby telephone booth, luckily found a dime in my pocket, dialed "Operator" and told her to write down: Michigan WN 69837. I explained, gave her my name and address, and hung up. Then I burst into tears. I didn't stop until Jane drove me home and Mother hugged me and comforted me. I don't know why I was terrified. Perhaps it was the realization that evil was as close as a passing car.

As you can see, this device enabled the writer to re-create the haste, panic, and immediacy of the action. In the following passage from *A Farewell to Arms*, Hemingway used simple sentences to achieve an effect of nervous tension as Lieutenant Frederic Henry leaves the hospital to get something to eat after watching Catherine Barkley suffer through a stillbirth. To help you realize the high frequency of simple sentences, we have marked the sentences according to type (S = modified or expanded simple sentence; C = compound sentence; CX = complex sentence); we shall discuss compound and complex sentences later.

I ate the ham and eggs and drank the beer [S]. The ham and eggs were in a round dish—the ham underneath and the eggs on top [S]. It was very hot and at the first mouthful I had to take a drink of beer to cool my mouth [C]. I was hungry and I asked the waiter for another order [C]. I drank several glasses of beer [S]. I was not thinking at all but read the paper of the man opposite me [S]. It was about the breakdown on the British front [S]. When he realized I was reading the paper he folded it over [CX]. I thought of asking the waiter for a paper, but I could not concentrate [C]. It was hot in the cafe and the air was bad [C]. Many of the people at the tables knew one another [S]. There were several games going on [S]. The waiters were bringing drinks from the bar to the tables [S]. Two men came in and could find no places to sit [S]. They stood opposite the bar where I was at [CX]. I ordered another beer [S]. I was not ready to leave yet [S]. It was too soon to go back to the hospital [S]. I tried not to think and to be perfectly calm [S]. The men stood around but no one was leaving, so they went out [CX]. I drank another beer [S]. The man opposite me had taken off his spectacles, put them away in a case, folded his paper and put it in his pocket and now sat holding his liqueur glass and looking out at the room [S]. Suddenly I knew I had to get back [S]. I called the waiter, paid the reckoning, got into my coat, put on my hat and started out the door [S]. I walked through the rain up to the hospital [S].

The tally: eighteen simple sentences with some modification, four compound sentences, and three complex sentences.

COMPOUND SENTENCES

In narrative writing, another useful sentence device is the compound sentence, which results from the combining of two sentences. As we have noted, simple sentences, regardless of any modification or expansion, retain their basic SVC structure, as in this sentence taken from the Hemingway example:

S	V	C
I	tried	not to think and
		to be perfectly calm.

But in a compound sentence, several SVC patterns can be combined, as in this sentence from the same example:

S	V	C		S	V	C
It	was	hot in the cafe	*and*	the air	was	bad.

A compound sentence consists of two or more SVC structures joined by a coordinate conjunction — *and, but, for, or, nor, yet,* or occasionally a semicolon. The SVC structures can also be linked by a pair of conjunctions — *either/or, neither/nor, both/and, not only/but also.* Structurally, these two compounding patterns look like this:

S V C
{ and
but
for
or
nor
yet
; }
S V C

{ either
neither
both
not only }
S V C
{ or
nor
and
but also }
S V C

Despite their usefulness in personal and narrative writing, compound sentences formed with *and* might be frowned upon in other kinds of writing because they fail to signal any special relationship between the two joined ideas. Note how the following *and* sentence merely reports what occurred, leaving it up to the reader to wonder about the connection between the two clauses:

He cut a full cord of birch and his wife called him into the house.

Is there a causal relationship (because he did it) or a temporal one (when he did it) or what?

It is precisely this imprecision that accounts for the conversational effect of the compound sentence. When we talk we are so busy thinking of what we want to say that we often neglect to furnish the necessary signals. Thus we use many compound sentences (particularly with *and* as the connecting conjunction) and depend upon the social context to supply the relationships. But in writing, too many consecutive compound sentences sound juvenile, as shown in this account by a child:

I was walking to school and a bird hit a tree. I ran to it and it tried to fly away. It could not move and I brought it to school. All my friends were sorry for it but the teacher was angry. She made me take it to the principal's office and he called someone on the phone. He told me the bird would be taken care of and I went back to class. I wonder what happened to it.

Richard Bradford uses the compound effectively in the second and third sentences in the opening paragraph of *Red Sky at Morning:*

We were using the old blue china and the stainless steel cutlery, with place mats on the big oval table and odd-sized jelly glasses for the wine. The good stuff was all packed and stored, and the Salvation Army was due the next day for the leftovers. My mother called this last dinner a picnic, but she didn't wear her overalls to it. She had on the blue hostess gown with the purple flowers.

QUESTIONS AND EXCLAMATIONS

In addition to simple sentences and compound sentences, other sentence types can help to provide a conversational tone in your narrative writing. Questions, particularly, are valuable in achieving a natural and informal voice. Once again, let your own conversation be your guide. Generally, the questions that you and your friends ask are short and direct, often no more than a grunt with a trailing question intonation: "How come?" "Why not?" "How much?" "What then?" "So what?" But in writing, questions should be used sparingly. Like expensive perfume or after-shave lotion, they are most effective when saved for special occasions.

The same goes for exclamatory sentences. You probably sprinkle these throughout letters to close friends to impart the stress and pitch you would use in talking to them. Although they should be used sparingly in other kinds of writing, what could be more natural than a few exclamations in autobiographical narratives or personal essays? But please use moderation! Like continuous going-out-of-business sales, exclamations lose their effectiveness when overused.

SENTENCE FRAGMENTS

Another device that can be used effectively in personal narrative— when used sparingly—is the sentence fragment. Starting with a capital and ending with terminal punctuation, but usually lacking a subject or a verb that shows tense, these nonsentences can add color and vigor to informal prose. Note how skillfully Dick Gregory used sentence fragments (italicized) in this passage from his autobiography, *Nigger:*

The teacher thought I was stupid. *Couldn't spell, couldn't read, couldn't do arithmetic. Just stupid.* Teachers were never interested in finding out that you couldn't concentrate because you were so hungry, because you hadn't had any breakfast. All you could think about was noontime, would it ever come? Maybe you could sneak into the cloakroom and steal a bite of some kid's lunch out of a coat pocket. *A bite of something. Paste.* You couldn't really make a meal of paste, or put it on bread for a sandwich, but sometimes I'd scoop a few spoonfuls out of a paste jar in back of the room. Pregnant people get strange tastes. I was pregnant with poverty. *Pregnant with dirt and pregnant with shoes that were never bought for me, pregnant with five other people in my bed and no Daddy in the next room, and pregnant with hunger.* Paste doesn't taste too bad when you're hungry.

The fragments here are all effective. In the first, the omission of the subject (*I*) shifts the emphasis from the writer to the reasons for the teacher's opinion of him and achieves a free, natural effect that would have been lost in the traditional counterpart:

The teacher thought that I was stupid because I couldn't spell, read, or do arithmetic.

The emphatic summary declaration of the next fragment ("Just stupid") conveys a decisive note of finality. The next two fragments ("A bite of something" and "Paste") focus attention on the boy's desperate craving for food: first on his urge for just "a bite of something" and then on the most unappetizing, unimaginable substance in the classroom—paste. The final fragment ("Pregnant with . . .") is a lengthy one that is in apposition with the previous sentence. Here the ironic repetition of the word *pregnant,* generally meaning fruitfully abundant, emphasizes the boy's barren predicament.

Sentence fragments, if they are to work for the writer, must in some way amplify what is said in the surrounding context, and the missing elements should be easily recoverable, as in the rewritten version of the first sentence. Of course, fragments that are idiomatic, such as "The sooner, the better," present no problems.

Any restrictions on fragments? Yes. Like questions and exclamations, they are dramatic, attention-getting devices and so should be used sparingly. However, some types of fragments would be unacceptable to most readers and should be avoided. Very often in these cases, student writers mistake a verb form in the construction for a main verb. Let's look at some of these puzzlers.

I had a perpetual clash with my mother. *A woman who was as stubborn as I was.*

The italicized fragment is a noun phrase modifying *mother* in the preceding sentence. Unlike the Gregory examples, this fragment detracts from the relationships involved rather than emphasizing them. Confusion of the verb in a relative clause ("who *was*") for a main sentence verb is the culprit here, as it often is. A comma or dash after *mother* solves the problem.

John lost his driver's license for two years. *For drinking while driving.*

This common type of fragment involves a prepositional phrase. It is often a problem for student writers because its verbal *-ing* form can easily be mistaken for a true verb.

He felt that he was capable of making his own decisions. *Being of sound mind and body.*

Here, use of the *-ing* form may again be at fault. You can avoid such fragments by making sure an auxiliary verb, such as *have* or *is,* precedes the form. Without an auxiliary, the *-ing* verb carries no tense and cannot be a main verb.

He wore a raincoat. *Although it was not raining.*

Here, a subordinate clause (an SVC structure introduced by a subordinate conjunction) is the culprit. Subordinate conjunctions, such as *although, because, whether,* and *if,* signal a close and dependent relationship between two sentence elements, and logically the two elements should not be separated by end punctuation.

Like other language devices, fragments can be highly effective when used properly; but they require that you understand their structure and their limitations. Fragments are certainly helpful in narrative writing as another means of adding the spice of naturalness to your prose. But like other spices, they should be used sparingly.

ACTIVE VERSUS PASSIVE SENTENCES

In personal writing, particularly in narrative, you can best establish a conversational tone and a sense of immediacy and action by making certain that most of your sentences are in the *active* voice—that the subject is the logical agent for the action in the predicate (the verb + the complement). Look at these three versions of the same sentence and note the difference in the dramatic immediacy generated by each:

1. Tom fearlessly chased the bear raiding the cooler.
2. The bear raiding the cooler was fearlessly chased by Tom.
3. The bear raiding the cooler was fearlessly chased.

You probably agree that example 1 carries more immediate impact. It is an *active* sentence; *Tom* is the logical agent or initiator of the action in the predicate ("fearlessly chased the bear raiding the cooler"). The other two versions are reordered to *passive* form. In both, the object of the verb ("the bear") is transposed to the subject position and the verb form is changed. In example 2 the subject *Tom* has been relegated to a less active role at the end of the sentence. Example 3 is least active of all: because English structure permits it, *Tom* has been completely removed from the action; in 3, there is no apparent human agent.

As you can see from the examples, changing a sentence from active voice to passive alters not only its psychological effect but also its form. The passive form is a result of two changes in the original sentence:

1. Reordering the object to subject position and putting the subject, now introduced with *by,* after the verb. This *by* phrase can be deleted, as in example 3 above.

    Tom fearlessly chased *the bear* ⇒
    (Subject)   (Object)

    The bear was fearlessly chased (by *Tom*).
    (Object)   (Subject)

2. Changing the active verb to passive.

    chased ⇒ was chased

Obviously, this reordering to passive can be performed only in sentences with a transitive verb and an object. Usually this rearrangement results in little change in meaning, but the action implicit in the sentence can become greatly diminished when an active sentence is made passive. The sense of direct action is weakened both by the loss of the close relationship between the subject and the action expressed in the verb and by the loss of the active verb. When used in narratives about people, these characteristics of the passive can obscure or de-emphasize the human involvement and action.

Because readers are generally more interested in who-is-doing-what than in what-is-being-done, you should emphasize the human action in personal writing by avoiding the passive. This will almost automatically produce a more natural tone, since people do not normally use passives in conversation or in writing to friends. Notice the differences in tone and action in these two versions of the same anecdote. Ask yourself which version you prefer.

1. Carol and I attended a movie last night. While we waited in line, Carol bought some popcorn. About half an hour later, after we had entered the theater and finished the popcorn, she nudged me and showed me something in her hand. I could see that it was a piece of a tooth.
2. Last night, a movie was attended by Carol and me. While we waited in line, some popcorn was bought by Carol. About half an hour later, after the theater had been entered by us and the popcorn had been finished, I was nudged by her and I was shown something in her hand. That it was a piece of a tooth could be seen by me.

Surely you prefer the first passage. That's generally how you and others talk. Most of us who speak English would find it unacceptably awkward to say "the movies were attended by Carol and me." Yet many people use such unnatural passives in writing because they think that this sentence structure is more formal or scholarly.

There is, of course, a time and place for the passive. In scientific writing, in dealing with abstract ideas, or in situations where the subject-agent is unimportant, the passive is preferable to the active. We will discuss effective uses of passive in later chapters. But to achieve a sense of action and immediacy in your personal writing, you should avoid the passive whenever possible.

DIALOGUE SENTENCES

Appearances are always important, even in writing. So it is well to consider using dialogue whenever appropriate because it enhances the appearance of the written, typed, or printed page. It permits writers of narrative to apply a key principle in advertising copywriting: leave a lot of white space. In contrast to pages covered with words, pages with white space or empty space appeal to people because they suggest reading that is restful to the eye and relaxing to the mind. The usual short statements and brief paragraphs in dialogue make it as inviting as driving early in the morning with few cars on the streets.

While dialogue is easy to read, it is anything but easy to write. Done skillfully, it creates the illusion of conversation even though it never accurately renders it. When we talk to another, well, when we talk, we—er—oh, yes—we often stop—that is, when we talk to one another—y'know—we may stop, maybe to light up a cigarette (even though, sure, cigarettes aren't good for us), or else we'll digress for a few seconds, yeah, and then, let's see, what were we talking about—oh, yes—when we talk we often ramble on—er—at great length, yes, with pauses, digressions, asides, retractions, qualifications, of course, not all the time, no, but you'd be surprised—yes, you would—at what comes out when people open their mouths. Readers would usually find a taped transcript of an actual conversation insufferable. Consequently, you must pare dialogue to the marrow, keeping statements short and the conversation itself brief. Although we do read continuous dialogue in plays, in other prose forms we expect it to be broken up by expository or descriptive passages. Otherwise, it may become monotonous, tedious, and artificial.

Brevity is indeed the watchword for writing realistic dialogue: short words, sentences, and statements. But in spite of its brevity, dialogue should depict the personalities of the speakers. Each person should be individualized and characterized by what is said, what is not said, how it is said, and what actions accompany the statements.

Direct Discourse

Let's study the following passage to note some techniques for writing dialogue in personal narrative. In the selection, Rube Marquard, one of the few major league pitchers to win more than two hundred games, who had been disowned by his father ten years earlier when he left home to play baseball, tells about the reunion with his dad.

One day when I was pitching for Brooklyn I pitched the first game of a double-header against Boston and beat them, 1–0. I was in the clubhouse during the second game, taking off my uniform, when the clubhouse boy came in.

"Rube," he said, "there's an elderly gentleman outside who wants to see you. He says he's your father from Cleveland."

"He's not my father," I said. "My father wouldn't go across the street to see me. But you go out and get his autograph book and bring it in, and I'll autograph it for him."

But instead of bringing in the book, he brought in my Dad. And we were both delighted to see one another.

"Boy, you sure are a hardhead," he said to me. "You know I didn't mean what I said ten years ago."

"What about you, Dad?" I said. "You're as stubborn as I am. I thought you never wanted to see me again. I thought you meant it."

"Of course I didn't," he said.

After we talked a while, I said, "Did you see the game today?"

"Yes, I did," he said.

"Where were you sitting?" I asked him.

"Well, you know the man who wears that funny thing on his face?"

"You mean the mask? The catcher?"

"I guess so. Well, anyway, I was halfway between him and the number one—you know, where they run right after they hit the ball."

"You mean first base?"

"I don't know," he said. "I don't know what they call it. I was sitting in the middle there."

"How many ball games have you seen since I became a ballplayer, Dad?"

"This is the first one," he said.

—Rube Marquard, "I Become a Big Leaguer," in *The Glory of Their Times*

Note the short sentences, the simple words, the question-and-answer rhythms, the reliance on the common verb *said*, and the frequent omission of tags to identify the speaker. Four dialogue devices are used in the conversation:

1. Bare statement:

"Well, you know the man who wears the funny thing on his face?"

2. Statement plus speaker tag:

"Where were you sitting?" I asked him.

3. Speaker tag plus statement:

After we talked for a while, I said, "Did you see the game today?"

4. Interrupted statement:

"Rube," he said, "there's an elderly gentleman outside who wants to see you."

Bare statements are particularly effective with two people, but may also be used with more participants as long as no confusion arises. In such situations, name tags may help to establish identities, and the context may also earmark the speaker. Here's an example:

"How about a movie, Bill?"
"Not tonight, Mike. Got a date. Maybe Joe will go with you."
"Sorry, Mike. Not tonight."
"How come?"

"Stephens is giving a chem exam tomorrow. Gotta study."

"Aw, no you don't. Does he, Bill?"

"Yeah. Joe's aiming for med school. He's gotta have the grades."

"Right. Have to crank out the grades for med school. No time for a flick tonight."

If you are not careful, too many consecutive bare statements, even those involving only two people, may confuse readers. But don't let this possibility deter you from using this dialogue device frequently. It is highly effective because it is lifelike, allowing readers to overhear conversations without being aware of the author's intervening presence.

In the Marquard passage, you may have wondered about the absence of interpretative tags with adverbs ("he said angrily") or with lively verbs ("he exclaimed"). In well-written dialogue, the feeling is conveyed in the words, not in the tags. Although we urged you previously in Chapter 3 to avoid overworked verbs, dialogue is an exception. Simple common verbs (*say, ask, tell*) should be relied on to de-emphasize the author's role and to focus on the actual conversation. Of course, it may be helpful occasionally to employ an interpretative tag such as the following:

He shrieked, "Dad!"

"This is the first one," he said, looking embarrassed.

Indirect Discourse

Thus far we have been discussing the most common form of dialogue, direct discourse, but as you know from Chapter 2, dialogue can also be expressed indirectly. Indirect discourse gains in brevity but loses in vividness, because readers are told about the conversation instead of hearing it for themselves. Here is an indirect-discourse version of the first part of the Marquard passage:

The clubhouse boy told me about an elderly man claiming to be my father who wanted to see me. I knew it couldn't be my father because he wouldn't go across the street to see me. But when the man came in, it was Dad. We were delighted to see each other. He told me that he hadn't meant what he said ten years ago. I was surprised. I said I thought he never wanted to see me again.

Although indirect dialogue usually lacks the freshness and vitality of direct dialogue, it may be especially effective in compressing conversation intended merely to provide a transition between two scenes or to save space for other purposes. Observe how Noel Perrin uses it in the following account of his efforts to sell in New York City the firewood that he had cut at his Vermont farm.

Finally, just as it's getting dark, we come to Diamond Ice Cube, at 201 East 33rd, and here our luck turns. They are still open, and they're buying wood. The boss looks my truckload over, and concedes that the logs on top are suitable. "Of course, I don't know what you've got under there," he says suspiciously. (More dry maple, that's what.) "How much you want for it?" he asks.

It's almost six o'clock, and I only want $30 for the entire five-eighths of a cord of maple. The birch? The birch would be extra. "Thirty for the lot," he says. "Thirty-five," I answer, and he agrees. This is about 9 cents a log, but at least I've got a sale.

What I don't have is delivery. It's quitting time, his drivers have gone home, and he wants me to come back tomorrow to unload. I explain that the wood will probably be stolen by then; he explains that that's my worry, not his.

> —Noel Perrin, "Getting Fired," *New York*

Questions in Direct and Indirect Discourse

It is sometimes difficult to distinguish between direct and indirect questions starting with question words (*who, what, when, where, why, how*).

> Direct: He asked, "How much will you sell it for?"
> Indirect: He asked how much I would sell it for.

You may have observed that the word order is the tip-off: the inverted word order of a question (question word + auxiliary + subject + verb) signals direct discourse:

> Direct: They asked me, "*Where   has   he   gone?*"
>   Question word   Auxiliary   Subject   Verb

Normal sentence order after the question word (subject + auxiliary + verb) signals indirect discourse:

> Indirect: They asked me *where   he   had   gone.*
>   Question word   Subject   Auxiliary   Verb

Note that *whether* nearly always signals an indirect question.

> Direct: The young man asked, "Will it be ready on Friday?"
> Indirect: The young man asked *whether* it would be ready on Friday.

Whenever you are writing dialogue—direct or indirect—watch for question words to crop up, and when they do, pay particular attention to word order.

A simple problem of this sort should not deter you from writing dialogue. No other single device provides such life to your papers and to the people you write about. Writing dialogue is fun, but difficult to bring off well. The suggestions presented above should assist you with matters of craft, but they will not help much in your developing an ear for the idioms, dialects, phrases, structure, pace, and sounds of speech. To become aware of these, listen carefully to the way people talk and study the dialogue in the fiction of such writers as John Updike, Saul Bellow, Norman Mailer, Philip Roth, Doris Lessing, and Bernard Malamud. If you really want to master dialogue, you might follow Benjamin Franklin's example: copy a passage from a good writer, reproduce it from memory, and compare your version with the original.

ASSIGNMENTS

For Discussion

1 Identify the sentence patterns that underlie the following simple sentences:

    a Emotions play a large part in dancing.
    b Next came the railroads.
    c About three houses down on the opposite side of the street lived a cute little girl named Kathy.
    d The present population of the world is four billion people.
    e Balance is the key factor in skiing.
    f The following year I dropped math.
    g One night I rode my bicycle on the fraternity house roof.
    h I held a small rock over the edge and released it.
    i Clarke gives us a picture of a world that is similar to today's society.
    j Waterskiing is very easy to learn.
    k I was in the senior band that winter.

2 Analyze the kinds of sentences (simple, compound, complex) used in this student narrative of an adventure on a railroad bridge. What advice about sentence choice could you give the student to make an effective description even more exciting? Can fragments be used to advantage anywhere?

HIGH BRIDGE

We parked the motorcycle on the side of the highway and climbed up. The hill was covered with limestone gravel, glittering in the bright sunlight. The loose stones rolled down the incline as our feet sought firm footholds. Finally, my hand grasped the rusted steel railing at the top and I pulled Robin up behind me. We were at High Bridge after a half hour of hard riding and climbing.

We looked all around us and tried to take in the beauty below us. There was even beauty and grace in the old, black and rusty railroad bridge spanning the open distance between two high rising cliffs. We could see the muddy water of the river below us, moving slowly in its sluggish course. The tall oaks and their neighbors in the river valley tried in vain to reach up to us. We were almost higher than the birds in their own territory.

I held a small rock over the edge and released it. We started to count, one, two, three . . . nine . . . ten, splash! In that brief span of ten seconds the small missile seemed to hang motionless in the atmosphere. I didn't see it move; it just shrank until it crashed into the water. All this time Robin held her breath and ended by just saying, "God!"

It all seemed so serene; we were just suspended in space by a network of steel. Whomp! WH OO MP! As soon as my ears picked up this deep bellow, I experienced a sickening realization. There was a train coming and we were both in the middle of the bridge. The diesel engines were thundering as it came churning ever closer. It was too late to get off the bridge, so we sat down on the catwalk clutching the handrail. Now came the monster . . . the bell was clanging constantly as his white eye flashed back and forth. The bridge began to shake violently to and fro. The metal struts were singing like telephone lines. I wondered if that structure of rusted steel could hold such weight on its back.

I looked around at Robin as if nothing was happening, but I really felt sick. Robin was still there—staring wordlessly at me. The cars rolled by as the caravan of steel picked up speed. All I could see was a blur of colors, letters, and numbers posted differently on every one. The wheels clicked monotonously over the small breaks where the rails had been joined. The springs on the cars creaked as they were pitched from one side to the other. Will this never end? How long have we been hanging here? Then we saw the red caboose. It looked like a small house on wheels chasing after the iron serpent ahead of it. We both knew that our ordeal was finally over. As the fire-breather snake wound back into the hills from where it came, the bridge became quiet and stable. We stood up and made our way back to the motorcycle. Neither of us spoke.

3   Identify the fragments in the following student examples. Be able to provide a possible explanation (other than punctuation) as to why the students may have confused them with complete sentence structure.

   a   The people are moving out of the cities to own homes with lawns. Places away from the bustle of the cities. Good farm land is being bought up and subdivided. Thousands of new homes are built every year. More and more mouths to feed with less land to produce the necessary crops.

   b   But if some parents think married students should be on their own and need help financially, then the young couple will have to work, but not make enough money to live adequately and save money, too. Which they will need desperately in the future.

c If we have disagreements about where to go or what to do. My wife does not insist that we do what she has planned.

d The great awakening started back in the 1950's when a mild form of violence made its way into films. For example, the Bogart movies of the 50's.

e The Puritans also had crime and mental disease among their ranks. Disease being the biggest problem they had.

f College athletic recruiters are as bad as advertising agents; they both have something to sell. The advertising agent selling his product, the college recruiter selling his school.

g The amateur golf player and the professional both have their own unique character and style of playing. Such as their clothes: one could be fancy and flashy, the other not so colorful. The individual way they swing and hit the ball.

h As I look over the green lush grass of the meadows and fields, I am aware that there are many beautiful things going on. There is new life and excitement everywhere. Rabbits crawling out of their winter homes in the ground. Rabbits taking their first breath of crystal-clear spring air. Also, the trees and flowers trying desperately to show their new beauty.

4 Sentences in the passive voice not only obscure the actor-subject but also frequently result in extremely awkward sentence structure. Discuss the problems involved in the following student examples and be able to change them into active sentences.

a Ships were the first form of transportation shown in the film as people were brought to America.

b One wonders if all the campus activities are only carried on during the week.

c The bow and arrow has been replaced by the gun for protection purposes.

d Also, John Lennon is constantly seen barefoot in these pictures and on their album "Abbey Road," which is the way they bury the House of Lords, which all Beatles are a member of.

e Because of the fear one would experience in coping with such extraordinary circumstances, emotions would be stirred.

f The paper must be written by him by tomorrow.

5 Discuss the techniques of dialogue sentence structure in the following examples. What advantage does each give the writer?

a Mr. Martin got to the office at eight-thirty the next morning, as usual. At a quarter to nine, Ulgine Barrows, who had never before arrived at work before ten, swept into his office. "I'm reporting to Mr. Fitweiler now!" she shouted. "If he turns you over to the police, it's no more than you deserve!" Mr. Martin gave her a look of shocked surprise. "I beg your pardon?" he said. Mrs. Barrows snorted and bounced out of the room, leaving Miss Paird and Joey Hart staring after her. "What's the matter with that old devil now?" asked Miss Paird. "I have no idea," said Mr. Martin, resuming his work. The other two looked at him and then at each other. Miss Paird got up and went out. She walked slowly past the closed door of Mr. Fitweiler's office. Mrs. Barrows was yelling inside, but she was not braying. Miss Paird could not hear what the woman was saying. She went back to her desk.

—James Thurber, "The Catbird Seat"

b "If you go, I'll tell," Jason said.

"We'll have fun," Nancy said. "They won't mind, just to my house. I been working for yawl a long time. They won't mind."

"I'm not afraid to go," Caddy said. "Jason is the one that's afraid. He'll tell."

"I won't tell," Jason said. "I'm not afraid."

"Jason ain't afraid to go with me," Nancy said. "Is you Jason?"

"Jason is going to tell," Caddy said.

—William Faulkner, "That Evening Sun"

c "Ah, you're — you're — a?" I began as soon as I had mastered my surprise. I couldn't bring out the dingy word "models": it seemed so little to fit the case.

"We haven't had much practice," said the lady.

"We've got to *do* something, and we've thought that an artist in your line might perhaps make something of us," her husband threw off. He further mentioned that they didn't know many artists and that they had gone first, on the off-chance — he painted views of course, but sometimes put in figures; perhaps I remembered — to Mr. Rivet, whom they had met a few years before at a place in Norfolk where he was sketching.

"We used to sketch a little ourselves," the lady hinted.

"It's very awkward, but we absolutely *must* do something," her husband went on.

"Of course, we're not so *very* young," she admitted with a wan smile.

—Henry James, "The Real Thing"

For Writing

1 Rewrite the sentences in exercise 3 above, replacing the fragments with complete sentences or with more effective fragments.
2 Rewrite the following student paragraphs, making use of short simple sentences or compound sentences to add a stronger air of immediacy and urgency to the action. Add details if you feel they would make the narrative more effective.

a I got a taxi and headed for the National Airport in Washington, D.C. I figured it to be about five miles away—it was more like thirty. "Damnation" was all I kept saying. The driver had been covered with perspiration from waiting outside the cab, but he was cooling off now in the air-conditioned cab, and loving it. I asked him to step on the gas and he did, quite readily. I think that he must have been drunk.

When I arrived at the National Airport, I ran up and down stairs to get to my terminal, dragging my bicycle behind me. A man asked me when I made it there what flight I was to be on. "Eastern Flight 547," I replied. "There she goes!" he said as he pointed out the window at the red tail-lights of my plane disappearing into the black sky. I was only five minutes late.

b Sunday morning at ten o'clock, Tony, Albert, and I were in the canoe ready for the "Great Canoe Race." The gun went off and we were on our way down the river. The first part of the race we were in the lead, but someone had drilled a hole in our canoe. I had to take my shoes off and start bailing the canoe. As we neared the finish it was obvious we would not win so Tony decided to tip the canoe. At which time I lost my shoes and car keys. The water was thirty-six degrees Fahrenheit. My skin turned a pale blue and I thought I was dying. We came in fourth in the "Great Canoe Race" and won absolutely no prize at all, but we did get our picture put in the school newspaper.

3 Using a different dialogue technique, rewrite this selection from a student narrative. Try to make your dialogue contribute more to the action than it does in the original.

We caught up with the hit-and-run car about a mile later, and Fritz immediately began writing the out-of-county license number down on a piece of cigarette rolling paper.

"What should we do now?" I asked Fritz.

"Let's pull up beside him, and get a good look."

Not knowing what good it was going to do, I changed lanes and speeded up until we were just beside the other car. Fritz then rolled down his window, and yelled to the man driving the car, "Hey, buddy—you know you hit a dog back there?" Having to watch the road, I didn't get to see the man's reaction, but heard Fritz scream, "He's got a gun, Rick!"

Knowing how accurately observant Fritz is, I didn't waste time to check him out, but down-shifted my car to third, trying to get away as fast as possible.

We were still in the lane adjacent to the other car, but in front of it by a few feet, when I heard a loud dull clap of gunshot, and felt pieces of the vinyl rear window of my convertible top fall on my neck. The bullet had entered from behind my head, and deflected off the window, up and out the top of the roof. I looked over at Fritz, whose mouth was hanging open, and eyes staring straight ahead in disbelief.

As I pulled back into the same lane the man was in, I grabbed Fritz's head and pulled him down in the seat. We were driving toward Main Street when I noticed the traffic light was red.

I couldn't stop for fear that the man would take another shot at my head. So I slowed and maneuvered my car through the cars on Main Street, and miraculously didn't hit any of them. Fritz looked up at me with his wide open mouth and eyes, and just shook his head, again in disbelief.

I looked in my rear-view mirror and watched the man with the gun take a right on Main Street. A feeling of relief flooded me.

6 Punctuation in Personal Writing

Punctuation is often a headache for even the most experienced writers. One reason for this is the often seemingly arbitrary or illogical way punctuation marks are used. A brief look at the historical development of punctuation will help to explain how present-day rules developed, sometimes without reference to the grammatical needs of the language.

Because many early English manuscripts were read aloud to a largely illiterate population, the earliest punctuation marks indicated breath pauses for church lectors or readers. As printing came into use and the literacy rate increased, more and more punctuation devices were invented. In the beginning, they were generally used arbitrarily by the typesetters, rather than consciously by the writers. By the nineteenth century a systematic effort was made to set off grammatical structures by punctuation. Although current punctuation practices are still moving toward that goal, many earlier arbitrary decisions remain a part of the conventions, or rules, of written punctuation. In spoken English, for instance, a breath pause almost always occurs between a long, complicated subject structure and the verb, as in:

The unique characteristic of the generation now passing through adolescence in America is that it is the first to be born into a technological society.
— Barry M. Schwartz

Few people could read this sentence aloud without pausing for breath between the last word in the subject, *America,* and the first verb, *is;* but it is conventionally unacceptable to place a comma between them. The general punctuation practice is not to place a comma between the subject and verb.

Another convention with no relationship to either structure or punctuation logic requires that quotation marks always be placed outside rather than inside a period:

They sang, "Let's all make it, this time around."

Under some circumstances, however, the writer can arbitrarily decide whether to substitute one punctuation mark for another or omit a device altogether. For example, in this sentence from a popular rhetoric textbook, the author rather arbitrarily decided on dashes rather than commas to separate the phrase "the concept of *net force*" from the rest of the sentence:

The subject which the author wished to explain—the concept of *net force*—is unfamiliar to most readers.

> —Edward Corbett, *Classical Rhetoric for the Modern Student*

The sentence is just as "correct" when commas replace the dashes:

The subject which the author wished to explain, the concept of *net force,* is unfamiliar to most readers.

As you can see, punctuation choices can be difficult and confusing. Often you, like other writers, are forced to bow to the rules of convention even when they seem unreasonable or arbitrary. But gaining a knowledge of the ways that features of spoken language relate to punctuation can give you more confidence and skill in effective written communication and can release you from some of the perplexity of conflicting rules. By understanding the possibilities inherent in spoken English, you can use punctuation in your writing not only to aid your readers but also to create the effects you desire.

THE "PUNCTUATION" OF SPOKEN ENGLISH

Years ago, Victor Borge, the pianist-comedian, devised a comedy routine in which he used oral punctuation. He ascribed to each punctuation mark a verbal equivalent—a grunt, a snort, a click. His audiences found the result hilarious not only because of his own comic antics but also because he was applying to spoken English, conventions that were devised for written English.

Borge was implying that there is a need for punctuation in spoken English, but obviously he was wrong. We do get along without punctuation in talking—but how? The answer is that people do not speak by consonant and vowel sounds alone. Other vocal noise is present, indicating word boundaries, terminating sentences, and signaling major grammatical devices within sentences. A brief discussion of these will enable you to understand how we can talk without punctuation.

English is primarily a *stress* language. That is, we rely strongly on the intensity, accent, or emphasis given to individual syllables in words, phrases, and sentences to give meaning to our utterances. You are probably most aware of stress in the way it can distinguish nouns from verbs in certain word pairs like *récord* (noun)/*recórd* (verb), *pérvert* (noun)/*pervért* (verb), *dígest* (noun)/*digést* (verb). In such instances, both meaning and function can be changed by shifting the primary (heaviest) stress to a different syllable. We also rely on stress variation to signal differences in meaning, as in these two sentences:

His uncle is a nice *old man.* (term of endearment)
His uncle is a nice old *man.* (statement of chronological age)

In addition to stress, we rely on *pitch* to signal our listeners. By varying the tonal quality of our voice, we affect the meaning of our sentences. By dropping from normal pitch to a lower one, we can state, for example, "You're the expert," without offending the hearer. But raising the pitch at the end of the statement might also raise the person's temper:

You're the expert ↘ (statement of fact, compliment)
You're the expert ↗ (insulting question)

Another intonation signal is *juncture,* or the length of the pause between two words, phrases, or clauses. Linguists have identified four distinct junctures in English, one of short duration that helps us to respond to word or syllable boundaries, and three of longer duration (called terminal junctures) that accompany both primary stress and discernible changes in pitch. The dramatic effect that terminal juncture can have on meaning is illustrated by an old linguistic joke. With normal question intonation, the following merely asks the listener to identify an object: "What's that in the road ahead?" But with juncture (J) before the last word, the question becomes macabre: "What's that in the road (J) a head?"

Although our discussion of these complex intonation signals—stress, pitch, and juncture—has been brief, you should now realize how we rely on these devices to communicate in speaking. To compensate for their absence in writing, we substitute punctuation marks. Thus to take Victor Borge seriously (which of course he did not intend), we can argue that we do not create punctuation devices for our spoken language because stress, pitch, and juncture are already available. But since we cannot transfer these three vocal devices to writing, we substitute punctuation marks for them. As you can see, punctuation, like a notation system in music, can help readers reproduce more accurately the writer's intended language tune.

INTONATION PATTERNS AND PUNCTUATION MARKS

What remains now is to relate the previous discussion of stress, pitch, and juncture to specific punctuation marks as they are most commonly used. Our purpose here is not to treat the marks in detail but to show you how they can serve a particular function in translating the spoken language to written form.

The Period

Periods signal the end of a complete utterance, a sentence or sentence fragment, and correspond to a lengthy breath pause and a drop in pitch, both accompanied by strongest or primary stress.

That was a great $^{\text{par}}_{\quad\text{ty.}}$

The Question Mark

Questions in English have several intonational possibilities, but one punctuation mark is used for all. A question that expects an answer supplying more information than a simple *yes* or *no* generally follows the same pattern as a statement ending in a period; that is, it ends with a drop to lowest pitch.

What did you expect to $^{\text{ga}}_{\quad\text{in?}}$

A question that expects a *yes* or *no* answer, however, usually exhibits rising pitch at the end:

Did you eat that $_{\text{cook}}{}^{\text{ie?}}$

These two question intonation patterns accompany two basic question structures in English:

1.   Are   you   planning to take the exam tomorrow?
     Auxiliary   Subject   Remaining predicate

2.   What   do   you   plan to do?
    Question word   Auxiliary   Subject   Remaining predicate

Because questions generally take these forms, there is no punctuation problem. But in writing personal narratives, particularly dialogue, unusual constructions may arise. Here are some of the problems:

1. Question in statement form:

> You're really serious about that. (intonation dictates use of period)
> You're really serious about that? (intonation requires question mark)

2. Indirect question:

> Jay asked if Bill was going to study for the exam tomorrow.
>
> > or
>
> Jay asked if Bill was going to study for the exam tomorrow?

Only the first form is acceptable. Although there is an indirect question inserted into it, the overall sentence is a statement and requires a period.

3. Sentence or sentence fragment added to statement or question:

> a. "Me, I don't study for exams."
>
> > or
>
> "Me? I don't study for exams."

Either punctuation is possible, depending on the context. The sentence with the comma could be a cocky, defiant declaration. The sentence with the question mark says in effect, "Are you talking to me? If so, then hear this: I don't study for exams," and "me" would probably be accompanied by a rise in pitch.

> b. "Bill—can you believe it—aced that exam without cracking a book."
>
> > or
>
> "Bill—can you believe it?—aced that exam without cracking a book."

The second sentence, with the question mark, is preferable. A question mark should be placed after any sentence element that can logically be separated from the rest of the sentence and that would be spoken inquiringly. Again, intonation would be a reliable indication of which punctuation mark is appropriate.

The Comma

The comma is more difficult to relate to intonation because it corresponds to junctures produced within a long utterance — within a lengthy, complicated sentence or question. What's more, the junctures can vary in length and can accompany a rise in pitch such as occurs in question intonation, a drop in pitch like that of statement endings, or a medium pitch sustained across the juncture. This line from a nursery rhyme demonstrates the possibilities:

Oa_{ts} (J) pe_{as} (J) be_{ans} (J) and barley $\text{gr}_{ow.}$ (juncture with falling pitch)

Oa^{ts} (J) pe^{as} (J) be^{ans} (J) and barley $\text{gr}_{ow.}$ (juncture with rising pitch)

Oa_{ts} (J) peas (J) beans (J) and barley $\text{gr}_{ow.}$ (juncture with sustained pitch)

However, it is not necessary to gain the linguistic skills to identify the specific accompanying pitch behavior of every utterance. It is necessary only to realize that the occurrence of juncture signals that a comma may be required (except, as we have seen, when the juncture occurs between subject and predicate). Comma usage will be discussed further in later chapters.

The Colon and the Semicolon

Even though they are both punctuation marks that occur within a sentence and never at the end, the colon (:) and the semicolon (;) exhibit intonation features similar to those associated with the period. Both are used to indicate points where a lengthy juncture, usually accompanied by a drop in pitch, is present. Also, both of them, but particularly the semicolon, often occur at places in a sentence that could be closed by a period. Each of the following sentences could be made into two; the colon and the semicolon, along with their spoken intonation features, indicate the dividing points.

Already it is clear that we have learned much from it [Watergate]; we can almost say we have profited by it. (Already it is clear that we have learned much from it [Watergate]. We can almost say we have profited from it.)

— Henry Steele Commager

The changeable, movable, disposable, available person feels cut off from possibility by marriage, and with good reason: Some possibilities are cut off. (The changeable, movable, disposable, available person feels cut off from possibility by marriage, and with good reason. Some possibilities are cut off.)

—Herbert Gold

Note that in the second example the author himself capitalized the first word after the colon, strengthening our contention that it is a natural point for end punctuation—a period. You should be aware, however, that in most writing, periods can be substituted only when the structure following the colon or semicolon is a complete clause with a subject and a verb.

PUNCTUATION MARKS OF SPECIAL IMPORTANCE IN PERSONAL WRITING

We have looked at how some of the most common punctuation devices function and how they relate to spoken English. We will discuss troublesome items like the comma and the semicolon later in the book when dealing with complex sentences where these punctuation considerations are especially relevant. Now let's turn to the punctuation devices that are of particular importance in personal writing. These are the dash, the exclamation mark, parentheses, and quotation marks. Although you are already familiar with these, a review of their functions and their relationships to intonation features will aid you in communicating more effectively in your journal entries, autobiographical narratives, anecdotes, and personal essays.

The Dash

The dash is indeed a dashing mark, dramatically signaling an interruption, surprise, or shift in thought. Frankly, we could get along adequately without the dash—as some writers do—because it serves mainly as a substitute for other punctuation marks, usually the comma. But the dash produces a stronger, more forceful pause than the comma. Note how the dash functions in the following statements from Claude Brown's *Manchild in the Promised Land,* making them more effective than their "dashless" counterparts:

They wouldn't put any good cops down there—if there is such a thing as a good cop.	Dash adds emphasis.
They wouldn't put any good cops down there, if there is such a thing as a good cop.	Comma could separate clauses, but shorter pause diminishes importance of second clause.

This was a real Sunday morning—a lot of blood and vomit everywhere and people all dressed up and going to church.

Dash highlights explanation.

> This was a real Sunday morning: a lot of blood and vomit everywhere and people all dressed up and going to church.

Colon could signal explanation, but accompanying drop in pitch more widely separates the two sentence elements.

Mr. Stillman—everybody but me called him Silly—had tiny red eyes that looked at people in a mean way from way back in his head.

Dash calls attention to interruption.

> Mr. Stillman (everybody but me called him Silly) had tiny red eyes that looked at people in a mean way from way back in his head.

Parentheses could enclose this optional aside. Here, the effect is visual rather than intonational.

But then I thought, aw, hell, it wasn't their fault—as a matter of fact, it was a whole lotta fun.

Dash accents idea.

> But then I thought, aw hell, it wasn't their fault; as a matter of fact, it was a whole lotta fun.

Semicolon could connect short, related ideas, but signals drop in pitch, thus sacrificing the immediacy of the relationship.

These examples illustrate how the dash can replace other punctuation marks and add emphasis. In addition, the dash has a few special—but rare—uses. In dialogue, it may indicate that the speaker is fumbling for words or is interrupted:

> "If you don't stop talking about the dash, I'll—I'll—." Her voice faltered.

> One student shouted, "You know what you can do with the dash, you can —." "That's enough," the professor interrupted.

We do not want to dash off without some final comments. Realize that the dash is particularly helpful in the relatively informal world of personal narratives. In most other forms of writing, this punctuation mark should be used with utmost caution. Most people in business, for example, approve of the dash in sales letters and advertisements but not in other letters, memorandums, and reports. But in personal writing, the added interest and color the dash can contribute justify its use.

The Exclamation Mark

The exclamation mark resembles the dash in three respects: it draws attention to a statement, it tends to be overused, and it appears more often in personal narrative than in other forms of writing. The exclamation mark usually suggests a speaking voice filled with strong emotion or agitation, sounding generally higher, more intense, and perhaps louder than the one used in normal conversation. In this connection, the exclamation point often ends noninterrogatory sentences beginning with *how, what,* or *why:*

> How fascinating!
> What a day for a discussion of punctuation!
> Why, if it isn't old meathead!

Note that the exclamation point is a solitary figure, appearing only one to a sentence. Only in the comics, informal letters, and other highly informal writings would the following be appropriate:

> I need next month's allowance, now, desperately!!! Wow!!!!
> Lucy, why don't you get back in center field where you belong!!!!!

Excessive use of exclamation points suggests a scatterbrained writer, one who is as irritating as a hard-sell car salesman on TV. But exclamation points may appear quite often in dialogue. There they are helpful when speakers interject comments ("Oh!"), talk in fragments ("If I'd only known!") or exclaim ("But you shouldn't have done it!"). When not writing dialogue, be certain you have sufficient reason to use an exclamation mark!

Parentheses

If you want to whisper privately to the student sitting next to you, you might cup one hand to your mouth and talk under your breath. Parentheses are like a pair of hands cupped to state quietly some incidental comment or explanation. Here's how they were used by one writer:

There, on the night of the full moon in August, fire walking climaxes a week's ceremonies in honor of the Hindu god Kataragama. From all over the island, worshipers and spectators (Buddhist as well as Hindu, although theoretically

Buddhists do not believe in gods) had been converging on the little settlement in the jungle of southeastern Ceylon.

—Leonard Feinberg, "Fire Walking in Ceylon"

When an entire sentence is enclosed by parentheses, be sure to place the terminal punctuation mark within the parentheses, as in this example from the same essay:

Our driver on the trip to Kataragama was a young Singhalese who told us that his name was Elvis. (He told Englishmen that his name was Winston.)

This example also shows that parentheses can be used to lighten the tone of written material, much as a person might lighten a serious conversation by making a wisecracking aside.

Quotation Marks

In narrative writing, quotation marks appear mainly to enclose spoken words in dialogue. Their use is illustrated in the following passage from Ernest Hemingway's "The Short Happy Life of Francis Macomber."

"We're going after buff[alo] in the morning," he [Wilson, the guide] told her.
"I'm coming," she said.
"No, you're not."
"Oh, yes, I am. Mayn't I, Francis?"
"Why not stay in camp?"
"Not for anything," she said. "I wouldn't miss something like today for anything."

We hope that in reading the selection, you have not missed these points about quotation marks in narrative writing:

1. They enclose only the actual words of the speaker, not any words about these words.
2. The closing quotation mark appears after (not before or above) the other punctuation marks. Note the placement of the commas, periods, and question marks in the passage.
3. Quotation marks must be used again each time the speaker's actual words are interrupted. Note how this practice is followed in the last sentence in the dialogue.

When a lengthy statement continues for more than one paragraph, a special convention can be used to help your readers. To signal that the same speaker is talking, use quotation marks to introduce each new paragraph, and use quotation marks at the end only of the last paragraph.

    ``_____

_____

_____.

    ``_____

_____

_____.''

In your first attempts at writing dialogue, check your drafts carefully against the instructions given here. After a while, you'll be able to use quotation marks with confidence.

ASSIGNMENTS

For Discussion

1 In the following sentences, discuss whether punctuation use was determined on the basis of established convention, arbitrary decision, or in response to breath pause or other intonational factors. Note the cases where the writer's punctuation forces you to read the sentence in a particular way.

    a Betrayal between strangers? A very unlikely idea. But does a kiss on the cheek make the persons less than strangers?   — Paul Velde

    b While bad stuff is flying in Vietnam, Chicago, our universities — and where not? — it matters to me whether a team of strangers wins or loses a game.
— Jonathan Baumbach

    c Looking back through the long past we picture the beginning of the world — a primeval chaos which time has fashioned into the universe that we know.   — Arthur Stanley Eddington

    d Human life does not "work," either.   — Herbert Gold

    e Therefore, I, for one, choose not to leave.   — Richard G. Hatcher

    f We often ask ourselves why life must be like this.

    g Sometimes I think I heard Waneko telling me, "It's almost over, baby, it's almost over — we got it beat."   — Piri Thomas

    h At this extreme of polarization, movies won't even be called movies anymore, but cinemah or filluhm (as in Philharmonic Hall).   — Andrew Sarris

    i Everything disappointed him [Lee Harvey Oswald]; nothing gave him a feeling of his own distinct being; he tried over and over again to find a situation in which he could experience himself as alive, productive, a person of consequence; and one of the most interesting clues to his personality lies in the odd fact of his always writing about his actions (in the Historic Diary) in the present tense.   —John Clellon Holmes

j It is almost as if while taking a walk through a green field, I espied a blade of grass with manure on it, and bending down to that obscure little blade I said to it scoldingly, "Naughty! Naughty!"   —Henry Miller

k So many decisions in life are of this kind: they fall in between.
—Joseph Fletcher

2 Discuss what punctuation is needed in the following passage:

This sentence and the following one give you an idea of the difficulty of reading a passage without punctuation marks reading would be even more difficult than it now is if we had no way to signal the end of clauses and sentences indeed under such circumstances reading and particularly oral reading would be almost impossible.

For Writing

Punctuate the following examples (in each of which dialogue is used). Justify your punctuation choices.

1 In the annals of Zen there are many cryptic answers to the final question What is the Buddha which in our terms means What is the meaning of life What is truly real For example one master when asked What is the Buddha replied Your name is Yecho Another said Even the finest artist cannot paint him Another said No nonsense here And another answered The mouth is the gate of woe My favorite story is about the monk who said to a Master Has a dog Buddha-nature too The master replied Wu which is what the dog himself would have said.   —Gilbert Highet, *The Mystery of Zen*

2 Ain't she cute Red Sam's wife said leaning over the counter Would you like to come be my little girl No I certainly wouldn't June Star said I wouldn't live in a brokendown place like this for a million bucks and she ran back to the table Ain't she cute the woman repeated stretching her mouth politely Ain't you ashamed hissed the grandmother
—Flannery O'Connor, *A Good Man Is Hard to Find*

3 I have heard said he you will not take this place any more sahib What are you going to do with it Perhaps I shall let it again Then I will keep it on while I am away   —Rudyard Kipling, *Without Benefit of Clergy*

Special Considerations in Personal Writing

In a very real sense, each piece of writing is a "happening." Like people, each develops not only its own characteristics, but its own problems that must be solved in unique ways. But, also like people, a piece of writing shares many things in common with others, and thus some general guidelines can help to prevent or cure any ills that might arise.

THE CONSPICUOUS "I"

The *I* is back. After being frowned upon in almost all writing for many years, the *I* has returned, even appearing in erudite papers in scholarly journals. But in personal writing, the problem is likely to be not the absence of *I*'s, but the presence of too many.

Because in autobiographical narrative you are writing about yourself and people you know, you may overuse personal pronouns, especially *I* and *we*. If you do, they can distract from the effectiveness of the narrative just as frequent coughing can destroy the impact of a fascinating speech or a beautiful concert.

If *I* appears as the first word in several successive sentences, the effect is generally childish. If this is what you wish, fine. It is the effect Malcolm X achieves in the following selection from his *Autobiography:*

One thing in particular I remember made me feel grateful toward my mother was that one day I went and asked her for my own garden, and she did let me have my own little plot. I loved it and took care of it well. I loved especially to grow peas. I was proud when we had them on our table. I would pull out the grass in my garden by hand when the first little blades came up. I would patrol the rows on my hands and knees for any worms and bugs, and I would kill and bury them. And sometimes when I had everything straight and clean for my things to grow, I would lie down on my back between two rows, and I would gaze up in the blue sky at the clouds moving and think all kinds of things.

In this passage, five of the seven sentences start with *I*. The voice is that of a child. If the writer had not wanted to achieve that effect, he might have written the passage this way:

1. According to my recollection, one thing in
2. particular that made me feel grateful toward
3. my mother was the day I went and asked her
4. for my own garden, and she did let me have my
5. own little plot. I loved it and took care of
6. it well, *especially growing peas.* I loved
7. especially to grow peas. Having them on the
8. table made me proud. I was proud when we had
9. them on the table. I would pull out the grass
10. in my garden by hand when the first little
11. blades came up *and* I would patrol the rows
12. on my hands and knees for any worms and bugs,
13. killing them and burying them and I would kill
14. and bury them. And sometimes when I had every-
15. thing straight and clean everything was straight
16. and clean for my things to grow, I would lie
17. down on my back between two rows and I would gaze
18. up in the blue sky at the clouds moving and think
19. all kinds of things.

Much of the childish charm of the original has disappeared along with seven of the eleven *I*'s.

If you wish to reduce the number of *I*'s or *we*'s, you can do so by applying any of these techniques that will work effectively in your writing:

1. Change the subject + verb to a prepositional phrase: "I remember" to "according to my recollection." See line 1.
2. Change the subject + verb to an *-ing* phrase: "I loved especially to grow peas" to "especially growing peas." See lines 6–7.
3. Change SVC clauses to *-ing* phrases to act as subject: "I was proud when we had them on the table" to "Having them on the table made me proud." See lines 7–8.
4. Combine sentences with the same subject: "I would pull out . . . I would patrol" to "I would pull out . . . and patrol." See lines 9 and 11.

5. Shift an object to subject position; this can be done by recasting the sentence from active to passive or, as in this case, by changing the verb *have* to *be:* "And sometimes when I *had* everything straight" to "when everything *was* straight." See lines 14 and 15. (Occasional use of the passive may be less harmful than piling up *I*'s.)

In summary, feel free to use the *I*, but keep an eye open to see that it doesn't sneak in at the beginning of several successive sentences; let it in only when you wish it to be there.

PARAGRAPHING IN PERSONAL WRITING

A new paragraph is like a Coke break — a pause that refreshes. Readers slow down, perk up, and prepare for a fresh start. Usually a new paragraph allows readers not only to catch their breath but also to get ready for a shift in the direction of thought. If you remember these two primary functions of paragraphing, you will realize the rhetorical opportunities available when considering whether or not to start a new paragraph in personal writing.

You probably have always used new paragraphs to introduce a new subject. But in personal writing, which is usually organized in chronological rather than logical sequences, and which conveys a more intimate and friendly tone, paragraphing may be more flexible. Often reader considerations override others. Generally, relatively short paragraphs (up to five or six sentences) appear lighter, easier, and quicker to read than lengthier ones. Therefore, rather than tax average readers with bulky paragraphs, writers often resort to shorter ones in relating personal experiences. Here, for example, is an excerpt from Erma Bombeck's popular newspaper column, "At Wit's End":

Teen-age runaways are serious business. But the Huckleberry Finn crowd is something else.

I had this friend whose preschooler ran away from home so often she rented his room.

There was scarcely a morning that Itchy Feet didn't announce dramatically, "I am leaving home," and grabbing a couple of essentials (a truck and a shoe box of baseball cards), he would start for the door.

These three short paragraphs could have been combined into one or two longer ones, but Bombeck probably wanted to attract readers, maintain a light tone, and quicken the pace by using several short paragraphs.

Sometimes in personal writing a long paragraph might be divided into shorter ones to emphasize a particular point. In the following examples from Stewart Alsop's *Stay of Execution,* an account of his life from the time he learned that he had leukemia to shortly before his death in 1974, the dread of being left alone is discussed in two paragraphs instead of one, giving the point greater emphasis.

In fact, I more than resented being left alone — I feared it. On the second page of my notebook, after the scribble "leukemia," there is a longer scribble: "Tish left briefly this afternoon and suddenly I was alone with an awful loneliness." These words tell something about what it is like to have a killing cancer, especially at first.

You become terribly dependent on other people, and the physical presence of other people becomes essential to you. Ordinarily, I rather liked being alone, but on rare occasions when I was alone during those first ten days at NIH [National Institute of Health] I hated it. I was even thankful for my roommate, the elderly farmer who shared my room. We had very little in common, and he was presumably dying too, but at least he was a warm body.

In dialogue, discretion may also be used in paragraphing. Usually, a new paragraph is required for each new speaker; related accompanying narrative and descriptive detail should be included in the new paragraph. The following passage illustrating this convention is from *To Teach, To Love* by Jesse Stuart. In it he relates how he was encouraged by his instructor, Dr. Alfred Crabb of Peabody College, to sell an assigned paper to a magazine.

This time Dr. Crabb asked me to stay after class. He said he wanted to talk to me about my paper. And I waited until all members of the class had left the room.

"Stuart, I've been at Peabody a long time," he said. "Each summer and each year I have my students taking philosophy of education do this paper. This is the best one I have ever received and I . . . ."

"Well, thank you, Dr. Crabb," I interrupted him. I was really pleased to have this compliment from him.

"And I think you might sell this paper to a magazine," he said.

"Which magazine would you suggest, Dr. Crabb?" I asked.

"Any of the quality magazines," he replied.

After talking to him, I hurried to my room, put the manuscript in an envelope with a self-addressed and stamped envelope for its return if it were rejected. I sent it to *Esquire*.

Note how the words of each speaker appear in a new paragraph, and how in the middle of the passage, Stuart's observation that he was pleased at the compliment follows his statement of appreciation in the same paragraph.

In the following passage from Richard Wright's autobiographical

Uncle Tom's Children, the novelist makes extensive use of paragraphs, often placing the speaker's words in separate paragraphs instead of after the speaker identification tag. We have italicized these instances to call them to your attention.

One night, just as I was about to go home, I met one of the Negro maids. She lived in my direction, and we fell in to walk part of the way home together. As we passed the white night-watchman, he slapped the maid on the buttock. I turned around, amazed. The watchman looked at me with a long, hard, fixed-under stare. Suddenly he pulled his gun and asked:
"Nigger, don't yuh like it?"
I hesitated.
"I asked yuh don't yuh like it?" he asked again, stepping forward.
"Yes, sir," I mumbled.
"Talk like it, then!"
"Oh, yes, sir!" I said with as much heartiness as I could muster.
Outside I walked ahead of the girl, ashamed to face her. She caught up with me and said:
"Don't be a fool! Yuh couldn't help it!"
    —Richard Wright, "The Ethics of Living Jim Crow," in *Uncle Tom's Children*

By placing the italicized statements in separate paragraphs instead of including them with the narrative material, Wright gains emphasis. The watchman's arrogant challenge—"Nigger, don't yuh like it?"—is highlighted by appearing on a separate line. Similarly, the woman's "Don't be a fool! Yuh couldn't help it!" emphasizes her acceptance of a life of oppression because it appears alone in a separate paragraph.

Occasionally, it may not be desirable to emphasize particular statements by individual speakers. For example, in the following passage from her autobiography, *Memories of a Catholic Girlhood*, Mary McCarthy incorporates into a single paragraph the following exchange between a priest and herself:

"You have doubts, Mother says," he began in a low, listless voice, pointing me to a straight chair opposite him and then seating himself in an armchair, with a half-averted face, as priests do in the confessional. I nodded self-importantly. "Yes, Father," I recited. "I doubt the divinity of Christ and the Resurrection of the Body and the real existence of Heaven and Hell." The priest raised his scanty eyebrows, like two little wigs, and sighed. "You have been reading atheistic literature?" I shook my head. "No, Father. The doubts came all by themselves." The priest cupped his chin in his hand. "So," he murmured. "Let us have them then."

These examples indicate that in personal writing you can be flexible about paragraphing. This does not mean that "anything goes" nor that "anything" will be effective. You should realize that new paragraphs traditionally signal the beginning of a new subject. But in personal writing, new paragraphs may also be used to emphasize a point or to make a passage appear lighter and easier to read. Your challenge is to decide how best to present your ideas in personal writing so that they will be attractive and clear to readers. Skillful paragraphing can help.

ASSIGNMENTS

For Discussion

1 Rewrite the following sentences, eliminating as many *I*'s as possible but preserving most of the original wording.

   a Because I am not accustomed to agreeing with Bill, I would like to point out that I do agree with him on this subject.
   b I had dolls that talked and cried and opened their eyes, but I never had a doll that I loved as much as I did the Betsy doll.
   c As I think back on the incident, I can realize now that I was being arrogant.
   d When I consider how my Sundays are wasted, I know that I could have studied more and I could have gotten higher grades.
   e I can remember vividly how I felt when I first drove off in the car alone.
   f I had not seen Terry for several weeks and as I thought about meeting her in an hour, I realized that I was worried about what I would say to her.
   g One night as I was returning from the library, I looked in the Chemistry Building and I saw a dog on the lab table, sniffing at the test tubes.
   h I felt I was too weak to continue. I thought I was going to pass out. I was afraid that I would not be found until it was too late.
   i I estimate that I must have thrown 36,700 newspapers onto porches during the days that I was delivering for the *News*.
   j I have always felt that if I were to receive an opportunity, I could become a famous spy.

2 Analyze the following selections to determine possible reasons why the writers paragraphed as they did.

   a You hear it said that fathers want their sons to be what they feel they cannot themselves be, but I tell you it also works the other way. A boy wants something very special from his father. I know that as a small boy I wanted my father to be a certain thing he was not. I wanted him to be a proud, silent, dignified father. When I was with other boys and he passed along the street, I wanted to feel a flow of pride: "There he is. That is my father."

But he wasn't such a one. He couldn't be. It seemed to me then that he was always showing off. Let's say someone in our town had got up a show. They were always doing it. The druggist would be in it, the shoe-clerk, the horse doctor, and a lot of women and girls. My father would manage to get the chief comedy part. It was, let's say, a Civil War play and he was a comic Irish soldier. He had to do the most absurd things. They thought he was funny, but I didn't.

I thought he was terrible. I didn't see how mother could stand it. She even laughed with the others. Maybe I would have laughed if it hadn't been my father.

— Sherwood Anderson, "Discovery of a Father"

b I had not seen don Juan for several months. It was the autumn of 1971. I had the certainty that he was at the house of don Genaro, a fellow sorcerer in central Mexico, and made the necessary preparations for a long drive to visit him. On the second day of my journey, however, on an impulse, I stopped at don Juan's place in Sonora, in the midafternoon. To my surprise, I found him there.

My surprise seemed to delight him. He was sitting on an empty milk crate by the front door. He appeared to have been waiting for me. There was an air of accomplishment in the ease with which he greeted me. He took off his hat and flourished it in a comical gesture. Then he put it on again and gave me a military salute.

— Carlos Castaneda, *Journey to Ixtlan: The Lessons of Don Juan*

c So much for Thanksgivings past. With that behind me, it's perfectly clear why I've made a small production out of Thanksgiving all the years I've been married. They call it Compensating. It began with my first little frozen and eviscerated turkey on West Ninth Street, and has been going on ever since. On the side of Norman Rockwell, The Pilgrims, and Nostalgia, it's always been a classic American meal, but everyone's always loved it; no one's ever complained. This year, when Jonathan did, I pounced on his request for something different, and it worked: George vanished. I pored over cookbooks and Jonathan's old *Gourmet* magazines, and when I finally had an impressive menu mapped out, threw myself into the marketing and cooking. I ran around shopping by foot, picking everything out myself and lugging it home—the sixteen pound bird, the vegetables and fruits. (I startled the hell out of them at the Nieuw Amsterdam Market, where, as Jonathan once informed me, "the clientele only orders by phone.") I even stood and watched the man in the fish store shuck the oysters for the stuffing, and walked all the way over to Schrafft's for the pumpkin pie, the one stand-by of the Nostalgia menu that intuition told me not to change this year. Then I cooked everything, from the soup, a *consommé double* which required two days of keeping a stock-pot bubbling on the stove, to the nuts, almonds I blanched, buttered, salted and roasted myself.

—Sue Kaufman, *Diary of a Mad Housewife*

For Writing

1   As an exercise, dash off the first draft of a few paragraphs about a recent experience, using as many *I*'s as come to mind. Then revise the passage, using the techniques for eliminating *I*'s suggested on page 113. Compare the percentage of *I*'s deleted with the results of your classmates.

2   Write an analysis of the paragraphing of John Updike's "A&P," a short story narrated in the form of a personal experience (reprinted in Chapter 30).

3   Write a short dialogue between yourself and some friends about a recent movie, television program, teacher, athletic event, party, or other subject. In a separate statement, explain why you deviated from conventional paragraphing at any point.

Revision
of Personal
Writing

WRITERS AND REVISION

Good writing results from careful, thoughtful, painstaking revision. Although it is probably the most important step in the writing process, most students overlook revision, apparently feeling that papers can be dashed off at one sitting and then copied in a neat final draft. Experienced writers know better. Tolstoy wondered how anyone could write without rewriting everything over and over again, a conviction that no doubt accounts for the fact that he revised *War and Peace,* his monumental masterpiece, five times. James Thurber has told of rewriting a short story fifteen times; Hemingway of redoing the last page of *A Farewell to Arms* thirty-nine times. James Michener never does even an important letter in one draft, because he considers himself to be "not a good writer" but "one of the world's great rewriters." And Truman Capote (*In Cold Blood, Breakfast at Tiffany's*) follows a set routine: a first draft in penciled longhand, a complete revision done the same way, a third draft typed on "a very special kind of yellow paper," and after a week or month, a final version typed on white paper.

In view of the example and advice of professional writers, why do most students fail to revise their papers? It may simply be that they do not realize the importance of revision. They may fail to view writing as a process, a system of achieving an objective through a series of step-by-step operations much like other processes, such as baking a cake, planting a garden, preparing lab equipment, or even waxing a car. The writing

120

process consists of five steps: selecting a subject, planning it, writing, revising, and proofreading. Newspapers and newsmagazines assign these steps to different people: an editor selects the subject, a reporter writes about it, a rewrite person revises it, and a proofreader checks it. You must play all these roles yourself. The first three roles will be considered later. Here we will be concerned with revision and proofreading.

BLOCKS TO EFFECTIVE REVISION

The main obstacles to effective revision are psychological ones. After you have received a writing assignment, stewed about it, labored over it, and eventually turned out an acceptable quantity of words, chances are that you will be elated. How great to be rid of that nagging worry about the assignment! Why fuss and fret further? Why not copy the paper neatly, and then dash off for a date, a beer, or a movie?

Added to this euphoria of completion is the satisfaction derived from the act of creation. Certainly there is a special joy in creating something with your own mind and hands, whether it is a sandcastle, a candle, a poem, an omelet, a piece of pottery, or a writing assignment. But often, in our enthusiasm, we are blind to our creation's imperfections. And so, blinded by pride and hope, we turn in a completed—but unrevised —paper. It is done—the impossible has been accomplished! And we are usually content.

APPROACHES TO EFFECTIVE REVISION

How to combat these two paralyzing psychological blocks—the euphoria of completion and the satisfaction of creation? The answer lies in transforming yourself from author to editor. In other words, you must reread your paper as you would someone else's. You must, in a sense, become another person, detached and objective, one who will not be kind, considerate, or generous about the writing, but will scrutinize it closely, noting every error, flaw, weakness, awkwardness. This transformation from author to editor can best be accomplished by getting away from the first draft for a period of time and by adopting a particular critical frame of mind.

The first draft should cool for as long as possible so that you can see it as others will. Like pie from the oven, its taste can't truly be judged while it's hot. The best suggestion is to write the first draft long before your deadline and get away from the paper for a day or two. But if you're working at the last minute, as most of us do, take a break to walk, make a phone call, watch TV, or work on an assignment for another course. When you return, you will be more likely to read your paper as a stranger.

Then you can see what you have actually written instead of what you intended to write. The longer you stay away from your first draft, the more likely you are to find faults.

And find faults you must. If you view revision as a perfunctory chore to be completed quickly, then don't waste your time. You must consider revision as a valuable opportunity to catch your errors, find your weaknesses, improve your strengths—in sum, to turn a so-so first draft into a first-rate paper. It means being harsh, ruthless in refusing to settle for less than perfection. It means consciously searching for imperfections, trying to spot weaknesses. Only in this frame of mind can you revise effectively.

STRATEGIES FOR REVISING PERSONAL WRITING

An effective way to revise any particular piece of writing is to formulate questions pertinent to the special needs and aims of the writing assignment. The following questions apply to the special characteristics of personal narrative.

Organization

1. Is my organization clear? If narrative, is the time sequence consistent? If personal essay, do I follow the direction set by my opening statement?
2. Is the paper organized so that it accomplishes what I had in mind when I started writing?
3. Is my paragraphing appropriate to the purpose of my paper?

Narration

1. Are the voice and language of the narrator consistent throughout?
2. Has my choice of narrative method—direct or indirect discourse—been the most effective for my purposes?

Language

1. Is the language of the dialogue as realistic as possible?
2. Is the language consistent with character and situation?
3. Have I provided enough specific details to describe the action adequately? Can my readers experience it for themselves, or are they forced to adopt my own reactions? Do all the details contribute to the action, or are there irrelevant passages?
4. Have I made effective use of figurative language? Active verbs?
5. Have I been careful not to overuse *I* and *we*?

Punctuation

Have I made effective use of the punctuation marks that are particularly important in personal writing: dashes, exclamation marks, parentheses, and quotation marks?

As you can see, brutally honest answers to some questions may lead to major revisions, such as rewriting the paper with a new approach. But other questions require only minor changes—additions or deletions throughout the paper. Painful as this process is, it is perhaps the most important of the five writing steps in fulfilling your writing commitment to yourself: to write the best narrative that you are capable of and to discover for yourself the real sense of satisfaction that comes from disciplining your creative powers.

PROOFREADING

So you've worked hard to revise your paper; you should be finished. You should be able to turn it in, confident you've done your best. But you can't. Still another step lies ahead: the fifth and last one, proofreading.

Proofreading a paper before turning it in is like glancing in the mirror before an important date to make sure that you look your best. But good proofreading requires more than a glance. Although this inspection is slow and tedious, it is an important step in all writing—but especially in personal writing because you may have taken a more relaxed approach to your paper and thus made more mechanical errors.

It's difficult to decrease your reading speed to about five miles an hour to scrutinize your final copy, noting whether words are missing, letters are omitted or juxtaposed, punctuation is right, words have not accidentally been repeated at ends and beginnings of lines and pages, and so on and on and on. It is easy to race through a paper, skim it quickly, and think that it is proofread. But most students find it difficult to inch through their papers patiently and painstakingly, maybe stopping to make certain that an *ei* should not be an *ie,* checking a style guide about the comma before *which,* seeing every letter of every word on every page. To help, you may want to read aloud slowly to yourself or start at the end and go through the paper backward, sentence by sentence, as some professional proofreaders do.

Proofreading is tedious, like fishing when they're not biting. It takes persistence, but the payoff is worth it. No one excuses careless writing, even when it is autobiographical. To most people, a slip of the pen is as serious as a slip of the mind. But even if your motivation is only to please yourself, then it's best to look carefully at your final draft. Proofread thoroughly; give your brainchild that final glance before you send it off to meet its public. Don't be careless!

ASSIGNMENTS

For Discussion

1   How do you go about the process of writing? And why do you do what you do? For example, to what extent do you think about the subject before writing? Do you write down ideas, jot an outline, make any notes? Where do you write—desk, library, bed, floor? With what— pen, pencil, typewriter? On lined or unlined paper; pads, loose pages, or notebooks? When do you write: mornings, afternoons, evenings? Do you revise or merely recopy? How carefully do you proofread?

2   Are you aware of the psychological blocks that keep you from revising effectively? How do you usually feel after you finish a first draft? How satisfied are you with your papers when you turn them in?

3   Had you realized that most writers place such importance on revising, spend so much time doing it, and revise so frequently? Do you know about any writers, other than those mentioned, who revise extensively?

4   Do you agree that proofreading is important? Should a careless slip affect your grade, or should it be overlooked because it indicates nothing about your writing ability?

5   Is it harder or easier to proofread your own writing than someone else's? Why?

6   How does proofreading differ from regular reading?

7   Is there anything wrong with the following?

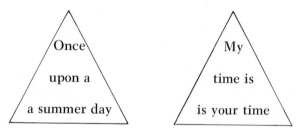

For Writing

1   Proofread the following student paper, correcting only the typographical and other careless spelling, punctuation, and similar mechanical errors.

When living in a dorm, you give up all your privacy. It seems like you are not alone for one minute. There is either somone talking at you or looking at you. This makes life difficult and exasperating at time.

Everyone likes to have the opportunity to do some studing sit and daydream undisturbed,or to have a private conversation with thier friends. The walls in the dorn, which are tissue-thin, conduct sound very well. This results in you're next store neighbor hearing all your most most valuable secrets. Besides accidental eavesdroping, there is the constant interruption of your thinking when someone plays there sterio or tv at full blast. Another difficulty is that guests alway arrive at the most inconvient monent. At home they would would call first. here they pop in whenever your a mess, at your worse.

Talking on the phone can also be a harrasing experience. There are no seperate lines, usually eight girls on a single one. And the the same number on the other line. Providing you are lucky enough to get the person that you want to talk to to on the line, then the invasion of privacy begins. Every ten second one of the other fourteen people on the too lines tries to place a call, Or, somone sits near you, listening, hopping you will hang up. You could go out of you mind?

That's not as bad as your date's being a topic of intrest and concern to all your dormitory friends. Take, for example, the "One O Clock Check-Up," which occurs on Friday and Saturdays nihgts when people return from their dats. Then the inspectors usally examine the new arrivals. They check for tale-tale signs such as drunken behavior, passion marks, overly red lips, wrinkled cloothing, messed hair, and and flushed faces. From this checklist they can detect what you did and what sort of time you had. You just cant keep anything a secret.

Usually the last stronghold of privacy is the bathroom, but in a dorm even this seem lost. The shower curtains do not insure privacy. they flap when the water is turned on, exposing all your fat and everything. Then there is the bathtub calamity. Every time you start you start daydreaming in a delicious, soothing, steeming tube of water, someone sticks her head in and tries to see if you are allmost done. Lying there, with faces peaking at your every few minites you want to scream.

Well, you finally realize that the privacy you had at home just isn't possible in the dorms. About all you can do is to expect the fact and enjoy invading the privacy of others. But then. if you get disparate, you can if you disire—go home again.

2   Revise the following student narrative, correcting mechanical errors and adjusting sentence structure and paragraphing where you think it's needed.

The rays of the Sun are breaking in again. Time to start another day of being stoned and lying around. Breakfast on another coke and English Muffin at Howard Johnsons. Here comes Harmon and Dale to play the days activities.

"How you doin Jimmy?"

"O'kay Harmon; what are we goin to do today?"

"Well, I got a hold of some nice hash, so lets go to the country and get high."

We signed for our meals, being employees, and headed for the country. We go out of the bussle of people going to work and preceeded to get stoned. After driving and smoking for about an hour we pulled off the road and walked through the meadow of new hay too the woods. Everything was comming alive from its winter sleep and seemed so fresh. The air was full of scents of clover, honeysuckle, mint, and trees. The birds gayly singing their songs to the world, as if they wanted a reaction.

The stream was clear blue, as was the sky. Rippling along and sings it's own song for who ever would listen. All around was life and freshness and beauty. We sat by the stream and started talking about what we were going to do. The discussion shifted and Harmon and Dale talked about the deals they were making, and how much money was comming in. As I listened I realized that all their life would ever be was a dope deal and the profits made from that deal. It had also dawned on me that I was the same way. Living from day to day selling a little dope to get more dope, and continuing in the same way. Was this the life I wanted? The next morning, climbing the hill to school, fear of what was to happen mounted. Acceptance back into the social order would be hard to accomplish, and failure was easy. Walking through the hall with reservation I made it to the rea door where people I knew stayed. Moving out and into the crowd I was greeted with the love and happiness of a travler being away on a journey. This was where I belonged, with people who care about life and the living of that life.

The Informative Voice: Descriptive Writing

8

Introduction
to Descriptive
Writing

My task . . . is, by the power of the written word, to make you hear, to make you feel — it is, before all, to make you see.

— Joseph Conrad

This is precisely the purpose of descriptive writing: to share with readers some object, scene, activity, person, or mood that you have experienced. When you re-create it in writing, you are trying to capture the way it is or the way you saw it, heard it, felt it, tasted it, or smelled it.

Why bother? Mainly to inform and interest others, either as the main purpose of a written work or as part of a personal, expository, argumentative, critical, or other essay. For example, you might describe the pollution of a stream in a political pamphlet, the attractiveness of a rug in an advertising brochure, the character of a person in a business recommendation, the beauty of a campsite in a college newspaper article, the taste of food in rating a restaurant, the outcome of a laboratory experiment in a scientific report, the damage to a car in an accident report, or the features of a person in a letter to a friend. Whether or not they are aware of it, people are constantly describing, and often their descriptive ability determines whether they are interesting or dull people. Some of your friends can go on a vacation and enthrall you afterward with a lengthy, vivid account of magnificent natural settings or quaint, charming towns; other friends can tell you little more than that they had fun. What accounts for the difference?

THE QUALITIES NEEDED FOR DESCRIPTIVE WRITING

Good description depends upon keen perception and a vocabulary adequate to convey the experience in concrete, specific words. To some extent, these two qualities—perception and vocabulary—are interrelated. Only as we become aware of and interested in flowers do we add such words as *forsythia, crocus, delphinium, snapdragon, iris, phlox, petunia, zinnia, dahlia, salvia,* and *marigold* to our vocabulary. Of course, we may pick up many words from conversation, reading, and watching television, but most of the concrete nouns so important in description come from our own experiences. Test yourself. If you know these words, how did you acquire them: *kettledrum, catfish, buttonhole, scissors, tachometer, split end?* Whether you learned the word before perceiving the object or perceived the object and then learned the word, you need to develop both your perception and vocabulary to write effective descriptions. In this chapter and the following ones, we hope to help you improve your power of observation and your skill in using words to describe what you perceive.

Perception

Perception depends on curiosity, on developing an interest in other people and the world you live in. It requires using all your senses, particularly sight, to observe what you have merely glanced at before. For example, take a close look at one of your new college friends. Observe the color, texture, thickness, and style of hair; the color, clarity, and movement of eyes; shape and thickness of eyebrows; size and protrusion of ears; color, texture, shape, and size of lips and mouth; size and shape of nose; bone structure and skin tones of face. Note the changes when your friend smiles, laughs, talks, broods, or gets angry. If you observe these features, you will be able to reply intelligently to your parents (instead of saying something nondescript and vague) when they ask you what your friend looks like.

Everyone and everything may look the same if you don't sharpen your senses to the world about you. A robin may look like a cardinal, homemade bread may taste like store-bought, wool may feel like cotton. And except for rock or other music, you may be completely oblivious to "background" sounds, not conscious of their quality, not noting how our ears are assaulted by noise. In *The Second Tree from the Corner,* E. B. White discusses sound:

Sound is not easily measured. Some of the loudest sounds wouldn't give a decibel machine the faintest tremor: a hushed voice in a house where someone has died; or a child's finger on the latch of a door where a man is trying to work, timorously testing the lock to see if the man won't come out and play. The quality of sound is much more telling than the volume, and this is true in the city, where noise is inevitable. A country sawmill is rich in decibels, yet the ear adjusts easily to it, and it soon becomes as undisturbing as a cicada on a suburban afternoon. New Year's noise, even in its low decibel range, has an irritating quality, full of sharp distemper. It is impatient, masochistic — unlike the noise of Paris, where the shrill popping of high-pitched horns spreads a gaiety and a slightly drunken good nature. Heat has an effect on sound, intensifying it. On a scorching morning, at breakfast in a cafe, one's china cup explodes against its saucer with a fierce report. The great climaxes of sound in New York are achieved in side streets, as in West 44th Street, beneath our window, where occasionally an intestinal stoppage takes place, the entire block laden with undischarged vehicles, the pang of congestion increasing till every horn is going — a united, delirious scream of hate, every decibel charged with a tiny drop of poison.

We suggest that you pay more attention to what you hear and taste and smell and touch and see, not merely to improve your writing of descriptions, but to add to your enjoyment of life. We experience life primarily through our senses, and as we increase or heighten our sense perceptions, so we enrich our lives. Much of the beauty in the world comes from nature — from the land, the trees, the flowers, the birds, the sky, the rain and snow. As we increase our awareness of nature, become more sensitive to its delicate and subtle colors, patterns, shapes, and sounds, we appreciate more of what life has to offer and live more fully and richly. Of course, everything in nature or in the world is not beautiful. Much is ugly. In *Hard Times,* Charles Dickens wrote about Coketown, a fictitious city modeled after the polluted industrial towns of England in the 1850s:

It was a town of red brick, or brick that would have been red if the smoke and ashes had allowed it; but as matters stood it was a town of unnatural red and black like the painted face of a savage. It was a town of machinery and tall chimneys, out of which interminable serpents of smoke trailed themselves forever and ever, and never got uncoiled. It had a black canal in it, and a river that ran purple with ill-smelling dye, and vast piles of building full of windows where there was a rattling and a trembling all day long, and where the piston of the steam-engine worked monotonously up and down like the head of an elephant in a state of melancholy madness.

Sometimes the ugliness of a place is internal, as in Rabbit Angstrom's apartment in John Updike's *Rabbit, Run:*

The clutter behind him in the room—the Old-fashioned glass with its corrupt dregs, the choked ashtray balanced on the easy-chair arm, the rumpled rug, the floppy stacks of slippery newspapers, the kid's toys here and there broken and stuck and jammed, a leg off a doll and a piece of bent cardboard that went with some breakfast-box cutout, the rolls of fuzz under the radiators, the continual crisscrossing mess—clings to his back like a tightening net.

Whether our personal world is ugly or beautiful or, more likely, some mixture of the two, we become more alive as we grow more aware of its sights, sounds, smells, tastes, and texture. And being more aware and more alert to what is going on about us, we become more interested in life and more interesting to others.

Vocabulary

In part, good description results from perception. But it also results in part from conveying this experience to others in words. Sometimes we may not know the precise term to describe what we have perceived, but often we are just too lazy or unwilling to search our minds or check our dictionaries or other sources for the exact word. For example, if you were writing about the odor of a kitchen, attic, cellar, or gym, would you use any of the following?

stale	smoky	spicy	rancid
musty	fragrant	rich	burnt
greasy	cloying	pungent	sour
damp	heavy	dusty	acrid

Most of these words are familiar, yet we might be too lazy or uninterested to use them. We would probably be content just to write, "The room smelled good" or "The room smelled bad." To write effective descriptions, we must take the trouble to search for the precise words that state exactly what we have perceived.

True, specific words are effective as we discussed in Chapter 3, but sometimes you may not know any. For example, when writing about horses, you might have difficulty if you were unfamiliar with such terms as *foals, colts, yearlings; geldings, mares, fillies, stallions; thoroughbred, quarter,* and *draft; palominos, roans,* and *pintos.* To describe a formal room, you would need to know the names of the different styles of furniture: Chippendale, Duncan Phyfe, Victorian, Windsor, Louis XVI, Queen Anne. To do justice to a basketball game, you should be able to use such words as *pick, press, dunk, charge, switch off, goal tend,* and *zone defense.* Of course, such specialized words are not always necessary. But when they are, and you don't know them, what can you do?

A lengthy discourse on vocabulary-building would be out of place in this introductory chapter about description. We do suggest, though, that you open your eyes and ears to the words in your books, magazines, newspapers, and textbooks, and in the talk, lectures, and conversations of friends, professors, and television personalities. You may want to jot down some of these words, check them in the dictionary, and try them out right away in your conversations to fix them in your memory.

You can also begin to anticipate your experience. If you're going to a dog show, talk to people in advance about it or read up on it in the library, looking at books about dogs, magazine articles, or encyclopedias. You can prepare yourself in the same way if you're going to California, a soccer game, or a local historic place. Of course, much of the information will be written in words you already know and use; some, however, will take the form of new words that you need to acquire to understand, appreciate, and describe the experience to others.

Others—they're the ones you are writing for. In a sense, you are like a newspaper reporter, presenting a picture of what you have perceived. It need not be a dramatic auto accident, a vicious murder, a magnificent church wedding, an exciting bank hold-up, or a blazing three-alarm fire. It may be a chaotic dorm room, a routine morning school bus ride, an eccentric professor, or noon at the local hamburger joint.

Whatever you select as a topic, all your senses must be alert so that you can perceive the experience clearly and completely, and you must translate and transform your perceptions into words that convey the experience accurately, vividly, and lucidly to others. That's what description is all about.

THE FORMS OF DESCRIPTIVE WRITING: FACTUAL AND PERSONAL

What exactly is description? What forms does it take? What are its characteristics?

Let's start with the philosophers, who have argued for centuries whether an object really exists or exists only in the mind of someone perceiving it. This metaphysical speculation gave rise to the classic question: Does a falling tree make a sound in the forest if no one is around to hear it? We mention this philosophical problem not to confuse you but to relate it to the two basic forms of description: factual and personal.

Factual description assumes that material substances exist independently of the beholder. It follows that people, places, animals, buildings, objects, and scenes can be accurately and objectively described as they truly are, regardless of the personal perceptions, associations, and impressions in the mind of a particular writer. What is important in such factual descriptions is fidelity to the subject. As a writer, you try to present the subject not as it seems to you alone, but as it exists to any objective observer. A factual description of toads, for example, would enable readers to recognize and learn about them. It would not mention your squeamishness about them. All such personal reactions should be omitted from factual descriptions. In a nutshell, the factual description proclaims: This is the way it *is*.

Not so the personal description. It assumes that material substances have no true reality because each is transformed by the minds and senses of people. Therefore, we each are entitled to our own reactions, responses, impressions, feelings about anything we see, hear, smell, taste, or feel. In the process of describing, we may reveal much about ourselves as well as our subjects. In another nutshell, the personal description proclaims: This is the way it is to *me,* the writer.

The distinction between a factual and personal description is somewhat like that between photographs and paintings. Although photographers do select the angle, light, composition, lens opening, and shutter speed, their freedom is greatly limited by the subject. And generally their purpose is limited: to represent the subject as it exists to most people. But in paintings, artists portray only what they observe and choose to represent. They may enlarge, diminish, discolor, or otherwise distort or transform the subject as they wish. The photograph is similar to factual description; the painting to personal description.

Of course, all is not that simple. Just as photographs may reveal much of the photographers' personal views and just as paintings may realistically portray their subjects, so descriptions may be neither purely factual nor purely personal but a combination of both. Therefore, we should think of descriptive writing as a broad spectrum, with factual description at one end, personal description at the other, and many shades in between.

Let's look at a couple of examples. Here is an excerpt from a factual description of the praying mantis:

The praying mantis, a member of the family Mantida, order Orthoptera, derives its name from the prayerful position it assumes with front legs raised while the mantis is waiting to attack its prey. A full-grown mantis varies from 2 to 5 inches in length, resembles in color the plants on which it rests. Behind the small, freely movable, triangular head with a biting mouthpiece is a long and thin prothorax, which is held almost erect. The rest of the body is thicker, although the general shape is long and slender. The wings are short and broad. The forelegs have sharp hooks for capturing and holding the prey, which consists mainly of injurious insects.

The purpose here is to present information objectively and clearly. The writer's attitude toward the insect is not revealed: the tone is matter-of-fact, the language simple, clear, exact. Anyone with a knowledge of the mantis might have written this description; there is no flavor to it, nothing personal, distinctive, individualistic.

Quite the opposite is this paragraph from Jean Henri Fabre's captivating descriptive essay about the praying mantis:

Apart from her lethal implement [the forelegs], the Mantis has nothing to inspire dread. She is not without a certain beauty, in fact, with her slender figure, her elegant bust, her pale-green colouring and her long gauze wings. No ferocious mandibles, opening like shears; on the contrary, a dainty pointed muzzle that seems made for billing and cooing. Thanks to a flexible neck, quite independent of the thorax, the head is able to move freely, to turn to right or left, to bend, to lift itself. Alone among insects, the Mantis directs her gaze; she inspects and examines; she almost has a physiognomy.

—Edwin Way Teale, ed., *The Insect World of J. Henri Fabre*

The purpose here is to convey an impression of the insect, particularly how this writer feels about it. To most people, the mantis is sinister; to Fabre, the mantis resembles an attractive, slender woman with an elegant bust, a dainty mouth, a head that turns to inspect and examine, and almost facial features. In the factual description, the mantis was referred to as *it*; here the mantis is *she*. Fabre provides his readers with a fresh, distinctive way of thinking about and visualizing the mantis. This personal description is distinctive, individualistic, interpretative, anything but objective. And, in language that is rich and suggestive (*elegant, ferocious, like shears, billing and cooing*), the description contains elements of both irony and droll humor as it points out the contrast between appearance and reality.

As we have said, some descriptions combine the factual and the personal. As in most writing, the purpose, audience, and context should determine the nature of a description. In much scientific, industrial, government, and business writing, the purpose of description is to present the facts to an audience interested in learning them; such descriptions take the form of speeches, reports, articles, memorandums, and books—all usually serious and formal. In novels, short stories, plays, poems, and personal narratives, the purpose is usually to evoke an experience to an audience interested in feeling and perceiving it under circumstances that are more relaxed and less formal. And in other writing—nonfictional books and articles about places, scenes, objects, people, and the like—the purpose is to interest and inform an audience in ways that vary considerably, from the light and casual to the serious and significant. Thus writers approach description in various ways and use it—

often in descriptive essays, but usually within narrative, informative, and persuasive works—according to their purpose, the audience's interests, and the communication situation.

What this means to you is that you need to weigh these three factors before writing a description. For example, if you describe your dorm room to your mother so that she can make curtains for it or bring you some furniture, you should stick mainly to the factual. If you describe it for a high school friend, you should usually present your personal impressions. And if you were to describe it for a family friend, favorite high school teacher, or clergyman, you should combine the factual and the personal.

At this point, you might find the following outline helpful as a summary to remind you of the differences between the two main types of descriptions.

	Factual	*Personal*
Purpose	To present information	To present an impression
Approach	Objective, dispassionate	Subjective, interpretative
Appeal	To the understanding	To the senses
Tone	Matter-of-fact	Emotional
Coverage	Complete, exact	Selective
Language	Simple, clear	Rich, suggestive
Uses	Writing in science, industry, government, professions, business	Novels, short stories, plays, poems, personal narratives, some essays

We shall elaborate on some of these distinctions in later chapters when we suggest ways of writing effective descriptions.

ASSIGNMENTS

For Discussion

Contrast the following descriptions as those of the praying mantis were contrasted.

DAISY (CHRYSANTHEMUM LEUCANTHEMUM PINNATIFIDUM)

A dicotyledon of the sunflower family (*compositae*), the daisy has flowers of dense heads, many florets, akene fruited, alternate and opposite leaves on stems 1–2 feet high. Its leaves are lobed with large blunt teeth. The flower heads, borne at the end of slender stems, are 1½–2 inches across. The central "eye" of disk flowers is surrounded by ray flowers. The disk flowers bear the style, stamens, and ovary.

THE DAY'S EYE[1]

Daisies come to bloom, whiten the roadsides and dapple the old pastures. Some people call them oxeye daisies, which is a redundancy, since the word "daisy" is no more than "day's eye" in the old English. Botanically the name is *Chrysanthemum leucanthemum,* which perpetuates another old English name, Whiteflower or Whiteweed. One old back-country name in New England is Farmer's Curse.

Weekenders and newcomers to the country pick daisies for bouquets. Farmers consider the daisy a pesky weed. But as long as it grows at the roadside it will grow in the meadow. It will grow in an ash heap, in a pile of rubble, in a crack in the city pavement.

The daisy is tough as an urchin, insistent as a beggar. And really a beautiful flower, unless one happens to be a farmer.

For Writing

1 Write a factual description of a clock-radio, this book, your shoe, or your English classroom.
2 Write a personal description of telephones, credit cards, bubble gum, contact lenses, or trains.
3 Write a factual description of any subject you wish. Then write a personal description of it.

---

[1] *New York Times,* 20 Aug. 1975. © 1975 by The New York Times Company. Reprinted by permission.

Writing Descriptions

It is one thing to know what goes into gazpacho soup, fettuccine, strudel, and crêpes suzette; it is another thing to create them. Similarly, it is one thing to know what makes effective factual and personal descriptions, but another to write them. In this chapter we shall discuss matters of organization, style, and tone that are pertinent to your descriptive papers. We shall assume from your reading of the last chapter that you recognize the differences between factual and personal descriptions and recognize when one kind or the other is appropriate. Although some writing situations may call for a hybrid of the two, our suggestions deal with each type separately because you can easily combine them once you have mastered each individually.

FACTUAL DESCRIPTION

Factual descriptions require you to present information clearly and objectively. To achieve these qualities in your writing, you should keep in mind the following recommendations about organization, style, and tone.

Organization

Factual descriptions are mainly concerned with visual observations of organic or inorganic matter, although other information may be included. Sometimes the organization must follow a prescribed pattern established by a particular discipline, publication, course, or company.

The following description of the cardinal from Roger Tory Peterson's well-known *Field Guide to the Birds* illustrates such an organizational scheme:

CARDINAL   RICHMONDENA CARDINALIS   Subsp. p. 214 illustration

Field marks: — *The only all-red bird with a crest.* Smaller than Robin (8–9). Male: — All red except for black patch at base of bill. Female: — Yellowish-brown, with a touch of red; at once recognizable by its crest and heavy bill.

Similar Species: — Summer Tanager (no crest); Special Tanager (black wings).

Voice: — Song, a series of clear, slurred whistles diminishing in pitch. Several variations: *what-cheer, cheer, cheer,* etc.: *whoit whoit whoit,* etc. Note, a short thin chip.

Range: — United States e. of Plains and n. to s. New York, Lake Erie (s. Ontario), s. Minnesota, and se. South Dakota; towns, farms, roadsides, edges, swamps, etc. Non-migratory.

This pattern (field marks, similar species, voice, range) would present you with no organizational problem: once you had established the sequence, you would simply follow it. In other factual descriptive assignments, realizing that sight is the main means of perception, you might use some form of spatial organization like top to bottom (see the description of the praying mantis, p. 134), left to right, main feature to less important ones, foreground to background. Like a cinematographer letting the audience observe every detail clearly, you should focus on each part before moving in an expected direction rather than confusing the audience by jumping back and forth unpredictably. But unlike the camera operator, you can reveal more than meets the eye and ear. In the preceding description, for example, note the information about where cardinals may be found.

Style

You can assume that readers are already interested in the subject of your factual description and wish to be informed about it as accurately, clearly, and completely as their needs indicate. Consequently, you need not attempt to arouse their curiosity or otherwise motivate them. But you should keep their purpose and reading interests in mind. The description of the cardinal, for example, was written mainly for people who just want to be able to identify a strange bird and learn a little about it. Of course, in such general factual descriptions, there are no imaginative opening lines like "Most glorious of all the winged creatures is the magnificent shocking-red male cardinal." And there are none of the scientific facts about eating, breeding, and the like that ornithologists would need.

In keeping with the objective approach, the language in factual descriptions is specific and simple. Naturally, an account of a breeder reactor producing plutonium would be couched in more technical terms for nuclear physicists than for nonscientists. Like most of the language, the sentences are relatively simple and short, featuring mainly forms of *be* and other common verbs, beginning with subject-verb combinations, and omitting the first person pronoun (*I*). Observe these characteristics for yourself in the following passage about the sassafras from Alfred Carl Hottes' *Book of Trees:*

The leaves are usually one- to three-lobed and turn orange-scarlet in the Autumn. The bark is a cinnamon-gray, and is deeply furrowed. The twigs are hairy when young, and yellowish-green, aromatic, and with very unequal internodes. The scanty fruits are bluish-black, with red stems, and surrounded at the base by thick, scarlet calyx.

Hottes presents only the facts, using precise adjectives and concrete nouns and emphasizing the details by avoiding almost any other verb but the colorless *be*. In some circumstances, verbs are so unimportant that they are omitted, as they were in the description of the cardinal.

Tone

The tone used must be appropriate to the objective, straightforward presentation of the material. Readers should be unaware of the writer. No judgment should be rendered, no opinion stated, no feeling expressed. A driver may smell of alcohol (a fact), but unless the results of a breath test are available, he or she should not be described as drunk (a judgment).

Complete objectivity is difficult but necessary if readers are to rely on what is written. This factual, impartial quality is best achieved by a matter-of-fact tone with no excesses, no emotions. Because the subject is serious, the attitude of the writer should be serious. Thus a factual description — whether of an eye, a rock formation, a television tube, or an engine — may be quite formal, even dull and dry. But otherwise it may not be trusted. The voice heard in the writing should be that of an authority speaking soberly and calmly, not that of an average person expressing opinions and emotions. Perhaps factual descriptions, as a result, do not make for exciting reading, but they do serve important, useful functions when readers need reliable information. And generally, if readers are at all curious about a subject, they will be interested in any intelligent, clear, carefully written description of it. Consequently, in this form of description, which implies "Here are the facts," only a sincere, straightforward, matter-of-fact tone is effective.

PERSONAL DESCRIPTION

In personal descriptions, which are based on your response to objects, scenes, situations, and persons, you attempt to share your experience with your readers, hoping to re-create it and thus evoke a similar response. What is important is the way you feel about the subject. Your organization, style, and tone, therefore, must be appropriate to the mood you wish to create.

Organization

Because writers wish to convey some dominant impression, they usually state it in the opening sentence or sentences. Note how Edgar Allan Poe achieves this effect in "The Fall of the House of Usher":

During the whole of a dull, dark, and soundless day in the autumn of the year, when the clouds hung oppressively low in the heavens, I had been passing along, on horseback, through a singular dreary tract of country; and at length found myself, as the shades of evening drew on, within view of the melancholy House of Usher. I knew not how it was — but, with the first glimpse of the building, a sense of insufferable gloom pervaded my spirit.

In these two beginning sentences, Poe has created a mood of oppressive melancholy and stated his dominant impression, one of "insufferable gloom." This early statement of a dominant impression is a fine example for you to follow in your personal descriptions. Occasionally, however, you may withhold your impression for the conclusion to give the effect of a summary.

In addition to stating the dominant impression, you must consider whether you wish to be a static or moving observer. If static, then you should select and follow consistently some logical order, just as in factual descriptions. If moving, then you must clearly signal readers with phrases or sentences that mark the shift from one location to another. To illustrate, here are some of the introductory sentences from paragraphs in John Ruskin's description of St. Mark's Cathedral in Venice:

And now I wish that the reader, before I bring him into St. Mark's Place, would imagine himself for a little time in a quiet English Cathedral town, and walk with me to the west front of its cathedral.

Think for a little while on that scene . . . . And then let us quickly recollect that we are in Venice . . . .

> We find ourselves in a paved alley . . . .
> A yard or two farther, we pass the hostelry of the Black Eagle . . . .
> Let us enter the church.
>
> —John Ruskin, *The Stones of Venice*

Writers, whether static or moving, generally organize their material spatially, describing the subject from left to right or from top to bottom. But occasionally a writer will organize a description in a time sequence, often utilizing contrast in a before-and-after pattern. This rhetorical device can be highly effective in personal descriptions, as this paragraph from Mark Twain's *Life on the Mississippi* shows:

Once a day a cheap, gaudy packet arrived upward from St. Louis, and another downward from Keokuk. Before these events, the day was glorious with expectancy; after them, the day was a dead and empty thing. Not only the boys, but the whole village, felt this. After all these years I can picture that old time to myself now, just as it was then: the white town drowsing in the sunshine of a summer's morning; the streets empty, or pretty nearly so; one or two clerks sitting in front of the Water Street stores, with their splint-bottomed chairs tilted back against the walls, chins on breasts, hats slouched over their faces, asleep—with shingle-shavings enough around to show what broke them down; a sow and a litter of pigs loafing along the sidewalk, doing a good business in watermelon rinds and seeds; two or three lonely little freight piles scattered about the "levee"; a pile of "skids" on the slope of the stone-paved wharf, and the fragrant town drunkard asleep in the shadow of them; two or three wood flats at the head of the wharf, but nobody to listen to the peaceful lapping of the wavelets against them; the great Mississippi, the majestic, the magnificent Mississippi rolling its mile-wide tide along, shining in the sun; the dense forest away on the other side; the "point" below, bounding the river-glimpse and turning it into a sort of sea, and withal a very still and brilliant and lonely one. Presently a film of dark smoke appears above one of those remote "points"; instantly a negro drayman, famous for his quick eye and prodigious voice, lifts up the cry, "S-t-e-a-m-boat a-comin'!" and the scene changes!

With these last three words, Twain signals his readers that he is moving from the "before" to the "after":

The town drunkard stirs, the clerks wake up, a furious clatter of drays follows, every house and store pours out a human contribution, and all in a twinkling the dead town is alive and moving. Drays, carts, men, boys, all go hurrying from many quarters to a common center, the wharf. Assembled there, the people fasten their eyes upon the coming boat as upon a wonder they are seeing for the first time. And the boat is rather a handsome sight, too. She is long and sharp and trim and pretty; she has two tall, fancy-topped chimneys, with a gilded device of some kind swung between them; a fanciful pilot-house, all glass and "gingerbread," perched on top of the "texas" deck behind them; the paddle-boxes are gorgeous with a picture or with gilded rays above the boat's name; the boiler-deck, the hurricane deck, and the texas deck are fenced and ornamented with clean white railings; there is a flag gallantly flying from the jack-staff; the furnace doors are open and the fires glaring bravely; the upper decks are black with passengers; the captain stands by the big bell, calm, imposing, the envy of all; great volumes of the blackest smoke are rolling and tumbling out of the chimneys — a husbanded grandeur created with a bit of pitch-pine just before arriving at a town; the crew are grouped on the forecastle; the broad stage is run far out over the port bow, and an envied deck-hand stands picturesquely on the end of it with a coil of rope in his hand; the pent steam is screaming through the gauge-cocks; the captain lifts his hand, a bell rings, the wheels stop; then they turn back; churning the water to foam, and the steamer is at rest. Then such a scramble as there is to get aboard, and to take in freight and to discharge freight, all at one and the same time; and such a yelling and cursing as the mates facilitate it all with! Ten minutes later the steamer is under way again, with no flag on the jack-staff and no black smoke issuing from the chimneys. After ten more minutes the town is dead again, and the town drunkard asleep by the skids once more.[1]

Although the main organization pattern here is the temporal one of before-and-after (or, if you wish, before-during-and-after), Twain has also relied on a spatial arrangement, moving from the Water Street stores to the wharf, then away to the river, and finally, far off to the point, where the sight of smoke prepares us for the change in the scene. Consequently, within the basic temporal framework, spatial organization is used effectively.

Style

In personal description, you should be concerned about interesting your readers. Strong, dramatic, intriguing, controversial, or provocative opening sentences can help, either at the beginning of a personal description paper or in introducing personal descriptive paragraphs. Here are some samples from Tom Wolfe's *The Pump House Gang:*

Her walk-up flat was so essentially dreary. . . .
    They have missed the Off Broadway's most extraordinary show, however, which is in the kitchen.
    The boys have the new Los Angeles car kids' look.

[1] Mark Twain, *Life on the Mississippi* (New York: Harper & Row, 1951), pp. 32–34.

One afternoon, however, about 2 p.m., I came back into the room, and boy, it was chaos in there.

Each of these sentences should arouse readers' interest, prodding them to satisfy their curiosity by continuing to read. The writer's enthusiasm or strong personal feeling can also spur readers on. The following examples from Henry David Thoreau's *Walden* are softer and more serene than Wolfe's, befitting the silence and solitude of life in the woods by Walden Pond, yet the sentences in context motivate readers effectively:

This is a delicious evening, when the whole body is one sense, and imbibes delight through every pore.
I rejoice that there are owls.
The scenery of Walden is on a humble scale, and, though very beautiful, does not approach to grandeur, nor can it much concern one who has not long frequented it or lived by its shore; yet this pond is so remarkable for its depth and purity as to merit a particular description.

Whatever the technique used, you should try to interest readers, arouse their curiosity, and compel them to want to share your experience. You should not assume that everyone wants to hear about your skiing trip, mountain vacation, or high school graduation; you should take pains to interest readers in the subject.

Attracting your readers' attention is the first step; maintaining it is the second. To do so depends mainly on details, on the small sensory impressions that combine to create vivid images in their minds. Here is where your sensitivity in observation counts heavily — as does your skill in using your other senses. In the previous passage, Mark Twain made the scene come alive for us by relying heavily not only on sights but on sounds and odors, some of which are listed here:

Sights:

one or two clerks sitting in front of the Water Street stores, with their splint-bottomed chairs tilted back against the walls
a sow and a litter of pigs loafing along the sidewalk
watermelon rinds and seeds
two or three lonely little freight piles
a pile of "skids" on the slope of the stone-paved wharf
a film of dark smoke

Sounds:

the peaceful lapping of the wavelets
the cry, "S-t-e-a-m-boat a-comin'!"

a furious clatter of drays
the pent steam is screaming through the gauge-cocks
a bell rings
such a yelling and cursing as the mates facilitate it all with!

Odors:

the fragrant town drunkard
great volumes of the blackest smoke [appeals to sight also]

The abundance of sensory details conveys the impression that Twain is standing on Water Street watching the scene unfold, instead of sitting in his study writing about it many years later. Such details may be perceived not only by great authors but by all who are alert to the sights and sounds and smells and tastes and textures of the world around them. Here is a student paper, rich and sensitive in its depiction of the scene, relying heavily on details (especially in the fourth paragraph):

POND CREEK

Walking through a hazy, warm October afternoon, in my mind I could see Pond Creek in the July sun as clearly as if I had been there only yesterday instead of years ago. Now, in another year, another season, and another place, the memory of Pond Creek comes sharply into focus and once more I feel that I'm ambling along its banks in a warm, redolent, unhurried midsummer afternoon.

It seems that days were never anything but beautiful at Pond Creek, or at least my memories always picture them so. It was always warm, but in a special way. I don't recall it being uncomfortably humid. Rather, there was a dry enveloping kind of heat that wrapped itself around you and seemed to dispel all memories of winter chills with its gentle pervasive warmth. It used to come in soft, sweet-smelling breezes that would tousle you like huge children ruffling up a puppy's fur and then swirl you about lethargically. All this glorious warmth seemed to be confined within a tent of sky that was perpetually the color of chicory blooms, a clear, soft, unobtrusive blue that seemed to have absorbed some of the warmth of the day into itself. The sky was an important part of Pond Creek and is prominent in my memories of the place. I can see it now, vaulting high above the whole scene, glowing in the warm July sunlight, and gathering the whole valley under its buttresses.

I could never quite figure out whether this sky held the hills about Pond Creek with its edges to keep them from undulating away like benign green sea monsters or whether the hills reached up and clung to the skirts of the sky to hold it and keep it from lifting away. At different times both have seemed appropriate. These hills about the creek weren't really outstanding as far as hills go but they always seemed to have a personality. Their green, rounded forms always reminded me of old, old creatures who have seen, experienced, and understood much life and who are patiently waiting for whatever the future has to distribute over their sinewy, weathered coils. These long, low-lying giants were always marked by a soft blue haziness that perhaps hid many scars that were evident of their having existed eons ago.

Bound among the coils of these ridges were the wide, rocky, grass-covered fields through which wound Pond Creek. Sloping from the hills to the very waterline of the creek, the land as I remember it teemed with things that stimulated every sense. I can remember vividly the sweet, dusty fragrance of hot, dry grass; the acrid, alive smell of sweating horses and cattle; the sharp tang of wood sorrel and the blandly sweet taste of honeysuckle nectar; the whipping of the blowing grass against my jeans; the playful snatching of the matted blackberry vines at my hands and ankles; and the exhilarating loss of balance as I trip in some hole or over a root; the warm contented chirring of the cicadas, the rustle of the tall grasses and the squeaky munching of the horses — all in a world of golds, browns, and greens interspersed with the brilliant flowers of later summer that are just beginning to bloom.

But most of all, I remember Pond Creek itself, flowing in a long, lazy, almost unvaried curve through these grassy fields. Even now I hear it babbling like a small baby as it trundles busily among the round, brown stones of its bed, a kind of clear, sparkling brown in color that catches the gold colors of the grass and reflects them back brightly. A coolness always seemed to rise off its waters as they'd pass beneath an overhanging bank, bringing with it the peculiar odor of mossy stones and water reeds and the suggestion of hidden crannies where minuscule animals cling in the dark to cool, wet rocks, safe from the sun's intrusion. The creek then deepens in the sunshine and takes on a more majestic flow, or rather a slower one, for Pond Creek was always a bit of a baby and never able to summon the dignity necessary for majesty. It then disappears around the bend, under the single-laned bridge and out of memory.

It's strange how real Pond Creek's memory is. I haven't seen it in a long while but the day, the season, the hills, the grass, and especially the creek are recalled whenever I experience the warm, hazy afternoons similar to those at Pond Creek.

Much of the effectiveness of this paper stems from its wealth of details and from its rich language. The writer's feeling for Pond Creek is conveyed in large part through similes (the breezes "that would tousle you like huge children ruffling up a puppy's fur," the hills that might undulate away "like benign green sea monsters"); through metaphors ("heat that wrapped itself around you," "long, low-lying giants"); and through the alliterative repetition of initial sounds ("the soft, sweet-smelling breezes," "the contented chirring of the cicadas," and "trundles busily among the round, brown stones of its bed"). The richness of the language adds not only vitality and interest to the description but evokes feelings of pleasure, enabling readers to share the joyful mood of the author as she describes memories of Pond Creek.

Also contributing to this effect are the sentences that often ramble lazily like the creek itself. Many flow on to great length, adding phrase upon phrase, packing in details, pointing out specific sights, impressions, sounds, and smells, all suggesting how meaningful and moving were the writer's summer days at Pond Creek and how poignant are her recollections of it.

Such well-developed sentences, along with the evocative language, the sensory details, and some attempt to create and maintain reader interest, are stylistic qualities of personal descriptions. This is not to say that every personal description must contain all these elements (note, for example, that "Pond Creek" does little initially to attract reader interest); but most of these characteristics may be found in effective personal descriptions and all can help you in your writing.

Consequently, before writing, you should list all the details you can, jotting down everything that caught your eye, came to your ears, and affected your other senses. Then add adjectives and adverbs so that through suggestion and association you arouse in your readers the same mood that you experienced. Finally, with this list as a guide, write the first draft of your paper.

Tone

In factual descriptions, tone is severely restricted; in personal descriptions, it is completely unrestricted. Your tone must clearly indicate your attitude toward your subject. Your writing "voice" may be filled with disgust and bitterness about filthy, rat-infested, underheated housing for the poor; with sadness about the destruction of grass and bushes and trees by a new highway; with rage about police brutality toward innocent people; with irony about the gaudy taste of the newly rich; with compassion about the infirmities of the aged; with reverence about a crocus blooming; or with excitement about a circus, rock concert, or championship game. Listen to the voice of crusty old Squire Bramble, Tobias Smollett's eccentric but lovable character in *Humphrey Clinker*, as he describes his visit to London in 1771:

I am pent up in frowsy lodgings, where there is not room enough to swing a cat; and I breathe the streams of endless putrefaction, and these would undoubtedly produce a pestilence, if they were not qualified by the gross acid of sea-coal. . . . I go to bed after mid-night, jaded and restless from the dissipations of the day—I start every hour from my sleep, at the horrid noise of thundering at every door . . . and by five o-clock I start out of bed, in consequence of the still more dreadful alarm made by the country carts, and noisy rustics bellowing green peas under my window. If I would drink water, I must quaff the mawkish contents of an open aqueduct, exposed to all manner of defilement, or swallow that which comes from the river Thames, impregnated with all the filth of London and Westminister—Human excrement is the least offensive part of the concrete, which is composed of all the drugs, minerals, and poisons, used in mechanics and manufacture, enriched with the putrefying carcasses of beasts and men; and mixed with the scourings of all the washtubs, kennels, and common sewers, within the bills of mortality.

As Squire Bramble registers his disgust at the dirt, noise, and discomforts of London, he becomes more and more emotional, undoubtedly exaggerating as we all do in such circumstances, pouring his fury out in a surging, powerful piling up of phrases, each providing more stomach-turning details as he rages on and on. But the tone is conveyed above all by his words.

HINTS FOR WRITING FACTUAL AND PERSONAL DESCRIPTIONS

Here is a checklist of suggestions that may be helpful to you in writing factual and personal descriptions.

Factual Descriptions

1. Organization: Usually spatial: top to bottom, left to right, large to small, and so on. Be logical, consistent: do not shift back and forth.
2. Style: No need to attract reader interest. Language should be simple and specific. Technical words that readers would understand may be used. Emphasis on nouns, adjectives—not verbs. The passive may be effective; the first person pronoun ineffective. Sentences should be short and simple.
3. Tone: Factual, serious, formal. The writer's voice should not be heard. The description should sound as if it were written by a scientific, objective, detached authority. The implication: here are the facts, only the facts.

Personal Descriptions

1. Organization: Logically organized by space, time, or both. But opening statements should attract readers and establish the dominant mood. The writer may be static or moving; if moving, clearly notify readers of position changes.

2. Style: Details are essential in picturing whatever is described. Also vital are rich and suggestive words and phrases to evoke emotional responses in readers. Listing details according to their sensory appeals is helpful. Sentences may be lengthy and involved, and the first person pronoun may be used.
3. Tone: The description should be written with feeling. The writer's voice — casual, warm, enthusiastic, caustic, bitter, or whatever — should be heard. The implication: here is how I feel about it.

Specifically, you might ask yourself these questions before writing:

1. What details shall I include?
2. How shall I organize them?
3. Should I interest readers or not? If so, how?
4. What is the dominant impression I wish to convey in my personal description?
5. What tone should I adopt?

Naturally, no list of suggestions or questions can solve all your writing problems. But by checking here before you write, you may be reminded of one or two helpful hints.

DESCRIPTIONS OF PEOPLE

People are different, and writing descriptions of people is different. You're probably already aware of some of the complications because you've often been asked, "What's so-and-so like?" In replying, you might resort to an identification, an impression, or a character sketch, depending on the situation. Let's examine each.

Identification

Although you might provide an identification, you'd probably want to go further than that. Used mainly in official records and documents, identifications consist only of certain statistical information (height, weight, age), visible characteristics (color of hair, skin, and eyes), and recognizable marks (scars, birthmarks). Here is a fairly typical example:

W A N T E D

Peter J. Serra

Description: Caucasian; age 42; ht., 5′10″; wt., 200 lbs.; eyes, brown; thinning black hair; usually wears mustache; pock-marked complexion; scars on inside left wrist; wears horn-rimmed glasses.

Impression

Unlike the identification, the impression may not identify a person, but it does convey an overall idea of him or her. Many details may be missing, yet the writer does provide in a few broad strokes a general feeling about the subject. Although an impression is usually less complete and informative than an identification, it may be more effective in capturing an individual's striking or distinctive traits. Here are two examples of what we mean.

Henry Mortimer, the former Chief Inspector, was long, lean, bald and spritely. At the sides and back of his head his hair grew thick and grey. His eyebrows were thick and black. It would be accurate to say that his nose and lips were thick, his eyes small and his chin receding into his neck. And yet it would be inaccurate to say he was not a handsome man, such being the power of unity when it exists in a face.

—Muriel Spark, *Memento Mori*

The man was large and broad-shouldered, but a little gaunt and drawn in the face underneath his sunburn. He had an open friendly expression and a wide forehead crossed by rows of regular lines. He had plenty of curly dark brown hair, going grey in places. His heavily veined hands were lightly crossed on his knees, and his gaze shifted easily along the row of passengers opposite, appraising each without embarrassment. He had the sort of face which can look full of amiability without smiling, and the sort of eyes which can meet the eyes of a stranger and even linger, without seeming aggressive, or seductive, or curious.

—Iris Murdoch, *The Bell*

These impressions do provide some factual details (curiously, both mention hair color), but they are more concerned with creating an idea of people than providing a means of identifying them. Muriel Spark's description provides some details, all shaped to portray the outlines of an older man, handsome despite his unattractive features. And Iris Murdoch furnishes more information, most of it designed to suggest the man's open friendliness.

Impressions seldom appear by themselves but are usually incorporated into written works, such as articles, novels, short stories, histories, and essays. In length, impressions may range from one sentence to several paragraphs.

Character Sketch

More complete descriptions of people are usually called character sketches; they may also be referred to as profiles, literary portraits, and biographical sketches. As its name indicates, a character sketch delineates the character of a person, or at least his or her main personality traits. In the process, it may include an identification and an impression, but it will do more than tell what people *look* or *seem* like: it will show what they *are* like.

A character sketch may be about a type rather than an individual, revealing the characteristics common to the members of a group, such as campus jocks, cheerleaders, art students, religious fanatics, television devotees. The purpose of writing about a type may be serious or satirical, either to inform readers about the group or to poke fun at it. In the following opening paragraph from Milton Birnbaum's article "Professor Scylla and Professor Charybdis," you can observe how a character sketch can be used for humorous effect to caricature a "mod" young professor:

Professor Scylla is still in his thirties but likes to think of himself as much younger looking in appearance. He tries to reinforce this impression by adopting the latest sartorial innovations — bell-bottom pants, vivid-colored striped shirts, worn open at the collar, ankle-top shoes; although tending to baldness, he lets his remaining hair grow below the neck and has recently sprouted some formidable looking sideburns. There is a sparkle to his eyes, a new spring to his gait, a general feeling of "it's good to be alive" exuding from his demeanor. He's never seen alone on campus. He's always followed by a coterie of admiring students; he eats with students instead of his colleagues, and his office is never closed; memoranda of seemingly grave import from students and to students are tacked onto the bulletin board outside his office. His home likewise is an oasis for the exchange of ideas and calls to action. He smilingly denies the allegation that he condones the use of pot and asserts that, after all, pot is not nearly so damaging to one's health as are cigarettes and alcohol.

In such character sketches about types, you should treat the subject as a composite of most members of the particular group. For example, if you were to write about "The School Bus Driver," you should include in this portrait the characteristics of most drivers, not a particular one. Descriptions of types, therefore, require more generalization than do descriptions of individuals, but both rely on essentially the same rhetorical techniques.

These techniques include narrative and expository as well as descriptive devices. Anecdotes, personal narrative, and dialogue are all important in vividly portraying someone or some type. One incident demonstrating a person's stubbornness is far more effective than a flat statement that the person is stubborn. But the character sketch often relies on expository techniques in presenting and illustrating an individual's most striking or memorable qualities. Thus, a character sketch has a rather formal structure, generally being organized into three parts:

an introduction, an identification and impression, and amplifying information.

INTRODUCTION

When a character sketch is not part of another literary work, such as a novel or essay, but an independent piece, the introduction should serve both to interest readers in the person and to present his or her most striking characteristic. In the following student examples, an intriguing or provocative opening paragraph catches the reader's attention and also establishes the person's dominant trait.

I guess the most exciting fellow I've ever known was a guy everybody called Little Steve.

Tough and mean. That's the best way to describe Bill Evans. When babies are born, they're sweet, soft, and cuddly. Not Bill Evans. He was probably fighting and clawing and scrapping from the start.

After six hours of being locked up in a classroom with a teacher during the class day, most kids don't want to have anything more to do with her. They beat it out of the room as fast as possible. But in Room 145 the kids linger after the school buzzer sounds. That's where Carol Sicars teaches. She's wonderful.

Sometimes the dominant quality about a person is presented in an opening anecdote, which by its very narrative form usually interests the reader. The following account by Carmen Mendez describes how she entered the Guatemala American Hospital as a fifteen-year-old girl just out of high school and met an unforgettable man.

A wiry little cricket of a man in old work clothes. . . . He was about 30 and stood only five-foot-seven, even counting his plume of black hair. He couldn't have weighed more than 110 pounds. His grin was the biggest thing about him.

Thinking that he was probably a hired man, I found it unexpectedly easy to ask, "Whom should I see about studying to become a nurse? My pastor says it's a good career."

"I think that you should see *me*," he answered with mock gravity, not in the least self-conscious about his poor Spanish with its heavy American accent. His light blue eyes twinkled. "And yes. How could anyone have a better, more satisfying career than to serve in the medical-missionary field, where the need is so great."

Thus, in the first moment of meeting Dr. Charles Albert Ainslie, I heard his favorite prescription for attaining the good and happy life—the formula that was to make him one of our country's most valuable and beloved medical pioneers.

—Carmen Mendez, "My Most Unforgettable Character," *Reader's Digest*

The key idea in each of these introductions commits the writer just as "I've got a funny story to tell you" commits the speaker. Each of the students has a clear assignment: to show why Little Steve was so exciting, Bill Evans was tough and mean, and Carol Sicars was wonderful. And Carmen Mendez has also indicated her thesis: to demonstrate why Dr. Charles Albert Ainslie was a valuable and beloved medical pioneer.

IDENTIFICATION AND IMPRESSION

After the introduction, writers usually provide an identification and impression of their subjects so that readers can formulate some image in their minds. Sometimes they include this material in the introduction, as Carmen Mendez did.

AMPLIFYING INFORMATION

The third part of the character sketch—the amplifying material—should be organized according to either a chronological or an analytical pattern. If the introduction describes a first meeting, then it would be logical to follow with a discussion of how this initial impression was later supported, modified, or reversed. Or the flashback technique could be used to review the subject's birth, family, and early life. But this biographical approach should be used cautiously because often it is uninteresting, inappropriate, or irrelevant. A paper about a teacher, for example, should generally not include such material unless it is unusual or illuminating. Yet you could still use the chronological plan by beginning with your first school day with this teacher and proceeding to the last, or starting with the last and flashing back to the first, or introducing a striking anecdote from a Christmas party and then flashing back to the first day and moving forward from that point.

The second option for organizing a character sketch, the analytical pattern, consists of dividing the main trait into parts and elaborating on each. The student paper about the exciting Little Steve, for example, was divided into three sections: his spectacular athletic feats, his impulsive whims, and his search for daring experiences. The writer thus organized his material by dividing it into units, each showing one aspect of why Little Steve was exciting.

Failure to use either the chronological or analytical pattern can confuse and irritate the reader. Despite some fine touches, the following paper illustrates how poor organization can weaken a character sketch.

Gail is a friend I wish I hadn't known so well last summer—wish I hadn't known at all. She has long brown hair falling gently over her shoulders. Her sparkling hazel eyes twinkling above an almost perpetual set smile make her very tempting.

Gail is different from most girls. She seems to be very grown up but is really two-faced. You're great when you're with her but behind your back, you're not so great.

Gail wants to be popular so she'll go with anyone to be seen in the right places by the right people. She used people like a ladder, walking over them until she reached the top — vice president of the class, homecoming queen, and various other honors.

Gail makes people feel good with her dumb honest manner, asking lots of questions, pretending that you're so smart, complimenting you and acting modest. It's a game which she plays well. After you know Gail, you'll know how to play it well too.

Some clear organizational pattern would have been helpful here, either a before-and-after plan, setting forth Gail's apparently attractive qualities and then exposing them, or an analytical approach, breaking down her deceitfulness into the ways she beguiles, dupes, and uses people.

Poor organization is not this paper's only weakness. Writers are obliged to show *why* they feel as they do. It is not enough to state their opinion: they must make readers realize the reasons for it. Lawyers do not go into court and merely declare that their client is innocent. They prove it. Similarly, you must prove that the subject of your character sketch is foolish or fascinating, compassionate or cruel, shy or sophisticated. It is not enough for the student writer to tell us that Gail is a phony; he should have shown us. Why not some dialogue illustrating how Gail asks lots of questions, plays dumb, and showers compliments? Or some evidence to support the statement that she wants to be seen in the right places by the right people? Or an example about how she used people to become homecoming queen? The failure to show Gail in action not only results in a weak depiction of her but also makes us question the accuracy of the portrayal. We wonder whether the writer is just bitter because Gail wasn't interested in him. In sum, the lack of specific detail, proof, and evidence results in an unconvincing paper.

Conviction in a character sketch is important because it is not an academic exercise concocted by English teachers to plague students but a valuable, practical writing experience. Chances are you will be writing letters about new friends; examinations and term papers about illustrious people; statements in behalf of other students for social or academic honors; recommendations for jobs or promotions; and testimonials for relatives, friends, or company or civic leaders. The importance of being able to write interesting and informative character sketches should certainly be evident when you consider how often you talk about people. And people are what character sketches are all about.

ASSIGNMENTS

For Discussion

1 Read the following paragraphs from George Orwell's essay "Some Thoughts on the Common Toad," and then answer the questions that follow.

Before the swallow, before the daffodil, and not much later than the snow-drop, the common toad salutes the coming of spring after his own fashion, which is to emerge from a hole in the ground, where he has lain buried since the previous autumn, and crawl as rapidly as possible towards the nearest suitable patch of water. Something—some kind of shudder in the earth, or perhaps merely a rise of a few degrees in the temperature—has told him that it is time to wake up; though a few toads appear to sleep the clock round and miss out a year from time to time—at any rate, I have more than once dug them up, alive and apparently well, in the middle of the summer.

At this period, after his long fast, the toad has a very spiritual look, like a strict Anglo-Catholic towards the end of Lent. His movements are languid but purposeful, his body is shrunken, and by contrast his eyes look abnormally large. This allows one to notice, what one might not at another time, that a toad has about the most beautiful eye of any living creature. It is like gold, or more exactly it is like the golden-colored semiprecious stone which one some-times sees in signet rings, and which I think is called chrysoberyl.

For a few days after getting into the water the toad concentrates on build-ing up his strength by eating small insects. Presently he has swollen to his normal size again, and then he goes through a phase of intense sexiness. All he knows, at least if he is a male toad, is that he wants to get his arms around something, and if you offer him a stick, or even your finger, he will cling to it with surprising strength and take a long time to discover that it is not a fe-male toad. Frequently one comes upon shapeless masses of ten or twenty toads rolling over and over in the water, one clinging to another without distinction of sex. By degrees, however, they sort themselves out into couples, with the male duly sitting on the female's back. You can now distinguish males from females, because the male is smaller, darker and sits on top, with his arms tightly clasped around the female's neck. After a day or two the spawn is laid in long strings which wind themselves in and out of the reeds and soon be-come invisible. A few more weeks, and the water is alive with masses of tiny tadpoles which rapidly grow larger, sprout hind-legs, then fore-legs, then shed their tails; and finally, about the middle of the summer, the new generation of toads, smaller than one's thumb-nail but perfect in every particular, crawl out of the water to begin the game anew.

I mention the spawning of the toads because it is one of the phenomena of spring which most deeply appeal to me, and because the toad, unlike the skylark and the primrose, has never had much of a boost from the poets. But I am aware that many people do not like reptiles or amphibians, and I am not suggesting that in order to enjoy the spring you have to take an interest in toads. There are also the crocus, the missel thrush, the cuckoo, the black-thorn, etc. The point is that the pleasures of spring are available to everybody, and cost nothing.[2]

a What is the basic organizational pattern?

b Has Orwell tried to arouse reader interest? If so, how?

c What rhetorical device does Orwell use twice in the second para-graph to make the toad seem attractive? What transition does he use to move from one device to the other? Could this descriptive paragraph appear earlier or later? Is it most effective here? Why or why not?

d What is the dominant impression Orwell wishes to convey about toads in the third paragraph? Does this impression serve any de-scriptive function? What transitions does Orwell use to switch from toads to tadpoles?

e What is the rhetorical function of the first sentence in the fourth paragraph? From your reading of this paragraph, what do you think is the thesis of Orwell's essay? Why is his description of the toad particularly effective in view of this thesis?

2 Writers are occasionally faced with the problem of how to provide a great deal of statistical descriptive information in an interesting manner. How does Ted Morgan try to accomplish this in the follow-ing paragraphs? Which details do you think best indicate the enor-mity of the luxury liner S.S. *France*? To what extent is the descrip-tion factual? To what extent personal? Discuss its organization, tone, style.

"To give you an idea of the size of the *France*," a ship's officer said, "it is the only ship in the world where you can travel with your wife and your mistress with the assurance that they will never meet."

The *France* is 1,035 feet long, almost as long as the Eiffel Tower, and 110 feet wide. It weighs 66,348 tons, can do better than 30 knots, and can carry

[2] From "Sone Thoughts on the Common Toad" from *Shooting an Elephant and Other Es-says* by George Orwell, copyright, 1945, 1946, 1949, 1950 by Sonia Brownell Orwell; copyright, 1973, 1974 by Sonia Orwell. Reprinted by permission of Harcourt Brace Jovano-vich, Inc. and Secker & Warburg.

up to 2,044 passengers. It has eight boilers that develop 90 tons an hour of steam pressure and four propeller shafts driven by a set of turbines that can deliver up to 160,000 horsepower. Each propeller weighs 27 tons. It has two autonomous engine compartments, with 14 watertight bulkheads—so that no damage can deprive the ship of more than half its propulsion machinery—and two pairs of antiroll stabilizers. Its red and black smokestacks, with fins that drive soot away from the ship, weigh 45 tons each.

All the fresh water, including the water for the boilers, is produced in four distillery plants capable of converting 300 tons of sea water in 24 hours. The ship has long lines and a terraced silhouette like the *Normandie*. The curves of her hull are so graceful that below the waterline there is not a single flat plate. The plates are welded, not riveted. There are 22 elevators serving 11 decks, and telephones in each cabin, linked by 18,000 miles of wiring. There are 46 miles of sheets, cut up into useful lengths; two padded cells; one prison cell; a hospital; a refrigerated morgue; a printer who stocks 80 different models of engraved invitations; 13 full-time firemen, and stainless steel kennels with wall-to-wall carpeting and five-course meals, and imitation fire hydrants for homesick American dogs.

On the two-class North Atlantic run, the segregation is horizontal. First-class passengers use the upper decks. The passengers in tourist class, which is called *Rive Gauche,* are spared the humiliating barriers with "first class only" signs as they take their turns around the deck.[3]

3 Discuss each of the five student papers that follow, pointing out the strengths and weaknesses of their tone, style, and organization, and indicating exactly what the writer might work on in revision.

a During the first few weeks of school, a student's roommate can greatly influence his or her outlook on college life. Many students, including myself, leave for college without knowing a single person going to the same school. If such is the case, it is of utmost importance to like and get along well with that person whom you are spending so much time with. I consider myself most fortunate in this respect. Judy has proved to be much more than just a roommate to me. She is already a really close friend. I have been very content here at school, and I am sure that Judy is one of the factors which add to my contentment.

poor details about Judy

b My roommate is definitely a unique character. He has a life style strictly limited to one human being—Jim Beard. I think no other person has such a combination of peculiarities as Jim does. Since I've known him, I've become accustomed to being prepared for anything. From my experiences of the last few weeks, there is nothing he could do that would shock me.

[3] Ted Morgan, "Vive la *France*," *New York Times Magazine*, 12 May 1974, p. 43. © 1974 by The New York Times Company. Reprinted by permission.

In appearance he seems to be average enough — six feet tall, straight blond hair and blue eyes. However, quite often his actions are to the contrary.

For example, the average college student living in a dorm normally sleeps on a bed, but not my roommate! Instead, he prefers to sleep on the floor without a mattress. He uses his mattress for lounging around in the daytime but not for sleeping.

Another peculiarity I'm becoming accustomed to is to see him walking down the corridors of the dorm at all hours of the night doing John Wayne imitations while dressed only in his underwear and cowboy boots. On our floor we have people from all over the country, but no one but Jim walks around at midnight in such attire!

Jim has a variety of odd eating habits to go along with his unusual clothing styles. He seems to be the only person I know who combines sweet pickles and beer, herb tea and pizza, and bananas with black coffee.

In addition to strange eating habits he constantly redecorates the room. He changes posters so often I barely have time to become accustomed to one before he changes it. His latest addition to the room is a black light which he uses to send Morse Code to the girls in Donovan Hall.

Jim may have some odd personal habits, but he is a decent person to have for a roommate. Very seldom is he unhappy, and he's one of the best-liked fellows on Haggin Hall's B-3. In spite of some of his more distinguishable habits, I feel I couldn't have found a better person with whom to share such close quarters.

c   In a student's lifetime, hopefully he will be fortunate enough to have one teacher who dedicates his whole being to his pupils. In high school, we were blessed with a man like this. Mr. Fiorucci taught biology and chemistry, and he made the whole realm of these courses come alive for every student. He made each class hour a fascinating new discovery into a world of science none of us knew or understood before. Mr. Fiorucci sincerely loved the students and wanted them to realize the total value of education. His influence certainly changed the lives of many teenagers. Many students went eagerly on to college because he had touched their lives. I myself am here today with inner thoughts of someday teaching students with that same thrill for learning Mr. Fiorucci always gave.

d   My roommate, in my opinion, happens to be a unique person with a well-rounded personality. Not one day goes by that I do not learn something new about him. He has an engaging sense of humor and can find something amusing about almost any situation. I do not stay depressed when he is around because of his positive disposition. He can always point out the brighter aspects of whatever may be bothering him. He is rarely discouraged but easily hurt. My roommate is sensitive to the feelings of other people and tender and kind to anyone who needs help. He has a logical solution to most problems that arise and is usually able to look at things objectively. I have chosen to present only his best personality characteristics, although as he is a human being, he does have a few imperfections. It is obvious that I admire him and in case you haven't guessed, he is not only my roommate, but also my husband.

   e   Most great men have their greatness recognized after their passing from this earth. Our Mr. Wesley was no exception. Now, after the shocking death of our beloved principal, do we take notice of his kind heart, Christian attitude and great love for the human race.

   Sometimes it seems to us that few stop to remember the deeds of Mr. Wesley. Some, however, remember his kind, heart-to-heart talks which, although seeming unreasonable at the time, now seem to stick in one's mind as a guide through life. Some also remember his undying faith in the student. He never gave up hope in a student. He worried about each individual from the valedictorian to the student who failed every subject. He didn't stop to think about nportance of a student, because the thing uppermost in his m or her become a better, more adapted Christian person. vould have liked to take Mr. Wesley's whistle and throw uld see. These people, however, didn't know of the love eap, dime store whistle. When he was a boy, this same his father to call him home. The significance of the whistle the usual teacher-student relationship held by most prin- held a parental relationship with each of his students. y was taken advantage of despite (or because of) his good icipal was mocked by many, but he returned this mockery rstanding. We are reminded of the Great Master who was lltitudes but gave love and understanding in return. passing, did not take his love with him. It will remain in person who knew him. His advice will be a guide through st of all his spirit will remain in the halls of our high school walk in them.

vity and write a personal description of it, recording , sounds, odors, and other sense impressions. Among night choose are a rock concert, a country fair, a church school dance, the locker room after the game, lunch cafeteria, or Saturday night at the high school hangout. nal description of a place. If one does not come quickly haps the following questions will help. If you could xt few hours anywhere, what place would you choose? most beautiful place you've ever been? The ugliest? sturbing? Most peaceful? Noisiest? Happiest? Most inspiring? Most terrifying? Most ornate? Dingiest? Oldest? Most charming? Most comfortable?

3 Write a factual description of the same place you selected in exercise 2.

4 As a child, you probably had some favorite hideaway where you could be all alone. Describe it, explaining your feeling of comfort and seclusion.

5 Describe the place selected in exercise 4 from the viewpoint of an adult.

6 You probably had or have some toy, object, or other "security blanket" that you were or are attached to. Write a factual description of it; then write a personal description.

7 If you have ever been in an automobile accident, write three factual descriptions of it: first, your own view as you might write it to your insurance company; second, the other driver's account as he or she might write to his or her company; third, the policeman's report.

8 Write a personal description of an automobile accident to a friend.

9 Most of us are creatures of routine, walking or driving the same way from our room to class every weekday. Write a personal description of what you see, hear, smell, touch, and experience as you proceed from door to door.

10 Using any of the following or similar sentences as your opening statement, write an appropriate description:

a It was thrilling to be there.
b For the first time, I was truly stirred by the beauty of nature.
c Man's disregard for the environment was evident everywhere.
d On a clear day you can see _____.
e The _____ was out of place in those surroundings.
f Bedlam broke loose after the game.
g It looked like a wreck.
h The old neighborhood had changed.
i At night my childhood room was filled with terrifying shapes and shadows.
j I had expected it to look different.
k Town springs to life on Saturday.
l I had looked at it many times but never really seen it before.
m Summer nights are a symphony of sound.

11 The following description appeared in the *New York Times*. Write a similar one about some other month of the year, a season (winter, football season, Christmas), or a traditional event (harvesting, ski weekends, Thanksgiving), or anything else that would be appropriate from a descriptive "Here Comes _____" paper.

HERE COMES MAY[4]

April thins away and here comes May. There is no question about what time it is by the clock of the year. It is spring, no longer a promise but not a performance, well along in its first act. The maples have started to bloom, and the shadblow is frothy with flowers. The haze of undergrowth-green in the woodland is spreading upward into the trees. There is a pastel-delicate mixture of pale green and pink and yellow in the birches and the poplars.

Wild flowers are in bloom. Bloodroot is opening its waxen-white petals and its big gray-green leaves. Jacks are appearing in their canopied pulpits. Wake Robin opens its liver-red blossoms to lure carrion flies. Violets begin to make the meadow's damp corner lush with fresh green heart-leaves and the purple of spring's royalty. Tulips open in the dooryard, and lilacs seem to be trying to beat the apple blossoms out of their buds. The farmer's pastures and hay fields are green as his dooryard lawn.

Back at the root of the word, April meant "the open air," the air outdoors. Maybe that is why we expect so much of April, after March. We yearn for May and June, and April is only the beginning, the preparation. But it is the commitment, complete. Here comes May, with June not far behind. Busy May, with all those buds to unfurl, all that grass to grow tall, all that chlorophyll to be spread. And there's nothing man can do to help, except to say, "Welcome May. Spring is all yours now. Make it pretty."

- 12   Write a character sketch about a certain type of person at high school — student, teacher, administrator, or other employee. Be certain to discuss at some length the appearance, interests, mannerisms, likes, and dislikes of such a composite individual, and to portray him or her in some characteristic incident. Your paper may be serious or satirical.

- 13   Write a character sketch about a certain type of parent whom you know from personal experience. For example, you might deal with the Permissive Parent, the Strict Parent, the Buddy Parent, the Camp Director Parent, the Boy Scout Parent, the Former Athlete Parent, or the Teacher Parent. Follow the previous suggestions stated in exercise 12 to present your character vividly.

- 14   From your experience in a summer or other job, write a character sketch about some person or type. For example, if you worked as a waiter or waitress, you might want to describe your boss or someone you worked with, or such customers as The Big Spender, The Indecisive Individual, The Wine Connoisseur, or The Spoiled Brat.

- 15   Write a character sketch either about a favorite relative, teacher,

[4] *New York Times,* 28 April 1974, Section 4, p. 20. © 1974 by The New York Times Company. Reprinted by permission.

neighbor, minister, friend, employer, or about someone you dislike or detest. Be sure to provide sufficient evidence to support your opinion.

16 Write a character sketch about a type of child recalled from your youth. You might select The Neighborhood Bully, Teacher's Pet, or The Rich Kid.

17 One of your friends has applied for a summer job as a camp counselor, giving your name as a reference. As a result, you have just received a letter from Mr. Outdore, Director of the Whispering Pine Camp, asking you to write a recommendation for your friend. Write the letter; do not worry about its business format.

18 Write a description of the most unforgettable character you have ever met. Realize that it might be someone you have been with only once, such as on an airplane or at a concert.

10

Language in Descriptive Writing

HOW DOES A WORD MEAN?
DENOTATION AND CONNOTATION

> A man was killed and his son was seriously injured in an automobile accident. The boy was rushed to a hospital. The surgeon took one look at him and said, "This is my son! I can't operate on him!" How could the boy have been the surgeon's son?

Most people are baffled by this question. Some reply with a timid, "The boy was adopted?" Others rack their brains, then give up. The answer is quite simple: the surgeon was the boy's mother. The reason people are puzzled is that they are so accustomed to thinking of a surgeon as a man, they do not consider the possibility that it could be a woman. According to the dictionary, the word *surgeon* refers to any physician, male or female, who "diagnoses and treats injury, deformity, and disease by manual and instrumental operations." This definition gives us the word's *denotation,* or dictionary definition. However, the total meaning of a word is not necessarily limited to its denotation. *Surgeon* conjures up in the minds of most people the word's associations, or its *connotation*—an image of a male, usually white, usually middle-aged, probably above average in height, garbed in a gown with a mask over his mouth and nose. But, obviously, surgeons can also be female. Thus, the connotation of a word may lead people astray, as it does in this story.

The advocates of women's liberation are right on target in showing how language can corrupt thought. But in most instances, such as the word *surgeon,* the fault lies not in the word but in society, perhaps the medical society in particular, for traditionally limiting the admission of women to medical schools. So it is natural to think of men when we talk about surgeons, or about pilots, professors, politicians, and business executives, just as we visualize women when we talk about nurses, secretaries, librarians, and housekeepers. But as times change, so will connotations and language. Our guess is that *mankind, countryman,* and *freshman* will not be replaced by *peoplekind, countrypeople,* or *freshpeople,* but as more women move into traditionally male occupations, we look for common acceptance of *policewoman, newspaperwoman,* and *chairwoman,* or perhaps even their unisex equivalents, *policeperson* (or *police officer*), *newspaperperson* (or just *journalist*), and *chairperson* (or *chair*). The dictionary already includes *Ms.;* other changes will follow.

Which brings us back to the dictionary and its definitions. To be fair and accurate to lexicographers, those alert and sagacious word-watchers, dictionaries are concerned with both denotations and connotations. The part of a dictionary entry that explains the meaning of a word is denotative. But the discussion of a word and its synonyms involves connotations, or the associations people have with words. Note how this concept is illustrated in the following discussion from the *American Heritage Dictionary* about words that have the same denotations as *fat* but different connotations:

Synonyms: *fat, obese, corpulent, fleshy, stout, portly, pudgy, rotund, plump, chubby.* These adjectives mean having an abundance of flesh, often to excess. *Fat* always implies excessive weight and is generally unfavorable in its connotations. *Obese* is employed principally in medical usage with reference to extreme overweight, and *corpulent* is a more general term for the same condition. *Fleshy* implies an abundance of flesh that is not necessarily disfiguring. *Stout* and *portly* are sometimes used in polite terms to describe fatness. *Stout,* in stricter application, suggests a thickset, bulky person, and *portly,* one whose bulk is combined with an imposing bearing. *Pudgy* describes one who is thickset and dumpy. *Rotund* suggests roundness of figure in a squat person. *Plump* is applicable to a pleasing fullness of figure, especially in women [note that dictionaries are not immune to sexism]. *Chubby* implies abundance of flesh, usually not to excess.

EUPHEMISMS

Euphemisms — words with overly favorable connotations — are often used to conceal what might be offensive or disturbing. The word *prison* is being replaced by *penal institution* and *correctional facility,* suggesting places less harsh and dehumanizing than those in which we actually incarcerate violators of the law. Another social problem is being made less poignant because the words *indigent, inner-city,* and *low-income* are commonly substituted for *poor,* a term with more explicit connotations. And we no longer have *poor* children; they are *disadvantaged, underprivileged,* or *culturally deprived.*

Euphemisms, or "language pollution," or "doublespeak," as some call it, is often intended to obscure or hide the real situation. Bureaucrats are especially skillful in selecting terms with inoffensive connotations, as was evident during the Vietnam war and in the Watergate affair: in Vietnam *waste* was used for *kill,* while the Watergate defendants' perjury and destruction of evidence were referred to as *stonewalling.* Government officials are not the only ones at fault. Big business no longer *lays off* workers, it *furloughs* them. And labor engages in *work stoppages,* not *strikes.*

Occasionally, but only occasionally, language pollution is reversed, the offensive terms replacing the more polite one. More newspapers now report that women are *raped* instead of *criminally assaulted,* a word substitution that may contribute to greater public concern about this offense. Similarly, *syphilis* and *gonorrhea,* formerly taboo words, are replacing the polite term *venereal disease* in an effort to arouse public concern.

Sometimes euphemisms are harmless. Like white lies, they may be kinder than the literal truth. One of our ugliest words for people is *crippled;* a pleasanter one is *handicapped.* To many people, being considered old is a terrifying experience, so they sometimes prefer to be called *senior citizens* instead of *old people.* And to give individuals a greater sense of prestige and importance in their work, we often refer to *hair stylists* instead of *barbers, beauticians* instead of *hairdressers, custodians* instead of *janitors, realtors* instead of *real estate salesmen,* and *morticians* instead of *undertakers.* These substitutions and others like them do little harm and make life more tolerable for the people involved. But you should be so alert to the use of words that you recognize when they are euphemisms. And you should try to see through euphemisms to the wrongs, injustices, and inequalities that they often camouflage.

EFFECTIVE USE OF WORDS IN DESCRIPTIVE WRITING

You may be wondering at this point what all this talk about connotations, denotations, and euphemisms has to do with writing, particularly descriptive writing. The general answer is that good writing always depends upon the effective use of words. As we have pointed out, you should develop a larger vocabulary to communicate precisely what you perceive and how you feel. But you should also develop a zest for words as such, even a love for them, if you wish to write well. You should share some of Dylan Thomas' feeling for words, which he dates from his childhood:

I tumbled for words at once. And when I began to read the nursery rhymes for myself, and, later, to read other verses and ballads, I knew that I had discovered the most important things, to me, that could ever be. There they were, seemingly lifeless, made only of black and white, but out of them, out of their being, came love and terror and pity and pain and wonder and all the other vague abstractions that make our ephemeral lives dangerous, great, and bearable. Out of them came the gusts and grunts and hiccups and hee-haws of the common fun of the earth. . . . And as I read more and more, and it was not all verse, by any means, my love for the real world of words increased until I knew that I must live *with* them and *in* them. I knew, in fact, that I must be a writer of words, and nothing else. I knew I had to know them most intimately in all their forms and moods, their ups and downs, their chops and changes, their needs and demands.

—Dylan Thomas, "Poetic Manifesto"

You need not develop so passionate a commitment to words, but you should learn to respect and enjoy words for the pleasure and power they give you. In personal description words must play a dual role: to communicate and to evoke, to let readers both perceive and feel. Even on a practical level, in a descriptive advertisement, this twofold responsibility is apparent. Read the following two ads and decide which one ran in *Playboy* (different wordings are in italics).

COPY A	COPY B
Whether *speeding* on the highway or *driving over curving country roads,* the Jaguar E-type *is the best.*	Whether *cruising* on the highway or *deftly stalking through twisting country roads,* the Jaguar E-type *dominates all it surveys.*
It is so handsome that it has been *shown* at the Museum of Modern Art.	*Its styling is so classically distinctive* it has been *displayed* at the Museum of Modern Art.
Beneath that *attractive exterior are engineering features that have enabled it to win* at the 24-Hour Race of Le Mans.	Beneath that *sculptured surface lurks engineering that traces its breeding to the legendary Jaguar victories* at the 24-Hour Race of Le Mans.
Jaguar's independent suspension front and rear *lets the car keep its four wheels on the road even when it's rough.*	Jaguar's independent suspension front and rear *lets the graceful cat keep all four feet on the ground, silky even on rough terrain.*
The four wheel disc brakes are ventilated in front and mounted inboard in the rear. All E-types are complete with Dunlop Sport 70 whitewall belted radials.	The four wheel disc brakes are ventilated in front and mounted inboard in the rear. All E-types are

The *excellent* Jaguar V-12 aluminum alloy engine is *exceptionally smooth*. Its 326 cubic inches of capacity is *much* smaller than the 468 cubic inches of capacity of the average American luxury V-8.

In addition to the luxury, comfort and instrumentation that you expect in a Jaguar, there is that *something else* in the Jaguar E-type that gave this automobile its name. Jaguar, *a fine animal, fierce but in full control of itself, excitable but restrained.*

complete with Dunlop Sport 70 whitewall belted radials.

The *incredible* Jaguar V-12 aluminum alloy engine *gives the word "smoothness" a new standard to live by*. Its 326 cubic inches of capacity is considerably smaller than the 468 cubic inches of capacity of the average American luxury V-8.

In addition to the luxury, comfort and instrumentation that you expect in a Jaguar, there is that *indefinable quality* in the Jaguar E-type that gave this automobile its name. Jaguar, *a magnificent beast, wild of spirit but in full control of its powers, exuberant yet disciplined.*[1]

Copy A describes a fine machine; Copy B (which is the version that appeared in *Playboy*) suggests an experience, an opportunity to own a car that will make driving an adventure and will win the admiration and envy of others. What creates the difference is the use in B of language that is rich in suggestiveness. From the opening "Whether cruising on the highway or deftly stalking through twisting country roads" to "wild of spirit but in full control of its powers, exuberant yet disciplined," the copy has been directed to the reader's imagination, implying that the Jaguar car is as alive, powerful, graceful, and exciting as the animal itself. Note the references to *stalking, breeding, cat, feet,* and also the evocative quality of the final sentence. Just the contrast between "a fine animal" in Copy A and "a magnificent beast" in B illustrates our point. Although *fine* expresses approval, *magnificent* suggests much more, conveying the idea that something is exalted, superlative, impressive, imposing. Similarly, *animal* is a vague, neutral term, while *beast* conjures up the picture of a powerful, wild creature, prowling for prey, alert for adventure, action, danger, excitement. Given the choice of buying a car that is likened to "a fine animal" or "a magnificent beast" (assuming that money is no object), most people under thirty would opt for the latter. That's what the Jaguar manufacturers are hoping.

Like language rich in connotations, similes and metaphors also evoke vivid impressions. The following passage from N. Scott Momaday's

[1] *Playboy,* June 1974, p. 5. Reprinted by permission of British Leyland Motors Inc., Leonia, N.J. and Bozell & Jacobs Advertising.

House Made of Dawn relies heavily on these figures of speech to describe Rainy Mountain, the name given to the knoll in Oklahoma where his people, the Kiowa Indians, live:

The hardest weather in the world is there. Winter brings blizzards, hot tornadic winds arise in the spring, and in summer the prairie is an anvil's edge. The grass turns brittle and brown, and it cracks beneath your feet. There are green belts along the rivers and creeks, linear groves of hickory and pecan, willow and witch hazel. At a distance in July or August the steaming foliage seems almost to writhe in fire. Great green and yellow grasshoppers are everywhere in the tall grass, popping up like corn to sting the flesh, and tortoises crawl about on the red earth, going nowhere in plenty of time.

This passage gains its power from the figurative language: the prairie like "an anvil's edge," "green belts along the rivers and creeks," the foliage seeming to "writhe in fire," the giant grasshoppers "popping up like corn." In a few sentences, Momaday has enabled us to see and feel and hear what living on Rainy Mountain is like, and made us realize that only a hardy people could endure living there in "the hardest weather in the world."

Connotative and figurative language are important in nearly all forms of writing, but particularly in personal descriptions. There, as in the examples about the Jaguar and Rainy Mountain, the writers are conveying an experience, trying not only to present information about an automobile or a geographical area but also showing how it feels to own and drive that car or live in that place. In such descriptions, words rich in associations are more effective than those that only transmit information.

Of course, words strike different people differently. Momaday's reference to "an anvil's edge" is evocative mainly to readers who know that blacksmiths hammer hot metal into shape on an anvil. Words like *mother, children,* and *home,* thought to be the most successful in triggering favorable responses, may backfire with people who have had bitter experiences with their mothers, children, or homes. And some people may find *house* more evocative than *cottage, street* more than *boulevard,* and *drunk* more than *wino.* But most would not. Thus, we are naturally referring to most readers when we talk about the need to select words and phrases appealing to their emotions as well as their reason.

But these words and phrases, rich in their ability to convey an experience vividly and imaginatively, have no place in factual descriptions. In scientific and technical writing, language should be exact and precise, selected mainly to convey a specific meaning, designed to communicate information, not feeling. A factual description of Momaday's Rainy Mountain would consist of statements about temperature averages and ranges, humidity, rainfall, and wind velocity. And the passage about the Jaguar would include other factual information in addition to the sentences about the disc brakes, tires, and engine. Indeed, there is a time and a place for words and phrases with little imaginative appeal.

How do you learn to use words skillfully — the right words in the right places? You can't learn overnight or in a few weeks or even in a few months. As we mentioned earlier, you have to develop a zest for words, cultivate an absorbing interest in them, develop a feeling for them, think and worry about them, struggle and play with them. That will take time. But what you can do in your next paper is to search for words in your dictionary or in a synonym book, substituting more effective ones for those dashed off in your first draft. Your job is always to find the right word, one that will say exactly what you mean, primarily denotative for factual descriptions, richly connotative for personal ones. By using the right word to perform the required task, you should improve your next paper and future ones. And by noting and pondering over and developing a fascination for words, by becoming more sensitive to their denotations and connotations, you should improve as a writer.

ASSIGNMENTS

For Discussion

1   Explain the following statements:

    a   Words do not have meanings; only the people who use them have meanings.

    b   If the language is debased or misused, if the meaning of words is obscured, the basis for common judgment is undermined, if not destroyed.

—Eugene McCarthy

    c   People go to dictionaries to find out what words mean while lexicographers (people who write and edit dictionaries) go to people to find out what words mean.

2   In *Confessions of an Advertising Man,* David Ogilvy stated that the two most powerful words a copywriter can use in a headline are *free* and *new.* His research indicates that other effective words include *important, sensational, miracle, bargain, hurry, last chance,* and *wanted.* Why do you think these words are appealing? What other words would you add to the list?

3   Perhaps because people often behave like animals, we often use animal names, such as *pig* and *chicken,* to refer to people. What other animal terms do we use and how appropriate are their connotations?

4   Explain why each of the following terms popular among the military forces during the Vietnam war is considered a pollution of the

language: *incursion, protective reaction strike, waste* (for *kill*), and *pacification.*

5   What do you think are the ten most beautiful words in the language? (Some suggestions: *dawn, mother, murmuring, nevermore.*) The ten ugliest? (Some suggestions: *scab, mud, gonorrhea.*) The saddest? Happiest?

6   Find a term in sports that has a different meaning in another context. In addition, suggest why the term is used as it is in sports. For example, the word *diamond* obviously refers to the shape of the playing field in baseball, but how would you account for *bullpen, dugout, strike,* and numerous other terms?

7   With the trend toward writing comments on report cards instead of giving grades, teachers have learned how to use euphemisms. For example, instead of telling parents that their child is cheating, a teacher might write that the child needs guidance in learning how to abide by the doctrine of fair play. What euphemisms can you suggest for the following qualities: *dirty, fights frequently, lies, steals, disliked by others, lazy, rude, selfish, noisy, usually late?*

8   Fill in the blanks and point out the connotation of each added term:

   a   When you tell me to do it, it's nagging; when I tell you to do it, it's _____.

   b   When you talk to your friends, it's idle chatter; when I talk to mine, it's _____.

   c   When you don't like something, you complain; when I don't like something, I _____.

   d   My dog is playful; yours is _____.

   e   I offered helpful suggestions; you offered _____.

   f   Our basketball team plays an aggressive game; your team plays _____.

   g   I am broad-minded; you are _____.

   Can you make up any additional sentences?

For Writing

1   Write a response to either of the following:

   a   Ed Lane, minister of the Unitarian Church in Westport, Conn., in the church newsletter *Echoes:*

Symbols are important and have their place, yet there is danger of focusing so much on a symbol that it becomes more important than the reality it represents. . . .

   In these terms, and in support of women's liberation, de-genderizing language is a diversion into trivia rather than a raising of consciousness and a mutilation of language rather than an accomplishment of equality in status.

The straw that broke the camel's back was the substitution of "chairperson" for "chairman." . . .

"Chairman did not ever have a sexual connotation for me. Because the word was neutral it was preceded by "Madame" or "Mister" when addressing a particular individual, just as "Jones" is sexually neutral unless preceded by Mr., Miss, etc. . . . and the last syllable of "chairperson" is just as masculine as that of "chairman." . . .

And while we're at it, why discriminate against last syllables? I'm sure that words like *man*agement, *man*date, and *man*datory had their origin in an era in which men made the decisions and gave the orders, so those will have to go also.

Imagine a world with no *brother*hood, hu*man*ness, and not even ro*man*ce.

b Harriet Duzet, letter in *Intercom*, a newsletter of the Society for Technical Communication:

I would like to go on record as a proponent of "chairperson" because it is, indeed, sexually neuter. In the business and professional world, I believe that women would prefer to be regarded as "people" and not given sexual or marital labels. Yes, the word "chairman" has survived many decades of use because it was apt in a male-dominated world. Now, however, a substantial proportion of the population working outside of the home is female. Semantic changes are overtaking us and what sounds strange today will be commonplace tomorrow. Who would have thought a year ago that "Ms." would not only be accepted but popularly used today?

I object to the terms "chairlady" and "chairwoman" for various reasons. My first objection is that their use forces you to distinguish by sex between chairpersons. My second is that the terms appear similar to the worn-out expressions "charlady" and "charwoman," who performed the most menial of tasks. Further use of "chairlady" suggests corollary use of the term "chairgentleman," which is obviously absurd.

2 In *Language in Thought and Action*, S. I. Hayakawa points out that, connotatively, words can be neutral—can "purr" (have a favorable effect), or can "snarl" (be insulting to the audience). These three sentences, all describing the same church breakfast, demonstrate how word choice can add different emotive color to description.

> Neutral: Every Sunday, between the church services, the women of the congregation serve a breakfast of scrambled eggs, bacon, grits, biscuits, juice and coffee for $1.25.
> "Purr": Every Sunday, between the inspiring services, the untiring ladies of this charming congregation offer an appetizing brunch of fluffy scrambled eggs, crisp bacon,

butter-laden grits, light, hot scones, fresh frothy nectar, and steaming *cafe au lait* for a reasonable $1.25.

"Snarl": Every Sunday, between the deadening services, the female do-gooders of this sleepy congregation ladle out a nauseating mess of leathery scrambled eggs, limp hogback, soggy hominy, heavy, cold buns, stale, flat, juice-flavored water, and tepid java for a presumptuous $1.25.

Write three paragraphs describing something from your own experience—a place, a person, something that has special meaning to you—describing it first in neutral language, then with "purr" and "snarl" connotations. As in the examples, make use of adjectives and synonyms to accomplish your purpose.

3   One way to force yourself into an awareness of word connotation and careful word choice is to write *haiku*. Originally Japanese, the *haiku* is a poetic form that has been somewhat successfully adapted to English. The most widely used form consists of exactly seventeen syllables (usually three lines of five, seven, and five syllables) and is a concrete description of an immediate experience from everyday life. The most successful *haiku* involve a single poignant scene from nature that strikes a responsive philosophical chord. Study these two examples and then try your hand at writing several of your own:

> On a barren branch
> A bird chirps piteously
> Fighting bitter cold.

> Down abandoned streets
> Lamp posts sported furry caps
> In the early dawn.
> —George K. Brady

4   Rewrite the copy of an advertisement, as we did in the Jaguar example, to show how and why the original language is more effective, or, if you wish, rewrite the copy to increase its effectiveness. Be certain to include the advertisement or write out its copy in your paper.

5   Henryk Skolimowski, a University of Southern California philosophy professor, has charged that highly emotional terms in advertising are applied to objects, thus making us consider them as if they were human beings. For example, soap is called *lovely,* cars *proud, bold.* The result, he contends, is that we have developed a strong emotional attachment to many objects, practically worshipping them. After looking at some advertisements, write a descriptive ad for one of your own prized possessions.

The Voices of Written English

In Chapter 4, we discussed the varied voices of spoken English—the dialects of different geographical regions and different social communities. We also pointed out that you, as a speaker of English, have many personal voices available to you—one for rapping to close friends, another for conversing with parents or grandparents, another for talking to strangers. Depending upon your audience and your circumstances, you shift freely back and forth among these different modes of speaking. Most of the personal writing you were asked to do in Part 1 of this book was in a style close to conversational English. But the chances are that as you moved through the assignments from journal writing to personal essay, your writing style automatically changed. You probably moved from the relaxed, conversational voice of the journal entry nearer to the voice you reserve for strangers: one characterized by relative freedom from regionalisms and community usages. If so, then you moved closer to another variety of English: the dialect of written English. As you move from the intimate audience of your personal writing to a more public one, you will need to operate more and more in that dialect.

As a "dialect," written English manifests certain characteristics. Generally tighter in structure and limited to usages generally accepted as standard to all varieties of English, it is, in a sense, a separate dialect from the spoken varieties—one permitting less freedom of choice from among all the available language options. And unlike most spoken varieties, written English is characterized by the avoidance of regionalisms, using instead universally accepted vocabulary and grammatical items. In addition, because the written form lacks the facial expressions, the body gestures, and the intonation features available to speakers, a writer must be more concerned with unambiguous sentence structure. For instance, the student who momentarily startled a harassed English teacher at registration with the statement, "I'm a freshman English major who needs an advisor," quickly clarified his intended meaning by repeating it and emphasizing the pause between *freshman* and *English,* thus communicating that he, a freshman, was an English major. But if this statement were written, the ambiguity would remain. The student could indeed be saying, as the astonished professor initially inferred, that he was majoring in freshman English. Obviously, more conservative and formal sentence structures are needed for accurate communication in written English than in its counterpart spoken forms. But this does not mean that when we write there must be absolute rigidity and strict conformity to rules, or that variety is not possible.

This variety, however, does not stem from exactly the same factors that operate in spoken dialects. We have seen that the speaker's distance from his or her audience has some influence on spoken English, but in written English this distance becomes highly significant. In writing, *situation* is paramount. Situation includes not only the *audience* written to—close or distant—but also the *purpose* for writing and the social *context* in which something is written. All play an important role in establishing the written varieties of English.

EXAMPLES OF VARIETIES OF WRITTEN ENGLISH

An analysis of three examples can help to clarify the relationship of context, purpose, and audience in determining appropriate usage.

1. Well, you just sour your dough. You start it off with a little yeast and flour and water, and you set it up close to the stove with the lid off, 'cause they say there's so much wild yeast in the air. Then you just set it up there and you leave it sit for thirty-six hours or so. And it gets a tang to it. And then when you get ready to make your pancakes, you pour a little bit of this in a bowl, the way I do it. Now most of the people don't do it this way. I keep quite a little sour dough on hand. Most of the people, just a cupful.

—Quoted in Carol Hill and Bruce Davidson, *Subsistence U.S.A.*

Even though taken out of its social situation, this paragraph contains clues to it. The purpose here is to give another person a general idea of how sourdough is made. The highly conversational tone indicates a face-to-face relationship between writer and audience; the choice of every-day, simple vocabulary and the use of the personal pronouns *I* and *you* add to the intimate tone. In the statement, "You pour a little bit of this in the bowl," the use of *this* indicates that the speaker is pointing to the mixture — speaker and listener are physically sharing the experience. This close relationship is additionally signalled by the simple sentence structure throughout and the fragment at the end, all conveying only minimal information. Sentence introducers, such as *now, well,* and the clipped word *'cause,* also bear witness to the informal, conversational quality characteristic of close social contact. All of these combine to produce a distinctive style of writing: a written variety that we call *Casual English.*

2. Sourdough ranks among the world's most controversial foods. Like fried chicken or spaghetti sauce, it has its factions and fanatics, each of whom knows more about it than the next fellow, or thinks he does. There is the old fashioned type who believes that the only real and effective starter is made from hops, water, and flour, and must be at least a couple of decades old — a kind of eternal flame that should never be extinguished. And then there is the type of aficionado who is convinced that potato water makes a better starter . . . with a boost from today's active dry yeast, and, though he will concede that a starter *can* improve almost indefinitely as it ages, he tosses his out at the end of each year. About the only point on which Phil and the others agree is that a starter should not be kept in a metal container, for its ingredients corrode almost all metals; thus Phil's kitchen boasts the ubiquitous earthenware crock of the true sourdough devotee.

— Dale Brown, *American Cooking: The Northwest*

Again on the subject of sourdough cookery, this paragraph has markedly different characteristics from the preceding one. The purpose is still to inform the audience about the topic, but the context of the writing situation is obviously not similar. Here, the writer speaks to a distant audience: an unseen listener. He cannot point to one sourdough batter and then another. Instead, he is forced by the situation to supply information, and in doing so must use more precise language. Too, in order to convey details, the sentence structure takes on complexity and length. The longest sentence in the previous example of Casual English contained twenty-three words, but, with the exception of the first, all sentences in paragraph 2 exceed that — the longest having forty-four.

Further evidence of the writer's distance from his audience is in his use of the neutral third person pronouns, resulting in a more formal tone than was projected by the *you* of the first example. However, some writers prefer to use the second person, impersonal *you* even when writing to a general audience to establish a more intimate relationship with the audience than is possible with the third person.

Other features of the second example that add formality and distance are the lack of conversational sentence openers such as *Well* and the choice of words. Although most words in the passage are suitable for a general audience, others are addressed to one with a fairly high level of education (note especially the words *aficionado* and *ubiquitous*). Formal grammatical structures such as *each of whom* also point to an educated audience.

Taken together, all these factors create a style of writing distinctively different from that of Casual English, one we call *General English.*

3. For the manufacture of yeast, most authorities have recommended that subsequent to the treatment with malt the mash should be "soured" by the action of lactic acid bacteria, a culture of which is added in the final stages of the process and allowed to act for a period of 12 to 15 hours at a temperature of 59° C. The precise effect of this treatment is obscure. It is claimed on the one hand to bring about a hydrolysis of the proteins present in the grain extract and thus render them more readily available for yeast growth.

—Magnus Pyke, "The Technology of Yeasts"

Again, essentially the same topic is dealt with, but purpose, audience, and context are drastically changed. The purpose of this excerpt from a scientific text is not to give a practical, general description, but a detailed technical explanation of the process. The social context is a classroom or laboratory. The audience is not a general one, but highly specialized, familiar with the scientific jargon. Note that the writer expects his readers to understand 59° C and *hydrolysis.* In addition, the writer separates himself from the audience as much as possible: *authorities* recommend, not the author; his quotation marks around *soured* almost apologize for the near-casual tone of this commonplace usage; colder impersonality is conveyed by introductions such as "It is claimed" instead of "I have observed" or even "This researcher has observed."

To convey precise information, the sentences are long and involved: the first sentence alone contains fifty-eight words. Most of the verbs are passive — "should be soured," "is added . . . and allowed," "is claimed" — contributing not only to the complexity of sentence structure but adding an even greater tone of impersonality by removing any human agents.

This paragraph represents a variety of written English characteristically different from the other two, one that we call *Specialized English.* In this book, any writing utilizing a special vocabulary as in this example, or that makes artistic use of figurative language (as in literary writing), will fit this category. In other words, Specialized English is a variety aimed at a particular audience with a special educational background or written primarily to appeal to the artistic senses of the audience in order to delight as well as inform.

DISTRIBUTION OF VARIETIES OF WRITTEN ENGLISH

We do not intend to imply that all writing falls neatly into these three categories; human nature and language usage do not permit such simplicity. But these are convenient starting points of classification. Little writing will be purely one variety or another. Instead, as do regional and social dialects, the three varieties tend to overlap.

This overlapping occurs when a writer who is using predominantly one style or variety dips into another to deal with a special problem or purpose. Particularly in dialogue sections, many autobiographical narratives are predominantly written in Casual English, but may exhibit some characteristics of General English in expository passages. Personal essays written to a general audience, like the Bombeck example on pp. 32–33, are basically in General English with a few features borrowed from Casual. In addition, autobiographies such as Eldridge Cleaver's *Soul on Ice* make extensive use of such a mix. Many quasi-scientific articles written for magazines with popular appeal, such as *Psychology Today* and *Scientific American,* are usually in General English, interspersed with some vocabulary items of Specialized English. Novels and short stories often employ features of all three styles, predominantly utilizing the figurative language and rhetorical structures characteristic of literary Specialized English, but including aspects of Casual English in dialogue and of General English in both dialogue and expository passages. William Faulkner and Flannery O'Connor are but two writers who effectively use all three varieties in their fiction.

As a student of writing, you should not only be aware of the general characteristics of each variety of written English, but you also should realize that each can be mixed with the others. To become an effective writer, you should be able to judge when mixing varieties is beneficial to your purpose and when it is detrimental. For instance, the word *soured* in the example of Specialized English did no real harm to the tone and level of its language usage. Likewise, a few slang words interjected into a paper written in General English might add life and interest, but an excess could seriously change the style you are attempting to establish. If you wish to maintain consistency, you must take care that the written variety you have chosen is not overshadowed by the inclusion of too many items from the others.

FEATURES OF THE VARIETIES OF WRITTEN ENGLISH

The following chart could help you to become familiar with the general characteristics of the three written varieties. But remember that even though writing can be broadly categorized, no two pieces of writing can be exactly the same. Each bears the stamp of a writer's own style.

WRITTEN VARIETY	USE IN WRITING	AUDIENCE	LANGUAGE FEATURES	TONE
CASUAL ENGLISH	Limited use: Personal narrative and essays. Dialogue. Letters to friends and relatives. Writing addressed to a peer audience.	Familiar; close in some way to writer. Mutual knowledge and experience with writer.	Vocabulary: simple words, slang, and localisms. Sentences: simple structure, short, simple sentences; fragments; coordinate sentences. Voice: first person, personal pronouns and references. Punctuation: individualized and relatively free from conventional rules.	Subjective: personal, intimate, friendly.
GENERAL ENGLISH	Unlimited use: Magazine writing. Books appealing to a mass audience. Newspaper writing. Term papers. Nontechnical reports. Letters to editors and business people. Argument pa-	General: distant, but acknowledged. Audience needs informative details.	Vocabulary: generally recognized and current. Sentences: longer and more complex than in Casual English; coordinate and subordinate structures. Voice: generally third person; impersonal *you*	Neutral

WRITTEN VARIETY	USE IN WRITING	AUDIENCE	LANGUAGE FEATURES	TONE
	pers. Written examinations. Most college assignments.		permitted for some purposes. Punctuation: tighter adherence to rules, less individualized choice.	
SPECIALIZED ENGLISH	Limited to a particular subject and audience. Specialized technical or professional writing. Academic writing: theses and dissertations. Legal drafts and documents. Literary writing.	Select audience: distant from writer. Audience has specialized background.	Vocabulary: specialized technical jargon; literary devices. Sentences: long and highly complex; high percentage of subordinate-coordinate structures. Voice: excluding literary writing, third person; strict avoidance of personal pronouns. Punctuation: rigid adherence to rules in all but literary writing.	Professional writing: objective, highly impersonal and formal. Literary writing: established by writer without reference to audience.

ASSIGNMENTS

For Discussion

1 Specify the written variety of each of the following passages and explain your choice.

a America is rather like life. You can easily find in it what you look for. If you look for skyscrapers or cowboys or cocktail parties or gangsters or business connections or political problems or women's clubs, they will certainly be there. You can be very hot there or very cold. You can explore the America of your choice by plane or train, by hitch-hike or on foot. It will probably be interesting, and it is sure to be large.

—E. M. Forster, *Two Cheers for Democracy*

b These are sweeping generalizations, yet they illustrate Frye's concern to establish, on the one hand, an autonomous conceptual universe while insuring, on the other, that this universe is not isolated from culture, society, and human letters. But how can criticism be both disinterested and engaged at the same time? Or, we might ask Frye, what is criticism really, the study of self-contained literary forms and their analogical relations or the inter-play between literature and social value? His system, of course, does not permit these kinds of questions to be easily asked, for he conceives of criticism as a dialectical axis, having "as one pole the total acceptance of the data of literature, and as the other the total acceptance of the potential value of those data" [Northrop Frye, *Anatomy of Criticism*, p. 25]. This dyadic framework permits him to pursue practically any critical problem he wishes, depending on whether his gaze is centripetal or centrifugal—to use the terms of the "Second Essay."

—Robert D. Denham, "Frye and the Social Context of Criticism"

c Look around you; what do you see? Long, stringy, greasy, smelly, lice-infested hair, patched and torn and patched again blue jeans and tie-dyed tee shirts. On which sex? Both! Unless there is a prominent mustache or beard, the males and females look the same. These kids think they are "cool" and "hip to the trick." They sit around and meditate or protest on the Court House steps for love and peace instead of war. They rebel against our established and wonderful way of life and try to destroy it. We who love our life style have to conquer the hippies.

—Student paper

d Like their relatives—leafhoppers, spittlebugs, cicadas, aphids, and scale insects—most of the treehoppers that one encounters in the United States are fairly ordinary-looking insects, the sort of things all but a naturalist or an orchard owner would very likely overlook. But move south towards the tropics and these insects become an array of elaborate monstrosities. They remain, in essence, the same humble insects, but carry around on their backs ex-

travagant structures, the purposes of which are by no means clear to scientists.
—Lewis L. Deitz, "Mild-mannered Minimonsters"

e Before I had gone that 50 yards, I noticed an uneasy feeling. Then, just as I realized I was getting dizzy, I fell. Sitting there in two feet of water, I couldn't get up. The world seemed to be moving back and forth. What I had not noticed before I began to walk was that the entire sheet of water was moving—mostly out, but with small undulations, unrippled. The moving water and the still land around had collided in my eyes and bounced off the ear balancers, so all I could do was fall. I sat there several moments, smiling into the sea, relieved to know why I was soaked.
—Charles Jones, "A Place Apart"

f In children the infection [osteomyelitis] is caused by organisms such as the staphylococci and less commonly by streptococci or pneumococci. The germs usually reach the bone through the bloodstream from a focus elsewhere in the body. Osteomyelitis can also be caused by direct spread from infected tissue in the vicinity of bone, or as a result of a wound or open fracture.
—Adrian E. Flatt, "Bones and Muscles and Their Disorders,"
Family Medical Guide

g Acute osteomyelitis of children starts as a localized infection of the yet-uncalcified ends of the shaft of a growing bone. This infectuous process rapidly extends to the medullary cavity of the shaft whence it may perforate through the cortex to the periosteum separating the latter from the bone by formation of a subperiosteal abscess; or it may dissect through the epiphysis (the end of the bone, developed separately as part of a joint, and which later unites with the shaft) into the near-by articulation, causing a purulent arthritis.
—Charles Phillips Emerson and Jane Elizabeth Taylor,
Essentials of Medicine

h *What* and I had an unpleasant time of it during my childhood. Like many of us I was told never to respond with "What?" "Tommy?" "What?" was to be replaced by "Tommy?" "Yes, Sir?" or "Tommy?" "Yes, Ma'am?" or to my peers, "Tommy?" "Yes?" "What?" meaning "What did you say?" was another no-no. I was told to say, "I beg your pardon?" I never understood why I should beg the pardon of someone if *he* was mumbling.
—Thomas H. Middleton, "What's What"

2 Why must writers be concerned about their audience when they choose a written variety of English?

For Writing

1 Write a brief narrative about a personal experience using the direct discourse method as described in Chapter 2, pp. 22–27. Write in Casual English.

2 Write the same narrative, using direct discourse and General English.

12

Usage in Descriptive Writing

In Chapter 4 we pointed out that narrative writing permits a wide range of language usage. In the writing of realistic dialogue all the stylistic options of spoken English are available, including regionalisms, slang, and even usages generally considered nonstandard. As a rule, the scope of language in descriptive writing is not that broad, except perhaps in descriptions narrated by a literary character. The colorful descriptions in *Huckleberry Finn* exemplify this possibility; because Huck is the narrator in the novel, the descriptive sections are expressed in his unique manner with the same social and geographical dialect characteristics of his dialogue.

Other descriptive writing, however, particularly factual or objective description, calls for an idiom characterized by standard usages, by avoidance of regionalisms, and generally by features closer to those of Casual or General written English than to those of free, conversational spoken English. But because you are often asked to write for a broader audience than you were with personal narratives, you are then committed to a more general use of vocabulary and grammatical structures. The voice in the writing should remain yours, but should not be the intimate one reserved for your journal or your closest associates. Strive instead to reproduce the voice you reserve for a friendly but less familiar audience, such as for an aunt or uncle you like.

To resolve possible confusion about appropriate language use, you might think of the varieties of written English as operating on a continuum from very informal usage to extremely formal usage:

Informal $\longrightarrow \longrightarrow \longrightarrow \longrightarrow \longrightarrow \longrightarrow \longrightarrow \longrightarrow \longrightarrow$ Formal

Casual $\longrightarrow \longrightarrow \longrightarrow$ General $\longrightarrow \longrightarrow \longrightarrow$ Specialized

On the continuum, the language style of most descriptive writing is closer to General than is much narrative writing. However, you should not find moving from one language style to another difficult in written English. You do it many times a day in spoken English. Remember how easily you shift from the intimate, relaxed style of your conversations in the hall to a more formal usage in classroom discussions? With practice, you will become equally proficient in changing modes in written English.

GLOSSARY OF USAGES FOR REFERENCE IN DESCRIPTIVE WRITING

In writing description, we make extensive use of special language structures: for making comparisons, for expressing spatial relationships, for indicating time, and for achieving special aesthetic effects (figurative language). English usage provides many options for these purposes, some more desirable than others in descriptions written to a wide audience. The following glossary is designed to serve as a reference guide to help you with many items frequently used in such descriptions.

all together/altogether

All together is used to refer to all members of a group gathered together:

At last, we're all together under one roof.

Altogether is an adverb meaning "wholly" or "completely."

The scene he encountered at the top of the hill was *altogether* delightful.

already/all ready

These two, although frequently interchanged, are not synonymous. *Already* is an adverb meaning "prior to a specified time."

The signs of spring were *already* in evidence.

All ready means "completely prepared."

The expedition was *all ready* to set forth.

a lot of/alot of

A lot of is an intensifier meaning the same as "many." It is frequently used with mass nouns or nouns having only a plural form.

A lot of sugar is wasted. (mass noun)

A lot of cattle become diseased every year. (noun having only a plural form)

Alot of is a spelling error, occurring when *a lot* is mistaken as one word.

allusion/illusion

Allusion and *illusion* are often pronounced alike, which causes them to be confused. *Allusion* refers to a casual reference to something; it should be followed by *to. Illusion* refers to a false impression; it should be followed by *of.*

Women resent *allusions* to feminine frailty.
Napoleon retained his *illusion* of power even after his banishment.

analogous in/analogous to

Analogous is a synonym for *similar* or *like.* It is followed by *in* when referring to the specific respects in which several things are similar:

The wings of airplanes and birds are *analogous in* shape and structure.

Analogous to indicates that two things are similar:

Airplanes are *analogous to* birds.

analogy between/analogy of . . . to/with . . .

You can make or draw an *analogy between* two things or an *analogy of* one thing *to* or *with* another.

He made an *analogy between* fads in curtains and women's fashions.
The professor drew an *analogy of* the structure of the inner ear *to/with* that of a conch shell.

anywhere/anywheres

We can't find one *anywhere.* (acceptable)
We can't find one *anywheres.* (unacceptable in written English)

appears that/like/like that
See **seems.**

as . . . as/so . . . as

As . . . as is a popular construction for comparison:

Mary is *as* proficient in math *as* John.

The negative version, *not as . . . as . . .* is also widely accepted, although in specialized writing some people prefer *not so . . . as . . . .*

Mary is *not as* proficient in math *as* John. (acceptable for most usage levels)
Mary is *not so* proficient in math *as* John. (Specialized English)

as, such as

As is not an acceptable substitute for *such as* in:

They had many things in common, *such as* a love of music and an appreciation of nature. (acceptable)

They had many things in common, *as* a love of music and an appreciation of nature. (unacceptable in written English)

at this point in time/at this moment in time

Both are overused clichés and are unnecessarily wordy. For more effective writing, avoid them in favor of *now*.

compare to/compare with

Compare to is used to emphasize the similarities between two things; *compare with* signifies relative values, whether similarities or differences or both.

In his article, Mailer *compared* the "happening" quality of graffiti *to* other forms of pop art. (similarities only)

He *compared* the effects of heroin *with* the effects of marijuana. (similarities and differences can be included)

comparison between

He made a *comparison between* students from large universities and students from small colleges. (similarities and differences can be included)

different from/different than

These two forms are frequently interchanged in spoken English at all social levels; however, in all forms of written English except Casual, the following usage is generally recommended:

The European cultural heritage is *different from* that of the American Indian. (use *from* as a preposition that is followed by a noun phrase)

The view from the mountain that morning was *different than* any we had seen before. (use *than* as a conjunction that precedes a complete clause)

except/accept

These two verbs are often confused. *Except* as a verb means to exclude or exempt:

Juniors and seniors are *excepted* from obligatory dorm residence.

Accept is to receive something offered:

He *accepted* the scholarship.

It might help to sort them out if you remember that *accept* has a higher frequency of use. Once you *accept* that fact, you can *except* most of the possibilities of *except.*

effect/affect

These are often confused when used as verbs. In relaxed speech, they sound alike, which adds to the confusion. *Effect* means to "bring something about":

The doctors were able to *effect* a cure for his disease.

Affect means to "influence in some way":

The disease *affected* him in peculiar ways.

It may also help to remember that *effect* occurs more frequently as a noun than as a verb; the opposite is true with *affect.*

farther/further

In contemporary usage, *farther* is preferred to express greater distance in space:

St. Louis is *farther* from New York than Cleveland is.
I won't carry this piano any *farther.*

In careful English, *further* is restricted to a sense of greater advancement in time:

He is *further* along in graduate school than Mary is.
I won't carry this argument any *further.*

However, the two have become so freely interchangeable that many usage experts look upon *further* as simply a variant of *farther,* so that "St. Louis is *further* from New York than Cleveland is" would be acceptable to most people even for written English. Adjust to the taste of your audience in making a choice.

fewer/less

Fewer is usually restricted to count nouns:

Fewer birds are now found in the swamps of Florida.

Less is generally used with mass nouns:

Less animosity toward the Establishment is apparent on campuses today.

In written English you should try to maintain this distinction, even though many people do not in conversational English.

former/latter

Former—the first-mentioned item; *latter*—the second-mentioned item.

They should be used only when there can be no confusion about which item in the preceding context each refers to.

> When it came to apples and oranges, he preferred the *former* to the *latter.*

Latter, because of a tendency to add voice to consonants between vowels, is often misspelled *ladder.* Despite the old superstition, if you have a choice between walking in front of a truck or under a ladder, choose the *latter.*

hardly/barely/scarcely

All three are weak negative adverbs meaning "not quite." Addition of another negative is considered unacceptable, as are other double negatives.

> Jim had *hardly* any appetite. (acceptable)
> Jim didn't *hardly* have any appetite. (unacceptable double negative)

in/into/in to

In and *into,* when used in a directional sense or to show movement, are in most cases freely interchangeable—

> Jerry drove the car *in/into* the parking lot. (either *in* or *into* is acceptable)

—except in instances like this, where no direction or movement is indicated:

> Jerry parked the car *in* the parking lot. (*into* not acceptable)

In is used also to express time in prepositional adverbs such as "in a few moments."

In and *to* can be compounded as *into* only when both are clearly prepositions. In situations such as the following, *to* is part of the infinitive *to see,* not a preposition:

> Jerry drove us *in* to see the play.

in/within

Both *in* and *within* as prepositions may convey the sense of "inside," but *within* is usually used when "inside" has the additional condition of limitation of space, substance, or time:

> I'll do it *within* the hour.
> He was trapped *within* the confines of the prison.
> They live *within* a mile's distance from each other.

Remember, *in* is more commonly used for "inside" jobs than *within* is.

like/as/as though/as if

Like, when used as a preposition, ruffles no one's usage feathers:

> She swims *like* a fish. (preposition — universally accepted)

But when used as a conjunction replacing *as, as if,* or *as though, like* becomes controversial.

> He has never acted *like* he should. (*like* as a conjunction — controversial)
> He has never acted *as* he should. (acceptable even in the most specialized usage)
> They act *like* they were the only drivers on the road. (controversial)
> They act *as if/as though* they were the only drivers on the road. (either is acceptable)

Like as a conjunction is acceptable in all forms of spoken English and in written Casual English, but because the usage disturbs many people, it is best to avoid it when writing to a wide audience. One word of caution, however: don't become so hyper-careful that you err in the other direction, substituting *as* for *like,* as in:

> *As* my mother, my roommate always tells me when to get up. (substitution results in ambiguity)

nowhere/nowheres

Nowheres is a dialectal variant of *nowhere* and is unacceptable in written English.

> Mary could find him *nowhere.* (acceptable)
> Mary could find him *nowheres.* (unacceptable in written English)

on/upon/up on

Even though they are freely interchangeable, *on* is generally used to emphasize a position of rest while *upon* carries the connotation of "movement to."

> The book lies *on* the table. (fixed location)
> Jack jumped *upon* the table. (movement involved)

Up on occurs when *up* and *on* are clearly not a compound preposition, as in:

> He threw the book *up on* the roof.

pretty

Pretty as an adverb — "The car was in *pretty* good shape" — is widely used in spoken English, and acceptable in written Casual English. However, for other purposes, some less overworked qualifier should be substituted: *moderately, fairly, somewhat, rather.*

seems like/seems as if/seems as though/seems that/seems like that

Like after verbs denoting sensation—*seem, look, feel, appear*—is as controversial as when used after other kinds of verbs (see **like/as**).

> He seems *like* an understanding person. (preposition—acceptable in all levels of usage)
>
> It seems *like* he doesn't know what he's doing. (*like* used as a conjunction—controversial)
>
> It seems *as if/as though* he doesn't know what he's doing. (preferred by many educated people to *like*, particularly in written English)

In many dialect areas, after verbs such as *seem, feel,* and *appear, like* may be paired with *that* in some situations, but only in spoken English.

> It seems *that* he doesn't know what he's doing. (acceptable for all levels of usage)
>
> It seems *like that* he doesn't know what he's doing. (dialectal variant—should be avoided in written English)

similar/similar to

Similar and *similar to* fill adjective positions:

> Another company offered me a *similar* job.
> Another company offered me a job *similar to* my present one.

But they should not be used as adverbs, as in:

> They ran *similar*. (unacceptable—use *similarly*)
> They ran *similar to* each other. (unacceptable—use *similarly*)

so/as

See **as . . . as.**

somewhere/somewheres

Somewheres is a dialectal variant of *somewhere* and is universally unacceptable in written English.

> They were sure to find it *somewhere*. (acceptable)
> They were sure to find it *somewheres*. (unacceptable in written English)

such/such a/such as/such . . . as

The adjective *such* can qualify plural nouns or mass nouns:

> *Such* men are rare. (plural noun)
> *Such* love is rare. (mass noun)

Such a is used with singular count nouns:

> *Such a* man had never been seen before.

After *no,* we can use *such,* but not *such a,* even with singular count nouns:

No *such* animal ever existed. (singular count noun)

But not:

No *such an* animal ever existed.

Such . . . as operates as a formula in situations *such as:*

Is there *such* an animal *as* a unicorn?
There's *no such* animal *as* a unicorn. (negative formula)

Such as can also be used in place of *similar to/like:*

In times *such as* these, no one is safe.

But, just as with *like, such as* is frowned upon when the formula is used so that *as* introduces a whole clause:

The army attacked with *such* force *as* nothing could withstand it.

Although you may encounter this latter usage in literature written before the twentieth century, it is not acceptable in modern usage; *that* replaces *as:*

The army attacked with *such* force *that* nothing could withstand it.

through/thru
Through has the general connotation of "from one end to another" in reference to time (*through* the day), space (*through* Europe), or agency (*through* faith). *Thru* is a variant spelling, acceptable in Casual English.

till/until
Till is an acceptable variant of *until.* Avoid, however, *til, 'til, 'till,* and *untill.*

used to/use to
Use to is a frequent misspelling of *used to* in statements like:

He *used to* be the mayor of New York.

Sentence Strategies in Descriptive Writing

In Chapter 5, we suggested ways in which short, simple sentences and compound sentences could be used for certain purposes in personal writing. But in descriptive and other kinds of writing, different sentence structures may be more effective. Because sentences are the vehicles for expressing ideas and for imparting information, you should search for the type best suited for the job at hand. It is somewhat like renting a truck: we select the size best suited to the load. The simple sentence works best when few details are needed and action is emphasized. But when you pack your sentences with specific details, or weighty, complex ideas, you need complex, expanded sentences. Fortunately, there are many kinds of English sentences, and we can choose among them to achieve certain effects, to carry details, or to achieve variety of sentence style.

Sometimes variety is obtained simply by rearranging or rewording some elements of the sentence—for special emphasis, for greater clarity, or occasionally just for the sake of breaking the monotony of too many similar sentences. Another way to achieve variety, while at the same time adding specific details, is by adding modifiers to structural elements within the sentence or to the sentence as a whole. The latter—the addition of sentence modifiers—can be accomplished in two ways: (1) by piling up modifiers before the main clause or (2) by adding modifiers after the main clause. The first is usually called a *periodic* sentence; the second a *loose* or *cumulative* sentence. Despite their usefulness to all kinds of writing, we will examine in this chapter the processes of reordering and inserting modifiers, as well as the characteristics of the cumulative sentence, as tools best suited for adding detail and life to description.

ACHIEVING VARIETY BY REORDERING

Even with short, simple sentences, however effective they might be for a particular writing situation, variety is desired. A series of sentences all beginning with the subject not only becomes monotonous but provides little opportunity for making transitions or connections from one sentence to the next. By comparing a rewritten paragraph from John Steinbeck's "The Chrysanthemums" with the original, we can illustrate the importance of varying the basic subject-verb-complement (SVC) sentence structure (see Chapter 5) and the special effects that can result. (Note that all but the fourth one are expanded simple sentences.) Be aware of the placement of the italicized phrases in each version.

Rewritten Version	*Steinbeck's Version*
1 The high gray-flannel fog of winter closed off the Salinas Valley from the sky and all the rest of the world. **2** It sat like a lid on the mountains *on every side* and made of the great valley a closed pot. **3** The gang plows *on the broad, level land floor* bit deep and left the black earth shining where the shares had cut. **4** The yellow stubble fields *on the foothill ranches across the Salinas River* seemed to be bathed in pale cold sunshine, but there was no sunshine in the valley now in December. **5.** The thick willow scrub along the river flamed with sharp and positive yellow leaves.	**1** The high gray-flannel fog of winter closed off the Salinas Valley from the sky and all the rest of the world. **2** *On every side* it sat like a lid on the mountains and made of the great valley a closed pot. **3** *On the broad, level land floor* the gang plows bit deep and left the black earth shining like metal where the shares had cut. **4** *On the foothill ranches across the Salinas River,* the yellow stubble fields seemed to be bathed in pale gold sunshine, but there was no sunshine in the valley now in December. **5** The thick willow scrub along the river flamed with sharp and positive yellow leaves.

Both versions exhibit the same basic SVC structure in sentences 1 and 5. But the other sentences in Steinbeck's paragraph differ from those positioning does not merely vary the SVC pattern; it also provides a sense of spatial transition—it allows the reader's "eye" to move in space from one part of the scene to another. It is precisely this quality that is most lacking in the rewritten version, which makes it less effective as description.

In English, we can take a number of liberties in the reordering of adjective and adverbial modifiers, but we should realize that adverbial phrases generally have considerably more flexibility than adjective phrases. The term *modifier* is almost impossible to define, and we probably can arrive at the true meaning of it only after an in-depth study of language structure. But for our purposes, we can say that modifiers are elements that expand or comment on other parts of a sentence such as a noun, a verb, or sometimes the whole sentence. Even though many adjectives or adverbs are movable, or *free,* others in the language are *bound,* not only to their head structure — that is, to the noun or verb they modify — but also to a certain position in the sentence.

As a speaker of English, you are intuitively aware of these restrictions; otherwise you would have trouble communicating. But in writing we often tune out our language sense, failing to listen to what we write. We need, therefore, to set up conscious warning signals alerting us to the wealth of language ability we already have. Let's look at a few examples of bound modifiers to jog your unconscious memory:

1. Adjectives in a noun phrase:

   ten little purple   marbles
   (Noun Modifiers)   (Noun Head)

   Try to shift any of these italicized modifiers without adding a breath pause. If you cannot, that means they are bound to their position before the noun head. And bound they are.

2. Bound adverbial modifiers:

   He was *totally* unprepared for the assignment.

   Again, reordering of the italicized modifier proves difficult. Some members of your class may argue that it is possible to place *totally* after *unprepared;* not everyone will agree on that, but either way it must remain close to the verb.

These examples should make you aware that we cannot freely move modifiers about, that there are grammatical restrictions on rearranging some elements in a sentence. But what of the ones that can be shifted?

Not all free modifiers are equally free, and some are more restricted in some contexts than in others. In general, adjective modifiers can be placed before or after a noun head, but cannot be moved to another position in the sentence. Let's look at some of the possibilities of several kinds of phrases that can serve as adjectives:

1. a. A large man *with a sneer on his face* threatened the porter.

Prepositional phrase modifying noun head *man*—normal word order.

    b. *With a sneer on his face,* a large man threatened the porter.

Prepositional phrase moved to front position for special emphasis.

But not:

    c. A large man threatened the porter *with a sneer on his face.*

This positioning shows the need for keeping noun modifiers as close to their noun heads as possible. In this version, who is sneering? Is it the *large man* (noun head) or *the porter?*

2. a. The man *standing near the door* held a gun on the crowd.

Here, an *-ing* verb phrase (participial phrase functioning as an adjective) modifies the noun head *man,* and appears in normal word order.

    b. *Standing near the door,* the man held a gun on the crowd.

This placement, desirable in some instances to put special emphasis on the location of the man, is not always possible. If the expanded noun phrase occurred in the context of the following sentence, the verbal modifier would be bound to its position after *the older man:*

The young man at the teller's desk demanded the money; the older man *standing near the door* held a gun on the crowd.

Here, the phrase is restrictive—that is, it is bound to the position after the noun phrase *the older man* because its main function is to distinguish him from the other man rather than to locate him.

3. a. Billie Jean King, *flushed with victory,* jumped the net to console her opponent. (past participle phrase modifying the noun head *Billie Jean King*)

    b. *Flushed with victory,* Billie Jean King jumped the net to console her opponent.

Moving the italicized phrase to the front of the sentence merely gives it greater emphasis; it still modifies *Billie Jean King.* But try placing the phrase at the end of the sentence. What happens?

4. Attempts *to reorder infinitive phrases such as this* are generally unsuccessful.

Can you reorder the italicized infinitive phrase, which modifies the noun head *attempts?* Is it bound or free?

You can probably see from these few examples that a good rule of thumb is to keep adjectival phrases close to the noun they modify. But what of adverbial modifiers? If, like adjectival modifiers, they are tied to a particular sentence element—verb or predicate—then these adverbials should not be allowed to lose their heads. Some adverbials, however, logically seem to modify the sense of the whole sentence, rather than just a single element. These *sentence modifiers,* as they are sometime called, have almost unlimited flexibility, depending upon your purpose, as in this example:

Martha sobbed soundlessly *standing there in the rain.*
Standing there in the rain, Martha sobbed soundlessly.
Martha, *standing there in the rain,* sobbed soundlessly.

The normal word order—placement of the italicized adverbial at the end—gives it only the same status that any other adverb of place would have in the sentence: "Martha sobbed soundlessly *there, under the tree, by the car,*" and so on. In the second sentence, placing the adverbial before the main clause gives added importance to the location where the sobbing was done, an emphasis only slightly lessened in the third version, in which *Martha* receives the positional emphasis.

This brief discussion of reordering modifiers has dealt with only one method of achieving sentence variety—using sentences that already contain inserted modifiers. Like reordering, the process of inserting modifiers is one that you generally perform without conscious thought. But often in revising you need to combine the ideas expressed in several short sentences to achieve a better finished product. If you are a little unsure about how to go about this, it is helpful to have some conscious knowledge of the process at your command.

EXPANDING SENTENCES BY INSERTION

1 The size of the picture is about 18″ x 18″. 2 The tiger is eating a rhinoceros. 3 The tiger is brown with black stripes. 4 The rhinoceros is black. 5 There are all kinds of plants. 6 You can see the blue sky. 7 The plants look as big as trees, but they are not trees. 8 Some of the plants are broken. 9 The picture has lots of green color in it, with black, some yellow-green, pink, and blue. 10 At the bottom the weeds aren't very tall.

This student description of a painting by Henri Rousseau exhibits, among other problems, a severe case of "basic sentence-itis," giving the prose a childish quality. This paragraph needs many changes before it can be called an effective description. But for our purposes here, let's look only at its short, simple sentences and at some ways that we can combine them by using the process of embedding, or insertion.

You may recall that in Chapter 5, we briefly discussed the basic sentence patterns of English and how we can make questions of them, omit some sentence materials to form fragments, or join two or more sentences together as compounds. But simply joining basic sentences is not the only way to combine them. It is also possible to omit some material from one sentence and insert the remaining structure into another. Let's revise this student paragraph to demonstrate some of the possibilities of this process.

Looking at the paragraph, we find that sentences 2, 3, and 4 share related information—a necessary condition for insertion.

2   *The tiger* is eating *a rhinoceros.*
3   *The tiger* is brown with black stripes.
4   *The rhinoceros* is black.

It's obvious that sentence 2 supplies the action and that 3 and 4 simply add information about topics introduced in 2. We'll use 2, then, as our base sentence and insert into the base the new information in 3 and 4 — the insert sentences—omitting information that is redundant, or repeated. Let's see how this looks (the structures to be inserted are italicized):

2   The tiger is eating the rhinoceros. (base sentence)
3   The tiger is *brown with black stripes.* (insert) → ~~The tiger is~~ *brown with black stripes.* (adjective phrase)
4   The rhinoceros is *black.* (insert) → ~~The rhinoceros is~~ *black.* (adjective)

Result: The tiger, *brown with black stripes,* is eating a *black* rhinoceros.

You probably realize that this resulting sentence is not the only possibility for inserting the adjective: "brown with black stripes" could be shifted to a position before "the tiger." Or the phrase could be split, resulting in "the brown tiger with black stripes is eating a black rhinoceros." All are stylistic options, and you make a choice on the basis of emphasis, situation, purpose, or sometimes just because it sounds better to you.

Let's look at another set from our paragraph:

5   There are all kinds of plants. (base sentence)
7   The plants *look as big as trees but they are not trees.* (insert) → ~~The plants~~ (that, which) *look as big as trees but they are not trees.*

Here we've changed the insert sentence to a relative clause; the relative pronoun *that* or *which* can replace the subject.

8   *Some* of the plants *are broken.* (insert) → *Some of* ~~the plants~~ (which) *are broken.*

Result: There are all kinds of plants, some of *which are broken, that look as big as trees but are not trees.*

This leaves us with a minor ambiguity created by the final relative clause, which could be referring to the size of the animals. Since it's the plants, not the animals, that are as big as trees, let's reorder the sentence elements to:

There are all kinds of plants *that look as big as trees but are not trees,* some of *which are broken.*

Now sentences **1** and **9** can be combined:

9   The picture has lots of green color in it, with black, some yellow-green, pink, and blue. (base sentence)
1   The size of the picture is *about 18″ x 18″.* (insert) → ~~The size of the picture is~~ *about 18″ x 18″.*

This leaves an adjective phrase—everything is omitted but the prepositional phrase.

Result: *About 18″ x 18″,* the picture has lots of color in it, with black, some yellow-green, pink, and blue.

Now let's put the paragraph together as we have revised it through these sentence changes:

About 18″ x 18″, the picture has lots of color in it, with black, some yellow-green, pink, and blue. You can see the blue sky. The tiger, brown with black stripes, is eating a black rhinoceros. There are all kinds of plants that look as big as trees but are not trees, some of which are broken. At the bottom the weeds aren't very tall.

Better, isn't it? But note that we have added no information or words. We have simply inserted some structures into the base sentences while deleting items not necessary to the meaning. Note, too, that the paragraph is no longer characterized by disjointed, haphazard statements; the description now moves in a consistent direction from one part of the painting to the next.

In revising the paragraph, we worked mainly with adjectival modifiers, both bound and free; but adverbial elements from insert sentences can also be put into base sentences. Let's look at some of the possibilities.

Bound adverbial modifiers:

The crisp winter air was cold. (base sentence)
The cold was *painful.* (insert) → ~~The cold was~~ *painful* + *ly*
Result: The crisp winter air was *painfully* cold.

The train arrived at the station. (base sentence)
The train arrived *on time*. (insert) → ~~The train arrived~~ *on time.*

Result: The train arrived at the station *on time.*

Both these examples illustrate bound adverbial modifiers, those that have little or no flexibility of placement: the first must precede the adjective it modifies; the second must follow its verb head. As a speaker of the language, you probably handle these without conscious thought. Free (movable) adverbial modifiers, however, often have several options, and, as indicated in the preceding section, you must sometimes make conscious choices about their placement. Here are a few of the possibilities:

Free adverbial modifiers:

She removed the books from the shelves. (base sentence)
She *lovingly dusted each volume.* (insert) → ~~She was~~ *lovingly dusting each volume.* (verb form changed to get an *-ing* form)

Result: She removed the books from the shelves, *lovingly dusting each volume.*

or

Lovingly dusting each volume, she removed the books from the shelves.

The house stood stark against the horizon. (base sentence)
The house was *charred by a massive fire.* (insert) → ~~The house was~~ *charred by a massive fire.*

Result: The house stood stark against the horizon, *charred by a massive fire.*

or

Charred by a massive fire, the house stood stark against the horizon.

or

There is a third possibility. What is it?

In summary, we have briefly described the process of insertion, a method used to expand sentences. It involves combining sentences by omitting repeated information, changing the remaining elements into new syntactical units, and inserting them into a base sentence at the appropriate places. The purpose of insertion is to eliminate unnecessary repetition and to create richness of detail and description by adding modifiers to sentences. Insertion is a language skill that you innately possess to a high degree. Our purpose in this discussion is to give you insight into ways that you can consciously tap this language resource to become a more proficient writer.

THE CUMULATIVE SENTENCE

John Erskine once wrote, "When you write, you make a point, not by subtracting, as though you sharpened a pencil, but by adding." Even though this is true for all forms of writing—adding evidence to an argument, specific information to an expository paper, or supporting detail to a research paper—it is perhaps most important in description. To describe a scene effectively, we strive to appeal to the reader's senses—sight, hearing, taste, touch, and smell. This calls for the inclusion of many specific details. In the preceding section we suggested that inserting adjective and adverb modifiers into a sentence is one way to add details. But too many inserted modifiers can produce sentences that are almost unreadable:

> All the ten thousand "catch-as-catch-can" spectators, old and young alike, standing with their heads thrown back and their mouths dropped in awe, emitting not a sound, not even the shuffle of feet nor the rustle of clothing, watched in frozen silence, a silence that seemed almost an entity in itself, the drama of life and death, of hesitation and despair, being enacted on the bridge.

This sentence is rich in detail, but it contains so many inserted modifiers that the base sentence—*all the spectators watched the drama being enacted on the bridge*—almost gets lost.

The late Francis Christensen, in his work on sentence analysis,[1] suggested that perhaps the best vehicle available for carrying a heavy load of modifiers is the *cumulative sentence*. In a cumulative sentence, the base clause is kept intact and modifiers are added after it, as in this example:

> *Writing is often a frustrating task,* demanding long hours of thought, requiring us to sharpen both wit and pencil, forcing us to discipline ourselves to inevitable criticism—personal and public.

As you can see, the italicized base sentence is followed, rather than interrupted, by a series of modifiers. This arrangement gives you the same advantage of clarity and focus possible in basic simple sentences, but

---

[1] Francis Christensen, "A Generative Rhetoric of the Sentence," *Journal of the Conference on College Composition and Communication,* October 1963, pp. 155–61.

at the same time allows you to add much detailed information at many
levels of generality.

Levels of Generality

Since the term *levels of generality* may seem new and confusing, let's
analyze some examples. We have seen that modifiers can add more specific information to a fairly general statement, permitting us to move
in the sentence from general to specific. A basic sentence pattern operates at only one level—a very general level—while an expanded sentence with many modifying structures can include many levels or layers
—general modified by specific, modified by more specific, modified by
even more specific, and so on. Let's look at an expanded noun phrase so
that you can see the principles involved. We will start with the basic
noun phrase *a cow* and add these modifying phrases:

> black and white
> with a bell around her neck
> that jangled raucously with every step

We can diagram the expanded phrase like this:

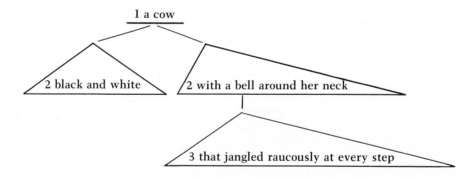

The numbers indicate the levels of generality of the various phrases. *A
cow* is the noun head in the expanded phrase and is its most general part,
so we have labeled it level 1; *black and white* and *with a bell around her
neck* both provide specific information about the head, *a cow,* so they are
at level 2. *That jangled raucously at every step* results in even greater
specificity by giving detailed information about the bell; because it modifies *bell* rather than *cow,* it is at level 3.

Now let's consider levels of generality in sentences, particularly in
cumulative sentences. Here is a diagram of our earlier example of a
cumulative sentence:

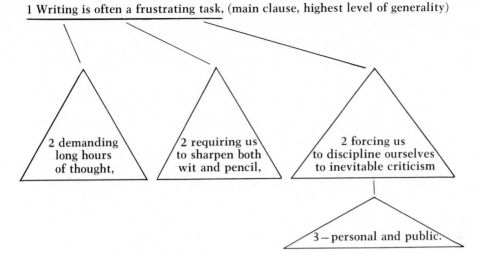

1 Writing is often a frustrating task, (main clause, highest level of generality)

2 demanding long hours of thought,

2 requiring us to sharpen both wit and pencil,

2 forcing us to discipline ourselves to inevitable criticism

3 — personal and public.

The main subject-verb-complement (SVC) clause, as the sentence head —the structure to which modifiers can be added—contains the most general information. The three *-ing* phrases at level 2 add specific details. Because all three modify the main clause (note that any of them can be omitted without damaging the logical sense of the sentence), they are all at the same level of generality. But the phrase "personal and public" refers to "criticism" rather than to the main clause and therefore adds a third dimension of detail—a third level of generality—to the sentence.

You are probably wondering, "Why make such an issue of all this?" Certainly, you have no difficulty in creating highly modified sentences laden with many levels of generality. But being aware of *how* you move from general to specific in your sentences can help you to provide signals to your readers that will enable them to sort out your sentence structure and understand your meaning more easily. For instance, in our example, all the items at level 2 have the same basic structure, each beginning with an *-ing* verb form; this parallelism in their structure indicates that they are at the same level of generality. Because not all of us have the innate sense of style to produce such parallelism consistently, some conscious knowledge of the modification levels and their relationship to writing style can improve our writing.

Because we'll be dealing in the next section with long, involved sentences that would make our example diagrams very unwieldy, and because we will use this same kind of analysis in Chapter 17 when we discuss paragraph development, let's look at the same sentence arranged as Christensen suggests to indicate the movement from general to specific:

1   Writing is often a frustrating experience,
  2   demanding long hours of thought,
  2   requiring us to sharpen both wit and pencil,
  2   forcing us to discipline ourselves to inevitable criticism
    3 — personal and public.

Varying Cumulative Sentences

Within the basic pattern of the cumulative sentence — main SVC clause followed by a series of modifiers — many variables are possible. Let's analyze some of these.

First, here is a sentence arranged to show its two levels of generality:

1   The village immediately repaired en masse to the house of the saint,
  2   to carry away holy relics,
  2   to divide up pieces of his garments among themselves,
  2   to carry off whatever they could find as a memento of the blessed martyr.

                         — Miguel de Unamuno, "Saint Emmanuel the Good, Martyr"

Note that here, as in the preceding example, the author has relied upon parallel structure to signal the reader that the three infinitive phrases (*to* + verbal) are *coordinate,* or equal to each other. One way to test whether the three modifiers are coordinate is to see whether you can omit one of them without changing the meaning of the sentence. Another test is to see if the modifiers can be switched. Can the third one precede the first without serious change in meaning? Obviously, it can. In this example sentence, any one of the three verbal modifiers could be omitted or switched about freely without seriously altering the meaning of the remaining information. Modifiers with this kind of parallel relationship to the main clause are said to be in *coordinate sequence:* they are not dependent upon each other for meaning.

What about this sentence?

1   All my people are larger bodies than mine,
  2   quiet,
    3   with voices gentle and meaningless
      4   like the voices of sleeping birds.

                         — James Agee, *A Death in the Family*

Here, the modifying additions to the main clause have a *subordinate* relationship to each other; that is, the information at any level is subordinate to — dependent upon — information provided in the preceding level. The phrase "with voices gentle and meaningless" (level 3), for instance, expands the "quiet" of level 2, rather than "larger bodies" (level 1). If you apply the switch test here, you'll find that the sense becomes garbled. And only level 4 can be omitted without seriously damaging the meaning. A cumulative sentence having modifiers with this dependent relationship is said to exhibit *subordinate sequence*.

Both of these sentences are fairly uncomplicated examples of cumulative sentences: the first limited to coordinate modifiers and the second to a series of subordinate ones. But cumulative sentences can be very complex and characterized by mixed sequences, as is this student example:

1 The Berlin street was alive with activity —
  2 everywhere people walking or riding,
  2 Volkswagens swarming like flies,
    3 black and noisy,
  2 young children with red cheeks playing on the sidewalk,
  2 elderly women walking slowly,
    3 huddled in their woolen coats
       4 clutched tightly against the bitter wind,
  2 all ages riding bicycles.

Notice the student's effective use of parallel structure to keep the level 2 coordinate modifiers sorted out: each has a noun phrase subject followed by an *-ing* verb form.

As with other sentence types, one way to achieve variety in cumulative sentences is to start the sentence with a transitional phrase:

Transitional phrase And for the players themselves,
  1 they seem expert listlessly,
    2 each intent on a private dream of making it —
      3 making it into the big leagues and the big money,
        4 the own-your-own bowling alley money;
  1 they seem specialists like any other,
    2 not men playing a game
      3 because all men are boys
        4 time is trying to outsmart.

                               — John Updike, *Rabbit Redux*

This sentence also illustrates another means of varying cumulative sentences: by stringing them together as compounds, using a comma and a conjunction or (as here) a semicolon to join the main clauses.

SUMMARY: THE CUMULATIVE SENTENCE AND INSERTION

Because of its structure—main clauses followed by modifiers—the cumulative sentence is a useful vehicle for carrying a heavy load of descriptive details. It permits us to write with clarity while adding rich texture to descriptive prose; details can be added and interwoven at many levels of generality, from the very general to the highly specific. We are not suggesting that only cumulative sentences be used in description, nor that they cannot be used in other kinds of writing. As with too many simple, basic sentences, too many cumulatives can become monotonous and artificial, and can interfere with communication and style, rather than enhance them. Descriptive paragraphs, like those in other forms of writing, are most effective when the sentences are varied and tailored to the needs of the writer and the reader, as in this student paragraph from which we took one of our examples of the cumulative sentence:

The Berlin street was alive with activity—everywhere people walking or riding, Volkswagens swarming like flies, black and noisy, young children with red cheeks playing on the sidewalk, elderly women walking slowly, huddled in their woolen coats clutched tightly against the bitter wind, all ages riding bicycles. Near a corner a small crowd stood waiting for the next bus. Along both sides of the street many sundry shops and pubs, gaily adorned in the typically Old German style, attracted wide-eyed tourists. The noise of construction was distinctly audible in the background. Here and all over the city new buildings were going up, new tunnels dug for the U-Bahn, and better "strasses" paved.

The paragraph is effective because the student has employed many of the sentence devices discussed in this chapter to recreate the scene on a Berlin street as he saw it: inserting adjective and adverbial modifiers into simple sentences, reordering sentence elements to break the monotony of SVC structure, and making effective use of the cumulative sentence.

Like this student, you can apply these principles easily in your own writing. Suppose that in your first draft you have written this basic sentence:

She was practically brought up at the tennis club.

In revising, you decide that this sentence is vague and anemic. What to do? First, you might insert some modifiers to the subject:

The daughter of two tennis pros, she was practically brought up at the tennis club.

Then to the verb:

> The daughter of two tennis pros, she was practically brought up—
> *first with tolerance, then with encouragement*—at the tennis club.

Then you might change the basic structure to a cumulative form:

> The daughter of two tennis pros, she was practically brought up—
> first with tolerance, then with encouragement—at the tennis club,
> *playing in a sandbox, taking lessons, working as a ball girl, and eventually*
> *winning club tournaments.*

Finally, you would need to insert modifiers in some of these:

> The daughter of two tennis pros, she was practically brought up—
> first with tolerance, then with encouragement—at the tennis club,
> playing in a sandbox *within sight of the courts,* taking lessons *all year*
> *round,* working as a ball girl *in her spare time,* and eventually winning
> club tournaments.

You would now have a sentence that is rich in descriptive detail but that, despite its length, is not at all awkward or hard to understand.

Our purpose in these analytical discussions of the inserting process and the cumulative sentence has not been to make you an expert at analyzing sentences, but to give you the background you need to employ these devices for sentence expansion and variation in your own writing. In the next section, we will look at some of the pitfalls you should avoid in creating richly modified sentences.

MODIFICATION BOOBY TRAPS

Is there anything peculiar about these sentences?

1. The mayor is a dirty street fighter.
2. A girl with a flag that was waving at us looked very familiar.
3. Rodolphe sent Emma Bovary a note that he was leaving town in a basket of apricots.
4. He knew Brahms as a young man.
5. Pedaling frantically and watching the bus barrel down on you from behind, a raucous voice pierces the air: "Don't you know what bicycles are for?"

You're right. They're all a little weird. In 1, the mayor could fight dirty streets or fight dirty in the streets. In 2, either the girl or the flag could wave at us. In 3, Rodolphe may have discovered a new way to travel—in a basket of apricots. In 4, are you sure that *he* was "a young man," or was it *Brahms?* And 5 presents the mind-boggling possibility of a raucous voice pedaling a bicycle down the street, dodging buses.

Though these sentence problems can be humorous, we rarely set out to create them; in fact, we often find them embarrassing—a slip of the pen, so to speak. But these ambiguous structures are not only disconcerting; they also seriously interfere with clarity of meaning. Except when we are writing poetry, in which we strive for multiple meanings, we avoid these kinds of booby traps, all of which involve ambiguous or dangling modifiers. But they often occur accidentally as a result of inserting modifiers into noun phrases, verb phrases, and sentences as a whole, because we tend to place structures into sentence positions natural to spoken English. But unfortunately, in written English, we cannot adequately indicate the stress, pitch, and pause features that keep them from being ambiguous when we speak. Understanding these structural ambiguities can help you to avoid them.

Ambiguous Noun Phrase Modifiers

As in examples 1 and 2, a very common source of ambiguity is the expanded phrase. The kind of double meaning illustrated in example 1 ("The mayor is a dirty street fighter") would not cause problems in a spoken language. The speaker's intonation features would clearly indicate the meaning intended (see Chapter 6, pp. 103–05). In writing, however, to clarify such structural problems, we must either rewrite the phrase or use punctuation devices to substitute for intonation features. The hyphen is useful for this purpose:

The mayor is a dirty-street fighter.

   or

The mayor is a dirty street-fighter.

In both of these versions, the hyphen indicates which compound the writer intended. Any remaining ambiguity stems from the multiple meanings of *dirty,* rather than from the structure.

This kind of ambiguity booby trap is often a problem in the process of adjective insertion because the resulting expanded noun phrase can be interpreted in more than one way. For this reason, when you insert an adjective into a noun phrase, you should be especially wary of the structure Adjective + Noun + Noun Head (*dirty + street + fighter*).

Another cause of crossed wires in a noun phrase is possessive nouns. The ambiguity in a statement like "Vassar is an old women's college" arises from two structural possibilities:

(Adjective + Possessive) + Noun Head
   (old-women's)   (college) = a college for old women

Adjective + (Possessive + Noun Head)
  (old)   (women's college)   = an old college for women

Again, either rewriting or inserting a hyphen can solve the problem.

Modifiers following the noun head can also cause trouble. In the noun phrase of example 2, "a girl with a flag *that was waving at us . . . ,*" the italicized relative clause could have derived from either of these insert sentences:

A girl was waving at us.
A flag was waving at us. $\rightarrow$ that was waving at us

The proximity of the relative clause to *flag* and the use of the neutral *that* exaggerate the ambiguity. A more careful choice of relative pronouns solves this problem:

A girl with a flag *who* was waving at us. (*who* is used to refer to humans)

A girl with a flag *which* was waving at us. (*which* is used to refer to nonhumans and inanimate objects)

Ambiguous Adverbial Modifiers

If such a strong risk of ambiguity lurks in noun modifiers, which are not easily moved, imagine the dangers inherent in the highly movable adverbial modifiers. One of the tricks that adverbial modifiers can play on unwary writers is illustrated in example 3:

Rodolphe sent Emma Bovary a note that he was leaving town *in a basket of apricots.*

Ordinarily, a place adverbial can appear at the end of a sentence without much danger of ambiguity, as in:

John gave her an engagement ring *at the County Fair.*

No problem here. There is no question about where John gave her the ring. But this end-of-sentence position can cause ambiguity if other structures are added between the main clause and the adverbial, giving the adverbial another modifying possibility, as in:

John gave her an engagement ring he had purchased *at the County Fair.*

Now there is confusion: did John *give* her the ring at the fair, or did he purchase the ring at the fair? In both examples, the basic problem is the same: the place adverbial could have originated in either the base or the insert sentence.

John gave her an engagement ring *at the County Fair.* (base sentence)
John had purchased the ring *at the County Fair.* (possible insert sentence)

Rodolphe sent Emma Bovary a note *in a basket of apricots.* (base sentence)
Rodolphe was leaving town *in a basket of apricots.* (possible insert sentence)

You can use this device to spot ambiguity, then solve the problem simply by placing the adverbial closer to the verb:

Rodolphe sent Emma Bovary a note *in a basket of apricots* that he was leaving town.

The same positional influence operates in example 4:

He knew Brahms *as a young man.*

The adverbial would create no problem in this position if the noun preceding it could not possibly serve as its head, as in:

He knew her as a young man.

In cases like this, moving the adverbial to initial position removes the danger of double meaning:

As a young man, he knew Brahms.

Dangling Sentence Modifiers

Perhaps the structural booby trap that most jeopardizes writers is the dangling sentence modifier, the culprit in example 5:

Pedaling frantically and watching the bus barrel down on you from behind, a raucous voice pierces the air: "Don't you know what bicycles are for?"

What makes these structures especially hazardous is that, unlike the other ambiguous modifiers we have been discussing, the problem may not be limited to the internal modification of a single sentence. Rather, with dangling initial modifiers, the preceding sentence may play a big part in creating the ambiguity. Let's look at this example as it appeared in the context of a student paper on the dangers of bicycling:

Motorists will actually vie for the honor of having you and your machine entangled in their front grills as trophies of a good day's work. *Pedaling frantically and watching the bus barrel down on you from behind,* a raucous voice . . .

The use of *motorists* as the subject of the first sentence sets up the expectation that *pedaling* and *watching* will refer back to it. Indeed, structurally they seem to do so, but logically they cannot; instead, they dangle.

A strictly traditional treatment of adverbials placed before the main clause requires that the modifier be logically tied only to the subject of the sentence. However, recent recognition that such movable modifiers can be related to the whole main clause has caused us to realize that not all traditionally identified "dangling modifiers" dangle. But how can you know when a sentence modifier really dangles? A good test is to change the *-ing* structure into a sentence that could be an insert sentence. If the subject of the insert sentence is different from that of the main clause, the modifier dangles. Let's look at an example:

Driving down the Interstate, the moon followed us at the same rate of speed.

Here, we can change the participle phrase to the insert sentence:

We were driving down the Interstate.

We is the logical subject underlying the *-ing* phrase; this is signalled by *us* in the main clause. But *moon* is the subject of the main clause, so the relationship of the modifier to the rest of the sentence is illogical and thus ambiguous. Note that both our examples involve *-ing* verbal phrases, the guiltiest structure in dangling modification—so guilty that they are often set apart by a special label: dangling participles. Writers need to be especially vigilant about these and other subjectless verbal phrases. Remember, if the subject of the insert sentence is different from that of the main clause, the modifier dangles.

Although not as troublesome as the participle, the infinitive phrase, one that contains an infinitive without a subject, often creates ambiguity:

To become a violinist, a good teacher is needed.

Restoring the deleted subject of the main clause remedies the ambiguity:

To become a violinist, you need a good teacher.

Does the following sentence seem ambiguous to you?

After the bill was passed, Congress recessed for a week.

Only the most puristic critic would deem this a dangling modifier. Although *bill* seems to be the subject of the passive adverbial clause, the logical subject, lost when the insert sentence was made passive, is still implicit in the sentence.

Congress passed the bill. (insert sentence) → The bill was passed [by Congress]. (changed to passive)

Normally in such situations, ambiguity is not a problem because readers automatically supply the logical subject.

There are a few exceptions where the logical subjects in the main clause and in the sentence modifier are different, but no ambiguity results because some other grammatical device signals the relationship. Look at this example:

When *John* was twenty-one, *his* father decided to retire.

Here, the possessive pronoun *his* shows an unambiguous relationship to *John*. But in this next possibility, we can't be sure whether *his* refers to *he* or *father*.

When *he* was twenty-one, *his father* decided to retire.

In summary, you should be especially cautious, in writing sentences, when these structures are involved:

1. Noun phrases exhibiting the structure Adjective + Noun + Noun Head or Adjective + Possessive + Noun Head.
2. Adverbial phrases at the ends of sentences expanded with inserted modifiers.
3. Sentence modifiers in initial position, particularly participial or infinitive phrases without subjects.

Here are some additional tips for eliminating ambiguity.

1. Sometimes you can add gender signals (*his, her, its*):

   Ambiguous: The boy on the horse with a patch over one eye.
   Clear: The boy on the horse with a patch over one of *his/its* eyes.

2. Occasionally you can change the verb form to show singular or plural (*is/are; was/were*):

   Ambiguous: one of the football players who seemed exhausted
   Clear: one of the football players who *was/were* exhausted

3. Sometimes a coordination signal (*and, but, or*) can be added:

   Ambiguous: a car that was parked in front of a garage that needed paint
   Clear: a car that was parked in front of a garage *and* needed paint

All this does not mean that you should avoid using certain structures just because they may result in ambiguity; they are much too valuable for that. If you are alert to ambiguity and apply the suggestions given here, you can avoid these modification booby traps.

PUNCTUATION OF EXPANDED SENTENCES

As you create more complicated sentences, you become more committed to furnishing punctuation aids to your readers. In a long, involved sentence, punctuation is needed both to indicate grammatical structures — such as the limits of the sentence — and to clarify meaning. So far in this chapter we have examined ways to rearrange and expand sentences; now let's turn to some of the punctuation problems that arise in the process.

Reordered Elements or Introductory Materials

Adverbials placed *before* the main clause are usually set off by a comma:

His face had been a long time healing *after the accident.* (normal order, no comma needed)
After the accident, his face had been a long time healing.
— Dorothy Canfield

The haunted landscape began to brighten *instead of darkening.*
Instead of darkening, the haunted landscape began to brighten.
— James Joyce

Occasionally, we dipped the oars into the lake.

Sometimes the comma after *occasionally* and other short adverbial phrases preceding the main clause are not set off by a comma:

For about ten years astronomers have been observing sites in the sky that are powerful emitters of x-rays.
— Ben Bova

However, if the omission of the comma in such instances results in ambiguity, leave it in:

In ten years time will have eroded away her youth.

Here, the reader may be forced to reread the sentence because of an initial confusion whether the opening adverbial is "in ten years" or "in ten years time." A comma solves the problem:

In ten years, time will have eroded away her youth.

Parenthetical Elements

Parenthetical elements, phrases that do not contribute directly to the meaning of a sentence but provide incidental information or function as transitional devices, are usually set off by commas:

The snow, *as we could see,* had covered all landmarks.
We could not, *of course,* find the way back to the lodge.
The fawn, *unfortunately,* stumbled into the trap.

Elements in a Series

NOUN PHRASES IN A SERIES

Commas may be used to separate each noun phrase in a series from all the others or to separate all but the last two:

The breakfast table was laden with *steaming coffee, fresh fruits, orange juice, and delicate crêpes.* (commas separate all four noun phrases)
The breakfast table was laden with *biscuits, fruit juices, jams, ham and eggs.* (no comma between the last two items)

Omitting the comma in the second example creates the sense that the last two items are a unit, rather than separate entities. Consequently, if they are not a unit, we prefer a comma before the *and,* though it is optional.

Instead of commas, semicolons are sometimes used to set off lengthy, complex items in a series. This helps to avoid confusion with other commas used for punctuation inside a lengthy modifier. This punctuation device is perhaps found more in expository writing than in description:

On the contrary, the trend to encourage the crash programs to get quick answers—*like the Manhattan project, which turned the laboratory discovery of uranium fission into a cataclysmic bomb in six years; the Computer/Automation Revolution; the Space Program; and now the Bioengineering Revolution, with its possibilities not only of spare-organ plumbing but of changing the nature of living things by gene manipulation. . . .*

—Lord Ritchie-Calder

ADJECTIVE PHRASES IN A SERIES

Adjective phrases following the noun head are always set off by commas:

Valley children, *with sunken, impudent eyes, quick tongues and singing voices, chests thin as shells,* gathered around the Punch and Judy.

—Dylan Thomas

Adjectives preceding the noun head do not need commas if they occur in normal word order. You can often determine this by reading the phrase aloud; if you can do it without producing a pause, or juncture, then a comma is not necessary, as in:

The *big bright summer* sun shone in her eyes.

(For further discussion, see page 105.)

However, if the adjectives are not in normal word order, commas set them off (again, reading aloud can help to indicate the comma sites):

The *beautiful, green, soft, luxurious* grass tickled between their toes.

Another test for commas is to insert *and* between the adjectives. If *and* seems natural, then a comma can substitute for it:

The beautiful *and* mysterious woman entered the room majestically.

    or

The beautiful, mysterious woman entered the room majestically.

Appositives

An appositive element functions as a device of definition or identification when inserted into sentences after noun phrases. An appositive may take the form of a noun phrase, as in "Beethoven, *the composer* . . . ," or of a relative clause, as in "Beethoven, *who wrote many symphonies* . . . ." These appositives are set off by commas only if they add information that is not necessary to the logical meaning of the sentence. Read aloud, there should be pause, or juncture, on either side of the phrase to indicate a comma; thus *two* commas are needed to separate the element from the rest of the sentence. If no pause is necessary for natural reading, *no* commas are needed. Appositives not directly tied to the meaning of the sentence are called *nonrestrictive;* those necessary to the meaning are *restrictive.* Let's look at some examples:

Patterson Tower, *the recently completed office building,* is a monument of concrete ugliness. (information in the appositive is not necessary for identification; it merely adds details — set off by commas)
The recently completed building *Patterson Tower* is a monument of concrete ugliness. (here *Patterson Tower* is the appositive, needed for identification — no commas used)

The distinction between restrictive and nonrestrictive elements is even more difficult to make when relative clauses are involved, as in:

An uncle in a panama smacked the ball to the dog, *who swam it out of reach.*

                                                             — Dylan Thomas

Here, by separating the italicized relative clause with a comma, the writer has signalled that he considers it to be only supplementary and not vital to the meaning of the sentence.

Relative clauses such as this, beginning with either *who* or *which*, can be treated as either restrictive or nonrestrictive. Relative clauses beginning with *that*, however, are always restrictive and are not set off by commas:

The dog *that carried the ball out of reach* belonged to my uncle.

Identifying restrictive and nonrestrictive appositives is difficult and confusing. If you remember these three points, you can avoid most of the punctuation problems that these structures pose:

1. You as the writer must decide how you want the reader to "hear" and understand the sentence. If you wish to make the appositive non-restrictive, you must provide the punctuation to set it off completely from the rest of the sentence. If you wish to make the appositive re-strictive, *no* commas are needed.
2. Read the sentence aloud and listen for breath pause, or juncture. If you produce juncture on either side or on both sides of the apposi-tive, set it off with commas.
3. If the appositive is a relative clause beginning with *that*, use no commas.

Appositives can also be set off by dashes and parentheses. For discus-sion of these possibilities, see Chapter 6.

PUNCTUATION OF CUMULATIVE SENTENCES

Cumulative sentences require punctuation between the main SVC clause and the added sentence modifiers. The punctuation can be a comma, a dash, or a colon.

Comma: It is a difficult country, *where the goats must drink seawater and the finches drink blood, where the people drink rainwater collected on roofs or brackish water drawn from wells near the sea.*
— Kenneth Brower

Dash: By day there were flies everywhere—*flies in the soup, flies in the tea; at night the buzz and bites of mosquitoes in the small, warm, overcrowded tents.*
— Ernest Hemingway

Colon: Though the clock on the living room sideboard says only 4:20, dark-ness has come: *dark carpets, thick drawn drapes, dead wallpaper, potted plants crowding the glass on the side that has windows.*
— John Updike

These examples should help with most of the punctuation problems you will encounter as you expand your sentences with specific details. The special difficulties created by other complicated sentence structures will be dealt with in later chapters.

ASSIGNMENTS

For Discussion

1   For what purposes do writers reorder sentence elements? Bring to class some examples of fairly simple, reordered sentences like those in the Steinbeck paragraph on page 192, and discuss the effect they produce.

2   In the following descriptive sentences, identify first the base sentence, then the modifiers. Are the modifiers adjectival or adverbial? Free or bound? (Aids: look for the head word being modified and test for reordering.)

   a   The water skier, his life-jacket a bright orange band, swerved suddenly.

   b   Disgusted with the turn of events, the cyclist propelled his machine toward the hills, purple in the distance.

   c   The silent birds sat motionless in the sand.

   d   He felt the impact of the blow throughout the length of his arm, jarring his flesh lightly.

—Richard Wright, *Native Son*

   e   Silently we unlatch the door, letting the drift fall in, and step abroad to face the cutting air.

—Henry David Thoreau, *Excursions*

   f   They are feeding it on to the conveyor belt, a moving rubber belt a couple of feet wide which runs a yard or two behind them.

—George Orwell, "The Road to Wigan Pier"

   g   Over a mouthful of spaghetti — delicious spaghetti — I peer at Janie with her newly red hair, the butterfly effect penciled out from the eyes, those pants, the gold chain dangling from hips to pelvis.

—Rasa Gustaitis, "Out-of-Sight Janie and Sequential Monogamy"

   h   The big cottonwood tree stood apart from a small grove of winterbare cottonwoods which grew in the wide sandy arroyo.

—Leslie Chapman Silko, "The Man to Send Rain Clouds"

   i   It had an amber tree against a blue-green background, resplendent with fruits and flowers and the all important roots.

—Jane Howard, "Help See Own Way Behave"

j   During the climb, I had seen the moss-covered boulders mottled by shafts of bright sunlight which fell through the canopy of green leaves overhead.

— Student paper

3   All of the following sentences are ambiguous. Explain the source of the trouble in each and rephrase to clarify.

   a   They are now experimenting on food to be shot with atomic rays that can stay under water as long as the submarine.
   b   They named me Mariam Buford after a heated debate.
   c   Reminiscing about 1964, my father had a heart attack and was taken to the hospital.
   d   A metaphor is a group of words usually found in poetry that means something else.
   e   In its concentrated form, a teaspoon could kill 30 million people.
   f   A person should try motorcycling so at least the love of riding by so many people could be understood.
   g   Looking down the waterway some more boats appear, adding more confusion and excitement which amazes the tourists.
   h   The passengers were herded into tubes that led to contraptions which resembled buses that moved to more tubes that led eventually to the airport terminal.
   i   Ever since grade school, I had looked forward to this occasion when I, with all my fellow classmates, moved my tassel from the right to the left.
   j   Other players came around and poured maple syrup in our hair with their right hand.
   k   Since the magic ring was devised by an evil power, it inevitably corrupted anyone who used it in the end.
   l   The drinking age had really nothing to do with the context of his letter, and it left me as one reader hanging on a short note.
   m   Surrounding Patterson fountain is a seat made of stone with the capacity of about fifty people.
   n   The second reason is that movies such as westerns in which the hero always wins the fight or argument tends to help a person imitate the thoughts and actions of those whom they admire in situations of the same nature.
   o   A woman was petting a horse with a big cartwheel hat.
   p   To get a good view of the stage, a box seat is needed.
   q   While a small child, my grandfather carried me on his shoulder.
   r   Driving through the Smokies, a bear stopped our car at a garbage can.
   s   Cutting down on the speed limit, it would probably affect truck drivers.

t   He didn't see how a woman had the ability to run the office without someone helping her like a man.

u   I sit here writing my autobiography, weighing two hundred and forty-five pounds.

For Writing

1   Add sentence modifiers to the following main clauses to produce descriptive cumulative sentences in coordinate, subordinate, or mixed sentences. Try to use parallel structures to indicate levels of generality, and watch your punctuation devices.

a   The girl walked slowly toward him . . .
b   He gazed out pensively at the passing landscape . . .
c   I remember my grandfather well . . .
d   On the balmy spring evenings, I must force myself to the library . . .
e   _____ Hall is the most unusual building on campus . . .
f   I looked around at my classmates . . .
g   I sauntered into the campus grill for breakfast . . .
h   I wearily carried the last load of clothing to my new dormitory room . . .
i   The sun suddenly broke through the clouds . . .
j   I dove into the cold water . . .

2   Add detail-bearing modifiers to make the following paragraphs more vividly descriptive. Use the sentence devices discussed in this chapter: reordering, inserting, and the cumulative sentence.

a   He paused at the corner to watch the work of the wrecking crew. The great metal ball swung at the walls. Everything it touched wavered and burst. There rose a cloud of plaster dust. The afternoon was ending. There was a fire in the area of demolition, fed by the wreckage. Moses heard the air, felt the heat. The workmen threw strips of molding. Paint and varnish smoked. The old flooring burned gratefully. Scaffolds walled with doors quivered as the trucks carried off fallen brick. The sun was surrounded by gases.

—Adapted from Saul Bellow's *Herzog*

b   The skier started down the slope. The main mountain range was behind him. He veered down the steep grade and he picked up speed as he went. He felt the cold air on the parts of his face exposed by the ski mask. The sun shone on the snow. The atmosphere and the exertion made him gasp for air. He gathered speed and experienced a sense of flying. Trees seemed to be rushing off in the opposite direction. He swerved to a stop at the bottom. He felt a sense of satisfaction and returned to the chair lift for another run.

3   Many contemporary poets are writing unrhymed and unmetered poetry, relying on the capacity of expanded sentences to create an image
rich in detail. Lawrence Ferlinghetti and others are shaping their
poems in a broken arrangement similar to the Christensen analysis
we have used in this chapter. Looking closely at the poem below,
you can see that Ferlinghetti goes a step beyond Christensen, isolating smaller grammatical segments. Even so, these smaller units are
related by grammatical form and modification levels, as in Christensen's method.

#17[2]

Terrible
　　　　　a horse at night
　　standing hitched alone
　　　　　　in the still street
　　　and whinnying
　　　　　　as if some sad nude astride him
　had gripped hot legs on him
　　　　　　and sung
　　　　　　　　a sweet high hungry
　　　single syllable

Ferlinghetti's poem is a sentence fragment, but his technique can be
applied to cumulative sentences as well. Here's a poem written by a student with knowledge of Christensen analysis—several cumulative sentences compounded as in our example on page 203. Using it as a model,
create your own "Ferlinghetti verse."

FORRER HALL LOBBY

Forrer Hall lobby
　is a small windowed center
　　　　　　of excitement
With a housemother at the front desk
　　　knitting an afghan
　　　　　Always in the classic pose
　　　　　　　of an all knowing mom
　　　　　faithfully watching over her girls

[2] From Lawrence Ferlinghetti, *A Coney Island of the Mind.* Copyright 1955 by Lawrence
Ferlinghetti. Reprinted by permission of New Directions Publishing Corporation.

And the step slide sound the rubber soled shoes
                    of the hump-backed janitor make
                    as they cross the polished tiled floor
While the house mother screams that a bulb
                                        must be replaced
                                        over the bathtub
                                        in the bathroom
                                        on first back
And the new color television set
                blares
                        the Sunday afternoon football game
                Over the calls of the guys
                        positioned
                                    on two brown sofas
                                    facing each other
Calling to girls as they walk
                        out the door
        As a loud crunch resounds from across the room
                        as an overweight coed devours the crust
                                    from a leg of chicken
And the man from Pasquales finally delivers
                    a mushroom and cheese pizza
                    to four starving girls
                    on fourth back
                    who've waited four hours
And the German shepherd takes over the men's restroom
As the speaker screams
                        visitation
                            is
                            over
And the guys are escorted down the front steps
                                    into the front lobby
And sorority corridor echoes the songs
                                of sorority girls
                                singing fraternity songs
While the staid, serene portraits of Mr. and Mrs. Forrer
                        peer down
                            over the
                        Sunday afternoon
                                    havoc
                                        of
                                        it
                                        all

Revision
of Descriptive
Writing

Having provided you with a checklist and questions (on pp. 148–49), we urge you to consult them not only before writing descriptions but also afterward to determine whether you have met your commitment to the audience, the purpose, and the context.

We also urge you in revising to concentrate particularly on your choice of words and your sentences. Can you substitute more effective words for the ones you have used? Can you rephrase something here or there to convey your picture more vividly to the minds of readers? And what of the sentences—can you use insertion to add vigor and richness to them? Can you add specificity by developing cumulative sentences from simple ones? Improving words and sentences in revision is important in all writing but perhaps most of all in descriptions.

Finally, because it is likely to be more of a problem in description than in personal narration, where your language is usually simpler, what about your spelling? Most of us have trouble with spelling because words are seldom spelled the way they are pronounced. This book is not the place for spelling lessons, but we do want to point out that even if you spell poorly, you can lick your problem. Simply check in the dictionary each and every word whose spelling you have the slightest doubt about. Yes, occasionally we know that you won't be able to find a tricky one like *facetious* or *pneumonia,* but you will avoid nearly all your other misspellings. As we see it, poor spelling results from laziness—the unwillingness to take the time and trouble to look up words. And that is catastrophic because nothing infuriates readers more than poor spelling. Be safe—look up the spelling of all words you wouldn't bet five dollars on!

220

And once again, work hard on revising your paper to improve it, not merely to recopy it and get it out of the way.

REVISION EXERCISE

The best revision practice is to rewrite your own material. However, it may help you develop better critical skills if you analyze and rewrite someone else's paper, because you don't have the emotional ties that you have to your own writing. Here's an excerpt from a student's journal. Rework it so that it is a true character sketch of either the teacher or the child and so that it would be suitable for a wider audience than journals usually reach.

When I was in the second grade, I had this teacher, a nun, and she was the most beautiful, wonderful person I had ever met or seen in my life. There wasn't anything I wouldn't do for her attention. I was in love with this young nun and I hoped to marry her some day. Of course I didn't know at the time they couldn't get married. I always tried doing things for her. I always brought her something every day when I came to school. One time I can remember I was coming to school and I saw this little frog, so I caught it and I thought it would be a nice gift for her and besides she could have a little pet of her own. As I lifted my hand and opened it to show her the gift it took a hop. I'll never forget her reaction, for that matter, I'll never forget all the other girls' reactions in my class. I'd never heard so much screaming and seen so many startled looks. I'll tell you one thing I learned and that's never to bring frogs to class.

One day it was getting close for school to let out. It started raining pretty hard and there were puddles all over the place. But when school was let out it stopped raining, just like a miracle. We had to come down some steps from our classroom. At the bottom there was this big puddle of water. So our teacher went down before us and made sure that we all jumped over the puddle and went our way. Anyway as we were coming down the steps and everybody was jumping the puddle and going on their way—you know what I did? I jumped right in the middle of it and splashed my teacher and a girl in front of me and a boy behind me. I didn't care what happened I just wanted her attention, and I got it. She made me go all the way back up the steps and come back down and jump the puddle. And if I didn't she was going to paddle my hands. I was really scared. All I wanted was for her to take me aside and dry me off and show me some attention. But she didn't and from that day on I became more interested in girls my age, and besides they were more fun.

3

The Explanatory Voice: Expository Writing

14

The Nature of Exposition

You've been writing and speaking exposition all your life!

Of course, you haven't called it that. You have probably thought of it as explaining or informing, or sounding off, or rapping. But all these are forms of exposition. Look at the term *exposition* itself. In a general sense, it means "a setting forth." You may recall that the World's Fair is often referred to as an exposition, a place where nations set forth their artistic or industrial works. In fiction, the author sets forth the background of the characters in the exposition. In a fugue or sonata, the composer sets forth the themes in the exposition. In your papers, when you set forth your ideas or opinions or views, you are engaged in exposition.

You may be wondering: Why not simply refer to expository writing as informative writing? Why not use the common word instead of the specialized one? And if there is some distinction, what does it matter?

There is a distinction, and it does matter. Nearly everything you write could be classified as informative: an account of your attending the wrong class the first day of college, a poem expressing your feelings toward a loved one, a letter describing your dorm room to your mother, or a handout urging students to vote for your friend in a campus election. Exposition differs from these informative writings because its purpose is not primarily to narrate, describe, or persuade; its main purpose is to explain. It does so in numerous ways: by classifying, defining, analyzing, exploring, interpreting, and evaluating, to mention a few.

In the process of writing exposition, you may be concerned with one extreme or the other: the relatively objective or the highly subjective.

An expository paper about kitchen knives, for example, would probably include general information about paring, boning, slicing, and carving knives and perhaps a few special kinds, such as a cook's knife, butcher's knife, cheese knife, filleting knife, and Chinese chopping knife. But a paper evaluating your high school or explaining why young people have lost faith in most politicians would mainly reflect your personal opinion. Of course, in a strict sense, every expository paper states your personal opinion, whether about the kind of kitchen knives or the quality of your high school. But in the following chapters we will treat exposition more generally, viewing it as comprising usually (1) the factual (classification, definition) and (2) the personal (analysis, opinion).

One final clarification of exposition. It differs from the other rhetorical forms in that it tries to draw a distinctive response. After reading narration, readers usually say or think, "We enjoyed that"; after description, "We saw, heard, and felt that"; after persuasion, "We're convinced of that"; and after exposition, "We understand that."

Although you now realize that the term *informative writing* might be applied to nearly all written work and that exposition is a subspecies of informative writing, your reaction may be, "So what?"

The answer is basic to this book and to your writing course. As we explained earlier, the more you know about writing, the better you should write—just as the more you know about weaving, the better you should weave. So it follows that if you understand expository writing—what its purpose is, how it should affect readers, and what its characteristics are—you should do a better job of it. This may result not only in higher grades on your college papers and essay examinations but also in greater pride and satisfaction in yourself and more success in your future career.

Those statements may strike you as a commercial for exposition. But unlike many commercials, this one, if it really is one, is true. The most common and important written work is expository. In college, you are called upon to write essay examinations, critiques, analyses, case histories, lab reports, recommendations, and research papers. After college, whether you work as an engineer, accountant, teacher, salesperson, nurse, or social worker, you will have to write letters, memorandums, reports, and papers explaining what you did, found, accomplished, proposed, concluded, or recommended. In a sense, expository writing is the writing of the working world and the writing that enables the world to work. It does this by providing answers to such vital questions as these:

What is _____ ?
What is the purpose of _____ ?
What are the causes of _____ ?
What are the effects of _____ ?

What is the value of _____ ?
How does _____ work?
How effective is _____ ?
How good is _____ ?
How could _____ be improved?
Why is _____ important?
Why should _____ be changed?
Where is _____ ?

In answering these questions, writers may include narrative or descriptive paragraphs or passages, but they rely mainly on exposition.

You now have some idea of why exposition is the most important mode of writing to understand and the most valuable to master. To begin, let's consider the audience and subject matter of expository writing.

ADAPTING THE PAPER TO THE AUDIENCE

Although, as pointed out previously, you should be particularly concerned about your readers in narrative and descriptive writing, you must be keenly aware of them and responsive to their needs in expository writing. You would probably explain coed dorms in one way to your kid brother, another way to your high school principal, and a third way to your friends. The words you use, the information you include, the approach you take, and the points you emphasize might all differ. Unless you adapt your paper to your readers by considering what they already know about the subject and what else they need and want to know, you generally cannot write an effective expository paper. For example, if you're going to explain how to play the banjo, should you assume that your readers are familiar with the instrument, can read music, or even know one chord from another? If you're going to discuss designated hitters in baseball, do your readers know what they are? And what about a paper on gourmet cooking? Will your readers know how to sauté?

In the two other modes of writing that we have discussed—personal writing and descriptive writing—you can assume that readers are unfamiliar with the subject and proceed accordingly. But in exposition, you must analyze the audience to realize what they already know, want to know, and need to know. And if your subject is not assigned, you must also consider the audience in deciding on a topic. Here's what we mean.

SELECTING A SUBJECT: THREE CONSIDERATIONS

In selecting a subject, you should remember these ABC's: appeal, breadth, complexity. We shall discuss breadth in Chapter 16 when we talk about topic restriction. Here we shall merely mention that many student papers never come to grips with their subject because it is too huge to handle. Understandably, students like to latch on to broad subjects, feeling secure that they will then be able to turn out the assigned number of words. Thus it may seem safer to write about cooking than about a narrower subject like crockery cooking. But this reasoning is faulty because no writer can possibly do justice in a short paper to a subject as vast as cooking. Breadth, consequently, is one consideration in selecting a subject.

Complexity is another, and it is a two-edged sword. Either blade can destroy a written work: if the subject is too complex for the audience, the paper will be a bore; if the subject is too complex for the writer, the paper will be a disaster. Let us explain.

Although many subjects can be adapted to almost any audience, some subjects require that the audience have a grasp of basic principles—as, for example, intermediate French requires a knowledge of beginning French. Consequently, there's little point in writing about adjustments in Federal Reserve requirements for readers who are unfamiliar with economics, or about Whitehead's alternative to dualism for readers who are ignorant of philosophy. And the same applies to writers. You cannot write well about a subject you do not understand well. For example, if you are mystified by the workings of the Electoral College, don't write about it. As a matter of fact, if you are the least bit uncertain about a subject, you should avoid it, unless you can do extensive research. If you can't, try to select only those subjects that you are chock full of information about, and forget about those that are too complex for you or your readers.

The third consideration, appeal, works practically the same way. The subject must appeal to you and your audience. We believe that you know what interests you and that if possible you will select such subjects to write about. But you may be tempted to forget your obligation to interest your readers. Sometimes we suspect a national student conspiracy to bore freshman English instructors because they are a captive audience who must read all papers. We would urge instead a campaign to interest all readers—instructors, classmates, or others.

Is it always necessary to be interesting? Generally, yes. In some situations, such as writing instructions to students for obtaining free football tickets, or reading a technical paper to accountants gathered specifically to hear it, you can assume you're dealing with a highly motivated audience. But if built-in motivation doesn't exist, you must try to create interest, and this is not easy.

You can start by searching for an appealing subject, one that is either inherently attractive or fascinatingly different. If you think about people's basic drives—for sex, food, beauty, power, money, health, and the like—you should be able to come up with an inherently attractive topic that few readers can resist. A paper on "How to Make Out on Dates" or "How to Improve Your Personality" will usually generate interest. It is not so easy, however, to be fascinatingly different. Generally it involves taking a common approach to a subject and then giving it an uncommon twist. Anyone can discuss the joys of childhood, but what about the fears? Instead of writing about cars, why not bumper stickers, decals, or dashboard gadgets? How about raising weeds instead of eliminating them, or driving carelessly rather than safely? The trick is to think of the obvious, reject it, but don't throw it away. Give it a slight twist.

If you can't twist a standard approach or find an inherently attractive or fascinatingly different subject, don't give up. Most of us can dig up only a few such diamonds, not enough to satisfy the demands of your freshman composition course. What to do then?

One answer is to look into your bag of interests, hobbies, gripes, worries, and passions. Think about what preoccupies you, your friends, father, mother, brother or sister, aunt or uncle, grandparents, neighbors, high school teacher, coach, mailcarrier, doctor, cleric, mechanic, druggist, supermarket checker, or any one of the many people that you talk to. What do you say to them after you've covered the weather and their health? Do you have an uncle you kid about whittling, an aunt with a green thumb, a grandparent suffering from loneliness, a friend with a thing for bluegrass music? If you can't write about your own interests, use theirs if you know enough to do so. But try to make the topic appealing to your readers.

One way to accomplish this is to ask yourself before you begin to write, "Why should someone read this paper?" For example, if you decide to write about your summer job waiting on tables in a motel restaurant, search for an angle that will either benefit readers or appeal to their natural curiosity about other people. You might discuss techniques for increasing tips, such as recommending the higher-priced meals to increase your 15 percent tip or letting your customers know that you're working your way through college. Most readers will be interested in reading about tricks of the trade—any trade.

Generally, you can attract readers by increasing their ability to understand or accomplish something that should interest them. You can create and hold their attention, for example, by informing them how they can become better at something: how they can dress more distinctively, perform in college more effectively, participate in sports more skillfully, gain popularity more easily, manage money more successfully, shop more economically, and enjoy life more fully.

You may protest that you don't know enough to write about these subjects. And as for other subjects, you may say that you haven't visited unusual places, hold no strong convictions about current issues, pursue no hobbies, have no interest in sports, see few movies, know no fascinating people, watch little television, and read even less. So there is nothing significant, distinctive, exciting, or interesting for you to write about.

But there is. You are different because you are you—unique and therefore interesting. Of course, in many respects, you are like the others in your class. You are about the same age, have studied similar subjects, share the same general life style, and possess similar fears, worries, hopes, and desires. But in spite of all these similarities, you are different. You look different, grew up in different surroundings with different parents, relatives, and friends, went to different places on vacations, attended different schools, studied with different teachers, had different jobs, and experienced different moments of embarrassment and anxiety and exhilaration and disappointment and fulfillment. Consequently, you see the world through different eyes and filter what you observe through a different mind. You may view the same object, person, or event that your classmates do, but these subjects will trigger different ideas or opinions in you. Your job in writing exposition is to capture this difference, write about it *honestly,* deal with it fully, and present it clearly, always keeping in mind the importance of interesting and informing your particular readers. What you write need not be earth shattering; it need mainly be appealing to your readers.

These are a few introductory words about the ABC's of selecting a subject—appeal, breadth, and complexity—about the general importance of the audience, and about the nature and importance of expository writing. This textbook itself is an example of exposition: its purpose is to inform you about writing and to show you how to improve your papers. In the process, we've tried to consider what you know, need to know, and want to know about writing. We've also tried to mind our ABC's.

ASSIGNMENTS

For Discussion

1 Do you agree or disagree with these statements from the chapter? Why?

    a Nearly everything you write could be classified as informative.
    b The more you know about writing, the better you should write.
    c The most common and important written work is expository.
    d You can create and hold your readers' interest by telling them how they can become better at something.

2 What groups of people (classified by age, sex, geographical location,

economic status, education, occupation, and so on) would probably be interested in the following articles? What groups would not? Why?

Technology, Nature, and Society
Fourteen Common Income Tax Mistakes
Hockey Fans Are Different
The Scholar in Public Life
Porno Flicks
The Characterization of Women in the Fiction of Norman Mailer
New York City Politics
Where Did Hollywood's Exciting New Male Star Get VD?
New Concepts in the Evolution of Complexity
Should You Invest in Mutual Funds?
Dinosaurs Were Dandy
Retirement Condominiums
The Counterculture in the South

3 Think of a different approach or twist that you might use in writing about each of the following subjects.

Sunday School	Children
Exercise	Drinking
Wealth	The City

4 Here are twenty broad subject categories that should trigger some ideas for papers. Select three and narrow them down to topics that could be treated adequately in themes of about 750 words.

Advertising	Family	Magazines
Animals	Feminism	Money
Automobiles	Future	Movies
College	Gripes	Music
Crime	Health	Nature
Drugs	Hobbies	Places
Education	Literature	

5 A list of questions often answered in various expository papers appears on page 226. See how many theme topics you can develop for your own possible use by filling in the blanks with specific subjects.

For Writing

Write an expository paper on one of the topics suggested in exercise 3, 4, or 5 above. Try particularly to interest your classmates.

15

The Forms of Expository Writing

Jack: Taken in any of the flicks in the Silent Film Festival at the Student Union?

Jim: Just the old Keystone comedies. The movie auto chase boggles my mind. You know, the Keystone Kops really began all that.

These two students are starting a serious discussion that could involve any or all of the common expository forms: classification, definition, analysis, and opinion. Jim could set up a *classification* dividing movie auto chases into several subcategories according to their purpose, such as for building suspense, illuminating character, or satirizing some situation. During the conversation, Jack might refer to a trucking shot, a term unknown to Jim, so *definition* would be in order. Jim might also *analyze* the movie chase for its realism or to express an *opinion* about the effectiveness of the chase scenes in such films as *Bonnie and Clyde* and *The French Connection*.

Even in such a casual discussion, Jack and Jim are utilizing expository forms that their subject and purpose naturally require. Similarly, in talks with your friends and in your writing assignments, you will be using classification, definition, analysis, and opinion. To employ them effectively, you should consciously understand them as conventions of the written language.

232

CLASSIFICATION

The Uses of Classification

Classification is essentially a sorting procedure that enables writers to come to grips with a broad subject by allowing them to divide it into its parts. Although often merely a part of expository papers, classification can be an end in itself. For instance, an agriculture student might write a paper classifying the corn planters available to farmers; or a Xerox executive might prepare a report that lists and describes that company's duplicating machines. In both assignments, classification would be used as a separate rhetorical form, itself classified as a subclass of exposition.

Classification, as a process and skill, is handy in other ways. It can be useful in planning a paper. In dealing with a broad subject that can be broken into several categories, or classes, your skill at classification can help to narrow the topic. For example, if your paper is about colleges, you might find it necessary to classify them according to type: Ph.D. granting universities, other universities, private four-year schools, and so on. If classifying colleges by type makes you realize that the subject is too diverse and complex to handle in a short paper, you might restrict your topic to Ph.D. granting universities.

Classification, as we will discuss later in this chapter (pp. 235–42), is also an important aspect of definition and other forms of expository writing. In defining *investments,* for example, it would be informative to include a brief classification of the various forms, like savings accounts, savings certificates, Treasury bills, stocks, bonds, and the like. In addition, classification can be useful in papers in which evaluation is the objective. If you were rating cars, you'd be wise to classify them first according to price, horsepower, gas mileage, and safety features. Here again, classification would be used not as a separate rhetorical form, but as a writing approach that can be used with other expository forms.

The Techniques of Classification

We have said that classification is a sorting procedure. Using the subject "college professors," you could begin the sorting process by recognizing that "college professors" constitutes a generally accepted and well-defined *class.* Then you must decide on a basis for categorizing "college professors" into *subclasses.* At this stage the purpose of your paper comes into play. If you are subclassifying professors at your college for a report to a dean who will use it to make promotion decisions, you would probably subclassify them on the basis of teaching ability and research. But if you are subclassifying them for summer jobs as advisors to new students, then you might prefer to categorize the professors by personality, interest in students, and ability to relate to them.

In planning your classification scheme, keep these suggestions in mind:

1. You should have a clear-cut basis for establishing *class.* For instance, "college professors" as a *class* could include only people who teach full-time; you could not validly include deans, registrars, teaching assistants, or counselors.
2. You should be able to divide your class into at least two subclasses. For example, suppose you decide to make the sex of the teacher your basis for classification. If all your professors are males, then a sub-classification by sex becomes logically impossible. You can deal only with male professors. "Male college professors" in your discussion thus becomes a separate *class;* no subclasses are possible.
3. You should determine subclasses according to the subject matter and the purpose of your paper.
4. You should include all pertinent subclasses. For example, it is distressing that many articles classifying drugs omit the most widely abused drug, alcohol. Also illustrative but less upsetting is the failure (in articles about American cars) to include the Checker, a passenger car used mainly as a taxicab.

Let's apply these four suggestions to a classification of sources of used cars, which might be the basis for a paper informing students about the advantages and disadvantages of buying from each kind of source. Here's a diagram of the paper:

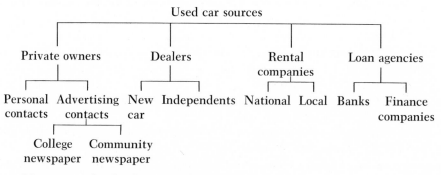

Now to apply the four suggestions:

1. Is there a clear-cut basis for establishing class?
   Used car sources as a class could include only individuals, dealers, and others who sell cars formerly owned by another person. The class could not include national discounters who sell new cars ordered by mail.

2. Is each class or subclass divided into at least two subclasses?

   In the diagram, the class *used car sources* is divided into four sub-classes, each of which is divided into at least two subclasses. One subclass (advertising contacts) is further divided into two. If the student were at a college that did not publish a newspaper or run used car ads in it, then this subclass could not be divided and would have to be re-designed *newspaper advertising contacts.*

3. Are the subclasses determined by the subject matter and the purpose of the paper?

   All subclasses include sources that students might contact in buying a used car. Excluded from the classification are auctions, a subclass that was omitted because ordinarily students cannot buy used cars this way.

4. Are all pertinent subclasses included?

   Except for auto auctions—estate, police, and wholesale dealer auctions—all sources have been included.

DEFINITION

As the preceding section indicated, classification is a relatively un-complicated process when there is general agreement about the scope and meaning of a term. But often a *class* term has several possible meanings, depending upon the context and the audience. In these situations, the writer or speaker must isolate and clarify the meaning intended. For instance, a professor in a psychology or education course might frequently use the phrase *exceptional children.* Without knowledge of the specialized definition, you might assume that the term refers to highly intelligent or gifted children. Other students might think the children are mentally retarded. Neither assumption would be accurate here. Thus your professor is obligated to explain in this context that *exceptional* refers to *any* child who does not meet the criteria for "normal." True, *exceptional children* does include both bright and mentally retarded children. But in education and psychology the term also refers to children with birth defects, children with acquired physical handicaps, and emotionally disturbed children.

The definition of a word or term, then, is often crucial to clear communication. And, as our examples and earlier discussion implied, the connotative meaning of a word depends on numerous factors: context, age of the user, geographical dialect, use in specialized jargons. To write clearly, especially in exposition, you will often have to define your terms, particularly abstract, technical, and new words. So you should be aware of the different ways of handling definition. Your choice depends upon your purpose and the word's complexity, or difficulty.

Synonym Definition

We used this technique in the preceding sentence by adding *difficulty* to indicate the meaning of *complexity.* This simple method of defining by adding one or more similar terms can clarify an unfamiliar word quickly and easily. Synonym definition is particularly helpful when you would expect most readers to understand a term but realize that some may not. In this situation, the synonym supplies a brief explanation for those who need it without boring or offending those who do not. Synonym definition, however, should not be used with key or complex terms because such words require more complete explanations.

Illustrative Definition

This definition relies on examples to explain the term. Often it consists of naming or pointing to a specific person, place, or thing to illustrate the meaning: "110 pocket cameras, such as the Kodak Instamatic, are convenient." An illustrative definition may also explain an unfamiliar term by referring to a familiar one, as when New England town meetings are used as an example to explain the direct democracy of ancient Athens.

Negative Definition

It is often necessary to define a term by indicating what it is not, as with *widow:* a woman whose husband is not living and who has not remarried. But except in such cases, negative definition is combined with other forms of definition. For example, in a paper about equal employment opportunities for minorities, you might define *minorities* as referring not to religious minorities (Jews) or national minorities (Japanese-Americans), but to economically deprived minorities (blacks, Indians, Chicanos).

Formal Definition

Frequently, in writing a paper, you will need a more accurate and precise definition than the ones previously described. This is particularly true when you plan to use a term in a very limited sense. In such a situation, a formal definition using classification techniques would be helpful. As you recall, in classification we start with a class and then divide it into its subclasses. Formal definition works differently. We first determine the class an item belongs to and then distinguish it from other items in that class by stating its distinguishing features. Sounds complicated, but it isn't. Here's the formula:

Item to be defined = class + distinguishing feature (df) 1 + df 2 + df 3 + etc.

And here's a simple example of how it works:

Item to be defined = designated hitter
Class = baseball player

The next step is to distinguish the item to be defined (designated hitter) from other members of its class (baseball player). We might proceed like this:

Distinguishing feature 1 = who bats for the pitcher

But this distinguishing feature is insufficient because a pinch-hitter might also bat for the pitcher. Hence:

Distinguishing feature 2 = each time the pitcher's turn at bat arrives

In addition, to accurately explain *designated hitter*, we should add:

Distinguishing feature 3 = does not play in the field

Work them all into a sentence and you have the formal definition:

A designated hitter (item) is a baseball player (class) who bats for the pitcher (df 1) each time the pitcher's turn at bat arrives (df 2) and who does not play in the field (df 3).

The following formal definition illustrates how the formula may be applied to a more complex subject:

A human act (actus humanus) is one of which man is master, one that is consciously controlled and deliberately willed, so that the agent is held responsible for it.
— Austin Fagothey, *Right and Reason*

As defined here, *human actions* (item) are distinguished from all actions (class) by being restricted to those done willfully (df 1) and intentionally (df 2) so that people are responsible for them (df 3). Excluded from this definition are acts committed by children, mentally retarded people, and people who are temporarily insane, delirious, or drunk — an important distinction in ethics and law.

Note that these two examples follow certain procedures recommended in writing formal definitions:

1. They use a form of the verb *be*. Such other verbs as *means* and *refers* are not acceptable.
2. The definition statements are positive. They avoid the vagueness often resulting from negative statements: "Beer is not a wine."
3. A synonym for the term or the term itself is not used in the definition.

Taboo: "A designated hitter is a hitter who . . ." However, you may refer to the class as Fagothey does in "A human act is *one (act)* . . ."

4. Figurative language and other poetic devices are avoided. Shakespeare's definition of *man* ("such stuff as dreams are made on") or *life* ("but a walking shadow") may be full of "sound and fury" but signify little to anthropologists concerned with primates, or physicians wrestling with the problem of when to declare a patient dead.

5. The definitions do not reflect personal bias ("Tenure is the system that provides lifetime jobs to incompetent teachers").

It is fun to write comic, caustic, or witty definitions, and easy to dash off inaccurate generalizations, but it takes dull, painstaking, hard work to define a term accurately and logically in a formal definition.

Extended Definition

Occasionally you will be compelled to develop a more complete, detailed definition than you can achieve in a single sentence. Let's say you are asked in a history course to write about the legislative branch of the American government. Extended definition is one form that such a paper could take. Your first task would be to distinguish between American and other legislative systems to establish the class: the legislative branch of American government. When the meaning of the class term has been clearly delineated, you could expand this formal definition by subclassifying the term into the legislative branches of the federal government, the state governments, and local governments. The result would be an extended definition, a rhetorical form with two main parts:

1. Establishment of *class.* This involves introducing the *term* and setting up distinctive features. Two common methods of distinguishing a particular meaning of a term from other possibilities are to examine the historical origin and meaning of a word (its *derivation*), and to describe some crucial aspect of the item in great detail. As an example of the latter, in defining the term *narcotics,* you would need to describe the medical effects of narcotics so that your intended meaning would be distinguished from the general misuse of the word as referring to all drugs. You could then limit the term to only those drugs that act as depressants. A reference to the origin of the word, borrowed from related forms in other languages and carrying the original meaning of "benumbing," might also help readers to understand the term.

2. A subclassification process. This involves subcategorizing the *members* of the class, by simply enumerating them; by expanding the meaning through comparison or contrast of the component subclasses; or by furnishing an extensive description of each, using subclass features that identify each as a separate subclass.

The following passage from an extended definition by Robert Brustein demonstrates the definition techniques we have been discussing.

THE RETREAD CULTURE [1]

We had fed the heart on fantasies,
The heart's grown brutal on the fare.
—W. B. Yeats

If it were possible to isolate a single identifying characteristic of American culture over the past decade, it would likely be the element of reproduction: The representative form of our time is a *remake*.

> Introduction of the term to be defined: the key idea in the article.

By a remake, I mean a cultural work based, however loosely, upon a previous construct of fiction or legend which refashions the characters, plot, situation or structure of the original, usually in the hope of arousing recognition.

> Formal definition of the term establishes *class*.

To take some obvious examples from the world of entertainment, the television series called "The Hot l Baltimore" was a remake of the play with the same name by Lanford Wilson. The television series, "M*A*S*H," does a similar thing with Robert Altman's film. TV's "Happy Days" is a thinly disguised remake of the George Lucas movie, "American Graffiti," in the way it exploits the music and mores of adolescents in the nineteen-fifties. Mel Brooks's "Young Frankenstein" is a comic sequel to the many Frankenstein monster movies based on Mary Shelley's book (Woody Allen's "Love and Death" is a comic remake of virtually the whole of Russian literature). And the film of "Jaws," not to mention the Peter Benchley novel from which it is drawn, is a disguised remake both of Ibsen's "An Enemy of the People"—the attempt by officials of a resort town to cover up a threat to its prosperity—and, more obviously, of Melville's "Moby Dick"—the pursuit of a malevolent white fish by a fanatical mariner who is eventually destroyed by it.

> Illustrative definition: examples clarify the formal definition and further define class.

[1] *New York Times Magazine*, 26 Oct. 1975, pp. 38–42. © 1975 by The New York Times Company. Reprinted by permission.

Much of contemporary American entertainment, in short, is not so much being created as re-created. It is a recycled commodity which moves in dizzying spirals through various media, generally losing depth and detail along the way. . . . Where audiences once were eager for what was novel and innovative, they now seem more comfortable with the familiar, as if they wished to escape from contemporary difficulties into the more reassuring territory of the habitual and the known.

This escapist side of the remake culture is certainly reinforced by the current nostalgia boom. Revivals of old stage hits like "No, No, Nanette" and "Irene"; retrospectives of films from the thirties and forties by auteur directors, authentic-looking reconstructions of period styles in new films like "The Sting" and "Godfather II"; revived musical forms like ragtime and fifties rock—all play off a deep American discontent with the present time. So do the "genre" films of industry favorites like Peter Bogdanovich—"What's Up, Doc?," "Paper Moon," "At Long Last Love"—which seem to be based less on the director's experience of life than on his experience of other movies, as if he had spent his first 30 years imprisoned in a screening room. . . .

Obviously, there are commercial reasons behind all of this [nostalgia], and I don't mean to suggest that remakes, revivals, sequels, or reproductions represent anything new. Entrepreneurs have always recognized that what was once successful is likely to be successful again, providing the time is ripe and the consumer is ready. Remakes, in fact, have been the foundation of American musical comedy since its postwar flowering with "Oklahoma!" (a remake of the Lynn Riggs play, "Green Grow the Lilacs"), where for every Broadway musical that used an original book, 10 others were drawn from successful novels, short stories and plays. "Cabaret," for example, began as an Isherwood book, then became a play, a movie

Distinctive feature 1: historical perspective separates the term from other possible interpretations of it; distinguishes the term from other possible members of the class.

Distinctive feature 2: escapist nostalgia is one of the distinguishing features.

Historical perspective again emphasizes the distinction between this definition and other uses of the term *remake*.

of the play, a Broadway musical and, finally, a movie of the musical.

What is different about the remake phenomenon today is its multiplicity and universality. D'Artagnan, after his initial appearance in Dumas, has repeated his adventures in stage plays, Douglas Fairbanks silents and Technicolor talkies, and will no doubt continue riding with his swashbuckling companions as long as entertainment lasts. But the recent Richard Lester version of "The Three Musketeers" consists of two movies, not one, while "The Godfather" appears in *three* parts, including a nine-hour television version of the first two movies with 90 minutes of deleted material restored. Apparently, America's appetite for entertainment is becoming simply insatiable, and, as a result, is far outstripping the industry's capacity to generate new products. With all that television time to be filled, all those movie theaters to be occupied, all those records to be sold, remakes have not only become essential to popular media like TV, films, musicals, recordings, fashions and advertising, but are also becoming an important element of scholarship, serious literature, drama and painting.

Distinctive feature 3: "multiplicity and universality." Subclass 1: Examples for distinctive feature 3 make up first subclass: remakes of remakes.

The article then goes on to spotlight the second subclass: films made about the lives of former media stars.

As you can see from this example, extended definition can utilize many different definition techniques. Distinctive features are used to limit and sharpen the meaning of a term for a specific purpose—to establish it as a distinct class that can then be divided into subclasses. It works like this:

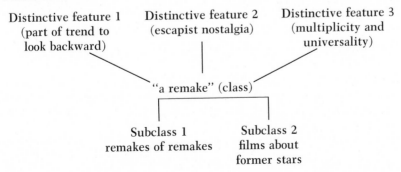

Distinctive feature 1 (part of trend to look backward)

Distinctive feature 2 (escapist nostalgia)

Distinctive feature 3 (multiplicity and universality)

"a remake" (class)

Subclass 1 remakes of remakes

Subclass 2 films about former stars

Later in this chapter we shall discuss the organizational scheme for writing an extended-definition paper like this one.

ANALYSIS

Like classification, analysis is a process of subdividing material for expository purposes. However, classification is concerned simply with identifying and describing a subject; the aim of analysis is not only to divide the item into its component parts but to study and evaluate the relationship of the parts. Like the other forms of expository writing discussed, analysis can be a separate rhetorical form, or it can serve as a writing technique used within other forms. In explaining the principle of the ten-speed bicycle, you could employ analysis for its own sake by breaking down the gear system into its component parts and discussing their relationships. But you might use analysis only briefly in an extended definition of an abstract idea to pinpoint the formal definition of the term that you intend to develop. In defining existentialism, for instance, you might spend the first few paragraphs looking at some of the basic component aspects of this abstract philosophy — the uniqueness of the individual, the importance of free choice, the significance of individual action, and so on — before looking at different versions of existentialism. Or you might employ analysis in the explanation of a process, such as the operation of a rotary engine or making a clay pot on a potter's wheel.

Analysis as an organizational and writing technique can be divided into two main categories:

1. Process analysis: separating a procedure or process into its component parts and examining the relationships involved in the steps.
2. Item analysis: breaking an item or concept into its component parts and analyzing the relationships between the parts.

Process Analysis

Writing itself is a process. Thus, your composition teacher might ask you to write an analysis of the procedure for writing a successful paper. The resulting paper would be a process analysis.

1. PLANNING STAGE (First step in process)
   Choosing a topic
   Limiting the topic
   Organizing the paper (making an outline)
2. INITIAL WRITING STAGE (Second step in process)
   Writing the rough draft
   Setting the rough draft aside for a period of reflection
3. FINAL DRAFT STATE (Third step in process)

Revising
Making the final neat copy
Proofreading

As you can see, process analysis is usually organized chronologically: first this is done, then this, and so on. A danger in writing such papers involves determining the logical starting point. In an analysis of an effective tennis serve, for instance, you would not need to describe the racquet or give advice about obtaining a court. But you would need to list the consecutive steps in the process of serving *and* to describe the relationships between these steps (the component parts of the act of serving)—hand grip on the racquet, stance, ball toss, swing, and follow-through.

Item Analysis

Item analysis shares some of the organizational tactics of classification. Suppose that in a political science course you were asked to explain the organizational structure of your university. You could construct an item-analysis outline like this:

> *Organizational Structure of a University* (Items to be analyzed)
> 1. The Board of Regents or Trustees
> 2. The President and executive staff
> 3. The deans and staffs of the colleges
> 4. The heads and members of departments
> 5. The Faculty Senate
> 6. The student government

A paper based only on this outline would be a classification. But in an analysis you would not merely describe the parts of the university organization, as in classification; you would go on to discuss the relationships between the parts. You would need to consider questions like the following:

> What role does the President play in relation to the Board of Trustees and the Faculty Senate?
> How much influence, if any, do student organizations have at each level?
> What influence do the various departments have on the other components?

Describing Relationships in an Analysis

The two most common methods of indicating how items or steps can be related are comparison and contrast, and cause and effect. The first involves comparing and contrasting your subject with items familiar to your audience. For instance, a general audience might better understand an analysis of the operation of the rotary engine if its combustion system is compared to the workings of a conventional internal combustion engine. The second method, cause and effect, might be useful in your paper on university organization. You might mention the sense of isolation many freshmen experience in a large university; this alienation would be an *effect*. Some *causes* for it might be determined by examining the relationship of the component parts in the university organization. Could the feeling of alienation arise from lack of individual student participation at each level of the system? Do the deans, department heads, or faculty committees welcome contact with individual students, or do they work only through a limited number of student representatives? Does the student government attempt to involve large numbers of students? All these questions get at the *why* of a problem. As you work through an analysis assignment, make sure that you address yourself to the questions *Why?* and *For what reasons?*

Because cause-and-effect analysis can involve complex logical reasoning, we will treat it more fully in Chapter 24.

OPINION

Returning to our friends Jim and Jack and their opening conversation about films, we find them now hotly discussing Jack's opinion that movies of the 1970s have created a new stereotype that is as damaging to today's blacks as the caricature of the Negro servant in earlier films. Jack has voiced an opinion involving a conclusion that he has drawn from his observation and knowledge of current movies and old ones he has seen on late, late TV shows. To defend his opinion statement successfully, he must give Jim an *exposition* of the examples that led him to formulate it. He might employ the techniques of classification or item analysis in describing the stereotype of the shuffling, happy-go-lucky servant depicted in early movies and persisting into the 1930s in such films as *Gone With the Wind* and those with Shirley Temple. Then he might use techniques of definition to show the image of the black man as a "honky-hating," violent superstud as first portrayed in such films as *Shaft* and *Super-Fly*. These tasks can be handled as dispassionately as any classification or analysis exercise. But then Jack must use these well-defined stereotypes to support his contention that the new image is as unrealistic and as damaging as the earlier one. At that point he must use objectively analyzed material to support a subjective reaction to the material—to support his opinion.

Like Jack, you may often find yourself struggling to furnish support for an opinion you hold. You are not interested in persuading someone else to adopt your point of view, merely in presenting your reasons for thinking as you do. The issue may involve nothing more than a simple conclusion about the unusual behavior of a friend or the difficulty of a physics course. But as a student, perhaps more frequently than you might wish, you will be asked to write a paper supporting an opinion statement similar to Jack's or to many that you encounter every day in places like lecture classes or the editorial page of the newspaper.

For example, in a typical editorial, you might find such opinion statements as:

> The slow progress of ratification of the Equal Rights Amendment is jolting women's groups into renewed action.
> Solid-waste disposal and recycling are still major environmental concerns of the nation's cities and industries.

Each of these statements expresses the writer's opinion, which was arrived at by examining and interpreting a series of facts, observations, and views of authorities. Both also serve as the thesis, or main idea statement, of the articles. The editorial writers support and defend their opinions by presenting the evidence that led to them.

As a student, you will probably write opinion papers in which you too will be expected to state a conclusion and support it. Much research writing falls into this category, whether the research conclusions are reached in the library or the laboratory. You will frequently employ this rhetorical form in papers to express a critical opinion of a piece of literature, a work of art, or a film; your response to a decisive event in history; or even your attitude toward some college or professional sport.

Because the opinion paper requires attention to logical relationships, the organization of such a paper is a bit more complex than that of the other forms discussed in this chapter. Papers based on opinion, classification, definition, and analysis have all been discussed in terms of their application and form. To make an analogy to sports, we have in this chapter described the character of the games. For classification, definition, and analysis, our descriptions of the "games" should suffice as organizational schemes for these kinds of papers. But for opinion papers, further strategy needs to be developed. In Chapter 16 we will explore the techniques that you as a writer can use in the prewriting stage of an expository paper based on opinion.

FROM FORM TO ORGANIZATION: A BRIEF REVIEW

In the previous pages, we have looked at the most commonly used methods of exposition: the ways that writers explain and order experience so that an audience can receive the message clearly. The relatively objective forms, classification and definition, have been discussed in terms of their usefulness for writing purposes and in reference to the rather restricted conventions that you should follow in handling them. The structure outlined in describing each form can also serve as an organizational pattern for writing your own classification and definition papers.

Following the suggestions on pages 233–35 for planning a classification scheme, you can organize a paper into two parts: the first should deal with the item you intend to classify in reference to your purpose for writing the paper. The second part should fulfill the guidelines given for subclassifying the item.

In like manner, the steps outlined on pages 235–38 for constructing a formal definition and the annotated example of an extended definition on pages 239–42 can serve as an organizational model for developing an effective definition paper. Again the task is essentially a twofold one and might look like this:

I. Establishment of *class* for item to be defined.
  A. Enumeration of distinctive features that all members of the class share in common.
  B. Exclusion of other possibilities.
II. Establishment of subclasses.
  A. Subclass A (distinctive features that distinguish this subclass from other subclasses to be included).
  B. Subclass B (distinctive features that distinguish this one from others).

As you can see, you are limited to the "game" patterns established for these two rhetorical forms. Papers that involve evaluative analysis or expression of opinion about a topic, however, must rely more heavily on the logical relationships of the material. For such a paper, therefore, strategy that goes beyond a mere outline becomes necessary. In Chapter 16 we will explore the techniques that you can use in the prewriting stage of an expository paper written either to evaluate and analyze an item or a process, or to explain an opinion you hold about a subject.

ASSIGNMENTS

For Discussion

1 This is a classification problem. First you must ascertain if all these critters will fit into a general class: establish the class by determining the features that they have in common. Then decide on the kind and number of subclasses by isolating the features not shared by all.

2   Indicate whether the following statements are adequate or inadequate as formal definitions and why.

   a   A chair is an object that a person sits on.
   b   A holiday is when you don't have to work.
   c   Communism is the form of government they have in Russia.
   d   A free person is not a hungry puppy.
   e   Love is the most beautiful emotion.
   f   Happiness is a warm puppy.
   g   A schlemiel is a person who falls on his back and breaks his nose.
   h   Obscenity is the state of being obscene.
   i   Life is just a bowl of cherries.
   j   Discord is disharmony.

3   Consider the following statements about war to determine their adequacy as formal definitions and also to note whether they contain anything that would be helpful to you in writing an extended definition of the subject.

a   War, more ancient than any history, is the outcome of passions, follies, fallacies, misconceptions, and defective political institutions common to the great mass of men. They are not incurable misconceptions, not incurable follies. But they may well become so if we persist in assuming that they don't exist.

—Sir Norman Angell

b   For a war to be just three conditions are necessary—public authority, just cause, right motive. . . . But those wars also are just, without doubt, which are ordained by God Himself, in Whom is no iniquity, and Who knows every man's merits.

—St. Augustine

c   War is a racket.

—Smedley Butler

d   To my mind, to kill in war is not a whit better than to commit ordinary murder.

—Albert Einstein

e   War is delightful to those who have had no experience of it.

—Desiderius Erasmus

f   Warfare is the means whereby the members of a parasitic ruling class of alien origin endeavor, while exploiting their own subjects, to dominate those surrounding peoples who produce wealth in a tangible and desired form.

—Havelock Ellis

g We have no adequate idea of the predisposing power which an immense series of measures of preparation for war has in actually begetting war.

—William E. Gladstone

h I have never advocated war except as a means of peace.

—Ulysses S. Grant

i War is a science, a series of mathematical problems, to be solved through proper integration and coordination of men and weapons in time and space.

—George Zhukov

j War alone brings up to its highest tension all human energy, and puts the stamp of nobility upon the peoples who have the courage to meet it.

—Benito Mussolini

4 Work out a possible scheme for item analysis of one of the following:

    a The organizational structure of your college or university
    b The organization of the marching band of your high school or college
    c A sorority or fraternity
    d A high school organization—debate club, athletic organization, Band Booster club, school newspaper

5 Work out a possible scheme for a process analysis of one of the following:

    a Buying a used car
    b Making a dress
    c Getting a date
    d Snowing a teacher
    e Assembling a stereo unit
    f Tuning up a car

6 The following passage is from the Student Code of the University of Kentucky. Analyze it as an extended definition. Does it include all the steps recommended in this chapter?

PLAGIARISM

All academic work, written or otherwise, submitted by a student to his instructor or other academic supervisor, is expected to be the result of his own thought, research, or self-expression. In any case in which a student feels unsure about a question of plagiarism involving his work, he is obliged to consult his instructor on the matter before submitting it.

When a student submits work purporting to be his own, but which in any way borrows ideas, organization, wording or anything else from another source without appropriate acknowledgment of the fact, the student is guilty of plagiarism.

Plagiarism includes reproducing someone else's work, whether it be a published article, chapter of a book, a paper from a friend or some file, or whatever. Plagiarism also includes the practice of employing or allowing another person to alter or revise the work which a student submits as his own, whoever that other person may be. Students may discuss assignments among themselves or with an instructor or tutor, but when the actual work is done, it must be done by the student and the student alone.

When a student's assignment involves research in outside sources or information, he must carefully acknowledge exactly what, where and how he has employed them. If he uses words of someone else, he must put quotation marks around the passage in question and add an appropriate indication of its origin. Making simple changes while leaving the organization, content and phraseology intact is plagiaristic. However, nothing in these rules shall apply to those ideas which are so generally and freely circulated as to be part of the public domain.

For Writing

1 Using the techniques of classification suggested in this chapter, write a paper of classification on one of the following:

race cars	recreation vehicles
male chauvinists	tents
feminists	back-packers
fishing lures	a type of popular music
bicycles	college roommates
TV heroines	campus dates
cola ads	TV heroes

2 Choose one of the following terms or one of your own and, using the method recommended in the chapter, write an extended definition of it.

designated hitter	sexism
screen pass	ripoff
phase elective	bugging
back-packing	X-rated
high school senioritis	condominium
Black Power	tachometer
school spirit	funky
phony	sisterhood
ghetto	cheating

16

Logical Organization of an Expository Paper

WHY PLAN AN EXPOSITORY PAPER?

We have said that in writing a paper, as in many other problem-solving endeavors, you are deeply involved in imposing order on experience. Before you can effectively explain to others the special meaning of an item, a process, an analysis of a problem, or your reasons for holding a certain opinion, you need to sort out your ideas and plan your strategy for presenting them. Earlier in the book we suggested methods of organizing personal narratives by chronological order, and descriptions by spatial arrangement. In Chapter 15 we suggested schemes for writing expository papers that involved classifying techniques. But in exposition where the aim is to explain or present a personal evaluation or opinion, you need another form of organization that will emphasize the relationships between items or ideas. Ordering your ideas by time sequence or spatial arrangement will not suffice; logical organization is needed.

Although in writing an analysis you might divide an item or process into its component parts and present them in a chronological order, it would also be necessary to compare and contrast the function of the parts and examine their relationships. In analyzing how the role of university president can effectively serve as an apprenticeship for an executive position in government, you might first determine the various functions that a university president serves in relation to the tasks of a state governor and arrange these as chronological steps in the training process. But you must also compare the various roles that people in both positions play and consider how these roles relate to each other. The latter requires logical reasoning and discussion.

Logical organization would also be necessary in a political science paper setting forth your opinion about how the Nixon Administration's "credibility gap" stemming from the Watergate affair contributed to a constitutional crisis. Simply listing the events in chronological order would not solve this paper's organizational needs. Rather, before you began to write you would need to consider questions like these: *In what ways* did the "credibility gap" manifest itself? Other than the Watergate break-in and the subsequent cover-up, what were the *causes*? *What influence* did the personality of Nixon and the people around him have? *What effects* did the publicity and attitudes of the press create? *What relationship* did the Vietnam war have to the establishment of the "credibility gap"?

In both these hypothetical papers you would be dealing with the questions, *Why? What are the reasons? What are the relationships?* Explanation of these questions demands logical organization. And logical organization requires planning the strategy of presentation before writing begins.

Students often find prewriting activity frustrating, and they often resent any imposition of form on their writing. They particularly resist any effort to convince them that the additional work involved in devising an outline or some other kind of organizational scheme can improve their writing. True, many professional writers do not work out elaborate outlines before they start to write; but they have spent so much time and effort at their craft that their organizational skills have become almost instinctive.

Learning to drive a car is a pertinent analogy. When you first start to drive, you consciously map out a chronological list of steps and a set of cause-and-effect relationships. You think about the sequence of turning the ignition key and then stepping on the accelerator pedal; at the same time, you are conscious of the relationship between the position of the automatic gear shift and starting the car. As you gain confidence and driving experience, you follow these steps and guidelines subconsciously. Even though you are unaware of them, they have become a part of you, and you use them every time you get behind the steering wheel.

Like learning to drive, or becoming proficient in any other new skill, writing requires meticulous, conscious organizational effort. And, as with driving, you will find you may discard much of the conscious planning when you have written as many papers as you have taken trips (in a car, that is!). You will also discover, as every writer does, that when preparing for a long, involved piece of writing, just as in planning a long motor trip, you need to be organized.

STEPS IN DEVELOPING A LOGICAL ORGANIZATION

Although you may disregard some of the following steps in some writing situations you would be wise to consider all of them in the planning, or prewriting, stage of most of your writing:

1. Find a topic.
2. Restrict or limit the topic.
3. Formulate a thesis statement.
4. Develop an organizational scheme or outline.

Let's consider each step in some detail.

Find a Topic

The search for a topic is frequently the most frustrating and time-consuming aspect of a writing assignment. Even if you sometimes resent it when a college instructor assigns you a topic, you should also realize that this frees you from a long, arduous task. But when you have to come up with a topic on your own, what should you consider? For one thing, you should note the situation involved in the assignment. A mathematics professor will be reluctant to accept a paper on "How to Be a Successful Pool Player" unless you include mathematical formulas for foolproof shots. Nor would you choose to write about Kurt Vonnegut, Jr., in a course on seventeenth-century literature—unless you wanted to flunk the course. If you decide to try your hand at professional writing, one ploy in finding topics is to look at some popular magazines to find the kinds of articles they accept. Topics that would appeal to editors of *Playboy* would probably be rejected by *The Christian Science Monitor*, and you wouldn't send an article on drag-racing to *Gourmet* unless you could somehow work the preparation of food into it!

As we mentioned previously, an effective method for selecting a topic is to start with a concern for the ABC's—appeal, breadth, and complexity—and apply these questions to each of the topics you are considering:

Appeal

1. Am I interested in it? If the subject is dull and uninteresting to you, your readers will also find it so.
2. Will it interest my audience? If you don't think this is an important consideration, remember all the times you've been bored when an enthusiastic supporter of a cause babbled on and on.

Breadth

3. Is the scope of the material within my time limitation? Sometimes a subject may require longer researching time than you have to com-

plete the assignment. Occasionally, you find that you must send away for data to a government agency or a library in another town. Be sure that you have time for this.

Complexity

4. Can I explain the subject adequately? If it's a topic about which you say, "I know what it means, but I don't know how to express it," back off from it. Or if the subject is too difficult for the audience, you'll probably have to devote too much space to simplifying it—assuming you are able to do so.

These basic points about finding a subject will serve as a helpful general guide for you. While they may not lead you to a stimulating subject, as some of the suggestions in Chapter 14 might, these questions should keep you from floundering with a dismal one.

Restrict the Topic

Jane: I have to write a paper this weekend for cultural anthropology.
Joe: What on?
Jane: I don't know for sure. Perhaps on the class discussions of the family as a social unit. They were pretty interesting.
Joe: Sounds good. But what are you doing with it?

Jane has obviously gone through some of the soul-searching suggested in the last section. She has decided on a topic that interests her, is relevant to the assignment situation, and will probably interest her audience—her anthropology instructor. But she still has a problem. How can she possibly discuss the family as a social unit adequately in 1,000 words or less? She is ready to enter phase two of the organizational procedure: restricting, or narrowing, her topic.

Joe's question, "But what are you doing with it?" is an appropriate one. In order to treat her topic with maximum efficiency and interest, Jane should limit it to a workable scope. She would be wise to concentrate on her own interests, her background, and her desire for new knowledge. For instance, if she is a native of southeastern Kentucky or eastern Tennessee, she might wish to discuss the *Appalachian* family as a social unit. If she has some knowledge of the commune family, she might restrict her topic to this recent phenomenon. Or if she is concerned with the effects of the nuclear family on American culture, she could limit it to that particular family organization.

But in restricting the topic, as in all else, common sense must prevail. A topic can be overrestricted. It can become so limited that it will be impossible to deal with even in a short paper without becoming tedious and repetitive. If Jane were to choose "My Family as a Social Unit" as her topic, the resulting paper might be interesting to Jane and fascinating as a personal narrative, but in exposition her chance of boring her audience is great—*unless* she manages to make her family appear representative enough to serve as a model for a paper written from an anthropological or sociological approach.

Formulate a Thesis Statement

A thesis statement, often referred to as the main idea of a paper, is probably the most important part of prewriting. In essence, it summarizes what the paper is about. It contains not only the topic and the restriction of the topic but also the approach of the writer to the topic. Its main function is to provide the writer with a device to maintain focus and restriction. Actually, the thesis statement is somewhat like the rudder of a ship. With it you can steer clear of the muddy shoals of indecisive writing and avoid floundering in the treacherous waters of disorganized ideas. Stated in plainer language, the thesis statement that will effectively guide you through a paper has the following characteristics:

1. It should be a simple, declarative sentence. You may, in the final version of your paper, formulate the thesis as a question leading into the rest of the paper, but in this prewriting stage, it should always take the form of a statement.

   The thesis should be as concise and straightforward as possible. Again, this is an exercise to force you to think very carefully. It will not always be possible to adhere to this rule of thumb; you cannot always avoid sentence complexity when dealing with complicated ideas. But you should make every effort to do so. Thesis statements containing subordinate clauses often set booby traps for inexperienced writers. For example:

   > In spite of the danger that many guilty parties may go unpunished by law because the resulting publicity may make a fair trial impossible, *the Senate is justified in holding public hearings on wrongdoing in government.*

   As you can see, there are really two possible thesis ideas in the senordinate material and then as a kind of afterthought sail quickly justified in holding hearings. The italicized main clause contains the idea your reader expects you to discuss and support. But all too often, inexperienced writers get mired down in a long exposition of the subordinate material and then as a kind of afterthought sail quickly through the real subject of the paper in the last paragraph. A simple declarative thesis sentence can usually prevent this false emphasis.

2. A thesis statement should indicate your purpose. However, it need not be explicitly stated. Inexperienced writers feel that they must hit their readers over the head by starting a paper with phrases such as, "My purpose in this paper is to . . . ," "I intend to show that . . . ," and "It is my purpose to . . . ." More sophisticated writers, except when writing scientific or technical papers, generally avoid such overt expression of purpose.

> Example: My purpose in this paper is to support the view that a college education is a life-long benefit.
> Rewrite: A college education is a life-long benefit.

The first version not only is formal and pretentious but may project a condescending tone to many readers. In the rewritten version, purpose is present, but implied. Your reader assumes that your purpose is to defend and support this view.

3. A thesis statement should suggest, but need not overtly state, the writer's attitude toward the subject.

> Example: I think that strip mining is only a short-term, environmentally destructive solution to the long-term problem of fuel shortages.

Sometimes, of course, you may wish to state that the view expressed is your own, particularly when you are discussing highly controversial subjects or when your purpose is to sell yourself in some way to your audience: perhaps in applying for a job or running for a political office. But an implicit statement of attitude is generally regarded as more subtle, sophisticated, and emphatic than an explicit one. For instance in this restatement of the thesis, the conviction of the writer is more vigorously expressed because of the absence of personal attribution:

> Rewrite: Strip mining is only a short-term, environmentally destructive solution to the long-term problem of fuel shortages.

In the absence of any reference to any source or person, this opinion is obviously the writer's. Moreover, there are clues to the writer's personal bias:

a. Word choice, or diction: words with great emotional impact, like *environmentally destructive,* strongly indicate writer bias. The tone of these words in this context indicates a hostile attitude toward strip mining.

b. Sentence structure: the use of *only* and the parallelism of *short-term solution* and *long-term problem* add weight to the writer's implicit negative opinion toward strip mining.

4. The thesis statement should reflect your concern for your audience. Of course, the subject matter itself often reflects the nature of the audience, but word choice can also play an important role. For instance, in the following thesis statement, the writer indicates by the specialized jargon that the intended audience is psychologists, familiar with the vocabulary of their profession:

> Children's play and imitation in the preconceptual stage show a predominance of either assimilation or accommodation.

On the other hand, the statement below, on the same subject, is aimed at a more general audience and would more likely appear in a magazine you'd pick up at a newsstand:

> The young learn to understand and digest new experiences by imitating them in play.

Remember that, like the focusing statement of the personal essay and the key idea in the opening of a description, the thesis statement in expository writing provides the focus of the paper. Once formulated, it acts as a rhetorical rudder to keep your paper and ideas on course. Our previous example of the thesis statement on strip-mining limits the writer to a discussion of the destructiveness of mining done by the strip method.

> Strip-mining is only a short-term, environmentally destructive solution to a long-term problem.

The terms *strip-mining* and *environmentally destructive solution* are the key terms or dominant ideas in the thesis that limit the scope of the paper. The juxtaposition of "short-term solution" and "long-term problem" helps to fix the organizational plan: the material in the paper must be focused on these concerns.

In short, a well-thought-out thesis statement is necessary to write an effectively restricted and focused paper. It controls and directs the paper; it indicates both the writer's purpose and attitude. In fact, it is so significant that many instructors who do not require their students to develop other formal organizational skills, such as outlining, do insist that students always formulate a thesis statement before writing.

Because it plays such an important role in determining the focus of a paper, a good thesis statement is hard to come by. So far, we have concentrated on the ingredients of a good thesis statement. Let's look at some weak ones through the eyes of a critical reader.

Thesis: I think that the registration system is abominable.

Critical Reader: Of course you think so, or you wouldn't have said it; why do you start out with "I think . . . "? It gives your paper an apologetic tone. Besides, what registration system do you mean? No restriction! And how can you logically support such an emotionally charged word as "abominable"? You're asking for trouble!

Thesis: The fuel crisis in America.

Critical Reader: Well, you have a topic—fuel crisis. And I suppose "America" provides some restriction. But what's your pitch? What do you have to say *about* the fuel crisis? If you don't know, then how will your readers figure it out? Half a thesis is *not* better than none.

The critical reader of this book could accuse us of trying, for the sake of conciseness, to make the search for a thesis statement seem easier than it really is. We may be guilty. In some ways, finding a thesis is like fishing: you may have to throw many back before you hook a satisfactory one. The function of a satisfactory thesis is analogous to a contention made by the poet Robert Frost: when a poet sets down the first line of a poem, he has committed himself to many things—the subject of the poem, the length of the line, the beginning rime scheme, and the purpose. The thesis, once formulated and written into the opening paragraphs of a paper, in a very real sense has committed the writer to the form the paper must take and the message inherent in it. Therefore, you may have to devote much time and effort to formulating an effective thesis statement, perhaps going through several versions before you are satisfied with it. Let's look now at two kinds of thesis statements especially useful for writing opinion or analysis papers.

INFERENCE THESIS STATEMENT

Thesis statements should be designed to fit the needs of your writing assignments. Often in expository papers explaining the reasons for your opinion about a subject, your thesis statement will take the form of an inference—a conclusion based on some kind of evidence or observation. Examples of inference statements that could serve as thesis statements for opinion papers are:

The present definition of clinical death is inadequate for modern medical practices.

The financial plight of the big cities may be a serious national economic threat.

Political rhetoric has contributed to the use of imprecise word usage, or "doublespeak."

Television commercials have become a pop art form.

All reflect the writer's opinion and can be supported with facts and observations.

ANALYTICAL THESIS STATEMENT

A second kind of thesis statement that is especially useful in writing analysis papers is the analytical thesis. It not only expresses the main idea in the paper but also outlines the main supporting evidence in stating a number of reasons, causes, main factors, and the like. However, it does impose restrictions. First, it forces you to decide on the order to follow in your paper. Second, the points must be parallel, both in grammatical structure and in relationship to one another and to the thesis idea. Here are two examples of analytical thesis statements:

Congress needs reform in committee structure, in committee assignments, and in subcommittee activity. (item-analysis thesis)

You can improve your tennis game by placing your serve more effectively, by perfecting your net game, and by developing a drop-shot. (process-analysis thesis)

Note that both imply that the writer has some convictions about the subject. Note also that the list of items following the main clause correspond to the suggested outline for analysis papers in Chapter 15, pages 242–43. There are two points to keep in mind as you write from such a thesis: (1) in the paper you should deal with each point in the same order as in the statement; (2) you need to discuss the relationships involved. The thesis statement does not explicitly reveal the relationships; you must do that in your discussion.

Develop an Organizational Scheme or Outline

In solving a problem, the first step is to identify it. If your car stops running, for example, you have to determine what's wrong before you can start to repair it. But in writing a paper, the problem has usually been defined for you. Your instructor has either assigned a paper on a subject or permitted you to choose your own, perhaps suggesting that it be related to the course work. Let's assume the latter situation.

Suppose that in your freshman composition course you have been reading essays about the current situation of American Indians and are assigned to write a paper expressing and supporting your opinion about some aspect of it. The first step in solving this assigned problem is finding a topic. You decide, in looking over the possibilities, that you and your readers (your instructor and perhaps your classmates) have no burning interest in the complex puzzle of broken treaties and the resultant litigation, nor in the influence of the Bureau of Indian Affairs on reservation life. But a reference to peyotism, the Indians' religious use of peyote, has aroused your curiosity and you would like to know more about it. Fine! You will find that the hard work of trying to instruct and interest your readers is lightened if you are enthusiastic about your subject.

In the initial stages, you might think out the problems in much the same way that we suggested for planning a descriptive paper: determine what information (details) to include; think of ways to interest your readers in the subject; and then consider the organization of your paper. However, as we have pointed out, the organizational problems of expository writing are more complex and require more sophisticated prewriting skills; thus we shall concentrate on them here. Though an opinion paper presents the same organizational problems as other kinds of expository papers, we will concentrate on that particular form as an example.

So, at this point, what do you have? A very general topic: peyotism (the use of peyote in Indian rituals). Since several of the articles you read and discussed in class dealt with this subject, you feel you have an adequate preliminary knowledge of it. Without such knowledge, you should not tackle any subject as a paper topic.

The first organizational step is simply to jot down all the ideas that come to you about the subject. These observations can be in any form: sentences, phrases, or even single words. They can express conflicting viewpoints about the subject. The purpose is just to get an informal listing down on paper. Here, in no particular order, are some ideas you might come up with:

1. Peyote is a cactus containing a hallucinatory drug, mescaline.
2. Hallucinatory drugs are generally harmful and their use should be controlled.
3. Peyote seems to be nonaddictive.
4. Peyotism has spread from the Indians of the Southwest to about fifty tribes all over the United States.
5. Peyotism is an essential rite in the Native American Church, a fundamentalist form of Indian Christianity.

6. Indians use the derived drug in small amounts to induce "visions" in religious ceremonies.
7. The Food and Drug Administration classifies peyote as a nonnarcotic drug.
8. The drug can be obtained by doctor's prescription.
9. No federal law prohibits the use of peyote.
10. Alcohol and tobacco contain proven harmful substances.
11. Tribal Councils have prohibited its use.
12. The Supreme Court has ruled that tribal legislation lies outside the jurisdiction of the United States.
13. The Supreme Court has expressed the opinion that tribal legislation discriminates against religious freedom.
14. Modern Indians use peyotism as a link to their past identity.
15. Wine, which contains a harmful substance, is used in many Christian rituals.

Obviously, other points could be made, but this list is sufficient to demonstrate the method. Your aim now is to classify these items into general categories. But first, you might decide what attitude you hold about the topic. If you have already formulated an opinion, then the problem is solved. But if you are uncertain about how you feel about the use of peyote, then it would be helpful to examine the tone in which your ideas are expressed: are they predominantly favorable or unfavorable to the use of peyote? In this instance, we can see that although many of the statements are neutral in tone, when they are divided into categories of approval or disapproval, the overall impression is favorable to the practice of peyotism. We will exploit this favorable attitude, first as we categorize the list and later when we formulate a thesis statement.

One possible set of general categories for these items is as follows:

Definition: 1, 3
Background information: 4, 7, 8
Use: 5, 6, 14
Legal aspects: 9, 11, 12, 13
Attitudes: 2, 10, 15

The next task is to cull out unnecessary material. Other subjects are familiar to many readers and would require little or no "definition" or "background," and so these could be eliminated in many writing situations. But since the subject of peyote is probably unfamiliar to most people, you will need to include background material. But it need not serve as material in the main part of the paper, acting as support for the thesis. Rather, it can be presented in the opening paragraphs of the paper and introduce the thesis idea. Therefore, it does not need to be an integral part of your outline.

The information in the other categories—"use," "legal aspects," and "attitudes"—can be generalized into statements supporting the thesis idea. And what of the thesis? You could devise a statement like:

> Some Indian tribes use peyote in many of their religious rituals.

But your assignment was, as you recall, to express an opinion and support it. True, the above thesis idea could be the basis of an expository paper, but one that would be descriptive in nature, simply illustrating the ways that peyote is used. Also, it would come closer to being a statement of fact rather than one of inference or opinion. Let's turn now to some inference thesis statements that could be devised from the material.

> The *prohibition of peyotism* by the *Tribal Councils* is a *violation* of Indians' *right* of religious freedom.
>
> Indians who use *peyote in rituals* are *justified* in regarding peyotism as a religion beneficial to its followers.

Because either of these two statements is suitable for a thesis, you are now ready to organize the material on peyotism. At this point, you must decide on the arrangement and logical relationships of the supporting evidence. To begin this process, ask yourself these questions:

> Does the subject require extensive definition or background discussion?
>
> Will I need to consider whether some readers may have misconceptions about my subject?
>
> Would it be more effective to hit my audience with the strongest points first or to put them at the end of the paper to provide a climax?
>
> Do any of the ideas require a special order to retain cause-and-effect relationships?
>
> Will any aspect of my supporting material turn off part of my audience?

You'll probably agree with our earlier contention that most readers will not be familiar with peyotism, so you will have to provide background information. Also, since peyote is a hallucinogenic drug, readers may react emotionally against it; if you approve of Indians using it, you will need to demonstrate to your readers that peyote is relatively harmless. These points must be included in the organization of your paper.

The most common device for organizing is the outline, which can be in either topic or sentence form. A topic outline using a thesis statement we constructed previously might look like this:

Thesis: The prohibition of peyotism by the Tribal Councils is a violation of the Indians' right of religious freedom.

Orientation: Definition of peyotism
History of peyote in Indian religious rites

Main Points:
  I. Use of peyote in modern ceremonies
 II. Misconceptions
    A. Emotional attitudes toward hallucinogenic drugs
    B. Acceptance of use of other legal—but harmful—substances: alcohol and tobacco
III. Legal aspects
    A. Tribal legislation
    B. Supreme Court rulings

Conclusion: The Tribal Councils have violated the right of religious freedom by denying Indians the use of peyote in religious ceremonies.

Many instructors will expect only a topic outline. However, many others believe that a sentence outline is a better tool for inexperienced writers. It does offer you the important prewriting advantage of forcing you to express the necessary logical relationships between your ideas before you begin to write. This frees you later to concentrate on all the other complicated problems of the writing process: sentence structure, word choice, paragraph development, and so on. Using the same thesis statement as above, we could develop the following sentence outline:

Thesis: The prohibition of peyotism by the Tribal Councils is a violation of the Indians' right of religious freedom.

Orientation: Definition—peyote is a form of cactus containing the hallucinogenic substance mescaline.
History—peyote has been used by certain Indian tribes since pre-Columbian times and has become a symbol of Indian identity.

Main Points:
  I. Peyote is now used in essential rituals in a fundamentalist Indian-Christian sect.
    A. It is an attempt by Indians converted to the white people's religion to retain their ethnic identity.
    B. Its use is strictly controlled during the ceremonies.
    C. No orgies have ever been reported at these rituals.
 II. Misconceptions about drugs have contributed to the prohibition of peyote.
    A. Indian leaders have been led to believe that peyote is addictive.

     B. None of the Indians using it have experienced harmful after-
effects.

     C. Alcohol and tobacco, although legal and not usually thought
of as "drugs," are both apparently more harmful than peyote.

     D. Alcohol in the form of wine is served in some church rituals.

  II. The Tribal Councils have denied the Indians the rights that
other American citizens have.

     A. The Supreme Court ruled that as separate governing bodies
the councils were within their rights, but were discriminatory in denying Indians rights granted to other U.S. citizens.

     B. Tribal legislation should be based on the privileges granted to
all citizens in the Bill of Rights and the Constitution.

Conclusion: The Tribal Councils have violated the right of religious
freedom by denying Indians the use of peyote in religious ceremonies.

Obviously, other outlines might be written from this material. The
material presented here to support the thesis could even be manipulated
to support the opposite view that Tribal Councils are justified in their
actions. This ability of the writer to slant or direct materials to almost
any point of view is a good justification for the time you spend outlining
before writing: it helps you make sure that all the material is focused the
way you wish it to be in the paper.

Note that in the outlines we suggest here, we have included the introduction and conclusion, a departure from the form frequently found in
rhetoric textbooks. We believe that the more planning you do, the easier
the writing will be.

The final step in all this, of course, is to transform your outline material into an expository paper. Here is how the parts match up:

1. Introduction of the paper
In the opening paragraphs, you provide orientation – background information, devices to stimulate your readers' interest – and, most
important, the thesis statement.

2. Body of the paper
This section comprises the discussion of all the main points and the
evidence that supports them.

3. Conclusion of the paper
This generally acts as a summary and includes a restatement of the
thesis idea.

We shall conclude with a few additional remarks about the use of an
outline.

1. The outline, whether it is in topic or sentence form, is a *tool* to help
you in the writing process. Constructing an outline after writing the

paper in order to satisfy an instructor's requirement is useless — unless you do the outline after the rough draft to catch weaknesses in your logic. But student writers are usually not proficient enough to do that, nor can they really bring themselves to completely rewrite a poorly organized first draft. It is almost always best to develop an outline before writing.

2. For convenience, the thesis statement is isolated from the rest of the outline. But in the paper, the thesis idea should be worked into the introduction. Only in scientific writing do you ever encounter a professionally published article with an isolated thesis. In such a case, the thesis serves as a brief abstract of the article.

3. The outline is the substructure of your final paper. If your paper is merely your outline put into paragraph form, then you are misusing this valuable tool. The outline can help you to organize your ideas, to indicate major partitions in the paper, and to set up logical relationships, but it is still only a skeleton. In writing the paper, you should add the flesh and form to make your subject aesthetic and exciting. A paper that goes no further than the outline is about as interesting and informative as someone else's botany notes.

4. The outline should serve you. Although your instructor may require it, the outline exists not as an end in itself but as a means to help you improve the final product, your paper. Consequently, you should benefit from the outline, not feel hampered or restricted by it. As you are writing, for example, if you are smitten with some inspiration, feel free to add the new idea. Don't let the outline strait-jacket you. But do check carefully to see that such a change fits logically into the organization of your paper.

ASSIGNMENTS

For Discussion

1 At the end of Chapter 14, page 231, there is a list of broad topics that you were asked to restrict so that they would be suitable for writing a short paper. Choose eight or ten of them and formulate for each a workable thesis statement for an expository paper expressing an opinion.

2 Discuss why each of the following sentences is inadequate as a thesis statement for an expository paper of opinion. Reword each to make it an effective, workable thesis.

   a The pollution caused by our technology has had an effect on everyone.

   b Classes are the toys of college freshmen, and drop-add is the traumatic procedure they must go through to purchase their toys.

   c Sports are a deciding factor in many peoples' actions and behavior.
   d There has been a great need for organized labor because working conditions were bad, with long hours, low wages, and few vacations.
   e Should we grant amnesty at all, or should we grant amnesty with punishment, and who should make the final decision on amnesty?
   f Riding a bicycle to, from, and on the campus can be disastrous.
   g Football and soccer are alike in many ways.
   h In selecting a college, students consider academic reputation, social atmosphere, and costs.
   i Because college freshmen have a hard time adjusting, they need to live in a dormitory and be forced to attend class.
   j The registration system at this college is lousy.

3 Discuss the weaknesses of the following two outlines.

   a   HOW CAN AUTO ACCIDENTS BE PREVENTED?

       I. Should driver's education be made compulsory?
      II. Should the age limit be changed from sixteen to eighteen years?
     III. Are hot-rod organizations of any value to the community?
      IV. Should there be a limit on the horsepower of a car?

   b   TEENAGE NONCONFORMITY
   Thesis: Teenagers in the United States are conforming less to society's norms.
       I. Parental care and guidance.
      II. School drop-outs hinder our society as a whole.
     III. Juvenile delinquency comes from broken homes.
          A. Teen gangs.
      IV. Teenage marriage is a serious problem.

For Writing

1 Use one of the following quotations as a thesis statement, or develop a thesis stating your own opinion of one of these ideas. Then construct a topic or sentence outline that could be used in writing a paper on the subject.

   a Though ambition is itself a vice, it is often the parent of virtues.
                                                              — Quintilian

   b Loyalty . . . is a realization that America was born of revolt, flourished in dissent, became great through experimentation.
                                                    — Henry Steele Commager

c   It is more convenient to follow one's conscience than one's intelligence, for at every failure, conscience finds an excuse and encouragement in itself.

—Friedrich Nietzsche

d   Freedom in general may be defined as the absence of obstacles to the realization of desires.

—Bertrand Russell

e   Patriotism is the passion of fools and the most foolish of passions.

—Arthur Schopenhauer

f   All work, even cotton-spinning, is noble; work is alone noble.

—Thomas Carlyle

2   Using the method outlined in Chapter 15 and an analytical thesis, write an item analysis of one of the topics suggested in exercise 4 under "For Discussion" (see page 249).

3   Write a process analysis of one of the topics suggested in exercise 5 under "For Discussion" in Chapter 15.

17

The Form
of the Expository
Paragraph

WHAT IS AN EXPOSITORY PARAGRAPH?

In Chapter 7, we dealt with special considerations in writing narrative paragraphs, pointing out that several factors might influence a writer's decisions about paragraphing: emphasis, clarity, conventions of dialogue, or even the writer's whim. Obviously, the highly personal, loose quality of narrative writing permits much variety. The paragraphs contained within expository papers, like the papers themselves, are generally more tightly constructed than their narrative counterparts. But that is not to say that all expository paragraphs are exactly alike.

In books, magazines, and newspapers, paragraph length varies greatly, often controlled more by the medium than the message. For instance, newspaper paragraphs tend to be short; that is because newspaper articles are usually reportive, containing only the essential facts about an incident or situation, and because newspaper columns are narrow, long paragraphs would seem endless on the page. If you examine a variety of magazines and books, you will probably find that their paragraph length often reflects the audience the material is aimed at. Magazines for general audiences, like *Time* and *Newsweek,* tend to have shorter paragraphs than those written for more educated readers, like *Harper's* and *The Atlantic Monthly.* Defining the nature of expository paragraphs is further complicated by the practice of interspersing short paragraphs for emphasis or transition, even in scholarly articles or books.

In spite of its elusive character and its infinite variety, the paragraph, like the sentence, does seem to be a recognizable convention of the language. Even though linguists and rhetoricians continue to debate the fine points of sentence definition, most people agree on what a sentence is. So, too, with expository paragraphs.

Try this simple experiment. Read this passage from a freshman paper, indicating where you sense that paragraphing is indicated. Then check your results with those of your classmates to find whether most of you agree.

1. The Amish Church is an Apostolic Church. **2.** The theology of the Amish and the practices based on this theology are derived from the *Books of the Apostles*. **3.** The Amish also base their behavior on the teachings of Christ in the Sermon on the Mount and on a strict adherence to the Ten Commandments. **4.** Practices based on these Scriptural verses, such as passive resistance, the refusal to take an oath, salvation through Christ and confession of sin, honesty and humility in all affairs, private prayer, and a deep faith in and dependence on God, characterize an Apostolic Church. **5.** The Amish Church is also a rural church. **6.** Members of the church are almost exclusively farmers. **7.** As in every other aspect of Amish life, there is a biblical basis for maintaining a rural church. **8.** Much of the Old Testament deals with people, such as Isaac, Jacob, Moses, and David, who led simple and rural lives. **9.** These were people whom God looked upon with favor. **10.** There are other reasons why the Amish maintain their rural way of life. **11.** Rural life encourages children to stay on the farm and within the sect. **12.** Amish children know little else but farming and how to serve God through their farms. **13.** Amish farms, recognized as some of the most beautiful, well kept, and productive farms in the world, stand as a tribute to God. **14.** Amish farms exemplify the Amish belief that, if one is in harmony with God's earth, one is in harmony with God. **15.** In rural areas, the Amish are less likely to draw attention to themselves and their children. **16.** Separatism can most easily be practiced on a farm, which is, for the most part, self-sufficient. **17.** Working side-by-side in the fields helps to unite families. **18.** It was in the cities that Christ encountered the suspicion and harassment of the Pharisees and Roman government. **19.** Jesus was tried and crucified in a city. **20.** William Cowper, an English poet of the eighteenth century, embodied the essence of Amish thought concerning a rural church in one of his poems when he said, "God made the country, but man made the town."

The chances are that you and your classmates will generally agree with the writer, who paragraphed before sentences 5 and 10.

This experiment has been tried successfully so many times with such a variety of forms, including nonsense-word paragraphs, that considerable evidence now exists that the paragraph is indeed a generally recognized convention of the language, at least the written language. (Linguists are trying to determine whether we recognize oral paragraph signals in the spoken language.)

Let's analyze the student example to see why you paragraphed as you did. Since most definitions of *paragraph* emphasize meaning as the basic concern in paragraphing, let's look first at the meaning clues. Sentences 1–4 all relate to the idea of the "Apostolic Church" mentioned in sentence 1. However, at sentence 5 the writer introduces a new idea, that of the "rural church," and discusses it through sentence 9; hence the need for a separate paragraph consisting of sentences 5–9. Consequently, sentences 1 and 5 might be referred to as topic sentences, which, as you may know, generally state the paragraph's central or summary idea in the same way that thesis statements present the main idea of a paper. What has occurred, therefore, is that we have responded to meaning clues in determining the scope of the paragraph. But meaning is not a sufficient criterion for paragraphing. By examining printed paragraphs, you could find numerous examples of a single idea discussed throughout several paragraphs instead of being confined to one, as paragraphing by close meaning relationships would indicate that it should be.

Consequently, many rhetoricians now rely more on structural signals than on meaning as a paragraph indicator. In our Amish example, even though the writer lacks the sophistication to supply the number and variety of structural devices employed by more skillful writers, we can still isolate some that you responded to, perhaps subconsciously. Note that the use of *this* (sentence 2) and *these* (sentence 4) in positions commonly occupied by the articles *a* or *the,* establishes a close relationship among sentences 1–4. Sentences 13 and 14 start with the same structure elements: *Amish farms*/Verb; this parallelism of structure and vocabulary helps to link these two sentences with the idea of "farming" in 12. Elsewhere, structure words like *also* (sentence 3) act as connectors of ideas from one sentence to another, and in doing so improve the cohesiveness of the whole paragraph. And adverbial materials, moved from the normal position in the sentence to the beginning as in sentence 15 (*In rural areas*), hook the sentences closer together.

So you see that in spite of the wide variations in paragraph length and content, there is evidence that the paragraph is a recognizable unit of discourse. Using our observations about the example and other writings, we can construct the following formal definition:

A paragraph is a unit of discourse containing a sequence of sentences closely related in structure and meaning. The main, or subject, idea may be expressed implicitly or explicitly; in the latter case, the subject idea generally takes the form of a topic sentence. A paragraph is also characterized by a complex set of structural or formal signals that help to establish relationships between the sentences.

The rest of this chapter will extend and develop more fully this formal definition to show you how to write effective paragraphs. You might keep in mind that we will be discussing the attributes of an ideal paragraph—sometimes referred to as a textbook paragraph. As you will see, good paragraph writing can result from the struggle to attain this ideal.

THE COMPONENTS OF THE PARAGRAPH: SUBJECT, RESTRICTION, AND ILLUSTRATION

A. L. Becker recently reported on research indicating that modern paragraphs consist of three components: TOPIC (or SUBJECT), RE-STRICTION, and ILLUSTRATION.[1] Becker and his colleagues concluded that a paragraph is a unit characterized by the presence of certain kinds of "slots": one that introduces a topic, one that limits or restricts it, and a third that illustrates or develops the restricted topic.

To clarify this theory, let's briefly glance back at sentence structure as discussed in Chapters 5 and 13. In a highly generalized sense, the components of a sentence (subject, verb, and complement) can be viewed as functional slots that can be filled with many different items. Here are a few examples:

Subject	Verb	Complement
Freshmen	study	composition.
Over the fence	is	out.
Whoever believes that	is	naive.
To be or not to be	is	the question.

Like the sentence, the paragraph can be thought of as a language form, can be analyzed at a very general or abstract level, and can be schematized as having certain functional slots: SUBJECT, RESTRICTION, and ILLUSTRATION (SRI).

These correspond to the component parts of an expository paper as outlined on page 264 in Chapter 16. The INTRODUCTION of the essay, which states the subject of the paper restricted to a workable scope, corresponds to the SUBJECT and RESTRICTION slots of the paragraph; the BODY of the paper, in which the supporting and illustrative ideas are presented, is analogous to the ILLUSTRATION slot of the expository paragraph.

Expository Essay	Expository Paragraph
INTRODUCTION————	{SUBJECT
(statement of	{RESTRICTION
thesis)	
BODY————————————	ILLUSTRATION

[1] A. L. Becker, "A Tagmemic Approach to Paragraph Analysis," *College Composition and Communication* (December 1965), pp. 237–43.

Having briefly looked at how paragraph structure relates to a smaller unit, the sentence, and to a larger one, the essay, let's examine the paragraph itself. Earlier in the chapter, the paragraph was defined as a unit of discourse containing a series of sentences and having as a central, focal point a topic or main idea, generally an explicitly stated topic sentence. How then does this summarized definition relate to paragraph *form?* Let us examine the following paragraph from the middle of a *Time* magazine article about current marriage experiments:

Versions of the 50–50 marriage are cropping up all over the country. In Detroit an industrial relations specialist does all the cooking and his social worker wife keeps the family books. In Berkeley a research economist quit his job so his wife could continue working as a radio program coordinator while he takes care of their two children. A Boston lawyer feeds and dresses his children each morning because his wife often works late for the National Organization for Women.

SUBJECT
RESTRICTION

ILLUSTRATION

In this paragraph, the opening sentence is the topic sentence, establishing both the SUBJECT—"50–50 marriage"—and the RESTRICTION of the subject—"versions . . . are cropping up all over the country." As is often the case, the paragraph SUBJECT refers back to the SUBJECT of the whole essay—in this case, cooperative marriages. The RESTRICTION is directed toward the paragraph itself. In longer, more complex paragraphs, the writer may use two or three sentences to establish SUBJECT and RESTRICTION, as in this example from an article whose general subject is competitive sports:

The competitive-sport experience is unique in the way it compresses the selection process into a compact time and space. There are few areas of human endeavor that can match the Olympic trials or a professional training camp for intensity of human stress. A young athlete often must face in hours or days the kind of pressure that occurs in the life of the achievement-oriented man over several years. The potential for laying bare the personality structure of the individual is considerable. When the athlete's ego is deeply invested in sports achievement, very few of the neurotic protective mechanisms provide adequate or sustaining cover. Basically, each must face his moment of truth and live with the consequences. The pro rookie usually gets only

SUBJECT

RESTRICTION

ILLUSTRATION

three or four chances to demonstrate ability before he is sent home. What sort of personality structure supports the person who can face this blunt reinforcement of reality?

—Bruce D. Ogilvie and Thomas A. Tutko, "Sport: If You Want to Build Character Try Something Else," *Psychology Today*

The paragraph on marriage and the one on sports both provide examples in the ILLUSTRATION slot to develop the topic idea set forth in the beginning. Thus, in these examples, as in all well-constructed paragraphs, there is a discernible flow: the material in the paragraph moves from a general statement of the topic (SUBJECT) to a more specific restatement of it (RESTRICTION) and then to a concrete discussion that often includes examples (ILLUSTRATION). In traditional rhetoric a paragraph characterized by this movement from general to specific is called *deductive*. But some paragraphs reverse this order: they begin with a series of sentences containing specific material, move to a general statement about the content, and then to an indication of that statement's relationship to a more general topic. Traditionally, this order is called *inductive*. Here's an example:

Under a canopy of hickory and oak trees file people of all ages and sizes, some neatly dressed in street clothes formal enough for lunch at the Tavern, others in sloppy jeans and fringed jackets, with huge, floppy, hand-crafted leather hats on their heads, and here and there, some older women in the long gingham dresses and sunbonnets characteristic of the Appalachian farm wife. They file past booths topped with red, yellow, and blue-striped canvas and filled with the handcrafts traditional to this fair: thin, beautifully polished wooden trays, brightly colored enamelware, rainbows of corn-stalk flowers, and macramé wall hangings sharing the limbs of trees with sand-cast candles. Near the gate the loud clatter of a corn-meal grinder can be heard, interspersed in the quiet pauses between customers with the plucking of dulcimer strings and the soft crooning of mountain singers. **ILLUSTRATION** This Mardi Gras scene, greeting the newcomer to the Berea Arts and Crafts Fair, is an annual rite of spring. **RESTRICTION** This gentle orgy, one of several in the area, is a reaffirmation that traditional craftsmanship is alive and well and still flourishes in Appalachia. **SUBJECT**

This kind of inductive, or IRS, paragraph can be used effectively to break the monotony of a long series of SRI paragraphs and often provides an interesting way to structure opening or closing paragraphs.

Other possibilities for ordering these components exist. You can restrict, illustrate, and then state your subject (RIS); or you can restrict, state the general subject, and then illustrate (RSI); follow the pattern of the sports paragraph (SRI plus TRANSITION to the next paragraph); or restate the subject at the end (SRIS). Besides the SRI forms, other discernible but less frequently used paragraph types occur: PROBLEM-SOLUTION, obviously, describes a paragraph that opens with a statement of a problem and then proceeds to suggest solutions; QUESTION-ANSWER follows a similar pattern. However, the SRI form seems most favored by modern writers. But the important thing to remember about any paragraph form is not that the components are restricted to any particular order, but that you must include all components if your paragraphs are to be complete and well-developed.

The workhorse paragraphs in your expository papers — that is, the informative and explanatory paragraphs — should be especially well-developed. If any of the component slots is empty or only half-filled, your paragraphs will be anemic. However, at times, like other writers, you may deliberately delete some parts of the paragraph for specific purposes. More about these possibilities later.

PARAGRAPH DEVELOPMENT

Earlier in the chapter we mentioned that a variety of fillers can occupy the functional slots — SUBJECT, RESTRICTION, and IL-LUSTRATION — of the SRI workhorse paragraph. The nature of these fillers and their relationship to the overall structure of expository SRI paragraphs might be diagrammed like this:

SUBJECT: General subject matter of both the paragraph and the paper. May be mentioned in a transitional sentence or in a topic sentence that takes the form of a generalization, a statement of opinion, or an inference.

RESTRICTION: The main, specific point of the paragraph. May be included in the topic sentence with the SUBJECT or restated in a generalization, opinion statement, or inference.
Definition of terms used.
Clarifying materials — background, history, orientation information.

ILLUSTRATION: Supporting material to demonstrate the validity of the RESTRICTION:

Examples
Anecdotes
Statistics
Reasons
Citing of authority
Enumeration

Inadequate Paragraph Development

We suggested previously that failure to provide enough material to fill any of the slots can result in a poorly developed paragraph. Let's consider inadequate development in each of the three basic paragraph slots.

DEVELOPMENT LACKING IN THE SUBJECT SLOT

At the turn of the twentieth century the American Indians were a demoralized people. Their population had decreased because of war, disease, and famine. This led to an increased belief that the Indians were unable to take care of themselves, and, in 1849 the Bureau of Indian Affairs was established to aid the Indians and help them improve their way of life. The Bureau is now in a difficult fix: from many outside sources comes pressure to make the Indians self-sufficient. But inside the Bureau, many employees see their role as paternalistic, and their main function to show the Indians the error of their ways.

Because this transitional paragraph introduces the paper's RESTRICTION (the conflict in the Bureau of Indian Affairs), the lack of ILLUSTRATION here is acceptable. But what is needed (and never supplied anywhere in the paper) is an explanation of the SUBJECT, the Bureau of Indian Affairs. The student assumes more knowledge about this organization than a general audience could be expected to have. Four or five detailed sentences of explanation would have not only developed the paragraph but improved the effectiveness of the entire paper.

DEVELOPMENT LACKING IN THE RESTRICTION SLOT

Some members of the Congressional Committee, in investigating the Watergate incident, seemed intent on proving presidential malfeasance. They questioned the witnesses closely on the President's possible knowledge of the events, the dates of their discussions with him, and the content of memoranda received from the White House. Dean, in particular, was kept on the witness stand for five grueling days, during which the committee attempted to establish the proof of his contention that the President not only had knowledge of the cover-up, but did, in fact, give permission and guidance to it.

Here the writer in the RESTRICTION has used the legal term *malfeasance*, which many readers may not know. A brief definition would pinpoint the meaning exactly and at the same time improve the paragraph development.

DEVELOPMENT LACKING IN THE ILLUSTRATION SLOT

ILLUSTRATION is the most frequently underdeveloped paragraph slot. One of the most frustrating tasks in writing is deciding how much development is enough. How many examples are needed? How many authorities should be cited? How many statistics are necessary? These questions can be answered only in light of the writing context, the nature of the material and the needs of your audience. Generally, complex or controversial material requires a great deal of supporting or explaining illustration. If you are writing about a specialized subject to a general audience, you should also supply more information than would otherwise be necessary.

Methods of Developing the Illustration Slot

The following student paragraphs illustrate some of the devices or kinds of fillers available for developing the ILLUSTRATION section of a paragraph.

DEVELOPMENT BY EXAMPLE

Information can be obtained from school catalogues to help a student select a college. After receiving a catalogue, the student can begin to flip through it for general details. For example, in scanning one from a large university and one from a small private school, he would find several differences. Two of these are costs and academic requirements. He would notice that the cost at the state university is approximately half the cost at the private college. In academics, the student who plans to enter the state university is required to take the American College Test (ACT) while many small colleges require the Scholastic Aptitude Test (SAT) plus several achievement tests. The catalogue also provides a general description of the academic subjects offered. From glancing over these, the student is able to get a general idea of the courses that suit his intended major. A student interested in medicine or home economics could tell by the catalogue of the small college that these two areas are not stressed as much as in the large university. A large university is designed to meet the needs of all students, so the programs are extensive, offering almost every course and discipline. The smaller, private colleges are designed for a general education, even though majors are offered in traditional fields.

Compare the extensive use and explanation of examples in the last paragraph with the skimpiness of this one:

The laws concerning marijuana are out of date. They are vague and hard to enforce. They need to be strengthened in some areas and completely changed in others.

The instructor's comment beside this paragraph was, appropriately, "What laws? Be specific. Laws vary from state to state." Some of these laws cited as examples and some discussion of the *ways* they should be changed or strengthened would have improved the paragraph. Note how statistics, reasons, and use of authority serve as ILLUSTRATION in the following student examples.

DEVELOPMENT BY STATISTICS

The air pollution of this area is largely due to the recent vast increase in the local population. The 1960 census showed the population of the city of Lexington to be 62,180 persons, but this has increased to well over 100,000 according to the 1970 figures, a 46 percent increase in the city alone. Fayette, the county to which Lexington belongs, has had the same proportionate increase as the city. All this does not include the university students residing here, which adds anywhere from 15,000 to 20,000 more people to the population. This huge influx of people along with their cars, fireplaces, and other pollutants has direly affected the purity of the local air.

DEVELOPMENT BY REASONS

It should be realized that Zero Population Growth is not an immediate answer. It will take time for its effects to become apparent. As Jacoby states, there will be 300 million people living in the U.S. by A.D. 2050 if Zero Population Growth is started in 1975. But even three hundred million people polluting the earth is preferable to the population possibilities if Zero Population Growth is not realized. As for Jacoby's economic fears, a large population inhibits economic growth, rather than enhances it. The United States has always been a leader in economic growth, while having a relatively small population when compared to poorer, more crowded countries, such as China and India. Obviously, the resources of India cannot handle the large population; starvation and disease are rampant there as a result. India and China provide vivid warning signs that should be considered by opponents of Zero Population Growth before they raise their voices against it.

DEVELOPMENT BY AUTHORITY

This paragraph cites several expert sources to make its point.

The in-patient program does not have a lot of these problems, i.e., the patient's dropping out of the program, or being thrown into constant association with drug pushers. It was reported in *U.S. News and World Report* that "one weapon against today's narcotics epidemic is to *lock up* drug users while they undergo treatment." A study was done for the federal government by psychologists of the University of California at Los Angeles. The survey indicated that confinement, combined with follow-up care, may be the most effective way to treat heroin addiction. Another study on the in-patient program was done by Dr. George Vaillant, a Harvard University psychiatrist. He traced for twenty years the activities of 100 New York City heroin addicts who had been patients at the U.S. Public Health Service Hospital in Lexington, Kentucky. The study, Dr. Vaillant said, disclosed that only 3 percent of the patients released in less than nine months kept away from heroin. The abstinence rate rose to 13 percent for those who served nine months or more, and shot up to 66 percent for those confined for more than nine months followed by parole. Another psychiatrist, Dr. Bejerot, of Sweden, also agrees that the only way to cure heroin addiction is to isolate drug addicts in treatment centers away from the urban areas and keep them there until authorities judge it is safe to return them to society.

DEVELOPMENT BY ENUMERATION

A method of paragraph development that may combine all the previous ones discussed is enumeration, which involves a numerical sequence of several examples, types, causes, effects, or reasons.

There are basically two types of cheating. One is plagiarism, which involves copying someone else's work without due credit and attempting to pass it off as your own. It sometimes gets to be a little fuzzy as to what is plagiarism and what is not. (It is generally agreed by most faculty members that, among other things, commercial term papers qualify as plagiarism.) If you're unsure at any time, your best bet is to check with the instructor you are doing the work for. The other form of cheating is the better-known kind, that of copying from the person next to you on a test, quiz, or other graded work. It *includes* copying homework *if* the homework is graded *and* counted in the final grade.

Note that in this type of development very often the enumeration is overtly indicated by using cardinal numbers (one, two), ordinal numbers (first, second), or some other numbering device.

DEVELOPMENT BY ANECDOTE

This anecdote paragraph in IRS form was an opening paragraph, with the final sentence acting also as the thesis statement for the paper. (See also the discussion on the use of anecdotes in Chapters 2 and 19.)

Four boys were driving home from the Kentucky State Fair one summer night. They were all a little drunk. About three miles from their homes they were pulled over because one of the headlights was out. Immediately the police detected the alcohol and quickly called another patrol car. Then began a series of ridiculous happenings which convinced me that at least some of the rumors about police treatment of teenagers are true.

Paragraphs developed by anecdote or by narrating a case study very often lend themselves readily to the IRS form.

We have listed several ways of developing paragraphs in expository writing. Other specific methods of paragraph expansion will be discussed in Chapter 27.

Deciding about the kind and amount of development you need is frustrating. It is easy to look at another writer's solution, but the sobering knowledge remains: you must still grapple with these problems alone with your pen or typewriter. The only real advice we can offer, once you have familiarized yourself with the possible kinds of solutions, is this: you must place yourself in the role of your readers. Then ask yourself these questions as you read over what you have written:

Where did you find this out?
How do you know this?
Why is it true?
Who says so?
Can you give an example?
What led you to this conclusion?

Remember that you obviously believe and accept what you have written. But your readers need to be convinced. You can get them to accept your opinion or explanation only by fully developing the ILLUS-TRATION slot of your paragraphs. Use examples, anecdotes, statistics, reasons, authorities, or enumeration to drive your point home.

FUNCTIONAL VARIETIES OF PARAGRAPHS

As you become more aware of paragraph structure and are exposed to more college level prose, you will realize that there are several varieties of paragraphs besides the previously discussed "workhorse" paragraph, in which all the component slots—SUBJECT, RESTRICTION, and ILLUSTRATION—are filled.

As we have indicated, there are times when writers employ a short, isolated paragraph to emphasize an important point that might be buried if it appeared within a fully developed paragraph. Sometimes writers break up a lengthy enumeration paragraph into several short, simple paragraphs, each containing a reason, cause, or other enumerated item. Writers also occasionally use short paragraphs to help readers by signalling an important transition, particularly when moving from one major idea to another in a lengthy paper. The following discussion will show you when, how, and why you should employ these paragraph forms, which are characterized by the absence of material in one or two of the function slots—SUBJECT, RESTRICTION, or ILLUSTRATION.

Transitional Paragraph

A transitional paragraph has an empty ILLUSTRATION slot. It usually performs two functions: it summarizes or evaluates previous material, and it foreshadows subsequent material.

A transitional paragraph introduces both SUBJECT and RESTRICTION, as this example shows:

And that's why welfare is a women's issue. For a lot of middle-class women in this country, Women's Liberation is a matter of concern. For women on welfare it's a matter of survival.
> —Johnnie Tilman, "Welfare Is a Women's Issue," *Ms.*

The first sentence summarizes the reasons presented in preceding paragraphs. The phrase "women on welfare" in the last sentence picks up the overall SUBJECT of the article. And "a matter of survival" introduces the RESTRICTION to be discussed in the paragraphs to follow.

Sometimes a transitional paragraph takes the form of a question, which moves readers from one idea to another and has the added advantage of making readers confront the material. Two examples follow:

How real and how general does the confusion seem actually to be?
> —Joseph Wood Krutch, "Is Our Common Man Too Common?"

This one-sentence paragraph bridges the writer's preceding discussion of the subject, "confusion," and the RESTRICTION of the discussion to follow, indicated by "how real" and "how general."

In the next example a question is asked and then the writer indicates the nature of the subsequent discussion by observing that no answer has been previously sought.

What happens inside the mind of a woman struggling with such a conflict? Since it has not been properly acknowledged until now, the question has remained unaddressed.

—Vivian Gornick, "Why Women Fear Success," *Ms.*

Our final example of a transitional paragraph states a value judgment pertaining to the previous discussion and then introduces the SUBJECT of the forthcoming paragraphs, indicated by the italicized words:

But not even those wonderful clergymen who pray in behalf of Congress, expressway ribbon cuttings, urban renewal projects, and testimonial dinners would pray for a demolition derby. *The demolition derby is,* pure and simple, *a form of gladiatorial combat* for our times.

—Tom Wolfe, *The Kandy-Kolored Tangerine Flake Streamline Baby*

Emphatic Paragraphs

A paragraph of emphasis consists of short declarative sentences (sometimes only one sentence) generally intended to shock readers, elicit a gut reaction from them, or ensure that they get the message, clear and unadorned. This example from a student publication probably accomplishes all three:

The last frontier is indeed gone—but this time it's not the dinosaur or the buffalo who are in danger of extinction, it's man himself, and at his own hand.

—Linda Hanley, "Ain't No Time to Wonder Why . . .
Whoopie We're All Gonna Die," *The Spectrum*

Sometimes the emphatic paragraph effectively ends a paper, providing an impact not easily achieved by a longer paragraph. Here is an effective two-sentence final paragraph that also serves as a general summary of the student paper's SUBJECT:

The Greek system has grown up, moving from a "teenie-bopper" mentality to a seriousness of purpose more appealing to young adults. Because of all the changes in the system, more students are choosing to be Greeks rather than freaks.

Here's an example of an emphatic paragraph set apart for the purpose of making a plea. It is from a student publication and appeared in an article requesting cooperation for a student-operated bookstore:

Textbooks are a priority, but it all takes money. So the expansion into textbooks depends on *you.*

Introductory and Concluding Paragraphs

Paragraphs that serve as openers and closers of a paper have many of the formal characteristics of the other kinds of paragraphs discussed in this section. Because they present unique problems, they are treated separately and at length in Chapter 19.

Enumerative Series of Paragraphs

Frequently in papers with complex subject matter, you may have to deal with several aspects of a problem, such as a recital of the factors that contributed to United States involvement in Southeast Asia. Or you may be faced with a situation like that of one student writer whose final paragraph was reprinted above: listing the reasons for the recent renewal of interest in fraternities and sororities. If you discuss each factor or reason in detail, the resulting paragraph with its many items will be too long to be read easily. What to do? The most common device is to divide the paragraph material into a series of paragraphs. For instance, the SUBJECT and RESTRICTION can be introduced in a short paragraph that is followed by a series of paragraphs, each dealing with separate aspects of the ILLUSTRATION materials. Here's how one student, writing on America's use of the atomic bomb, solved the problem:

In spite of much information from reliable intelligence sources that Japan's defenses were rapidly weakening, President Truman listened to the pro-bomb advocates and went ahead with the bombings. There were several major factors which were considered by the pro-bomb factions as overwhelming reasons for the use of the bomb.

First paragraph in the series introduces SUBJECT and RESTRICTION

The first was that the entire research and building projects had been geared toward their eventual use. [The student supports this *factor* in the rest of the paragraph.]

Second paragraph in the series: ILLUSTRATION 1

The second factor was the cost in money and resources which the production of the bombs had required. [The rest of the paragraph develops this *factor*.]

Third paragraph in the series: ILLUSTRATION 2

In this section of the book we have explained some of the ways in which the various paragraph forms can be used. Paragraphs in which only one or two of the function slots are filled can serve important rhetorical functions—to provide a bridge from one idea to another, to emphasize an important point, to enumerate a list of items, to summarize, or to introduce a new aspect of the paper.

ASSIGNMENTS

For Discussion

(1) Find the SUBJECT – RESTRICTION–ILLUSTRATION partitions in the following student paragraph. What devices has the student used in developing the paragraph? Does he convince you that his opinion is valid?

WHO'S BOSS?

Men are more capable for being the head of a household than women. As men are stronger than women it is only right that the responsibility of such a position should be upon their shoulders. A man should be the dominant influence of the family and have the final word on important matters. A man is less timid than a woman and as it takes a certain amount of boldness to face any authoritative job, a man's brisk manner is called for. A man is better able to cope with the many business matters essential to the efficiently run home. In business details a man has the upper hand due to a working knowledge of such things as mortgages, banking procedures, insurance premiums and numerous other items in business. A man is the best decision maker because he is less gullible, doesn't get hysterical, or do things rashly as women do. A man shows more protective qualities towards his family and home and is concerned with its well-being as a whole. If back in pioneer days a woman took matters into her own hands and set herself up over her husband as head of the household, she might suddenly find herself homeless, because the husband had built the house and it was rightly his to be boss in. The pioneer wife was a woman who knew she was lucky to have a roof over her head and was content to keep house and not to be the head of it. Although there are exceptions the usual situation finds that the man is the head of the household and until the reverse becomes true, this proves man is the better boss.

2   Do the weaknesses inherent in the following student paragraph result from faulty paragraph organization, weak development, or both? What kinds of materials could the writer have used to develop his ideas?

One might say our ambition has been hampered by the idol of security. Security has become our ultimate goal. Our existence revolves around our new idol and gives us nothing more than a stable job and group security. We conform to group standards and find ourselves being expressed through a group rather than individually. Everything is thought out and laid before us so no individual mental exertion is necessary.

3 Identify the organizational technique used in each of the following paragraphs. Is it SRI, IRS, SRIS—or is one slot missing? Can you determine the subject of each paragraph's essay? Are they paragraphs of development or transition?

a In the past two decades, however, a combination of new technology and sociopolitical changes has overturned the classic balance of privacy in the United States. On the technological front, microminiaturized bugs, television monitors, and devices capable of penetrating solid surfaces to listen or photograph have dissolved the physical barriers of walls and doors. Polygraph devices to measure emotional states have been improved as a result of space research, and increased use has been made of personality tests for personnel selection. The development of electronic computers and long-distance communication networks has made it possible to collect, store, and process far more information about an individual's life and transactions than was practical in the era of typewriter and file cabinet.

—Alan F. Westin, "Privacy"

b The sinister fact is not that most citizens are taking drugs; people have always done that, although never as many or as much. The real terror implicit in our current drug culture is that so many, incredulous about official pronouncements, are experimenting, sometimes lethally, with very dangerous ones.

—Joel Fort, "The Drug Explosion," *Playboy*

c For a time, the television industry comforted itself with the theory that children listened to children's programs and that, if by any chance they saw programs for adults, violence would serve as a safety valve, offering a harmless outlet for pent-up aggressions: the more violence on the screen, the less in life. Alas, this turns out not to be necessarily so. As Dr. Wilbur Schramm, director of the Institute of Communication Research at Stanford has reported, children, even in the early elementary school years, view more programs designed for adults than for themselves; "above all, they prefer the more violent type of adult program including the Western, the adventure program, and the crime drama." Experiments show that such programs, far from serving as safety valves for aggression, attract children with high levels of aggression and stimulate them to seek overt means of acting out their aggressions. Evidence suggests that these programs work the same incitement on adults. And televiolence does more than condition emotion and behavior. It also may attenuate people's sense of reality. Men murdered on the television screen ordinarily spring to life after the episode is over: all death is therefore diminished. A child asked a man last June where he was headed in his car. "To Washington," he said. "Why?" he asked. "To attend the funeral of Senator Kennedy." The child said, "Oh yeah—they shot him again." And such shooting may well condition the manner in which people approach the perplexities of existence. On television the hero too glibly resolves his problems by shooting somebody. The *Gunsmoke* ethos, however, is not necessarily the best way to deal with human or social complexity. It is hardly compatible with any kind of humane or libertarian democracy.

—Arthur M. Schlesinger, Jr., *Violence: America in the Sixties*

d What about the interactions among social organizations, world order, and human nature?

—Elisabeth Mann Borgese, "Human Nature Is Still Evolving"

For Writing

1 Rewrite the following paragraph, developing it by adding detailed information that would make the statements apply to your own college's catalogue.

The Catalog is a fantastic collection of information that is at least one year old and is organized to confuse and bore almost everyone. The course descriptions are occasionally partially accurate. The stated requirements are not up to date and you should check with your advisor for changes (practically every undergraduate college in the University changed its requirements in some way during the past year and NONE of this is reflected in the Catalog).

2 Write a well-developed paragraph, using SRI form, agreeing or disagreeing with the paragraph in exercise 3 in the Discussion section.
3 Choose a topic about which you have some opinion. Develop a topic sentence and write two paragraphs, using the same topic sentence and supporting material—one in SRI form and the other in IRS form.

18

The Movement of the Expository Paragraph

THE INTERNAL STRUCTURE OF THE PARAGRAPH

An architect must consider not only the external shapes, colors, and relationships that make a building attractive but also the internal features that make it comfortable, pleasant, and functional. Similarly, writers should be aware not only of the basic external form of the paragraph but also of the internal organization, particularly the direction of movement or modification within the paragraph and the part played by the relationships between sentences.

Francis Christensen, whose concept of levels of generality in sentences was discussed in Chapter 12, sees the paragraph as a series of sentences that move from general to specific — from one level of generality to another — in much the same way that sentence modifiers do. In our discussion of sentence sequence in Chapter 12, we outlined cumulative sentences with modifiers in *coordinate* relationship as follows:

1 The swallows fed on insects, (main clause)
  2 swooping down at breathtaking speeds, (sentence modifier)
  2 wheeling back to dizzying heights, (sentence modifier)
  2 and soaring aloft for the next dive. (sentence modifier)

Modifiers occur in *subordinate* relationship in sentences like:

1 The swallows fed on insects, (main clause)
  2 swooping down at breathtaking speeds (sentence modifier)
   3 that dazzled the watchers (modifier)
    4 — the envious humans below. (modifier)

As you remember, both these sequences can be combined in a single sentence—resulting in a mixed sequence.

This principle can also be applied to paragraph structure, since sentences in a paragraph exhibit relationships to one another similar to those that sentence modifiers have. We can analyze paragraphs by the same method used earlier to analyze sentences. The number 1 signifies the most general level in the paragraph (usually the topic sentence); 2 less general; 3 even less; and so on. Just as a sentence modifier labeled 2 meant that it modified the main clause (1), so too, sentences at level 2 in a sense "modify" the main idea or topic sentence of a paragraph. Let's look at the various kinds of paragraph structures.

Coordinate Sequence

Paragraphs in coordinate sequences usually have only two levels of generality. Let's look at a paragraph by a professional writer.

1 The evil that has produced what we now call the "environmental crisis" is arrogance or, to use the ancient Greek term that is more accurate, *hubris,* the assumption by men of divine prerogatives.

 2(a) It is the willingness to use more power than one can control.

 2(b) It is the ignorant use of power.

 2(c) It is a sin the consequences of which are invariably visited upon the descendants of the sinner, as the Greek myths tell us over and over again.

 2(d) It is the reason why humility and modesty and self-restraint and temperance have been recognized as essential virtues through all of human history.

 2(e) The man who assumes and uses the powers of the gods must in his ignorance inevitably reduce the common fund of life and fortune on which his children will have to live.

        —Wendell Berry, *The Unforeseen Wilderness*

The first sentence is the topic sentence for the paragraph and contains both SUBJECT ("environmental crisis") and RESTRICTION ("arrogance or . . . *hubris*") and is the most general statement in the paragraph. The subsequent series of sentences, even though they are all coordinate to one another—that is, at approximately the same level of generality—are less general than the topic sentence is and together serve as ILLUSTRATION. Berry's topic sentence introduces the idea of *hubris;* the subsequent sentences pinpoint fairly specific qualities of *hubris.* Note, too, that none of the sentences numbered 2 is dependent upon any of the others. Deletion of any one of them would not seriously impair the meaning or logical arrangement of the paragraph, but only thin it out. Also, there is a certain amount of flexibility in the order. 2(a) and 2(b) could easily be reversed, as could 2(c) and 2(d), without changing the meaning or tampering too seriously with the climactic effect of the series. As you can see, the writer frequently has a choice in the internal arrangement of the coordinate paragraph.

A striking characteristic of this and many other coordinate paragraphs is the parallel structure used for the "modifying" sentences, here four beginning with "It is . . . ." However, in paragraphs as in sentences, writers do not utilize this rhetorical technique simply for aesthetic effect, but to help the reader respond to the relationships that the writer sets up. Parallelism of structure is one of the devices used by good writers to convey meaning accurately.

Experienced writers apparently use coordinate-sequence paragraphs for rather limited purposes. In Wendell Berry's book we found only two paragraphs demonstrating this form; both were used as this one is, to drive home a point. However, writers occasionally use this paragraph arrangement in defining a complex or controversial idea, or in a concluding paragraph when they wish to summarize their points. Unfortunately, the coordinate sequence is not always used so skillfully in student papers, as this student example demonstrates:

1   There is certainly no hobby more intriguing than that of pyrotechnics.
    2(a)   One reason for its intrigue is that the work is creative and requires extensive use of the imagination.
    2(b)   In few other hobbies does one witness the thrilling beauty and power which the pyrotechnist can create singlehandedly.
    2(c)   In addition, one derives a sense of achievement in seeing an instrument which he has created function as planned.

The choice of coordinate sequence here is unfortunate. The paragraph is thin and lacks conviction because each of the level 2 sentences needs further development. For example, the writer should have discussed in at least one more sentence *why* pyrotechnics is creative and requires extensive use of the imagination. Similarly 2(b) and 2(c) need support from subordinate-sequence sentences. In addition, the level of generality in 2(b) is confusing. Because it contains the word *create*, the reader is likely to link the sentence to 2(a) with its *creative*, thus suggesting a subordinate relationship between the two. However, the student writer evidently regarded sentence 2(b) as coordinate and made it serve as the second of three reasons.

Unless the student writer deliberately avoided parallel structure for some reason that the rest of the paper might make obvious, he might have revised the paragraph using parallelism to identify the coordinate relationship of the ideas. One way to accomplish this is by enumeration or use of a numbered sequence ("One reason . . . Another reason . . . A third reason . . . "). Another device is to begin each sentence in the same way, like this:

1   There is certainly no hobby more intriguing than that of pyro-
      technics.
2(a) It requires creativity and extensive use of the imagination.
2(b) It demands a knowledge of explosives and how to utilize
      them to blend color, light, and noise effectively.
2(c) It entails not only conceiving but also producing an in-
      strument that functions as planned.

This revised paragraph is clearer to readers, but it is still anemic, lacking the subordinate sequence of sentences that would give it power and conviction.

Subordinate Sequence

A paragraph in subordinate sequence contains sentences at dimin-ishing levels of generality, each dependent upon the preceding one for meaning. Here is a paragraph containing such a sequence:

1 The tolerant attitude of the state government in Pennsylvania has helped
   to guarantee the continued presence of the Amish community at Lancaster.
   2 The state constitution, modeled after Penn's Articles, ensures that no
      religious practice of the Amish or any other sect will be interfered
      with.
      3 Although there is a national law which states that a child must
         attend school until the age of 16, Pennsylvania tends to favor its
         state law where the Amish children are concerned.
         4 Consequently, in Pennsylvania, the Amish are permitted their
            own schools, usually taught by one of their own sect, where at-
            tendance is anything but mandatory.
            5 When the children are not needed on the farm, they are
               sent to school to learn enough reading to be able to read
               the Holy Bible, enough writing to be able to write their
               names, and enough arithmetic to be able to keep household
               and farm accounts.
               6 This is in accordance with the Amish belief that the only
                  real education their children need is in the ways of God
                  and of the sect and this is best discovered in the ways of
                  keeping a house and working a farm.
                  7 These things are best taught at home.

Here we are concentrating on the meaning relationships; later in the chapter we will discuss the structural, or formal, devices of paragraph unity. Note, however, that despite the differences in the internal organization of these two sequence types, both exhibit the same overall form: both are SRI paragraphs. In the example of subordinate sequence, the first sentence introduces the SUBJECT ("tolerant attitude"); the second states the RESTRICTION (Pennsylvania follows state rather than federal law); and the remaining sentences constitute a detailed ILLUSTRATION. Note, too, that unlike the Berry example, deleting a sentence or reordering the levels here would interfere with meaning and logical relationships.

Paragraphs in subordinate sequence are especially useful for the full development of a single idea. But what of the many times when you want to write about a fairly complex idea or to show the relationship between two ideas? Obviously a more complex paragraph organization would be necessary. Writers solve this problem by mixing the two sequences within a single paragraph.

Mixed Sequence

Consider this student paragraph:

1 In general, men share the same attitude about sex.
  2 For men, sex is only an animalistic drive.
    3 Man looks for sex to ease his animal nature.
  2 Man loves to dominate woman and uses sex to accomplish this.
    3 He experiences a superior feeling when he engages in the sex act.
      4 The phrases "She melted in my arms," or "She was like a puppet on a string," or "I wore her out" emphasize the way in which a man uses a woman to build up his own ego.
      4 It is common knowledge that when a man does "conquer" a woman, he tends to boast about his "victorious campaign."
        5 The act itself sometimes doesn't give a man enough of a superior feeling, so he must tell others about his venture.
        6 In this way, he makes up for any lost feeling of superiority by courting the envy of his male counterparts.

The sentence numbers indicate how the internal organization of this paragraph combines coordination and subordination. Note also that here we have a more complex version of the SRI paragraph, with the writer dividing the RESTRICTION into two sentences and two segments of the paragraph (marked by level 2) and providing some ILLUSTRATION for each. Our example is fairly simple, but you should realize that mixed sequences can become very complex.

We suggest that you try your hand at analyzing some of the paragraphs in the exercises at the end of the chapter. However, the purpose of the discussion and the exercises is not to instruct you how to analyze other people's paragraphs, but to teach you how to perceive the inner workings of the paragraph so that you can improve your own. This understanding of paragraph structure can help you to see that paragraphs are not made up of randomly ordered sentences, but are structures containing sentences clustered and arranged according to their contextual and rhetorical relations to one another and to a central unifying idea, a subject. The levels of generality that a writer assigns to sentences help to maintain the integrity and unity of the paragraph as a rhetorical form.

PARAGRAPH UNITY

We have discussed the roles of both contextual meaning and levels of generality in establishing paragraph unity—the sense of cohesiveness necessary to identify a unit of discourse as a paragraph. Both of these center more on the meaning of the content than on the structure (although it is sometimes very difficult to separate the two). However, we hinted that there are other structural, or formal, devices of paragraph unity that readers respond to, sometimes without consciously realizing it. Parallel structure is certainly one clue to paragraph unity, but there are others. Before categorizing these formal paragraph signals, we would like you to try a simple experiment: try to reconstruct the following paragraph as the student writer originally wrote it, placing the scrambled sentences in proper order. (One hint: the paragraph is in SRI form with sentences arranged in mixed sequence.)

1. This erosion removes precious topsoil, making the ground unfit for anything to grow—not rabbit's tobacco, not sassafras, not corn, not beans.
2. But now the pasture is filled with boulders from the strip mine up the hill, and never again will cattle graze nor meadow birds nest there.
3. I have seen creeping spoil banks topple towering oak trees and cover the lush shrubs and vines carpeting the ground.
4. The land dies.
5. Finally, I know of a pasture where partridges once nested after the cattle were removed.
6. Not only the waterways but the land itself has been a victim of strip mining.
7. And because there is no ground cover, erosion occurs.
8. Rabbits also lived there, as did many other ground creatures.

9.   Erosion, in the form of monstrous landslides, resulting from locating strip mines close to highways, blocks the roads and makes it impossible for school children and workers to reach their destinations.

10.   Because the trees are toppled, squirrels, birds, and possums can't nest there and the habitats of the wildlife are crowded; more squirrels must nest in fewer trees.

You should not have had too much trouble unscrambling this paragraph. Except in sentence 4, the student writer has provided you with many formal signals. Here is the original paragraph with the signals marked to show how the various elements are linked to chain the sentences together.

6 Not only the waterways but the land itself has been a victim of strip mining. **3** I have seen creeping spoil banks topple towering oak trees and cover the lush shrubs and vines carpeting the ground. **10** Because the trees are toppled, squirrels, birds, and possums can't nest there and the habitats of the wildlife are crowded; more squirrels must nest in fewer trees. **7** And because there is no ground cover, erosion occurs. **1** This erosion removes precious topsoil, making the ground unfit for anything to grow — not rabbit's tobacco, not sassafras, not corn, not beans. **4** The land dies. **9** Erosion, in the form of monstrous land slides, resulting from locating strip mines close to highways, blocks the roads and makes it impossible for school children and workers to reach their destinations. **5** Finally, I know of a pasture where partridges once nested after the cattle were removed. **8** Rabbits also lived there, as did many other ground creatures. **2** But now the pasture is filled with boulders from the strip mine up the hill, and never again will cattle graze nor meadow birds nest there.

Note that the circled words are synonyms for or refer in some way to *land* in the topic sentence; these are then woven throughout the paragraph, creating a unifying chain. Rectangles enclose words that tie together clusters of sentences having significant relationships: *erosion* in 7 to *erosion* in 1 to *erosion* in 9, for example. Both circles and rectangles indicate a general class of paragraph unity signals that use words generally equivalent or related in meaning. We will refer to these signals as *meaning links*.

The underlined words in the student paragraph do not function as vehicles of meaning. Instead, they provide transition from one idea to another (*not only . . . but, and*) or allow the reader to move from one relationship to another (*because, also*). Other underlined words act as signals of time or place: *there, now, never again, finally.*

In summary, structural, or formal, signals of paragraph unity can be classified thus:

1. Meaning links.
   Series of words having equivalent meaning: synonyms, pronouns, and the demonstratives (*this, these, that, those*) are most common.
2. Transitional words.
   a. Subordinate conjunctions such as *because, if, when, thus, although.*
   b. Coordinate conjunctions—*and, or, either . . . or* are most common.
   c. Transitional phrases or adverbials such as *furthermore, for example, in other words, on the other hand.*
3. Signals of time or place.
   a. Time: *now, then, later, sooner, previously.* Also prepositional phrases such as *at that time, in the past, in the future, last week.*
   b. Place: *Here* and *there.* Also hundreds of prepositional phrases such as *over the hill, in that place, outside the window.*
4. Verb sequences.
   We did not discuss this in reference to the student example, but frequently a shift in verb tense is a signal that a new paragraph is needed. In our sample paragraph (except where the student writes about the past condition of the meadow), all the verbs or auxiliaries of the main clauses are marked for present tense: "*has* been," "*is,*" "*blocks.*" But suppose the student had added this sentence at the end of the paragraph: "Strip mining *was* outlawed in Illinois." You as the reader would have immediately responded as much to the shift to past tense as to the abrupt shift in content; you would have been disturbed that the writer included this statement as part of the paragraph. This may help to explain why English professors react to this in your papers by writing "tense shift" in blood in the margins of your papers.

The omission or skimpy use of these signals is an easy trap for any writer to fall into, but it is especially hazardous for inexperienced writers. That is because, as you write, you are mentally aware of all the relationships, so you may not feel compelled to supply helpful signals to your reader. But this is a part of your commitment to your readers. You have an obligation to help them quickly discern your meaning, unhindered by the illogic and the fuzzy references that so often result from omitting these signals.

Writing unified paragraphs, then, is essentially a matter of communication, and effective communication can result only from sending out and receiving clear signals. If you, the writer, provide the proper signals, readers should get the message loud and clear.

ASSIGNMENTS

For Discussion

1 Following is a paragraph in which the sequence of sentences has been scrambled. Try to put it back together as the student wrote it. State what form the paragraph takes (SRI, IRS, or whatever) and indicate its levels of generality. If you find that, like Humpty-Dumpty, it can't be put together again, analyze the weaknesses of the paragraph that prevent the reassembly.

1   The members of the group all go to a designated place and sit in a circle around the fire.

2   Each member then partakes of the peyote and goes through his "experience."

3   These ceremonies always follow a set pattern.

4   This was described in a brief statement on how the ceremony is set up.

5   Peyotists do not deviate from this pattern, unless absolutely needed, and then only rarely.

6   He starts the group through by chanting songs and prayers to Mescalito, who is the god of peyotism.

7   These experiences or "trips," as the modern drug culture terms them, are how a peyotist learns from his religion.

8   There is a leader to guide the group through the ceremony.

9   The ceremony usually breaks up in the morning when the ceremonial feast is eaten.

2 What sentence sequence does each of the following three paragraphs exhibit—coordinate, subordinate, or mixed?

a Adopting the Korean pattern of waging war without declaring it, of nominating only a few to do the killing while the rest stayed home to make a killing, we corrupted a whole generation. Young men were openly counseled in ways to beat the system; innumerable college men took education courses so they could become elementary-school teachers when they had no vocation for such work but only a desire to evade the draft. The poor went to war and the rich stayed home. Ghetto youths were sent to Vietnam while members of professional athletic teams were provided with escape hatches. Young men joined the National Guard to avoid service overseas, and girls were coached on how to marry quickly and become pregnant even more quickly so as to help their men beat an evil system.

— New York Times Magazine

b However, one important aspect of the college that is often considered early in the planning stage is the particular college's general reputation. This general reputation is made up of the picture one sees of the college in academics, sports, and social life. The image that is thus presented of what the school is like is quite often a prerequisite to trying to find out more about the college. For example, perhaps a young man in junior high school read an article in a sports magazine about the outstanding athletic program at college "X." After reading it, he decided that this school was one that interested him. So, he then tried to learn about other aspects of the college. In a similar manner, what a student has read or heard about a school's academic, athletic, or social life can be the initial factor in his beginning to select a college.

c   The grading system also contains penalties and rewards, but that's what makes people tick. Would any student write a term paper, read a textbook, or attend a lecture in a field outside his interest if he were not motivated by grades? Because studying and learning are hard work, students need penalties and rewards. Of course, this results in pressure. Certainly, this produces competition. But without them, few people would strive to let their learning exceed their intellectual reach. Oh yes, there are a few students who are highly self-motivated and are genuinely interested in learning. But most students would rather see a basketball game, rap in the Grill, or watch a movie. Let's face it—that's why we need the present grading system. Anything else would result in a lowering of the standards and a fifth-rate university.

3   Classify the various kinds of focusing signals—meaning links, transitional words, signals of time or place—in the three paragraphs in exercise 2.

For Writing

1   Choose three paragraphs that you've recently written and expand them, experimenting with coordinate, subordinate, and mixed sentence sequences.

2   Write a paragraph-length extended definition of the word *scholar,* using the following distinctive features:

  a   a seeker of truth and knowledge
  b   a possessor of an insatiable curiosity
  c   a practitioner of critical thinking
  d   a citizen of the world of discovery

First write the paragraph in coordinate sequence. Then add descriptive details to each distinctive feature, creating a mixed sequence. Then check to see if parallel structure helps the reader to determine the levels of generality. Last, revise for effective use of the structural signals listed on page 293.

19

Introductions and Conclusions in Expository Writing

ON WRITING INTRODUCTIONS

Starting papers usually seems as impossible as unscrambling eggs. That's why many people postpone writing until the deadline is about to strangle them. But once you perceive what options are available and what pattern you will follow, writing the opening paragraph should not be so nerve-wracking.

Although long articles and term papers may call for introductions of several paragraphs, short papers usually require only a one-paragraph introduction. Yet these introductory four or five sentences are so exasperatingly painful to write that some teachers suggest that you postpone the torture, waiting until you've completed your paper. You may do this if you're in a bind about getting started. As for us, we've always liked the Red Queen's advice in *Alice in Wonderland:* "Begin at the beginning, keep on going until you get to the end, and then stop." We've found that skipping the opening paragraph and returning to it later is like starting a meal with dessert and eating the main course afterward.

What complicates the introduction are the decisions required and the challenges posed. Here are some of the questions you usually have to consider:

1. How can I get my readers' attention?
2. How can I interest my readers?
3. How should I state my thesis?
4. Should I state the plan of my paper?

5. What voice should I employ?
6. What point of view should I use?

Let's tackle these one by one.

How Can I Get My Readers' Attention?

The opening sentence is somewhat like the introductory "tease" in a television commercial: both hope to attract people's attention so they will not turn away. Although advertising writers may rely on such standard visual devices as ravishing girls, virile athletes, appealing children, or breathtaking scenery, writers have none of these options. But they have others. By considering these other choices, you may find one that strikes your fancy if your own inspiration fails. Here are some possible attention-getting approaches, with examples about graduate teaching assistants:

1. A controversial statement

    Some students swear that graduate teaching assistants are inexperienced, ignorant, and uninteresting; others insist that they are enthusiastic, friendly, and inspiring.

2. An element of surprise

    That slightly older dude, garbed in jeans and sweatshirt, sometimes with beard, often with pipe, nearly always with a sack of books, who strides in late the first day of freshman class, is neither student nor professor but a peculiar species known as a graduate teaching assistant.

3. A note of contradiction

    Graduate teaching assistants are neither fish nor fowl, neither completely students nor teachers, neither really graduates nor assistants.

4. A short, dramatic statement

    Beware of graduate teaching assistants.

5. The use of statistics

    Most of the two million freshmen entering colleges and universities this fall will be instructed by graduate teaching assistants.

6. A figure of speech (simile or metaphor)

    A graduate teaching assistant is like a pilot on a new route: each is capable, but each is unfamiliar with the course.

7. The use of a quotation

> "Although they are inexperienced, most graduate teaching assistants are generally effective instructors because they relate well to their students," state the authors of *The Writing Commitment*.[1] [In a footnote you would cite the source from which you took this quotation. See the discussion of footnotes in Chapter 33.]

8. A reference to a current event

> The recent debate in the freshman dorm about graduate teaching assistants was almost as heated as the one at the United Nations about the Middle East.

9. Proof of your authority

> Having had seven graduate teaching assistants in my first two semesters at college, I feel well qualified to discuss their strengths and weaknesses.

These nine openings may not all be appropriate for your subject, your readers, or the occasion of your paper, but they do suggest some possibilities. If not, here are three others to consider: the rhetorical question, the definition, and the anecdote.

We separated these three from the others because they require some discussion. The *rhetorical question* has been employed so frequently that many sophisticated readers resent it as condescending or trite. Our advice is to use it only in a pinch, and then not as a single question but as a series. The danger with the single question is that it represents a desperate gamble. If readers reply "Yes" to the question, you've got them; but if "No," you've lost them. Here's what we mean:

> Have you ever thought about what it would be like to have a graduate teaching assistant for an instructor?

Because most readers haven't thought about this—and don't see any reason why they should—they might discard the paper instead of reading further. With a series of questions, however, the odds on hooking your readers' interest increase:

> Should you sign up for a course taught by a graduate teaching assistant? How effective are they? How do they grade? Are they interested in their students? Do they have time to see students in conferences?

The multiquestion approach may not always succeed, but the chances that it will are greater.

Another possible opening involves the *definition*. Here, too, some words of caution. If we had a dime for every paper we've read that began with "According to Webster," we could retire to Hawaii tomorrow. Definitions are deadly unless you're addressing highly educated readers or unless the subject lends itself to an interesting use of a definition. For example:

> Patriotism is generally defined as love of country, but to Samuel Johnson it was "the last refuge of scoundrels."

> The dictionary definition of a graduate teaching assistant as "a graduate student with part-time complete or partial college teaching responsibilities" says a lot but explains little.

The third possible opening that warrants a word of caution is the *anecdote*. Most readers enjoy jokes and short narratives, but these are effective only when they relate to the subject being discussed. In other words, the point of the anecdote must be closely related to the thesis of the paper. After-dinner speakers often violate this injunction with their "While I was coming to this meeting tonight . . . ." But after-dinner speakers have a captive audience. You don't.

Up to this point we've been discussing ways to write an attention-getting introduction. Now we'd like to mention what not to do. Here are some ways to turn readers off:

1. The apology

> Although I don't know much about graduate teaching assistants, I thought that I'd write a paper about them.

(Says the reader, "You may write it, but I'm not about to read it.")

2. The complaint

> I started thinking about this paper after dinner and couldn't come up with an interesting subject because we were told that we could write about anything, but I finally decided to discuss graduate teaching assistants for lack of something else.

(Says the reader, "Dullsville. I'll skip this one.")

3. The platitude

> Some graduate teaching assistants are good and some graduate teaching assistants are bad.

(Says the reader, "Some papers are good but this one sounds bad.")

4. The reference to the title

> The title of this paper, "Graduate Teaching Assistants," indicates

that it is concerned with graduate students who are teaching in college while also pursuing their own graduate work.

(Says the reader, "So what else is new? Why waste time reading this?")

And there you have it—what to do and what not to do to gain the attention of readers. Do you always have to be concerned with getting their attention? No; there are some occasions when you can assume that people will be highly motivated to read what you've written. But generally you'd be wiser not to take your readers, even your instructor, for granted.

How Can I Interest My Readers?

Let's assume that you've written that horrendously difficult first sentence or so and are confident that it will get your readers' attention. Now to develop readers' interest in your subject. This requires answering these questions: Why is my subject important? Why should people read about it? How will it benefit them?

In our earlier discussion about selecting an interesting subject, we talked about various appeals to motivate people. You may assume, for example, that most people would like to save time, effort, or money; to improve their knowledge, looks, and health; and to gain prestige, praise, and popularity. Does your subject appeal to any of these motivations? Or, can you suggest why a reasonably intelligent person should be concerned about it? For instance, not everyone is interested in cats, but most readers have developed a fondness for some pet at some time in their lives. You can build on this interest in writing about cats.

But you must keep your specific readers clearly in mind. If you were writing about graduate teaching assistants to a general audience of taxpayers, you would appeal to their curiosity in one way; to parents, in another; to entering college students, in a third. Unless you have your readers' interests at heart, you may be unable to attract their minds.

How Should I State My Thesis?

In Chapter 16, we discussed the thesis statement and suggested how to formulate it. But we did not discuss specifically where to place it in the paper or how to introduce it. We shall deal with these matters here.

As we mentioned, the formal statement of thesis is usually appropriate only in scientific or formal papers, such as research reports or dissertations. It is generally signalled by the words *subject* or *purpose:*

It is the purpose of this paper . . .

The subject that I plan to discuss . . .

Because your purpose generally is to treat the subject less formally, the thesis should be stated or implied without such explicit signals.

Next, where should it appear? Many students state it as the first sentence as if it were too hot to hold on to longer. But the introduction should function to introduce a subject graciously, not to dump it on readers. You probably wouldn't introduce two friends to one another by simply saying, "Mary Anderson, I want you to meet Fred Clarkson" and then leave them alone. You'd undoubtedly mention their mutual acquaintances or interests to indicate why they should enjoy knowing each other. Similarly, you should introduce your thesis to readers instead of merely announcing it in your opening sentence and leaving it practically alone in a skimpy paragraph.

You might conceive of an introduction as following the lines of a gaff, an iron hook with a handle that is used to land large fish.

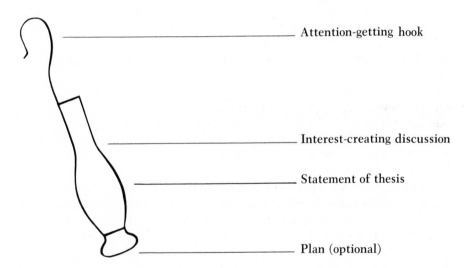

———————————————— Attention-getting hook

———————————————— Interest-creating discussion

———————————————— Statement of thesis

———————————————— Plan (optional)

By following this pattern, you start with a general indication of the subject and then zero in on the thesis. Here's the gaff in action:

DON'T LET THEM FOOL YOU!

Television commercials are often as irritating as an unanswered ringing telephone. Although any of the millions of viewers can turn off the blasting advertisements for deodorants, detergents, denture

     Attention:
figure of speech

adhesives, girdles, or hair washes, dyes, and lo-   Interest: appeal
tions, most people endure them or flee to the re-   to mutual dislike;
frigerator for a snack. If commercials were only   then to pocketbook
annoying, perhaps serious complaints could not be
registered. But what is wrong affects not people's
taste but their pocketbooks. *Television commercials*   Thesis
misrepresent products by employing deceptive devices.

Should I State the Plan of My Paper?

Particularly in writing a long paper or one with a complicated organizational plan, you would be wise to indicate the plan to your readers. This practice is helpful because the plan serves as a road map, showing readers where you are taking them. For example, the following sentence could be added to the preceding example:

These commercials rely on trick photography, misleading experiments, and false testimonials.

This statement helpfully notifies readers that your paper will deal with these particular subtopics and in the order announced. Although most readers welcome such help in long or complicated papers, it is usually unnecessary in short ones. Let common sense be your guide.

What Voice Should I Employ?

Occasionally you're introduced to a stranger: a friend of a friend, an acquaintance of your parents, a teacher, or the parents of the person you are dating. Usually you adapt your manner to theirs: if they are polite, reserved, and detached, then you are too. But in writing, you call the shots. You must establish in the first paragraph, and to some extent in the first sentence, the voice that sets up the relationship between you, your subject, and your readers. We've already talked about this subject of voice several times, pointing out how it depends on numerous factors such as choice of words, sentence structure, verb form, and pronoun choice. What is important to realize now is that in the introduction you will need to decide *which* voice to use. For example, the following opening sentences are arranged in the order of increasing formality. Note how each launches readers into the subject in a slightly different way.

1. So you're getting ready to go on vacation.
2. If you want to make a clean getaway to your vacation hideaway, here is a way to do it.
3. The best-laid vacation plans need not go astray.

4. Before you go on vacation, you should spend some time planning.

5. Most people can't wait to go on vacation.

6. Though the daily activities of people in various stages of life may differ, nearly all engage in the ritual of relief and relaxation known as a vacation.

7. It is my opinion that people must not only plan their vacation but plan what must be done before they leave.

8. One should be aware that preparations for departure on a holiday may assume an importance proportionate to the deliberations for the holiday itself.

Whichever voice you choose, it must be maintained throughout your paper. Decisions, decisions—but that's what writing is all about. And while you may sweat over a few initial sentences, trying to establish just the appropriate voice, remember the plight of the great historian Edward Gibbon, who three times rewrote the entire lengthy first chapter of his classic work, *The Decline and Fall of the Roman Empire,* searching for just the proper tone of voice to introduce readers to his monumental study.

What Point of View Should I Use?

In Chapter 2 we indicated that you have several choices of point of view in narrative writing. In expository writing you have three possibilities—first, second, or third person pronouns and their noun antecedents.

FIRST PERSON—*I*

Generally, the first person *I* or *we* strikes a personal, intimate note, which is especially appropriate when your experience lends authority or credibility to what you are saying about the subject. If your parents are divorced and you are writing about the effects of divorce on children, then by all means use *I* in referring to your own reactions. Take care, however, because, as Chapter 7 pointed out, one *I* can lead to many *I*'s, distracting and annoying readers, who may consider you egotistical or turn away from the subject to speculate about you, the writer. To avoid *I*, some students resort to such bloated substitutes as "your reporter" or "the author of this article," which are usually more distracting. There is nothing wrong with using *I*. If you choose it, stick with it—but be temperate.

Sometimes *I* may be employed less personally, as when you present yourself as representative of a group:

Like other college students, I am concerned about the scarcity of jobs.

Here and in similar situations, you are writing as a member of a group, not as a unique person. You may be tempted to slip into *we* on these occasions, but remember that the use of *we* instead of *I* in a personal context is affected:

> Sitting in our room, we stared at the walls, looking for a subject for our paper.

This editorial *we* is acceptable in editorials, where it usually represents the views of the editors, but it should be avoided elsewhere, particularly in situations where it may establish a condescending tone. Just remember the teacher who always annoyed you by saying, "We are going to do our arithmetic homework" or the nurse who insisted, "We will take our medicine now."

These warnings do not mean that *we* is out. It can be perfectly proper and effective when used for two major purposes—to establish writer-reader togetherness:

> We all struggle in writing the first sentence of a paper.

and to refer to an actual group:

> As new freshmen on campus, bewildered by the strange buildings, dazed by the hordes of students, and confused by new routines, we felt lost and unimportant.

The "togetherness" *we* establishes a natural, friendly relationship. The "group" *we* is less personal but still far from formal. Occasionally, a third situation calling for *we* arises: when two or more writers are collaborating—as we are so well aware in this book.

SECOND PERSON—*YOU*

The second person *you* is highly controversial. As you may know, many instructors forbid students to use it in their papers. We're usually on their side even though we ourselves use *you* throughout this book and accept it in some student papers. What's wrong with *you*? For one thing, it establishes a note that may often be too informal for exposition. Readers may resent being addressed as *you,* which sometimes they visualize as a finger pointing at them as in the old recruiting posters, "Uncle Sam wants YOU!" Then, too, the *you* viewpoint is closer to speech usage and is thus considered less formal and acceptable than the third person pronoun. Therefore, some instructors feel that students need the practice of writing in the more demanding formal style required in their work in other courses and often in business, industry, and the professions. Some instructors also feel that because much high school writing calls for *I* or *you,* college writing should require the third person.

Finally, *you* is dangerous, subject to being "over-yoused." Like *I*, one *you* frequently leads to many more:

> If you will take my advice, you will find that you do not have to spend much of your time studying for your final exam.

In defense of *you*, it is perfectly acceptable and effective when used sparingly and skillfully. It need not grab the reader ("Hey, you!"), but it can serve as a valuable impersonal or indefinite reference:

> As citizens interested in the community, you should inquire into the policies, practices, and politics of the zoning board.

In this textbook, we have generally employed *you* in this generic sense, hoping that you would find it a refreshing and pleasant departure from the dreary solemnity and impersonality of most college textbooks.

THIRD PERSON—*HE, SHE, IT*

The last point of view, the third person pronouns or their antecedents, is the one used most frequently in expository writing. The subject itself—poets, garbage collectors, birth control pills, or organic farming—stands in the spotlight, attended by its appropriate personal or indefinite pronoun (*he, she, it, they, anyone, each, everybody,* and so on). The main warning when using this point of view is to avoid the stilted, deadly *one*. When one is writing exposition, one often wishes to impress others by showing how important one can sound. But after one has encountered this use of *one* in one's reading, one would plead with others to shun it entirely or else resort to it only when one is without any viable alternative. You can see how *one* can drive a reader up the wall.

A last recommendation about point of view: after determining your point of view, stick to it throughout your paper. Ralph Waldo Emerson stated that "A foolish consistency is the hobgoblin of little minds," but in writing, there is nothing foolish about maintaining consistently the point of view established in your introduction.

A Final Word About Introductions

After this discussion of getting readers' attention, maintaining their interest, stating the thesis, announcing the plan, establishing a voice, and deciding upon a point of view, you can realize why the introduction is so agonizingly complicated to write. But don't despair. Most experienced writers struggle too. Probably the best advice is to jump in and get started, remembering that you can always return to polish up the introduction later. And in an emergency, if you can't get started, skip the introductory paragraph and begin by writing the second paragraph. It's more important to get going than to wait until you have hit upon the perfect beginning, because it may never come.

ON WRITING CONCLUSIONS

The conclusion of a paper serves two functions: it signals the end and leaves readers with something important to remember. The first is necessary for readers' sense of completeness, suggesting that they have just finished a well-planned, carefully conceived paper. The second is necessary for readers' sense of the subject, leaving them to think about what is important and appropriate. To fulfill both these functions in only a few sentences is no mean achievement.

Perhaps the first point to make is that the conclusion should not be long. Lingering goodbyes may be enjoyable with a loved one, but they bore readers. In short papers, a conclusion may even be omitted when enumerating a series of reasons in climactic order, the most important being reserved for last. In other instances, about three or four well-worded sentences should do the trick.

You may look either backward or forward in these concluding sentences. In looking backward, you may return to some metaphor or other motif in the introduction, restate the thesis, or in longer papers, summarize the main points. In looking forward, you may forecast the future, call for action, discuss implications, or point out the significance of the ideas. Here are some examples of these options.

Looking Backward

1. Return to the introduction (the italicized words refer to a comparison made in the introduction).

> Despite all these suggestions, finding a summer job may still be as difficult *as locating an inexpensive apartment near campus.* But at least you can be confident that you have gone about it efficiently and looked into all the possibilities. The rest is up to luck.

2. Restate the thesis.

> You can see that looking for a summer job need not be a hit-or-miss process. It can be conducted in a systematic, efficient manner that should produce results. Almost always, it will.

3. Summarize the main points (only in longer papers).

> What is important is to start looking for a summer job early and to follow the specific suggestions noted here. You may not want to investigate all the possibilities—employers overseas, federal agen-

cies, local or state governments, industries in other areas, and local businesses. But you should realize it is better to have too many opportunities than too few. That is why all these suggestions have been offered.

Looking Forward

4. Forecast the future.

> Despite these suggestions, you may not find summer work. The growing demand for these positions and the diminishing supply of them means that many young people will be unemployed. The result may be a return to the campus to attend summer sessions, which could double present enrollments. The end product might well be many three-year bachelor's degrees. And that is what the future may hold.

5. Call for action.

> The important point to remember is to get started looking for that summer job today. You can write letters to federal agencies, check into local and state government possibilities, get a copy of the *Summer Employment Directory,* and follow the suggestions about seeking work in local businesses. They who hesitate may be lost this summer.

6. Discuss implications.

> The implications of these suggestions should be apparent. Summer jobs will be more difficult to find this year than last. You may wait for Lady Luck to smile upon you or roll up your sleeves and start searching for yourself. You may follow these suggestions or your own. You may even decide to chuck the idea of getting a job — and enroll in summer school.

7. Point out the significance of ideas.

> Perhaps what is more significant than these specific suggestions is that even such an undertaking as finding a summer job can be carefully researched and planned. Some people go through life haphazardly, meeting problems with hastily conceived, last-minute answers. Other people anticipate problems and study how to meet them. To do so is usually more rewarding.

These examples suggest how the same paper might be concluded in various ways. Obviously, depending on the context, some would be more appropriate than others. Before concluding this discussion about conclusions, let us note a few rhetorical considerations brought out by the examples.

1. Not one of the examples starts with the overworked words *In summary* or *In conclusion*. We suggest that you discard these feeble mechanical signals. They are as jarring to your audience as the ringing of an alarm clock.
2. No apology is offered, no afterthought included, no extraneous note sounded. The conclusion should be like a parting handshake: firm and brief. Both present a final impression. It should be favorable.
3. In several examples, short sentences end the paragraph. These are effective in snapping it to a close. Sometimes an uncommon sentence pattern is also helpful, as in example 7, which begins with an infinitive. Even punctuation, such as the dash in example 6, can be utilized to achieve a sense of finality.
4. Another effective way to conclude is with a rhetorical question or with a catchy statement, as attempted in example 5. A possibility not exemplified here is to use an anecdote, but keep it short and make certain it is pertinent.

These suggestions should help you in writing the concluding paragraph of your paper. If you're stumped, look through them to find one that strikes your fancy and work it appropriately into your paper. After writing the paragraph, check to determine whether it conveys a sense of finality and leaves the reader with something vital to remember. (That is what we have just tried to do.)

ASSIGNMENTS

For Discussion

1   To avoid facing up to the cold reality of the blank page in getting started to write, many people play little games with themselves. For example, one of the authors of this book keeps postponing the ordeal by searching for inconsequential notes written to himself days or weeks ago and now misplaced. What games do you play—phoning a friend, dropping in to visit someone, getting a snack, having a few beers, waiting until inspiration strikes at 3 a.m., or what? What advice should you give yourself?
2   As a writer, have you used the opening rhetorical question, and what do you think of it? As a reader, what do you think of it? Apply these questions also to the definition introduction.
3   Discuss the writing situations in which it is not necessary to attract the attention of readers.
4   What appeals would you use to interest the following groups of readers in the essays listed on the next page: (a) senior high school students; (b) homemakers; (3) retired people?

Hypertension Is Deadly
Safety Tips for Bike Riders
Cable Television in the Future
Confused About Tires?
How to Eat Less and Like It
Give the President a Six-Year Term!
A Review of No-Fault Auto Insurance

5 Why should the thesis sentence not be the first sentence in most papers?
6 Analyze the introductions to chapters in this book or in other textbooks you have with you in class. To what extent do they follow the "gaff" approach? Discuss whether they are effective or not, supporting your conclusions with reasons.
7 Evaluate the following introductions from student papers:

a The automobile, a four-wheeled transportation vehicle, was initially a great blessing. It was a source of pleasure for people and an indication of one's prosperity. Its invention has allowed society to become very mobile and distant places to become far more accessible. The auto industry has been a tremendous boon for the economy of the United States over the past one hundred years. Yet today it is a menace.

b There is always at least one television commercial on your set that will disgust you. When you come home after a hard day's work and flip on your TV set, the last thing you want to see is a lady caressing and singing to her box of detergent. I've watched people practically ram their feet through an expensive color portable just because a certain obnoxious commercial was on the air. The television commercial is an ineffective means of advertising a product.

c Even though freshman dormitory hours are a much debated issue among new students at the university, I feel they are essential.

d Surveys and statistics show that there has been an increase in the number of people who have experienced college life, and this is due in part to the fact that a college education has become more and more vital in succeeding in today's world. Because of the increase in recent college enrollment, more people have become informed about the Greek system and its advantages. People today realize there's more to get out of a college education than knowledge from books, and a fraternity or sorority helps a student to acquire this knowledge.

8 Compare your past instructions from teachers and your own attitude about the use of *I*, *we*, and *you* with the views presented in this chapter.

9 What are the two functions of the conclusion? Why are they both important?

10 Why do the authors of this textbook use *you* throughout but advise you not to use it in papers for this course?

11 Evaluate the following conclusions from student papers:

a Considering both the advantages and disadvantages of the automobile today, it is evident that the country needs to develop a mass transit system to relieve traffic in and around the major cities. This system will take years to build, and much time and effort will be needed to persuade people to use it. In the meantime, they will continue to curse at and be cursed with the automobile.

b Insulting, shocking, and deceiving the public should not be effective ways of selling products. Yet products sell or else they would not continue to be advertised on television. Perhaps the continued use of these deplorable techniques says something about the American public. Perhaps people are not as intelligent as we would like to think they are.

c For these reasons I feel freshmen should be required to be in their dorms at certain hours from the opening days of school until the Thanksgiving vacation.

d According to a recent survey, there has been an increase in membership in social sororities and fraternities, so apparently more and more people have come to believe that the Greek system is good. Knowledge obtained from books is important, and just as important is the Greek system in promoting character, scholarship, and student involvement.

For Writing

1 Rewrite one of the introductions in discussion exercise 7 and the corresponding conclusion in exercise 11 and add a statement explaining why your revision is more effective.

2 Write an analysis of several attention-getting devices used in television commercials or magazine advertisements.

3 Write three introductory paragraphs, one for each of the audiences mentioned in discussion exercise 4, about any subject.

4 Write three different conclusions for a single subject, using a different technique in each.

5 Select one of the topics in discussion exercise 4 and write at least six opening sentences for it, each modeled after a different approach suggested in this chapter.

6 Choose one of the introductions in discussion exercise 7 or write one of your own on any topic. Restate the introduction several times, using an increasingly formal tone, as exemplified on pages 302–03.

Language in Expository Writing

THE NEED FOR CLARITY

Clarity—the word should be uppermost in your mind as you search for language to express your thoughts in expository writing. After all, the main purpose of this form of writing—to explain—could not be achieved if your language were murky or misleading. In a sense, writing exposition is like showing someone your ideas through a glass window. If the glass is dirty or distorted, the reader cannot see clearly. But replacing a pane or cleaning a glass may be easier than attaining clarity in writing. In fact, the word itself—*clarity*—is anything but clear. Just what do we mean?

In the mid-eighteenth century, the great English letter writer Lord Chesterfield advised his son to write *clear* business letters and explained what he meant by adding that "every paragraph should be so clear and unambiguous that the dullest fellow in the world may not be able to mistake it, nor obliged to read it twice in order to understand it." We wouldn't go as far as Chesterfield does in requiring that "even the dullest fellow in the world" be able to understand your writing. Instead, we urge you to write so that your readers do not have to struggle over your words, or reread them, or wonder what you meant, or be misled. What you've written should be as easy to digest as Jell-O.

But once again, who are your readers? Your answer to this question is crucial because what is clear to an adult might not be to a child; what is clear to a nurse might not be to an engineer; and what is clear to a college student from a Wyoming ranch might not be to one from Detroit's inner city. Thus you must first realize who your readers are and aim your writing at them.

Sometimes we like to talk about the writer as a quarterback aiming a message at the reader cutting down field. The writer is successful only if the message gets across to the reader. It is of little interest whether the writer stays in the pocket, or scrambles, throws when set or on the run, flips a hard or soft pass. The readers must catch on. If they don't, then the effort is worthless; there is no gain—in yardage or understanding. That is why we have emphasized repeatedly that you must write for your readers, which requires you to think about who they are.

Often you do know who your readers are. When you write a paper for a history professor, instructions for a Boy Scout hike, a speech for a high school class, an autobiography for a scholarship committee, or a letter for a college newspaper, you have a general idea of your readers. In other writing situations, you may know little about them and have to guess more. What should you do? How much can you take for granted about your audience? How high or low should you aim?

There is no all-purpose answer. Often you must make an educated guess at the schooling, interests, experiences, life styles, and backgrounds of readers. Then we suggest that you write just below this level, thus not taking too much for granted. It's better to err on the side of simplicity than complexity, as this old example illustrates:

> A plumber wrote to a Washington government department asking whether any damage was done to sewer pipes that he had cleaned with hydrochloric acid. He was informed that "The efficacy of hydrochloric acid is indisputable, but the corrosive residue is incompatible with metallic permanence." The plumber thanked the department for letting him know that no damage had been done. The department replied in dismay: "We cannot assume responsibility for the toxic and noxious residue of hydrochloric acid and suggest you use an alternate procedure." Again the plumber thanked them for approving. Finally, the department wrote the plumber, "Don't use hydrochloric acid. It eats hell out of the pipes."

You may not wish to give your readers hell and you may be leery of writing so simply as to seem to be talking down to them. If so, you might use some of the following devices instead to make certain that your writing is clear.

1. The explanatory *such as*.

> Critics of business assert that it is stacked in favor of private goods, *such as* food, cars, cigarettes, hair sprays, soaps; and against public goods, *such as* parks, libraries, beaches, clean air.

2. The explanatory *or.*

> Passive restraints (*or* air bags, as they are commonly called) may add hundreds of dollars to the price of retail cars.

3. The flattering *which, as you know.*

> Plea bargaining—which, as you know, is the practice of pleading guilty to a less serious offense instead of being tried for a more serious one—is increasing in our overburdened courts.

You might ask whether the simpler words could not always be used. Why such specialized terms as *private* and *public good, passive restraints,* or *plea bargaining*? Sometimes such terms are necessary because no suitable synonyms exist. For instance, we use *a fair catch* in football to refer to the act of signaling by the receiver of a kicked ball to indicate that he will not run with it and to notify opposing players that they will be penalized if they interfere with him. Imagine having to use this explanation instead of the specialized term!

But using such terms poses a problem—specifically, whether to define them or not. When informing do-it-yourself carpenters how to frame a basement or attic wall, you could assume that they would be familiar with such terms as *studs, plumb line, toenailed, joist,* and *lag screws.* You could assume that camera buffs would understand such terms as *XL cameras, reflexes, automatic metering, zoom lens, fixed-focus lens,* and *built-in exposure meters.* But if you were writing for beginning carpenters or photographers, you would need to clarify these words.

You may argue that all these examples are for real people in the real world and have little to do with you in freshman English, writing assignments for your English instructor. In one sense, you are correct: your English instructor will evaluate your paper. But generally, you are writing for your classmates or people like them, trying to interest and inform them, and your instructor determines how well you do this. These readers should be easy for you to identify with because most of them are about your age, they have many of your interests, they share many of your ideas, and they have undergone many of your experiences. But they are also different—in career plans, attitudes, values, knowledge, family relationships, social awareness, sensitivity, political views, personal outlook, life style, sophistication, aspirations, religious beliefs, and morals. You must be aware of these differences and consider them when you write to these readers.

Of course, you can't explain everything to every one of them. But you can try to make your ideas clear to most of them. This means being careful not only about specialized terms but also about any other troublesome ones. For example, we used to talk about bright, lively people as being *gay*; now we realize that most people are apt to misunderstand us, thinking that we are referring to these people as homosexuals. Perhaps more prevalent than such misleading words are obscure ones that may be troublesome to some readers. To show you what we mean, we have re-written the following paragraph from *The New York Times Magazine* to make it clearer to a general audience. The changed words are in italics.

Original	*Revision*
Although the beaver is an air breather, it is beautifully adapted to an *amphibious* life. Its oversized liver and large lungs enable it to hold its breath for as long as 15 minutes. Its ears and nose are *valvular* and can be shut off at will. A *transparent membrane* protects its eyes when it dives. Its mouth is constructed so that fur flaps close behind its front *incisors,* allowing it to chew wood underwater without choking.	Although the beaver is an air breather, it is beautifully adapted to *a life in the water as well as on land.* Its oversized liver and large lungs enable it to hold its breath for as long as 15 minutes. Its ears and nose *work like valves* and can be shut off at will *like a faucet. A thin layer of tissue* protects its eyes when it dives. Its mouth is constructed so that fur flaps close behind its front *cutting teeth,* allowing it to chew wood under-water without choking.

Some of these changes might be unnecessary for your classmates. You must be the judge. The important point to remember is that you must write to them and for them. This requires that you develop a double vision, looking inward to see what the words mean to you and outward to see what they mean to your audience. You may do this when writing your first draft or when revising. But you must do it, and you must see to it that your readers see clearly what you mean.

THE NEED FOR ACCURACY

But words may fail to communicate clearly for reasons other than that they are difficult or specialized. Sometimes we fail to use words accu-rately, selecting not the proper one but one almost like it. This may be done deliberately, as it often is by Archie Bunker ("You're invading the subject") for comic effect in the tradition of Mrs. Malaprop, the humor-ous character in Sheridan's eighteenth-century play *The Rivals.* But if you inadvertently create malapropisms such as *respectfully* for *respec-tively, condemn* for *condone, irreverent* for *irrelevant,* then you would be laughed at, not laughed with. The trick in avoiding errors of this sort is not to submit a paper until you have checked every word whose meaning you have any doubt about. We have found that our students usually admit they had been unsure of words they misused, but hadn't bothered to check them. Recklessness in some human endeavors may be desirable, but not in writing. Our advice: take a minute to check doubtful words, in either the writing or revising stage.

You can miss the right word by a mile, as when you use *imminent* for *eminent,* or you can miss by inches, as when you use *dislike* for *loathe.* In either example, you strike out because you confuse the point for the reader. Accuracy in selecting words demands that you hit squarely each time. Thus you need to be careful not only of confusing words that look or sound the same but of those that mean almost, but not quite, the same thing. You remember that we pointed out in Chapter 10 that even the same word can carry different connotations. To communicate effectively to a reader (or a victim), you should use *rob, mug,* and *burglarize* precisely. *To rob* is to steal from someone, usually in person; *to mug* is to steal from and injure someone; and *to burglarize* is to steal something from a house, usually when the residents are out. In each case, the victim loses, but each word connotes a different act.

Flaubert, the great French novelist, told how he spent hours searching for *le mot juste* (the precise word) when writing. You will not have the time or the inclination to do that, but you can strive for accuracy, particularly in revising, by trying to substitute a more precise term for the one that popped into your head while writing your first draft. To do so, a thesaurus, a synonym book, or a dictionary may be helpful. But be careful about using a thesaurus, because it merely lists words and does not distinguish their connotations or different shades of meaning. A dictionary or synonym book is safer and more helpful.

Above all, to write exposition well is to strive constantly to write accurately and clearly. If friends look over your paper and tell you it is well written, beware. Usually they mean that it sounds impressive, elegant, erudite. Much more desirable would be the statement, "It's clear. I understand exactly what you mean." For in expository writing, accuracy and clarity are nearly all.

ASSIGNMENTS

For Discussion

1 We often think of specialized words as strange new terms, but sometimes they are simple words used in new ways. Here, for instance, are the opening sentences of a political editorial.

Congress may be getting ready to do a better job on the long-neglected task of legislative oversight. It would be a mistake to expect too much. Strong practical and institutional barriers remain. Nonetheless, new chairmen, new members, new rules and new grass roots pressures all push in the direction of an expanded oversight effort.

—*Wall Street Journal*

What does *oversight* mean to you? To the writer? If you do not know, see if you can figure out the meaning from the following sentence, which appears later in the editorial:

The new effort also stems from a belief that closer oversight of agencies and programs may help rebuild public trust in government, persuading many citizens that someone up there is at last fighting their battles.

If you were writing the editorial, would you substitute another word for *oversight*? If so, what?

2 Many words in sports, like the term *stealing* as used in baseball, have entirely different meanings in other contexts. See how many you and your classmates can think of. For example, a *diamond* in baseball isn't a girl's best friend, and a *shortstop* isn't a brief layover at an airport.

3 One of the most colorful and imaginative forms of slang is that used by short-order cooks. We were startled at breakfast one morning to hear our waitress cry out, "Wreck two and roast the English!" Soon afterward we received our two scrambled eggs and English muffins. Are you familiar with contexts other than sports where slang terms can be misleading to outsiders?

4 Many words and phrases mean almost the opposite of what they say. For example, "Speed Zone" really means slow zone and "heads up" means to duck, or put your head down. What other examples can you think of?

5 What does this statement mean: "When he throws a party, he throws a party"? How do you know what it means? How can any meaning be conveyed by the same words as the words being explained?

6 Discuss the following:

The word *love* has by no means the same sense for both sexes, and this is one cause of the serious misunderstandings which divide them.

—Simone de Beauvoir, *The Second Sex*

7 A pun is a play on words, often creating an effect of pleasure (or pain) from different meanings of the same word. For example, in *Romeo and Juliet,* the dying Mercutio quips, "Ask for me tomorrow and you shall find me a grave man." Do you know any pungent puns that illustrate how dual meanings can produce humor?

8 How would you rephrase the following statements if you were using them in a talk to a business club?

    a Students with a three point average have developed good study habits.

    b Most freshpersons are required to live in the dorms.

    c Some soc. courses are snaps.

    d One of the joys of the library is wandering around in the stacks.

    e A few profs like to give pop quizzes.

    f Many of the first-year courses are taught by teaching assistants.

    g If we started Thanksgiving vacation on Tuesday, students would probably cut on Monday.

9 What is the meaning of the word *round* in each of the following sentences?

    a He rounded off the bill at $23.

    b The bout ended in the tenth round.

    c The round trip cost $47.

    d He bought chuck instead of round.

    e He paid for the round of drinks.

    f Just then he came round the corner.

    g The earth turns round.

    h He was a funny, round fellow.

    i The library is open all year round.

Usage in Expository Writing

THE INFLUENCE OF AUDIENCE AND PURPOSE ON USAGE

In personal writing and in much descriptive writing, you either write directly to yourself or to someone else from a highly personal point of view. But in exposition you would not be likely to write a comprehensive explanation to yourself. Therefore, an extensive written explanation presumes an audience—one rather far removed from your immediate personal circle. In order to communicate with that audience, you as a writer are forced to search for words whose meaning is generally recognized. In addition, you must use more complex paragraphs and sentences and more widely accepted language usages. Your explanatory writing then takes on the character of General English (see the chart on pages 178–79). You shift from the relaxed language dress of Casual style to the more conservative General English required for a general audience—the language apparel you don along with a business suit and take to the classroom or office with you.

The following paragraphs—from Michael Rossman's *The Wedding Within the War*, a book in journal form about the author's experiences in Berkeley during the riots after the Cambodia bombings—demonstrate how both audience and purpose can influence writing style. The first paragraph is in narrative form:

Clatter of pans, running water. I pulled myself up again, weary, and went into the kitchen. She was standing over the stove, stirring instant mashed potatoes.

318

I couldn't read her back. I held her. "I think we're tearing ourselves apart because the world is coming apart," I said. "I think you're right," she said. "Water the plants," I told her, as I went back into the front room, grimly ignoring the radio, the phone, "that's the thing to remember now, remember to water the plants."

Written in Casual English, the paragraph exhibits short, simple sentence structure, conversational vocabulary, personal pronouns, and a highly personal tone.

The next paragraph from the same book, written for the same audience but for a different purpose, has many features of General English:

And I know where it's going, for a little way at least. For Berkeley is truly a barometer. Every college in the country is undergoing an evolution in the culture and politics of its captive transient population; and each evolution is essentially like Berkeley's. I have watched it happening on every kind of campus, from upperclass Catholic girls' schools to working-class junior colleges. Activism begins, diversifies to departmental organizing, anti-draft work and guerrilla theater; the dance of confrontation proceeds in growing ranks; the administration gets slicker but finally blows its cool; dope culture spreads, the girls chuck their bras—wow, you wouldn't believe the wealth of data. And then beyond the campus the voluntary ghetto forms. Freak community seeks roots and begins to generate communes, families, head-shops and food co-ops, freak media, friendly dog packs and dog shit, links with the farm communes— there are ten within fifteen miles of Rock Island, micro-sample of Amerika. O, it is happening everywhere just like in Berkeley, only faster now; long-haired kids on the street, merchants' complaints, heavy dope busts, teachers fired, kids suspended, leash laws, narcs and agents and street sweeps and riot practice for the neighboring precincts and dynamite at the farmhouse.

Note that the sentence structure in this explanation of campus activism is more complex, interlaced with subordinate ideas and their accompanying structures, and note the addition of detailed examples. The language, with the exception of the subculture slang appropriate to his audience of student sympathizers, is appropriate for a socially concerned, educated reader. A few minor changes in vocabulary and grammatical structure could shift this from an explanation aimed at a special audience to one directed to a general audience. The purpose would remain the same; the audience would change. Following is a list of the specialized slang words and general words to replace them, resulting in a more formal voice:

"I have watched it happen"   ⟶ It has happened (removal of
                                personal voice)

"gets slicker and finally blows
    its cool"   ⟶ becomes increasingly devious
                                       and ultimately hostile
"dope culture"   ⟶ drug culture
"freak community"   ⟶ alienated community
"head-shops"   ⟶ drug paraphernalia shops
"freak media"   ⟶ subculture media
"dog shit"   ⟶ accompanying debris
"dope busts"   ⟶ narcotics raids
"kids"   ⟶ students
"narcs"   ⟶ narcotics agents

These changes, as you can see, are minor. But the paragraph can now be addressed to a general audience—people less conversant with the jargon of the student subculture. Slang terms have been replaced by more general ones, and some words that would not shock a college-age audience have been replaced by those less likely to turn off an older, more conservative one.

GLOSSARY OF USAGES FOR REFERENCE IN EXPOSITORY WRITING

As we have just pointed out, exposition requires more complex sentence structure than narrative and description. We also noted in earlier chapters that signals of relationship between ideas are necessary for maximum clarity and that English furnishes a wide variety of such signals in the form of connecting words—words used to subordinate some ideas to others. These subordinators are so numerous that many times several choices are available for the same purpose; thus, they become usage problems. Many of these subordinators are included in the glossary that follows, as are some vocabulary items used frequently in exposition.

as follows
The singular form of the verb, *follows,* is always used even when several items are listed:

> Before we can review the case, we need more information, *as follows:* the amount contracted for, the payment received, and the nature of the commitment.

as well as
As well as usually introduces a nonrestrictive phrase (a grammatical aside) and makes no change in the verb number in the main clause. Although the subject of this sentence seems plural, grammatically it is singular:

The state university system, *as well as* the private schools in the state, *has* an open admissions policy.

awhile/a while

Although these mean the same and are both acceptable in all forms of writing, they are not interchangeable in usage. *Awhile* is an adverb similar in function to *anytime, anywhere; a while* is a noun phrase.

I played tennis *awhile* on Sunday. (adverb)
I played tennis for *a while* on Sunday. (noun phrase, object of the preposition)

being as/being that

Used in some spoken dialects as a replacement for *because* or *since*, they should be avoided in written General English.

bring/take/carry

It is standard in some dialect regions to use *bring* and *take* interchangeably. In others, *carry* replaces *take* in sentences such as:

I'll *carry/take* you home after school.

In General English, *bring* and *take* both mean "to convey something from one place to another." *Bring* usually connotes the sense of conveying something *back* to the speaker's point of origin; *take* to go the opposite direction.

I *took* a shopping bag from home to the store to *bring* home the groceries.

but however/but nevertheless/but yet

All these fat subordinators are socially acceptable, but their use results in redundancy and excessive wordiness. For writing economy, use either *but* or one of the other words.

consists of/consists in

Consists of connotes "made up of components or parts":

Each chapter *consists of* instructional material, a summary, and exercises.

Consists in means "to have a basis in" or "inherent in":

Statesmanship *consists in* being in the right place at the right time and saying the right things to the right people.

correspond to/correspond with

Correspond to means "to be similar or parallel to something":

Some authorities believe that the twentieth-century disenchantment with social institutions *corresponds to* that of the fourteenth century.

Correspond with means "to exchange letters":

I have *corresponded with* my mother's aunt for many years.

criterion/criteria

Criterion is the singular form:

A single *criterion* has been established.

Although frequently used as a singular form in spoken English, *criteria* should be treated as a plural in written, General English:

Several *criteria* have been established.

data

Data, the Latin plural of *datum,* is now used interchangeably as a singular or plural form:

The data *are* conclusive, or The *data* is conclusive.

Data as a plural form and *datum* as a singular are preferred in scientific writing. *Data* as a singular is acceptable in all writing, except in a few forms of Specialized English, such as scholarly writing. Just be sure to keep your data consistent.

due to

Due to has traditionally been restricted to adjective use:

The basketball team's poor performance was *due to* the illness of the starting center. (adjective following *be*)

Although formerly frowned upon, its use as an adverbial is now widely accepted:

Due to the illness of the starting center, the basketball team did not win the game. (sentence adverbial)

However, for scholarly writing, the adverbial usage may be unsuitable; substitute *because of, on account of,* or *owing to* in such cases.

during the course of

A padded version of *during.* Acceptable but prose-fattening; elimination of *the course of* is an excellent way to shed excess verbiage.

first/firstly, second/secondly . . .

The *-ly* forms are awkward and unnecessary. Like fur-lined boots at a formal dance, they're acceptable, but who needs them?

hardly . . . when/hardly . . . than

Hardly . . . than is an acceptable variant for *hardly . . . when* in spoken English; however, in written General English, *hardly . . . when* should be used:

The vows had *hardly* been uttered *than* the church bells began to chime.

The vows had *hardly* been uttered *when* the church bells began to chime. (preferred in written General English)

however/how ever

However is a subordinator and is movable within the clause:

She could have prevented the tragedy; she, *however,* was not aware of that.

How ever is a question word + adverb—two separate words and not movable:

How ever did she manage to escape death in that wreckage?

if and when/when and if

A pair of wordy clichés. For economy's sake, use only *if* or *when,* not both.

inside of/outside of

When these words are used as prepositions, the *of* should be omitted in written General English.

Inside the building, people went about their business as usual.

Of course, if you use *inside* or *outside* as a noun, the *of* may be necessary:

The *outside of* the building was painted a drab gray.

previous to/prior to

Although both are acceptable usages, they often lend an overly pompous tone to your prose. If your natural tendency is to substitute *before* in speaking, do so in your writing as well.

Previous to/prior to that time . . . *Before* that time . . .

proceed/precede

Proceed means "to go forward," in the sense of continued action; *precede* means "to go before":

The army *proceeded* to the enemy camps.
She *preceded* her husband down the aisle of the theater.

Caution: Watch the spelling—*precede,* not *preceed!*

reason is because/reason is that

In writing, *the reason is because* has been traditionally frowned upon as redundant, and *the reason is that* preferred. However, *the reason is because* is widely used and accepted, even in scholarly writing. You need to realize, though, that fussy people consider this usage unacceptable:

> The *reason* he didn't go is *because* [*that*—preferred by some] his car broke down.

so/so that

So if often overused in spoken English as an intensifier for emphasis:

> You are *so* right.
> She looked *so* attractive in her new suit.

Generally, you should avoid this practice in writing.

So is just as vague and overused sometimes as a conjunction; in writing, generally, substitute *therefore, consequently,* or *thus* for *so.*

So that is a handy subordinator, but you should make sure that it carries the meaning of "in order that," rather than merely substituting for *so.*

> The farmer plowed the new field in the late fall *so that/in order that* he could plant an early crop.

while/although

Because the subordinator *while* can be used either to indicate time (when, during) or as a replacement for *although,* there is danger of creating ambiguity:

> *While* the rest of the family eats at five, she dines alone. (Does *while* mean *when* or *although?*)

You can realize from this discussion that as your writing becomes more impersonal, aimed at a more distant audience, your usage options change. Some of those presented in this glossary were described as more appropriate than others because of social acceptability; other choices, such as *during* for *during the course of,* were suggested for stylistic reasons. But you should be heartened by the knowledge that our language is rich in choices for all purposes; you will never need to feel constrained. Remember that you will spend a good part of your college education developing your ability to use all the facilities that the language has to offer. Language is both a delight and a tool. Learn to enjoy it and to create with it.

USAGE EXERCISE

Identify the usage "problem" in each of the sentences below. Discuss the current attitude toward the usage of each item.

1 A college education consists mainly of disciplining yourself to study regularly and of attending classes.

2   She couldn't be happy because she was so envious of others.
3   John has earned enough money working summers so that he can attend college.
4   The United States government, as well as all the others in the world, have to learn to stay out of civil wars.
5   While you are asleep, you can solve troublesome problems.
6   We packed these items for our camping trip, as follow: sleeping bags, extra socks, an axe, and cooking equipment.
7   The main criteria for acceptance to graduate school is a high score on the Graduate Record Examination.
8   You can't get enough pieces from that cake to feed this crowd, how ever you slice it.
9   If and when you make up your mind, let me know.
10 After awhile, we all went for cokes.
11 Being that unemployment is up, the Social Security fund is getting low.
12 I brought her to the threshold of her new home.
13 The police could have ended the dispute then, but nevertheless, they continued it the next day.
14 The American Revolution corresponded with the French Revolution in many ways.
15 They knew inside of an hour that they had won the tournament.
16 Prior to the Indian uprisings, many treaties had been broken.
17 The teacher preceeded to lecture to the class.
18 During the course of his investigation, Pasteur tried many ways to sterilize milk.
19 The data does not substantiate the conclusions.
20 Hardly had the door closed behind him than a great uproar arose.
21 The reason for much of the failure in college is because students have not developed self-discipline.

CHAPTER

Sentence Strategies in Expository Writing

When explaining, you place special demands on sentence structure. In narrative, to express immediacy and action, simple and compound sentences work effectively; in description, sentences expanded by inserted modifiers add vivid and colorful details. Certainly all these are also useful in exposition. But to explain and clarify difficult ideas and to express and support opinions, subordinate sentences that permit counterbalancing of complex ideas are needed. Consideration of the following paragraph by Bruno Bettelheim, rewritten so that the subordinate sentences of the original are omitted, helps to demonstrate the usefulness of these complex sentence structures in expository writing:

> **1** The present situation is the logical result of developments that began in the nineteenth century. **2** In the past seventy years, women have achieved biological and technological liberation. **3** The advent of contraception did not greatly reduce the actual number of children reared to maturity, which was formerly decreased by miscarriage, stillbirth, and childhood diseases. **4** Contraception did put an end to the incessant pregnancies that had drained women's time and energy. **5** Technological progress led to general economic prosperity, and women in the upper classes of the Western nations became able to lead lives of ceremonial futility. **6** Economist Thorstein Veblen saw that. **7** In the early years of the twentieth century, the popular notion of normal life was that man did the productive work. **8** Woman was an ornamental consumer.
>
> Bruno Bettelheim, "The Roots of Radicalism," *Playboy*

In this paragraph, the only real clue to any relationships between sentences is in their order: the expanded simple sentences and the one compound sentence (5) contain few signals about how the information in one sentence relates to that in another. Let's look now at the various sentence sequences and how they correspond to the original version. Since the first two sentences of the rewritten version are the same as in the original, we will start with sentence 3.

Rewritten Version	*Original*
3 The advent of contraception did not greatly reduce the actual number of children reared to maturity, which was formerly decreased by miscarriage, stillbirth, and childhood diseases. **4** Contraception did put an end to the incessant pregnancies that had drained women's time and energy.	**3** The advent of contraception, while it did not greatly reduce the actual number of children reared to maturity (which was formerly decreased by miscarriage, stillbirth, and childhood diseases), **4** did put an end to the incessant pregnancies that had drained women's time and energy.

As you can see, sentences 3 and 4 of the rewritten paragraph were combined in the original, the predicate of 3 introduced by *while*. Thus, the information given there is subordinated in order to give the material in 4 greater significance in relation to *the advent of contraception*.

Here's another sequence:

Rewritten Version	*Original*
5 Technological progress had led to general economic prosperity, and women in the upper classes of the Western nations became able to lead lives of ceremonial futility. **6** Economist Thorstein Veblen saw that.	**5** And with the general economic prosperity resulting from technological progress, women in the upper classes of the Western nations became able, **6** as economist Veblen saw it, to lead lives of ceremonial futility.

Here 5 and 6 of the rewrite were fused: 6 inserted into 5 and introduced by *as*. This permitted the writer to acknowledge Veblen's idea without giving its source the importance that a separate sentence conveys.

And finally:

Rewritten Version	*Original*
7 In the early years of the twentieth century, the popular notion of normal life was that man did the productive work. **8** Woman was an ornamental consumer.	Thus, **7** in the early years of the twentieth century, the popular notion of normal life was that of man doing the productive work, **8** while woman was an ornamental consumer.

Inserting sentence 8 into 7 introduced with *while* established a clearer relationship and contrast between the ideas expressed in the two sentences.

Through the devices discussed, Bettelheim clearly signals the relationships for his readers. They neither have to puzzle over meanings nor call upon any clairvoyant powers to interpret the paragraph. To explain exactly what he meant, the writer merely utilized various subordinating devices; the resulting clauses not only indicate causal relationships but help to emphasize information most important to his explanation. Subordination permits him to "accentuate the positive" and the pertinent.

COMPLEX SENTENCES: SUBORDINATE SEQUENCES

In Chapter 5, we indicated that one way to join sentences or clauses was to compound them by adding coordinate conjunctions such as *and* or *or,* formulated thus:

SVC and SVC and SVC.

In compound sentences, as you recall, the SVC clauses are independent, or main, clauses, restricted only by a relationship of chronological or logical order. All the clauses are at the same level of generality; none serves to modify any other, as in:

1 The pitcher stepped up to the mound and
1 the fans fell temporarily silent as he started his wind-up and
1 by the time he released the pitch, he had whipped them into a crescendo of sound.

Although superficially similar in structure to compound sentences, complex sentences differ greatly in the relationships established between clauses. If you experiment a bit with the following examples, you can see why sentences with subordinate clauses are called "complex." Decide which choices are possible and which are not.

1. The weather was very bad; (Main clause)

therefore,
so,
however,
but
nevertheless,
as
otherwise,
furthermore,
whether

the men did not hesitate to go fishing. (Subordinate clause)

2. The men did not
   hesitate to go fishing,
   (Main clause)
   $\left\{ \begin{array}{l} \text{therefore,} \\ \text{moreover,} \\ \text{however,} \\ \text{because,} \\ \text{although,} \\ \text{in spite of} \\ \quad \text{the fact that} \\ \text{whether} \end{array} \right\}$
   the weather was very bad.
   (Subordinate clause)

You probably discovered that only these choices are logically possible for the first example:

The weather was very bad; $\left\{ \begin{array}{l} \text{but} \\ \text{however,} \\ \text{nevertheless,} \end{array} \right\}$ the men did not hesitate to go fishing.

Conversely, none of these possibilities is appropriate for example 2, which permits only these:

The men did not hesitate to go fishing, $\left\{ \begin{array}{l} \text{although} \\ \text{in spite of} \\ \quad \text{the fact that} \end{array} \right\}$ the weather was very bad.

Even from this simple exercise, you should realize that you do not have free choice of joining possibilities: that some subordinators work better for some purposes than for others.

Using the same examples, let's look at some of the other peculiarities of subordinate sentences. Asking yourself these questions will help you to write this kind of sentence more effectively.

1. Can the final clauses in both these examples be shifted to initial sentence position? Obviously not; it works for the second, but not for the first.

> However the men did not hesitate to go fishing, the weather was very bad.
> Although the weather was very bad, the men did not hesitate to go fishing.

You can see from the examples that shifting the clause beginning with *however* is not grammatically possible; shifting the *although* clause is no problem.

2. Can the subordinator be moved to positions other than the initial one in the clause?

> The weather was very bad; the men, *however,* did not hesitate to go fishing. OR The weather was very bad; the men did not

> hesitate to go fishing, *however.* (Both are grammatical possibilities.)
> The weather was very bad; the men, *although,* did not hesitate to go fishing. (not grammatical)

In these examples, *however* has a property that subordinators like *although* do not: it can be moved freely within the clause.

As you can see, clauses can become subordinate in different ways, depending upon the subordinator. Traditionally, these have been called *subordinate conjunctions* and *conjunctive* or *transitional adverbs,* but we will refer to them as *conjunction subordinators* and *transitional subordinators.*

Conjunction Subordinators

The classification *conjunction subordinator* includes all those that can be moved only by taking the whole clause; the most commonly used are *after, although, as, because, before, since, if, whether,* and *while.* Remembering that all subordinators signal that a complete SVC clause follows, let's look at an example (the conjunction subordinator is italicized):

> Inflation and recession hit the country *after* we had ended our military involvement in the Vietnam war.
> *After* we had ended our military involvement in the Vietnam war, inflation and recession hit the country.

Note: In "After the Vietnam war, inflation and recession hit the country," *after* would be a preposition followed by a noun phrase. You should realize that many subordinators, like *after,* can function both ways.

The conjunction *but* behaves like a subordinator in that it cannot be shifted around within the clause; however, clauses introduced by it, unlike others introduced by subordinators, cannot be shifted to initial position.

> Many environmentalists opposed the bill, but Congress passed it anyway. (grammatical)
> But Congress passed it anyway, many environmentalists opposed the bill. (not grammatical)

Transitional Subordinators

A transitional subordinator relates two clauses somewhat differently from the conjunction subordinators previously discussed. Although still in subordinate sequence (at level 2 — see Chapter 18), the clause added with a transitional subordinator can become an independent sentence. Also, a transitional subordinator can be moved freely within the clause, but the whole clause cannot be shifted, as these examples show:

The eastern portion of the United States is dependent upon imported oil; *therefore,* its economy would suffer greatly from a higher oil tariff.

or

The eastern portion of the United States is dependent upon imported oil; its economy, *therefore,* would suffer greatly from a higher oil tariff.

or

The eastern portion of the United States is dependent upon imported oil; its economy would suffer greatly from a higher oil tariff, *therefore.*

but not

Therefore its economy would suffer greatly from a higher oil tariff, the eastern portion of the United States is dependent upon imported oil.

In complex sentences, whose clauses are joined by conjunction subordinators, the added clause is clearly subordinate in the traditional sense; the two clauses cannot be made into separate sentences without creating a fragment:

Many students still seek a baccalaureate degree. *Because* they believe in a liberal education. (fragment)

Sentences joined by transitional subordinators, on the other hand, can be broken into two complete sentences. In this respect they resemble compound sentences, but unlike compounds, the two clauses retain their relationship and a subordinate sequence:

1 The eastern portion of the United States is dependent upon imported oil. **2** *Therefore,* its economy would suffer greatly from a higher oil tariff.

Used this way, these subordinators function as transitional words, but they always establish a close relationship with the preceding sentence, or even, in many cases, with the preceding paragraph. But at the same time, a subordinate sequence is created.

Note the sentences with transitional subordinators are punctuated with a semicolon (;) before the subordinator, rather than a comma. But frequently a comma follows the subordinator. These are the possibilities:

Main Clause;   Transitional Subordinator,   SVC Clause.
Main Clause;   S,   Transitional Subordinator,   VC.
Main Clause;   SVC, Transitional Subordinator.

This punctuation practice varies from that used with conjunction subordinators, which are not movable within the clause. With those, if any punctuation is needed in lengthy sentences, a comma does the job:

Main Clause,   Conjunction Subordinator   Subordinate Clause.

Relationships Established by Subordinators

English is rich in words that function as joiners, particularly subordinators. Although we use relatively few of these in everyday, spoken English, we lavish them throughout our writing. But because they are fairly specialized, you should realize the kinds of relationships they signal. The following list does not include all the subordinators, nor does it indicate all their complexities, but it should help you in making decisions about appropriate choices.

RELATIONSHIP	CONJUNCTION SUBORDINATOR	TRANSITIONAL SUBORDINATOR
Information about the topic in addition to that given in the main clause		likewise, morever, also, furthermore
Separation or exclusion of the main clause material from that in the added clause	else, lest, whereas	otherwise, alternatively
Contrary condition or alternate possibilities	but	however, nevertheless, on the contrary, on the other hand
Causal	so, because, since, as, for	therefore, for this reason, then, consequently, thus
Purpose	that, in order that, so that, for the purpose of	
Limitation or restriction	though, although, in spite of the fact that, notwithstanding that	
Time	after, as, as soon as, while, before, until, since, when	
Special conditions	if, whether	

You can add these subordinate structures to your supply of tools for effective writing. Remember that because complex ideas often require complex sentences, subordinators play a key role in how you meet your writing commitment—to communicate ideas exactly and precisely to your reader.

SENTENCE ECONOMY

Most Americans hurry. Whether driving, eating, shopping, dancing, vacationing—or reading—we seldom do it slowly. While we may read narration and description at something approaching a slow pace, savoring the experiences they convey, we generally speed through exposition. In looking at information about assembling a bicycle, buying insurance, or enrolling in summer school, Americans want it to be to the point.

That's what is meant by economy. In our writing and teaching, we used to try to convey this concept with words like *conciseness* and *brevity*. But the trouble with these terms is they suggest that writing should be concise or brief. They imply that all sentences should be short, simple sentences, rather than the expanded ones we have discussed. But that's not what we mean by economy. Your writing must be complete enough to communicate everything necessary to help your reader understand the subject fully, but it's almost equally important to omit anything unnecessary. Achieving sentence economy is like dieting: the purpose of both is to remove fat. What's left should be strong, firm, and muscular. To diet, you've got to cut down on calories; to achieve sentence economy, you've got to cut down on words. You can do that by asking yourself the following questions when revising your paper:

1. *Can I cut out any material?* Deleting something from your paper is as painful as throwing out old possessions stored in the attic. If you've just struggled to write a first draft of the required length, it's almost asking too much of you to chuck out a section, a paragraph, a sentence, or even part of a sentence. But as you become more creative in combining sentences and adding modifiers, it becomes even more important to weed out any superfluous information cluttering your sentences. Keep only the necessary information.

2. *Can I omit the relative pronouns* which, who, *or* that? These three little words—*which, who, that*—are likely to clog your sentences unless you are alert. Note that one or two words are saved in the revised version of each of the following sentences, making each that much more economical.

Original: The fumes *which* come from millions of cars fill the air with pollutants.

Revision: The fumes from millions of cars fill the air with pollutants.

Original: Thousands of people *who* want to own luxury cars borrow at high interest rates from banks and finance companies.

Revision: Thousands of people wanting to own luxury cars borrow at high interest rates from banks and finance companies.

Original: Many automobile parts *that* are now made of plastics and other synthetic materials do not last long.

Revision: Many automobile parts now made of plastic and other synthetic materials do not last long.

Note when the relative pronouns are omitted, we also delete part or all of the verb phrase in the clause as in the first and third examples. Another common device is to change the verb to an *-ing* form, as in the second example.

Of course, you cannot always delete *which, who,* and *that* because sometimes they are essential to your desired effect. But when you can remove them, do so. Your writing will be more economical and more vigorous.

3. *Can I remove the introductory* there is *or* are, *and* it is? Just as inexperienced writers often lead up to the subject of their papers slowly, so they do with the subject of their sentences, resulting in the unnecessary introducers—*there is, there are,* and *it is.* Sometimes you may need them for stylistic purposes, but usually they can be eliminated.

Original: *There is* an increase in membership in sororities and fraternities this year.

Revision: Membership in sororities and fraternities has increased this year.

Original: *It is* one of the new policies of the Greek system to encourage civic projects.

Revision: One of the new policies of the Greek system is to encourage civic projects.

The savings in eliminating *there is, there are,* and *it is* may be small in each sentence, but this reduction and others will achieve significant overall economies in your paper.

4. *Can I delete prepositions?* Prepositions will swarm all over your papers unless you are vigilant. Most dangerous is *of,* a creature that has to be as carefully screened out as the housefly. But also be on guard against *in, on, by, to,* and *with.* Here's how they operate:

Original: At the time *of* registration, students are required to make payments *of* their fees.

Revision: At registration time, students are required to pay their fees.

Original: Because of the increase *in* enrollments, some classes *in* sociology are closed by early *in* the morning.

Revision: Because of increased enrollments, some sociology classes are closed by early morning.

Note that often the remedy for eliminating these prepositions involves changing the post-noun prepositional phrase into a pre-noun modifier, as in the first example. Other times, as in the second example, the problem can be solved by using a verb form rather than a noun derivative.

You should also guard against some prepositional phrases. They come in clusters: the *fact* cluster, the *regard* cluster, and the *reference* cluster are the main ones to watch out for. Here are all three clusters in one monstrous sentence:

Due to the fact that she inquired *with reference to* the dormitory hours, specifically *in regard to* when the girls had to return at night, we sent her a copy of the new regulations.

Here is the sentence without the preposition clusters:

Because she inquired about the dormitory hours, specifically when the girls had to return at night, we sent her a copy of the new regulations.

In reference to this subject and in regard to these prepositional phrases, and in view of the fact that you can improve your writing by eliminating most of them, do so!

5. *Can I omit any* -ion *words?* Unfortunately, the desire to impress others in writing often results in the piling up of the sonorous sounding *-ion* words. But they are all sluggish, overweight dreadnoughts likely to sink readers, sentence, and all.

Original: The chair made a recommendation that students should be given an invitation to provide information to faculty members about proposed new courses.

Revision: The chair recommended that students be invited to inform faculty members about proposed new courses.

6. *Can I combine sentences and omit repetitious material?* Using the techniques of insertion discussed on pages 195–99 in Chapter 13, you can combine a series of sentences:

Original: I decided to attend the university because of its fine academic program. The university has a good faculty. Athletics at the university are also excellent, particularly basketball. And the university has a lovely campus.

Revision: I decided to attend the university because of its fine academic program, good faculty, lovely campus, and excellent athletics, particularly basketball.

7. *Can I eliminate dead nouns?* Worn-out, meaningless nouns were listed and discussed on pages 44–45 in Chapter 3, so we won't bore you by repeating them here. But we do want to remind you that they too cause waste.

8. *Can I do away with deadwood?* After you have provided money for certain regular items in your budget, such as room, food, clothing, and fun, numerous miscellaneous expenses still exist. Although we have already classified seven regular wordy patterns, numerous others elude these categories, so we have adopted a miscellaneous category termed *deadwood.*

Deadwood is so prevalent in freshman papers that they constitute a serious fire hazard. We'd like to have a Coke for every time we've cut the ponderous "in this modern world of today" down to "today" or else crossed out the entire phrase. Why is it that expressions involving time bring out the wordiness in us?

By the time that the end of our vacation arrived, we were completely exhausted. (By the end of our vacation . . .)

In this day and age of inflated prices, five dollars does not go far. (In these inflationary times . . .)

And then there are those phrases using *number* ("five in number"), *color* ("blue in color"), *shape* ("round in shape"), and the like. Also on the deadwood list are certain unnecessary modifiers, particularly *very* and *really,* which can provide emphasis in speech but lose their effectiveness in writing. See for yourself:

Original: It is really necessary to return the library book very soon.

Revision: It is necessary to return the library book soon.

The unnecessary modifiers have probably immigrated from advertising, a world of raucous excesses.

Most deadwood defies classification. Thus you must become economy-minded, scrutinizing your sentences to strip the waste away. Naturally, you can't adopt a telegraphic style, but you can attack your sentences as if you were being charged for each word. Here's how we attacked one student sentence:

Original: He contracted in the sociology course to fulfill the requirements for an *A* grade as established by the professor.

First revision: He contracted in the sociology course to fulfill the professor's requirement for an *A* grade.

Second revision: He contracted in the sociology course to fulfill the professor's requirements for an *A.*

Third revision: He contracted to fulfill the sociology professor's requirements for an *A.*

Fourth revision: He contracted for an *A* with the sociology professor.

Perhaps, in some other contexts, the pruning might have stopped at the second or third cut. Sometimes, for stylistic or semantic reasons, all deadwood cannot be completely cut away. That's a conscious decision you should make after becoming aware of the unnecessary words and phrases in your own work.

What is most important is to keep your eyes and your mind alert to wordiness. If you do, you will find numerous opportunities to economize in your work. The eight questions, repeated here for your convenience, should serve as guidelines:

1. Can I cut out any unnecessary material?
2. Can I omit the relative pronouns *which, who,* or *that?*
3. Can I remove the introductory *there is* or *are* and *it is?*
4. Can I delete prepositions?
5. Can I omit any *-ion* words?
6. Can I combine sentences and omit repetitious material?
7. Can I eliminate dead nouns?
8. Can I do away with deadwood?

The key factor in achieving sentence economy is your frame of mind. You must realize that it's not the number of words you write that matters, but what you say. If you clutter your work with unnecessary words, you will probably confound your readers, resulting in their either deciding not to finish your paper or else finishing it and being finished with you. That's how aggravating it is to read padded prose. So don't be wasteful—eliminate any unnecessary word. Doing so may almost kill you, but it will bring life and clarity to your writing.

ASSIGNMENTS

For Discussion

1 Create complex sentences from these pairs of disjoined sentences, adapted from an article by Norman Cousins, using the subordinators suggested after each pair. How should each be punctuated? Which can be made into two sentences without creating fragments? Which subordinators will not work? Why? Which can be shifted to different positions?

   a The fouling of the environment probably produces fewer headlines than wars, earthquakes, thunderbolts, and flash-floods. It is potentially one of history's greatest dangers to human life on earth. (but, however, nevertheless, moreover, therefore, because, although)

b   Environmental poisoning will accomplish what no war to date has. Present trends continue for the next several decades. (if, however, as, because, though)

c   In 1948, a "killer smog" snuffed out 20 lives in Donora, Pennsylvania, and made 6,000 other townspeople so sick that they probably wished they were dead. Meteorologists reported that Donora got off easy. (on the other hand, because, due to, however, if)

d   The greatest danger comes not from this kind of "particulate matter" with which the human body can usually cope. Our respiratory passages are linked with thousands of lashing, hairlike *cilia* that beat back most invading particles and prevent them from entering the lungs. (although, because, however, otherwise, also)

(2) Remove the unnecessary words from the following sentences and indicate the technique used: omitting the relative pronoun, removing the introductory words, deleting prepositions, avoiding the *-ion* word, combining clauses, eliminating dead nouns, doing away with deadwood, or any combination of these.

a   ~~There are~~ two screws ~~which are~~ included in the package ~~that~~ attach the handlebars to the frame.

b   In some cases, students do not know whether they will have enough money to pay for registration at the university next semester.

c   The chairman received your letter ~~in~~ which you informed him that due to the fact ~~that~~ you were ill, you did not take the final exam.

d   I wish to invite you to the first meeting of the Philosophy Club ~~this year. This meeting~~ will be held in the conference room of the Student Center ~~It will~~ occur on Wednesday, September 20, ~~and start~~ at 8 p.m.

e   He gave consideration to the recommendation that students should submit their applications before spring break.

f   In view of the fact that few women apply to the College of Engineering, ~~there are~~ few women students admitted.

g   It is the opinion of most women employees that the university is engaged in discrimination against them.

h   Many faculty members who have had extensive experience at other schools claim that discrimination of this kind also exists there.

i   The investigator conducted an examination of the records in a hurried manner.

j   The number of applications to the College of Education is on the decrease.

k   The president addressed the faculty with regard to this matter of decreasing enrollments.

l   He was doing well in the course until the time during the semester when the research report was due.

For Writing

1   Write a letter home explaining why you need a car; why you didn't make the dean's list; why you need money; why you want to get married; or some other explanation. Make effective use of subordinators in your paper.

2   Write a paper explaining how you have become a waster of words, perhaps including a few sentences or phrases that you especially regret. Make use of complex sentences.

3   Draft a letter to the author of a textbook, pointing out how he or she might have eliminated unnecessary words from a particular paragraph and urging the author to write more economically in the future.

4   Find a "fat" paragraph in a newspaper, article, or book. Write a paper for your instructor, showing how you would reduce the paragraph and identifying the techniques you would use.

Revision
of Expository
Writing

Revision is a process not available to you when you speak. True, as you talk, you can stop to correct a grammatical error or replace a mispronounced word, but the advantage of writing over speaking is that you have the time to bring your critical judgment to bear. You've surely experienced the embarrassment after a party of remembering something that you wish you hadn't said and wishing that there were some way to take it back. Writing, on the other hand, allows you to reconsider, to return, to redo. You hold all the cards: to stand with what you have written, to revise, to revise again, to return to the original version, or to the second, or to revise yet again. Whatever you finally decide to use will result from deliberate, conscious thought, which is almost always superior to impulse. Certainly, as you rework and rework material, it may lose its novelty and effectiveness in your own mind. But a reader, encountering it for the first time, will view your final draft as a fresh one and probably think that it appears on the page as it originally poured out of your mind.

Of course, it didn't—just as this book didn't pour out of our minds but resulted from planning, making several false starts, writing, revising, and revising again and again. And because this book is an example of expository writing we had certain questions in mind as we revised each chapter. These questions not only may help in revising your expository papers but also should provide a summary of much of the material discussed in this section on exposition. We have omitted some general questions about the subject—about its appeal, breadth, and complexity — because we assume that with the paper already written, you would probably decide to go with it at the revision stage instead of writing a completely new one. Otherwise, here are the questions:

340

1. Audience
   Is the paper directed effectively to a particular audience?
   Are there any assumptions about the audience's knowledge that might be erroneous?
   Is the tone appropriate for the audience?
   Has an effort been made to interest the audience?
2. Form
   Does the paper mainly fall under one general category: classification, definition, analysis, opinion?
   If the paper consists of several of these or only one, does it adhere to the discussed techniques appropriate to the form?
3. Logical Organization
   If the paper was based upon an outline, does it follow the outline fairly closely, so that its organization is logical?
   If the paper was not based on an outline, would an outline reveal that it had been logically organized?
   Is the thesis sentence clearly stated or implied?
4. Paragraphs
   Do most of the paragraphs fit some variation of the SRI format?
   Is the development (ILLUSTRATION) sufficient?
   Have all the appropriate resources been used for developing paragraphs—examples, statistics, authorities, and so on?
   Do the paragraphs have various levels of generality? Or do they all follow the same basic pattern with only two or three levels?
5. Sentences
   Does the sentence structure help to emphasize and focus the subject matter?
   Are clear relationship signals provided for the audience?
   Could any of the sentences be written more economically?
   Is it possible to eliminate any *who, which,* or *that* constructions, *There is* or *There are* sentence openings, *-ion* words, or any of the other unnecessary words and phrases discussed on pages 333–37?
6. Language and Usage
   Are words with special meanings defined?
   Are usages avoided that would be restricted to a particular group?
   Have the meanings of any difficult words been checked?
   Have any idioms been used that might confuse or irritate members of a general audience?
7. Introductions and Conclusions
   Is the introductory sentence attention-getting?
   Does the rest of the paragraph contain a general exploration of the broad subject to interest readers?
   Does the thesis appear near the end of the introduction?

Does the conclusion indicate that the paper is ending?
Does the conclusion leave readers with an important idea to remember?

You may feel by now that we are overemphasizing the importance of
revision. But revision in writing is like ripping apart a sewing project
or repainting one wall of a room because it does not yet meet your standards of excellence. It's how you go about improving a piece of writing.
Granted, there are times—examinations, in-class themes, routine letters
—when you can't revise. Realize, however, that under such conditions,
you are not writing at your best. You can do that only when you revise.
And you can revise effectively only when you properly psych yourself up
for the job and when you develop a systematic approach to it. To revise or
not to revise? In writing, that is the crucial question. Your answer will
determine whether you write your best. It's your choice.

REVISION EXERCISE

Revise a written paragraph that you prepared in a hurry and that
received a grade you're not satisfied with. As you revise, recopy the
paragraph so that you can use it later for comparison purposes. Put it
away for a few days and then revise the revision, again recopying it as
you go. Now analyze the three versions as we did the student sentences
on pages 336–37. List the major changes made. Which seems more
fluent and spontaneous? Ask your composition instructor to evaluate
your final draft.

The Argumentative Voice:
Persuasive Writing

23 The Nature of Persuasive Writing

THE PREVALENCE OF PERSUASION

If there were such a place as an average college, such a creature as an average male student, and such a thing as an average day, then here is how they might average out:

7:32 a.m. Tries to persuade roommate about benefits of attending eight o'clock class.

8:10 a.m. In English class, argues that Gene deliberately pushed Phineas in *A Separate Peace*.

10:18 a.m. Over coffee in Student Center, contends that English instructor favors women, especially sexy ones.

11:27 a.m. Tries to convince others in philosophy class that killing incurable patients is ethically the same as letting them die by withholding medication.

1:28 p.m. Analyzes arguments in favor of and against genetic control.

3:06 p.m. Attempts to coax ticket manager into better seats for Saturday's football game.

5:57 p.m. Holds forth on the glories of the fast hair dryer, the best invention since the wheel.

6:06 p.m. Between segments of TV news, watches commercials for deodorant, bath soap, denture adhesive, toothpaste, coffee, car, bra, dog food, razor blades, tires.

7:27 p.m. Urges roommate to go out for a few beers.

7:31 p.m. Attempts to talk roommate into taking in a movie.

7:33 p.m.	Convinces roommate to go out on blind double date.
9:26 p.m.	Argues with blind date that women should pay alimony.
10:17 p.m.	Disputes with waiter about bill.
11:46 p.m.	Tries to coax date into goodnight kiss.
12:33 a.m.	Induces roommate to help with math homework.
1:17 a.m.	Prevails on stereo nut next door to turn down volume.
1:59 a.m.	Points out to roommate the many reasons why they should not go out on any more blind dates.

All this suggests that each of us can spend much time either persuading others to do or believe something, or listening to others with similar designs on us. So it follows that we can benefit from becoming more adept at presenting and analyzing arguments, logical skills that can be improved by studying the art of persuasion.

THE REWARDS OF PERSUASION

Mastering the art of persuasion can be very rewarding and satisfying to you in your academic, social, and career roles. In college classes and in papers and exams, you will often confront controversial issues that require you to analyze and reason logically. In your social life, you will often want to stake out a position on a number of subjects: political, economic, cultural, educational. In less serious moments, you will try to persuade your parents and friends to accept your tastes in pets, clothes, eating places, television programs, film stars, vacation spots, and the latest hit songs. And after college, no matter what field you enter, you will spend much of your time trying to sell people some product, service, or idea, whether it be to accept an out-of-court settlement, to buy an annuity, to follow a diet more carefully, or to reject a proposal to build a new highway near homes. And when you sell people, you persuade them. Persuasion is a form of power. To convince others how to think or act is to exert control over them. And while few of us would like to dominate others completely, most of us would like at least occasionally to change the opinions and influence the actions of others.

In this respect, persuasion differs from exposition. Even in expository opinion papers, you need not worry about readers' prejudices or their inability to act. Generally, before you provide an explanation of your opinion, you consider what readers already know about the subject and what they need to know. But in writing persuasion, you must also consider how readers feel about the subject, why they do feel that way, and when their views are contrary to yours, whether they can be changed or modified and if so, how. Then you are ready to convince readers by countering or negating their arguments and advancing your own. This tactical planning and the ensuing verbal combat characterize persuasion, not exposition.

But all the planning in the world about how to persuade others cannot accomplish miracles. Facts and predispositions may thwart even the most effective arguments. After all, you cannot persuade your instructor to give you a million dollars, because the *fact* is that he doesn't have it, and even if he did, he would have a few other uses for the money. Nor can you talk him into giving you an *A* for the course if you haven't earned it. His professional commitment to evaluate your work honestly would predispose him against your request. You should realize that no skillful argument or emotional appeal can change the minds or actions of some people on some subjects. And you would be wise to consider this possibility before you begin to argue.

The study of persuasion may benefit you in ways other than winning arguments and influencing actions. It should help you in your relationships with others, in understanding yourself better, and in protecting you from the daily barrage of blatant and sneaky advertising attacks on your mind and pocketbook conducted over radio and television and in the newspapers, magazines, and mails.

How can the study of persuasion improve your relationships with others? By enabling you to discern the issues in an argument, to perceive basic assumptions and personal prejudices, to narrow the subject to the area of controversy, to eliminate any threat to the other person's security, to reduce hostility, and to realize at some stage that you have reached a stalemate or a point of diminishing or little return. Thus you may argue but not antagonize, persuade but not provoke, and even fail but still not lose friendship or respect, gaining in understanding as you come to know and appreciate another's position, and that person yours.

Of course, sometimes we engage in arguments as dispassionate participants, playing an intellectual game whose outcome concerns us little. We might argue about the merits of a movie, singer, football team, or concert, enjoying the give and take of lively discussion, the thrust and parry of keen wits. The study of persuasion enables us to relish the game more, to perceive its direction and dimension, and to play at it more skillfully and enthusiastically.

Sometimes our arguments are internal. You may debate with yourself about matters as trivial as whether to carry an umbrella to class or as serious as whether to spend the weekend with someone of the other sex. The study of persuasion will allow you to focus on the issues, to avoid deceiving yourself, to sift the true from the false, and to arrive at a more rational conclusion. Certainly you may disregard that conclusion, but at least you will know what you are doing and why.

Deciding on a course of action is often complicated by the beguiling pleas, appeals, admonitions, and entreaties from others in the form of political speeches, television commercials, charity appeals, mail offers, radio spots, newspaper and magazine ads, organization membership drives, and sales pitches, as well as proposals from friends and acquaintances to go, do, think, and act as they would like you to. How to decide? Sometimes there are no rational grounds for a logical decision. Then you may rely on chance—the flip of a real or imaginary coin—or your gut reaction to the person or the proposal. But on other occasions, you can weigh the facts, evaluate the evidence, discern the use of misleading data or unreliable testimonials, and see through the many phony, deceptive, and distorted persuasive devices. You may still be fooled some of the time—but you need not be fooled most of the time.

Thus the study of persuasion is not unrelated to your life but very much a part of it, whether you are speaking or writing or listening or reading. To think clearly, to analyze skillfully, and to reason effectively are all skills that will contribute greatly to your intellectual growth and will prove to be invaluable, whether you major in physical education, home economics, journalism, civil engineering, or some other field.

THE TYPES OF PERSUASION: LOGICAL AND EMOTIONAL

Before proceeding further, we should distinguish between the two types of persuasion: logical and emotional. Seldom are they found in their pure states: some emotion generally intrudes into even the most carefully reasoned argument, and some reason generally penetrates into even the most wildly emotional tirade. But to write and analyze arguments effectively, you will find it easier to understand the techniques employed if they are discussed according to whether their basic appeal is to logic or to the emotions.

Logical persuasion—or *argumentation,* as it is called—is exemplified on such formal occasions as debates and higher court trials but occurs also in serious discussions of important controversial issues in books and magazines and in newspaper articles and editorials. In argumentation the treatment of an issue is thorough, the tone factual, the subject significant, and the purpose to aid justice, truth, fairness. Argumentation appeals to reasonable people to accept what is reasonable and is based on reasoned evidence.

Emotional persuasion, on the other hand, plays on the self-interest and passions of people. The subject is not treated fully but is modified to suit the prejudices of the audience. For example, a politician may discuss an issue from one standpoint before urban voters and from the opposite standpoint before rural ones. The tone may also vary: it may be indignant, humorous, angry, scornful, pleading, threatening. The sky is the limit; often anything goes that works well. Like atomic energy, emotional persuasion may be used for right and wrong purposes. We trust you will use it wisely and justly, being ethically bound to avoid deception and misrepresentation.

As we mentioned, argumentation and emotional persuasion occasionally overlap. Lawyers may present logical cases for their clients but resort to emotional appeals in summations to juries. And emotional Fourth of July oratory about the glories of our country may contain many logical arguments. The twain can and do meet, but they may generally be distinguished by the way the conflicting ideas are treated. The formal technique of logical argumentation requires a thorough refutation of contrary points, thus imposing more rigid requirements of organization and development. Not only must you cite the reasons in favor of your conclusion, but you must negate the opposing evidence. Not so in emotional persuasion. Conflicting evidence need not be discussed, or if so, not necessarily in detail.

The presence or absence of detailed refutation should help you to distinguish between emotional and logical persuasion, but when do you use one and when the other? As in many writing situations, there is no blanket answer. Much depends on the subject, occasion, and audience. An important, complex subject may be best handled by the techniques of argumentation; a simple, relatively unimportant one, by emotional persuasion. If you are writing about your views on "mercy killing," you might treat it formally as an argument because of its highly controversial nature. You might find emotional persuasion more appropriate for advocating a longer Thanksgiving vacation or better football seats for students.

Even so, the choice isn't that simple. The argumentative approach is not always determined solely by your subject matter. For example, the full formal treatment of argumentation might be given to the matter of better football seats for students if you present it in a written statement to your college's Board of Trustees or Regents. On such an occasion, you should consider the major counterarguments: the contributions and the good will realized from the public or alumni sale of fifty-yardline and adjoining seats. To ignore these points would weaken your case.

There is another consideration besides the seriousness of the subject and the gravity of the occasion: the audience. When dealing with welleducated people, logical persuasion is usually more effective than emotional. Although all people respond to emotional appeals because all have emotions, sophisticated audiences are likely to be more critical, better able to recognize emotional techniques, more likely to disapprove of them, and more favorably inclined toward logical ones.

Once again, based on the subject, occasion, and audience, you will have to decide on your rhetorical strategy in using either emotional or logical persuasion. Then you will need to employ certain techniques and to avoid certain pitfalls. We will take up these matters in the chapters that follow.

SELECTION OF A SUBJECT FOR PERSUASION

You may be ready to engage in formal argumentation about some subject, but before doing so, you should determine whether it is worth your time and effort. Be careful about rolling up your sleeves and leaping into the fray until you have examined the issue to see whether it can be settled easily or at all.

You should avoid the kind of subject that can be decided by factual information. It is a waste of time to argue about such matters as the cost of college tuition, state appropriations for public education, supermarket profits, population figures, divorce statistics, or even the weather, because the answers are contained in encyclopedias, almanacs, or other reference sources. Why dispute about whether Russia or the United States has the greater number of atomic submarines when the information is accessible? Why debate about the resale value or gas mileage of different cars when the figures are available? Why quarrel about the grounds for divorce in your state when the regulations are printed? Or why try to persuade others that it is legal to melt down United States coins when lawbooks can be consulted? All these issues can be resolved by referring to sources available in most college or community libraries. There is no sense in wasting your time or effort on such matters.

Other subjects should be avoided because no conclusions can be reached. These usually involve matters of personal taste, either literally ("My mother is a better cook than yours") or figuratively ("My dog is more beautiful, more loyal, smarter than yours"). Sometimes these disputes are fun and illuminating, but more often they end nowhere, being based solely on personal opinion. To cite one example, people have been arguing for years whether men or women are better drivers. Statistics indicate that women are involved in fewer accidents and receive fewer citations for major traffic violations, such as drunken driving and speeding. But men do far more driving than women, on the average. If men drive five times as many miles as women do, they could be expected to receive five times as many major traffic violations and be involved in five times as many accidents. But how can you weigh the more difficult driving done by many women, carting playful children and household pets on errands in bumper-to-bumper city traffic, against the many miles driven by men on safer thruways and turnpikes? Are men or women better drivers? Better skip the subject or pursue it for fun, realizing that you will probably not persuade anyone.

Some matters involving aesthetics and morality may be sensibly argued only when you can suppress your feelings ("I like" or "I approve") and can instead advance reasons that are based on generally accepted standards or that can be defined and agreed upon. While it may be impossible to decide which beer tastes best, which store carries the most attractive clothes, or which perfume smells sexiest, it is possible to contend that a novel, movie, play, painting, concert, or student paper is superior according to established critical standards. There is a world of difference between personal statements like "I don't want my brothers and sisters to play around with drugs" and a well-constructed argument setting forth the psychological, social, and physiological reasons against experimentation with drugs. Similarly, an unsupported value judgment like "My high school is better than yours" cannot be logically justified, unless some objective standards can be agreed upon (student-faculty ratio, curriculum, extracurricular opportunities, comparable student test scores, number of dropouts, percentage of seniors entering college, library facilities).

SPECIAL CONSIDERATIONS IN PERSUASIVE WRITING

In persuasive writing it is particularly crucial to define your criteria. In Chapter 15 we discussed the importance and methodology of definition from the simplest type, the synonym definition, to the most complex, the extended definition. In no other form of writing is definition as vital as in argumentation. Probably more than half the disputes that occur every day could be avoided if both parties would agree first on their use of terms. For instance, if you argue with your parents that "People have a right to do their own thing," exactly what do you mean? Cheat on examinations? Play a stereo at full blast? Run nude on a public beach? Throw beer cans out of car windows? Unless you define your terms, you and your parents cannot debate the subject intelligently.

But defining terms carefully is not sufficient to win the case in formal logical arguments. You must know not only why you favor a particular position but also why others oppose it. If you wish to argue that college sports should be de-emphasized, for example, your points might be negated by a factor that you failed to consider, such as the influence a college's winning football team can have on the state legislature, which allocates funds to educational institutions. To present your case effectively, you should be fully informed. You can usually find excellent material in your college library, particularly if you ask a librarian for help. But remember that other sources of information are available on campus. Discussing a subject with some of your classmates and friends may reveal numerous arguments for and against it. Also, many faculty members are well informed in their respective fields: locate the proper person (a constitutional law professor on constitutional law issues, an agricultural economist on food prices, a mining engineer or physicist on coal gasification, a Russian specialist in political science on the Politburo); make an appointment to see that person; and take notes during the interview. Consult athletic coaches about college sports, college newspaper editors about various college events and issues. Then there are campus police, foreign students, psychologists, physicians, and others—all with special knowledge about particular subjects. Interviewing them can be valuable in gathering information and in helping you to formulate your ideas about the subject.

No matter how convincing your gathered information may be, only when your case is well reasoned will it be effective with a critical, intelligent audience. To determine whether it is or not, you need to have some understanding of the tactics of logical reasoning, particularly the processes of induction and deduction. The next two chapters will give you a background in the nature and use of these skills and the ways in which they relate to writing.

ASSIGNMENTS

For Discussion

1 It is often necessary in a persuasive paper to provide factual information as support for your argument. Students sometimes find it difficult to design such informative material so that it is persuasive rather than merely explanatory. To help you with this writing problem, examine the following pairs of examples and determine which is argumentative and which is expository. Determine which characteristics of language use and sentence structure influence your identification in each.

   a The usual explanation, that the stone giants were moved to their present sites on wooden rollers, is not feasible in this case, either. In addition, the island can scarcely have provided food for more than 2000 inhabitants. (A few hundred natives live on Easter Island today.) A shipping trade, which brought food and clothing to the island for the stonemasons, is hardly credible in antiquity.

   —Erich Von Daniken, *Chariots of the Gods?*

   One explanation for the Easter Island statues is that large numbers of people rolled the huge stones to their present sites. But it is believed that the island itself could not have supported so many people, nor could merchants from another place have brought food and supplies to the stonemasons on the island.

b The act provided that after every Indian had been allotted land, the remainder would be put up for sale to the public. But the loopholes with which the act was punctured made it an efficient instrument for separating the Indians from this land. The plunder was carried on with remarkable order. The first lands to go to whites were the richest—bottomlands in river valleys or fertile grasslands. Next went the slightly less desirable lands, such as those that had to be cleared away before they could produce a crop. Then the marginal lands were taken, and so on, until the Indian had left to him only desert that no white considered worth the trouble to take. Between the passage of the Allotment Act in 1887 and a New Deal investigation in 1934, the Indians had been reduced to only 56,000,000 acres out of the meager 138,000,000 acres that had been allotted them—and every single acre of the 56,000,000 was adjudged by soil conservationists to be eroded. At the same time that the Indians were being systematically relieved of their lands, their birth rate rose higher than the mortality rate, and so there were more and more Indians on less and less land.

— Peter Farb, "The American Indian: A Portrait in Limbo,"
Man's Rise to Civilization

The act provided that after every Indian had been allotted land, the remainder would be put up for sale to the public. But the many provisions in the act permitted the separating of the Indians from the land. The first lands to go were the richest—bottomlands in river valleys or fertile grasslands. Next went the slightly less desirable lands, and then the marginal lands. Finally, the Indian was left with desert land that no one else wanted. Between the passage of the Allotment Act in 1887 and a New Deal investigation in 1934, the Indians retained only 56,000,000 eroded acres out of the 138,000,000 acres that had been allotted to them. During this same period, the birth rate rose higher than the mortality rate, so there were more Indians on less land.

c All men are capable of procreation. Besides the power to think and will, man has the ability to create new life. These generative powers are possessed by all normal men and women for the purpose of perpetuating the human race. It is axiomatic that those who bring such life into existence should assume responsibility for it. And since this obligation is not a light one, mankind must be encouraged to assume it and be rewarded for doing so.

— John S. Banahan, "What a Catholic Wishes to Avoid in Marriage"

Besides the ability to think and will, all normal people have the ability to procreate. However, human reproduction involves heavy responsibility.

2 From the following list of general topics, choose those that would be most suitable for a persuasive paper. Be prepared to give a rationale for those you choose and those you reject. Some might be suitable for more than one kind of paper: explain.

   a Inequities of the income tax system
   b The beauties of a sunset
   c A report to stockholders
   d Art galleries in the major cities of the United States
   e Legalization of marijuana
   f The extent of executive privilege in the federal government
   g Busing for racial integration of schools
   h Student population and distribution in the United States
   i Extrasensory perception
   j Animal life on a coral reef
   k Competition for grades
   l The Third Reich in the Second World War
   m The incidence of liver cancer in plastics workers
   n The history of the Khmer people of Cambodia
   o The role of the news media in politics

3 Why is it important to define terms and to deal with opposing viewpoints in argument? Explain, using your own examples.

CHAPTER 24

The Tactics of Logical Persuasion: Induction and Deduction

We have said that persuasion is a form of power. Presenting one side of a controversy so effectively that you win people over to your way of thinking or encourage them to take action makes you a leader and a guide for others. But to do this, you must increase your persuasive force—the energy behind effective argument. Persuasive force is a result of the interaction of the many factors in the communication process: the critical judgment or the interest of the audience, the time, the place, the social circumstances, or the projected "voice" of the speaker or writer. The most persuasive and logical of arguments can lose its force if, for instance, the audience has no understanding of the subject matter: the advantages of nuclear energy over hydroelectric power would have little significance to an audience of Amazon Indians. A beautifully structured argument on the desirability of continuing foreign aid to Taiwan might prove ineffectual if the place—say, the Senate chamber—was so hot and stuffy that the audience was too drowsy to pay attention. And, in the past, many well-documented and effectively argued editorials on the excesses of air pollution had little effect on the American public: the time was not yet ripe.

Persuasive force is a result of the total argumentative situation: it is most effective when everything works together. But how can you control all these factors? In speaking, you can do so fairly easily. If your audience stops listening, becomes hostile, or is distracted by outside noises, you can do something to regain their attention: switch to another approach or close a window. But how can you gain control in a written argument? The answer is you can't, at least not in the same ways; in writing you must rely more heavily on logical reasoning, which can exert more influence on your readers than emotional appeal can. The latter may work best in a face-to-face situation where the audience interacts with the speaker. But in written argument, you should depend upon sound reasoning to sway your audience. Logical force—the power generated by tracing sound reasons through to logical conclusions—supplies your persuasive thrust. Thus, because written persuasion depends so greatly on logical reasoning, you need to have some knowledge of its tactics so that you can sharpen your tools of persuasion to energize your own persuasive force.

Logical reasoning involves two basic processes of thinking and organization: induction and deduction. Although closely interrelated, each has its own forms and methods of organizing the thinking process. Let's take a look at how they work and how you can use them to write more persuasively.

The processes of induction and deduction both lead to conclusions but in different ways. Inductive reasoning proceeds from a number of particular cases to a generalized conclusion; deductive reasoning proceeds from the application of a general principle to a particular case and then to a particular conclusion. To illustrate:

Induction

Particular cases	Each of twenty-seven supermarket brand items examined was cheaper than the comparable name-brand item.
↓	
Generalization	Supermarket brand items are cheaper than comparable name-brand items.

Deduction

General principle	Supermarket brand items are cheaper than comparable name-brand items.
↓	
Particular case	This is a supermarket brand can of peas.
Conclusion	It is cheaper than the comparable name-brand can of peas.

Now let's examine these reasoning processes, noting the characteristics and the special problems of each.

INDUCTION

Induction, the process of reaching a conclusion based on facts, observations, and testimony, is often referred to as the scientific method because scientists rely on it in their work. But it is also the basis for much of the reasoning in our daily lives. If we find after a few purchases that one bookstore charges more than another, we conclude that it is more expensive than the other. If we observe that there is a frost late in April for a number of years, we conclude that there is no point in planting tomatoes before then. And if each time we eat a hamburger at a certain restaurant we get a stomachache, we conclude that we ought not to eat hamburgers there. As you can see, you have been thinking inductively all your life.

Some Dangers in Inductive Reasoning

HASTY GENERALIZATION

Induction comes naturally; we all tend to generalize about our experience. But there is danger whenever we make what is known as "the inductive leap," such as concluding that all supermarket brand items are cheaper on the basis of examining twenty-seven of them, thus jumping from a few observations to a generalization. Scientists in laboratories are careful to run numerous experiments before announcing their results. But many other people are in such a hurry to draw conclusions that they make an inductive leap to a *hasty generalization,* one that is based on insufficient evidence. Prejudices about minorities usually arise from observing or hearing about a few individuals in a group and then leaping to a conclusion about all members of that group. Often this stereotyping results from our response to conduct that confirms a prejudice. For example, having heard that redheads are quick-tempered, we recall this generalization when a redhaired friend excites easily. Unfortunately, we often ignore the generalization or fail to discard it when other redheads react calmly and coolly in a similar emotional situation. Thus prejudice continues, based on myths about blacks, Indians, Jews, Catholics, Polish-Americans, women, and many others.

Numerous other hasty generalizations about people are not necessarily based on prejudice, but on misinformation, such as that all college professors are radicals, all poets are impractical dreamers, all Cadillac owners are wealthy, all politicians are dishonest, and all Italians are Mafia members. We should be particularly careful in generalizing about human beings, remembering that each is a unique individual, influenced by genetic, environmental, and other factors—but not completely determined by any of them. Thus we should subject these generalizations to the most intense scrutiny, requiring that they be based on a sufficient number of cases and that the information be reliable.

UNRELIABLE INFORMATION

Unreliable information often comes from biased or incompetent sources. Although print causes an assertion to appear factual, we should realize that statements are written by human beings, often with vested interests in their subjects. We should be suspicious about assertions against cutbacks in defense spending by Pentagon figures, against strip mining restrictions by coal companies, against cable television by television station owners, against abolition of the depletion allowance by oil companies, against national health insurance by doctors. These people and organizations find it difficult to be impartial about such issues because their profits, salaries, lives, and futures are involved in decisions about them. Because the truth may be obscured by self-interest in any situation, relying on information from a particular source can be dangerous unless you know something about the source's relationship to the subject.

Sources may also be unreliable because of their incompetence, or false authority. This frequently occurs when well-known figures in one field issue statements in areas outside their expertise. For example, athletes frequently provide testimonials in advertisements for products. But there is no reason why a professional quarterback should be a greater authority on deodorants than other men or why a tennis star should know more about cosmetics than other women. Of course, if she endorses tennis racquets, balls, or shoes, that's another story. But even then, we should remember that she's being paid for her testimonial and therefore cannot be impartial. Of course, athletes are not the only culprits. Film stars speak out on politics, economists about education, doctors about crime, lawyers about traffic problems, clergymen about economics, and college professors about everything. All these people are entitled to an opinion, but we should question their authority in one field when their reputation has been made in another.

Thus far we have discussed induction as a reasoning process leading from *some* to *all,* from particular cases to a generalization about them. We have focused also on the difficulty of inductive reasoning, specifically the dangers of hasty generalization and of relying on incompetent or biased sources. Let us now consider the forms that inductive reasoning can take.

Forms of Inductive Reasoning

SAMPLING

Induction is frequently used to arrive at a conclusion about a group based on questioning a *sample,* or a certain percentage, of that group. This method of induction is called *sampling.* The Gallup Poll, for example, works inductively with a small sample of the population to inform us about how people feel about political issues, the economy, potential presidential candidates, and other matters. Although you will probably have few occasions to do any sampling yourself, you should be generally aware of proper sampling methodology, if only to discern errors in the evidence used to support or oppose your argument.

Basic to the concept of sampling is the fact that it is impossible or impractical to poll the whole group. Consequently, instead of interviewing every owner of a television set, the TV pollsters question a number of people who represent a cross section of the population. In any sample, it is essential that the number of people be large enough and the nature of the people be representative. Unless you have taken a course in statistics and know how to determine a sufficient statistical sample, you must use common sense in judging whether a sample is large enough. Obviously, if you wanted to find out something about the average freshman in a class of one thousand you should not poll ten; about 10 percent, or one hundred students, would be more acceptable. Next is the problem of determining that the sample is representative. If all one hundred students were fraternity members, or veterans, or scholarship students, the sample would be biased. A more representative group would result from some form of random sampling, either selecting names out of a barrel or following some pattern of chance selection, such as taking every tenth name in a roster of the freshman class. Professional pollsters usually follow a modification of this random procedure, dividing the group being sampled into subgroups and giving each subgroup a weight corresponding to its proportion in the entire group. Within each subgroup, individuals would be selected randomly. Although this is the most complicated process, it is the most exact. For example, to learn about the church-going habits of students, pollsters would probably divide the student body into religious groups and then randomly sample each group—Baptist, Methodist, Catholic, Jewish, and so on—according to its weighted proportion. But whatever the method, a sample should be large enough and representative enough to ensure objectivity and accuracy.

ANALOGY

Another form that inductive reasoning may take is *analogy,* a comparison between two things that are alike in some respects and that therefore are inferred to be alike in another. Analogical reasoning occurs quite often in business, where planning is based on the hypothesis that a profitable product in one city will sell as well in a similar community, a technique successful in one factory will work also in a similar plant, and a site that attracts customers in one part of the country will do so in another. But just as businesses are not always successful in applying analogies, neither does analogy always benefit an argument, particularly when what is compared is not basically similar. For example, it may be true that you can't teach old dogs new tricks, but this adage cannot be extended to old people.

Reasoning by analogy carries great persuasive force but is not logically sound because what is true of something at some time in some place is not necessarily true of something else at another time and in another place. Yet analogies can appear to be quite convincing, as this letter to *Newsweek* by James C. Simmons illustrates:

Death, taxes, and the prohibitionists are always with us. The last naively believed they could cure a host of social vices by outlawing liquor, gambling, prostitution, drugs and pornography. They were wrong, of course. And if gun control goes on the books, the result will be the same: people who want guns for illegal purposes will have no difficulty getting them—they will simply pay more on the black market.

The suggestion here that gun control must fail because control of liquor, gambling, prostitution, drugs, and pornography have failed is a clever use of analogy but is logically unacceptable. These social vices are viewed as victimless crimes that provide some pleasure to users while not usually harming others. But guns kill thousands of innocent people every year. Thus the analogy, like all analogies, fails. Of course, Simmons has a point in stating there will be a black market for guns. It is just that solely on the basis of the analogy, there is no sound reason why guns will be as easy to get as liquor was during Prohibition or as illegal drugs are today.

Certainly, you may employ analogy to add interest and illustration to your argument, but don't depend on it for logical proof.

CAUSAL GENERALIZATION

Inductive reasoning is also used to establish causal relationships. When we observe that all the plants in our house are healthy except for one in a dark corner, we conclude that its condition is caused by lack of light. Here is how we arrived at a causal generalization by reasoning inductively:

> Plants: All plants in our house are alike and receive similar care.
>
> Sick plant: This plant is treated the same as all the others except that it gets no light.

Causal generalization: The sick plant (and any others treated like it)
will not grow well and be healthy because of
the lack of light.

Like other forms of inductive reasoning, causal generalization is
fraught with dangers. In our example, the causal connection was simple
and direct. In other instances, the relationship may appear to be causal
but may only be temporal, coincidental, or correlative; or it may indeed
be causal but the cause may not be the only one or not a direct one.

Most common of all the dangers inherent in causal generalization is
the relationship that appears to be causal but is actually *temporal*. Popular superstitions best illustrate this point. A student who fails an exam
on Friday, the thirteenth, blames the failure on the date. Another who
walks under a ladder on the way to class and later stumbles on the stairs,
bruising a knee, blames the injury on the ladder. A third who has a rabbit's foot in hand when an unexpected check arrives from home attributes the windfall to the lucky talisman. And millions of people consult
their horoscope every day, believing that a causal relationship exists
between their birthdate and their daily fortunes. Such examples may
seem silly, but innumerable people swear by these and other superstitions. Unfortunately, they remember only the instances when there
was a *coincidental* relationship. How often, for example, has the horoscope been wrong, Friday the thirteenth passed without incident, no
accident resulted from walking under a ladder, or bad luck occurred
despite the rabbit's foot?

Rationally analyzed, superstitions are examples of hasty generalizations: they belong to a subgroup consisting of one kind of cause-and-
effect relationship. If one occurrence follows another closely, the first
is interpreted as the cause of the second—a type of faulty, or fallacious,
reasoning so common that it bears a special name, *post hoc* (abbreviated
from the Latin *post hoc, ergo propter hoc,* meaning "after this, therefore
because of this"). *Post hoc* reasoning is exemplified not only in superstitions but in other situations, even medicine. For centuries, ill persons
were subjected to the practice of bleeding. Because many of them responded well to this treatment, bleeding was believed to have caused
their recovery. This *post hoc* reasoning and "the cure" were finally
abandoned when the medical profession realized that patients recovered
from diseases because of their bodies' natural recuperative powers or
because the disease had run its course, not because of the bleeding. But
even today many people credit various patent medicines or folk remedies
for curing common colds when they would probably recover in the same
time without any treatment except resting and drinking extra liquids.

One way to test causal relationships is to determine whether they are regular—that is, whether a particular cause always produces the effect. Here are three questions to ask:

1. Does the cause always produce the effect?
2. Without the cause, is the effect different?
3. When the cause varies, does the effect change?

Now to apply these as a test for causal relationships. Let's say that for several Christmas holidays you've given your friends loaves of fruit bread made from your mother's old recipe with yeast, cinnamon, eggs, flour, raisins, citron, maraschino cherries, and other goodies. This year you're a little short of yeast so you omit it entirely from one loaf, add only one package to another, and use the regular two packages in a third. After you've given the dough time to rise, you note that the one with the right amount of yeast has doubled in bulk, the one with half the amount has increased somewhat, and the one without yeast has not risen at all. Under these circumstances, assuming that each loaf otherwise contained the same ingredients and was treated the same, you could conclude inductively that the yeast caused the fruit bread to rise.

But, alas, some conclusions, particularly those involving people, are not this simple and do not readily lend themselves to this test. Let's take a look at some examples.

As you know, there is a link between cigarette smoking and lung cancer. A high proportion of males who smoke heavily die of this disease, a lesser proportion who smoke moderately contract the disease, and relatively few nonsmokers are afflicted. Statistics indicate, therefore, that the cause (heavy smoking) often produces the effect (cancer), that without the cause the effect is different (those who do not smoke seldom get lung cancer), and that when the cause varies (light smoking) the effect changes (fewer cancer deaths). In such situations, scientists and other careful observers call the relationship a *correlation* rather than a cause because a direct causal connection has not been proven. There is a possibility, for example, that some third factor—physiological or psychological—may be responsible both for the desire to smoke and for the lung cancer.

Mention of this third factor suggests another problem in dealing with causal relationships: a cause may not be the only one or the direct one or even a possible one. Recent figures about rape in our country reveal that this crime has been increasing greatly. But some authorities wonder whether the increased number of rapes is due to more rapes being committed or more rapes being reported. Formerly, authorities estimated that in only one rape out of ten were the police notified. Recently, as a result of the consciousness-raising efforts of the women's liberation movement and more sensitivity by the police in dealing with rape victims, more victims may be reporting the crime and the incidence of rape may not have increased significantly.

Finally, our tendency to oversimplify sometimes results in a failure to perceive that a cause may not be the only one or the direct one. Too often we rush in with simple answers to complex problems. We might talk of a friend's dropping out of school because of low grades, a person's divorce because of financial problems, or our country's economic difficulties because of increased oil prices. These may all be examples of oversimplification. The friend's dropping out of school could stem from financial problems; the divorce may have resulted from sexual tensions; and the inflation may have been caused by numerous other factors, particularly government spending during the Vietnam War. Or, in one of these examples, the apparent cause may have been only an indirect one. Low grades may have been a cause for your friend's leaving school, but the direct cause may have been his lack of money, which required that he work forty hours a week, leaving him too tired to study or attend classes regularly. In this situation, your friend's financial problem is the direct cause, his poor academic record the indirect cause.

At this point you may feel that induction is a lost cause. You should not. But you should be more cautious and critical when reasoning inductively and when analyzing inductive arguments. You should make yourself aware of the perils of hasty generalizations, the dangers of incompetent or biased sources, the risks of an insufficient or an unrepresentative sample, and the pitfalls of analogy. And then there are the hazards of causal generalizations: the temptations of *post hoc* reasoning; the possibility of confusing a correlation with a cause; or of failing to identify the importance of the cause—whether it is the only one or the direct one.

You may feel that we have caused this subject to be difficult and complicated. Let us assure you that we are not the cause: logical thinking is a complex human activity that often requires strenuous intellectual effort, hard work, and self-discipline. Yet it is particularly necessary and rewarding in argumentation, which involves not only inductive reasoning, but deductive. And now, on to that.

DEDUCTION

As we indicated previously, deduction, the other major form of argumentation, follows a different reasoning pattern. Induction leads us to a conclusion after an examination of the evidence. Deduction, on the other hand, is based mainly on assumption; no discernible evidence has to underlie the assumption: it is a statement accepted as true. Assuming a certain premise, then you logically arrive at a conclusion, as this example illustrates:

All freshmen enroll in freshman English. (assumed premise)
All fraternity pledges are freshmen.
Therefore, all fraternity pledges enroll in freshman English. (conclusion)

From the first two statements, you can logically conclude that all fraternity pledges enroll in freshman English. Note that you reached this conclusion simply by thinking about the assumed premise; you did not have to interview students, talk to the registrar, consult with the dean, examine records, or for that matter, stir from your seat. Instead, you can rely completely on the logical relationships between a given assumption and the statements following it.

But the distinction between induction and deduction is not quite that simple. Induction can play a role in a deductive argument. In our example, how did we arrive at the assumption that all freshmen take freshman English? We probably based it on the college's rule or took someone's word for it. But we might have inspected a number of transcripts and concluded inductively that all freshmen take the course. Similarly, our second statement about the freshman status of fraternity pledges could have been based on hearsay or reached inductively by examining their records.

While induction and deduction may be combined to arrive at a conclusion, each is a distinct process. In inductive reasoning, we rely on evidence discovered or believed to be true, as, for example, we relied on the studies leading to the generalization that heavy smokers more frequently develop lung cancer. But realize that in inductively arriving at such a conclusion we cannot examine all the possible evidence; much has to be skipped over. So we move from some of the evidence to the conclusion, assuming that the remaining evidence will support the same conclusion. This reasoning process, as mentioned earlier, is called the inductive leap. But the omitted evidence might have forced a different outcome; therefore, induction may not always lead to absolutely accurate conclusions. Heavy smoking might be only one of the factors in lung cancer, and the missing evidence might have illuminated that. Deduction, on the other hand, when based on a true premise, must lead to an indisputable conclusion. Also, deductive reasoning follows a special pattern not necessary to induction, and the form of this reasoning must be *valid* if the reasoning is to be sound. The concept of validity is so crucial and complicated that we will spend the rest of this chapter on it.

We assume that you have a common-sense knowledge of truth and that you understand that true premises are a necessary ingredient for acceptable deductive reasoning. These points are important because it is possible to construct a valid argument based on false premises. Here's how:

> All typed papers will receive an A.
> All the students in Professor Brown's class turned in typed papers.
> Therefore, all the students in Professor Brown's class will receive an A.

There's nothing wrong with the form of the reasoning here; it's valid. Yet, despite its validity, the conclusion is worthless because it has been derived from a false premise: all typed papers do not automatically receive A's. Thus a deductive argument can be valid but false. Keep in mind as you read this discussion that we assume deductive reasoning is based on true premises.

On now to the concept of validity, a subject considered in such detail by Aristotle and later logicians that a thorough study usually requires at least an entire semester. Consequently, we can only introduce you to the fundamentals, enough to help you in most arguments.

The Categorical Syllogism

You have probably noticed from the previous examples that deductive reasoning often follows a particular form, a unit of three statements; first, one that sets up the general terms or conditions, then one that presents the particular terms or conditions, and finally a conclusion that must logically follow from the preceding statements. This form is called a syllogism. In a categorical syllogism, the first two statements are referred to as the premises; the third, as the conclusion. Although syllogisms take many forms—some constructed on premises, some on relationships between statements—the most common kind, the categorical syllogism, looks like this:

	Categorical Syllogism	*Shorthand Form*
Major premise:	All in-state students are registered voters.	All A's are B's.
Minor premise:	All freshmen are in-state students.	All C's are A's.
Conclusion:	Therefore, all freshmen are registered voters.	All C's are B's.

Not only can you reduce syllogisms to a shorthand form, you can also draw pictures of them to show their validity. Traditionally, overlapping circles (called Venn diagrams) have been used for this purpose, but we believe that you will find simple sketches like these more helpful:

Major premise: All freshmen are dorm residents.

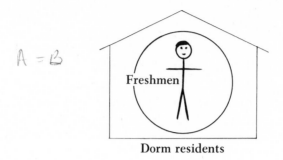

Minor premise: All the members of the college tennis team are freshmen.

Conclusion: Therefore, all members of the college tennis team are dorm residents.

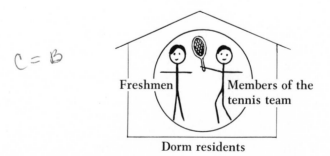

   Look at a picture of another categorical syllogism, this one based on a negative major premise. In this syllogism, we have a single individual in the minor premise, but because each individual person is one of a kind—the only one making up that particular class—we assume that *all* precedes the name:

Categorical Syllogism	Shorthand Form
Major premise: No graduate students are dorm residents.	No A's are B's.
Minor premise: Carol Smith is a graduate student.	(All) C is A.
Conclusion: Therefore, Carol Smith is not a dorm resident.	(All) C is not B.

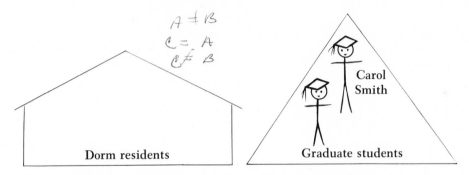

This syllogism is valid, as our drawing shows; Carol Smith is included in the group "graduate students," but not in "dorm residents."

Let's move on to a more complex syllogism:

Categorical Syllogism	Shorthand Form
Major premise: Some older students are dorm residents.	Some A's are B's.
Minor premise: No graduate students are dorm residents.	No C's are B's.
Conclusion: Therefore, some older students are not graduate students.	Some A's are not C's.

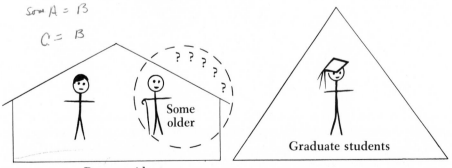

The "some" qualifier in a syllogism indicates that the assertion is only about that part of the group; it says nothing about the other members of the group. In this syllogism, the writer knows that some older students are dorm residents, but knows nothing about where the other older students live. The writer also knows that older students living in dorms are not graduate students. The sketch indicates that the writer's reasoning about this information is valid.

Now let's use a graphic illustration to test an invalid syllogism:

	Categorical Syllogism	Shorthand Form
Major premise:	All married students are car owners.	All A's are B's.
Minor premise:	All teaching assistants are car owners.	All C's are B's.
Conclusion:	Therefore, all married students are teaching assistants.	All A's are C's.

As you can see, the illustration of the syllogism reveals that it is not valid. Both the groups—teaching assistants and married students—may own cars, but all teaching assistants need not be married students.

Our purpose in using illustrations for these syllogisms is to help you gain a clearer understanding of them and to suggest a technique you may use in deciding whether they are valid or not. Some people do well with pictures, some with shorthand formulations, some with complete statements. Choose whichever works best for you.

Syllogism Fallacies

A syllogism is valid only if the reasoning process is sound—that is, if the conclusion follows logically from the given premises. The conclusion cannot go beyond the boundaries set up in the premises. If it does, the reasoning is unsound. An instance of unsound reasoning is called a *fallacy*. Here we shall consider three of the most common kinds of fallacies.[1]

[1] You might be interested to know that in traditional logic, these three fallacies are called, in the order in which they are discussed here, the Fallacy of Four Terms, the Fallacy of the Undistributed Middle, and the Fallacy of Illicit Process.

If a syllogism contains more than three terms, the logical bounds of the syllogism form are overstepped and a fallacy is the result:

A   B

Major premise: *The dictionary* is *a guide to the language.*

C   D

Minor premise: *The thesaurus* is *a book of synonyms.*
Conclusion: None possible because one of these four terms would have to be left out in the logical cold.

Generally, you won't be deceived by a syllogism like this one, with its four clearly distinct terms. A more common problem arises when what appear to be three terms are actually four because one term is used with two meanings. Here's an example:

Major premise: All liberals favor large government social programs.
Minor premise: Professor Green is liberal about attendance and late papers.
Conclusion: Therefore, Professor Green favors large government social programs.

Obviously, the word *liberal* here is used in two senses, one political and the other academic. The syllogism, consequently, is invalid because it contains four terms (*liberal* in the political sense, *liberal* in the academic sense, *Professor Green,* and *large government social programs*).

Syllogistic reasoning can also be invalid if the conclusion attributes characteristics to a whole class or group when the premises have assigned these qualities only to a part of the class or group. Some examples will clarify this fallacy:

Major premise: All property owners favor reduced real estate taxes.
Minor premise: Janet favors reduced real estate taxes.
Conclusion: Therefore, Janet is a property owner.

The premises here do not validly allow the conclusion. They tell us that Janet and the property owners agree about real estate taxes, but not that Janet is a member of that group, sharing *all* its characteristics. You may better understand the illogic of the fallacy by laughing at it in this nonsense syllogism:

Major premise: All goats have beards.
Minor premise: Santa Claus has a beard.
Conclusion: Therefore, Santa Claus is a goat.

It's easy to see the faulty reasoning here but often harder to spot it in unethical advertising copy or a political speech, such as the following:

Now you good folks don't need no college degrees to figure out just where me and my opponent stand. I'm for making people work and not paying them for sitting around doing nothing. My opponent, he favors giving them welfare just like all those ignorant do-gooders and big-spenders do. In my book, that makes him one of those ignorant do-gooders and big-spenders. And that sure ain't the kinda fellow us folks here want to vote for, is it?

The political opponent here, like Janet and Santa Claus in the previous examples, has been falsely associated with a group when he shares only one characteristic of that group.

A related fallacy occurs in this form of syllogism:

Major premise: All faculty members belong to the Credit Union.
Minor premise: All faculty members belong to the Faculty Club.
Conclusion: Therefore, all Credit Union members belong to the Faculty Club.

The conclusion here is not valid because nothing in the premises states anything about *all* Credit Union members. Of the three groups mentioned there (*faculty members, Credit Union,* and *Faculty Club*), we know something only about all faculty members. Possibly, members of the business office could belong to the Credit Union but not the Faculty Club, while administrators like assistant deans could belong to the Faculty Club but not to the Credit Union. We cannot know from the premises. Consequently, this form of syllogism, which contains an *all* statement about a class or group (Credit Union members) in the conclusion, cannot be valid unless there is an *all* statement about that class or group in the premises. This simpler example should help you to spot this fallacy:

Major premise: All rings are luxuries.
Minor premise: All rings are small, circular metal bands.
Conclusion: Therefore, all luxuries are small, circular metal bands.

The Conditional Syllogism

In a categorical syllogism, validity stems from the logical relationships between the terms in the subject and predicate components (or slots) of the two premises in the conclusion derived from them, as in:

All men are spiritual brothers.
John and Mac are men.
Therefore, John and Mac are spiritual brothers.

There are other kinds of deduction involving syllogisms in which certain conditions are set up and if these conditions are met, the conclusion is valid. One of these is sometimes known as an *if/then* syllogism:

> *If* the stadium is finished, *then* the team will open its season there.
> The stadium is finished.
> Therefore, the team will open its season there.

Another kind of "conditional" syllogism is the *either/or* type:

> *Either* the Common Market succeeds *or* Europe falls.
> The Common Market is succeeding.
> Therefore, Europe will not fall.

Both these forms are tricky and can be valid only if the conditions and the alternatives as stated in the syllogism are scrupulously met. We need not go into great detail about them here; we mention them only because they occur so often in written argument. Because they are frequently at the core of fallacious reasoning, we will deal with them at greater length in our discussion of other logical fallacies in Chapter 25.

Validity, Truth, and Form

You may wonder why we have given space to formal considerations of logic in a composition textbook. The answer is that just as you naturally express your thoughts and ideas in certain sentence patterns, so too you naturally formulate arguments in logical patterns. But in persuasive writing, mere ability to create logical patterns is not enough. As you probably realize by now, the logical form—the syllogism—has persuasive power of its own, aside from the information or conclusion that it carries. As we've indicated, even a nonsensical or blatantly false argument appears persuasive if presented in a valid, logical form. You might say that using logical deductive argument without realizing the power inherent in its form is like firing a gun without knowing whether it's loaded or not. In like manner, people can easily be deceived if they do not know that there is a difference between truth and validity. Who knows, for instance, how many people are persuaded by the "truth" of a slogan like "If guns are outlawed, only outlaws will have guns," when they are really responding to the persuasive force of a valid syllogism? The form camouflages other obvious possibilities; after all, policemen also carry guns. Many experienced writers capitalize on the persuasive force of syllogistic reasoning; but responsible writers, in addition, avoid using deductive reasoning for unethical purposes. They are careful to arrive at conclusions that are both valid and true.

In order for a syllogistic argument to be true, the conclusion must stem from true premises; truth is not dependent on validity—on whether the reasoning is sound or not. To demonstrate, let's look at this syllogistic argument:

All feminists are against motherhood.   A's are B's.
Joan is a feminist.   C's are A's.
Therefore, Joan is against motherhood.   C's are B's.

The reasoning is ironclad; it proceeds validly from premise to premise to conclusion. But because the major premise is false—a gross over-generalization—the conclusion is false. However, because it "sounds logical," the unwary might be convinced that the conclusion is true, just from the force of the logical argument. And it is precisely this character-istic of deductive reasoning that demagogues and unethical advertisers exploit. Making their task simpler is the fact that validity is always easier to establish than truth—even when the audience understands the mechanical processes of deductive reasoning. Perhaps that is because "truth" is so elusive; people hold radically different attitudes about abstract ideas such as religion, love, socialism, and justice. Therefore, in your own writing, you are probably on safer logical grounds to operate from premises that can be supported by factual concrete evidence. This syllogism demonstrates some of the problems confronted in reasoning from abstract ideas:

All things derived from God are capable of love.   A's are B's.
Human beings are things derived from God.   C's are A's.
Therefore, human beings are capable of love.   C's are B's.

Even though they might recognize such a syllogism as valid, your audience could accept the conclusion as true only if they believed that (1) God exists, (2) all things are derived from God, and (3) all things, including human beings, are capable of love. So you see, when we speak of "truth," we can speak only in relative terms; thus we can surely argue more effectively if we avoid abstract premises whose truth can be questioned.

The aim of this discussion has been to show you that in deductive reasoning, truth and validity are two separate entities, but they are equally important. Unlike love and marriage in the once-popular song, you *can* have one without the other. But you should realize that you can achieve maximum persuasive force only when your arguments are both valid and true. Otherwise, you will be guilty of reasoning that is either untrue or unsound. In either instance, your reasoning will be unac-ceptable.

ASSIGNMENTS

For Discussion

In the following examples, determine whether the paragraphs de-pend upon inductive or deductive argument. Remember, induction moves from the particular to the general, deduction from the general to the particular. Also, how does each paragraph relate to the SRI principle of paragraphing (Chapter 17)?

a The reputed lush jungles of Central America exist in only a few places, where enough rain falls to support heavy vegetable growth, and even there soils are notoriously poor. Most of Central America is high, rugged and mountainous. In these regions there are only two seasons—wet and dry—and the dry is searing. No rain falls for six long months, streams dry up, vegetation withers, and agriculture and vegetable growth in general come to an end. This type of high and seasonably dry mountain country is sadly depleted by erosional processes. It is in this area where ignorance and indifference are causing the plunder of these nations.
—James B. Packer, "Slash and Burn Below the Border," *Smithsonian*

b The primary function of a university is to discover and disseminate knowledge by means of research and teaching. To fulfill this function a free interchange of ideas is necessary not only within its walls but with the world beyond as well. It follows that the university must do everything possible to ensure within it the fullest degree of intellectual freedom. The history of intellectual growth and discovery clearly demonstrates the need for unfettered freedom, the right to think the unthinkable, discuss the unmentionable, and challenge the unchallenged. To curtail free expression strikes twice at intellectual freedom, for whoever deprives another of the right to state unpopular views necessarily also deprives others of the right to listen to those views.
—Yale Committee, "Freedom of Expression at Yale,"
The Chronicle of Higher Education

c Each year over four million Americans take "aptitude," "achievement" and "proficiency" tests. They include 1.8 million high-school students who take the College Board exam required by most colleges for admission; 500,000 students seeking admission to graduate schools, law schools, and business schools; and people seeking certification or placement in more than 20 different occupations and professions—teachers, architects, auto mechanics, CIA agents, medical technicians and policemen. Their performance on these tests will determine, largely or in significant part, the schools they will attend and the professions they will enter.
—Ralph Nader, "Reports," *Ladies' Home Journal*

d But if those skills were more than salable, if the study made them better citizens and made them happier to be human beings, they have not been cheated. They will find some kind of job soon enough. It might even turn out that those humanizing and liberating skills are salable. Flexibility, an ability to change and learn new things, is a valuable skill. People who have learned how to learn, can learn outside of school. That's where most of us have learned to do what we do, not in school. Learning to learn is one of the highest liberal skills.

—Robert A. Goodwin, "Should College Teach Salable Skills?"
The Chronicle of Higher Education

Induction

1   Discuss whether the following persuasive paragraphs rely primarily on emotional or logical argument. What audience would they best appeal to?

a   In the philosophy of semantics there is a standard rhetorical question: Is it progress if a cannibal eats with a knife and fork? Similarly, if society is sexist is it altered when its language is revised? Or do its attitudes remain when its platitudes change? The prognosis is not good. Words, like currency, need to be reinforced with values. Take away the Federal Reserve and its dollar bill is waste paper. Take away meaning and a word is only noise. Changing chairman to chairperson is mock doctrine and flaccid democracy, altering neither the audience nor, in fact, the office holder. Despite its suffix, chairman is no more sexist than the French designation of boat as masculine, or the English custom of referring to a ship with feminine pronouns. Chairman is a role, not a pejorative. Congressman is an office, not a chauvinist plot. Mankind is a term for all humanity, not some 49% of it. The feminist attack on social crimes may be as legitimate as it was inevitable. But the attack on words is only another social crime—one against the means and the hopes of communication.

—Stefan Kanfer, "Sispeak: A Msguided Attempt to Change Herstory," *Time*

b   Teachers are overworked and underpaid. True. It is an exhausting business, this damming up the flood of human potentialities. What energy it takes to turn a torrent into a trickle, to train that trickle along narrow, well-marked channels! . . . Do not blame teachers if they fail to educate. The task of *preventing* children from changing in any significant way is precisely what most societies require.

—George B. Leonard, *Education and Ecstasy*

c   Thus Women's Lib may achieve a more peaceful society on the way towards its other goals. That is why the Swedish government considers reform to bring about greater equality in the sex roles one of its most important concerns. As Prime Minister Olaf Palme explained in a widely ignored speech delivered in Washington this spring: "It is *human beings* we shall emancipate. In Sweden today, if a politician should declare that the woman ought to have a different role from man's, he would be regarded as something from the Stone Age." In other words, the most radical goal of the movement is egalitarianism.

If Women's Lib wins, perhaps we all do.

—Gloria Steinem, "What It Would Be Like if Women Win," *Time*

d The political struggles ahead are for increasing shares of government largesse. The opposed forces are numerous. On one side are powerful lobbies such as the industrial-military complex, the agro-business lobby, and the highway lobby. These have powerful spokesmen. The poor, the unemployed, and the disemployed are opposed—and they are not well organized.

The use of violence as an instrument of persuasion is therefore inviting and seems to the discontented to be the only effective protest.

William O. Douglas, *Points of Rebellion*

e Such a rally here will serve not only to organize for the national fight, but also to show tangible support for the embattled Black students whose very right to enter certain parts of this city has been challenged. It will say to them that "you are not alone in this national struggle." It will encourage their parents to hold on. It will make all those who would gather in mobs to intimidate our children think twice.

Today only 80 of Boston's schools are involved in desegregation. In September all 200 will be involved. We have already been told by the anti-desegregation forces that they will renew their opposition and their resistance this spring, and that their numbers will grow. I believe them.

If school desegregation cannot be brought about in Boston, then it won't happen anywhere else in the North. That's why this fight *must* continue. And that's why we must win.

—Thomas Atkins, Speech before the National Student
Conference Against Racism

2 Identify the inductive weaknesses (weak analogy, unreliable information, insufficient sampling, inductive leap) in the following:

  a Many students who dislike and fear courses in mathematics have learned to respect mathematical theory in logic courses. Therefore, students who are not proficient in languages might profit from a general linguistics course.

  b I wakened to the sound of a loud crash above my head. It was followed by a scream of pain and outrage and another crash quickly ensued. A moment of silence, then came a series of curses and finally a long period of weeping. My neighbors upstairs were engaging in their usual Saturday night brawl.

  c Ralph Nader has quoted the president of the Educational Testing Service as saying that "charging the tests with bias against minority and poor students is like criticizing the bathroom scales because some people are fat and others don't get enough to eat."

  d After interviewing the women on the third floor of the women's dorm, I concluded that most students drive home for the weekend.

e   The Army Corps of Engineers and the law firm representing the investors in a proposed marina issued figures that "proved beyond doubt" that a new dam would be an economic asset to the state.

f   Every summer, the academically motivated new freshmen register early. Composition classes offered at prime times—9:00 a.m. to 12 noon—close out first. Therefore, these classes will have a higher grade average than classes offered at unpopular times.

g   Jobs for engineering graduates are almost impossible to find. My brother, who graduated last year, hasn't found a job yet.

h   The president of a national fraternity reported that students who live in fraternity houses have a happier college experience than those who reside in dormitories.

3   Examine the causal relationships in the following passages. Identify the effect and the cause or causes. Does the writer consider the cause(s) the direct one, the only cause, or merely a correlation?

a   Ironically enough, this sinister and threatening phenomenon [overpopulation] has been caused by the beneficent and praiseworthy activities of medical science and public health in preserving life. It is the result of death control. Mortality has gone down, especially infant mortality, which not so long ago in many countries accounted for the deaths of a third or even a half of all babies born before they had reached the age of one. The expectation of life of a Roman citizen even at the height of the Empire was only 30 years; in tropical countries less than a century ago, it was often only 20. Today it is rising everywhere, and in some Western countries is over 70.
—Sir Julian Huxley, "The Age of Overbreed," *Playboy*

b   All the federal legislation in the world won't help this country if its citizens are not aware of their invaluable function to keep our communities safe. Many of you are aware of some strange trends which have developed in this country. There are people willing to overlook crimes which imperil us each and every day. Many shirk their responsibility for the crime rise by "scapegoating" the police and other law enforcement officers.
—Congressman Bill Chappell, "Some Call It Dissent," from *Juxtaposition: Encore*

c   Clearly *Playboy's* astonishing popularity is not attributable solely to pin-up girls. For sheer nudity its pictorial art cannot compete with such would-be competitors as *Dude* and *Escapade*. Rather, *Playboy* appeals to a highly mobile, increasingly affluent group of young readers, mostly between eighteen and thirty, who want much more from their drugstore reading than bosoms and thighs. They need a total image of what it means to be a man. And Mr. Hefner's *Playboy* has no hesitancy about telling them.

—Harvey Cox, "*Playboy's* Doctrine of Male," *Christianity and Crisis*

d Even Winston Churchill, who is looked upon by older whites as perhaps the greatest hero of the twentieth century—even he, because of the system of which he was a creature and which he served, is an arch-villain in the eyes of the young white rebels.

—Eldridge Cleaver, *Soul on Ice*

e As you can readily hear, if you listen to any jazz performance (whether of the Louis Armstrong, Benny Goodman, or Charlie Parker variety), the rhythmical effect depends upon there being a clearly defined basic rhythmic pattern which enforces the expectations which are to be upset. That basic pattern is the 4/4 or 2/4 beat which underlies all jazz. Hence the importance of the percussive instruments in jazz: the drums, the guitar or banjo, the bull fiddle, the piano. Hence too the insistent thump, thump, thump, thump which is so boring when you only half-hear jazz—either because you are too far away, across the lake or in the next room, or simply because you will not listen attentively. But hence also the delight, the subtle effects, which good jazz provides as the melodic phrases evade, anticipate, and return to, and then again evade the steady basic four-beat pulse which persists, implicitly or explicitly, throughout the performance.

—John A. Kouwenhoven, "What's American About America?"
Harper's Magazine

Deduction

1   The following statements could serve as major premises in a categorical syllogism. What kind or kinds of inductive reasoning—sampling, analogy, or causal generalization—might have contributed to each generalization? Add a possible minor premise and conclusion to each to form a deductive categorical syllogism.

    a All public school teachers are people certified by state education departments.

    b All cold-blooded animals are hibernating creatures.

    c All West Point cadets are eligible for combat duty.

    d Constitutional laws are those laws that ultimately can be approved by the Supreme Court.

    e Home-canned food is a potential health hazard.

    f Disease can be eradicated by educating people about it.

    g Undergraduate men's colleges tend to overemphasize sports.

    h Great literature is a mirror of human relationships.

    i Hippies are nonconformists.

    j A martyr's cause is never lost by an assassin's bullet.

2 Decide whether the following categorical syllogisms are valid. If a syllogism is invalid, explain why.

a All human societies are doomed to deteriorate.
America is a human society.
America is doomed to deteriorate.

b No philosophers are evil.
Some Greeks are philosophers.
Some Greeks are not evil.

c All students are eligible for student government.
No teachers are eligible for student government.
No teachers are students.

d No Republicans are Democrats.
Some Republicans are supporters of George Wallace.
Some supporters of George Wallace are not Democrats.

e All barbiturates are drugs.
Marijuana is not a barbiturate.
Marijuana is not a drug.

f All rational people are believers in rule by law.
Some rational people are college professors.
Some college professors are believers in rule by law.

g All women are potential mothers.
Betty is a potential mother.
Betty is a woman.

h God is love.
Love is blind.
Homer was blind.
Homer was God.

For Writing

1 Write two versions of a paragraph, one deductively argued and the other inductively argued, to persuade your audience to your viewpoint about a controversial topic.

2 Suppose you received the following letter from your brother in high school. Answer the letter, explaining the significance of "truth" and "validity" in reference to his reasoning.

Dear _____,

Life at home is really a hassle these days. Mom and Dad treat me like an infant—hassle me every time I go out at night, set time limits and wait up for me. Mom is constantly at me for not eating right. Then I go to school and it's the same crap—the teachers act as if I'm a baby freak. I guess the truth is that all grownups think teenagers are babies. The only valid conclusion I can come to is that Mom and Dad are just like all the other grownups in the world. Teachers too. Sometimes I feel like splitting the whole scene. You sure are lucky to be in college where you get treated like an adult.

The inherent syllogism here is:

Mom and Dad (and teachers) are grownups.
They treat teenagers like babies.
All grownups treat teenagers like babies.

Remember, "truth" and "validity" are difficult concepts — define them carefully.

The Uses
and Abuses
of Logical Reasoning

LANGUAGE AND PERSUASION

Even though some persuasive devices such as logical syllogisms can be reduced to abstract formulas, effective persuasion is best accomplished through effective use of language. You can achieve maximum persuasive force only after you have learned to express your logical reasoning in language that can attract your audience to the problem, can convince them that your viewpoint is valid, and can appeal to their better emotional instincts. This task requires not only a writing commitment, but also an ethical one. Making use of tactics that are persuasive because they appeal to the baser instincts of readers, or somehow deceive them, is dishonest. Unscrupulous politicians who deliberately play upon their constituents' racial or ethnic hostilities to sell themselves as candidates, and advertisers who exploit their readers' desires to be socially or sexually attractive, are using unethical persuasive tactics. Usually these involve calculated and deliberate methods.

But often there is a narrow distinction between honest and dishonest persuasion. You want to shape your ideas and language so that they best present your argument, but if you carry this too far, omitting information that might weaken your point, then dishonesty can be the result. You do want to appeal to the emotions of your audience—to foster sympathy, respect, or appreciation toward the subject of your argument—but too strong an emotional appeal may obscure the logical reasoning in the paper. Obviously, the best way to make sure that your arguments are presented rationally and ethically is to be aware of the ways that persuasive language can be used and abused. In this chapter we will examine some of these.

Slanting

One of the tactics of persuasive writing is the use of slanting—shaping your language and ideas to most effectively enhance your particular viewpoint about a subject. Used wisely, it can help you to place your ideas clearly before your readers. Unfortunately, however, slanting can also be used unscrupulously, as shown in this speech by a fictitious congressman. Which side is he really on? He uses slanting so blatantly and unethically that his own views are completely lost.

CONGRESSMAN OILEY'S POSITION ON WHISKEY

I had not intended to discuss this controversial subject at this particular time. However, I want you to know that I do not shun a controversy. On the contrary, I will take a stand on any issue at any time regardless of how fraught with controversy it may be.

You have asked me how I feel about whiskey.

Here is how I stand on this question:

If when you say whiskey you mean the devil's brew, the poison scourge, the bloody monster that defiles innocence, dethrones reason, destroys the home, creates misery and poverty, yes, literally takes the bread from the mouths of little children; if you mean the evil drink that topples the Christian man and woman from the pinnacles of righteous, gracious living into the bottomless pit of degradation and despair, shame and helplessness and hopelessness, then certainly I'm against it with all my power.

But if when you say whiskey you mean the oil of conversation, the philosophic wine, the ale that is consumed when good fellows get together, that puts a song in their hearts and laughter on their lips and the warm glow of contentment in their eyes; if you mean Christmas cheer; if you mean the stimulating drink that puts the spring in an old gentleman's step on a frosty morning; if you mean the drink that enables a man to magnify his joy and his happiness and to forget, if only for a little while, life's great tragedies and heartbreaks and sorrows; if you mean that drink whose sale pours into our treasuries untold millions of dollars which are used to provide tender care for little crippled children, our blind, our deaf, our dumb, our pitiful aged and infirm, to build highways and hospitals, and schools, then certainly I am in favor of it.

This is my stand and I will not compromise.

Do you really know which side Oiley is on? No, because he has effectively kept his own position from you by exploiting to the fullest the connotative possibilities that words have. Playing on their emotional effects, he employs words and phrases to support and heighten first one position, then the other.

In aligning himself with the temperance advocates, he woos their support by such words of condemnation as "devil's brew," "poison scourge," "misery and poverty," "evil," and "topples Christian man and woman from the pinnacles of righteous, gracious living." But to ensure the vote of his drinking constituents, he shifts to language of approval: "oil of conversation," "Christmas cheer," "when good fellows get together," "stimulating drink that puts spring in an old gentleman's step." Manipulating language in this way is one way to accomplish slanting.

The kind of slanting used by our fictitious congressman is irresponsible. However, when used responsibly, slanting is an acceptable technique for shaping your material so that it emphasizes and supports your argument. Because persuasive writing requires you to present your point of view as forcefully and convincingly as possible, it is natural that you shape your presentation both to your point of view and to the character of your audience. Slanting involves (1) organizing of your material—selection and arrangement of supportive information, (2) constructing sentences so that their structure helps to emphasize your main points, and (3) choosing language that will set the mood and tone best suited to the purpose of your argument and to the audience you address. But employing these tactics, as Congressman Oiley does, to twist your information into falsehoods or half-truths and to use emotionally charged words that appeal to baser human passions, results in distortion. Argument then becomes diatribe and demagoguery, and slanting becomes a vice.

In Chapter 10, we talked of the importance of considering the connotations of words in writing effective descriptions. In persuasive writing, you need to be even more alert to the effect of words on your audience. In descriptive writing, you made word choices for aesthetic reasons—reasons that required no ethical decisions on your part. But in persuasion, there is often a fine line between using words to achieve responsible slanting and twisting words to cater to the prejudices of the audience. Remember, a deliberate attempt to sway an audience emotionally may work for a small limited group, but an appeal to a broader audience can succeed only when logical reasoning is expressed in responsible language.

The following paragraphs from a newspaper demonstrate some of the degrees of slanting that are possible on a single controversial subject

—in this case, the Equal Rights Amendment. The first is from an editorial:

The equal-rights business just doesn't make sense when screened against tradition and mores and personal identity. But ERA agitators are hell bent for action, and as Alexander Pope said, "Oh woman, woman! When to ill thy mind is bent, all hell contains no fouler fiend."

For the record, one does not quarrel with such ERA concepts as equal pay for equal ability. Nor does one take exception to the basic precept in the amendment's terse language: "Equality of rights under the law shall not be abridged in the United States or by any state on account of sex." . . .

What bothers us are the interpretations being placed on the proposition of equal rights and what this is doing and will do to our traditional way of life. Family, marriage, morality—these, for example, are threatened by libertinism already being practiced in the name of freedom.[1]

These paragraphs, though colorful, are obviously biased in favor of the "woman's place is in the home" point of view. Words and phrases like "business doesn't make sense" and "ERA agitators are hell bent for action"; the derisive quote from Alexander Pope; and the appeal to fears that the ERA threatens "our traditional way of life"—all are highly emotive and serve to slant the material to an extreme point of view. The language begs for confrontation, not compromise.

The second example, from a response to the editorial, uses more neutral language, but still expresses a strong opinion—this time on the other side of the issue. The writers, a group of newspaperwomen, attack the editor's contentions rather than relying upon emotive language. The slanting in this instance is less offensive, being more dependent upon content than on language: the language is neutral; no single word or phrase would elicit a strong emotional response.

[The editor] mentions "the best of all possible worlds" in reference to the traditional view of women. Some women prefer this, and we respect them for that, but some women today question whether they should have "easier jobs" because they are thought to be the weaker physically. We question the assumption that a physical job is harder than a nonphysical job.

Most professional jobs are not easy jobs, neither are they physical jobs. They are jobs demanding integrity, ability to assimilate, innovation and imagination: a fine mind. We question the assumption that men's minds are of a higher quality than women's or vice versa. We concur that there will always be minds greater and lesser than all people's, but some will belong to men and others to women.[2]

[1] Lexington (Ky.) *Herald-Leader*, 27 April 1975. Reprinted by permission.
[2] Lexington (Ky.) *Herald-Leader*, 3 May 1975. Reprinted by permission.

Here, the writers respond to the editor's concern about women's traditional role by expressing respect for a point of view that conflicts with their own—the preference of some women for that traditional role. Then they turn to another point that the editorial stressed—that women need to be excluded from certain kinds of "physical jobs" for their own protection. Generally, the writers' plea is a rational one: that men and women be hired according to individual ability instead of disqualifying women because of their supposed inferiority. The writers achieve responsible slanting by restraining the emotional impact of the language and relying upon rational, logical content.

As in this example, language use in slanting should be responsible and disciplined, thus enhancing the writer's voice and the logical tactics of the argument. You certainly may use emotive language in slanting, but it should appeal to the reasonable and humane instincts of your readers. It should not insult them, or taunt them, or appeal to their basest emotions. The latter tactics may occasionally have a dramatic impact, but their persuasive force is greatly limited and with many readers, they may backfire.

Ambiguous Language

Just as responsible slanting can add to your persuasive voice, so too can precise and unambiguous word choice. In Chapters 6 and 13 we discussed how ambiguity can result from the lack of intonation clues in written English or from the confusing word order of inserted modifiers. But there are other sources of ambiguity that you need to be aware of. In persuasive writing, clarity is of primary importance; in addition to defining any uncommon terms, you must also take care that each word has exactly the meaning you intend: words used in ways that permit several interpretations can weaken the force of your argument. Word ambiguity can derive from two main sources:

1. The word may have several dictionary meanings and appear in a context that gives no clues to the intended meaning, as in this sentence from a student argument paper:

     The want of independence is a common urge within us that often tends to make some people act hastily and without proper thought.

   Here, the problem is with *want,* that can be a synonym for either *desire* or *lack.* Even if the context provided clues to the intended interpretation, the reader still might puzzle over it or be amused—resulting in a break in the communication track.

2. A word may have more than one function (for example, some words can function as either a noun or a verb, or as an adjective or a verb),

and appear in a context where its intended function is unclear, as in this sentence:

> In the early 1970s, campus unrest about the Vietnam war reached a desperate peak; everywhere students were revolting.

Here, *revolting* creates ambiguity because it can function either as an adjective form or as part of the verb phrase (*be + revolting*). Often this kind of word ambiguity is inadvertently humorous and may seriously undermine the effectiveness of your argument.

Vague Language

Vagueness results from either the overuse of abstract language or the use of poorly defined words. This student paragraph from a paper persuading students to seek a liberal education demonstrates both characteristics:

The rags to riches ideology that Horatio Alger instituted in the 1900's has been perpetuated past reality. Climbing the "ladder of success" can no longer begin on the bottom if one hopes to reach the top. And a college degree is a means of starting in the middle. The increased technological advancements and growth of bureaucratic business have complicated our lives to the point that a specialized education is of paramount importance if one hopes to live with a certain degree of financial security and luxury. A student's primary concern is succeeding within America's economic system after graduation. Students, for the most part, are no longer interested in studying the humanities, but only what is able to qualify them for a good job. The purpose of education at the university level has been altered; the quest for knowledge is secondary and the quest for a degree is primary. In viewing a major university's faculty–student relationship one can see that education has been atomized and organized to the point that it has almost become a commodity.

Even though the paragraph is potentially effective, it is so vague that you might have had to read it several times to get the message. Ask yourself whether an argument can be convincing if the reader is forced to reread and decipher meaning, in the meantime losing track of the point being made. Highly abstract terms such as *increased technological advancements, bureaucratic business, paramount importance,* and *financial security* combine with poorly defined terms such as *humanities, atomized,* and *commodity,* producing a vague, weak statement and confusing the issue.

In this revision, we substitute more specific, concrete words wherever possible and provide some definition of specialized terms.

The Horatio Alger "rags to riches" concept has invaded the realm of college education. Unlike the Horatio Alger heroes, we can no longer start at the bottom rung on the ladder of success. Instead, we must start in the middle in order to reach the top. A college degree is a way of starting in the middle. But the demands of an ever-expanding technology and an international business system have forced many students to seek not a liberal education, but a highly specialized one. Pre-med students, for instance, must specialize early in the natural sciences—chemistry, biology, anatomy—if they are to assimilate the number of scientific discoveries and techniques they will encounter in their graduate work. Without a specialized education, there is little chance of getting a professional job and making a decent living. Therefore, to achieve financial security, students search out the professional courses, not the courses in literature, music, philosophy, and language that have traditionally been the core of the humanities. Thus, the purpose of education at the university level has been altered: the quest for knowledge is secondary to the quest for a certifying degree. Even faculty–student relationships reflect the change; instructors and students alike look upon education as a commodity—a package of merchandise to be bought over the counter and resold in the marketplace.

Notice that in the revision we have not altered the student's meaning nor strayed very far from the original wording. The "ladder of success" metaphor has been more specifically related to the topic; a specific example (pre-med students) has been provided; brief definitions have been added; specific courses have been mentioned to indicate what is meant by professional and humanities courses; the word *degree,* which could cover all college degrees, is now limited in meaning by the addition of "certifying"; and *commodity* has been explained by adding a descriptive phrase. Not only is the point made clearer, but the concreteness of the paragraph adds authority to the writer's voice. In persuasive writing, then, as in narrative and description, concrete language generally better serves your purpose than words that are so abstract or so general that they mean nothing in particular.

FALLACIOUS REASONING

In a world where you are constantly bombarded with advertising slogans and political speeches, you may well challenge our contention that valid logical reasoning is the best aid to persuasive force. After all, the public is persuaded to buy everything from disposable diapers to waterproof coffins every day—persuaded by argumentative devices that are logically fallacious. But logical fallacies, despite their persuasive force, should be avoided in reasoned argument. They are the tools of the advertising con artist, the political demagogue, and the unscrupulous evangelist. Anyone persuaded by these tactics will sooner or later feel cheated and belittled—hardly the relationship you want to establish in persuading someone to your point of view.

Logical fallacies derive from several sources. One involves deductive validity, as we saw in the discussion of deductive reasoning in Chapter 24: these "formal" fallacies occur when there are more than three terms in a syllogism or when the conclusion does not logically follow from the premises. Other kinds of logical fallacies occur in inductive reasoning; three of these—insufficient sampling, hasty generalization, and *post hoc*—were discussed in Chapter 24. A third kind of fallacy, the most blatant abuse of logical reasoning, involves an appeal to the emotions of the audience. These "emotional" fallacies are probably most damaging to a reasoned argument, but ironically are most persuasive. The following lists of additional logical fallacies and emotional fallacies can help you to recognize common fallacies not previously discussed so that you can avoid them in your writing.

Other Logical Fallacies

STEREOTYPING

Stereotyping results from reaching a conclusion about a whole group based on observations about part of that group. People who think that blacks have natural rhythm, Poles are stupid, or women are hyper-emotional are guilty of stereotyping.

NON SEQUITUR

Non sequitur (Latin for "it does not follow"; pronounced "non se′kwiter") is evident in a statement like this: "X will make an excellent President because he's a good family man." Underlying this is the syllogism:

All good family men make good Presidents.
X is a good family man.
Therefore, X will make a good President.

The problem lies in whether being a good President logically follows from the premise about family men. In actuality, the very qualities that make a good President—strong leadership, decisiveness of action, single-mindedness of purpose—might be disastrous to family relationships. When tempted to use *non sequitur*, remember that this fallacy is Edith (Dingbat) Bunker's stock in trade.

BEGGING THE QUESTION

You commit this fallacy when you present questionable premises as uncontestable truth. The premise "Abortion is wrong, because it's murder," is obviously not accepted as truth by everyone in modern society; otherwise, there would be no court cases trying to decide the issue. Premises involving opinions require factual support; without it, you are begging your audience to accept your premises simply on your authority or on faith.

A common form of begging the question is the circular argument. A categorical syllogism constructed from the "abortion" premise illustrates this:

Abortion, a form of murder, is wrong.
All forms of murder are wrong.
Therefore, abortion is wrong.

Arguing in a circle, the question-begging conclusion echoes the question-begging premise.

You can also beg the question and argue in a circle using an *if/then* form. In this statement from a letter to a newspaper editor, the writer both assumes that everyone accepts the truth of his reasoning and restates the major premise in the conclusion: "If God is left out of the schools completely, then the schools will be without God."

EITHER-OR

This fallacy results when two conditions or positions are falsely presented as the only possible alternatives. This fallacy (sometimes called False Dilemma) can be highly persuasive, as in Patrick Henry's famous "Give me liberty or give me death!" But it can also lead to dangerous oversimplification, as in the slogan, "America—love it or leave it." Another example of this is an argument presented by the Army Corps of Engineers to justify the building of a dam that would destroy a uniquely scenic area: "Either build the dam or have yearly destructive flooding."

There might be other alternatives in these three situations or any other. Your argument will have greater strength if you recognize all the alternatives and discuss them, rather than relying on the *either-or* fallacy.

Emotional Fallacies

Emotional fallacies appeal directly to the human frailties of the audience: some to their prejudices, some to their vanity, some to their national pride, others to their desire to emulate people they admire. Because of this, they exert great persuasive force. There is certainly a place for emotional appeal in argument and persuasion, but responsible writers avoid using these fallacies to achieve it.

AD HOMINEM

Ad hominem, or an appeal "to the man," involves attacking a person instead of that person's stand on an issue. A politician who, when challenged by an opponent to discuss military spending, instead accuses the opponent of alcoholism is arguing *ad hominem.*

AD POPULUM

Ad populum is an appeal to "the people" — particularly to their prejudices or fears — rather than to the merits of the issue. A politician who exploits the racial hostility generated in a community over an explosive busing issue is guilty of this fallacy.

NAME-CALLING

When Valerie Solanas wrote her *S.C.U.M. Manifesto,* her name-calling tactics helped to polarize the women's liberation movement: "He (the male) is a half dead, unresponsive lump, incapable of giving or receiving pleasure or happiness; consequently he is at best an utter bore, an inoffensive blob, since only those capable of absorption in others can be charming." This kind of verbal attack really persuades no one; it repels rather than attracts. Engaging in this kind of name-calling, however, may be less reprehensible than resorting to names intended to trigger an automatic negative response: *commie, pinko, Nazi, fascist,* and racial and ethnic slurs — *nigger, kike, Canuck,* and the like.

GLITTERING GENERALITY

A glittering generality is a stock statement or phrase that appeals to the patriotic or family feelings of an audience: "the American way of life," "life, liberty, and the pursuit of happiness," "the joys of motherhood," "the American dream," are all perfectly acceptable when used in a relevant context and clearly defined. But when used specifically to elicit an emotional response, they become fallacious devices.

BANDWAGON APPEAL

How many times in high school did you persuade your dad to let you have the car to go to a party because "everybody else" was going? Simi-

larly, many advertising slogans urge readers to jump on the bandwagon —
to buy something so that they become associated with the majority of
people or with a particular prestigious group: "Beer belongs," "Camels
aren't for everybody (but then, they don't try to be)," "Join the Pepsi
generation," "The car for the people who think."

THE SYLLOGISM IN PERSUASIVE WRITING

Syllogisms are all around us, in newspaper and magazine letters and
editorials, in advertising, in public speeches, in ordinary conversation,
on bumper stickers, and even in poetry. But rarely are they obvious. The
syllogisms discussed in Chapter 24 are the forms that logicians use; in
written discourse, however, syllogisms can appear in many forms. With
only a little practice, you can see through their disguises and recognize
them as *bona fide* logical syllogisms.

Occasionally syllogisms are complete; but their three-statement form
is perhaps disguised by some added explanatory material, or their conclusion worded differently from the main premise, or their statements
arranged in an order that differs from the usual logical form. Most frequently, however, syllogisms are either shortened in form or expanded
to include several syllogisms within one paragraph. Let's look first at
two passages that contain complete, three-statement syllogisms.

The Complete Syllogism

Our society has moved illogically in this direction by virtually institutionalizing
adultery; a growing number of spouses permit each other complete sexual
liberty on the conditions that there shall be no "involvement" and that the extracurricular relations are not brought to their attention. It is beginning to in-
stitutionalize ritual spouse exchange.

— Alexander Comfort, "Sexuality in a Zero-Growth Society," *Center Report*

Here the form of the syllogism is hidden in a reordering of its essential
elements: the terms of the major premise appear in the opening and
closing sentences of the argumentative sequence. Here's one way to put
it into a tighter syllogistic form:

A society that encourages ritual spouse exchange is a society that
institutionalizes adultery.
Our society is a society that encourages ritual spouse exchange.
Our society is a society that institutionalizes adultery.

A valid, and probably true syllogism. Here's another, supported by specific experiences, that has an underlying syllogism:

> The cases of Adolf Beck, of Oscar Slater, of the unhappy Brooklyn bank teller who vaguely resembled a forger and spent eight years in Sing Sing only to "emerge" a broken, friendless, useless, "compensated" man—all these, if the dignity of the individual has any meaning, had better have been dead before the prison door ever opened for them. This is what counsel always says to the jury in the course of a murder trial and counsel is right: far better to hang this man than "give him life."
>   —Jacques Barzun, "In Favor of Capital Punishment," *The American Scholar*

Here's how the syllogism might be constructed:

> An experience that takes away individual dignity is worse than death.
> Long imprisonment is an experience that takes away individual dignity.
> Therefore, long imprisonment is worse than death.

The Shortened Syllogism and the Hidden Assumption

On Washington's Birthday, a man interviewed by a roving reporter was asked if he thought George Washington was really truthful. His answer was, "Of course not, he was a politician, wasn't he?" This cynical reply was actually a shortened syllogism with the main premise missing —but easily supplied:

> Major premise: (All politicians are untruthful—unstated)
> Minor premise: George Washington was a politician. (stated)
>   Conclusion: Therefore, George Washington was untruthful. (stated)

This is a common shortened syllogism, one in which the major premise is missing, but in spite of that omission it still carries logical force. In fact, one of the reasons that shortened versions occur so often in writing is that they frequently carry more persuasive power than complete, explicitly stated syllogisms do. This power stems mainly from their dependence upon hidden assumptions—the assertions missing along with the omitted statement. In this dependence lies both the strength and the danger of shortened syllogisms. These abbreviated forms can be persuasively effective because they flatter your audience: your readers can demonstrate their knowledge and logical facility when you permit them to supply the missing part. But shortened syllogisms can also obscure premises or conclusions that are invalid or untrue; in a very real way, they often beg the question. For instance, in our George Washington example, are you really willing to accept as absolute truth the hidden assumption in the missing premise—that *all* politicians are untruthful? We hope not.

Hidden assumptions accompany all variants of the shortened syllogism. Let's look at some of these possibilities and their underlying hidden assumptions:

SHORTENED FORM	SYLLOGISM (unstated premises italicized)	HIDDEN ASSUMPTION
Of course he writes poorly—he's a football player.	*Football players write poorly.* He's a football player. He writes poorly.	All football players write poorly. (sweeping generalization)
"Folger's coffee is mountain-grown."	*Mountain-grown coffee is the best coffee.* Folger's is mountain-grown coffee. *Folger's is the best coffee.*	All coffee grown in the mountains is superior to other coffee. (begging the question)
Part-time students don't get free football tickets, and poor Connie's a part-time student.	No part-time students get free football tickets. Connie is a part-time student. *Connie won't get a football ticket.*	Projected conclusion that Connie is analogous to all other part-time students and won't get a free ticket. (probably valid)
CAUTION: WOMAN DRIVER (bumper sticker)	*All women drivers demand caution.* *This driver is a woman driver.* This driver demands caution.	All women are dangerous drivers. (stereotyping)

As you can see, any part of the categorical syllogism may be missing. Your task in writing and analyzing arguments is to realize this, probe for the hidden assumptions, and check the complete syllogism for both truth and validity.

The Expanded Syllogism

Occasionally, it is necessary to reason through a series of syllogisms in order to arrive at a valid conclusion or to illustrate an argument more vividly. At such times you can combine several syllogistic forms. Let's look at such a situation:

The man who is not at peace with himself cannot be trusted to lead his fellow-men in the ways of peace. The unbalanced leader is certain to unbalance the society in which he functions. Even the leader who is intent on the side of the good but who is a fanatic will stimulate fanaticism in his followers, arouse dogmatism and bigotry, and induce oppression and cruelty. When he is on the side of evil, he will lead his followers into such excesses and wickedness as will shame all humanity, and which even the innocent will wish to forget as soon as possible.
— Marten Ten Hoor, "Education for Privacy," *The American Scholar*

The assertion made in the first sentence establishes the major premise for all the syllogisms implicit in the sequence. First we construct a formal syllogism from the first two sentences. This then supplies an underlying major premise for the others:

Syllogism 1

Major premise: *The man not at peace with himself is unable to lead.*
Minor premise: The unbalanced man is a man not at peace with himself.
Conclusion: The unbalanced man is not able to lead.

Syllogism 2

Major premise: (Same as above)
Minor premise: The good leader who is a fanatic is a man not at peace with himself.
Conclusion: The good leader who is a fanatic is unable to lead.

Syllogism 3

Major premise: (Same as above)
Minor premise: The man on the side of evil is a man not at peace with himself.
Conclusion: The man on the side of evil is unable to lead.

As you can see from this example, the expanded syllogism is a handy stylistic device; once the major premise and the form are established, you can expand the idea and at the same time retain the full persuasive force of the categorical syllogism. And you can avoid unnecessary repetition by letting one premise work for several syllogisms.

The purpose of our discussion on logic is not to make you masters of all the intricate argumentative devices. Actually, we've touched on only a few. But if you are aware that syllogistic reasoning in some form usually crops up in persuasive writing and if you become adept at recognizing its possibilities, then you will be able to use it effectively in your own writing.

ASSIGNMENTS

For Discussion

1 In these examples, identify the words or phrases that signal the writer's opinion or bias about the subject.

   a Grades are the play money in a university Monopoly game. As long as the tokens are offered, the temptation will be largely irresistible to play for them. Students are so busy taking notes, doing tests, and getting tokens that they have forgotten to ask: Of what worth is all this? Or perhaps they ask and the grade is their answer.

   One certainly learns something in the passive lecture-note-read-note-test process: how to do it all more efficiently next time (in the hope of eventually owning Boardwalk and Park Place). As Marshall McLuhan has said, we learn what we do. In this process most students come to view learning as studying and remembering what other people have learned. They assume that knowledge is logically and for practical reasons divided up into discrete pieces called "disciplines," and that the highest knowledge is achieved by specializing in a discipline. By getting good grades in a lot of disciplines they conclude they have learned a lot. They have indeed, and it is too bad.

   Such harsh judgment seems unjustified to many professors. From their viewpoint a great deal of thinking goes on; they generate most of it themselves and then hear their own echo, often disguised, on tests and papers.

   —Roy E. Terry, "Dialog," *Change*

   b And I noted a recent Congressional committee's report pointing out that for comparable services New York's cost of doing business is roughly the same as that of most large American cities. But that is not what is really important to me now, any more than is the knowledge that weaknesses, mistakes and mismanagement in frontline city government have long been there and still are.

   What *is* important is the appalling insensibility of the leader of our country to such a major part of American life as the American city. One would hope that such myopia is only confined to this one critical aspect of America and its history. Mr. Ford has never faced a large and diverse constituency. A safe and homogeneous Congressional district is hardly the school of hard knocks.

Twenty-five years in the marbled cocoon of the House of Representatives can be a far more isolating experience than that of the average person trying to "make it" in almost any neighborhood in America today. And being on the Committee on Armed Services for most of that 25 years is worse than con-finement in a cocoon — it's being sealed in a tank, unless one is to adopt the unsafe and uncomfortable course and ask hard questions of the Pentagon and its management, its uses, and abuses. Enormous cost overruns of taxpayer-funded contracts, millions in waste, to say nothing of Vietnam and other ex-orbitant junta alignments and adventures, were none of Mr. Ford's critical con-cern for waste, mismanagement or policy; from him, we got only unquestioning and uncritical support.

— John V. Lindsay, "Speaking Up for New York," *Newsweek*

c   Of the products of the human intellect, the scientific method is unique. This is not because it ought to be considered the only path to Truth; it isn't. In fact, it firmly admits it isn't. It doesn't even pretend to define what Truth (with a capital T) is, or whether the word has meaning. In this it parts company with the self-assured thinkers of various religious, philosophical, and mystical persuasions who have drowned the world in sorrow and blood through the conviction that they and they alone own Truth.

— Isaac Asimov, "When Aristotle Fails, Try Science Fiction," *Intellectual Digest*

d   The murders within five years of John F. Kennedy, Martin Luther King, Jr., and Robert F. Kennedy raise — or ought to raise — somber questions about the character of contemporary America. One such murder might be explained away as an isolated horror, unrelated to the inner life of our society. But the successive shootings, in a short time, of three men who greatly embodied the idealism of American life suggest not so much a fortuitous set of aberrations as an emerging pattern of response and action — a spreading and ominous belief in the efficacy of violence and the politics of the deed.

— Arthur M. Schlesinger, Jr., *Violence: America in the Sixties*

e   A university, as a center of learning rather than as a manipulator of land, is a place of realism and ferment. Inevitably, performance of the aca-demic mission has an effect on students who claim that knowledge has a moral force which dictates action. Naive as this claim is, it has led to a lot of earnest effort — if poorly planned and often bungled — toward changing the anteroom.

— William Ellet, "The Overeducation of America," *Models for Writing*

2   Identify the main weakness of the following sentences: vagueness or ambiguous language. Try to reword each so that the meaning you think the writer intended is more clearly expressed.

   a   Many attempts have been made to force athletic teams to drop nicknames and mascots symbolizing the Indians.

b   The people are the church, but in their fear of involvement they have ironically used the church as a hideaway.

c   One reason for people's loss of faith is their inability to relate to the intangible.

d   Nurse Ratched is McMurphy's persecutor. She turns him into a vegetable but his essence still lingers on.

e   Almost all prejudicial views yield a lack of knowledge of the facts about prejudice.

f   Talking about sex dealing with children, people and parents should be more open-minded.

g   I think that the highest appreciation should be given to parents, because what they have done for their children was done because they wanted to and not because they had to.

h   The Russian divisions advance toward Berlin as the Eighth Army push bottles up the Germans.

i   While there is accent on skills and methods, as there would be for any disciplined studies, the aims are to come to an understanding of language as fundamental to what it means to be human, and to the ability to synthesize and utilize that understanding in a variety of human concerns.

j   Does your business suit fit the needs of modern merchandising?

k   More schools have failed dropouts than dropouts have failed schools.

l   When these gun control laws failed to control crime, these groups, instead of looking toward the real cause of the problem, simply asked that more of the same type laws be passed as if the number of laws would aid in fighting crime.

3   Identify the logical or emotional fallacies in the following examples:

a   I was with the FBI for twenty years. My son can't be a bigot.

b   The Imperial Wizard maintained in a newspaper interview that the Ku Klux Klan was the best organization in America — the only one organized for the purpose of maintaining Americanism.

c   American taxpayers are going to have to support the reorganization of our rail system in terms of mergers, abandonments and the elimination of parallel trackage and redundant yards, or they will be saddled first with subsidies and soon thereafter by a nationalized rail system.

d   If the Pope were a woman, he'd be for abortion.

e   It all adds up to the fact that throughout history women have preferred at heart to paddle their own canoe, having what might better be called a mind of their own, however poorly it may work. Do we really want to change the interesting, exciting and beautiful nature of women through legislation, by ratifying the ERA?

— Letter to the editor

f It's the foxiest station-wagon on the road.

— Ad for Audi Fox

g Finally, say those who want weather war outlawed, even the most limited uses of weather modification tend to open up a Pandora's Box of horrors. If we accept weather modification as a very limited battlefield weapon, the next step is a slightly less limited operation — and the next step is the use of the same techniques to alter the climate of an entire country.

— Phil Stanford

h Rare taste. Either you have it or you don't.

— Scotch ad

i There is a certain kind of person who knows how to live. He knows how to get just a little extra out of every precious minute.

— Boat ad

j In this friendly, freedom-loving land of ours, beer belongs — enjoy it.

— Beer ad

k Middle America is concerned about law and order.

l Making [basketball] points wasn't always easy for a girl. But now you can do anything. Make the team or color your hair.

— Hair dye ad

m Bob True, in my opinion, is the best qualified candidate. I have known him since 1963, and in my opinion, he is an honorable, Christian man, an upstanding family man.

— Letter to the editor

n Men are all alike: selfish creatures who every weekend plant themselves in splendid isolation in front of a TV set. They substitute vicarious touchdowns, birdies, chip shots, and home runs for family participation and fun.

o The pinkos and weirdos at the state university naturally are against my legislative programs.

4 Below are examples of shortened and expanded syllogisms. Complete the syllogisms and state the hidden assumption in each.

a Wars are not "acts of God." They are caused by men, by man-made institutions, by the way in which man has organized his society. What man has made, man can change.

— Fred M. Vinson

b All those millionaires who pay no income tax can eat their hearts out; they won't get any rebate.

—Newspaper filler

c Football coaches can't expect to hold the job forever. After all, they weren't elected by the people.

—Newspaper filler

d Determination comes from keeping one's mind on something. This determination can result in good or ill but there's no doubt that without determination and drive, little greatness would have come out of this civilization.

—Letter to the editor

e Everything positive is accomplished in terms of negatives. You can become branch manager by not sticking your neck out. You can make it to the vice-presidency of the corporation by not contradicting and by not being too egghead grammatical. The man who knows says nothing controversial.

—Eve Merriam, "The Matriarchal Myth"

f But legislation which would funnel money to families who adopt [handicapped or retarded] children is not the right way of getting them into homes. People could start adopting children because of the money rather than because they really want a child. Children with special defects need special love and attention, and a subsidy from the federal government is not the way to get it.

—Newspaper editorial

g The real job will have to be done by the public. If it won't seek out and elect candidates capable of making moral distinctions, it's fated to continue being victimized by a system in which the ends too long have justified the means.

—Newspaper editorial

h "Milk-drinkers make better lovers."

—Bumper sticker

i The company may discharge any employee whose conduct on the job is disruptive. Joe's conduct is certainly disruptive.

j Of course he was under surveillance. Anyone with a job in government who dates foreign women is suspect.

k I could not love thee, Dear, so much,
Loved I not honour more.

—Richard Lovelace, "To Lucasta, Going to the Wars"

l Of course freshman English is boring; it's a required course.

m The tax cuts sound good until we grasp the over-all picture. Energy is industries' life-blood. When the oil industry is burdened with added tax to compensate for some of our tax cuts, not only will gasoline prices soar, but personal tax cuts will be re-collected threefold through more energy costs involved in producing all commodities.

—Newspaper editorial

For Writing

1 In the following editorial, the writer exposes a hidden assumption in an argument to ban commercials on candy and soft drinks. Write a similar brief exposé of an advertising or campaign slogan.

JUNK FOOD ADS[3]

The Federal Trade Commission recently turned down a request from a consumer group that wanted a ban on commercials for candy and other sugar-laden foods on TV programs aimed at children. The petitioners claimed that such products pose a health hazard, but the FTC ruled that it would defer any action until the Food and Drug Administration completes its current review of the sugar question.

The nation's nutrition obviously would improve considerably if children could be persuaded to eat fruit, vegetables and nourishing snacks, rather than sugar-coated cookies, candy and cakes. But claiming that these are a health hazard, except in the very narrowest sense, is stretching the meaning of that word pretty far.

The gist of this argument seems to be that children exposed to such ads soon start clamoring for the advertised products, a not unreasonable assumption. But the tacit premise of all this is that parents are then obliged to cater to Junior's wishes by buying junk food they know is of little value.

TV may well raise expectations that youngsters would be better off without, but adults who can't firmly dampen those expectations will have parental problems far worse than the effects of bad nutrition.

2 Choose one of the following syllogisms (or construct one of your own) and write a paragraph that incorporates the syllogism. Reword the syllogism so that it is not so obvious.

a The guarantee of a stable society is a desire of middle-class America.
Enforcement of law and order is a guarantee of a stable society.
Enforcement of law and order is a desire of middle-class America.

---

[3] Reprinted with permission of The Wall Street Journal, © Dow Jones & Company, Inc. (1975). All Rights Reserved.

b All people are members of the human family.
Blacks and whites are people.
Blacks and whites are members of the human family.

c All forms of marriage are risky.
The commune marriage is a form of marriage.
The commune marriage is risky.

d No people should be victims of oppression.
The American Indians are people.
No American Indians should be victims of oppression.

e All societies educate their children in compliance with societal values.
The people of the United States are a society.
The people of the United States educate their children in compliance with societal values.

f If congressional steps are not taken soon, then the governmental weaknesses exposed by Watergate can destroy our country.

3 Write a paper discussing the use of emotional fallacies in advertising. You may choose to concentrate on one kind of ad—automobile or liquor ads, for example—or on advertising tailored to a specific magazine—*Playboy, Ms., Gourmet,* or *Ebony,* for example.

Organizing the Persuasive Paper

Now that you have an understanding of the reasoning tactics of argument and the way to formulate specific arguments, we need to look at the tactics of organizing an argument paper. Just as anecdotes, definitions, and SRI paragraphs can be either brief or extended pieces of writing, so too arguments can be two- or three-statement syllogistic structures or expanded to a full-blown article or book. A book such as *The Assassination Tapes* by George O'Toole, arguing that President Kennedy's assassination resulted from a conspiracy, is an example of argument expanded to book length. In a composition course, because your argument paper will probably not exceed 1,000 to 1,500 words, you are forced to restrict your subject carefully.

You can't discuss any subject intelligently until you have narrowed it down to manageable size and formulated it precisely. Both these points have already been discussed in Chapters 14 and 16, but they are so important that they bear repeating. You should steer clear of broad subjects such as national health insurance or the environment unless you can treat them at length. The different features of various proposals about these issues are so numerous and complex that you could not do justice to either in a short paper. On the other hand, a proposal to change the academic grading system would be appropriate because it could be treated in about 1,000 words.

But the subject or proposition must be spelled out precisely. If you wish to advocate a change in the grading system, you must propose a specific plan. Do you want professors to submit written evaluations, switch to a Satisfactory–Unsatisfactory marking system, eliminate failing grades, or what? Moreover, the plan you decide on needs to be precisely stated in your thesis. For example, you could recommend that the *D* grade be eliminated from the grading system. But you should never vaguely argue that the system should be changed somehow.

Obviously, to write an effective argument paper, much planning is necessary. Once you've decided on your subject—preferably one you have strong convictions about—and what you intend to propose about it, and have gathered your informational ammunition, then you should spend time organizing it. Actually, argument virtually requires that you experiment with the organization—that you try ordering your supporting material or evidence in several ways. It would be frustrating and time consuming to write two or three different drafts. The solution? The writer's faithful servant, the outline. An outline for a persuasive paper is similar to that for an expository one (see Chapter 16), but with some important differences and special characteristics imposed by the difference in purpose. In exposition, you explain, inform, clarify, define; your thesis statement is a simple explanatory summary of your subject matter. But in argument, you persuade, cajole, seek to bring about change; your thesis statement must reflect that purpose.

THE THESIS STATEMENT OF ARGUMENT: THE PROPOSITION

Whether the purpose is emotional or logical persuasion, the thesis statement of an argument is called a *proposition*. It has this sentence structure: SUBJECT + *should/must/can/would* + VERB + COMPLEMENT; for example, "All freshman courses *should* be offered on a pass-fail basis," "Congress *must* limit the foreign policy powers of the Presidency," "A better solution than abortion *can* be found for the population explosion," "Cooperation, not containment, *would* be the best foreign policy for the 1980s."

As you can see, the proposition thesis strongly states your personal opinion. Although the proposition should be expressed forcefully in your outline so that you can keep it in focus, you would be wise to soften the wording or the presentation in your paper. In an outline, as we'll demonstrate later, a strongly worded thesis statement can help your reasoning processes, but in the finished paper it may irritate your audience. There are several techniques for blunting the dogmatic edge of propositions. One is to phrase the proposition as a rhetorical question, as in the following example:

Can scientific research and technology help mankind create a more decent society? I think so . . .

—Jerome B. Weisner, "Science and Technology in a Decent Society"

Writing about a controversial subject in the next example, Gloria Steinem begins by allaying the fears of the males in her audience, and then presents her thesis, which we have italicized:

Any change is fearful, especially one affecting both politics and sex roles, so let me begin these utopian speculations with a fact. To break the ice.

Women don't want to exchange places with men. Male Chauvinists, science fiction writers and comedians may favor that idea for its shock value, but psychologists say it is a fantasy based on ruling-class ego and guilt. Men assume that women want to imitate them, which is just what white people assumed about blacks. An assumption so strong that it may convince the second-class group of the need to imitate, but for both women and blacks that stage has passed. Guilt produces the question: What if they could treat us as we have treated them?

That is not our goal. *But we do want to change the economic system to one more based on merit.*

— Gloria Steinem, "What It Would Be Like If Women Win," *Time*

These are only a couple of the techniques for cooling possible audience hostility toward your argument. In expository writing, you were urged to introduce your thesis in an introductory paragraph primarily to interest your reader. In persuasive writing, you are advised to soften the impact of your proposition upon your readers. The more difficult *Not necessarily.* the controversial pill is for readers to swallow, the more palatable you need to make it. *Argue paper need to be firm.*

OUTLINING THE PERSUASIVE PAPER

Like the thesis statement in exposition, the proposition in a persuasive paper serves as a focusing device. In addition, it can offer a solution to a problem or make a recommendation, but it also acts as a conclusion derived from the presented evidence. Thus the proposition serves the same purpose as the conclusion of a syllogism: it should logically follow from your proofs, from your premises. The outline for a persuasive paper with its proposition-thesis and supporting arguments, then, can be viewed as an expanded syllogism. Let's see how this works.

Suppose you have decided to write about changing the college grading system. Remembering earlier warnings, you have narrowed the subject and intend to argue in favor of a pass-fail system in freshman courses to help eliminate the stigma of the low grades often earned by freshmen with high academic potential. The proposition is stated as simply and directly as possible. Its form is that of a strong recommendation that can double as a logical conclusion:

Freshman courses should be offered on a pass-fail basis.

Now let's randomly list possible supporting points or evidence — factors that could result in poor grades in the freshman year:

1. The shock of a freshman student's transition from home to college life.
2. Change from high school courses to college.
3. Lack of motivation.
4. Indecision about career plans.
5. Psychological pressure of grades.
6. Lack of self-discipline.

You now have the beginning of a topic outline: you might combine 1, 2, and possibly 6; also you note that points 3 and 4 seem related and could be generalized as one main point. The result is a topic outline:

Proposition: Freshman courses should be offered on a pass-fail basis.
    I. The difficulty of adjusting to the college experience.
   II. Lack of career motivation.
  III. Psychological pressure of grades.

This outline provides the general points, but what of their logical relationship to the proposition — and to one another, for that matter? In a topic outline no relationship is indicated, but the points can be restated and slanted so that they act as syllogistic premises, and after the license of a logical leap over the implied minor premise, they can lead to the conclusion as stated in the proposition. Let's look at them in a series of shortened syllogisms that show how the main points can have a *therefore* relationship with the thesis:

    I. The qualitative grading system unnecessarily penalizes those freshmen having difficulty adjusting to the college experience. (*Therefore*) Freshman courses should be offered on a pass-fail basis.
   II. The qualitative grading system unnecessarily penalizes those freshmen with unformulated career plans. (*Therefore*) Freshman courses should be offered on a pass-fail basis.
  III. The qualitative grading system unnecessarily penalizes those freshmen suffering from the psychological pressure of grades. (*Therefore*) Freshman courses should be offered on a pass-fail basis.

As you can see, the supporting arguments are now shaped or slanted so that they have a cause-and-effect relationship with the conclusion; they pass the "therefore" test. In the sentence outline, main points I, II, and III now consist of possible reasons why it would be advantageous to offer freshman courses on a pass-fail basis. The conclusion (the proposition-thesis) logically follows from each premise as evidenced by the "therefore" relationship. The outline, then, is in essence an expanded syllogism: a cluster of three syllogisms. The three main points each serve as a major premise; the proposition is a conclusion derived from any of the premises. The implied minor premise of each syllogism is the same and one that needs to be supported with specific evidence in the discussion, even though it is only implied. The minor premise is: "Freshman courses offered on a pass-fail basis do not penalize freshmen having trouble adjusting to the college experience." Using the first of our three main points and stretching the form a bit, a syllogism might look like this:

> Major premise: (I) The qualitative grading system unnecessarily penalizes freshmen having difficulty adjusting to the college experience.
>
> Implied minor premise: Freshman courses offered on a pass-fail basis do not penalize freshmen having trouble adjusting to the college experience.
>
> Conclusion: Therefore, freshman courses should be offered on a pass-fail basis.

Each of the other two main points could be treated the same way.

So much for the logical form. In rhetorical structure, both the outline and the finished paper resemble the Subject-Restriction-Illustration form we established for expository papers in Chapter 17. With the SRI slots indicated, our outline now looks like this:

SUBJECT   RESTRICTION

Proposition: Freshman courses should be offered on a pass-fail basis.

> I. The qualitative grading system unnecessarily penalizes those freshmen having difficulty adjusting to their new life style.
>
> ILLUSTRATION   II. The qualitative grading system unnecessarily penalizes those freshmen with unformulated career plans.
>
> III. The qualitative grading system unnecessarily penalizes those freshmen suffering from the psychological pressure of grades.

All that is needed now is to supply the specific information or evidence for each of the main arguments: statistics about freshman failures for point I; possible handicaps in being accepted into graduate school for point II; evidence to show that pass-fail permits students to concentrate on adjusting to college and developing good study skills rather than on grade point averages for point III.

Besides establishing cause-and-effect relationships, such an outline has great flexibility: it can be used for either inductive or deductive presentation. For a deductive paper, follow the form illustrated; the proposition appears in the opening paragraphs. This organization works best with a friendly or neutral audience with no hostility to the proposition that must first be allayed. For induction, reverse the order: present the supporting premises first and conclude with the proposition. Inductive organization is very useful for presenting controversial issues to a potentially antagonistic audience: the evidence is offered before the audience can react emotionally against the proposition. The outline can also serve as the organizational scheme for an argument based on emotional persuasion or on logical persuasion. For the latter, you must include and deal with refutations of your proposition.

What are some of the possible refutations, or opposing arguments, that might be voiced against pass-fail courses? Some critics in your audience might be concerned that college standards will be lowered; some might think that graduate programs cannot intelligently screen candidates without qualitative grades; some hold the hard-nosed view that not all students should be in college and that freshman grades should be used to weed them out. You could choose to ignore all these opposing views in a paper relying mainly on emotional persuasion, but in logical argument you must deal with them.

HANDLING REFUTATION

In classical rhetoric, the argument had a rigid, conventional form: refutation (*refutatio*) was always dealt with early in the argument before the writer's own views or counterarguments were presented. In modern argument, however, writers can choose to follow the classical convention, taking care of the refutations early in the paper; they can deal with them one by one as they present their own views; or they can present them in the closing paragraphs. Each approach has its advantages. Making refutation a part of the introduction is most effective when writing on highly controversial subjects: the Steinem example illustrates how refutation can be used in the opening paragraphs to soothe or disarm the audience. This approach can also help to catch the readers' attention or shock them into action, as in this argument intended to prod lawyers into approaching an old problem in a new way (we have italicized the proposition).

The purpose of law is to regulate human behavior — to get people to do what we want them to do. If it doesn't, it's a failure, and we might as well admit it and try something else. Laws should be goal-oriented; they must be judged by their results, or we're just kidding ourselves. Any time we pass a law that more than a handful of people violate, the law is probably a bad one. Man is the only animal capable of shaping his own society, of changing his own destiny.

We must use this capability to build a society in which laws become guide-lines rather than threats, guidelines so strong that no one would want to do anything other than follow them.

Liberal doctrine assumes that crime is society's fault, not the fault of the individual who happens to commit the crime. So you shouldn't punish the individual, you should try to change the sick society that spawned the crime in the first place. The conservative tends to see mankind as basically evil, born with genetically determined instincts that force man to behave wickedly when-ever possible. The only way to stop this innate immorality is to stamp it out. Stomp on it. Catch the criminal and beat the living hell out of him; that will make him a much better person. We've molly-coddled the bastards long enough.

Both positions are terribly, terribly naive and ineffective. *Somehow we've got to learn how to* force *people to love another, to* force *them to want to be-have properly. I speak of psychological force.* Punishment must be used as precisely and as dispassionately as a surgeon's scalpel if it is to be effective.

— James V. McConnell, "Criminals Can Be Brainwashed—Now,"
Psychology Today

Oversimplifying the attitudes of two opposing views concerning crime and punishment—extreme views that members of the audience may share to some degree—helps this writer to prepare his audience psycho-logically to consider the solution he is offering, which could be repugnant to many in his audience.

The second and probably the most prevalent way to present refuting positions in modern argument is to deal with them side by side with your own opinions and proofs. In the following paragraph taken from the body of a persuasive article, the writer introduces possible opposing views in a series of questions that immediately follow his own plea for government action on environmental pollution:

We can have anti-pollution auto engines, but they will still have to run on some kind of energy, which will require mining or offshore oil drilling or electric plants. Can we really afford to let individuals have cars at all? Or all the cars they buy?

We can build lower-pollution electric power plants at acceptable cost, very probably, for a while. But even they will cause some pollution and re-quire smokestacks that tower over landscapes and peaceful rivers. U.S. power needs are now doubling every ten years, far faster than the population. Can we really let everyone consume all the electricity he wants—for electric type-writers, electric pencil sharpeners, electric can openers, hair driers, knife sharpeners, shoe polishers? Do we really need endless miles of neon signs, scarring the roadsides and confusing drivers as well as eating up scarce energy? Do we really need air conditioning on days in the pleasant 70's, just because big buildings are now being erected with sealed windows (to keep out the pollution that this overuse of energy causes)?

—Victor Cohn, "But Who Will Pay the Piper and Will It Be in Time?"
Smithsonian

Note that Cohn begins each paragraph with a possible solution to the problem of pollution—first anti-pollution auto engines, then lower-pollution power plants—and goes on in each paragraph to present a counter-argument to that solution—first that energy to run anti-pollution auto engines will result in another kind of environmental pollution, then that smoke pollution and increasing use of electrical appliances will nullify the advantages of lower-pollution power plants.

Also note Cohn's use of questions, which flatter his readers by appealing to their rationality and intelligence; with them he guides his readers to his way of thinking, rather than forcing it upon them.

A third, less common way to handle refutation is to conclude with it. This is most effective when the audience is uninformed or neutral and there is little danger of alienating them from your proposition. Occasionally a summary of the counterarguments you presented earlier can add to the effectiveness of your conclusion.

In short, refutation can be handled by presenting refutations and counterarguments in the introduction, the body, or the conclusion of your persuasive paper. As these examples indicate, you choose the method of presenting refutation according to your material, your purpose, and, most importantly, the attitude of your audience. If you expect your readers to be hostile to your subject or to your recommendation about it, then you must first build a bridge of mutual agreement. You should search for a view you probably hold in common with most of your readers that you can present first. For instance, in addressing an audience that may be hostile to a birth control measure you advocate, you might begin your paper by emphasizing how the quality of family life could be improved with birth control; all of us desire happy families. Similarly, in arguing for increased Medicare benefits, you could remind the dissenters in your audience that they too will benefit someday; all of us grow old. On the other hand, if your audience is likely to be neutral or uninformed, you might move immediately into background information and skip the attitude-softening process.

AUDIENCE AND THE FORM OF THE PERSUASIVE PAPER

The Introduction: Appealing to the Audience

The introduction of a persuasive paper shares some features with that of an expository one: you attract readers' attention, interest them in the subject, and present the thesis. But in argument, because you seek to change your readers in some way, not merely to inform them, you need to be constantly aware of the needs and attitudes of your audience. In personal writing, the writer is paramount, but as writing becomes more public, the audience becomes increasingly dominant. Persuasion is perhaps the most public of all forms. In argumentative writing, therefore, the audience has top priority. Once you realize this, you can see the need for shaping your whole paper so that it constantly reaches out to the audience. As a writer, you should strive to convince your readers that a problem or a situation needs changing, that there are reasons for concern about it, and that you have a strong interest in the situation and something to propose about it. Let's look at some ways that writers have used an introduction to achieve these goals:

At 9:15 on the morning of August 6, 1945, an American plane dropped a single bomb on the Japanese city of Hiroshima. Exploding with the force of 20,000 tons of TNT, the Bomb destroyed in a twinkling two-thirds of the city, including, presumably, most of the 343,000 human beings who lived there. No warning was given. This atrocious action places "us," the defender of civilization, on a moral level with "them," the beasts of Maidanek. And "we," the American people, are just as much and as little responsible for this horror as "they," the German people.

So much is obvious. But more must be said. For the atomic bomb renders anticlimactical even the ending of the greatest war in history. (1) *The concepts "war" and "progress" are now obsolete.* Both suggest human aspirations, emotions, aims, consciousness. "The greatest achievement of organized science in history," said President Truman after the Hiroshima catastrophe— which it probably was, and so much the worse for organized science. (2) *The futility of modern warfare should now be clear.* Must we now conclude, with Simone Weil, that the technical aspect of war today is the evil, regardless of political factors? Can one imagine that the Bomb could ever be used "in a good cause"? Do not such means instantly, of themselves, corrupt any cause? (3) *The Bomb is the natural product of the kind of society we have created.* It is as easy, normal and

Paragraph 1:
Relates bombing of Hiroshima—emphasizes killing of "human beings," not merely statistics. Compares "atrocious action" of U.S. bombing of Hiroshima with German atrocities.

Paragraph 2:
The writer has numbered and italicized his opinions about the effects of the bombing. In the discussion, he refutes possible conflicting viewpoints about each.

unforced an expression of the American Way of Life as electric iceboxes, banana splits, and hydromatic-drive automobiles. We do not dream of a world in which atomic fission will be "harnessed to constructive ends." The new energy will be at the service of the rulers; it will change their strength but not their aims. The underlying populations should regard this new source of energy with lively interest—the interest of victims. (4) *Those who wield destructive power are outcasts from humanity.* They may be gods, they may be brutes, but they are not men. (5) *We must "get" the national State before it "gets" us. Every individual who wants to save his humanity—and indeed his skin—had better begin thinking "dangerous thoughts" about sabotage, resistance, rebellion, and the fraternity of all men everywhere. The mental attitude known as "negativism" is a good start.*[1]

Statement of the writer's proposition.

Macdonald appeals to his readers' guilt and self-interest—emotions shared by writer and audience alike. Other argument papers open with an appeal to universal emotions such as sympathy and humanitarianism.

The welfare rolls in the United States currently number 15 million Americans, and the annual cost is approximately $20 billion. But welfare is not just statistics. It is synonymous with poverty, and poverty means drugs, crime, and deteriorating cities. A drug addict dies on a lonely Harlem street. A building superintendent bashes down a door in a dank tenement and rapes a woman. A welfare mother screams obscenities because she cannot get the money to feed her children.

Appeal to sympathy and humanitarian instincts of the audience.

   Despite the massive social and economic effects of welfare, no solution seems forthcoming, partly because sharply conflicting analyses logjam reform. Liberals see the problem as economic: those on relief are excluded from the mainstream, unable to help themselves; higher payments are in order. Conservatives see the problem in moral

Introduction of opposing viewpoints —pinpoints complexities.

---

[1] Dwight Macdonald, "The Bomb," *Politics*, Sept. 1945. Reprinted by permission of Dwight Macdonald.

terms: those on relief are "cheaters" and "loafers"; financial cutbacks and stricter regulations are in order.

Some of the contradictory attitudes are no doubt illusions believed by various people for political or personal reasons. *My own opinion is that there are indeed many myths about welfare, and that these must be exploded before a solution to the problem of public assistance can come into sight.*
—Clayton Thomas, "The Welfare Dollar Goes 'Round and 'Round," *National Review*

Introduction of the writer's proposition, that myths must be exploded before solutions can be found.

Both examples are effective introductions to persuasive papers: they dramatize a problem, appeal to an emotion or attitude held by most people, state the thesis, justify the case, and explain the writer's reason for discussing it. And both attract readers' attention—a prime requisite for any effective introduction.

The Body: Ordering of Supportive Arguments

Your audience must also be considered when you determine the order of the main points in the body of your paper. An extremely controversial idea that will automatically alienate your audience should be dealt with last, not first. For instance, if you are writing a paper advocating zero population growth, you would be wise to make abortion as a device for birth control the last point in the paper—thus permitting your less volatile arguments to have an effect on readers who are so hostile to abortion that they might not finish a paper that advocated it.

Another consideration in deciding on the order of your supporting evidence is rhetorical emphasis, the relative importance of your arguments. If your arguments build on each other, one strengthening the position of another, then you might gain persuasive force by presenting them in climactic order. In a paper arguing against the practice of dumping mercury wastes into our waterways, for instance, your strongest argument—that it damages and can destroy the human nervous system—would receive more emphasis if discussed after you show the effect of mercury on plants and fish. Thus, arrangement of your material can help you slant it toward your own position on the subject.

In exposition, you cite statistical information, historical or sociological background, and authority and precedent mainly to explain and to develop your topic. In effective persuasion, however, these become evidence, or proof, and need to be slanted toward your position. Remember that by slanting we do not mean falsifying; we mean using objective evidence so that it effectively supports your proposition. Let's compare some examples illustrating the expository and argumentative use of similar evidence.

USE OF STATISTICS

Expository

What has happened, simply, is that the baby-boom has ended. When the GIs came home after World War II, they began begetting large quantities of children, and Americans went on begetting at high rates for about 15 years. The best index of population growth in the U.S. is the fertility rate, that is, the number of babies born per thousand women aged 15–44. In 1940 the fertility rate was 80, just a few points above the 1936 Depression all-time low of 76. Ten years later, in 1950, the baby-boom had begun and the fertility rate had soared to 106, an increase of 32 percent in just ten years. It kept climbing. In 1957, it reached 123, up more than 50 percent in two decades.

— Ben Wattenberg, "Overpopulation as a Crisis Issue:
The Nonsense Explosion," *The New Republic*

Argumentative

An American, on the other hand, can be expected to destroy a piece of land on which he builds a home, garage, and driveway. He will contribute his share of the 142 million tons of smoke and fumes, seven million junked cars, 20 million tons of paper, 48 billion cans, and 26 billion bottles the over-burdened environment must absorb each year.

— Wayne H. Davis, "Overpopulated America," *The New Republic*

Wattenberg states his statistics interestingly, but they are not shaped to his point of view: the language is neutral, not emotive. Davis, on the other hand, slants his language even in presenting figures to support his argument.

SOCIAL AND HISTORICAL BACKGROUND

Expository

That Americans have changed their nature since Andrew Jackson's day or Theodore Roosevelt's or even Harry Truman's is now taken as self-evident — at least among Americans. No visiting European from Crèvecoeur to Somerset Maugham would have reported us to the world in the way in which we now report ourselves, nor would Charles Dickens, who liked us least and used almost every other derogatory term to describe us, have used the word we repeat most frequently today. Arrogant, perhaps. Self-conscious and bump-tious, certainly. But frustrated? If there was one people on earth incapable of frustration it was the people who inhabited the United States . . . a hundred years ago.

— Archibald MacLeish, "The Great American Frustration," *Saturday Review*

Argumentative

For centuries, men here have been discovering new ways in which the happiness and prosperity of each individual revolves around that of the community. Now suddenly we are witnessing the explosive rebellion of small groups, who reject the American past, deny their relation to the community, and in a spiritual Ptolemaism insist that the U.S.A. must revolve around each of them. This atavism, this New Barbarism, cannot last, if the nation is to survive.

— Daniel J. Boorstin, *The Decline of Radicalism*

In both these opening paragraphs, background material is used to introduce the subject of the paper, but in the argument example, the writer shapes it to foster reader acceptance of his proposition in the last line.

AUTHORITY AND PRECEDENT

Expository

The U.S. Civil Rights Commission's 1961 Report *Justice* noted that the U.S. Department of Justice received 1,328 complaints alleging police brutality in the two-and-a-half-year period from January, 1958 to June, 1960. One-third of the complaints were from the South, and somewhat less than one-half of the complainants were Negro. Police officials note that few, if any, of these cases investigated by the F.B.I. have resulted in prosecution and certainly not conviction of any police officer. Still, the Civil Rights Commission concluded that "police brutality in the United States is a serious and continuing problem."

— Burton Levy, "Cops in the Ghetto: A Problem of the Police System,"
from *Riots and Rebellion*

Argumentative

Clearly the university is under no obligation to collaborate with the CIA simply because it is a government agency. This conclusion has not only the sanction of centuries of the history of universities; it has legal sanction as well. For to the argument that the university should not look beyond the official credentials of an agency of the government — an argument advanced with considerable earnestness by those who wish to avoid the moral issue — we must consider the counterargument of the legal principle adopted by the United States at the time of the Nuremberg War Crimes trials. The official American position, submitted by Supreme Court Justice Robert Jackson, was quite simply that no citizen is bound to accept as legal and valid every act of his government, nor can he avoid responsibility for his conduct by placing responsibility on the government. This position was accepted by the Tribunal, and under it men like Albert Speer, Minister of Munitions, were found guilty. It is not necessary to argue that the CIA is violating international law; it is enough to recognize the validity of the principle that institutions, such as universities, are not precluded from inquiring into the credentials of such branches of the government as make demands upon them.

—Henry Steele Commager, "The University as a Recruiting Agency," *The New Republic*

Both of these passages present authoritative information in unimpassioned language. Levy cites authority to indicate a problem; Commager, on the other hand, cites authority to support the strong opinion expressed in the opening topic sentence and reiterated in the final sentence.

As you can see from these examples, evidence in expository writing is handled objectively; whereas in effective persuasion evidence is shaped by subjective language to support the writer's point of view. Other kinds of evidence—factual information (case histories or scientific discoveries), citing reasons for causes, using analogy or comparisons —would be handled in much the same way in argument.

The Conclusion: The Final Appeal to the Audience

The conclusion of a persuasive paper should summarize the argument and restate the proposition. In addition, to be most effective, it should make some appeal to the audience for action. This appeal can be emotional, capitalizing on the sympathy or indignation that you have stirred in readers. Or you may appeal to the decency and fairness of your audience. In some instances, you can present them with a choice: they must either accept your proposal or suffer unpleasant consequences. This *either-or* approach as used effectively in the following passage is ethical as long as there truly are no other alternatives.

The next question usually is, "So—can it work, can the ghettoes in fact be organized?" The answer is that this organization must be successful, because there are no visible alternatives—not the War on Poverty, which was at its inception limited to dealing with effects rather than causes, and has become simply another source of machine patronage. And "Integration" is meaningful only to a small chosen class within the community.

Counterargument to other solutions

The revolution in agricultural technology in the South is displacing the rural Negro community into

Northern urban areas. Both Washington, D.C., and Newark, New Jersey, have Negro majorities. One-third of Philadelphia's population of two million is black. "Inner city," in most major urban areas, is really predominantly Negro, and with the white rush to suburbia, Negroes will, in the next three decades, control the heart of our great cities. These areas can become either concentration camps with a bitter and volatile population whose only power is the power to destroy, or organized and powerful communities able to make constructive contributions to the total society. Without the power to control their lives and their communities, without effective political institutions through which to relate to the total society, these communities will exist in a constant state of insurrection. This is a choice that the country will have to make.

Either-or choice

Summary of thesis and the writer's arguments

   —Stokely Carmichael, "Toward Black Liberation,"
from *Black Fire*

   In the next example, the writer appeals to the sense of fairness inherent in an intelligent audience and relies on people's ability to empathize with other people:

As I have said, I think pornography is necessary to many people. Although personally I am bored by the bizarre deviations and sickened by the sado-masochism, I can accept that, however extreme and grotesque, it provides a catharsis for many whose sexual and emotional needs are otherwise unsatisfied. If at times I seem casual or flippant it is because my concern is with the literature and not with the conditions which promote it; with the written word and not with the personal despair, of which perhaps one of the saddest aspects is the guilt incurred. Even so, if one is amused at the gargantuan breasts and buttocks which many men find stimulating—and whose needs are easily catered for by the many legal publications which specialize in such fetishes—one has a deeper commiseration with the transsexualist who finds his body alien to his mind. If the research for this book has taught me anything, it is an increased

Restatement of proposition

Appeal for understanding of behavior different from one's own sympathy for my fellow human beings whose erotic needs can only be served by fantasy literature which is often difficult to find, expensive, and illegal.

    There, but for the grace of Aphrodite . . .

— Gillian Freeman, "Pornography as a Necessity," *The Undergrowth of Literature*

Emphatic close; paraphrase of "There, but for the grace of God, go I"

In argument papers, as in other kinds of writing, conclusions often evolve as they are being written. If at the outset you are aware of what you want to achieve with the concluding paragraphs, you'll have little trouble formulating them as you write.

SUMMARY

The organization of a persuasive paper should demonstrate the same kinds of logical relationships between the proposition and its supporting arguments that exist between the conclusion of a syllogism and the premises that logically lead to it. A paper written from such an outline would be similar in overall design to that of an expository paper: SUBJECT and RESTRICTION handled in the Introduction, ILLUSTRATION forming the body of the paper, and a conclusion restating the SUBJECT and RESTRICTION. This order would be characteristic of a deductively organized argument. An inductive paper would present the supporting arguments first and then conclude with a statement of the proposition. Schematized, a persuasive paper looks like this:

INTRODUCTION (SUBJECT and RESTRICTION)

    Orientation: Introduction to the problem or recommendation.   For logical persuasion:

    Proposition: (In inductive papers, proposition appears in the conclusion.)   Strongly stated solution or recommended course of action.   Refutation/counterargument if classical form is followed.

    BODY (ILLUSTRATION)

      I. Supporting argument
        A. Evidence (proof)
        B. Evidence (proof)
     II. Supporting argument
        A. Evidence (proof)
        B. Evidence (proof)

Refutation/counterargument usually handled here in modern argument.

CONCLUSION

Restatement of proposition	Refutation/counter-
Appeal for action	argument can be
	presented here if
	topic is noncontro-
	versial.

Like the model organizational scheme presented for the expository paper, this one is intended not as a restriction on your writing, but only as a guide for structure. Perhaps your paper will need only two supporting arguments, or perhaps four, or a different introductory approach.

Supporting evidence can consist of statistics, authority, facts, case studies, historical or social background, analogy, and explanation of causes. These should be so presented that, along with the language you use and the way you order your material, they help you develop your argument as forcefully as possible.

As in expository writing, the outline is only a tool, a skeletal version of your final paper. It permits you to experiment with the order of your supporting arguments and to work out the logical relationships among them before you begin to write. If your main points lead logically to the proposition, passing the "therefore" test at the outline stage, your final version should pass all other tests.

ASSIGNMENTS

For Discussion

1 The following are thesis statements—expanded and rephrased propositions—from argument papers. State each one as a proposition. What advantages does the writer of each gain from the original, expanded version?

a We are precipitated into a war which, I think, cannot be justified, and a war which promises not a benefit, that I can discover, to this country or the world.

— William Ellery Channing, "Sermon on the War of 1812," from *American Protest in Perspective*

b A great many folks admit that many of the people in jail ought to be there, and many who are outside ought to be in. I think none of them ought to be there.

— Clarence Darrow, "Crime and Criminals"

c Legislation against manufacture and export of DDT, particularly in the United States, can bring a major international disaster: the return of malaria epidemics—suffering and debilitation from hundreds of millions of cases—deaths from tens of thousands of them.

—James W. Wright, "DDT: It Is Needed Against Malaria, but for
the Whole Environment . . . ," *Smithsonian*

d   It seems to me that our ideals, laws and customs should be based on the proposition that each generation, in turn, becomes the custodian rather than the absolute owner of our resources—and each generation has the obligation to pass this inheritance on to the future.

—Charles Lindbergh

2   **What is the nature of the audience that each of the following introductory paragraphs is addressed to? Does the writer consider the audience neutral, supportive, or antagonistic? What tactics does each writer use to appeal to the audience?**

a   If I looked at jails and crimes and prisoners in the way the ordinary person does, I should not speak on this subject to you. The reason I talk to you on the question of crime, its cause and cure, is that I really do not in the least believe in crime. There is no such thing as a crime as the word is generally understood. I do not believe there is any sort of distinction between the real moral conditions of the people in and out of jail. One is just as good as the other. The people here can no more help being here than the people outside can avoid being outside. I do not believe that people are in jail because they deserve to be. They are in jail simply because they cannot avoid it on account of circumstances which are entirely beyond their control and for which they bear in no way responsibility.

—Clarence Darrow, "Crime and Criminals"

b   People of Yale University! What's happening around you? I'm becoming convinced that the rampant, out-of-touch intellectualism in which you immerse your daily lives is leading you down the path of inert oblivion. In the two and a half years I've been here, I have never seen so many people out of touch with themselves, their bodies, and maybe even life itself.

What good is your jammed-up intellectualism to you when you can't relate together the things that are happening around you, the things that are shaping your lives? I have never seen a place with so many talented people where inaction is actually valued, where people think that they can control their lives by thinking out something devoid of action. To think that this docile, jammed-up institution is to produce "1000 male leaders per year"! If so, then someone should seriously consider what it is that we will be leading.

—Robert Wesley, "All About Production"

c   Speaking of the different kinds of treatment accorded to the affluent and to the marginal citizen, as I was the other day, reminded me that Barry

Goldwater has lately come out for gentler penalties against marijuana offenders.

This hardest of hard-liners in the law-and-order field admitted that his view of the subject had been changed by "personal considerations." All this can mean is that somebody close to him was puffing on pot and got his hand caught in the act.

    —Sydney J. Harris, "Pot Moves Up in Class," Louisville (Ky.) *Courier-Journal*

3 Outline the following short arguments. What is the implicit proposition for each? The main arguments? Is the appeal emotional, logical, or a combination of the two? How is refutation handled? How effective is the conclusion? What kind of proofs does the writer rely on?

a Autos are the number one cause of air pollution, as well as energy wastage. They kill 50,000 to 60,000 people a year—needlessly, from unsafe design. Highways and parking lots drain available agricultural and industrial land. The exercise of which they deprive us (walking, bicycling) is a major contributor to death from heart disease. The 7.6 million we throw away each year, like beer cans, clog our landscapes and city dumps. The steel, rubber, glass, plastic and energy used in building eight to ten million new ones each year squanders scarce resources.

Urban design, inadequate public transportation and physical health make automobile transportation a necessity for many Americans. We can't forbid their sale. But how about a ban on advertising cars? Isn't it incongruous for a nation claiming concern over energy to spend millions of dollars (especially on television licensed to serve "the public interest") encouraging the consumption of more and more thirteen-mile-per-gallon autos?

Half of all auto use is for distances under five miles. Bicycle sales (fifteen million a year) have already soared ahead of the sluggish auto market. Once the auto ads are banned, how about building on this citizen sensibility with a media campaign (à la World War II bond sales) to encourage further walking and bicycling—thereby saving our air and our health as well as our oil? (Reports and public-service spots on cars' gas mileage would be useful, too.) It worked (while we tried it) with anti-smoking spots on TV. . . .

    —Nicholas Johnson, "Ban Auto Ads," *ADA World*

b Ten years ago this month the U.S. surgeon general brought forth his Report on Smoking and Health. The report climaxed ten years of controversy over the relationship between cigarettes and lung cancer, and it precipitated a second decade of controversy on the same issue. The story merits a backward look.

In truth, the controversy over smoking and health probably dates from the time that Columbus first saw the Indians puffing their tabacas. Efforts to ban smoking can be traced to the edicts of James I against the "sot weed." From time immemorial, little boys have been warned against coffin nails. The cigarette has had many lovers, but very few friends.

Even so, it wasn't until the mid-'50s that statistical evidence began to accumulate on the cigarette-cancer relationship. By the time Dr. Luther L. Terry's study commission went to work, some 10,000 professional papers were available. From these papers—the commission did no independent research of its own—came the conclusion that heavy smokers are more likely to die of lung cancer than nonsmokers. Six additional reports have followed the first report of 1964, each of them identifying new perils and raising new warnings.

These cries of alarm have wrought considerable changes within the cigarette industry and within the advertising industry also. Back in 1963, the ten leading brands, headed by Pall Mall, included such non-filter labels as Lucky Strike and Chesterfield. Now Pall Mall has slipped to third, behind Winston and Marlboros; sales of Camels have dropped in half; Luckies and Chesterfields have disappeared from the top ten, and some new brands, relatively low in tar and nicotine, have taken their place. Cigarette advertising has vanished from radio and television; smokers are exhorted in public service announcements to "kick the habit" instead.

The anti-smoking campaign also has led to the ignored and familiar on every package and in every magazine ad: "Warning: The Surgeon General Has Determined That Cigarette Smoking Is Dangerous to Your Health." The decade has seen airlines divide their passenger compartment into sections for smokers and nonsmokers. The man or woman who lights up in public has become acutely self-conscious of the offense that may be inflicted on others.

Yet these years of intensive effort have had little effect on the smoking habit. Per capita consumption in 1963 amounted to 217 packs; last week it was 205 packs. Over the decade, cigarette sales have increased from 524 billion to 583 billion. Ironically, sales of cigars and pipe tobacco, thought to be less harmful, have significantly decreased in this period.

Why has the typical smoker been so indifferent to the warning and appeals? One answer may lie in the unconvincing nature of the evidence. After ten years, scientists have yet to identify what substance in the cigarette, if any, causes cancer. They have yet to demonstrate how smoke or tar or nicotine converts a normal cell to a malignant cell. The one major effort to prove that cigarettes cause cancer in dogs produced a publicity splash four years ago, but the experiment has run into professional criticism and has not been replicated.

The palpable fact remains that most smokers die from causes apparently unrelated to smoking. There may be lessons in all this, in terms of the power of government to control the personal habits of the people. Such a lesson should have been learned in the long, dark night of Prohibition. The nation even now is receiving instruction in such areas of the law as marijuana, homosexuality, and pornography: criminal sanctions may have some suppressive effect, but on the whole, not much. So, too, with tobacco: Men have smoked it for 500 years, and whole platoons of Surgeons General are not likely to dissuade them now.[2]

c   A letter in Time magazine a few weeks ago, from a reader who opposes gun laws, was typical of the kind of illogical thinking that supports such arguments. The letter said:

"A gun has no will of its own. A gun does only what its owner causes it to do. The root of the problem is within the human heart. Cure the cause rather than treat surface symptoms."

Let me transpose this argument to a similar term to demonstrate how absurd it is:

"An automobile has no will of its own. An automobile does only what its driver causes it to do. The root of the problem is within the human heart. Cure the cause rather than treat surface symptoms."

Therefore, dispense with automobile laws. No more speed limits, no more traffic signals, no more registration of cars, no more tests for drivers, no more fines or jail terms for offenses.

Instead, we try to reform and change human nature. We work at making most people kind and considerate and attentive and rational and model citizens.

Meanwhile, what is happening on the streets and highways? Slaughter, that's what's happening. While we're slowly "curing the human heart," we're speedily killing thousands of human bodies.

Why bother to make cars safer, either? Since it's obviously the motorist, and not the car, that causes accidents, let's also dispense with stronger bumpers, roll-over bars, seat-belts, impact-bags, or anything else designed to protect in a crash. When people's hearts are warmer, the highway homicide rate will go down to practically nothing.

All we have to do is improve the human race—it may take a few thousand years—and the auto will be no more of a threat, or fatal weapon, than the tricycle.

This is what the gun people imagine is rational thinking. Another of their themes is "infringement of liberty." But what would they think of a drunk driving a car down the road, without a license, without plates, without the slightest responsibility or obligation to others?

The automobile, at least, serves a useful purpose when its ownership and operation are carefully supervised. The handgun serves no purpose except the taking of human life.

True; guns don't kill—but people with guns do. And far too often.[3]

[2] James J. Kilpatrick, "Government Meddling Can Be Hazardous to Freedoms," © The Washington Star Syndicate, Inc. Reprinted by permission.

[3] Sydney J. Harris, "Illogical Thinking in Gun Law Debate." From *Strictly Personal* by Sydney J. Harris. Courtesy of Field Newspaper Syndicate.

4 Rewrite the parts of the following topic outlines so that each outline can act as an expanded syllogism. You will need to construct a proposition and main arguments. Your outline can reflect a position either for or against the issue.

a Legalized gambling
  I. Alternative to income tax
  II. People always gamble
  III. Possibilities for revenue for charitable organizations

b Banning of automobiles in national parks
  I. Pollution damage
  II. Overcrowding
  III. Preservation of wild life

c School busing
  I. Concept of neighborhood schools
  II. Integrated housing
  III. Fuel crisis
  IV. Educational advantages

5 Determine which groups in your audience would be most likely to be hostile to your views about the subjects in exercise 4. What refuting arguments would you have to deal with in logical persuasion? How would these influence the way you order your supporting arguments?

6 Discuss the effectiveness of the following conclusions. What kind of appeal is made? Is any syllogistic reasoning involved?

a From an argument for reopening the Kent State case:

By the time the Kent cases are completed, the ACLU and its foundation will have expended well over $100,000 in the quest to hold public officials accountable for their acts. Whenever someone asks why we are devoting so much time and effort and so many resources toward accountability for events that happened so long ago, I tell them that just four months ago—a few days before he was again sworn in office after a mandatory four-year hiatus—Governor Rhodes was questioned under oath by ACLU attorneys. He was asked, whether, in retrospect, there was anything he would have done or would now do differently at Kent.
  His reply: "None whatsoever. . . . Nothing."
  —"Kent State Five Years Later," *Civil Liberties*

b From an argument for learning the history of black people in the United States:

We weep for the true victim, the black American. His wounds are deep. But along with their scars, black people have a secret. Their genius is that they have survived. In their adaptations they have developed a vigorous style of life. It has touched religion, music, and the broad canvas of creativity. The psyche of black men has been distorted, but out of that deformity has risen a majesty. It began in the chants of the first work song. It continues in the timelessness of the blues. For white America to understand the life of the black man, it must recognize that so much time has passed and so little has changed.

> —William Grier and Rice M. Cobbs, *The Shadow of the Past*

   c   From an argument against the pursuit of status:

Finally, I think we must learn to transcend the pettiness of scrambling for the symbols of status. We should recognize the true strength that lies in being individuals who think for themselves and are independent in mind and spirit. We would all lead more contented and satisfying lives if we judged people not by the symbols they display, but by their individual worth.

> —Vance Packard, "The Pursuit of Status"

   d   From an argument that the space age can bring about a twentieth-century spiritual and social renaissance:

The choice is ours, it must be made soon, and it is irrevocable. If our wisdom fails to match our science, we will have no second chance. For there will be none to carry our dreams across another dark age, when the dust of all our cities incarnadines the sunsets of the world.

> —Arthur C. Clarke, "Space Flight and the Spirit of Man"

For Writing

From the following list of topics, determine which would be best suited for emotional persuasion and which would require logical persuasion. Choose one of each kind, restrict the topics, and construct two outlines for persuasive papers: one designed for emotional persuasion, the other for logical persuasion. Write a 1,000–1,500 word argument based on one of your outlines.

a   Inequities of the income tax
b   Poverty in the United States
c   Watergate
d   The role of the media in government
e   Violence as a political tool
f   Social change
g   Enforced busing

h   Marijuana legalization
i   Treatment of drug addicts
j   American foreign policy after the Vietnam war
k   National defense and military spending
l   Conformity and American education
m   Competition for grades
n   Co-ed housing on campus
o   Academic records—public or private information?
p   Women and the law
q   Gun control
r   Birth control
s   Malpractice insurance
t   Juvenile criminals
u   Striking—a tool for professional people?

Sentence and Paragraph Strategies in Persuasive Writing

In earlier chapters we presented certain kinds of sentences as especially useful to particular kinds of writing and for specific purposes: the simple sentence for personal narrative; the cumulative sentence for description; and the subordinate sentence for expository writing. We also discussed ways of organizing paragraphs and tactics for expanding them —for instance, the spatially ordered paragraph developed through descriptive detail and the SRI expository pattern expanded with examples and statistics. Persuasive writing, too, has special characteristics and requirements that benefit from some sentence and paragraph strategies more than from others.

You are probably familiar with the old story about the farmer who had much success in persuading his mules to perform their mulish duties. When asked his secret, he replied that there was no magic involved: before telling the mules what to do, he hit them in the head with a stick to get their attention. Argumentative writing requires a similar tactic; but the "stick" is the point of view you are trying to impress your audience with. Your success in persuading your audience will be largely a result of your ability to keep their attention on the subject. Your skill in devising ways to sustain focus on both the topic and your attitude toward it will determine the effectiveness of your argument.

SENTENCE STRUCTURE AS A MEANS OF FOCUSING THE TOPIC

Sentence structure can play an important role in sustaining readers' attention. Sentence elements can be reordered to focus your topic; transitional elements can provide logical links from one sentence to the next; and sentence structure can be manipulated to emphasize and de-emphasize certain points — all of which give you extra persuasive power. Let's turn now to more detailed discussions of these devices.

Reordering Sentence Elements

In the following paragraph, taken from the body of an article arguing that new sexual patterns emerging out of a zero-growth society must be accompanied by a new kind of moral responsibility, the writer makes use of reordered sentences to focus his topic. To note the writer's sentence tactics, compare his version to a rewritten one showing normal sentence order. Pay special attention to the italicized elements.

Original Version	*Paraphrased Version*
1 *In the zero population growth world* we are all "clan brothers" and will have to find ways of expressing the hippy ideal of universal kinship. **2** *For many of the young today,* a wider range of permitted sexual relationships seems to express this ideal, and even the rather compulsive wife-swapping of middle-aged couples in urban America seems to be reaching towards the same solution. **3** *What is clear* is that we cannot reimpose the old rigidities. **4** *In going forward to newer and more varied patterns,* our sense of responsibility and our awareness of others is to be severely tested if we are not to become still more confused and unhappy. **5** *If we pass the test,* we may evolve into a universal human family in which all three types of sex have their place, in which we are all genuinely kin, and in which all but the most unrealistic	**1** We are all "clan brothers" *in the zero population growth world* and will have to find ways of expressing the hippy ideal of universal kinship. **2** A wider range of permitted sexual relationships seems to express this ideal *for many of the young today* and even the rather compulsive wife-swapping of middle-aged couples in urban America seems to be reaching towards the same solution. **3** That we cannot reimpose the old rigidities *is clear.* **4** Our sense of responsibility and our awareness of others is to be severely tested *in going forward to newer and more varied patterns* if we are not to become still more confused and unhappy. **5** We may evolve into a universal human family in which all three types of sex have their place, in which we are all genuinely kin, and in which all but the most unrealistic inner needs can be met in

inner needs can be met in one form   one form or another *if we pass the*
or another.   *test.*

    — Alexander Comfort, "Sexuality in a Zero-Growth Society," *Center Report*

    To reinforce the main points in the arguments, adverbials and sub-
ordinate clauses are placed out of their usual order. Placing the phrase
"In the zero population growth world" at the beginning of sentence
1 not only supplies transition from the preceding paragraph but re-
introduces the subject of the paper. In sentence 2, placing "For many
of the young today" at the beginning of the sentence does not simply
help achieve sentence variety; referring to "the young" first helps the
writer to emphasize the widespread occurrence of new and changing
attitudes. Note that his comparison between young and middle-aged
people becomes more emphatic because of the reordering. In sentence 3,
transposing the predicate "is clear" gives added emphasis to the reordered structure and greater importance to an earlier argument. In
4, the initial position of "In going forward to newer and more varied
patterns" provides emphasis as well as a transitional summary of the
previous examples. Finally, the decision to open sentence 5 with "If
we pass the test" creates an effective transition from the "test" in the
previous sentence while automatically producing a shortened syllogism:
"*If* we pass the test [*then*] we may evolve into a universal human
family . . ."; this device adds great logical force to the argument.

    Few writers consciously analyze the order of each sentence in this
way. Usually the writing skills involved are accumulated over a long
period of trial and error. But being aware of some of the persuasive advantages of reordering sentences can help you reduce some of that
practice time.

Transitional Devices

    Another sentence strategy that could benefit you in argumentation is
the use of transitional structures. Probably the most effective transitional
devices are the kinds used in the Comfort paragraph — sentence elements
that contribute to meaning as well as to movement from one idea to the
next. But there are other transitional adverbials that can specify the
logical relationships between two sentences just as the transitional
subordinators discussed in Chapter 22 join the ideas in the two clauses
of a complex sentence. As we mentioned in that discussion, transitional
subordinators can and often do not only function as connectors within
sentences but also show relationships between sentences. Here's an
example using one of them:

Such differences [in the mathematical ability of boys and girls] could, of course, be genetic. *However,* it seems equally or more plausible to suggest that they are related to social pressures operating differently on women and men to mold them into the adult roles they are assigned by tradition to play.

—Marijean Suelzle, "Woman in Labor," *Transaction*

In addition to subordinators such as *however,* other adverbials can bridge relationships between two sentences: *in addition (to), obviously, fortunately, in truth, conversely, in fact, in much the same way, unlike this, in similar fashion* — these are but a few of the most widely used adverbial idioms. Good writers, however, avoid overusing them and rely instead on supplying short phrases to act as meaningful bridges and on reordering sentence elements to serve as transitional devices.

When you employ these transitional devices in your writing, you need to be aware of the conventions of punctuating them. Such devices are almost always set off from the rest of the sentence by commas, regardless of what position they have in the sentence:

Initial: *Moreover,* they were unable to determine a cause for the epidemic of measles.

Middle: They were unable, *moreover,* to determine a cause for the epidemic of measles.

Final: They were unable to determine a cause for the epidemic of measles, *moreover.*

Passive Sentences

In an earlier discussion of the passive, we pointed out that active sentences are more effective in narrative writing. In persuasive writing, if the passive construction is not abused, it places strong focus on the topic when other devices are inadequate. It can also be useful in other ways. In the following example, the writer effectively uses the passive for topic-focusing. But in addition, note the subtle diplomacy resulting from the omission of the agent *by* phrase and how it contributes to the persuasive power of the sentence. By the use of the passive, the writer can imply blame but not place it on a definite agent, thus avoiding a defensive reaction from the men in her audience.

The journeywoman [in a union] *is given* less training [than a journeyman], her promotional ladder is shorter or nonexistent, and she *is paid* less.

—Marijean Suelzle, "Woman in Labor," *Transaction*

The following sentence demonstrates another advantage of the passive: the omission of the agent when it is unimportant to the point. This results in added emphasis to the reordered subject.

Women *were asked* to write a story. . . . *Men were given* the same task.
— Marijean Suelzle, "Woman in Labor," *Transaction*

This use of the passive, when added to the many active sentences in the argument all beginning with the word *women* or *men,* helps the writer to keep constantly before her audience the contrast basic to her argument—the discrepancy between men and women in employment opportunities.

Used wisely and sparingly, passive sentences can be a valuable tactic for topic-focusing.

Cumulative Sentences

In persuasive writing, all sentence types are brought into play—simple sentences for stark emphasis; compound for listing causes, relationships, and proofs such as statistics; complex for indicating logical relationships, particularly those in which the clauses are joined by *if . . . then; either . . . or; therefore;* or a dash. But one type of sentence that is of special use in argumentation is the cumulative sentence.

In descriptive writing, you used cumulative sentences for handling colorful details. But the structure of the cumulative sentence can also be advantageous in persuasion: the main clause at the beginning can carry an uninterrupted, emphatic statement of a supporting argument, which is then strengthened by the additional proofs or alternatives that follow:

Ask yourself what might happen to the world of tomorrow if there is complete automation, if robots become practical, if the disease of old age is cured, if hydrogen fusion is made a workable source of energy.

— Isaac Asimov

The cumulative structure can also enable a writer to add descriptive details that qualify the stated point without breaking up the close grammatical relationships of the main clause:

The treatments are worse than the sickness: insulin shock, electroshock, and even psychosurgery, during which the frontal lobes of the brains of unmanageable patients were quickly disconnected.

— Wesley C. Westman, *The Drug Epidemic*

Periodic Sentences

As you see, the cumulative sentence can be an effective persuasive tool, but its use in argument is limited. Of greater advantage for some persuasive purposes is the periodic sentence. Unlike the cumulative sentence, which presents the main statement first, the periodic sentence either places the modifiers at the beginning and the main clause at the end, or places the subject first, then the modifiers, and finally the rest of the main clause. This structure's value in argument is that its climactic effect can enhance persuasive force: it gives the same advantages as inductive organization does. Note in the following examples how the message in the italicized material gains importance through the piling up of convincing details beforehand.

> As long as students whisper among themselves, look at their watches, read newspapers, and write letters in class, *little learning can take place.* (Main clause at end)

But the widely publicized estimates that one in seven, one in four, or one in two of the seven million college students in America can be considered a "drug abuser" *are vastly exaggerated.* (Subject at beginning; predicate at end)
> —Kenneth Keniston, "Heads and Seekers," *The American Scholar*

The main weakness of the kind of periodic sentence in the second example is that the interruption between the subject and predicate can make it difficult to read and comprehend. So use it only when you want the climactic emphasis it offers.

Balanced Sentences

A balanced sentence can take the form of two main clauses that are equal in content, length, and grammatical structure, such as Pope's:

To err is human; to forgive, divine.

Or the balance may be between the subject and the predicate:

The difference between tragedy and comedy is the difference between experience and intuition.
> —Christopher Fry

The balanced sentence can be used to emphasize a point, as in the Fry example, or it can permit the counterbalancing of two opposite points —which is probably its greatest contribution to argument. Using balanced sentences in this way also lends a psychological dimension to persuasion: the symmetry of the sentence form can lend an air of rationality and logic to the argument contained within. For this reason, perhaps, many writers like to use it as the closing line in an argument paper or to dramatize a central point.

PARAGRAPH STRUCTURE AS A MEANS OF FOCUSING THE TOPIC

We have just seen how sentence structure can serve to maintain focus on the main arguments in a paper. Paragraph structure, too, can enhance the kinds of reasoning necessary to a logical argument. In persuasive writing, you will often need to deal with effects and their causes — in arguing for remedies to a problem, or in rooting out the causes of a situation you want changed. You may also need to compare and contrast two similar or opposite ideas or remedies or recommendations. These tasks require special patterns of paragraph development — patterns additional to those we discuss in Chapter 17. Let's consider them now.

Cause-and-Effect Paragraphs

For some purposes in a logical argument, you may want to deal mainly with effects, as Marvin M. Katz does in this paragraph from his essay "What This Country Needs Is a Safe Five-Cent Intoxicant." As you read, note that he moves from a discussion of the diverse human needs for drugs (CAUSE) to the diverse EFFECTS of drugs.

Man's needs, it turns out, vary in kind and in pattern from person to person and within the same man. In view of this diversity of needs the accomplishments in drug development have been remarkable. The span of effects man can attain with drugs extends from such minor alterations as relief from tension, to major psychological changes that include escape from lethargy, from boredom and from aggressive inhibitions and, ultimately, to altered states of consciousness. They may even transport a person to an entirely different emotional or psychological state.	CAUSE EFFECTS

In another paragraph from the same article, Katz discusses at length one cause projected for the use of marijuana (EFFECT):

The most parsimonious of explanations, however, comes from sociologist Howard Becker. In discussing possible reasons for the use of marijuana he proposes that there is nothing unusual or deviant about the motives that lead to its use; it is rather the use that may lead to deviant behavior. He proposes that a person usually comes upon marijuana by chance and experiments with it simply out of curiosity. He maintains the habit only if he derives pleasure from it. Becker concludes that if someone learns to derive pleasure from marijuana, more com-	EFFECT CAUSE

plex explanations are unnecessary; he continues to use marijuana simply because it is a new kind of pleasurable experience.

You can see that cause-and-effect paragraphs can move from effect(s) to cause(s) or from cause(s) to effect(s). In a long, complex argument, the effect may be introduced in a separate paragraph followed by a series of paragraphs, each dealing with a single cause. In your own papers, as you work out the organizational and writing problems of handling cause and effect, make sure your logic is sound. Be careful to avoid the fallacies to which this kind of reasoning situation is especially vulnerable: *post hoc,* hasty generalization, and confusion of a correlation with a cause (see Chapter 24).

Comparison-and-Contrast Paragraphs

Paragraphs of comparison and contrast can be organized in two basic ways. The outlines and sample paragraphs below illustrate the possibilities.

Scheme I. Topic sentence: A and B can be compared/contrasted on certain points.
1. Point 1
   A
   B
2. Point 2
   A
   B
3. Point 3
   A
   B

There are two Americas. One is the America of Lincoln and Adlai Stevenson; the other is the America of Teddy Roosevelt and the modern super-patriots. One is generous and humane, the other narrowly egotistical; one is self-critical, the other self-righteous; one is sensible, the other romantic; one is good-humored, the other solemn; one is inquiring, the other pontificating; one is moderate, the other filled with passionate intensity; one is judicious and the other arrogant in the use of great power.

— J. William Fulbright, *The Arrogance of Power*

Scheme II. Topic sentence: A and B can be compared/contrasted on certain points.
1. A
   Point 1

         Point 2
         Point 3
      2. B
         Point 1
         Point 2
         Point 3

Like every other instrument that man has invented, sport can be used either for good or for evil purposes. Used well, it can teach endurance and courage, a sense of fair play and a respect for rules, coordinated effort and the subordination of personal interests to those of the group. Used badly, it can encourage personal vanity and group vanity, greedy desire for victory and hatred for rivals, an intolerant esprit de corps and contempt for people who are beyond a certain arbitrarily selected pale.

—Aldous Huxley, ''Ends and Means''

Each scheme has its own advantages and each lends itself to different purposes. If you wish to emphasize individual comparisons or differences, then Scheme I will work better. But if you are seeking an overall comparison in order to classify the two items, Scheme II will be better.

Another kind of comparison involves the use of analogy. In a logical context, analogy refers to metaphorical comparison. In the kind of comparison discussed in the previous paragraphs, two equivalent features shared by two similar items are compared. Fulbright contrasts the opposing attitudes of "the two Americas"; Huxley contrasts different purposes arising from the same activity. In analogy, however, a comparison is usually made between two things that are not ordinarily compared. In literature, where aesthetic quality rather than logical soundness is the aim, such analogies abound: "My love is like a red, red rose," "No man is an island," and so on. But though logically questionable (see page 360), analogy is often used in argumentative writing. When used judiciously, it can add interest and persuasive force to your arguments. Here are two examples: in one the whole paragraph is used to develop the analogy; in the other an analogy is used to support the paragraph's argument.

The rich nations of the world are adrift in lifeboats. ''In the ocean outside each lifeboat swim the poor of the world, who would like to get in, or at least to share some of the wealth. What should the lifeboat passengers do?'' We could try to take everyone aboard, but we would sink the lifeboat if we did, [Dr. Hardin] says. The boat swamps, everyone drowns. Complete justice, complete catastrophe. ''For the foreseeable future,'' Dr. Hardin concludes, ''our survival demands that we govern our actions by the ethics of the lifeboat, harsh though they may be.''

—Wade Greene, ''Triage,'' *New York Times Magazine*

Some people feel that letting an industry-funded body such as the NAB [National Association of Broadcasters] act as the conscience of the entire electronic media is not unlike letting the lions decide which Christians are too small or weak to eat. Others argue that in the face of a historically shortsighted government regulating body like the FCC, the NAB has performed heroically. Whatever your view, the Television Code is what keeps TV on its toes.

—Louisville (Ky.) *Courier-Journal*

SUMMARY

The strategies for sentence and paragraph development presented in this chapter can be added to your ever-expanding stock of writing skills. Because of the importance of appealing to an audience in persuasive writing, you should strive to gear everything in your argument to the particular needs of your audience. Your paper will carry strongest persuasive power if your logic, organization, language, and sentence and paragraph structure all work toward the same end. Difficult? Yes. But the satisfaction of creating a piece of writing that influences others is well worth the effort.

ASSIGNMENTS

For Discussion

1   Reorder the sentences in the following paragraph from a student argument paper so that there is stronger focus on the topic.

Hunger and famine will become a world-wide problem unless some form of population control is developed and enforced. The amount of food produced will decrease considerably because of the lack of fertile agricultural land, as the population continually increases. The land presently used for food production will have to be utilized for living space because of the increasing number of people. Much farm land will also be used for highways and parking lots to accommodate the growing numbers of automobiles.

2   Revise the following student paragraphs by changing sentences to passive or by adding transitional devices to improve the focus on the topic.

   a   Water pollution will cause disease and death while soil pollution will destroy vegetation which the animals depend on for existence. We will slaughter the animals that do survive long enough in massive numbers to feed an ever-increasing population. Animals that we can use for food will quickly disappear.

b One must understand what strip-mining is and how reclamation of strip-mined land can best be carried out in order to understand the problems associated with strip-mining and reclamation. Strip mining is a process of obtaining coal that is lying close to the surface of the ground. Coal is found in seams sometimes hundreds of yards wide and miles long. Coal companies can obtain the coal when it is near the surface of the earth by using bulldozers and other mining machinery to strip the layers of topsoil and subsoil that lie on top of the seam of coal. They remove a strip of soil and pile it in a ridge beside the stripped portion and then remove the coal. The machines then move over a few yards and remove another strip of soil and pile it up on the previously mined strip. This process leaves behind a series of steep ridges and narrow valleys which we call spoil banks. Strip-mined land looks different in different areas of the country depending on the original contour of the area, depth of the coal vein, nature of the subsoil, method and machinery used, and the average temperature and rainfall of the area.

3 Identify the kinds of sentences below (cumulative, periodic, or balanced) and discuss their effectiveness in handling the job the writer gave them to do.

a He calculated that if only one star in a thousand of these had planets at a suitable distance, and if an atmosphere developed on only one in a thousand of these, and if the right chemicals were present in the oceans and atmospheres of only one in a thousand of these, we would still be left with a hundred million planets suitable for life.
  — John P. Wiley, Jr., "Don't Bet Everything on the Big Bang," *Natural History*

b The earth rotates on its axis at one thousand miles an hour; if it turned at one hundred miles an hour, our days and nights would be ten times as long as now, and the hot sun would then burn up our vegetation each long day while in the long night any surviving sprout would freeze.
  — A. Creasy Morrison, "Seven Reasons Why a Scientist Believes in God,"
  from *Man Does Not Stand Alone*

c If one person alone refuses to go along with him, if one person alone asserts his individual and inner right to believe in and be loyal to what his fellow men seem to have given up, then at least he will still retain what is perhaps the most important part of humanity.
  — Joseph Wood Krutch, "The New Immorality," *Saturday Review*

d We no longer think of our life span as a steady, desperate accretion of money, but more as an arc, after a certain point tapering down into easy retirement.
  — Thomas Griffin

e There, for approximately a week, this teeming, milling mass of sun and sex worshippers swims, sleeps, flirts, guzzles beer, sprawls and brawls in the sands.

—Alvin Toffler

f You are not in charge of the universe; you are in charge of yourself.

—A. Bennett

g American parents, to the extent that they are Americans, expect their children to live in a different world, to clothe their moral ideas in different trappings, to court in automobiles although their forebears courted, with an equal sense of excitement and moral trepidation, on horsehair sofas.

—Margaret Mead

h To have a quiet mind is to possess one's mind wholly; to have a calm spirit is to command one's self.

—H. Mabie

i Style, to define again by example, is when a brother is wearing his gators (alligator shoes), fine vines (clothes), a slick do (process), in the old days, or an "uptight" natural today; style is having a heavy rap (verbal display), like the preacher, the young militant and the pimp (three strong and admired characters in black communities); style is driving an Eldorado; style is standing on a street corner looking cool, hip and ready; style is diggin on Yutsef Lateef rather than Johnny Cash; style is the way a black man looks at a woman and says, "Come here with your bad self."

—Johnnetta B. Cole, "Culture: Negro, Black and Nigger"

4 The following are cause-and-effect paragraphs. Identify whether they move from cause to effect or from effect to cause. How is each focused toward the argument inherent in the paragraph?

a The pursuit of excellence in scholarship is inherently a lonely business and traditionally college life compensated by providing intimacy-producing relaxation, clubs, and other activities. As universities and colleges have grown at an explosive rate, creating an uprooted environment in the process . . . as they have become more depersonalized with television lectures, machine grading, and compulsory ID cards . . . as they have drawn more and more students from distant places . . . and as clubs have become less a part of the college scene, much of the old intimacy of college life has disappeared.

—Vance Packard, "Collegiate Breeding Ground for Transients," from *A Nation of Strangers*

b In place of the traditional family has come the activist family in which each member spends the majority of his time outside the home "participating." Clubs, committees, and leagues devour the time of the individual so that family activity is extremely limited. Competition among clubs is keenly predicated upon the proposition that each member should bring his family into its sphere. Thus Boy Scouts is made a family affair. PTA, the YMCA, the country club, every activity, competes for total family participation although it demands entry of only one member of the family.

—Vine Deloria, Jr., "Indians and Modern Society"

c The militancy of young people, both white and black, eager for social change is often accounted for by saying that they have lost faith in the slow processes of democratic discussion and decision-making. This argument seems to me highly questionable. It is my impression that militant young people, far from being "disillusioned" with democratic processes, are totally unacquainted with them, since they are rarely shown on television. To be sure, national conventions are shown on television every four years, but the arduous, day-to-day debates, fact-finding, and arguments by which social decisions are arrived at by every democratic body from town councils to the Congress of the United States are never shown.

—S. I. Hayakawa, "Who's Bringing Up Your Children?"
A Review of General Semantics

5 In the following comparison-and-contrast paragraphs, identify the type of comparison scheme used.

a The device used to limit competition is that of assigning different roles to the different groups within the American society. White males have assigned to themselves such roles as President of the United States, corporate executives, industrialists, doctors, lawyers, and professors at our universities. They have assigned to white women roles such as housewife, secretary, PTA chairman, and schoolteacher. Black women can now be schoolteachers, too, but they are most prominently assigned to domestic roles—maid, cook, waitress, and baby-sitter. Black men are thought to be good porters, bus drivers, and sanitation men.

—Shirley Chisholm, "The Politics of Coalition"

b Those who are for busing at all costs simply don't give a hang about the hostility, hatred, disaffection, and indifference generated among people who are expected to implement the educational and racial gains that are wanted: they are, typically, inclined to say that "at least we have an improved balance in the classroom." Consequently, they are miracle workers, do-gooders of the worst sort, who dream of transforming the country in accord with their entirely admirable vision, by means of cumulative but purely formal and administrative arrangements. Just bus them and the education of blacks as well as race relations will be improved—or, at any rate, a measurable gain will be added to previous, comparable gains, and the objectives will be brought a step nearer. Nonsense! On the other hand, those who are against busing at all costs simply don't give a hang for whatever deterioration appears within their own communities as a result of their imposed isolation, rigidity, and resistance to any but selected local concerns. Just throw the carpetbaggers out, keep the old traditions, let the neighborhoods manage their separate affairs, and education and relations between the races throughout the country will flourish in their most natural way. Again, nonsense!

— Joseph and Clorinda Margolis, "Busing"

6   How has the writer used analogy effectively in each of the following paragraphs?

a   Living together without any sense of permanency or legality is no more like marriage than taking a warm shower is like shooting the rapids in your underwear.

— Sydney J. Harris

b   But the area of urban and suburban planning is only one instance of environmental crusaders rushing in where more reasonable men would tread more warily. In just about every aspect of American life, the environmentalists are imposing their regulations with all the indiscriminate enthusiasm of Carrie Nation swinging a baseball bat in a saloon. Common sense seems to have gone by the board, as has any notion that it is the responsibility of regulators and reformers to estimate the costs and benefits of their actions.

— Irving Kristol

c   The only way to promote freedom is to devise a set of rules and thus construct a pattern which the various members of that society can follow. Each can then determine his own acts in the light of his knowledge of the rules. On this basis each can predict his field of action in advance and what results are likely to ensue from his acts; and so he gains freedom to plan and to carry out his plans. The more you attempt to administer society, however, the less free it becomes. There is opportunity for freedom of choice only in acting subject to the rules, and then only if the rules are freed of any element of will or dictation. If these rules are just rules that tell you what method or act will yield what results, like the rules of a game, you can then freely determine your own play. You can use the rules to win the game. The more abstract and objective the rule, the freer is the individual in the choice of his alternatives. The rules must be so written as to cover every possible eventuality of choice and action.

— A. Delafield Smith, "Law as a Source of Notions of Freedom"

For Writing

1   The following statistics are a result of a survey of college students taken by George Gallup in 1975. Construct a comparison-and-contrast paragraph using the figures.

"Do you think the use of marijuana should be made legal or not?"

	Yes	No	Don't know
Freshmen	47%	49%	4%
Sophomores	46	49	5
Juniors	58	36	6
Seniors	64	30	6

"Do you drink alcoholic beverages?"

	Yes	No
Freshmen	64%	36%
Sophomores	72	28
Juniors	83	17
Seniors	88	12

2   Write a paragraph of emotional persuasion using analogy as your main tactic.

3   Write a paragraph discussing the causes of some condition in your community — for example, air pollution, water pollution, poor support of public schools, or the high dropout rate in the local high school.

Revision
of Persuasive
Writing

Previously, we have offered various suggestions for revising your papers. By now, you should be aware that revision is an important aspect of the writing process. If you have practiced good revision habits throughout, you should now be able to identify mechanical errors, question your choice of words, and in general criticize your papers more objectively than you could at the beginning of the course. These are skills that you can apply to any writing assignment. But since persuasive writing involves a new set of writing tactics, this checklist of questions may help you in revising an argument paper.

Organization and Support

1. Is my thesis in the form of a proposition?
2. Do my main points have a "therefore" relationship with the proposition—that is, does the proposition logically follow from the main points?
3. Have I supported my arguments with significant evidence?
4. Have I kept my audience in mind, refuting contrary opinions where necessary?

Logic

1. Have I relied on sound logical reasoning throughout rather than on fallacious appeal to emotion?
2. Have I used analogy? If so, is it reinforced by other kinds of evidence?
3. Have I used syllogistic reasoning effectively and truthfully?
4. Have I avoided unethical slanting and ambiguous language?

Sentence and Paragraph Structure

1. Does my sentence structure help me make my points clearly and forcefully?
2. Have I effectively used comparison-and-contrast and cause-and-effect paragraph structure when needed?

Check through your paper, asking yourself these questions. If you can answer "yes" to each, then you can be reasonably certain that you have written a successful argument.

REVISION ASSIGNMENTS

1 Write two more versions of your introduction to your argument paper, using a different approach in each. Decide which would be most effective for the audience you are trying to reach.

2 Do the same for your conclusion. In one, appeal to the sympathy or sense of fair play of the audience; in another, suggest a favorable result from intelligent action on the problem. Decide which conclusion is most effective.

5

The
Critical
Voice:
Writing
About
Literature

Introduction: Critical Reading for Writing

The scene opens on four freshman students sitting in the lounge at the Student Center. They have just finished reading Ken Kesey's novel *One Flew Over the Cuckoo's Nest* for English class.

George: Man, that's the craziest book! That Big Nurse character is something else. We were told to figure out her function in the book. What did you all make of her?

Ann: I think Kesey means her to be a kind of symbol of our mechanized society—a huge, sterile, monster machine that tries to dehumanize the others. She's often described as a machine— motors purring, and all that. Even her name, Ratched, could be a play on the word *ratchet*. That's some kind of machine part, isn't it?

Bill: Yeah, you could look at it that way. But I see her as a conformist. She goes by the rules no matter what. Always trying to make the crazy nonconformists in the book do things her way. Either they conform or get lobotomies.

Ruth: Well, you'll probably say this is pretty Freudian, but I think she's a universal mother figure—a professional "mom" who tries to castrate all the men in the novel.

George: Wow! That's pretty far out! I guess you could defend that idea from the book. But my theory's even wilder. I think she's a symbol of the white race. Notice her attitudes toward the Indian and the black orderlies.

Our four freshmen are engaged in an informal critical analysis of a literary text; they are interpreting some aspect of a novel—discussing what it means to each of them. And each interpretation, though startlingly different from the others, is valid and has been advanced by respected literary critics.

Literary writing demands this kind of personal interpretation. In exposition and argumentation, writers attempt to clearly and accurately communicate information and opinions about a world they share with readers. But in literature, the writer attempts to create a new world, akin to the one shared with the readers but still unique, filled with people, actions, and relationships that permit the reader some creative license. Thus, when you read exposition, it is essentially a learning and thinking process; but when you read literature, it is a creative one. That's why four students could arrive at four interpretations and why you can read a good literary work several times and find something new in it each time. To appreciate it most, and certainly before you can write an interpretative paper about it, you should read literature creatively; you should bring to it the art of critical analysis.

In this part of the book, we introduce you to the craft of reading and writing critically. This chapter will discuss the importance of critical reading and the functions of critical writing. In addition, to help you develop the skills for both, we will briefly examine the craft of writing literature: the skills and techniques that authors use to create a literary world. In Chapters 30 and 31, we shall suggest ways in which you can convey your critical interpretation of a literary work to an audience.

WHY CRITICAL ANALYSIS?

By *critical* analysis of a literary work we do not necessarily mean a negative or disapproving interpretation. Rather, the word *critical* as used here refers to the making of discriminatory evaluative judgments. The key word here is *discriminatory*. Students frequently complain to English teachers that they can't see why stories and poems have to be discussed in class. "Why," they ask, "can't we just read it to enjoy it?" Since reading is sometimes analogized with eating, let's look to that common human activity to find an answer to the question. How do you "enjoy" eating? Do you walk into a restaurant and instruct the waiter to bring just anything on the menu? Of course not. Rather, you choose the foods you "enjoy"—you browse through the menu to find something you have developed a discriminatory taste for. To some extent, this discrimination is personal; it results from years of random sampling of foods. But it is also a guided, learned preference; the people you have eaten with—your parents, brothers and sisters, friends—have all influenced your choice in foods.

So with reading. Even a glutton for reading, one who indiscriminately reads everything, should eventually acquire some taste for a really fine literary meal. A faster way to develop this taste is through critical discussion in English class. Here you have the opportunity to sample the dishes savored by the teacher and your fellow classmates.

"We can see that," our reluctant students might answer, "but why do we have to take literature apart? Why can't we just enjoy the story, responding emotionally to it?" The answer is that emotional pleasure is only one aspect of the enjoyment of anything. We appreciate a literary work just as we appreciate any human accomplishment: by understanding what the problems are and how they are solved. In baseball, we can admire a shortstop's artistry as he takes the throw on a dead run from the second baseman, touches the bag, veers off slightly to dodge the base runner, and then manages to throw to first base in time to complete the double play. Only by analyzing what he has done, by becoming aware of each decision he makes, and by realizing all the possibilities involved in the situation can we fully and truly appreciate the feat. You can apply a similar analysis to any human activity that requires skill. When a master does something, it looks easy. But master critics know that this ease is an illusion, because they are aware of the artistry and effort required at each step of the process. Just as judges of diving events analyze how divers handle the approach and other aspects of a dive, so critical readers examine the parts of a literary work. To evaluate the parts, they must take the work apart.

Analytical discussion of literature, then, can improve both your reading and writing skills. You are introduced to the methods of critical reading by an expert "coach," a teacher who is trained in the special reading skills needed for literature. In discussion, you practice the analytical skills that can aid in gaining an intelligent understanding of the art and craft of the literary writer. As you may know from experience with other activities, when intellectual awareness is heightened, so is pleasure. But critical analysis can do more than increase your enjoyment of reading; it can add a new dimension to your understanding of the real world and the motivations of the people you know. This humanizing effect is possible because literature is real, real in the sense that the people and the events are believable even though they might never have existed.

Consequently, literature, and an understanding of it, provide not only a way for you to while away a few hours of enjoyable escape from life, but give you an experience of life in a very real sense. Literature enables you to participate vicariously in a fictional universe, whether it be a mechanized world of the future, a sleepy Southern town, the court of Queen Elizabeth, or a distant battlefield. Encountering these fictional worlds can add to your understanding of the real world. Perhaps the most valuable means of achieving all this—of developing your own literary taste, increasing your critical abilities, and learning to use literature as a humanizing experience—is the writing of critical papers.

THE READER OF CRITICAL ANALYSIS

So far we have emphasized the value of critical analysis for you, the writer. But what of the audience that will read your critical papers? You may be asking yourself, what can my interpretations of a literary work do for other people? What can I contribute? These are questions that plague all would-be critics. Perhaps you can arrive at some answers by considering the following questions about your own individual reading habits. You probably haven't spent much time reading literary criticism, but haven't you often picked up magazine articles discussing movies or TV programs you have seen or want to see? Why? Is it because you want to verify your own interpretation or because you were puzzled by the plot and want to find out what someone else thinks of it? Or is reading a critical article merely a substitute for the kind of discussion our four students at the beginning of the chapter were having about Kesey's novel? Perhaps you missed seeing a movie that everyone is discussing, so you read something about it to avoid feeling left out. These are all valid reasons for reading criticism about literature, too: for reinforcing your own interpretation or obtaining a quick summary of the story. But as a reader of these articles, what do you demand of the people who write them? First, you expect them to have a first-hand, authoritative knowledge of the work. Also, you expect the critics to be analytical, perceptive, and sensitive—to be intelligent and discriminating in order to give you a better understanding of the work. And you expect the critics to support their opinions with specific references from the work itself— to refresh your memory of the plot and reassure you that the writer has first-hand knowledge of the material.

When you become a writer of literary criticism, then, you should try to satisfy these demands that you as a reader make on other critics. The first step in this process is a careful reading of the work. But how to go about this? We made the point earlier that you have a better appreciation of any skill if you have extensive knowledge of the process. Perhaps an understanding of how writers ply their craft can aid you in reading and analyzing a literary work in a more systematic and critical way.

THE ROLES OF THE WRITER OF LITERATURE

As we said, writers of literature create a new world, limited, for the special purpose of their work, in time and space. Alexander Solzhenitsyn's novel *One Day in the Life of Ivan Denisovich,* for instance, is an isolated world limited in time to a single day from dawn to dark and in space to the narrow confines of a Siberian prison camp. Other works may cover the span of a lifetime and encompass a whole continent. But whatever the scope, once the limits of time and space have been set, authors can then people a literary universe with their own created characters, direct the actions of their make-believe people, and determine their fates.

If Shakespeare's Macbeth could see real life as a stage and real people as players who "strut" their allotted time on it, then certainly we can view a literary work in that light. In writing a novel, a play, a short story, or even a poem, a writer creates a dramatic situation—a staged universe, peopled by characters who react to a situation and to one another in much the same way as real people in the real universe do.

In designing this fictional world, writers fulfill different roles. Earlier in the book we suggested that when you revise, you can separate the task into component roles—proofreader, editor, and so on—so that you can concentrate on one aspect of the job at a time. We can apply this same principle to the reading of a literary work, by assuming vicariously the different roles played by writers as they ply their craft. By doing this, we can outline a method for analyzing a literary work that can help you not only in reading literature but in developing the analytical skills needed to write about it. Of course, literary writers do not always consciously separate these functions any more than you do in writing; so in a sense we are creating an artificial situation when we use the analogy to the stage and separate each task from the whole writing process.

The Writer as Stage Manager

As "stage managers" writers are concerned with the technical aspects of their works. They plot out the action and decide on the chronology of events—how time is to be handled: whether to use flashbacks, whether the handling of the time will be realistic (events occurring in a normal sequence) or psychological (memory associations, flashbacks, dream sequences). In Part 1, on narrative writing, we discussed some of the techniques for creating time sequences. But in addition to the decisions about chronology, writers as stage managers must be concerned about spatial relationships—when and where to introduce each character, how many people to put in a scene at one time, how close in space they should be. To see the importance of these matters, consider the situation in Joseph Conrad's *The Secret Sharer*. The "sharer" of the captain's quarters could not have remained "secret" from the rest of the crew without the limited spatial possibilities of the isolated cabin. If the captain had lived in an open bunkroom with people going and coming all the time, readers would not be left at the end of the novel wondering if the secret sharer really existed or was a hallucination: his secret presence on the ship would have seemed implausible. The spatial strategy of an isolated cabin was essential to the writer's purpose in the novel and required careful thought and planning.

Related to spatial considerations is setting, and a third function of the stage-manager role is to decide how it is to be used. Is this place merely a backdrop for the action, or does it become an organic part of it, contributing to mood, motivation, and characterization? For example, Tennessee Williams' choice in *The Glass Menagerie* of a run-down flat in a once-opulent side of town reflects the condition of the characters themselves—once genteel, but now blemished by poverty and dying hope. Even in poetry, setting is often of particular concern to the writer: Robert Browning's staging of his dramatic monologue "My Last Duchess" in a beautiful, tastefully decorated palace makes the Duke's evil nature seem even more satanic by contrast.

Writers also make decisions about props and costumes—how are the characters to dress, what physical objects are necessary to the action of the story, play, or poem? How can these details be revealed to the audience so that they see the relationship to the action and the characterization?

Aware now of these technical devices, as you read any literary work, try to be conscious of how the writer employs them and how they contribute to the situation, the meaning, the action, and the development of character. By being constantly aware of these aspects of the writer's craft, you can gain insights as you read—insights that can contribute to a significant critical paper. Let's turn now to another role that writers play as they create a fictional world on a fictional stage.

The Writer as Scriptwriter

POINT OF VIEW

As a scriptwriter, the literary artist is concerned with the rhetorical aspects of the work. One of these involves perspective, or what is traditionally called point of view—how the story is told and from whose bias. We mentioned in Chapter 2 that writers have several options for handling point of view other than the first-person approach most frequently used in personal narrative. However, this "I" technique is often used in literary writing as well. If you are familiar with Mark Twain's *Huckleberry Finn* or J. D. Salinger's *The Catcher in the Rye,* you remember that each is narrated by the central character. Much modern poetry also employs first-person perspective. But unlike writers of personal autobiography, who themselves tell the story from their own point of view, literary artists can create a character who narrates the story in the first person. This narrator can be one of the main characters, not necessarily the central one, but one who is involved in the main action and tells the story. Or a minor character—outside the main action and either neutral or sympathetic to the main characters and the situation—can be the pervasive "I" who tells the story. Nelly Dean, the housekeeper and the "I" in Emily Brontë's *Wuthering Heights,* demonstrates this use of a minor character, narrating events of twenty years past as a fairly objective observer. By contrast, Marlow, Joseph Conrad's narrator for both *Heart of Darkness* and *Lord Jim,* does become emotionally involved with the main characters; his admiration for them as people overcomes his basic disapproval of their actions, and in the course of the story he becomes sympathetic to them. Writers using this device can present a story from a point of view not necessarily their own. As a reader, you need to make yourself aware of the way the author uses a narrator. Perhaps diagram 1 will help to clarify this point of view.

1

1. First-person point of view. Permits the author to tell the story through the mind of one character. But the writer must be constantly aware of the limitations placed upon the narrative and the perspective: the action and all other characters must be interpreted from the viewpoint of the narrator.

   The other main way literary writers handle point of view is through third-person narration, and this can be done in several ways. One device is called the "omniscient" point of view: the author, like a god or unembodied eye, stands outside the literary universe, observing all the actions and "seeing into" the motives of all the characters, using third-person pronouns in the narration ("he said," "she sang," "they went"). There is no pervasive "I," only the normal *I*'s and *me*'s of dialogue. Obviously, this technique allows the writer the most freedom in portraying the characters—each can be seen fully. The unfolding of the plot and revelation of character take place in the context of the action just as it does in drama—a literary form that is usually characterized by the omniscient approach because of the difficulties of creating a narrator on stage. Occasionally, playwrights do use a narrator. For example, in the ancient Greek plays and a few modern ones such as *Our Town* and *J. B.,* a chorus or an individual comments on the action. But most modern playwrights find that a narrator who must step out of a role on stage to address the audience detracts from the realism preferred by contemporary audiences. The omniscient narrator solves the problem; the device is used not only in plays but also in poetry, short stories, and novels. For instance, novels such as Thornton Wilder's *The Bridge of San Luis Rey* and short stories like Arthur Miller's ''The Misfits'' and Ray Bradbury's ''The Illustrated Man'' are narrated in this way.

Another advantage of using an omniscient narrator is that writers are not forced to rely on a single character to present their own philosophical or political position, but can create several who represent different aspects of it. Through the narrator's all-seeing position, the author can provide equal development of these representative characters, as Dostoevsky does in *Crime and Punishment.* In that novel, the main character (protagonist), Raskolnikov, professes the superman theory that fascinated Dostoevsky; Raskolnikov's sister Dounia and his friend Dmitri personify the author's beliefs in salvation through love and generosity. As diagram 2 indicates, the omniscient point of view permits the writer great freedom.

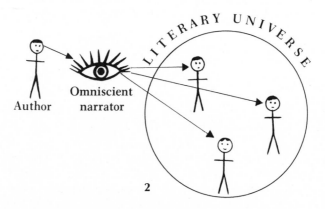

2. Omniscient third-person point of view. Writers freely illuminate the motivations of all the characters. Plot and character interaction are used to show character development.

In another device, known as the limited third-person point of view, everything is revealed through the mind of one character. Because the author knows everything in that character's mind, this perspective is related to omniscient point of view. But because the story must be told from the perspective of only one character, it is also limited. In this respect, then, it is closer to the restrictions of first-person narration, permitting a thorough exploration of only one character. With the actions and motives of other characters viewed through the narrator's eyes, everything is restricted to that character's limited, subjective point of view—as in real life. This point of view is exemplified in John Steinbeck's *The Pearl,* the author speaking of Kino in the third person but viewing everything through Kino's mind. The story is told from Kino's perspective, not the author's. This enables readers to see Kino's thoughts as well as his actions; but like Kino, they can only observe his wife Juana's behavior and hear her words; they, like him, are unable to get inside her mind. The limited third-person point of view is schematized in diagram 3.

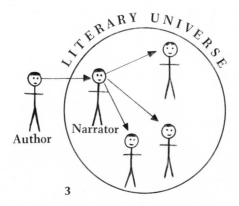

3

3. Limited third-person point of view. Allows the writer the advantages of first-person character narration, but adds a dimension of objectivity: the author can reveal unconscious motivations as well as conscious ones.

These are the three basic tactics for handling point of view in the telling of a story. You should realize, however, that this subject is more complex than it may sound. You cannot always determine easily the writer's central point of view, even by examining the narrator's pronoun usage. If first-person pronouns (*I, we*) are used by the narrator throughout, then it is easily discernible. But if the writer chooses third-person technique (*he, she, they*), the point of view can either be omniscient or limited third person. A further word of caution: when the omniscient "eye" narrates, you should not automatically assume that the perspective is necessarily the author's; omniscient narrators can be sympathetic to a specific theme in the book or to a particular character, or possibly act as a foil to one of the characters. A good critical rule of thumb is to remember that authors create and write stories; someone else—a narrator created by the author—tells them. As a reader, you must distinguish between the writer and the narrator.

Another complexity stems from the practice of some writers to combine point-of-view techniques. Rarely will you as a reader need to ponder all the possible ramifications of point of view—that is a task for professional critics. But a necessary aspect of critical reading is to determine the storyteller's perspective, regardless of the device used. You can get at this by keeping these questions in mind as you read: What does the narrator think of the other characters and their actions? What ethical standards does the narrator seem to have? How are these revealed? Is the narrator's personality so flawed that the reader is forced to doubt the honesty and reliability of the narration?

The last question is a significant one. Sometimes literary writers create narrators who are conspicuously unreliable, like Chief Bromden, who narrates Kesey's *One Flew Over the Cuckoo's Nest.* He is so obviously psychotic that the reader is never sure whether he is rational or hallucinating. At other times writers may use the narrator as a foil whose weaknesses and flaws illuminate the virtues of the central character. In a short story by Henry James, "The Liar," the narrator Lyons tells a story that challenges the integrity of the main character, but in the process reveals himself to be a liar about so many minor points that finally the reader is left with the gnawing suspicion that his whole tale is a lie. Since the narrator or narrators telling the whole story usually supply the central point of view, it is important that you as a critical reader determine how emotionally involved the author has made the narrators and how trustworthy they are as witnesses; otherwise, you may arrive at a false interpretation of the work.

LANGUAGE

Another rhetorical aspect of the author's scriptwriter role is using language to create a pervasive tone or mood and formulating dialogue that shows the characters' relationships and interactions. The writer's careful use of language can set a mood that is straightforward or satiric, sympathetic or disapproving, objective or emotionally charged; language can set the mood for a horror scene, a love scene, or a battle, despair, or hope.

Another use of language is to signal the theme of a character. If you know opera, you are aware that often a melodic strain accompanies the entrance of a certain character or foreshadows an imminent event. Writers can use language to produce this musical effect by having a character frequently repeat an identifying phrase: perhaps the most familiar

leitmotif is the one created by Charles Dickens for the miserly Scrooge—
"Bah, humbug!"

CHARACTERIZATION

Also as scriptwriter, the author determines the functions of the characters. Are they to be realistic or stock characters (stereotypes)? Which will act as foils to the main character and which as confidants? Which will serve as antagonists or enemies of the main character? Writers must not only devise ways to signal these relationships but to lead the reader to an awareness of the author's own assumptions about the characters. By being aware of these signals, you, the reader, should be able to determine whether the writer is hostile or sympathetic to the characters and their actions. To become conscious of all the ramifications and meanings of the characters' motivations, you must be aware of a third role that a literary writer plays: that of director.

The Writer as Director

To continue with our analogy of a literary work to a dramatic production, the writer's role as director is to unfold the levels of meaning inherent in the work. By using metaphorical language, by exploiting ambiguity of language and situation, and by capitalizing on the readers' psychological associations, a skillful writer-director takes the reader beyond the literal meaning of a work to a nonliteral or symbolic meaning. Many modern literary works—novels, short stories, plays, and poems— are written so that multilevel interpretation is possible, but because of limitation of space, let's use a short, lyric poem by Wendell Berry to illustrate how a writer can lead readers to this multilevel meaning.

FEBRUARY 2, 1968[1]

In the dark of the moon, in flying snow, in the dead of winter,
war spreading, families dying, the world in danger,
I walk the rocky hillside, sowing clover.

In this poem, the literal part of Berry's created literary universe is encapsulated in a single action: "I" sows clover on a barren hillside. The poet tells us that the literal action takes place during a winter month ("in flying snow, in the dead of winter") sometime after the full moon ("the dark of the moon") and at a time when the world is at war. By lan-

---

[1] From *Farming: A Hand Book* (New York: Harcourt Brace Jovanovich, 1970), p. 17. Reprinted by permission of Harcourt Brace Jovanovich, Inc.

guage choice and juxtaposition of ideas, the poet "directs" the reader beyond the literal setting of the poem to a larger universe embracing all people. "I" plants clover seeds in the worst possible environment for life to germinate: farmers planting by "signs" would never plant clover in the "dark of the moon"; it is "in the dead of winter," not the spring; and the farmland is not flat and fertile, but hilly and rocky. What do we know about "I" just from this information? In addition to these incongruities of planting, the poet uses other devices to direct us. The information in the second line seems irrelevant to the literal setting and action of the poem. But it is that line that directs the reader to the nonliteral universe of the poem. "Clover" in the third line, in contrast to the world calamities of the second, becomes symbolic of *life*. And the person sowing *life* on the rocky hillside in the face of almost hopeless farming odds becomes representative of humanity's need to nurture life in the face of the almost hopeless sociological odds of war and universal destruction. Thus, because of the writer's selection and organization of his material, coupled with his reliance on readers' psychological associations, "sowing clover" becomes both an affirmation of life and a symbol of humanity's ability to survive. This interpretation can now lead to others: many people associate prevailing against hopeless odds with hope and faith, and for them "clover" becomes symbolic not only of life but also of these human virtues. As you can see, the poet has directed his readers to meanings far beyond the literal one.

Although not so compressed and perhaps not so obvious, the same skills of direction can be applied to longer works; you simply need to become conscious of them as you read. Note that in analyzing the steps the poet takes in the poem, we moved from the literal to a more abstract meaning, and in the process we discovered the "theme" of the poem — the human affirmation of life. Like Berry's poem, all literary works contain a particular theme — a main idea expanded and developed in the body of the works — around which the action takes place. Some long works may exhibit several themes; Steinbeck's *Grapes of Wrath,* for instance, not only portrays the exploitation of migrant workers in the United States but also develops the themes of the dehumanization of extreme poverty and the will of people to survive against all odds. If, like Steinbeck and Berry, writers perform their role as director well, readers will almost unconsciously be led to a recognition of the theme or themes of the work.

THE CRAFT OF CRITICAL READING

We have looked fairly closely at the various components of literary craft; the technical aspects of plot, chronological organization, tactics of space and setting; the rhetorical aspects, the writing problems inherent in handling characterization, choosing a narrator or storyteller, creating special language and situational effects; and the symbolic aspects, the tactics for creating levels of meaning beyond the obvious, literal one. All of these are concerns of writers as they ply their craft. But readers need to be involved with these, too, as they practice the craft of critical reading. In the preceding section we pointed out some of those aspects of literature that you as a critical reader should be aware of. Let us now discuss the actual techniques of critical reading—skills that can also be applied to writing about literature.

As a reader of literature, you can read actively or passively. You can be aware or unaware of what is occurring in the story, play, or poem, just as you can be when viewing a painting, listening to a concert, admiring a piece of pottery—or watching a ball game. What makes the difference? As we mentioned, much awareness comes from understanding the literary craft and from critically reading and discussing literature—becoming actively involved in the process. How to start? We offer two suggestions: read closely and carefully; inquire constantly as you read.

But before pursuing these tips, let's return to the ball game analogy for a moment. The baseball fan notes the second baseman or shortstop edging toward second, depending on whether the batter is right- or left-handed. Then with the crack of the bat and the sight of the ball bouncing out to second, the fan watches the shortstop scoot to the bag, take the toss in stride while touching the bag, and evade the runner while throwing to first. The knowledgeable fan observes every action on the diamond; the casual spectator misses most of it. Similarly, the literary critic is alert to what is occurring in the story, play, or poem; the casual reader misses most of it.

We can't help you with basic reading problems, but in the preceding section we have tried to make you more aware of what generally goes on in a literary work. And we can suggest some specific questions that you can ask yourself as you read and when you've finished. By trying to answer these questions, many of which deal with the craft of the writer, you should obtain a clearer understanding of the work.

A few preliminaries. Just as the fan studies what is occurring on the field, so the critical reader studies what is occurring in the book. It might be interesting for a baseball fan to know where and when all the players were born and how they got involved in playing baseball and whom they had love affairs with and what other teams they had played for and so on. It might be informative to know where each team finished in the last five years and how each is doing in the current pennant drive. It might even add to an appreciation of a current game to know how the form of the game has changed over the years. But the game's the thing. What is happening on the field is most important. Everything else is not particularly relevant. You might ask, How does an analogy to a ball game relate to literature? As with background knowledge of baseball, biographical information about the author or historical information about the author's age or the social, political, intellectual, and other influences on the author may be interesting and informative. Or gaining a background of the history of the form—novel, play, short story—might add to your general literary knowledge. But like the game, the work is the thing. Everything else is not particularly relevant. All you really need to support your opinions about a work is evidence from its printed pages. That's what you must concentrate on.

But unlike a ball game, where chance may play a major role in a bad bounce or some other occurrence, in a literary work the author has complete control over the existence and actions of each character, what happens to them, where they go, how they dress, what they say. The author has selected every word on every page. Realizing this, we must take nothing for granted; nothing can occur without the author's design. As a result, we may profitably question everything, particularly the major issues:

The Questions	*The Areas*	*The Issues*
Who?	Character	The function, traits, and credibility of the people in the work.
What?	Plot	The series of related actions involving some problem that builds to a crisis and is resolved.
Where?	Setting	The physical location and the general environment, including the social, political, and other conditions affecting the characters.
When?	Time	The time structure of the work and the period it is set in.
Why?	Theme	The central or controlling idea that is conveyed mainly through the character and plot.
How?	Technique	The author's use of language devices to gain an effect.

These six questions—the journalist's classic lead of who-what-when-where-why-how—are just the tip of the iceberg. In the next chapter we will plunge deeper into these matters, but let's once again point out the method in our madness: by asking such questions of a literary work and by searching for satisfying answers, you should be better able to analyze and understand it.

In the following chapter we will discuss each of these six main questions in detail, exploring issues involved in answering each of them and indicating how these questions can help you organize and develop a critical paper on literature. But keeping these questions in mind as you read a work of literature can make you a more perceptive and critical reader as well.

ASSIGNMENTS

For Discussion

1   This chapter discusses *critical reading* and *critical writing*. What is meant by the two terms? What other kinds of reading skills are there? How does the purpose for reading relate to reading skills?
2   What are the special characteristics of literary writing that authors must be concerned with? How do they relate to the art of critical reading and writing?
3   Discuss the major techniques by which an author can handle narration. What are the advantages and disadvantages of each?
4   Consider the following passages, taken from literary works and representative of the narrative device used in each. Identify the kind of narrative point of view used in each.

a   Gene's brow wrinkled again in irritation; he thought she was deliberately not helping him, whereas in truth she did not know he wanted her help.
"The point is, Mother, I haven't the money to go."
Now for something as important to him as this Ruth would never have denied him the money, and Gene knew it. But Ruth herself did not know it, though he thought she did. He thought not only that she knew it but that the long process of reasoning herself into it, which she always went through, was a method of reproaching him. She had nothing like reproach in her mind; though she did not know it she was providing her conscience with good reasons for giving this money to him.
—George P. Elliott, "Children of Ruth" from *Among The Dangs*

b   Yesterday afternoon the six-o'clock bus ran over Miss Bobbit. I'm not sure what there is to be said about it; after all, she was only ten years old, still I know no one of us in this town will forget her. For one thing, nothing she ever did was ordinary, not from the first time that we saw her, and that was a year ago. Miss Bobbit and her mother, they arrived on that same six-o'clock bus, the one that comes through from Mobile. It happened to be my cousin Billy Bob's birthday, and so most of the children in town were here at our house. We were sprawled on the front porch having tutti-frutti and devil cake when the bus stormed around Deadman's Curve. It was the summer that never rained; rusted dryness coated everything; sometimes when a car passed on the road, raised dust would hang in the still air an hour or more. Aunt El said if they didn't pave the highway soon she was going to move down to the seacoast; but she'd said that for such a long time. Anyway, we were sitting on the porch, tutti-frutti melting on our plates, when suddenly, just as we were wishing that something would happen, something did; for out of the red road dust appeared Miss Bobbit. A wiry little girl in a starched, lemon-colored party dress, she sassed along with a grownup mince, one hand on her hip, the other supporting a spinsterish umbrella. Her mother, lugging two cardboard valises and a wind-up victrola, trailed in the background. She was a gaunt shaggy woman with silent eyes and a hungry smile.

—Truman Capote, "Children on Their Birthdays," from *Selected Writings of Truman Capote*

c Though sometimes through the wavering light and shadow
He thought he saw it a moment as he watched
The red deer walking by the riverside
At evening, when the bells were ringing,
And the bright stream leapt silent from the mountain
High in the sunset. But as he looked, nothing
Was there but lights and shadows.[2]

d But though my mother and I felt that I was fulfilling my part of the bargain all right, Lothar Swift's promise that I would go to Chicago with the band seemed far less reliable. There were rumors going around that he was having plenty of trouble raising money to move his horde so far, let alone to shelter them once he got them to the city.

Presently a form letter came for me. It said that band members had been put on either an *A* list or a *B* list, according to merit. While it was still the band's intention to pay travel and lodging expenses for all its members, it appeared necessary to ask that all *B* members sell two excursion tickets to "band supporters" who might wish to go along to Chicago. The tickets cost $47.50 apiece. Naturally, of course, I was on the *B* list.

—R. V. Cassill, "The Biggest Band," from *The Father and Other Stories*

e The Wedding-Guest he beat his breast,
Yet he cannot choose but hear;
And thus spake on that ancient man,
The bright-eyed Mariner.

"And now the storm-blast came, and he
Was tyrannous and strong:
He struck with his o'ertaking wings,
And chased us south along."

—Samuel Coleridge, "The Rime of the Ancient Mariner"

[2] From "The Mythical Journey" from *Collected Poems* by Edwin Muir. Copyright © 1960 by Willa Muir. Reprinted by permission of Oxford University Press, Inc. and Faber and Faber Ltd.

f Tom remembered that outside the hospital under the stone and brick carriage porch of the *Sanitarium,* on the newly curving and richly planted driveway which the old self-taught doctor had just had redone commemorating that his one son had just graduated from Harvard Medical School, the men had shouldered into their topcoats in the chilly September night and got into their cars, switched on their lights and pulled away. His father had been the last to pull away, in his brand new Studebaker. As he did, his wife, Tom's mother, had begun to sob and cry again. She had hated the old man, the grandfather, ever since she had first met him; and he had equally disliked and detested her. Tom and his sister had whispered together in the backseat about this new state of things where they were no longer grandchildren. They knew all about the active dislike between their mother and the grandfather, since she had told them over and over how miserable and unhappy he made her life having to live so close to him, so they did not put too much stock in her weeping and grief. They were much more interested in where people went when they died.

—James Jones, "The Ice-Cream Headache," from *The Ice-Cream Headache and Other Stories*

g It little profits that an idle king,
By this still hearth, among these barren crags,
Matched with an aged wife, I mete and dole
Unequal laws unto a savage race,
That hoard, and sleep, and feed, and know not me.
I cannot rest from travel; I will drink
Life to the lees. All times I have enjoyed
Greatly, have suffered greatly, both with those
That loved me, and alone; on shore, and when
Through scudding drifts the rainy Hyades
Vext the dim sea. I am become a name.

—Alfred, Lord Tennyson, "Ulysses"

h And as I was green and carefree, famous among the barns
About the happy yard and singing as the farm was home,
In the sun that is young once only,
Time let me play and be
Golden in the mercy of his means.[3]

5 In his play *Desire Under the Elms,* Eugene O'Neill gives an explicit, detailed description of the setting he wishes for the play and for each scene. Here is the setting description for the opening scene, followed

[3] Dylan Thomas, from "Fern Hill," from *The Poems of Dylan Thomas.* Copyright 1946 by New Directions Publishing Corporation. Reprinted by permission of New Directions Publishing Corporation; J. M. Dent & Sons Ltd.; and the Trustees for the Copyrights of the late Dylan Thomas.

by the appearance of one of the main characters. What can you sur-
mise from it about O'Neill's use of setting in the play?

*Exterior of the farmhouse. It is sunset of a day at the beginning of the summer
in the year 1850. There is no wind and everything is still. The sky above the
roof is suffused with deep colors, the green of the elms glows, but the house is
in shadow, seeming pale and washed out by contrast.*

A door opens and EBEN CABOT *comes to the end of the porch and stands
looking down the road to the right. He has a large bell in his hand and this
he swings mechanically, awakening a deafening clangor. Then he puts his
hands on his hips and stares up at the sky. He sighs with a puzzled awe and
blurts out with halting appreciation.*

EBEN. God! Purty!

*He spits on the ground with intense disgust, turns and goes back into the
house.*

The Form
of Literature
and Critical Writing

After finishing a book, viewing a television drama, or seeing a movie or play, generally we have an overall feeling of liking or disliking it, enjoying or not enjoying it, considering it time well spent or wasted. Translating this gut reaction into reasons and finding specific subjects to discuss or write about involves analyzing the work. At the end of Chapter 28 we mentioned one systematic way to proceed. In this chapter, we shall explore that "who-what-where-when-why-how" approach in greater detail and in reference to writing about literature. Our emphasis in the discussion here and in the next chapter will be on the technical, thematic, and interpretative aspects of literature, rather than on examining a work as representative of a certain literary form (*genre*) or on viewing it in reference to other works of its time. These considerations are best left for an advanced course in literature. Also, since formal criticism of poetry is a highly specialized skill, we shall concentrate mainly on those analytical techniques that could best apply to novels, drama, short stories, and possibly narrative poetry. In our sample analyses, we will use specific literary works for illustration. These examples should be self-explanatory, and though prior familiarity with the works would be helpful, you will not need to read the works to understand the discussions of them. We hope that in using these specific works we can not only suggest a method for planning and writing critical papers, but also indicate ways for you to handle similar material.

CHARACTER ANALYSIS (WHO?)

Other people—on the screen, stage, page, or in life—fascinate us. Observing them in literature may be most absorbing because we can know characters better than friends. You should realize that you never know exactly and fully what your friends are thinking and you seldom, if ever, see their private selves, the side they prefer not to expose to others, perhaps not even to themselves. But literature allows us to tap into the characters' minds and souls, enabling us to understand and know people better than we do in real life.

Yet we need to raise some questions about literary characters that we would not about real people. Real people exist and are what they are, for genetic, environmental, and other reasons; literary characters exist and are what they are, for literary reasons. These questions should help us to realize what those reasons are:

1. What is the character's function?
2. What traits does the character reveal?
3. Does the character change?
4. What is the overall impression of the character?
5. How credible is the character?

Let's discuss each of these questions in turn.

What Is the Character's Function?

Authors are creators, but the literary worlds they create must approximate the real world. For example, even in science fiction and fantasy literature, men and women are necessary to produce children—although there may be a rare exception to prove the rule, as Huxley's *Brave New World* exemplifies. While parents are necessary for birth, they need not remain on the scene afterward. Dickens often got rid of them, writing about orphans; other authors dispense with a mother or father. Why? How does their presence or absence affect a child, the events that take place, the view of life in the work, or anything else?

These are the kinds of questions to ask about the role of all characters. But to obtain a better perspective about their functions, you can classify fictional people into three groups: central, supporting, and background characters.

Literature is memorable for the characters who have walked from its pages into our cultural consciousness, appearing frequently in our minds, discussions, and writings. For example, how many of the following have you heard about: Oedipus, Antigone, Hamlet, Macbeth, Tom Jones, Heathcliff, Oliver Twist, Huck Finn, Captain Ahab? Like most central characters, all were involved in and generally dominated by a series of events from which they emerged either winner or loser, happy or unhappy, richer or poorer, better or worse; but all were wiser for the experience and became somewhat more admirable people even in death or defeat. Because these literary personages are compelling, we speak of them informally as heroes and heroines, but the more appropriate term is central character or, if you wish, main or principal character. In such a category would appear Brutus, Lady Macbeth, or Gatsby, yet we would not think of these characters as individuals of great nobility, nor even worthy of emulation. But insofar as they are prominent in a literary work and command our attention and interest throughout most of it, to some extent we identify with them, feel sympathy toward them, and are attracted to them. Occasionally, a central character may repel us, as does Jane Austen's Emma, who in the early part of the novel is cruel, snobbish, malicious, and overbearing. Sometimes, a work may have not one, but several main characters, such as the Joad family in *Grapes of Wrath.* Usually the title of the work indicates the main character, but there are exceptions: Brutus, for example, dominates *Julius Caesar;* Captain Ahab is the hero of *Moby Dick.* Our point is that central characters come in all sizes, shapes, sexes, races, and creeds. In popular escape literature, they are golden heroes and heroines, the good guys and the good gals, who win out and live happily ever after. In serious literature, they are absorbing individuals who command our interest and attention, though not necessarily our admiration.

At the other extreme in importance are background characters, people who populate literary works to provide an illusion of the real world. They are usually the common folk: the citizens in Shakespeare's *Julius Caesar,* the seamen in Herman Melville's *Moby Dick,* the rustics in Thomas Hardy's Wessex novels. They may serve some minor purpose in some scenes, but their main function is to contribute to the work's setting, providing a sense of place and atmosphere.

Between these two extremes — the central and background characters — are the supporting characters. Some, particularly in humorous works, may do a solo turn, contributing little to the development of the plot or of other characters but providing a few moments of relief or laughter or interest. Among these characters, who are truly "characters," are the porter in *Macbeth,* many of the clowns in Shakespeare's plays, and Dickens' eccentrics, notably Mr. Micawber in *David Copperfield.*

Another subgroup of supporting characters serves as foils, whose contrasting actions and opinions to those of the central characters, usually in parallel situations, reveal much about both. So it is that the practical Sancho serves as a foil to the impractical Don Quixote, and the scheming Cassius to the idealistic Brutus.

Other supporting characters may play major or minor roles, appearing throughout a work or disappearing after one scene. *The Catcher in the Rye,* for instance, is populated with minor characters who function to reveal Holden's compassion for others; they range from the innocent and virtuous (the nuns) to the shrewd and vicious (Stradlater and the bellboy, Maurice). Unlike these characters, who arrive and depart never to return, some supporting characters, such as the slave Jim in *Huckleberry Finn* or Nick Carraway in *The Great Gatsby,* are very close to being main characters.

What Traits Does the Character Reveal?

Once you have determined the functions of key characters, the next step is to analyze them individually. One way to do this is to list their traits as revealed by what they do, say, and think and what others say and think about them. Often in older novels, the all-knowing storyteller describes a character before bringing him or her on stage, as Dickens does with Bounderby in *Hard Times:*

He was a rich man: banker, merchant, manufacturer, and what not. A big, loud man, with a stare, and a metallic laugh. A man made out of coarse material which seemed to have been stretched to make so much of him. A man with a great puffed head and forehead, swelled veins in his temples, and such a strained skin to his face that it seemed to hold his eyes open, and lift his eyebrows up. A man with a pervading appearance on him of being inflated like a balloon, and ready to start. A man who could never sufficiently vaunt himself a self-made man. A man who was always proclaiming, through that brassy speaking trumpet of a voice of his, his old ignorance and his old poverty. A man who was the Bully of humility.

The description proves apt: Bounderby is an obnoxious braggart in the novel, a perfect bounder; the storyteller is reliable. But as we have mentioned, this may not always be so. In D. H. Lawrence's *Sons and Lovers,* the portrayal of Walter Morel is one-sided, showing him to be a coarse, insensitive, brutal husband but giving little attention to his filthy, dangerous, bestial labor in the mines, and his wife's lack of understanding. In literature, as in life, we must collect all the evidence but give more weight to what we ourselves see and hear, and carefully consider the source of all other information.

In amassing this information, you might find it helpful to jot down some notes. For example, if you were writing about Brutus in *Julius Caesar,* here are some traits you could note:

1. Foolishingly trusting, naive (fooled by Cassius; tricked by Antony)

2. Respected (all conspirators originally pay tribute to him; becomes leader)
3. Irritable (quarrels with Cassius; peevish with poet)
4. Tender, kind (loving husband to Portia; considerate of Lucius)
5. Idealistic (duty to Republic; failure to plan for successor)

And so on. Notes of this sort help because they force you to base your opinions on evidence within the work.

Does the Character Change?

You may have assumed from this discussion of character traits that people in literature are the same at the end of a work as they were at the beginning. Not at all. Some characters, particularly most central ones, change as a result of their experiences. Young people initiated into the realities of life gain maturity and insight, as Gene (*A Separate Peace*), Henry Fleming (*The Red Badge of Courage*), and Frankie Addams (*The Member of the Wedding*) all attest. And older people are altered—from kings (Oedipus) to housewives (Nora in *A Doll's House*). Look for a change, determine whether and how and why it takes place—or does not—and you will obtain more insight into the character.

Note, however, that some central characters do not learn from their experiences. One such is Harry Angstrom, the former high school basketball star, who is trapped in his marriage, his job, and his community in John Updike's *Rabbit, Run*. But like his nickname, Rabbit, he is more unthinking animal than responsible human, running away at the beginning of the novel only to return, wreck the lives of his lover and wife, and then run away again—no better, no wiser, no different—as the novel comes full circle.

What Is the Overall Impression of the Character?

After determining a character's function, traits, and change, you are ready to run a tally. What does it all add up to? Is the character admirable or not, or, more crudely, does the character belong with the good guys and gals or the bad ones? Sometimes the answer is simple. Obviously, Fagin in *Oliver Twist* is a villain and Antony in *Julius Caesar* is a hero. But most central characters and those in conflict with them are not pictured as black or white, all good or all evil. Most are drawn in shades of gray. Trying to arrive at some conclusion about them, therefore, forces you to analyze them in some depth.

A case or two in point. Earlier, we mentioned that Updike's Rabbit is irresponsible. Yet he is far from being completely repulsive. An individualist, he refuses to accept his sorry plight and seeks instead to recover the lost glory and the ideal life he enjoyed as a basketball star. On the surface Rabbit is admirable in his struggle for a better life as he finds himself trapped in a dull marriage, mired in a distasteful job, dominated by overbearing in-laws, caged in a dreary town, understood by no one. But basically, Rabbit emerges as an unethical person, using and misusing people, treating women as sex objects, and trying to find sensual enjoyment everywhere. Hardly admirable traits. But the portrait of Rabbit is in gray, not black. Updike depicts him in such a way that we often find ourselves sympathizing with Rabbit in spite of his detestable qualities.

More difficult to reach some conclusion about is "the noblest Roman of them all," Brutus, whose traits we itemized earlier. What do they add up to? Do his honorable motives excuse his dishonorable act? Is his sincerity sufficient? Can a noble death compensate for ignoble deeds? The answers are not simple; great literary figures have the same complexity as real people.

So, as judge and jury, you should find for or against your characters, see them as complete human beings at the end of a literary work, and arrive at some verdict about them, just as you arrive at conclusions about your friends on the basis of your knowledge and observations of them.

How Credible Is the Character?

So far we have been concerned primarily with the nature of characters, suggesting a method for you to follow in analyzing what they are like. Our purpose is to enable you to understand the characters—and, of course, the work—better. Now we suggest that you consider how well the characters are depicted. Essentially, this requires that you determine how realistic they are.

Because this textbook is designed for a course in writing and not in literary study we shall skip over the tricky theoretical problems of whether all literary works should be true to life and to what extent literary characters must be. Nor do we have space for a philosophical discussion about the nature of reality. We shall merely suggest that in considering whether characters are credible and realistic, you apply some of the traditional, common-sense views about people: that they have motives for their actions, are reasonably consistent, and are essentially individualistic. Not all the characters in literature must demonstrate all three of these qualities, but the central character and other important ones should do so to be credible. Let's consider each of these aspects of credibility.

MOTIVATION

Readers must be able to understand why characters act as they do. And actions must stem from probable causes, not possible ones. Life is stranger than fiction partly because people's true natures are hidden. Several times a year, for example, we read about gruesome murders committed by quiet young men who have led exemplary lives as Boy Scouts and Sunday School teachers. In literature, such characters would be unbelievable unless there was some previous suggestion of their potential hostility and violence. In other words, characters must be adequately motivated for readers to view them as credible.

Usually the crucial point for examining motivation occurs late in a work when the central character is confronted with a decisive choice. In popular escape literature—westerns, gangster and cop stories, cheap romances, and the like—often some accident occurs or some character changes for no valid reason. Usually a bad guy or gal suddenly turns good, allowing the hero to wed the heroine or kiss his horse and ride off into the sunset as virtue triumphs. Certainly, people may change in life, but if they do in literature, the transformation should occur over a period of time and the reasons should be both apparent and plausible. Generally speaking, selfish people just don't suddenly become unselfish—unless it's in their own self-interest to do so. But we can accept the change in a character like Arthur Dimmesdale in Hawthorne's *The Scarlet Letter,* having seen him wrestle with his conscience until finally, unable to bear his guilt any longer, he confesses his adultery from the pillory with his illegitimate daughter and her mother at his side.

CONSISTENCY

Although characters may change, we still expect them to be as consistent as real people. Generally, we know how our friends will respond in new situations. Similarly, we should be able to anticipate what characters will usually do. In *Sons and Lovers,* we realize that Paul Morel cannot marry either Miriam or Clara because of his strong attachment to his mother. To be consistent, Paul cannot love anyone but her. While readers may prefer literature to end happily, it would have been out of character for Paul to marry Miriam or anyone else. Characters must be true to themselves: this consistency is necessary if they are to be credible.

INDIVIDUALITY

If consistency is carried too far, characters will lack the complexity necessary for individuality. People are born equal, but they are also born different. Good literature portrays people as individuals, bad literature as stereotypes. Stereotypes often become faddish, as recent gangster and cop films illustrate. Gangsters, formerly depicted as ugly, cruel, stupid animals, have been transformed into suave, soft-spoken, and sophisticated business executives and loving family men, as in *The Godfather*. Policemen, formerly all-American boys, clean looking, clean thinking and clean loving, have become bearded, alienated loners, cynical and ruthless supercops, resorting to criminal ways to fight criminals, like the central characters in *The French Connection* and *Serpico*.

Although in good literature central characters are complex individuals, most of the supporting and background characters usually cannot be treated in such great depth, particularly in brief works such as plays and short stories. But occasionally in longer works these characters are portrayed with such vividness, flavor, and intensity that they take on individuality. Dickens' comic and satirical characters come readily to mind, as do other memorable figures like the Duke and King in *Huckleberry Finn* and Juliet's nurse in *Romeo and Juliet*.

PLOT (WHAT?)

The related actions or episodes in a literary work are called its *plot* (although this term is not generally applied to poetry). When someone asks us what a work is about, we tell them its story—its plot. But as a critical reader writing about literature, you should be able not only to summarize the plot but to analyze its structure.

The Elements of a Plot

Most plots follow the traditional pattern diagrammed here:

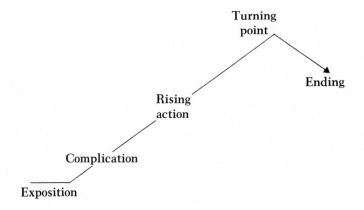

Let's first define the terms used in the diagram and then discuss and illustrate them.

1. Exposition: introduction of characters, establishment of relationships, setting of scene, creation of atmosphere, presentation of point of view.
2. Complication: the initial incident that creates some problem, conflict, difficulty, or change.
3. Rising action: the heightening of interest, excitement, or involvement as difficulties increase.
4. Turning point: the crisis or climax, the point of greatest emotion and interest, when the difficulty or problem is confronted and resolved.
5. Ending: explanation of events, how characters were affected, and what happened to them.

The *exposition* exposes you to the universe of the literary work, providing information about the characters and their relationships, the setting, and the time. It allows you to discover where you are, who these people are, and what kind of physical, social, and cultural surroundings they live in. And, equally important, it informs you about the narrator's point of view.

The *complication* closely follows the exposition because readers require that some problem or conflict become apparent soon to stimulate interest. Thus the conspirators plan to kill Caesar or Romeo and Juliet fall in love despite their feuding families. Something occurs or someone arrives to disrupt the routine and to intensify the lives of the characters.

Rising action is a term that describes the increased emotional effect created by additional events or ramifications of the original one. Theoretically, our interest rises as the action does. For example, in *Romeo and Juliet* we become more involved as major events occur: Romeo kills Tybalt, the wedding of Paris and Juliet draws near, Juliet swallows the potion, Romeo hears about her "death," Romeo kills Paris. In John Knowles' *A Separate Peace,* the rising action involves the first jumps from the tree, Gene's failing a test, Finney's fall from the tree, Gene's trial, and Finney's fatal second fall down the stairs.

The *turning point,* or *crisis* as it is often called, is the decisive incident that resolves the problem or conflict. Usually the point or scene of greatest interest, it is exemplified in popular escape literature by the courtroom trial; the "let's re-create the crime" episode in detective stories; the big game, match, or meet in sports stories; the showdown at high noon in cowboy yarns; the shootout chase in cop films; and so on. It is the point of no return; once reached, the outcome is settled. The central character usually makes a choice from which there is no escape: Romeo drinks the poison, Laertes fatally wounds Hamlet, Dimmesdale confesses.

The *ending* may be presented in a paragraph, a page, a chapter, or more, depending on what is needed to explain previous events and to account for what happens later to various characters. It is used for tidying up, straightening out, unraveling, cleaning up. There may literally be dead bodies to be hauled away (four in *Hamlet*), or a death to be revealed (Huck's father), a marriage (Eppie to Aaron Winthrop in *Silas Marner*), or other events signaling a termination or resolution.

Of course, no formula can be applied to all literary works, and the preceding simple diagram does not provide for episodic plots, subplots involving supporting characters, and other complexities. And just as readers interpret literature differently, so they may differ in diagramming a plot's structure. It would be possible to show, for example, that the turning point of *A Separate Peace* occurs when Finney falls from the tree limb instead of when he falls down the stairs.

Even though a diagram may not represent a plot structure with great accuracy and other readers may differ with your interpretation, you should find that it clarifies your understanding of a work to outline the plot visually. The accompanying diagram shows one way in which James Joyce's *A Portrait of the Artist as a Young Man* might be outlined, with its rising series of complications (C) to the turning point (TP).

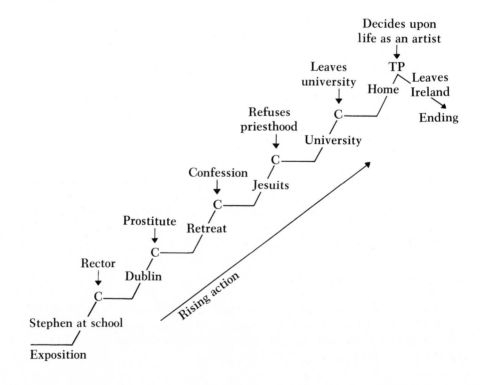

Please realize that not all plots conform to this pattern. Some works may be completely or mainly episodic, with a series of incidents involving the central character but with no overall rising action or turning point. If, for example, you took Jim out of *Huckleberry Finn* and merely recounted the numerous adventures that befall Huck, you might have the kind of "charm bracelet" outline shown in the accompanying diagram:

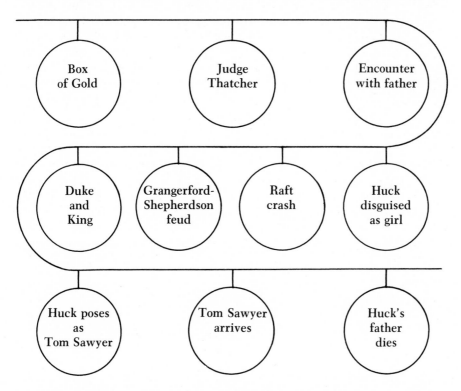

In an episodic work, several incidents might be removed without seriously affecting the plot, just as several charms might be removed without damaging a bracelet. Generally, episodic plots are constructed around an entertaining central character whose actions and reactions are fascinating and colorful.

Evaluation of a Plot

Having understood the plot, realized its structure, you should be ready to consider how skillfully it is conceived. Your evaluation should take into account such factors as foreshadowing, reliance on chance, unity, and the plausibility of the ending.

FORESHADOWING

The word *foreshadowing* becomes self-explanatory when you think of the way shadows appear in front of people to alert others of their approach. In literature, foreshadowing is a device to prepare readers for what follows. It may take the form of a strange remark, a prophecy, or some foreboding note. The terrors of childhood in the opening section of *Portrait of the Artist* foreshadow the problems of young Stephen; the supernatural signs and warnings early in *Julius Caesar* foreshadow his fate. To what extent is foreshadowing necessary? Obviously, in a detective story in which a plumber kills a homeowner, you would feel cheated if you never heard of the plumber until the last chapter. As a rule of thumb, the greater the element of surprise in the story, the greater the need for foreshadowing. Consequently, in Shirley Jackson's classic short story "The Lottery," there is ample preparation for the execution by stoning: the formality of the occasion, the black box, the strictness of the procedure, the quietness of the people, the remark about the quick passage of time between lotteries, Mrs. Delacroix's holding her breath, the nervous handling of the slips, the hints from Mr. and Mrs. Adams to Old Man Warner about putting a stop to the lottery, and Tessie's protestations when her husband opens his slip. The savage ending still comes as a shock—and no one who has read the story can forget it—but the ending is acceptable because it has been foreshadowed.

RELIANCE ON CHANCE

Another factor to consider in evaluating the plot of a work is the extent to which authors rely on chance to manipulate the lives of characters. Chance may take the form of unusual and unpredictable occurrences (death, automobile accident, sudden fortune, and the like) or coincidences (unexpected meetings, lucky or unlucky timing, discovery of unknown relationships, and so on). While we realize that chance plays a role in all our lives and anything can happen to any of us at any time, we expect a literary world to be more probable than the real world. If fact is stranger than fiction, as we noted previously, then fiction must be more normal than fact.

This does not entirely rule out chance from literature; it simply suggests that you question its use. Generally, chance may be accepted at the beginning of a work to develop the complication. And it should not be disapproved of in the rising action unless the author has unrealistically used death or some other device as a pat solution to some plot problem. There should be little concern, for example, that Jim O'Connor in Tennessee Williams' *The Glass Menagerie* turns out to be Laura's high school idol, because this coincidence does not materially change the action in the play. But it is highly implausible that Pip's benefactor in

Dickens' *Great Expectations* proves to be the escaped convict, and this coincidence does significantly affect what happens at the end of the novel.

Particularly at the turning point and the ending, we must deplore an author's resorting to chance. When one member of a romantic triangle is killed in an auto accident, when an unknown wealthy uncle dies leaving the desperately poor main character a fortune or when the villain drowns, we should indeed find fault. Ideally, chance should play little or no role in a literary work. Characters should meet under certain circumstances and the work should unfold, generated from the conflict created by this initial situation.

But in literature chance may certainly play a major role when the author's intention is to show that chance is the controlling influence in the lives of people. In the novels of Thomas Hardy, for example, the forces of nature constantly plague men and women; strange, often improbable events and unlucky meetings also occur to spoil their happiness. In his works and those of writers with similar views, chance is almost the central character, playing a major role in affecting human destiny.

UNITY

A third matter to consider in evaluating a plot is unity, whether all the episodes in a plot are necessary and contribute to its development. In popular escape literature and films, there is a tendency to add juicy sex scenes. We should ask whether they serve any function. Do they disclose something important about the characters involved, or are they included only to appeal to people's sexual instincts and thus to sell more copies or tickets? Generally, a work of literature should not contain digressions of any kind, unless included for some comic effect. The work should be as well unified as your themes.

PLAUSIBILITY OF THE ENDING

A final plot consideration is the ending of the work. It should be both logical—growing naturally out of what has gone before—and satisfying—concluding the issues raised in the work. You should be particularly wary of happy endings brought about illogically by chance or by sudden character transformations, like the convenient rehabilitation of a drug addict or the sudden religious conversion of a hardened criminal. And you should question the use of marriage to end a plot happily. After all, how many weeks would you give Cinderella and the prince? Let's not settle for marriages in which the couple will probably live unhappily ever after.

In this section we have raised a number of issues to help you understand the structure of plots and to enable you to evaluate them better. Let's summarize this material in these questions you should ask about a literary work:

1. How effectively is the exposition handled?
2. What is the complication? What issues does it raise?
3. What other issues or problems are developed in the rising action?
4. Where is the turning point? What is resolved and how?
5. Are explanations provided and loose ends tied up in the ending?
6. Are events, particularly surprising ones, properly foreshadowed?
7. What role does chance play? How acceptable is the use of chance?
8. Is the work unified? Are there scenes or characters that could be eliminated?
9. Is the ending logical and satisfying? Has the author resorted to chance or sudden character transformations to bring about the ending?

SETTING (WHERE?)

Every literary work takes place in a particular setting consisting of a spatial area (house, community, region, country) and the beliefs and values (social, moral, economic, political, psychological) of the people there. In few works, if any, is setting insignificant, but its importance may vary considerably according to the extent of an author's belief that environment shapes and controls human lives or that a work should depict the manners and morals of people.

On a simple level, literary works derive a vivid sense of realism from the inclusion of descriptions of such details as the natural surroundings, the architecture of a house, the decor of rooms, and the dress and physical appearance of characters. The popular fiction of Ian Fleming gained a touch of authenticity in an improbable world by specifying the commercial products James Bond and other characters used—the brand of cigarettes they smoked, the after-dinner liqueur they sipped, and the expensive perfume the women wore. Few other authors carry realism as far as that, but most supply enough graphic details that readers can sense, for example, a battlefield in *The Red Badge of Courage*, farm labor camps in *The Grapes of Wrath*, Harlem in *The Invisible Man*, and Civil War Tara in *Gone with the Wind*.

The setting can also create an atmosphere, playing on the feelings we experience about a location. In many of Poe's short stories, especially "The Fall of the House of Usher" and "The Cask of Amontillado," the strange surroundings contribute greatly to the suspense and to the mood of gloom, melancholy, and apprehension. Such poems as Grey's "Elegy Written in a Country Churchyard," Goldsmith's "Deserted Village," and Wordsworth's "Tintern Abbey" all establish a pervading mood through a description of the setting. And in Emily Brontë's *Wuthering Heights,* the setting with its wild moors and fierce storms serves as a cosmic background for the passionate love of Heathcliff and Catherine.

The setting of a work can serve an even more important function: as a force in conflict with human desires and endeavors. Often the struggle is an emotional one between people and nature. In James Dickey's *Deliverance,* men battle the Cahulawassee River as well as one another, and in *The Old Man and the Sea,* Santiago fights nature and its creatures. But perhaps no author focuses on nature as frequently and powerfully as Thomas Hardy in his many Wessex novels and stories. For example, in *The Return of the Native,* Egdon Heath might be viewed as the central character, dominating the work as an evil force: some people are the heath's victims, dying from drowning and snakebite, while others become its disciples by practicing witchcraft and succumbing to the primitive emotions it evokes.

Setting is not confined to the physical location of a work; it also includes the human environment. Characters are born, raised, and live among other people. The values of these other people — in the family, the community, the schools, the churches, and businesses — may influence a character's behavior. As discerning readers, we should be aware of the part environment plays in shaping the characters' lives. In both Arthur Miller's *The Crucible* and Nathaniel Hawthorne's *The Scarlet Letter,* the repressive religious beliefs of the seventeenth-century Salem and Boston communities establish a rigid code that cannot forgive the adulteries of John Proctor and Hester Prynne. The twentieth-century world of F. Scott Fitzgerald's *The Great Gatsby* reflects a materialistic society that cares only about a person's wealth, not how it is obtained. Jay Gatsby is a product of his age; in another society he might have been a different person with different values.

Such considerations give rise to the following questions, all of which should be asked in evaluating the setting of a literary work.

1. Could the setting be changed without seriously affecting the work?
2. Does the setting contribute significantly to the lifelike quality of the work?
3. Does the setting contribute to the atmosphere of the work by establishing a particular mood?
4. Does the setting play an important role in shaping or controlling the lives of the characters?

TIME (WHEN?)

Time in a literary work is important in relation to the author's selection both of a time sequence for presenting the work and of an era or period to set the work in. In discussing personal narratives in Part 1, we described the two main kinds of time sequences that writers use: chronological and flashback. But analyzing *how* an author has handled time may be more complex — and more rewarding — than merely determining which sequence has been used.

In Arthur Miller's play *Death of a Salesman,* the past is mingled with the present as we follow the associations in the mind of Willy Loman, the central character. Although the action takes place in only two days, his life is revealed through numerous flashbacks, starting with the decision not to follow brother Ben to Alaska years before. But Willy's sin, alluded to on several occasions, is not revealed until the turning point later in the play, although it occurred sixteen years before the stage action. At that time Biff, Willy's son, discovered him with another woman in Boston. The study of how an author handles time may not always be as interesting and significant as it is in this play, yet you should always take note of it in analyzing a literary work.

Also important is the use of time in the sense of the age or period when the action occurs. Although Arthur Miller does not provide a date for the events in his play, numerous references establish that it takes place during the Depression of the 1930s. Willy's failure — his inability to admit his own shortcomings — is certainly a personal one, but the play takes on social significance by portraying through Willy how the dreams and hopes of many Americans were destroyed by the breakdown of the economic system.

The time of the action in any work may be helpful for a complete understanding of its significance. Kurt Vonnegut, Jr., a prisoner of war in Dresden, Germany, when it was fire-bombed by American planes in 1945, included this incident in his 1969 novel *Slaughterhouse-Five* as the kind of senseless apocalyptic event that typifies human experience and may well bring about the end of the world. The time of the action in *A Separate Peace* is similarly significant because Gene's aggression toward Finney parallels the aggression between nations in the Second World War, which disrupts the peacefulness of the isolated prep school and affects the lives of all its students.

An author must decide both how to handle time in the work and at what time to set the action. By considering the following questions, you should understand the significance of both:

1. How does the author handle the movement of time in the novel? Which of the two main time sequences is used — chronological or flashback? What are its advantages or disadvantages?
2. In what period of time does the work take place? What difference would it make if the work were set in another time? What is the significance of its being set at that time?

THEME (WHY?)

Before embarking on our discussion of theme, or central idea, we must deal with two fallacies: the affective and the intentional. The first occurs when readers express how a literary work affects them personally. Instead of looking closely at what the work itself means, they dash off subjective interpretations that relate the work to their own experiences. For example, in discussing Ray Bradbury's *Dandelion Wine,* these readers might carry on about how moving the novel is because it brought back exhilarating memories of flying around in new sneakers as a child in the spring. Or in evaluating Richard Bradford's *Red Sky at Morning,* some readers might react favorably to it on the grounds that it reminded them of a similar experience growing up while their fathers were away in Vietnam. Although it is natural to identify with a central character and to experience vicariously the events in a work, you should detach yourself when writing critically, suppressing your personal grievances and preferences and responding objectively and intellectually. Focus on the work itself, not on your own emotional (affective) reaction to it.

Thus the affective fallacy is committed by slighting the novel, story, play, or poem to stress its effect on the reader; the intentional fallacy is committed by slighting the work to stress the author's intention. Although the author's intention in writing may have been to make money, win fame, or achieve fulfillment, some readers ignore these and other possible reasons in the belief that authors wish only to pronounce their views about life. Usually, trying to discern what an author intended requires psychoanalysis, not literary analysis. Even when authors have later declared their purpose, this explanation should not be accepted as the only possible interpretation because the authors may not remember clearly what they intended at the time, they may not have achieved what they set out to do, or they may subconsciously have introduced other ideas. This is not to say that their statements should be ignored; just that they should not be accepted blindly but should be examined in the light of the work. The work speaks for itself, louder and clearer and more accurately than the author can speak for it.

Consequently, we urge you to write in terms of the work's meaning, not the author's. Our question "Why?" as it applies to a literary analysis commits you to examine the ideas, particularly the main idea, in a work to determine what statement it makes about life. Does every work contain some such statement? If so, how do you discern it?

Even the simplest nursery rhyme or story can have a thematic message: "Jack and Jill" shows how dangerous life's routines can be; "Little Red Riding Hood" indicates the need for vigilance against disguised evil. Every work, no matter how slight, contains some basic observation about the nature of people, the freedom of the individual, the opportunity for happiness, the role of society, the importance of love, the discovery of self, the existence of evil, or some other subject. On a simple level, if the central character finds happiness, then the view of life is optimistic; if not, it is pessimistic. But usually it is far more important to analyze *why* and *how* the work ends as it does rather than merely to note the ending.

The theme grows out of the ending—or, more specifically, out of how the turning point is resolved. Often at this point, either the action may exemplify the central idea or a favorably presented character may express it. In *The Grapes of Wrath*, Tom Joad talks to his mother about the universal soul after the Christ-like preacher Casy has been murdered.

Guess who I been thinkin' about? Casy! He talked a lot. Used ta bother me. But now I been thinkin' what he said, an' I can remember—all of it. Says one time he went out in the wilderness to find his own soul, an' he foun' he didn' have no soul that was his'n. Says he foun' he jus got a little piece of a great big soul. Says a wilderness ain't no good, 'cause his little piece of a soul wasn't no good 'less it was with the rest, an' was whole. Funny how I remember. Didn' think I was even listenin'. But I know now a fella ain't no good alone.

In Anthony Burgess' *A Clockwork Orange*, an admirable minor character (the husband of the raped woman) utters the thematic statement to Alex, the central character:

You've sinned, I suppose, but your punishment has been out of all proportion. They have turned you into something other than a human being. You have no power of choice any longer. You are committed to socially acceptable acts, a little machine capable only of good. . . . A man who cannot choose ceases to be a man.

Thus, thematic statements usually are expressed by characters who are portrayed favorably, whether the central character or some other, including the omniscient narrator. Occasionally, the theme may be stated or reinforced ironically by an unattractive character. For example, when the odious Bounderby in Dickens' *Hard Times* argues strongly in favor of all work and no play and deplores anything that appeals to the imagination instead of the reason, the reader realizes that almost the opposite is being advocated.

How do you come to such a realization? And how can you support your opinion about a work's theme?

Nearly everything within a work should point to and contribute to the theme. In *The Grapes of Wrath*, Tom's statement, quoted previously, sums up the change from the Joad family's concern only for themselves to concern for others: first for the Wilsons, then for the people in the government camp, and finally in Rose of Sharon's giving the milk of her breast to the starving stranger. In *Hard Times,* Bounderby is exposed as a cruel man and a fraud, and Tom Gradgrind realizes that there is more to life than learning facts as a result of his daughter's unhappiness, his son's crime, and the kindness of Sissy and the circus people. Just as you can check an answer in algebra, you can check a theme in literature by applying it to incidents and character changes. And quite often in literature the theme will be suggested symbolically or literally in the title (*The Red Badge of Courage, Pride and Prejudice, For Whom the Bell Tolls*).

In some works, thematic ideas are not stated by characters or suggested in titles. What then? Your task is more difficult—but not impossible. Asking yourself these questions should help:

1. What happens to the central character and why?
2. Was what happened the character's own fault or due to forces beyond control?
3. If it was the character's own fault, what weakness did it reveal?
4. If the character overcame the difficulty, what new realization or trait did the resolution require?
5. Did other characters have similar problems? What do their actions reveal?
6. If the central character's problem cannot be attributed to human weakness, what was it due to?
7. Can this force be overcome? If so, how? If not, how can human beings cope with it?
8. Are people portrayed as basically evil or good, selfish or unselfish, kind or cruel?
9. Do the characters find happiness? If not, why not? If so, why? How?
10. Is nature favorable or unfavorable to people?
11. Does the literary work make any statement about ethical, religious, economic, social, political matters?
12. Does the work provide any insight into psychological problems about sex, love, death, guilt, alienation, or others?

Applying these and similar questions to a work to perceive its ideas should help, but you must be cautious in deciding on answers. Remember that a work—particularly a novel—may contain numerous ideas, but the theme is like a thread, tying together most of what occurs. *The Grapes of Wrath,* for example, contains numerous views about big business, charities, religion, private ownership of property, and the role of the government. But only the theme of human community runs throughout and sums up the entire work.

In deciding on a theme or stating it, you should avoid the imperative. The theme is not a moral, a commandment, a directive about how to live or what to do. Rather, it is a statement about life and people, an observation, a pronouncement, a verdict. Ralph Ellison's *The Invisible Man* points out how white people fail to see and treat blacks as human beings, using and exploiting them instead. George Orwell's *1984* shows how the human desires for love, freedom, and dignity can be eliminated or suppressed in a totalitarian society that controls communication and technology. And the theme of Robert Frost's poem "The Road Not Taken" is that a choice made at a crucial point in life may affect everything that happens to one afterward. These works are not sermons exhorting us to action. They are representations of people and life that we may not have experienced before. We should, therefore, enjoy the literary work as we enjoy other experiences; but at the same time we should become wiser from reading it just as we become wiser from our significant real-life experiences.

Of all the elements in a literary work, the theme is the most difficult to perceive. The problem stems from the work's presentation of specifics: certain characters in certain places at certain times engaged in certain actions. On the other hand, the theme is an abstraction, a generalization. Consequently, you need to consider all the other elements in a work to arrive at its theme. You should do this cautiously, testing your conclusion against specific characters and events in the work. Only when you have done this thoroughly should you feel confident about your interpretation of the work.

TECHNIQUE (HOW?)

No analysis of a literary work would be complete without a study of the writer's technique, the artistic devices that shape the content. Of importance to you in freshman English papers are such technical concerns as the special use of language for aesthetic purposes, particularly to establish tone and mood and to add symbolic significance. Not only can a knowledge of literary language devices help you in your critical papers, but it should make you aware of ways to use language more effectively in all written work. Throughout this book, we have encouraged you to write concrete and figurative language in order to achieve greater clarity or to add interest. But in literature, language imagery comes to full fruition. It is here that the beauty and grace of the language share equal importance with the message conveyed. In the most literal sense, the literary medium is the literary message. Language imagery is not designed merely to catch the reader's interest or to enhance or decorate, but to function as an organic part of the work. Concrete descriptions take on symbolic importance beyond contributing to clarity or adding "spice." Analogy serves not only to compare but to suggest multiple levels of meaning, taking on various forms and functions. Figurative language, occurring only sporadically in expository prose, becomes a fine art in literature. In fact, these language devices function as such an integral part of a literary work that a knowledge of them is often necessary to full understanding and enjoyment of it.

Throughout this book, we have emphasized the importance of tone in conveying the appropriate voice to achieve your purpose. We have urged you to strive by careful language choice for an authentic, intimate tone in personal writing, for an objective one in expository prose, and for a careful, studied one in argument. A literary writer must be even more aware of the tone set by the language in a work, not because of the nature of the audience but because of the artistic effect desired. The author may wish to create a tone of dread and foreboding, or one of color and light and optimism, or an ironic or satiric one. Although the characters and actions contribute to it, tone is by and large the result of language. We have already discussed many language devices and their use in your own writing; let's turn now to some that, although they exist outside literature as well, have special importance in literary writing.

Irony

Irony is achieved by incongruity: a pairing of opposites or perspectives, one of which may mask or reveal the real truth. It can be created by relying on a single statement (verbal irony). Or language and situation may work together to create it (situational irony).

Related to sarcasm and innuendo, verbal irony can be achieved through understatement or exaggeration. Sometimes the writer uses words of praise to imply criticism or censure, much as you may do when you say to a boastful friend, "Don't be so modest!" In situations such as this, irony is distinguished from sarcasm mainly by tone: the tone of irony is wryly humorous; sarcasm is biting and sharp. Another technique for creating verbal irony is through a reversal or twist; the writer, by exploiting the connotations inherent in the language, creates an expectation of one thing, then presents the opposite—as this student poem shows:

> Coke
> Cold, good,
> Refreshing, reviving, quenching,
> Drive-ins, picnics, snacks, all the good times,
> Pimples.

Situational irony often depends upon the interplay of language and event; in such cases ambiguity plays an important role. For instance, in *Oedipus Rex,* the blind seer speaks in ambiguous riddles to Oedipus—

"Today you will see your birth and your destruction"—making an ironic play on the word *see*. The riddle masks the real meaning that Oedipus' true identity, his birthplace and his parents, will be revealed (seen) and he will realize that he has murdered his father and committed incest with his mother. At another level, the word *see* ironically reminds the audience, already familiar with the legend, that Oedipus will lose his sight. When he finally "sees" what he has done, he blinds himself.

Dramatic irony can be enhanced by the language use of verbal and situational irony throughout the story. In Ibsen's *A Doll's House,* for instance, the central irony results from the fact that Nora's loving sacrifice for her husband Torvald leads unexpectedly to her disillusionment in him. This change is reinforced by frequent verbal and situational irony, such as Torvald's fatuous praise of Nora's industry in creating Christmas ornaments for the family—an activity that becomes offensive to him when he discovers she has been selling them to repay an illegal loan.

As you can see, irony, like other literary devices, does more than contribute to tone; it becomes an integral part of the meaning of the work as well. Other language devices not only serve this dual function but also become tools for creating imagery.

Paradox

Like irony, paradox is often a product of both language use and situation, and, like irony, its effect depends upon a kind of incongruity, a logical inconsistency. In paradox, this is achieved by the juxtaposition of two seemingly contradictory possibilities, which nevertheless share some plausible relationship. In verbal paradox, it is often a single statement or phrase that appears on the surface to be contradictory, implausible, or absurd but which may contain a truth. The Simon and Garfunkel song title "The Sounds of Silence" is a good example of verbal paradox. Like all instances of paradox, it forces us to change our perspective of something; *silence* is not usually associated with *sounds*, but pairing them in this way makes us realize that in reality silence does have its own peculiar sound.

Situational paradox depends upon the same contradictory elements; something in the situation or in the characters involved in the events is seemingly inconsistent and yet proves plausible. The terrible brutality of Don Corleone in *The Godfather* in his "business" dealings seems totally out of character with his gentleness toward his grandchild. Yet his behavior is believable. Situational paradox is a common device in modern poetry and drama; sometimes it operates hand in hand with irony, as in the opening lines from T. S. Eliot's "The Waste Land":

April is the cruelest month, breeding
Lilacs out of the dead land, mixing
Memory and desire, stirring
Dull roots with spring rain.[1]

The poet's opening line is both ironical and paradoxical: ironical in the incongruity of associating gentle April with cruelty; paradoxical in proving, in subsequent lines, the plausibility of the seemingly contradictory condition, implying that along with the new, lovely spring lilacs come old memories and desires that can perhaps be painful and sad.

Symbolism

Symbols are not restricted to literature: humans are symbol-making creatures, and symbols play an important role in our everyday lives. In addition to the symbolic characteristics of language itself, we are surrounded by objects that have taken on abstract meaning and value. A wedding ring, for instance, is a widely accepted symbol in our culture: its meaning moves out from our literal, concrete concept of it as a circular finger band made of silver or gold to a symbol of marriage and all its attendant connotations and values—love, marital happiness, close companionship, fidelity, family, romance, commitment. Even colors become symbolic: red in our society is associated with heat, anger, passion; white with innocence and purity; green with life and growth. These are some of the many symbolic associations shared by most people in our society; these are called *public symbols.*

Literary writers use such public symbols, but they also create *private symbols,* which are significant to the particular work: the green light on Daisy's dock across the bay in *The Great Gatsby* suggests Gatsby's will-o'-the-wisp search for acceptance in high society; the shark who battles the old fisherman for his catch in Ernest Hemingway's *The Old Man and the Sea* becomes representative of the forces of nature against which humans must often pit themselves. The writer creates these private symbols to achieve a particular purpose and transmits their imaginative meanings to the reader by situation or association with certain characters or behavior. But to be effective, these private symbols must have some relationship to actual ones; otherwise, they may have meaning only to the writer. Also, to be effective, they must be part of the realistic telling of the story: the shark is a natural predator in the waters where the old

---

[1] From *Collected Poems 1909–1962* by T. S. Eliot, copyright, 1936, by Harcourt Brace Jovanovich, Inc.; copyright, © 1943, 1963, 1964, by T. S. Eliot. Reprinted by permission of Harcourt Brace Jovanovich, Inc.

man fishes; thus the attack is a logical possibility as well as being representative of the symbolic associations of survival of the fittest, struggle for existence, and human encounter with unpredictable and overwhelming problems. If private symbols are well conceived, you as a reader will not need to go on a symbol hunt; they will make themselves known to you as you read. But to confirm their presence, be aware how they're used each time — what the circumstances are, what characters are involved — so that you can realize all the possible levels of meaning.

Occasionally, in a literary work, a symbol will be so important and dominant that it becomes a central, unifying force. In Conrad's *Lord Jim,* Stein's butterfly-collecting mania supplies the central symbol for the novel: the butterfly chase becomes symbolic of the romantic striving for an elusive and unattainable ideal — the striving that brings about Jim's destruction. Occasionally, the title of a work gives a clue to the central symbol; Joseph Heller's title *Catch-22,* for instance, refers to a fictitious Air Force rule that by the end of the novel has become symbolic of the stupid workings of bureaucracy and the frustration of trying to cope logically and reasonably with the corporate mind. In this way, the central symbol can be used to communicate the writer's "message" in a way very similar to the operation of a shortened syllogism — by permitting the reader to supply the missing material and the logical connections.

Metaphor

Symbols often take the form of obvious or implied metaphors. As you recall from Chapter 3, a metaphor is a kind of analogy, a comparison of two things that are alike in some way. In literature, although many kinds of metaphor are used, we shall examine only the more common ones. Earlier, we talked of *simile,* an explicit analogy introduced by *like* or *as* (*like* a soft breeze; *as* gentle as a butterfly touch), but there are others not so immediately apparent as these.

Personification: This metaphorical device treats inanimate or non-human objects as human or animate, as these lines from poetry illustrate: "The sea contains the hottest blood of all"; "'Come!' cried the granite wastes"; "The clock just now has nothing more to say."

Synecdoche: Metaphoric shorthand in which a single significant part becomes symbolic of the whole or the whole is made to represent a part. For example, in "our daily bread," the word *bread,* although only one food source, represents all forms of sustenance; "the law" is a common synecdoche for a single police officer.

Metonymy: A closely associated item is substituted for an object or group as in "He lives by the sword." *Sword* substitutes for the profession of soldiering. In the phrase, "gown and town," *gown* is a cover term for an educational institution and its professors.

SUMMARY

In this chapter we have presented a method for you to follow in writing papers about literature. The "who-what-where-when-why-how" approach is certainly not the only effective one, nor has our discussion of its various elements been complete. We have not had space to discuss myth criticism or other approaches, for example. But now you do have a simple, clear, and handy way to analyze a literary work, to develop stimulating theme subjects, and to write interesting, informative critical papers. Our purpose in this chapter was not to involve you in literary study as such. If you enjoy reading and discussing stories, plays, and poems, we suggest that you enroll in an introduction to literature course or one of the other literature courses offered by your English Department. Our purpose was to help you to understand literature in order to write more intelligently and effectively about it.

Special Considerations in Critical Writing

SOME APPROACHES TO THE CRITICAL PAPER

Despite all the discussion in the last chapter about ways to analyze literature, points to consider, and questions to ask, you may still be uneasy. Our suggestions may have sounded helpful, but you have a queasy feeling in the pit of your stomach that when you run up against a literary work, you still won't be able to formulate a subject for your paper or know how to go about organizing it. All right. Let's tackle an assignment together to see how you should proceed. First read this short story by John Updike, a leading American novelist, poet, and critic.

A & P[1]

John Updike

In walks these three girls in nothing but bathing suits. I'm in the third checkout slot, with my back to the door, so I don't see them until they're over by the bread. The one that caught my eye first was the one in the plaid green two-piece. She was a chunky kid, with a good tan and a sweet broad soft-looking can with those two crescents of white just under it, where the sun never seems to hit, at the top of the backs of her legs. I stood there with my hand on a box of HiHo crackers trying to remember if I rang it up or not. I ring it up again and the customer starts giving me hell. She's one of these cash-register-watchers,

[1] Copyright © 1962 by John Updike. Reprinted from *Pigeon Feathers and Other Stories*, by John Updike, by permission of Alfred A. Knopf, Inc. This story originally appeared in *The New Yorker*.

a witch about fifty with rouge on her cheekbones and no eyebrows, and I know it made her day to trip me up. She'd been watching cash registers for fifty years and probably never seen a mistake before.

By the time I got her feathers smoothed and her goodies into a bag—she gives me a little snort in passing, if she'd been born at the right time they would have burned her over in Salem—by the time I get her on her way the girls had circled around the bread and were coming back, without a pushcart, back my way along the counters, in the aisle between the checkouts and the Special bins. They didn't even have shoes on. There was this chunky one, with the two-piece—it was bright green and the seams on the bra were still sharp and her belly was still pretty pale so I guessed she just got it (the suit)—there was this one, with one of those chubby berry-faces, the lips all bunched together under her nose, this one, and a tall one, with black hair that hadn't quite frizzed right, and one of these sunburns right across under the eyes, and a chin that was too long—you know, the kind of girl other girls think is very "striking" and "attractive" but never quite makes it, as they very well know, which is why they like her so much—and then the third one, that wasn't quite so tall. She was the queen. She kind of led them, the other two peeking around and making their shoulders round. She didn't look around, not this queen, she just walked straight on slowly, on these long white prima-donna legs. She came down a little hard on her heels, as if she didn't walk in her bare feet that much, putting down her heels and then letting the weight move along to her toes as if she was testing the floor with every step, putting a little deliberate extra action into it. You never know for sure how girls' minds work (do you really think it's a mind in there or just a little buzz like a bee in a glass jar?) but you got the idea she had talked the other two into coming in here with her, and now she was showing them how to do it, walk slow and hold yourself straight.

She had on a kind of dirty-pink—beige maybe, I don't know—bathing suit with a little nubble all over it and, what got me, the straps were down. They were off her shoulders looped loose around the cool tops of her arms, and I guess as a result the suit had slipped a little on her, so all around the top of the cloth there was this shining rim. If it hadn't been there you wouldn't have known there could have been anything whiter than those shoulders. With the straps pushed off, there was nothing between the top of the suit and the top of her head except just *her*, this clean bare plane of the top of her chest down from the shoulder bones like a dented sheet of metal tilted in the light. I mean, it was more than pretty.

She had sort of oaky hair that the sun and salt had bleached, done up in a bun that was unravelling, and a kind of prim face. Walking into the A & P with your straps down, I suppose it's the only kind of face you *can* have. She held her head so high her neck, coming up out of those white shoulders, looked kind of stretched, but I didn't mind. The longer her neck was, the more of her there was.

She must have felt in the corner of her eye me and over my shoulder

Stokesie in the second slot watching, but she didn't tip. Not this queen. She kept her eyes moving across the racks, and stopped, and turned so slow it made my stomach rub the inside of my apron, and buzzed to the other two, who kind of huddled against her for relief, and then they all three of them went up the cat-and-dog-food-breakfast-cereal-macaroni-rice-raisins-seasoning-spreads-spaghetti-soft-drinks-crackers-and-cookies aisle. From the third slot I look straight up this aisle to the meat counter, and I watched them all the way. The fat one with the tan sort of fumbled with the cookies, but on second thought she put the package back. The sheep pushing their carts down the aisle—the girls were walking against the usual traffic (not that we have one-way signs or anything)—were pretty hilarious. You could see them, when Queenie's white shoulders dawned on them, kind of jerk, or hop, or hiccup, but their eyes snapped back to their own baskets and on they pushed. I bet you could set off dynamite in an A & P and the people would by and large keep reaching and checking oatmeal off their lists and muttering "Let me see, there was a third thing, began with A, asparagus, no, ah, yes, applesauce!" or what-ever it is they do mutter. But there was no doubt, this jiggled them. A few houseslaves in pin curlers even looked around after pushing their carts past to make sure what they had seen was correct.

You know, it's one thing to have a girl in a bathing suit down on the beach, where what with the glare nobody can look at each other much anyway, and another thing in the cool of the A & P, under the fluorescent lights, against all those stacked packages, with her feet paddling along naked over our checker-board green-and-cream rubber-tile floor.

"Oh Daddy," Stokesie said beside me. "I feel so faint."

"Darling," I said. "Hold me tight." Stokesie's married, with two babies chalked up on his fuselage already, but as far as I can tell that's the only dif-ference. He's twenty-two, and I was nineteen this April.

"Is it done?" he asks, the responsible married man finding his voice. I forgot to say he thinks he's going to be manager some sunny day, maybe in 1990 when it's called the Great Alexandrov and Petrooshki Tea Company or something.

What he meant was, our town is five miles from a beach, with a big summer colony out on the Point, but we're right in the middle of town, and the women generally put on a shirt or shorts or something before they get out of the car into the street. And anyway these are usually women with six children and varicose veins mapping their legs and nobody, including them, could care less. As I say, we're right in the middle of town, and if you stand at our front doors you can see two banks and the Congregational church and the newspaper store and three real-estate offices and about twenty-seven old freeloaders tearing up Central Street because the sewer broke again. It's not as if we're on the Cape; we're north of Boston and there's people in this town haven't seen the ocean for twenty years.

The girls had reached the meat counter and were asking McMahon something. He pointed, they pointed, and they shuffled out of sight behind a pyramid of Diet Delight peaches. All that was left for us to see was old McMahon patting his mouth and looking after them sizing up their joints. Poor kids, I began to feel sorry for them, they couldn't help it.

Now here comes the sad part of the story, at least my family says it's sad, but I don't think it's so sad myself. The store's pretty empty, it being Thursday afternoon, so there was nothing much to do except lean on the register and wait for the girls to show up again. The whole store was like a pinball machine and I didn't know which tunnel they'd come out of. After a while they come around out of the far aisle, around the light bulbs, records at discount of the Caribbean Six or Tony Martin Sings or some such gunk you wonder they waste the wax on, sixpacks of candy bars, and plastic toys done up in cellophane that fall apart when a kid looks at them anyway. Around they come, Queenie still leading the way, and holding a little gray jar in her hand. Slots Three through Seven are unmanned and I could see her wondering between Stokes and me, but Stokesie with his usual luck draws an old party in baggy gray pants who stumbles up with four giant cans of pineapple juice (what do these bums *do* with all that pineapple juice? I've often asked myself) so the girls come to me. Queenie puts down the jar and I take it into my fingers icy cold. Kingfish Fancy Herring Snacks in Pure Sour Cream: 49¢. Now her hands are empty, not a ring or a bracelet, bare as God made them, and I wonder where the money's coming from. Still with that prim look she lifts a folded dollar bill out of the hollow at the center of her nubbled pink top. The jar went heavy in my hand. Really, I thought that was so cute.

Then everybody's luck begins to run out. Lengel comes in from haggling with a truck full of cabbages on the lot and is about to scuttle into that door marked MANAGER behind which he hides all day when the girls touch his eye. Lengel's pretty dreary, teaches Sunday school and the rest, but he doesn't miss that much. He comes over and says, "Girls, this isn't the beach."

Queenie blushes, though maybe it's just a brush of sunburn I was noticing for the first time, now that she was so close. "My mother asked me to pick up a jar of herring snacks." Her voice kind of startled me, the way voices do when you see the people first, coming out so flat and dumb yet kind of tony, too, the way it ticked over "pick up" and "snacks." All of a sudden I slid right down her voice into her living room. Her father and the other men were standing around in ice-cream coats and bow ties and the women were in sandals picking up herring snacks on toothpicks off a big glass plate and they were all holding drinks the color of water with olives and sprigs of mint in them. When my parents have somebody over they get lemonade and if it's a real racy affair Schlitz in tall glasses with "They'll Do It Every Time" cartoons stenciled on.

"That's all right," Lengel said. "But this isn't the beach." His repeating this struck me as funny, as if it had just occurred to him, and he had been thinking all these years the A & P was a great big dune and he was the head lifeguard. He didn't like my smiling — as I say he doesn't miss much — but he concentrates on giving the girls that sad Sunday-school-superintendent stare.

Queenie's blush is no sunburn now, and the plump one in plaid, that I liked better from the back — a really sweet can — pipes up, "We weren't doing any shopping. We just came in for the one thing."

"That makes no difference," Lengel tells her, and I could see from the way his eyes went that he hadn't noticed she was wearing a two-piece before. "We want you decently dressed when you come in here."

"We *are* decent," Queenie says suddenly, her lower lip pushing, getting sore now that she remembers her place, a place from which the crowd that runs the A & P must look pretty crummy. Fancy Herring Snacks flashed in her very blue eyes.

"Girls I don't want to argue with you. After this come in here with your shoulders covered. It's our policy." He turns his back. That's policy for you. Policy is what the kingpins want. What the others want is juvenile delinquency.

All this while, the customers had been showing up with their carts but, you know, sheep, seeing a scene, they had all bunched up on Stokesie, who shook open a paper bag as gently as peeling a peach, not wanting to miss a word. I could feel in the silence everybody getting nervous, most of all Lengel, who asks me, "Sammy, have you rung up their purchase?"

I thought and said "No" but it wasn't about that I was thinking. I go through the punches, 4, 9, GROC, TOT — it's more complicated than you think, and after you do it often enough, it begins to make a little song, that you hear words to, in my case "Hello (*bing*) there, you (*gung*) hap-py *pee-pul* (*splat*)!" — that *splat* being the drawer flying out. I uncrease the bill, tenderly as you may imagine, it just having come from between the two smoothest scoops of vanilla I had ever known were there, and pass a half and a penny into her narrow pink palm, and nestle the herrings in a bag and twist its neck and hand it over, all the time thinking.

The girls, and who'd blame them, are in a hurry to get out, so I say "I quit" to Lengel quick enough for them to hear, hoping they'll stop and watch me, their unsuspected hero. They keep right on going, into the electric eye; the door flies open and they flicker across the lot to their car, Queenie and Plaid and Big Tall Goony-Goony (not that as raw material she was so bad), leaving me with Lengel and a kink in his eyebrow.

"Did you say something, Sammy?"

"I said I quit."

"I thought you did."

"You didn't have to embarrass them."

"It was they who were embarrassing us."

I started to say something that came out "Fiddle-de-doo." It's a saying of my grandmother's, and I know she would have been pleased.

"I don't think you know what you're saying," Lengel said.

"I know you don't," I said. "But I do." I pull the bow at the back of my apron and start shrugging it off my shoulders. A couple customers that had been heading for my slot begin to knock against each other, like scared pigs in a chute.

Lengel sighs and begins to look very patient and old and gray. He's been a friend of my parents for years. "Sammy, you don't want to do this to your Mom and Dad," he tells me. It's true, I don't. But it seems to me that once you begin a gesture it's fatal not to go through with it. I fold the apron, "Sammy" stitched in red on the pocket, and put it on the counter, and drop the bow tie on top of it. The bow tie is theirs, if you've ever wondered. "You'll feel this for the rest of your life," Lengel says and I know that's true, too, but remembering how he made that pretty girl blush makes me so scrunchy inside I punch the No Sale tab and the machine whirs "pee-pull" and the drawer splats out. One advantage to this scene taking place in summer, I can follow this up with a clean exit, there's no fumbling around getting your coat and galoshes, I just saunter into the electric eye in my white shirt that my mother ironed the night before, and the door heaves itself open, and outside the sunshine is skating around on the asphalt.

I look around for my girls, but they're gone, of course. There wasn't anybody but some young married screaming with her children about some candy they didn't get by the door of a powder-blue Falcon station wagon. Looking back in the big windows, over the bags of peat moss and aluminum lawn furniture stacked on the pavements, I could see Lengel in my place in the slot, checking the sheep. His face was dark gray and his back stiff, as if he'd just had an injection of iron, and my stomach kind of fell as I felt how hard the world was going to be to me hereafter.

If you were asked to write a paper about Updike's "A & P," what subjects could you consider? We shall offer several here, but realize that a longer and more complex work of literature like a novel or play would yield many more than this short story does.

A PAPER ABOUT CHARACTER

1. *The Character Sketch*
   This paper analyzes a central or major supporting character, pointing out traits, discussing motivation, arriving at an overall evaluation, and commenting on the author's skill or lack of it in depicting the character.

   Examples: "Sammy—Hero or Fool?"; "What Makes Sammy Quit?"; "The Alienation of Sammy"; "Sammy: Regrets Only?"

2. *The Function of a Supporting Character*
   A supporting character is discussed to explain what purpose his or her presence serves in the work.

   Examples: "Lengel—Protector of Community Morality"; "Stokesie's Role"

3. *Character Comparison*
   This paper describes two characters, usually the central one and a supporting one, to show how they are similar or different, or alike in some ways but unlike in others.
   Examples: "Sammy and Lengel"; "Different Girlwatchers: McMahon and Sammy"

4. *The Attitude of the Central Character Toward People, Subjects, Values*
   The central character's ideas are explored, usually to provide a better understanding of his or her nature or actions.
   Examples: "Sammy and the Community"; "Queenie's World Through Sammy's Eyes"; "Sexist Sammy"

5. *The Language of the Central Character*
   The language of the central character is closely examined as a means of revealing his or her nature.
   Examples: "The Slanguage of Sammy"; "The Comic Undertone"

6. *The Character as Narrator*
   When the story is narrated by or through the mind of a character, the reliability of the narrator and the possible distortion of his or her views can be a fruitful subject.
   Examples: "Through Sammy's Eyes Darkly"; "As Lengel Saw It"

A PAPER ABOUT PLOT

1. *Plot Structure*
   This paper analyzes the organization of a literary work or its parts to provide a better understanding of it.
   Examples: "The Function of the Lengthy Exposition"; "The Significance of the Ending"

2. *Plot Evaluation*
   The artistry of the plot is considered.
   Examples: "The Chance Arrival of Lengel"; "The Uncomplicated Complication"

A PAPER ABOUT SETTING

1. *The Role of Setting*
   This paper discusses the significance of the place where most of the action occurs.
   Examples: "Inside the A & P"; "The A & P and Middle Class Morality"

2. *Setting as Mood*
   A discussion of how setting establishes an appropriate or inappropriate mood.

Example: "The Plastic World of the A & P"

3. *Setting as Environment*
An analysis of how the environment influences the central or other characters.
  Examples: "The Town and the Summer Visitors"; "The Sexist World of the A & P"

A PAPER ABOUT TIME

1. *The Author's Treatment of Time*
A consideration of how time has been handled in telling the story, whether by strict chronology, flashback, or some variation.
  Examples: "A Sad Break in the Present Tense?"; "Action Time and Telling Time"

2. *The Time of the Setting*
This paper considers the date when the story occurs to determine its impact upon the characters or the action.
  Examples: Not significant in "A & P"

A PAPER ABOUT THEME

1. *Theme and Character*
An analysis of the way a theme is introduced by the actions or problems of a character.
  Examples: "Sammy's Confrontation with the Values of the Marketplace"; "Sammy and the Facts of Life"

2. *Theme and Plot*
This paper examines how a theme develops from the events presented in the plot.
  Examples: "Public Policy and Individual Humanity"; "The Practical Consequences of Idealism"

A PAPER ABOUT TECHNIQUE

1. *Language*
Usually the language of the central character is studied in detail to indicate how it is consistent or inconsistent with his or her character or how accurate or inaccurate it is when compared with the language of similar real people.
  Examples: "Teenage Characteristics in Sammy's Language"; "Sammy's Outdated Slang"

2. *Irony*
Verbal and situational irony may be considered together or separately to contribute to an understanding of the literary work and the artistry of the writer.

Examples: "The Ironic Ending"; "Verbal Irony in Sammy's Narration"

3. *Symbolism*

The use of symbolism is described, particularly if it contributes significantly to the work.

Examples: "The Queen and Her Court in the Grocery Store"; "The Metaphoric Depiction of Lengel the Lifeguard"

We are not suggesting that all these subjects would yield either fruitful or lengthy papers about Updike's "A & P." Our purpose is merely to suggest some approaches to writing about literature, using "A & P" as an example. With such a short story, several of these approaches might be better combined for a long paper. Most of them would certainly be suitable for short studies. But we hope we have indicated some answers to the question you might have asked after reading "A & P" or any other literary work — "What shall I write about?"

THE ORGANIZATION OF THE CRITICAL PAPER

Papers about literature take the same forms as those on nonliterary topics. Although the subject matter is literary, the critical paper is essentially descriptive, expository, or argumentative. As we've indicated with the Updike story, you might choose to write a character sketch (similar to those in Chapter 9) of one of the leading characters, choosing descriptive details from the work itself to produce a compressed picture of a character. Or you might employ the techniques of analysis discussed in Chapter 15 in tracing a theme or examining technical aspects such as the use of irony, imagery, or symbolism. Or you could develop an interpretation inferred from your reading and support it with those "facts" from the work that led you to it, using the organizational skills recommended in Chapter 16. Still another possibility is to convince your readers that your interpretation is valid even though it might be controversial; then you should couch your paper in argument form as illustrated in Chapter 26. Yet another approach is to compare several aspects of the work, extending the techniques suggested for comparison-and-contrast paragraphs in Chapter 27 to encompass a whole paper. So you see, the rhetorical problems involved in writing about literature are basically the same as those for other subject matter.

Thesis and Support

As with all well-organized writing, the critical paper needs a controlling thesis, or central idea. This can take the form of an inference statement that reflects a strong opinion or conviction you derive (infer) from the work. Let's look at some student examples of critical thesis statements, discussing the kinds of support and organization each requires.

1. Inference thesis requiring a character sketch of a main character for support:

In *The Bridge over the River Kwai,* Colonel Nicholson's dedication to military discipline and duty saves the morale of his men but results in his treason to the British cause.

> This "opinion" thesis requires that the writer support both contentions: Nicholson's dedication saves morale and leads to treason. Attitudes of other characters toward Nicholson and incidents portraying his growing fanaticism about the building of the bridge are necessary in developing a causal framework that explains the ultimate effect — treason of a dedicated, loyal soldier.

2. Inference thesis requiring comparison-and-contrast techniques for support.

The language of the schoolboys has both an identifying and an excluding power in Kipling's *Stalky & Co.* and in Knowles' *A Separate Peace.*

> Here, the thesis sets up a four-fold writing assignment for the student: to show how each of the two novels uses language to provide group identity and to exclude outsiders. The organization of the paper could follow either of these patterns:

I. *Stalky & Co.*	I. Identifying devices
A. Identifying devices	A. *Stalky & Co.*
B. Excluding devices	B. *A Separate Peace*
II. *A Separate Peace*	II. Excluding devices
A. Identifying devices	A. *Stalky & Co.*
B. Excluding devices	B. *A Separate Peace*

3. Inference thesis requiring techniques of analysis for support.

The turtle in *The Grapes of Wrath* is symbolic of the Joad family and their fight for survival.

> This thesis idea requires an analytical paper — a classifying of the adventures and characteristics of the turtle that are related in some way to the plight of the Joads. Remember that adequate support of an in-

terpretation involving symbolic meaning requires strong supporting evidence from the text.

4. Argument thesis:

Despite Tolkien's denials, *Lord of the Rings* can be interpreted symbolically as a Christian struggle between good and evil.

This argumentative thesis requires strong support from the novel backed up perhaps by the opinions of reputable critics. Since the author himself refutes the proposition, the student writer, remembering the possibility of intentional fallacy, must prove that Tolkien's use of symbols, conscious or unconscious, leads the reader to this interpretation. Careful citation of such symbols is of course required to substantiate the proposition.

A Sample Organizational Scheme

Now that we have looked at examples of thesis statements and discussed generally how these could be supported, let's devise an organizational scheme for a critical paper on the setting of Updike's story. This topic could be organized thus:

Thesis: In John Updike's "A & P," the supermarket triggers the action in the story. (Inference thesis)
I. The contrast of the polished, artificial store to the careless naturalness of the girls sets up the "complication."
(Here, it would be necessary to illustrate the effect of the contrast on Sammy and how this establishes the tension in the story: comparison-and-contrast technique is needed. You should pick up Updike's own contrasts: the girls "under the fluorescent lights," silhouetted against the neatly stacked packages, bare feet on the polished, "checkerboard . . . rubber-tiled floor," their curves contrasted to the straight aisles, their openness contrasted to the mazelike layout of the store.)
II. The location of the store helps to reinforce Lengel's values and behavior, thus contributing to the turning point in the story.
(You should emphasize the location in the "middle" of town, within sight of the banks, churches, real-estate offices, all evidence of the middle-class values held by Lengel—he is the arbiter of those values in the store. The proximity of the businesses and churches supports his values.)
III. The contrast of the girls to other customers in the store contributes to Sammy's decision.
(You need to prove that the customers are more a part of the

setting than they are characters—do they participate in the action much or are they merely part of the backdrop? The contrast between the aging women in hair curlers and the natural beauty of the girls—plus the effect of this contrast on Sammy and his decision—should be discussed.)

A paper written from this outline would require the skills of both analysis and comparison and contrast. Let's turn now to two student papers on other works, one using analytical techniques, the other comparison and contrast.

Student Paper: Tracing a Central Theme Through Character Analysis

In the following paper, the student demonstrates the most effective use of character analysis: not merely to describe a character, but to relate the character to a major theme in the work. In this case, the student develops a limited character sketch choosing only those aspects that support her inference thesis: that a postwar conflict of values is a major theme in Ernest Hemingway's novel *The Sun Also Rises*. The student's organizational scheme is indicated at the side.

JAKE BARNES' LOSS OF VALUES IN *THE SUN ALSO RISES*

Gail Gardenhire

One of the most overwhelming problems that Jake Barnes, the major character in Ernest Hemingway's *The Sun Also Rises*, has to face is adequately stated by a somewhat minor character in the book when Count Mippipopolous advises Jake, "That is the secret. You must get to know the values." Indeed, it seems that throughout this novel, Jake constantly searches to define his values and to see which ones will survive.

Inference thesis

Perhaps the greatest influence on Jake's increasing loss of values is his "old grievance." There are, however, several connotations that could apply to this phrase, the most obvious being Jake's impotence produced by an injury incurred "on a joke front like the Italian." Lady Brett Ashley might be another of Jake's "old grievances," which drags him farther and farther away from a definition of his values. Brett's "circle" of friends and even her very presence

I. Jake's sexual impotence and his love for Brett contribute to his loss of values.

seem only to reinforce Jake's realization that he is incapable of enjoying or satisfying any physical "value" which he might hold, and this, consequently, leads him to seek superficial values as substitutes for human ones.

Also essential to Jake's search is his exposure to a varied set of values characterized by two types of people in the novel and to the transition that these values undergo as these people are introduced to new situations. Perhaps the best example of this idea is the abrupt change in the values of the peasants when confronted with a fiesta in which "everything became quite unreal finally and it seemed as though nothing could have any consequence." These peasants, with their pure and simple ties to the soil and the uncomplicated measure of values in yield of crops or animals raised, quickly lose their pure and simple values, though perhaps only temporarily, when they become involved in the fiesta. Before, "money still had a definite value in hours worked and bushels of grain sold," whereas, "Late in the fiesta it would not matter what they paid nor where they bought." They have assumed the values of the city.

II. Shifting values of others in the novel contribute to his moral confusion.

Similarly, Jake goes through some transition in what he thought to be things most dear to him prior to this fiesta. His enthusiasm for bullfighting had been most precious to him and served as his greatest emotional involvement. As the fiesta progresses, however, and Jake becomes involved in the decaying values of all those about him, he loses, due to his bitterness about inability to give Brett sexual satisfaction, the last of his "precious" values.

III. Jake reexamines his values.

As a result, Jake is forced to redefine his values in terms of money. Here lies the power he lost in his war accident. Here lies a way to satisfy his senses, through adequate food and plentiful wine to dull his inner awareness that these new values are meaningless. Jake reaches the conclusion that life is, after all, "just exchange of values." Everything that life has to offer must be paid for "by experience, or by taking chances, or by money,"

IV. Jake redefines his values.

but "the bill" always comes. If you strive to "pay your way into enough things," then you'll eventually enjoy life and "get your money's worth."

In essence, Jake has learned that in order to make friends, and in order to survive in this hopelessly "lost generation," one must value only things that can be replaced. Money can be replaced. Friends or acquaintances can be replaced through the use of money, and superficial needs can easily be satisfied with money. Jake has finally decided that he must *not* value his once-in-a-lifetime love for Brett or his enthusiasm for bullfighting, because these are values that cannot easily be replaced with a "simple exchange."

Sadly enough, any glimmer of hope for the survival of values honestly valuable to Jake is lost by the time the fiesta is over, and he succumbs to all of the "lost generation" by admitting that "I did not care what it was all about. All I wanted to know was how to live in it." He makes that final compromise, that final exchange of a life of substance for one of mere existence.

V. Jake exchanges his value system for that of Brett's "circle."

Conclusion: Restatement of thesis and the theme of values.

Note that the student writer not only works in significant quotes from the novel throughout her own prose, but effectively introduces her subject with one—a reference to the values that have thematic importance in the novel. Not only does this add interest, but it helps also to substantiate her interpretation.

Student Paper: Tracing a Central Theme Through Comparison and Contrast

This second critical paper, also on *The Sun Also Rises,* compares two characters for the purpose of illustrating an important theme in the novel. Note that the writer includes only those characteristics relevant to the discussion. She doesn't give us a detailed physical description of the two men because their appearance is not significant; only their physical virility is important to the thesis.

IMPOTENCE, MANHOOD, AND VIRILITY IN *THE SUN ALSO RISES*

Elizabeth V. Henderson

"You are all a lost generation," said Gertrude Stein about the French veterans of World War I.

Introduction

When Ms. Stein made this statement, she could have been referring either to the tragic French casualties of World War I or, more likely, to the political and social impotence of France in the aftermath of the war. Even though France, as one of the Allied countries, had been victorious, it was an anti-climactic victory because France's losses, both human and financial, made it virtually impossible for it, as a nation, to have any measurable effect on the history of the period — to play a creative role in rebuilding the postwar society.

As the major character in *The Sun Also Rises,* Jake Barnes, like France, epitomizes the impotence of the era. A veteran of the war, Jake gave more than his life when he sacrificed his manhood for the Allied cause. The traditional concept of masculine virility is put to an ironic test as Jake fights to regain his manhood — a fight made even more ironic when contrasted to the animal virility of another character, Robert Cohn.

Thesis: comparison and contrast

Although Jake tries to see the wry humor of his impotent condition, he is constantly reminded of the tragedy in it. For example, he curses the homosexuals who pervert their manhood but are still able to win the attention of Brett Ashley, the woman Jake loves but with whom he will never be able to share a normal physical relationship.

I. Contrast of virility and manhood

A direct opposite of Jake is Robert Cohn, who is cowardly, materialistic, yet so vain about his masculine prowess that he is constantly ridiculed and used by the other characters and is the brunt of much of Jake's sarcasm. Cohn did not participate in the war and still possesses an adolescent's idealistic outlook on life. He lives his life passively, shallowly, traveling back and forth within the painted illusions of his literary world. He was "married by the first girl who was nice to him" and fathered children — an ability bitterly envied by Jake, who so much wanted to father Brett's children. Jake realizes, however, that there is more to marriage and fatherhood than just physical equipment, and that it takes a mature inner strength to make it last.

Cohn shows immaturity in the face of responsibility. When the problems of his relationship to Frances and his new novel grow too large, he plans to flee to South America on the pretense of loving travel. Jake sees the South American flight as another illusion—a motion picture solution to a real problem. But Cohn is innocently oblivious to Jake's sarcasm.

II. Contrast of Jake's maturity and Cohn's immaturity

Another difference between Cohn and Barnes lies in their respective concepts of life and death. Cohn, a trained boxer who detests the sport, uses it only to ward off threats. He has no apparent ideals or values, believing that life is for amusement, and death the force that will bring his amusement to an end. He knows nothing about facing death firsthand; he is only aware that statistically he is halfway through the years supposedly allotted for his life.

III. Contrast of Jake's and Cohn's philosophies of life

Jake Barnes, on the other hand, is a tragic victim of the war and has faced death directly. The knowledge that he has evaded but not conquered death gives him a great appreciation for the controlled confrontation of death that occurred in the bullfight. He realizes that Cohn considers the bullfight as brutal, not recognizing its place in the culture, but Jake feels that the bullfight arena is no different from real life, where death is brought to center stage and is a challenge for even the bravest man. He looks to the discipline of the bullfight as a model for the discipline and control necessary to his own life. When his love for Brett removes this discipline, he becomes helpless. Cohn, on the other hand, is repulsed by bullfighting, seeing only the brutality that somehow threatens his naive illusions about life. Cohn, too, is hurt by Brett, but it is his vanity that suffers. He cannot play her game by her rules; he cannot see that she uses his virility as she uses all men to satisfy her nymphomania.

IV. Comparison of Brett's effect on the two men

At the fiesta, Jake recognizes that Cohn's philosophy is an unrealistic protective bubble that seems divorced from reality and therefore void of consequences. It is also at the fiesta that Jake reexamines his own value system. He curses the church, whose ready-made, right-or-wrong distinctions make his own attempts at achieving a value system seem small and insignificant, then curses Brett, and finally himself for becoming so dependent on her friendship—a dependence as damaging as his impotence. Even though he finally realizes that he is the ultimate victor over Cohn because Brett loves him in ways that she could never love Cohn, he finds no comfort in the knowledge. This victory, like that of France in the war, is painful and anti-climactic, because it epitomizes his loss.

V. Contrast between Jake's intellectual and emotional reactions to Brett's love for him.

Jake's loss is great, perhaps more than if he had been killed. The loss suffered by France is tremendous. But Robert Cohn's loss is nonexistent because what has never been had cannot be lost. Although Cohn possesses the virility which attracted Brett briefly, he lacks Jake's true manhood. His narrow vision of life does not even permit him to perceive the "loss." In this sense, Robert Cohn is as impotent as Jake Barnes.

Conclusion: Restatement of thesis. Summary ties France, Jake, and Cohn together. Comparison and contrast sustained.

THE INFLUENCE OF AUDIENCE ON CRITICAL WRITING

Because students tend to write critical papers in a class where all the members have read, discussed, and are writing about the same work, they sometimes assume that the class and the instructor characterize their audience: that the audience has complete knowledge of the work and that no explanatory materials need to be included. This assumption, however, can breed dangerous writing habits. Unless your teacher directs otherwise, you should write to your classmates, but should include in the audience group some outsiders who may have read the book some time ago and have only a cursory knowledge of it. Having an audience such as this in mind will negate a tendency to bore your classmates with too much plot summary, but will also force you to provide enough information to enlighten the outsiders. You should include:

1. Identification of the work in the opening paragraphs. Note that both student examples mention the title early in the paper. Generally, the author's name is also given.
2. Enough plot information to illustrate the points you make. Resist the common trap of beginning the paper with an extensive plot summary

before launching into the real subject of your paper. Unless the assignment is to write a plot summary, such detail can be kept to a minimum. Both student examples strike a happy balance in this. Including only enough detail to "fill in" the less knowledgeable members of your audience can also serve the purpose of providing specific detail to support your inferences.

3. Definition or explanation of unusual terms or concepts. This is needed as much in critical writing as in other forms of exposition. Any of the methods of brief definition suggested in Chapter 15 can be utilized.

In general, then, critical writing follows the same patterns and commits the writer to the same considerations as do other forms of writing. Only the subject matter and the specialized skills and vocabulary of literary criticism differ from other forms of writing discussed in this book. The organizational matters, maintaining focus and logical relationships throughout the paper, and sustaining awareness of audience and purpose are as much a part of literary criticism as they are of extended definition or an argument. But literary writing does demand special attention to some technical aspects of writing that may be absent in other forms of writing. Let's look at some of these.

USAGES IN CRITICAL WRITING

Narrative Past Versus Chronological Past

How often in telling a personal anecdote to a friend have you lapsed into the habit of using the present tense: "Then the car salesman *says,* 'Why don't you take it out for a test drive?' He *knows* he *has* me hooked." All of us find this a convenient device when speaking to friends in a relaxed, intimate situation. In more formal speech and in most writing, you would undoubtedly substitute past tense for these present tense verb forms. "Then the car salesman *said,* 'Why don't you take it out for a test drive?' He *knew* he *had* me hooked." In written English, however, this use of present tense to mean past time is discouraged, particularly in exposition and argument. But in writing about literature, the present tense—referred to in this context as the narrative past—is generally acceptable. Astute critics often employ it when summarizing events in the story or in speaking of the effects the author attempted. However, they generally return to the conventional chronological past forms when making references to the book or in quoting materials to support their interpretation. Students often find that adapting this practice to their own writing is confusing. Perhaps a look at the use of present tense for narrative past and past tense for chronological past in the following paragraph can aid you to unravel the complexities of this specialized tense shifting. To make it easier to identify the significant verbs, we have underlined the present tense forms and circled those in past tense:

The only possible support for the idea that Kino may have experienced some sort of victory <u>comes</u> from a sentence concerning the townspeople who <u>observe</u> the return of Kino and Juana near the end of the book: "The people say that the two (seemed) to be removed from human experience; that they (had gone) through pain and come out on the other side." But these <u>are</u> the same neighbors who, on the day the pearl was found, (anticipated) that they (would remember) the day for years to come as the day of the great marvel, the day they (saw) Kino transfigured. They <u>are</u> also the people who, we <u>are told</u> in the headnote, (retold) all stories only in terms of "good and bad things and black and white things and good and evil things and not in-between anywhere." No, the neighbors transfigured Kino because that (was) their tradition. It is more likely that they (admired) his defiance than that they (discerned) any transformation of character, something completely unprepared for in the novel. The things that Kino <u>sees</u> in the pearl before he <u>discards</u> it—reminders of the ugly experiences he <u>has</u> just <u>passed</u> through—<u>symbolize</u> the success of the community of exploiters in warping the means to a new and better life into a means of death. To say that in throwing the pearl into the sea Kino <u>is</u> symbolically divesting himself of false values <u>is</u> to sentimentalize his character by attributing to him qualities which are inconsistent with his earlier actions and statements. This interpretation also <u>implies</u> that Kino (was) wrong and the exploiters (were) right, something hardly in harmony with the rest of the novel. We should not forget

Narrative past— present tense forms used to lead into a quote from the work.

The two verbs quoted from the novel cannot be changed.

When the writer talks about the novel, he uses the chronological past (past tense forms). But when he shifts to telling the story, he shifts to narrative past (present tense forms).

Narrative past— present tense forms —used in this combined summary of events and the writer's refutation of other interpretations.

Past tense again used in "talking about" the events.

that Kino <u>hangs</u> on to his newly acquired rifle
when he <u>returns</u> to La Paz.

—Roland Bartel, "Proportioning in Fiction: *The Pearl*
and *Silas Marner*," *English Journal*

As you can see, this device is fairly complex. For this reason, many writers of criticism and teachers of English prefer to avoid the problem by consistently employing past tense forms throughout except where present tense is necessary, as in the first sentence of this brief summary, taken from a book review in *Saturday Review*.

This too-slender novel <u>is</u> the story of a mother's life seen through the eyes of her son. A suicide in her early 50's, she had grown to womanhood in Germany in the years just before World War II. She had felt the excitement of the new order under the Nazis, the pleasure of feeling at one with everyone in the nation, of having a purpose. But her nature and the nature of her society were such that she was not long destined to enjoy purpose or happiness of any kind. She was different from those around her, her son <u>thinks</u>: a careful but rebellious woman in ways that showed themselves rarely.

—Review of Peter Handke's *A Sorrow Beyond Dreams*

Chronological past— past tense forms are generally used in plot summaries.

Present tense *thinks* relates to writer's use of *is* in opening sentence (writer's discussion of the novel)

In critical writing, then, you have two acceptable choices: you can use the narrative past or the chronological past. The important thing is to be consistent throughout. If you employ narrative past (that is, present tense forms) for plot summary, make sure that you don't shift to past tense forms.

Verb Accord

Closely related to this matter of verb tense is the problem of verb accord. In sentences it is necessary to be concerned with agreement of subject and verb. You must make sure that singular and plural subjects are followed by the appropriate verb form: in the present tense, *-s* forms (*hears, knows*) for third person singular subjects; plain forms (*hear, know*) for plural and other singular subjects. But in longer units of discourse, it is important that the verb tenses be in accord — that they all follow the same tense pattern throughout. Working with the following paragraphs adapted from Katherine Mansfield's "A Cup of Tea" can help you with this complex feature of English grammar. In each sentence except the first, we have omitted the part of the verb phrase that carries the tense signal, but have indicated the auxiliary or verb you should use to fill in the blank. Note that the verbs in the first sentence of each version determine the subsequent forms:

Version A

The other [girl] *did* stop just in time for Rosemary to get up before tea *came*. She (HAVE) the table placed between them. She (PLY) the poor little creature with everything, all the sandwiches, all the bread and butter, and every time her cup (BE) empty she (FILL) it with tea, cream, and sugar. People always (SAY) sugar (BE) so nourishing. As for herself, she (DO) not eat; she (SMOKE) and (LOOK) away tactfully so that the other (SHALL) not be shy.

Version B

The other [girl] *does* stop just in time for Rosemary to get up before the tea *comes*. She (HAVE) the table placed between them. She (PLY) the poor little creature with everything, all the sandwiches, all the bread and butter, and every time her cup (BE) empty she (FILL) it with tea, cream, and sugar. People always (SAY) sugar (BE) so nourishing. As for herself, she (DO) not eat; she (SMOKE) and (LOOK) away tactfully so that the other (SHALL) not be shy.

   In performing this exercise, you have no doubt realized that the past tense verb forms in the first sentence in Version A set the pattern for the verbs throughout the paragraph: *had, plied, was, filled, said, was, did, smoked, looked,* and *should.* In Version B, on the other hand, the initial present tense verbs resulted in *has, plies, is, fills, say, is, does, smokes, looks, shall.* Obviously, the opening or topic sentence in the paragraph sets up the verb accord requirements, and that is usually the case. Remember that although verb accord is important in all kinds of writing, it can become especially problematical in critical writing, particularly if you make use of the narrative past with its inherent problem discussed in the previous section.

Handling Quotations in Critical Writing

   There are times in critical writing when it is necessary or useful to quote directly from the work you are writing about. If you wish to use supporting material for a controversial interpretation, the author's original words might carry more weight than your own. Or sometimes, lengthy quotations are used for comparison purposes: a critic may wish to compare a segment of the author's published version with an earlier draft, or contrast two passages from the same work that has had several translations. But such tasks are rarely assigned in freshman English classes. For most of the critical writing tasks you will be given, brief quotations incorporated into your own discussion about the work will be sufficient and effective. Here are some examples from student papers that demonstrate some of the ways quotations can be effectively worked into critical papers.

1. To demonstrate a representative theme in the work:

Toward the end of D. Keith Mano's *The Bridge* a character observes: "Shakespeare was wrong: there are only two ages of man. Childhood and senility. Savage youth or a self-hating, self-destructive civilization. In between, a few moments—no more, a few—when the balance is held, when he is a god." That glum judgment is at the core of *The Bridge,* and like a number of the novel's thematic assumptions is highly debatable.

> Note that because this quote of several lines has been made an integral part of the student's comments about the novel, it is not necessary to separate and indent it, as is normal for longer quotes.

2. To support an interpretation (again discussing *The Bridge*):

In a literal interpretation of the communion, Priest developed a craving for "blood and flesh," and it was this hunger that reawakened his determination to survive. When Priest reached home, he found that Ogilvy, the state guard who had provoked the anger that sent him to prison, had killed his wife and child. Insane with grief, Priest jumped on the tormentor and devoured his arm "to the sweet flesh around its bone." Not only was Priest literally partaking of communion, but enacting the "eat or be eaten" law of the jungle. By this, Priest reasserted his right to live, not as a man whose cannibalism is only symbolic in communion, but as a beast who literally devours another. It was only in the most reductive natural context that he could find any support for the desire to live.

> Here the quotes are phrases incorporated into the sentence structure without "example signals"—*such as, for instance, like, Priest says,* and so on. Instead, the quotes flow naturally into the student's prose and only the quotation marks indicate that they come from the work itself.

3. To quote significant words from the text in support of an interpretation:

The author has tried to carry over his feeling for nature by his use of color. In "the force" the stem of the flower is green, of course. But then life is also labeled the same way. It must mean that age is alive and growing, and something beautiful, not to be thought of in a vegetative, passive way. In "Fern Hill" Dylan Thomas was "green and carefree." He has used the color to describe the boy, green and growing, learning, having fun.

Most literary references can be punctuated as in these examples: by setting off the quoted phrases or words with quotation marks. But there are several punctuation problems peculiar to critical writing that deserve attention: quoted lines of poetry, quotations that contain quoted material themselves, and quotations with omitted sections (ellipsis). Here's how you handle these matters.

1. Several lines of poetry:

The fact that Icarus, in the painting, is so small compared to the plowman and the ship, implies the insignificance to other people of what is undoubtedly the most significant event in the life of Icarus. "How everything turns away/Quite leisurely from the disaster; the ploughman may/Have heard the splash, the forsaken cry." To the plowman, however, Icarus' failure is unimportant since it has no direct effect on his life.

In this student paper on a poem by W. H. Auden, slanted lines are used to indicate the end of the poetic line, which does not always coincide with the end of a sentence. Of course, quotes of more than two or three lines can be separated from your text and indented in the same fashion as lengthy prose quotes. The slanted lines are not needed because you would then follow the line arrangement of the original:

> . . . How everything turns away
> Quite leisurely from the disaster; the ploughman may
> Have heard the splash, the forsaken cry.[2]

2. Quotations containing quotations.

It is the need for her daughter's love that causes the Marquesa's unhappiness. "She wanted her daughter for herself; she wanted to hear her say: 'You are the best of all possible mothers.'" Consequently, she wrote her famous letters to Dona Clara, although "her daughter barely glanced at the letters."
—Student example quoted in "12,000 Students and Their English Teachers," *CEE*

---

[2] From "Musée des Beaux Arts." Copyright 1940 and renewed 1968 by W. H. Auden. Reprinted from *Collected Shorter Poems 1927–1957*, by W. H. Auden, by permission of Random House, Inc.

The quoted material as it appeared in the original work looked like this:

She wanted her daughter for herself; she wanted to hear her say: "You are the best of all possible mothers."

Because the whole quote requires quotation marks in the student's paper, the original punctuation of the material quoted in the work ("_____") was changed to ('_____'). This device helps you to signal your reader which quotations are yours and which the author's.

3. Ellipsis.

As the American prisoners and their guards move across the treacherous ruins of Dresden, "Billy did not meet many eyes . . . most of the people would soon be dead." He knew that Dresden "would be smashed to smithereens and then burned. . . ."

Omission or ellipsis of material is indicated by three spaced periods (. . .). If the ellipsis occurs in the middle of a sentence, follow the pattern of the first quotation in the example: quotation marks are needed only at the beginning and end of the whole quotation. If material at the beginning of a sentence is deleted, a quotation mark is placed first, then the three periods (". . .). If the ellipsis occurs at the end of a sentence, the three periods appear first, then a fourth period to punctuate your sentence, then a quotation mark (. . . ."). Other punctuation problems involving ellipsis are discussed in Chapter 33, pages 550–51.

Informal Documentation in Critical Writing

Unless you quote from secondary sources (critical articles or books written by professional critics), you do not need to provide the kind of formal documentation that will be discussed in Chapter 33. Instead, since most of your quotations come from the work you are writing about, you need only give enough information to enable the reader to find the quotation—page numbers for fiction; act and scene for drama; and line numbers for poetry:

Novel or short story:

After this display of weakness, Ozzie "started to feel the meaning of the word control; he felt peace and he felt power" (p. 123). Ozzie is no longer a little boy.

For citations involving more than one page: (pp. 123–124) or (pp. 123–24).

Play:

Even Shylock's daughter expresses disapproval of her father's behavior: "But though I am a daughter to his blood,/I am not to his manners" (I, iii) or (I.iii).

Poem:

The poet describes the movement of the express as "gliding like a queen" (l. 3). This simile not only describes the movement . . . .

When several lines are quoted, the form is: (ll. 3, 4) or (ll. 3–5).

Frequently in critical writing even this informal documentation is not necessary. But if your instructor requires it, these models can be useful.

ASSIGNMENTS

For Discussion

1 What kind of critical paper should result from each of the following student thesis statements: character sketch, comparison and contrast, analysis, argument, other? What are the key terms in the statements that require discussion and support? What weaknesses do they manifest?

    a The Joad family in *Grapes of Wrath* possesses the same kind of unselfish love that the biblical "good Samaritan" had.

    b In the novel *The Bridge*, the baptism of Priest serves as a transitional bridge from the ending of one era to the beginning of a new one.

    c In *Waiting for Godot*, Samuel Beckett explores Christian symbolism in the guise of garment and nature imagery to support the central themes in his play.

    d In "Bright and Morning Star," Richard Wright illustrates the maturation of the protagonist by contrasting two rebels—one old and one young.

    e In *The Secret Sharer* the young captain as an outsider struggles to overcome his external isolation by correcting his internal, self-imposed isolation.

    f In *Matryona's House*, both Matryona and the narrator are quiet social rebels.

    g In Salinger's *The Catcher in the Rye*, Holden Caulfield can be seen both as a social rebel and as a victim of society.

2 Compare the use of quoted materials in the following three student paragraphs. Which do you think is most effective? Why?

[handwritten: platronic]

[handwritten right margin: read, note quoted material jot down if you think material is quoted effectively]

a Vladimir and Estragon, representing the metaphysical couple, have no society-oriented relationship. They are simply of equal status in a friend-to-friend relationship. Their relationship shows no class distinction or consciousness. This friend-to-friend relationship can be seen in two passages. The first passage is when Estragon falls asleep.

(Estragon sleeps, Vladimir gets up softly, takes off his coat and lays it across Estragon's shoulders, then starts walking up and down, swinging his arms to keep himself warm. Estragon wakes with a start, jumps up, casts about wildly. Vladimir runs to him, puts his arms around him.)

The second passage showing Vladimir and Estragon's relationship is in the scene where they talk about their relationship.

ESTRAGON: You see, you feel worse when I'm with you. I feel better alone too.

VLADIMIR: Then why do you always come crawling back?

ESTRAGON: I don't know.

VLADIMIR: No, but I do. It's because you don't know how to defend yourself. I wouldn't have let them beat you.

b The most obvious indication of Henry's insignificance is apparent from the beginning of the novel. It seems rather ironic that the primary character is not actually introduced until a large portion of the book has been covered. We know him only as the "youth." He has earned no name, no "badge" of distinction or accomplishment and, thus, no identity. While struggling with his initial anxieties about bravely facing combat or shamefully fleeing, the youth is merely one of a multitude of soldiers, "a part of a vast blue demonstration." Only when he is actually confronted with battle and succumbs to what he had feared, are we allowed to meet him as Henry Fleming. He has finally taken some definite action, perhaps not particularly admirable, but nevertheless decisive; and for this, he has earned some form of identity. He, in fact, now fears that everyone knows him as a coward. He is "a slang phrase."

c Humanity has lost its will to live by 2035. Man has been ordered to terminate his own life. Walters, Priest's fellow inmate at Yankee Stadium, states, "It's been coming to this. Dead by our own free will. Thank God — we didn't deserve to live." Xavier Paul and Priest witness a mass suicide on their way to New Loch. Xavier Paul "hates these people who hate their own lives. People who are guilty when they breathe with the lungs God gave them, who have no way to expiate their guilt. The world's polluted with despair. They deserve to die."

[handwritten: make amends for]

3 The following excerpts from student papers contain some mechanical flaws — either in verb accord or in punctuation of quotations. Find the flaws and revise them.

pick out
flaws &
correct
them

a Hawthorne's tales usually end with a moralistic view of life. Each character learns something about human nature that virtually destroys him. Sin is inevitable and is deeply rooted in human experience. Father Hooper in "The Minister's Black Veil" recognizes this and is obsessed by it. At his death he felt that every person wears a "Black Veil" to conceal his innermost thoughts and feelings from the rest of the world. Young Goodman Brown found that people wear hypocrisy as a veil to cover their evil natures. Yet each man at his death will have to bare himself to his Maker and face the consequences. Aylmer in "The Birthmark" and Ethan Brand are similar in that both end in having found an ultimate truth. Aylmer should have accepted the imperfection of life and been content with the anticipation of the perfect future. Ethan Brand searched the world over for the "Unpardonable Sin" and finally found it in himself. He discovered it to be egotism, which tends to separate man from his fellow man. Roderick Elliston in "Egotism; or, The Bosom Serpent" suffers from a terrible egotism which stems from jealousy. It manifested itself in the form of a serpent which was eating out the heart. Feathertop alone immediately recognized himself for what he really was, "a wretched, ragged, empty thing," and resolved that he would "exist no longer." Many such others live in "fair repute" and "never see themselves for what they are."

b Gandalf could be called a Christ-figure. In the beginning he has limited power, he is still learning. After the duel with Balrog, Gandalf is transformed and appears in white: I have passed through fire and deep water, since we parted. Gandalf had returned to life, more powerful than ever. He was beyond all harm: Indeed, my friends, none of you has any weapon that could hurt me.

c Lucky's soliloquy reflects the alienation of God from man. When Lucky spurts out, ". . . of a personal God . . . . with white beard . . . . outside time without extention who from heights of divine apathy . . . . divine aphasia . . . .," it signifies that God exists, but neither understands nor cares.

d By saying that the ships, theaters, domes, temples, and towers lie "open unto the fields, and to the sky; All bright and glittering in the smokeless air," Wordsworth contradicts the generally held belief that the city is nothing more than a cluttered, cramped collage of concrete buildings barely visible through a thick blanket of dingy smog.

(Note: The poem reads:

Ships, towers, domes, theaters, and temples lie
Open unto the fields, and to the sky;
All bright and glittering in the smokeless air.)

The Authoritative Voice: The Research Paper

Introduction to the Research Paper

The thought of writing research papers is frightening to many students. Some avoid courses requiring them; others drop the course at term paper time. True, writing these papers does require more sustained work and intellectual effort than other papers do. True, they demand that a writer work more efficiently and organize material more skillfully. But—also true—research papers are more rewarding. Writing them can be interesting, stimulating, and satisfying. They offer a unique opportunity to learn. And learning how to write research papers is one way to learn how to learn. Let us explain.

From time to time this semester, week, or perhaps even today, you've probably speculated about some person, event, issue, problem, or subject you wish you knew more about. It might be Alfred Hitchcock, the Chappaquiddick incident, ESP, the Loch Ness monster, the Watergate tape erasure, witchcraft, IQ, heart transplants, solar heating, monorails, the electric car. Whatever you are curious about, wonder about, or want to know more about can be your subject. By doing research, you are learning what you want to know about your subject. And by learning how to locate, select, arrange, evaluate, and present information about this subject, you are learning how to learn.

And learning is rewarding. Whether it merely satisfies your curiosity or builds your ego, learning makes life more interesting to you and makes you more interesting to others. You become the local expert, specialist, authority on some subject. Whatever the subject, you probably will know more about it after writing your research paper than do others in your class or perhaps in the entire freshman class. Knowledge is power.

But it does not come quickly or easily; it requires work, time, effort, and skill to master the process of research.

THE RESEARCH PROCESS

The research process is not entirely new to you. You have probably already conducted or been involved in some research. You may have combed the newspaper classified ads before looking for a regular, part-time, or summer job. You may have consulted consumer guides and spoken to numerous people before buying a stereo, television set, or used car. You may have boned up on automobile insurance before deciding what coverage to get, how much to buy, and what company to deal with. You may have investigated group plans, compared charter rates, and studied travel literature before going on vacation. And you probably pored over college catalogs before deciding which school to attend. In these and similar pursuits, you were engaged on a small scale in the same information-gathering activity that goes into a research paper.

Just as the process of research is not an academic exercise confined to English classes, neither is the writing of research papers. Chances are that in other college courses during the next few years you will be asked to investigate a subject and communicate your findings. And after college, you may join the many people constantly doing research and writing about it: government experts, lawyers, journalists, business executives, engineers, scientists, economists, and others in such professional fields as medicine, education, social work. Like you, these people are involved in the process of defining a subject or problem, consulting the available sources, and reporting the conclusions. Of these three activities, reporting is the most important because unless the significance and results of the research are clearly stated and communicated to others, all the defining and investigating are worthless.

Of course, your research differs from what some of these people do. That's why the research paper should more accurately be termed a *library* research paper, because your information is derived from books, magazines, journals, newspapers, and similar library materials. Other research papers may be based on interviews or questionnaires, or examinations of human beings, animals, insects, natural objects, chemical substances, or other things animate or inanimate in their natural environment or laboratories. These studies generally involve observing, measuring, experimenting, formulating and testing of hypotheses, and verifying. Library research involves working with primary and secondary sources. The former consists of consulting original documents such as official records, diaries, letters, manuscripts, and fictional and nonfictional works. The latter involves consulting second-hand sources—in other words, reading what others have written about a subject. Since you will be writing this second type of research paper in your composition course, you may wonder what there is for you to do besides string together the information you have gleaned.

THE RESEARCH PAPER

Much depends on whether the research paper is informative or persuasive. In the informative paper, you are a collector and clarifier, amassing facts and opinions from different sources, sifting through and evaluating them, and presenting them clearly and interestingly for your readers. You perform a valuable service by enabling readers to understand all aspects of a subject or issue, information that might be otherwise inaccessible or incomprehensible. For example, people might wonder why public school teachers are paid according to seniority rather than merit. Why aren't superior teachers given higher salaries? Why should more money go to those with longer rather than better service? A reading of the literature on this subject—both pro and con—could result in an interesting, informative paper presenting the arguments on both sides. Or, as many instructors prefer, the research paper could be persuasive: you spell out the reasons for and against payment of teachers according to merit and then advocate a particular position on the issue. But whichever paper you write—informative or persuasive—you take a fresh look at the existing facts and opinions, filtering this information through your mind, and presenting the subject in a new way. Writing a research paper is like furnishing a room: both involve selecting, assembling, arranging, adapting, treating, and presenting items according to your own particular taste. Like the room, your paper is an original creation.

It is also original because it is shaped to the needs and interests of your audience. Your instructor should indicate whether you should write for all the students in class, students majoring in your field of study, or some other group of readers. Whoever your readers are, you will have to consider their needs, interests, and knowledge in order to adapt your paper to them. How much background information will they require? What can they be counted on to know? Which terms must be defined? How much will they want to learn? How thoroughly will you have to document your paper? Your answers to these and similar questions demand you make certain decisions that contribute to the paper's originality.

Actually, the research paper is like many other original papers you have written in your composition course, except for the personal and descriptive ones. Most of your facts and ideas about the subjects of your other papers came from what you had heard or read, not from first-hand knowledge. But, in another respect, the research paper is different. As the very word indicates, you are to search again (re-search) the evidence about a subject, subjecting it to close scrutiny and examining it thoroughly and critically. And the information you present in this paper to support your views cannot be accepted on good faith, but must be documented point by point. In addition, certain formal conventions involving quotations, footnotes, and a bibliography must be followed to the letter.

So the research paper may be frightening, but it need not be if writing it is viewed as a process to be undertaken one step at a time. That is exactly how we suggest you go about it, as the next two chapters will reveal.

Preliminary Steps in Preparing the Research Paper

There is never enough time. At least, not for the research paper. Even though you may have two or three or four weeks, it will vanish in a twinkling unless you cherish every moment. That means you must get started, ignoring the nearby distractions and the comforting thought of the faraway deadline. And it means getting started by setting up a schedule for the ten-step process. Like this sample three-week one:

The Process	*The Schedule* (3 weeks)
Preliminary Steps	
1. Subject Selection	Days: 1–2
2. Preliminary Reading	3–4
3. Preliminary Bibliography	5–6
4. Preliminary Outline	7
Writing	
5. Note-taking	8–11
6. Final Outline	12
7. First Draft	13–16
8. Revision	17–18
9. Final Draft	19–20
10. Proofreading	21

By dividing the work for the research paper into a series of steps and by establishing and meeting a deadline for each, you will write a better paper with less work. And you'll sleep well the night before it is due.

521

Let's go through the process one step at a time. We'll cover the preliminary steps in this chapter and the writing steps in Chapter 33.

STEP 1. SUBJECT SELECTION

Selecting a subject may be a snap for you. Perhaps your instructor will assign one arbitrarily or let you choose from a list. Perhaps you have something on your mind that you would like to explore. For example, at this writing, New York City is on the brink of bankruptcy. We wonder whether any city has ever actually gone bankrupt, and if so, what happened. That might be our subject. But what if no subject is handy?

Subject Search

We suggest that you spend a day or two thinking, reading, listening, questioning, and writing down any interesting possibilities. Think about issues and people in the news or anything associated with them; arguments you've had with friends, relatives, family; historical events or persons you have been curious about; famous people you admire; ideas, movements, opinions, beliefs that have puzzled or concerned you. Glance through newspapers, magazines, books, textbooks with the idea of hitting upon a subject. Listen to what people around you are talking about, to what personalities on radio or television are discussing, to what instructors in your classes are lecturing about. Raise questions in your mind about places you have been or wanted to go to, hobbies you pursue or would like to, careers you are interested in or fascinated by, unusual experiences you have had or heard about. And whenever you have a scintilla of an idea, scribble it down before it slips your mind. If you stay alert to possibilities, brood about finding a subject, sit down and concentrate for periods of time, or discuss the problem with a friend, we think you'll have at least several topics in a day or two.

Subject Suitability

When reviewing these subject possibilities, you should eliminate any that do not lend themselves to library research, such as personal subjects and descriptions of processes or places. The former could not be located in any source; the latter would be easily available in a single source. In addition, most libraries probably would not have sufficient materials for research papers on very recent or local events. What you should keep in mind when considering subjects is the need to select one that will lend itself to various interpretations or different opinions—that is, the need to obtain information from different sources. For example, the operation of the Wankel engine would be an inappropriate subject: the necessary information could be found in one book or article. But the advantages, disadvantages, and future of this engine would require gathering information from various sources and thus would be an appropriate subject for a research paper.

You must be practical, therefore, and select a subject that can probably be researched. But even after you have decided on one, you must answer two questions before making it your final choice: (1) Does the library contain sufficient information about the subject? (2) Does the library contain so much information that the subject should be restricted in scope? To answer these questions, move to Step 2.

STEP 2. PRELIMINARY READING

The purpose of preliminary reading is to obtain an overview of your subject so that you can zero in on it. You may know, for example, that you want to write about the Pearl Harbor disaster in the Second World War, but you may be uncertain whether to tackle the problem of military unpreparedness there or the United States general unreadiness for war. And you also need to learn, as we just mentioned, whether there are too few or too many available sources.

The library has the answers to these questions (and to numerous others, as you can see from the illustration on page 524). We assume you are generally familiar with this building either from a tour of it, which many colleges offer, or from your instructor's description of its facilities. Consequently, we shall limit our remarks about the library to suggestions about using it for your preliminary reading.

Reference Works

Your first goal is to obtain additional knowledge or an overview of your subject. Consequently, you should head for the reference room, where certain standard works are kept: dictionaries, encyclopedias, biographical dictionaries, almanacs, yearbooks, and indexes.

DICTIONARIES

You probably don't think of a regular dictionary as a reference work, but often it is the fastest and most convenient source. If you were considering that paper about the Japanese attack on Pearl Harbor, a dictionary would provide the location and date; for one on Greta Garbo, it would furnish her original surname, date of birth, and occupation; and for one on chastity belts, it might give you an illustration! A dictionary is

How to bathe a boa.

Who we should call Ishmael.
Who won the battle of Culloden.
Who discovered Cleveland.
Who invented schnapps.
Who said, "Cogito ergo sum."
Who that actress was.
Who Gutenburg was.
Who Beau Brummel's tailor was.
Who invented aspirin.
Who has class.
Who Lincoln's first date was.
Who plays for the Who.
Who put Saks on Fifth Ave.
Who has a job for you.
Who plays tackle for Detroit.
Who said, "Don't give up the ship"
Why outhouses have moons.
Who the Jazz Singer was.
Who invented gunpowder.
Who wrote Shakespeare.
Who makes parts for your Stanley.
Who the Zealots were.
Who wrote that TV show.
Who Carl Reiner's first boss was.
Who Peach Melba was named after.
Who stood in the snow at Canossa.
Who invented the calendar.
Who figured out arithmetic.
Who signed the Mayflower Compact.
How to fix your car.
How to build a telescope.
How to bake a cake.
How to make a million.
How to get into college.
How to sew a dress.
How to do your taxes.
How to forge a Rembrandt.
How to beat Bobby Fischer.
How to raise gloxinia.
How to fix a leak.
How to land a man.

How to land a woman.
How to get a raise.
How to understand Faulkner.
How to buy a house.
How to train your dog.
How to get a patent.
How to type a letter.
How to find Borneo.
How to buy stocks.
How to ride a horse.
How to wash your house.
How to write a poem.
How to bathe a boa.
How to get a job.
How to throw a party.
How to run for Congress.
How to cut a diamond.
How to build a tepee.
How to blow glass.
How to predict the weather.
How to cast a horoscope.
How to find God.
Where they keep the Hope Diamond.
Where Bora-Bora is.
Where Murano glass comes from.
Where they teach palmistry.
Where gypsies live.
Where the world came from.
Where "The Night Watch" is.
Where Capt. Cook was going.
Where Haley's Comet goes.
Who Cookie Lavagetto is.
Where they speak Esperanto.
Where St. John went.
Where Astroturf is made.
Where the yellow went.
Where to go on vacation.
Where the world's
 tallest structure is.
Where the sun goes at night.
Where they made "Ben Hur."

Where to get a deal.
Where to find gold.
Where to dig for worms.
Where they speak Swahili.
Where to grow mushrooms.
Where they have dog races.
Where Sonnets from the
 Portuguese were written.
Where to get your Nikon fixed.
Where to get a business loan.
Where to take a date.
Where to have a party.
Where to complain about potholes.
Why E =MC².
Why the sky stays up.
Why Ike won.
Why deserts are dry.
Why bread rises.
Why litmus changes color.
Why England slept.
Why the Mets won in '69.
Why Peter Pan never grew up.
Why Falstaff was a coward.
Why the ocean is blue.
Why the dollar was devalued.
Why the Beatles split up.
Why the Tower of Pisa leans.
Why they eat spaghetti in China.
Why the Dodgers left Brooklyn.
Why the sword was in the stone.
Why Lincoln grew a beard.
Why Chicago is the Windy City.
Why there is smog.
Why it rains.
Why leaves are green.
Why sugar tastes good.
Why John Wayne is called "The Duke."
Why they created West Virginia.
Why outhouses have moons.
Who said, "Don't give up the ship"

Your library has all the answers. Stop in.

American Library Association 1975

far more than a spelling book, pronunciation guide, or synonym source; it is a storehouse of information about a wide range of knowledge: historical, biographical, geographical, mathematical, scientific, medical, and linguistic, to mention a few.

You should own a recent edition of an abridged dictionary (one that contains about 150,000 words in contrast to the huge unabridged dictionaries of about 450,000 words). But make certain you know how your dictionary is arranged. For example, in *Webster's New Collegiate Dictionary,* biographical and geographical names, and foreign words and phrases appear in separate sections at the end; this information is included with the regular entries in other dictionaries. In the *American Heritage Dictionary,* the central meaning of a word is given first; in most other dictionaries, the earliest meaning is first. For example, in the *Webster New World* and the *Webster New Collegiate* (the word *Webster* is not copyrighted and appears on many dictionaries less respected than these), *saloon* is first defined as a large room or hall for receptions, exhibitions, or entertainments—the word's earliest meaning. A later definition indicates that it is a bar—the central meaning today. But in the *American Heritage Dictionary,* the first definition gives this latter meaning. Our purpose in pointing out these differences is not to recomment one dictionary over the others but to alert you to the importance of reading the explanatory notes or guide to whichever dictionary you own.

An unabridged dictionary, such as *Webster's Third New International,* not only contains more words, especially scientific and technical terms, than an abridged dictionary but also provides more information about each word. Another useful dictionary is the *OED (Oxford English Dictionary),* a work developed on historical principles to show when, in what form, and with what meaning a word originally appeared in the language and how it has changed since. This information is particularly helpful in understanding the use of a word at a particular time between 1150 and 1933.

Among other dictionaries in the reference room are specialized ones on slang, quotations, rhymes, clichés, and acronyms.

ENCYCLOPEDIAS

A dictionary will furnish a date, location, and one or two sentences of information. An encyclopedia will enable you to obtain a better grasp of the subject. But you should realize that different encyclopedias are written for different readers. The *World Book,* for example, is generally designed for high school students. Its simple explanations of difficult scientific concepts are particularly helpful. Also useful are its cross references to related subjects, suggested readings, and short descriptions of books about the subject. The *Encyclopedia Americana,* written for college-educated readers, features American subjects and recommends supplementary readings. Especially important is its Index Volume, which lists not only the main subjects presented in the alphabetically arranged articles but minor subjects discussed in these articles, as well as other references to the main subject. The most scholarly and respected general encyclopedia is the *Britannica.* Formerly it was organized alphabetically and, as such, its ninth and eleventh editions are held in particularly high esteem. The latest edition, the fifteenth, is divided into three sections: (1) the *Propedia,* a one-volume subject index and outline of knowledge; (2) the *Micropedia,* a ten-volume set of short articles; and (3) the *Macropedia,* a nineteen-volume set of long, detailed scholarly articles. Thus you can check the *Propedia,* turn to the *Micropedia* for a short article on your topic, and then consult the *Macropedia* for a lengthier examination of it. Although more difficult to use at first, the new *Britannica* can be especially valuable in providing a broad perspective on a subject.

Numerous other general and specialized encyclopedias may be found in the reference room. Among the most valuable are encyclopedias in education, philosophy, social sciences, science and technology, and world art.

BIOGRAPHIES

If your subject is a living person, you might find it most helpful to turn to biographical reference works. *Current Biography,* issued annually and in monthly supplements, provides information about living people, including their addresses and a list of articles and books about them. Another source of information about living people is the *Who's Who* series, which appears in different volumes according to classification, ranging from individual countries (*Who's Who in America, Who's Who in England,* and so on) to sex (*Who's Who of American Women*) to subject area (*Who's Who in Art*). Two other biographical sources that deserve mention are *Contemporary Authors* and *American Men and Women of Science.* The content of these two works, like that of other biographical reference books, differs considerably: the first provides information not only about authors' careers, honors, and works but also about such personal matters as parents, children, religion, political affiliation, and early schooling; entries in the second are brief, consisting mainly of each scientist's place and date of birth, year of marriage, number of children, degrees, positions held, publications, and address.

The most helpful works about people no longer living are the *Dictionary of American Biography* (1958) and the *Dictionary of National Biography* (British, 1950). Naturally, both these works are limited to individuals who died prior to the publication dates of the main volumes and supplements.

ALMANACS

For statistical information, chronological listings, major developments in science and technology, and summaries of political events, almanacs are useful. Facts abound about athletics, climate, economics, employment, farm prices, famous people, foreign countries, and innumerable other subjects in these handy paperback volumes with their tissue-thin pages jammed mainly with figures, charts, tables, and lists. Two of the most helpful, the *World Almanac* and the *Information Please Almanac,* are published annually. The former probably contains more data; the latter more interesting articles, particularly because of its review of the year's events. To some extent, the *Information Please Almanac* is more like the annual supplements published by the encyclopedias mentioned previously, and the informative digest *Facts on File.*

Our purpose in discussing these reference works has been to suggest how you can obtain a general knowledge of your subject. But we do not want to imply that these books should be used only for that purpose. Often in working on minor points in your paper, you can locate significant information quickly by consulting dictionaries, encyclopedias, biographical sources, almanacs, and yearbooks. And of course, all of these works need not be examined in your preliminary reading; perhaps only one or a few will give you a sufficient overview of your subject.

Now you may be able to decide whether the subject should be restricted in scope. Let's suppose that you've been curious about Galileo, who you have been told was the creator of the modern scientific method. After looking at the material about him in several reference books, you may realize that this subject is too broad and that you had better limit it to his work with the telescope.

But we would not deceive you. A general reading may not be helpful except to arm you with more confidence about the subject because you now know more about it than you did before. And so, whether you have decided to limit your topic or not, you should next check on the adequacy of the library's information about it.

You have a choice: the card catalog or the indexes. If your subject is likely to be treated in a book, which usually takes at least a year to write and publish, then start with the card catalog. If your subject has been in the news more recently, consult the indexes (*New York Times Index:* one-month lag; *Reader's Guide:* three to six months). Of course, you may end up examining both the card catalog and the indexes.

The Card Catalog

No doubt you already know something about the card catalog from your public library or from your high school days. But since your college

Cards 1–4 Subject, title, and author cards.

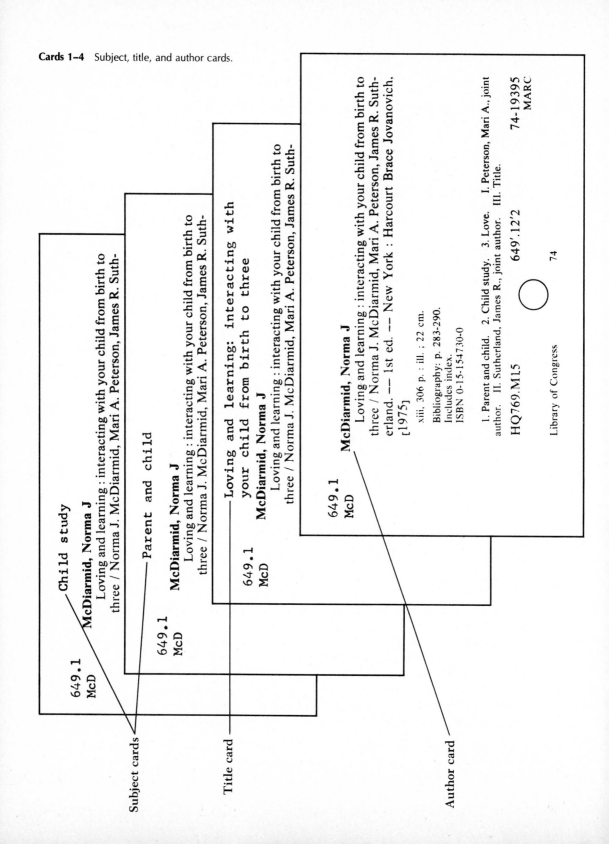

Subject cards

Child study

McDiarmid, Norma J
    Loving and learning : interacting with your child from birth to three / Norma J. McDiarmid, Mari A. Peterson, James R. Suth-

649.1
McD

Parent and child

McDiarmid, Norma J
    Loving and learning : interacting with your child from birth to three / Norma J. McDiarmid, Mari A. Peterson, James R. Suth-

649.1
McD

Title card

Loving and learning: interacting with
    your child from birth to three
McDiarmid, Norma J
    Loving and learning : interacting with your child from birth to three / Norma J. McDiarmid, Mari A. Peterson, James R. Suth-

649.1
McD

Author card

McDiarmid, Norma J
    Loving and learning : interacting with your child from birth to three / Norma J. McDiarmid, Mari A. Peterson, James R. Suth-erland. — 1st ed. — New York : Harcourt Brace Jovanovich. [1975]
    xiii, 306 p. : ill. : 22 cm.
    Bibliography: p. 283-290.
    Includes index.
    ISBN 0-15-154730-0

    1. Parent and child.   2. Child study.   3. Love.   I. Peterson, Mari A., joint author.   II. Sutherland, James R., joint author.   III. Title.

HQ769.M15   649'.12'2   74-19395
                                                              MARC

Library of Congress   74

649.1
McD

library probably contains many more cards, you can save time and un-earth information more easily by learning more details about how to proceed.

You should first find out whether your college library has one card catalog or two: one with all cards listed alphabetically; or two, one for author and title cards, the other for subject cards. If all the cards are in one place, relax. But if they are divided (which does make life easier once you've learned the system), then you must decide where to turn first. For a paper on the geodesic dome, you would consult the subject catalog; for a book by its inventor, Buckminster Fuller, you would look in the author-title catalog. The only trick is to realize that if you wish a book *about* Buckminster Fuller—not by him—then you must turn to the subject catalog. If you do not discover a card there about your subject, do not panic. Instead, consult the huge index volume—*Subject Headings Used in the Dictionary Catalogs of the Library of Congress*—to determine the heading used for your topic. For example, if you were seeking books about writing, you would not find them under that heading. By looking in the index, you would learn that these books appear under the heading "Authorship."

Realize that you might find the same card in both subject and author-title catalogs because at least two and often three or more cards are made for each book (see cards 1–4). These cards not only inform you whether the book is shelved in the library but also provide numerous helpful hints once you understand and interpret the notations on the card (see card 5). What information does this card provide? Let's list some points that may not be obvious.

1. The author is still living (birth date but no death date if card is ac-curate). Biographical information about him should be available in current indexes.
2. The number of pages (303—see "Descriptive information") suggests that this book treats the subject in some detail.
3. The date of publication indicates that the work should be based on recent materials.
4. The inclusion of a five-page bibliography points to some scholarly treatment. This list of source materials could be helpful in your own further research.
5. The Arabic numbers in the "Tracings" refer to information about the main focus of the book (college attendance and school sites), the scope of the treatment (United States colleges only), headings in the sub-ject catalog under which additional material can be found (college attendance, school sites, junior colleges), and, in some instances, the reading level (not pertinent here). The Roman numerals refer to ad-

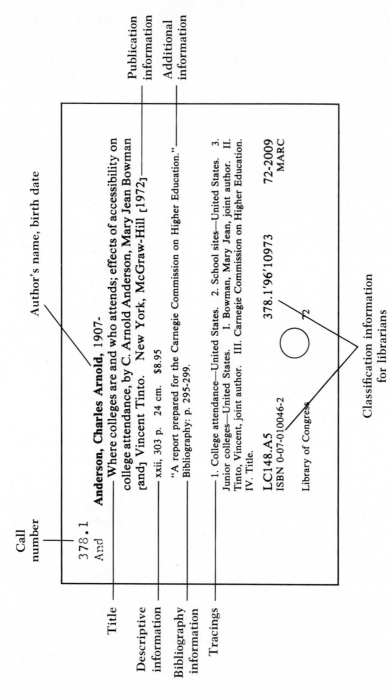

Card 5 Catalog card notations.

ditional catalog cards for the same work (joint author cards, title card).

When used thoughtfully, the catalog card can be more helpful than you might have realized. It can save you time and effort by eliminating certain sources from consideration. And it can suggest certain other sources. It's all in the cards.

Indexes

Indexes do for newspapers and periodicals what the card catalog does for books. A novice researcher can use the catalog; you must be a veteran to know your way around the indexes.

It's mainly a question of what you want to know and in what type of publication it may be found. If your subject has probably been treated in a widely read magazine, the most helpful index is likely to be the *Reader's Guide to Periodical Literature,* which catalogs 160 publications, such as the *Atlantic Monthly, Time, U. S. News, Redbook, Ladies Home Journal,* and *Sports Illustrated.* The entries in this invaluable work may seem baffling at first, but a thoughtful study of several of them for a few minutes and a reading of the introductory guide in the front of the book should clarify any problems. Here's how one entry on modern art looks:

The painted word: what you see is what they say. T. Wolfe. il Harper 250:57– 92 Ap '75

The entry begins with the title and the author's name. The rest of the information indicates that the article is illustrated and appeared in the April 1975 issue of *Harper's* magazine, volume 250, pages 57–92. It's simple when you know how!

The *Reader's Guide* began publication in 1900; for information in nineteenth-century periodicals, see *Poole's Index to Periodical Literature.* And for more specialized articles in scholarly journals, consult the appropriate subject index, several of which are listed below:

Applied Science and Technology Index: A subject index to about 225 periodicals in aeronautics and space science, chemistry, electricity and electronics, engineering, mathematics, physics, and related fields.

Art Index: An author-subject index to about 150 periodicals and museums' bulletins about archaeology, architecture, art history, arts and crafts, fine arts, graphic arts, industrial design, interior decoration, photography and films, planning and landscape design, and related subjects.

Biological and Agricultural Index: A cumulative subject index to about 150 periodicals in agricultural chemicals, economics, and engineering;

animal husbandry; bacteriology; biology; botany; ecology; forestry; conservation; and related fields.

Business Periodicals Index: A cumulative subject index to about 170 periodicals in accounting, advertising, banking, economics, finance, management, taxation, and related fields.

Education Index: An author-subject index to about 240 educational periodicals and other materials. Indexed according to professional areas (administration, pre-school, elementary, exceptional children, and so on) and academic fields (arts, applied science and technology, business, and so on).

Social Sciences Index: An author-subject index to 263 periodicals in anthropology, archaeology, economics, environmental science, geography, law and criminology, political science, psychology, religion, sociology, and related fields. Formerly, the *Social Sciences and Humanities Index.*

These and indexes like them in other fields are designed mainly for specialists, but you may find some articles valuable and illuminating.

Another helpful reference tool is the newspaper index, the most widely available, up-to-date, and useful being the *New York Times Index.* Published twice a month and also in a cumulative volume once a year, the index not only refers to news articles, speeches, editorials, essays, and reviews in the *Times,* but also often summarizes their contents. The index entries will look mystifying at first, but the introductory guide should help to unravel them. For example, the citation "D 27, 8:2" simply means "December 27, page 8, column 2." Also, once you find out the date of an event from the *Times Index,* you can use it to consult other newspapers or newsmagazines for their treatment of the story. But realize that the *Times* is not just an excellent newspaper that covers national and international events fully. It is a valuable document of the day and age with its interesting, comprehensive obituaries; complete texts of speeches and important statements; reviews of books, films, concerts, plays; and its own fine magazine published with the Sunday edition.

We should also mention some specialized indexes:

The Book Review Digest: presents a list of selected book reviews and excerpts from a few of them. Also, states lengths of reviews.

The Book Review Index: no excerpts but a more complete list of reviews.

Essay and General Literature Index: subjects treated in essays, chapters, or sections of books. Particularly valuable in the humanities and social sciences.

Biography Index: indexes biographical information appearing in over 1,000 magazines, books, and newspapers.

Consumer's Index: lists of articles from 100 periodicals about the financial or physical well-being of consumers.

Abstracts

Similar to the index but often even more helpful is a reference tool you may know little about — the abstract journal. Published mainly for scholars who do not have adequate time to read all the articles in their field, the abstract journals provide summaries of articles. Among the ones you might find useful are the following:

Abstracts of English Studies: summaries mainly about literature from articles in American and English periodicals.

America: History and Life: A Guide to Periodical Literature: summaries of articles on the history of the United States and Canada.

Historical Abstracts: summaries of articles on political, diplomatic, economic, social, cultural, and intellectual history.

Sociological Abstracts: summaries of national and international books and articles.

Psychological Abstracts: summaries of national and international articles, books, reports, and dissertations.

Pamphlets and Government Publications

Finally, let's mention two other sources of materials: pamphlets and government publications. Because these are often handled differently in various libraries, your reference librarian will help you locate information in these sources. Incidentally, if you are ever stumped about finding anything, consult the librarian. This person is professionally trained to help students and scholars use the library and usually enjoys working on research problems.

And now where are you? With these suggestions about how to obtain a general knowledge of your subject and how to find what information the library has about it, you should be able to zero in on your subject, knowing that sufficient material is available to write a research paper on it. In an afternoon or two, you should be able to check the encyclopedia, find and flip through some books and articles, and decide where you're going. In glancing through books, check the table of contents, preface, and introductory and concluding chapters. For articles, start with the most recent long ones and read the opening and closing paragraphs.

To begin, suppose you're interested in Mary Wollstonecraft, among the first feminists. A library check reveals that several books and numerous articles have been written about her. Obviously, you cannot treat her entire life adequately in a research paper. As you poke through some of the sources, however, questions begin to formulate in your mind. Did this woman who argued and fought so publicly and persuasively for women's rights practice what she preached? What about her sexual liaison with the American Gilbert Imlay? And her pregnancy by the political philosopher William Godwin, who despite his public pronouncements against matrimony did become her husband? Why her two suicide attempts? You might not want to probe into all of these but, instead, confine your paper to the fascinating relationship between Wollstonecraft and Godwin.

Once you have limited your subject and discovered what information the library has about it, you are ready to step ahead.

STEP 3. THE PRELIMINARY BIBLIOGRAPHY

The word *bibliography* sounds impressive, but it refers simply to a list of sources about a subject. You might have proceeded to compile one in your preliminary reading if you had definitely selected a subject. But assuming that you have only hit upon a topic after some general reading, you are now ready to work on your preliminary bibliography.

We refer to it as a "preliminary" bibliography to distinguish it from the final bibliography that usually appears at the end of research papers. The preliminary one helps you to pinpoint sources that might prove valuable. Because the final bibliography must be typed in alphabetical order, we recommend you do your preliminary work on 3″ by 5″ cards or similar slips of paper that you can rearrange easily as you discover additional sources from time to time. Frankly, for your relatively short freshman English paper, you could get by with notebook paper; but by working with the cards or slips, you will be learning the most efficient method for writing lengthier papers in your later advanced classes.

Your mission in this step is to track down sources that will best serve the purpose of your paper. Before, you mainly wanted to know whether sufficient material about your subject was available. Now you want to select the most informative books, articles, or other publications about it. Remember to discriminate by thoughtfully studying the catalog cards, as we discussed previously. In looking at possible magazine articles, note the title, date, and number of pages, as well as the name of the publication. Exercise some judgment. For example, a seven-page article about teaching chimpanzees to use language in *Scientific American* would undoubtedly be more informative than a four-page condensation in *Reader's Digest* or a one-page account in *Newsweek*.

Also, learn to snoop around a bit, play detective. Investigate related topics, say the family and friends of your subject, or topics related to yours. For a paper on the Presidency of Hiram Ulysses Grant, who came to be known as Ulysses S., scan the biography of his wife. For one on "General Patton—Hero or Heel?" look through autobiographies or biographies of his colleagues—Eisenhower, Bradley, Clark, MacArthur, and Montgomery. For a paper on state-operated lotteries, check into such related topics as the Irish Sweepstakes, state-run off-track betting, English soccer pools, and lotteries in European countries. A glance at the index of a book on a related subject might unearth a treasure of information.

Whenever you find a promising source, jot it down, one to a card. Most handbooks and rhetoric textbooks advise you to transcribe the bibliographical notation according to the highly complicated form prescribed for the final bibliography. We think that until you are more familiar with bibliographical style, you may take down the information in any form you wish, but you must note all of the following:

Book	*Article*
Name of author, editor	Name of author
Title	Title
Subtitle	Name of publication
Edition (if more	Volume of professional or
than one has been published)	scholarly publication
Place of publication (first city	Date
only, if several are given)	Page numbers
Publisher	
Date	

This information is generally available from the catalog card if the publication is a book, or the index entry if it is a periodical.

Three helpful hints about your preliminary bibliography:

1. Write the author's last name first to help you in alphabetizing later.
2. Copy down the call number and, if it might be a problem later, the location of the work. You may have to check something in it at the last moment—like the spelling of a name or the exact words of a quotation.
3. Write a comment or two about the material either from the information on the catalog card or from your glancing through it. This note may help later after you have examined many sources and wondered about some you looked at a week or two earlier.

The preliminary bibliography will probably keep growing as you keep reading. One reference source may refer you to another or mention a related subject to investigate. Some may prove to be dead ends, seemingly worthless. But jot down your evaluations and file the cards because you may see new possibilities in these references later.

You may wonder at this point whether you could have combined the previous step—the subject selection—with the compilation of the preliminary bibliography. You might have if you were sure of your subject and confident that materials about it were available. But our experience indicates that most students select subjects that are so broad they must be trimmed and trimmed again. It might be wasteful to work up a preliminary bibliography before checking the library and doing some reading.

And now, armed with your subject and a stack of bibliography cards, you are almost ready to enter the writing stage. But first, to give direction to your reading and note-taking, we recommend a preliminary outline.

STEP 4. THE PRELIMINARY OUTLINE

As its name indicates, the preliminary outline is a tentative plan for your paper, a general roadmap showing where you are going and how you think you will get there. As you proceed, you may want to alter your trip: detouring here, staying longer there, skipping some places entirely. For example, if the film *The Day of the Locust* intrigued you, you might read the novel and decide to write a research paper on what critics have thought of the novel over the years. A preliminary outline might look like this:

   I. Publication reviews, 1939.
  II. Critical attitudes: post-publication to pre-movie, 1940–74.
 III. Critical re-evaluation, 1975–76.

But later, observing some change in the critical reaction toward Nathanael West after the Second World War, you might divide point II in two, prewar and postwar, thus getting four sections.

Your preliminary outline is not a binding contract: it can be changed and changed again. But it does help in structuring and focusing your reading. In the West example, you would start with the initial 1939 reviews instead of reading anything you could get your hands on. Or, in a paper not organized chronologically, you would not read earlier materials before later ones but would concentrate on one aspect of the subject at a time. A paper on the economic woes of institutions of higher education might be originally conceived in three parts—junior and community colleges, private colleges and universities, and public colleges and universities. A restriction of the subject because of its length could result in a tentative outline that included only private colleges and universities:

   I. Church-affiliated institutions
  II. Private black institutions
 III. Independent institutions
      A. Major universities
      B. Other universities
      C. Liberal arts colleges

You might begin by selecting all your bibliography cards about church-affiliated schools and reading those sources; then you would do the same for black colleges; and so on down the line.

A tentative outline also helps in note-taking. That subject and others relating to the actual writing of the research paper will be discussed in the next chapter.

ASSIGNMENTS

For Discussion and Library Research

1 How appropriate would the following subjects or titles be for a research paper?

The Recent Pension Law	The Future of Detroit's Auto Industry
Cheating at Your College	The Impact of TV Violence on Children
Women's Athletics	How No-Fault Insurance Works
Child Abuse	Movies Are Sexier Than Ever
Life Today Is Better	Affirmative Action in Your Community

2 How many of the following would you expect to find in an abridged dictionary?

Months of the three principal calendars (Gregorian, Hebrew, Moslem)
Diagram of beef cuts
Table of alphabets (Hebrew, Arabic, Greek, Russian)
Currency of foreign countries
Geologic time scale
Diagram of car ignition
Manual alphabet for deaf-mutes
Proofreader's marks
Map of the United States
Books of the Old and New Testaments
Periodic table of chemical elements
Metric system
Morse Code
Ship's bells
Zodiac signs
Radio frequencies
List of U.S. colleges and universities
Punctuation guide
Tables of weights and measures
List of capital cities of the United States

3 What information is missing from the catalog cards on pages 538–39? What hints can you glean from information on the cards?

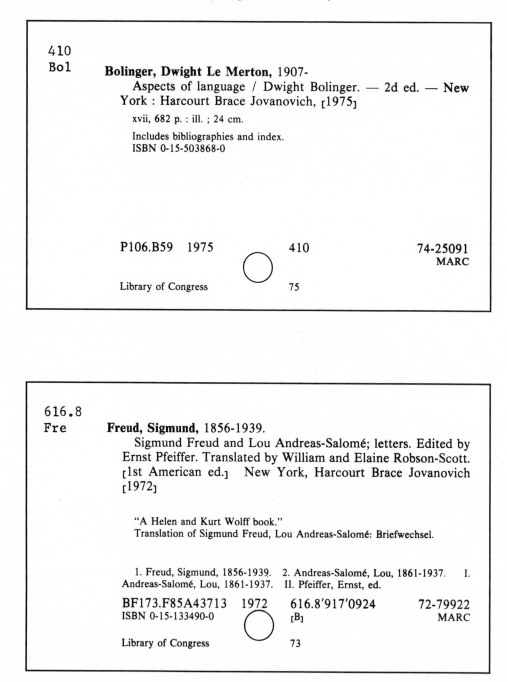

410
Bol

Bolinger, Dwight Le Merton, 1907-
    Aspects of language / Dwight Bolinger. — 2d ed. — New
York : Harcourt Brace Jovanovich, [1975]
      xvii, 682 p. : ill. ; 24 cm.

      Includes bibliographies and index.
      ISBN 0-15-503868-0

P106.B59   1975   410   74-25091
                                              MARC

Library of Congress   75

616.8
Fre

Freud, Sigmund, 1856-1939.
    Sigmund Freud and Lou Andreas-Salomé; letters. Edited by
Ernst Pfeiffer. Translated by William and Elaine Robson-Scott.
[1st American ed.] New York, Harcourt Brace Jovanovich
[1972]

      "A Helen and Kurt Wolff book."
      Translation of Sigmund Freud, Lou Andreas-Salomé: Briefwechsel.

      1. Freud, Sigmund, 1856-1939. 2. Andreas-Salomé, Lou, 1861-1937.   I.
    Andreas-Salomé, Lou, 1861-1937. II. Pfeiffer, Ernst, ed.

BF173.F85A43713   1972   616.8'917'0924   72-79922
ISBN 0-15-133490-0   [B]   MARC

Library of Congress   73

340.07
Pac **Packer, Herbert L**
New directions in legal education, by Herbert L. Packer and
Thomas Ehrlich, with the assistance of Stephen Pepper. A report
prepared for the Carnegie Commission on Higher Education.

xviii, 384 p. 24 cm. $10.00
Bibliography: p. 87-91.

1. Law—Study and teaching—United States. I. Ehrlich, Thomas, 1934-
joint author. II. Carnegie Commission on Higher Education. III. Title.

KF272.P3 340'.07'1173 72-5311
MARC

Library of Congress 72

Rutherford, William E
Modern English / William E. Rutherford. — 2d ed. — New
York : Harcourt Brace Jovanovich, c1975-

v. : ill. ; 24 cm.

Includes index.
ISBN 0-15-561059-7

1. English language—Text-books for foreigners. I. Title.

[PE1128.R83 1975] 428'.2'4 75-10765
MARC

Library of Congress 75

4 Name some possible reference sources for material about the following subjects. Your instructor may also wish you to determine whether your library contains sufficient information for a research paper about one of them.

Mass transit	The kidnapping of Patricia Hearst
Day-care centers	The plight of Soviet Jews
Women priests	The Turkish invasion of Cyprus
Attica prison riot	Confidentiality of student records in public schools
Kidney transplants	Normalcy of homosexuals
Rosenberg case	Campaign finance reform
World famine	New political alignments in the United States
Polygamy today	Coed college dormitories
Gambling	Fair trade laws
Hypnosis	The zeppelin

5 In what specialized indexes might you find information about the following? Your instructor may also wish you to determine whether your library contains sufficient material for a paper about them.

Dutch elm disease	Student recruiting in college
Acne remedies	Design and construction of school buildings
Video records	CATV (Community Antenna Television)
Psychiatric nursing	Effect of sexual activity on academic performance
Television advertising	Collective bargaining for public employees
Tax shelters	Military applications of lasers
Solar batteries	Giacometti exhibits
Educational games	Attitudes of college students
Cold remedies	Feeding of sheep

6 Suppose the following people are coming this year to speak to groups on your campus. As a student working in the public relations office, you have been asked to prepare biographical sketches on each. What sources would you consult? Your instructor may require you to write a biographical sketch on one of these people.

William Buckley	Sammy Davis, Jr.	Kris Kristofferson
Warren Burger	Valéry Giscard d'Estaing	Gunnar Myrdal
Anthony Burgess	Jane Fonda	Nolan Ryan
Cesar Chavez	Art Garfunkel	John J. Sirica
Norman Cousins	Barbara Jordan	Pierre Trudeau
Walter Cronkite	Henry Kissinger	Kurt Vonnegut, Jr.

For Writing and Library Research

1   Evaluate the entries about the following people in two encyclopedias and two biographical reference works. According to your
instructor's preference, prepare an oral report for the class or write
a short paper.

Hank Aaron	Jomo Kenyatta
Ethan Allen	Leadbelly
Wernher von Braun	Norman Mailer
Amelia Earhart	Sir Thomas More
Albert Einstein	Florence Nightingale
F. Scott Fitzgerald	Marquis de Sade
Hermann Hesse	Adlai Stevenson

2   Evaluate the encyclopedias in your library on the basis of their information about one of the following subjects. According to your instructor's preference, prepare an oral report for the class or write a
short paper.

Sacco–Vanzetti trial	Zen
Adolph Hitler	Martin Luther King, Jr.
Madame Curie	Korean War
Zelda Fitzgerald	Nuremberg war crimes trials
Dinosaur	Nuclear submarines

3   Evaluate encyclopedias, yearbooks, almanacs, and *Facts on File* on
the basis of the information each provides about one of the following
during the past year. According to your instructor's preference, prepare an oral report for the class or write a short paper.

Major political events	Information about literature
Deaths of important people	Significant athletic events
Scientific advances	Economic news

4   Write a short paper based on the most recent almanac information
about one of the following:

Baseball attendance figures
Crime rates in metropolitan areas
Contributions to the United Nations
Degrees awarded women
Magazine circulations
Public school cost per pupil by state

Writing
the Research
Paper

Most students writing a research paper at a typical high school suffer through the ordeal of copying lengthy passages from books and magazines, and then frantically trying to gather the passages and their own thoughts together in an all-night typing orgy. A nightmare of an experience.

Sound familiar? If so, if your high school experience was like this, you may be wondering, what was wrong with it? First, innocently or not so innocently, you probably plagiarized. Second, you were disorganized, having to scramble through pages and pages of notes looking again and again for information that you knew was there but could never find when you wanted it. Third, you probably turned in a mish-mash of statements, indirect quotations, direct quotations, and plagiarized passages, few of them integrated with connecting transitions, all designed to fulfill the assignment and satisfy the teacher, but not written to interest readers or to clarify the subject for them.

If your high school experience was different, fine: you are better prepared than most of your classmates to tackle the research paper. But even so, you can benefit from a review of the techniques that numerous scholars have developed to save time and to improve papers. The writing of a well-organized, worthwhile research paper begins with note-taking.

STEP 5. NOTE-TAKING

As your notes go, so goes your paper. If you learn to take notes carefully and thoughtfully, you should have little trouble writing a fine paper. But skillful note-taking requires an efficient system and disciplined habits.

The Mechanics of Note-Taking

Efficient note-taking involves setting up an information retrieval system that enables you to find a particular note easily. To accomplish this, we recommend using 4″ x 6″ cards (to avoid confusion with the 3″ x 5″ bibliography cards) or slips of paper; we urge you not to use notebook pages. Because the note-taking process requires that a single note contains information from only one source about only one aspect of the subject, many of your notes will consist of one or two sentences. Using a sheet of notebook paper for each brief note is impractical and cumbersome.

The note-taking process may seem wasteful, but in practice it may save hours. As an example, for a paper about the Babe Ruth legend, you might read about his funeral, one of the largest ever held in New York City. After writing this information on a note card, you would check your preliminary outline to see where it would best fit and then identify the entry with a "slug," a shortened subdivision heading from your outline. For the Ruth example, your slug might be "Folk Hero—Death." Later, when you have read all the source materials, you would shuffle through the cards, deal them into stacks according to their slugs, arrange the stacks in the order of the outline, and begin your paper. When you reach each section, such as "Folk Hero—Death," all your notes are readily available to you. As you can see, the beauty of this system is that it requires you to organize your notes and prepare for writing as you read. Nor do you have to endure the frustration of hunting through notebook pages for information, a chore that becomes harder as your papers grow longer.

In addition to the slug and the note, each card must contain some indication of the source. Usually the last name of the author and page number is sufficient (as on the sample note card below) because complete information is already available on the bibliography card. But if you are using sources by two authors with the same last name or if one author has written two sources cited in the paper, then add a first name or a short title to avoid confusion. Or use any other system you find helpful and accurate; the notes are for your use only.

In summary, each note card should contain three entries: a subject

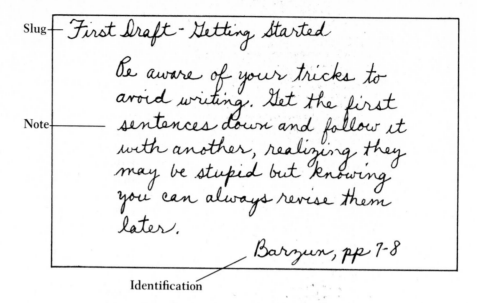

Slug

Note

Identification

heading, a note, and an identification of its source. So much for the mechanics of the system; now for the techniques of note-taking.

The Art of Note-Taking

At the beginning of the chapter we mentioned plagiarism. We do not want to lecture you about it or to write a lengthy, legalistic definition. Simply stated, plagiarism involves using someone else's words or ideas without acknowledging the debt. Actually, plagiarism is stealing— improperly taking someone else's property, someone else's written work. This problem is especially likely to develop in a research paper, because in it you rely on informative work that others have written. Consequently, you may think, everything in your paper is plagiarized in a sense. Not so. You are entitled as a researcher to include common knowledge without documentation (citation of its source). If certain information is generally known, as is evident by the fact that it appears in several sources or in an encyclopedia, then you need not document it unless you use the author's exact words. For example, numerous anthropology sources relate that the bones of prehistoric Peking Man were discovered in a quarry outside the Chinese capital in 1926, and in 1941 were sent to a U.S. Marine base near Chingwangtao, where they were stolen or lost when the Japanese invaded during the Second World War. This information is common knowledge and need not be documented. But opinions about the significance of Peking Man should be. As you can realize, this principle of common knowledge means that you will have to exercise your judgment. As a guide, when in doubt, document anything that might be controversial or questionable, such as a statement that Peking Man is unimportant in view of anthropologist Mary Leakey's recent findings in Kenya of fossils about 3.5 million years old. But if the information is not startling, dubious, or provocative and appears to be reasonably well known, it is yours to use freely.

Be careful, though—you may use this information but not the exact words. That is where the difficulty arises. As you sit taking notes from books or magazines, you become so seduced by the impressive appearance of the printed words that you convince yourself there is no other way of stating the idea. And before you realize fully what you are doing, you may copy the author's words onto your note cards without using quotation marks. A week or so later you may copy the words from your note cards onto your paper without citing your source. The result: plagiarism.

The main solution to the problem is not to rely so much on direct quotations, because few people are willing to read a paper cluttered with quotations from your sources; they are more interested in *your* statements about the subject. What you should do is avoid taking word-for-word notes and rely instead on writing summaries in your own words. But remember that the summaries should be documented unless the information is common knowledge.

Writing a Summary in Note-Taking

Learning to write summaries in taking notes is difficult but rewarding: difficult because you must convey the author's ideas not only in your own words but in fewer words; rewarding because this task requires you to learn and understand what is stated in order to rephrase it. Once you have struggled to reduce several sentences or paragraphs, you will have mastered the author's idea and will retain it in your mind.

The trick in writing a summary is to exclude all examples, secondary comments, unrelated references, and superfluous words, and to concentrate on the topic idea. We suggest you read the passage several times, look away from it, and write out the main thought in your own words. Then check and revise your summary against the original. Here's an example of a summary note:

Original Quotation
Research has shown that it is all but impossible to develop mental fatigue by studying, even by studying hard. We get "tired" readily enough but this happens because we are bored with the subject, not because bodily wastes accumulate in the brain, or even in the muscles. You may push away a textbook with the comment, "I'm exhausted! I can't read another word," then

casually pick up a magazine or newspaper and read avidly, without any signs of fatigue, for an hour or so. Obviously, we have confused *fatigue* with *boredom*.

—Walter Pauk, *How to Study in College*

Summary Note

According to research, it is almost impossible to become mentally fatigued by studying hard. People think they get tired, but actually they become bored.

Although the first sentence in the summary is close to a paraphrase, or rewording, the entire passage is not. We mention this point because students often believe that note-taking consists of changing words and sentence structures, as is often done in paraphrasing a poem. A paraphrase of the last sentence in the original, for example, might look like this:

It is apparent that we have mistaken *ennui* for *exhaustion*.

Paraphrase accomplishes little in note-taking: the author's original is probably stylistically better, so why not quote it? And the paraphrase requires nearly as many words as the original, and sometimes more, so what is its advantage? And isn't it possible to paraphrase and yet not truly understand the original?

Of course, a summary demands more work. You must read and reread the passage, select the key idea, write out a few sentences, and perhaps even revise them, knowing that you may have to rework them later to fit smoothly into your paper. But remember to check your summary against the original for accurate expression of the idea. And be certain to document your source because even though the words may be yours, the ideas are not.

Here is another example of a summary to show you how a lengthy passage can be reduced, primarily by focusing on the topic sentences (which we have italicized):

Original Quotation

Two things were outstanding in the creation of the English system of canals, and they characterise all the Industrial Revolution. *One is that the men who made the revolution were practical men.* Like Brindley, they often had little education, and in fact, school education as it was then could only dull an inventive mind. The grammar schools could only teach the classical subjects for which they were founded. The universities also (there were only two, at Oxford and Cambridge) took little interest in modern or scientific studies; and they were closed to those who did not conform to the Church of England.

The other outstanding feature is that the new inventions were for every-day use. The canals were arteries of communication: they were not made to carry pleasure boats, but barges. And the barges were not made to carry luxuries, but pots and pans and bales of cloth, boxes of ribbon, and all the common things that people buy by the penny-worth. These things had been manufactured in villages which were growing into towns now, away from London; it was a country-wide trade.

—Jacob Bronowski, Ascent of Man

Summary Note

Two unique qualities characterize the English canal system and all the Industrial Revolution: the inventors were practical people often with little formal education, and their inventions were designed to serve practical, everyday needs.

You could have worded this summary differently, of course; nothing is sacred about our version. But the point and the beauty of a summary note is that it forces you to read carefully and thoughtfully, requires that you write about the information while it is fresh in your mind, and results in your having written a statement that can be easily integrated into your paper later without your having to rewrite it then. But remember—even though the words are yours, the idea belongs to another. Consequently, you must indicate the debt by citing your source.

Should you ever copy a passage down word for word? Yes, in special instances when the wording is particularly striking, memorable, or characteristic of the author's style. It would be a shame, for example, to summarize Sir Kenneth Clark's stirring declaration of belief:

I believe that order is better than chaos, creation better than destruction. I prefer gentleness to violence, forgiveness to vendetta. On the whole I think that knowledge is preferable to ignorance, and I am sure that human sympathy is more valuable than ideology. I believe that in spite of the recent triumphs of science, men haven't changed much in the last two thousand years; and in consequence we must still try to learn from history. History is ourselves. I also hold one or two beliefs that are difficult to put shortly. For example, I believe in courtesy, the ritual by which we avoid hurting other people's feelings by satisfying our own egos. And I think we should remember that we are part of a great whole, which for convenience we call nature. All living things are our brothers and sisters. Above all, I believe in the God-given genius of certain individuals, and I value a society that makes their existence possible.

—Civilisation [sic]

When such a lengthy quotation (about fifty words or more) is included, it should be set off in block style—that is, indented slightly from the left-hand margin, and single spaced. This typographical treatment is sufficient to signal that the material is quoted; no quotation marks should be used, as the Clark example illustrates.

It might be helpful in this connection to remind you that when quotation marks are used with selections under fifty words, these marks should *always* be placed *after* commas and periods, but may come before or after other punctuation marks depending upon their function (see pages 109–10).

But our general advice, as mentioned previously, is to avoid numerous quotations, especially lengthy ones. Just as you often skip over long quoted passages in your own reading (and may have done just that with our example), so you should be cautious about including them. The crucial time to decide not to use them is in note-taking. Later, when writing, you may not have the strength and time to resist inserting quotations to pad your research paper.

STEP 6. WRITING THE FIRST DRAFT

Writing the first draft of a research paper is similar to writing any other first draft, except it is even tougher to get started. That's because you know the task ahead is harder, so the temptation is greater to postpone it in order to acquire more information—or to wait for inspiration. But start you must. Once you settle down to it, you are likely to be so full of the subject and so well organized that the writing will be easier than you thought. But the opening sentences are always excruciating! Just plod ahead, realizing that if you do not like them, you can redo them later.

Depending on your own inclination and the length of your paper, you might either write the first draft at one sitting or space the work over several days, perhaps allowing, for example, an evening for each one of your three main divisions. Some writers complete their first draft of one part of the paper before they even do research on others. For example, in a paper on the bombing of Hiroshima, the section about the military situation in the summer of 1945 might be written before doing the research about the decision to drop the atomic bomb and the opposition to it by prominent scientists. Or, in a paper on sources of energy, divided into sections on hydroelectric power, solar energy, geothermal energy, nuclear fusion, nuclear fission, oil, natural gas, and coal, it might be best to write about one of these at a time. If you can block out your paper in this way, you might find it easier to research and write each section of the paper individually. Usually, however, people postpone the writing as long as they can, either because the topic does not lend itself to such neat division or because they want to delay the moment of truth. We recommend that you write as much as you can, as early as you can. You can always revise later.

Quotations: Two Techniques

We realize that you may not heed our previous advice about summarizing long quotations in your note-taking, and we understand. Often the author's exact words are irresistible. But suppose you are confronted with note cards containing such quotations and you do not want to include the entire quotation in your paper. Let us show you two techniques for handling them in the first draft: assimilation and reduction.

ASSIMILATION

The process of assimilation consists of using summary along with key words and phrases from the original quotations. You present the idea in your own style, but weave in a few short phrases from the original because of their unusual force and flavor. In the following illustration, note how much more appealing the assimilated version is than the original.

Original Quotation

When the oriental mystery cults took root in Greece, one of the hallmarks of that era was the turning away from objective knowledge and the rejection of the rational, twin tendencies apparent in this country at least since 1948, when ouija boards first outsold Monopoly games by a substantial margin. Wrenched apart by profound changes in attitudes and custom, Greek civilization with all its complex ambivalence provided fertile ground for the mystery cults, and the parallels between that ambivalence and our own present us with an ominous message from the past: Faith in the occult flourishes in societies that are crumbling, endangered, or in the throes of radical change.
— Marjorie Clay, "The New Religious Cults and Rational Science," *The Humanist*

Assimilated Version:

Like the ancient Greeks, according to philosopher Marjorie Clay, we are turning away from objective knowledge and rationalism. Just as their "complex ambivalence provided fertile ground for the mystery cults," so, she claims, have our similar attitudes made us ripe for belief in the occult. Such a faith "flourishes in societies that are crumbling, endangered, or in the throes of radical change."

REDUCTION

Another useful technique for dealing with quotations involves using ellipsis to reduce them. This punctuation device allows you to substitute three dots (...) to inform readers that words have been omitted. When the omitted words appear at the end of a sentence, the three dots follow the customary period. Here's how a quotation might be reduced by using ellipsis:

Original Quotation

In *The Politics of Rape* (Stein and Day), one of the most recent studies to be published, the author, Diana Russell, advances the extremely questionable theory that "In the North today reverse racism sometimes operates, usually at the expense of a white woman, not a white man." She attempts to argue that a black man is much more likely to get off or receive lenient treatment on a rape charge because courts and other institutions fear being labeled racist, and describes a case in which a California district attorney appealed a "lenient" sentence of a black man convicted of raping a white woman. On retrial, however, this defendant received two consecutive three-years-to-life terms; an argument for the presence of the traditional prejudice, not the reverse.

—Angela Davis, "Joanne Little—The Dialectics of Rape," *Ms.*

Reduced Version

In *The Politics of Rape* (Stein and Day) . . . the author, Diana Russell, advances the extremely questionable theory that "In the North today reverse racism sometimes operates. . . ." She attempts to argue that a black man is much more likely to get off or receive lenient treatment on a rape charge because courts and other institutions fear being labeled racist. . . .

A writer using ellipsis must be careful not to distort the original by eliminating important material. In the previous example, omitting the reference to the specific case and to Davis' convincing rebuttal is a serious distortion because it allows Russell's theory to stand unrefuted. Similarly, advertisements for films and books may be suspect when they resort to ellipsis in quoting reviews. Here is what could happen:

Original review: In his latest, the author takes aim at the finance business and hits that fat, juicy target with a feather, failing to dent it.

Ad with ellipsis: In his latest, the author takes aim at the finance business and hits that fat, juicy target. . . .

Original review: The film is pretty silly, but it captures a certain scruffy, seamy side of big city life.

Ad with ellipsis: The film . . . captures a certain scruffy, seamy side
of big city life.

Quotations should not be distorted nor for that matter should they be
tampered with in any way. They should be copied honestly, even if the
original contains an error or something that might be construed as an
error by readers. To deal with that situation, you may use brackets and
the Latin word *sic* (meaning "thus") to inform readers that the previous word appears this way in the original. For example, in quoting
from Sir Kenneth Clark's *Civilisation* on page 547, we inserted [sic] to
point out that the title of his book was spelled with an *s* (the English
spelling) in the original, not a *z* (the American spelling), indicating that
neither we nor the typesetter had erred. Brackets can also be helpful in
inserting your own comments or explanations into quotations:

Our contemporary writers, artists, and philosophers are not appreciably more
effective than those of the golden age of Greece [about the fifth century
B.C.], yet the average high-school student understands much more of nature
than the greatest of Greek scientists.
— B. F. Skinner, *Science and Human Behavior*

Integrating Quotations

The final point we would like to make about quotations is most important: they should be skillfully woven into the paper, not crudely
patched into it. Here are some examples:

Patched: In her article, "The Myths of Homosexuality," Sister Jeannine Gramick, SSND, states: "There are, undoubtedly,
effeminate male homosexuals and masculine-type lesbians,
but these constitute only a small minority of the gay population."

Woven: Sister Jeannine Gramick, SSND, concedes in her article,
"The Myths of Homosexuality," that there are effeminate
male homosexuals and masculine lesbians, but she emphasizes that these stereotypes form "only a small minority."

And then there is the painful "tell 'em, quote, and tell 'em what you
quoted" technique:

Patched: James V. McConnell, a psychology professor at the University of Michigan, is in favor of brainwashing people.
In his article "Criminals Can Be Brainwashed—Now,"
he advocates: "We should reshape our society so that we

would all be trained from birth to want to do what society wants us to do. We have the techniques now to do it." He claims that we should brainwash everyone and that we already know how to do it.

Woven: James V. McConnell, a psychology professor at the University of Michigan, favors training people from birth "to want to do what society wants" and states that we have the techniques now to accomplish this.

Our point is that quotations should not be thrown at readers, but woven into the fabric of the paper. A paper should not be a patchwork quilt of statements and quotations, but a carefully woven blanket.

You may wonder by this time why we have discussed the use and abuse of quotations to such an extent. The answer is that all expository and persuasive papers require evidence to support their theses. In research papers, this evidence is generally formulated from notes based on the authority of others and often appears as quoted material. Thus the way you take notes and use them in your paper is crucial to its effectiveness. Also, in no other writing assignment will you encounter the problems of quotation to such an extent as in the research paper.

STEP 7. DOCUMENTATION

The research paper requires documentation to allow writers to acknowledge their indebtedness to other writers and to permit readers to verify information or learn more about the subject. This documentation takes the form of footnotes (placed at the bottom of the page, where the source is referred to) or endnotes (placed all together at the paper's conclusion) and usually a bibliography. One problem is that there is no standard documentation form: not only do the conventions differ among the humanities, sciences, and social sciences, but often they differ within a field.

What should you do? The answer depends—as in all writing—on who your readers are. Documentation for psychology, history, and sociology instructors may differ. You must follow whatever documentation form they require, just as scholars and writers follow whatever form editors impose. What we shall do here is to explain and help you with one of the most widely used systems, that established by the Modern Language Association and published in its *MLA Style Sheet* (2nd ed., 1970). We have taken a few very minor liberties with this system to simplify it for you. But once again, check with your instructor before writing up your footnotes.

What all this preliminary discussion adds up to is that you must find out what is required of you and then follow those instructions precisely. This should not be difficult because you can refer to this book or a style sheet instead of memorizing the details. But most students fail to realize how meticulous and careful they must be. Take heed.

Footnote Form

Although a footnote may add a comment or an explanation,[1] its most common function is to provide information about a source. If the material comes from a book, follow this form:

Book

1. Author entry
    First name, middle name or initial, last name, comma.
2. Book entry
    Title of book underlined (to indicate italics), parenthesis, place of publication, colon, publisher, comma, year of publication, parenthesis, comma.
3. Page entry
    Abbreviation p. or pp., number(s), period.

Here's how it looks:

[1] Erich Fromm, *The Art of Loving* (New York: Harper & Row, 1956), p. 23.

Please note: no mark of punctuation precedes the first parenthesis, but a comma follows the second. Also, like a sentence, a footnote begins with a capital letter and ends with a period.

For an article, the form is similar but the differences are important:

Article

1. Author entry (same)
    First name, middle name or initial, last name, comma.
2. Article/publication entry
    Quotation marks, title of the article, comma, quotation marks, title of the publication underlined, comma, day, month abbreviated (if more than five letters), comma, year, comma.
3. Page entry (same)
    Abbreviation p. or pp., number(s), period.

Here's an example:

[1] Such footnotes, like this one, should be kept at a minimum. Use them mainly to present additional information, such as a definition, reference to something else in the paper, or supporting or differing views in other sources.

[2] Stuart Baur, "First Message from the Planet of the Apes," *New York,* 24 Feb. 1975, pp. 30–37.

Note: the military date form is used, giving day-month-year instead of the usual month-day-year. Also, this entry contains no volume number because popular magazines are published by the calendar year and bound in the library accordingly. But because many scholarly journals are published and therefore bound by the academic year (September–June), their volume number should be presented in the footnote entry (see 5 below) to help readers locate issues more easily.

Here are examples for other sources you may encounter:

Article in Newspaper

[3] "College Hunt," *New York Times,* 11 May 1975, p. 29, col. 1.

Note: no author; *col.* = column.

[4] Mitchell C. Lynch, "Shaking up the G-Men," *Wall Street Journal,* 15 May 1975, p. 14, cols. 4–6.

Article in Journal

[5] Carl F. Strauch, "Kings in the Back Row: Meaning Through Structure—A Reading of Salinger's *The Catcher in the Rye,*" *Wisconsin Studies in Contemporary Literature,* 2 (Winter 1961), 5–30.

Note: a book title in the article's title is underlined; volume number of journal appears before date; when volume number is listed, no page abbreviation is used; date appears in parentheses.

Article in Collection

[6] Zellig S. Harris, "Discourse Analysis," in *The Structure of Language,* eds. Jerry A. Fodor and Jerrold J. Katz (Englewood Cliffs, N.J.: Prentice-Hall, 1964), pp. 355–83.

Note: *eds.* = editors; because Englewood Cliffs is not widely known, abbreviation of state follows.

Article in Weekly Magazine

[7] Roger Angell, "The Sporting Scene (Baseball)," *New Yorker,* 14 April 1975, pp. 90–95.

[8] "Year of the Ear," *Newsweek,* 19 May 1975, p. 93.

Note: No author given.

Article in Monthly Magazine

[9] Betsy Langman and Alexander Cockburn, "Sirhan's Gun," *Harper's,* Jan. 1975, pp. 16–27.

Note: two authors.

Book — More Than One Edition

¹⁰ Hans P. Guth, *Words and Ideas,* 3rd ed. (Belmont, Calif.: Wadsworth, 1969), pp. 326–36.

Book — Edited edition

¹¹ William Makepeace Thackeray, *Vanity Fair: A Novel Without a Hero,* eds. Geoffrey and Kathleen Tillotson (Boston: Houghton Mifflin, 1963), p. 89.

Book — Translation

¹² Miguel de Cervantes, *Don Quixote,* trans. J. M. Cohen (Harmondsworth, Middlesex: Penguin Books, 1950), p. 916.

Book — Two Authors

¹³ Christopher Jencks and David Riesman, *The Academic Revolution* (New York: Doubleday, 1968), pp. 55–59.

Commission Report

¹⁴ U.S. Commission on Civil Rights, *The Excluded Student: Educational Practices Affecting Mexican-Americans in the Southwest,* Report III (Washington, D.C.: U.S. Government Printing Office, 1973), p. 54.

Essay in Collected Works

¹⁵ Ralph Waldo Emerson, "Literary Ethics" (1838), in *Works,* ed. James Elliot Cabot, 12 vols. (Boston: Houghton Mifflin, 1883–93), IV. 171.

Note: The 12 volumes were published over the years indicated. The essay appears in volume four (note Roman numeral); the reference is to page 171 (note Arabic numeral) of that volume.

This list exemplifies only some of the many possibilities. If it does not help you with a particular source, consult the *MLA Style Sheet* in the reference room of the library, check with your instructor, or as a last resort model your footnote after the closest example to it here.

Additional Information About Footnote Form

When you sit down to write your first draft, you may have questions about handling footnotes. Some can be answered by looking at the student research paper reprinted at the end of this chapter; a few we will try to anticipate here.

1. Number

   The number follows the material being quoted, referred to, or commented on. Type it slightly raised above the line, *after all* punctuation marks except a dash. The footnotes should be numbered consecutively throughout the paper.

2. Placement

   Footnotes are typed under a line at the bottom of the page to which they refer. Each is treated like a separate paragraph: indented five spaces, headed by its number (raised slightly above the line), followed by the entry, which is single spaced, and ended with a period. When footnotes are placed at the end of the paper, they should appear on a separate page. Double space between footnotes no matter where they are placed.

3. Capitalization in titles

   As you may remember, the first word in a title should be capitalized and so should all other words except articles, conjunctions, and prepositions of four letters or less.

4. Titles—quotation marks versus underlining

   As is customary, enclose in quotation marks titles of such generally short works as articles, chapters, essays, poems, short stories, songs, and also unpublished writings of any length. Underline longer works, which are usually published individually, such as books, plays, magazines, pamphlets, reports, and films. Such titles would be italicized in print.

5. Second and later references

   Once you have provided all the required information in the first footnote reference to a source, you need not repeat it. Merely use the author's last name and the page number (Simon, p. 124). In those rare instances when two authors have the same last names, use their full names (Edwin Simon, p. 124); when the author has written two or more works previously mentioned, use the last name and a shortened title (Simon, *N.Y. Birds,* p. 124).

   As an alternative form, you may use the once required "Ibid." (a Latin abbreviation now Americanized and no longer underlined) for "in the same place as" and meaning, in this context, "in the same place as the work cited just previously." It can be used only when the work is cited in the preceding footnote. Also, "Ibid." cannot appear on a different page than the initial citation because it would require the reader to turn back to a previous page.

   Here are examples showing how "Ibid." works:

   [1] Mary Ellen Gale, rev. of *Capital Punishment,* by Charles L. Black, Jr., *New York Times Book Review,* 5 Jan. 1975, p. 1.

   [2] Ibid. [refers to Gale article, same page]

[handwritten margin note: forget about Ibid — keep on using ordinary footnotes]

³ Andrew Hacker, "Who Killed Harry Gleason?" *Atlantic,* Dec. 1974, p. 53.

⁴ Ibid., p. 55. [refers to Hacker article, different page]

⁵ Gale, p. 2. [refers to Gale article, different page]

⁶ Ibid. [refers to Gale article, same page as in footnote 5]

⁷ Hacker, p. 55. [refers to Hacker article; intervening footnotes require that page number be given, even though it's the same page as in footnote 4]

(next page of your paper)

⁸ Hacker, p. 55. [*Ibid.* cannot be used because the source has not been identified on this page of your paper]

6. Shortened First Reference

Often the first footnote itself may be shortened to avoid duplication: whenever possible, you should use at least the name of the author in the text of your paper; and if it appears there, it should not be repeated in a footnote. For an example, see footnote 6 on page 574.

At first reading, all these conventions may seem incredibly complicated and complex. They are. But bear in mind that they have been designed to enable readers to obtain maximum information in minimum space and at the same time to avoid distracting other readers who are not curious about your sources. Just as baseball, backgammon, or bridge might have seemed impossible to understand when you first started to play but proved easier afterward, so, with practice, documentation makes more sense and gets simpler. And what you should always realize is that you need not memorize or guess about documentation form. Merely consult this textbook or a style sheet. There is little excuse for errors except laziness or the unwillingness to look up the proper form.

Now it's time to look up and move on to the next step in writing the research paper.

STEP 8. REVISION

After completing your first draft, revise it carefully, scrutinizing it closely for organizational, stylistic, and mechanical weaknesses. In addition, examine it with these questions in mind:

1. Could the introduction be more interesting and informative?
2. Do transitions enable the reader to move easily from one section of the paper to another and to see clearly the relationship between the sections?

3. Are the quotations smoothly woven into the text?
4. Can lengthy quotations be eliminated or shortened by using ellipses? Can they be clarified by inserting a few of your own words in brackets?
5. Are footnotes numbered properly? Is the reference information presented correctly?
6. Can the number and length of footnotes be reduced by shifting the names of authors and the titles of their works from footnotes to the text without creating awkwardness?
7. Does the paper end with a summary and, if appropriate, a call for action?

STEP 9. WRITING THE FINAL DRAFT

Four matters may be left for the final draft: the title, the title page, the final outline, and the bibliography. This is not to say that these may not be attended to earlier if you wish, just that they may be postponed.

The Title

Although a research paper requires a serious, scholarly investigation of a subject, it need not sport a deadly title. Everyone enjoys a touch of humor, as these titles of articles in professional journals indicate:

Sheila Shaw, "The Rape of Gulliver: Case Study of a Source," *PMLA*, 90 (Jan. 1975), 62–69.

Elizabeth Wooten, "English Up Against the Wall," *College English*, 36 (Dec. 1974), 466–70.

Or, if not amusing, the title should at least be interesting, even intriguing:

Gregory Rabassa, "If This Be Treason: Translation and Its Possibilities," *American Scholar*, 44 (Winter 1974–75), 29–40.

Tony Tanner, *City of Words: American Fiction 1950–1970* (New York: Harper & Row, 1971).

Note that in three of these examples, subtitles provide a way to explain a clever but uninformative title.

The Title Page

The title page should appear attractive and well balanced. The following two styles are popular:

```
┌─────────────────────────────┐   ┌─────────────────────────────┐
│                             │   │                             │
│   FLIPPING OVER GYMNASTICS  │   │ FLIPPING OVER GYMNASTICS    │
│                             │   │                             │
│             by              │   │           by                │
│                             │   │                             │
│        Ann  Acrobat         │   │       Ann  Acrobat          │
│                             │   │                             │
│                             │   │                             │
│                             │   │                             │
│                             │   │                             │
│                             │   │                             │
│                             │   │                             │
│                             │   │                             │
│   English 102-15            │   │ Research Assignment   Ms. Korbut │
│                             │   │                             │
│   May 5, 1976               │   │ English 102-15     May 5, 1976 │
│                             │   │                             │
│                             │   │                             │
└─────────────────────────────┘   └─────────────────────────────┘
```

Note that the title is capitalized (not underlined) and that no periods appear on the page. Also, you should bear in mind that the title is repeated at the top of the first manuscript page.

The Final Outline

Some instructors may request that you hand in a formal outline with your final paper. This outline consists mainly of a revision of your preliminary outline. Be sure, however, that any changes you have made between your preliminary investigation and your completed paper are incorporated into the formal outline. An illustration of the formal outline accompanies the student research paper reprinted at the end of this chapter.

The Bibliography

The title page is what the reader encounters first; the bibliography, last. And it may be written last, too. Although some writers like to postpone adding footnotes until the last minute, we suggest that you write them in an early draft to find out how much space they will occupy on a typed page and, more important, to discover quite early whether you have all the information required for them. But the bibliography can wait until last.

The bibliography may take two forms: it may list all the works you relied on in writing the paper or only those works not mentioned in the footnotes. But under no circumstances should the bibliography be padded to impress readers by including works merely glanced at or listed somewhere. Many instructors and discerning readers have resorted to this sophomoric trick themselves in high school, or at any rate can readily see through it. Therefore, list only books and other materials you have actually used, not merely looked at or found on the shelves in the library.

Study the following examples to determine how bibliography entries differ in form from footnote entries:

Bibliography entry: Edel, Leon. *"Walden:* The Myth and the Mystery." *American Scholar,* 44 (Spring 1975), 272–81.

Footnote: [1] Leon Edel, *"Walden," American Scholar,* 44 (Spring 1975), 272–81.

Did you note these differences?

1. Bibliography entry begins flush with left-hand margin; footnote begins indented like a paragraph.
2. Bibliography entry is not numbered; footnote is numbered.
3. Bibliography entry uses author's last name first; footnote, first name first. (Easy to remember: footnotes and the first names in them come first; bibliography comes last in the paper and the last names in them come first.)
4. Bibliography entry uses periods to separate author, title, and publication data; footnote, commas.
5. Bibliography entry lists title and subtitle; footnote may list only title.

Can you find the two additional differences distinguishing a bibliography entry from a footnote for a book?

Bibliography entry: Drucker, Peter F. *Management: Tasks, Responsibilities, Practices.* New York: Harper & Row, 1973.

Footnote: [2] Peter F. Drucker, *Management* (New York: Harper & Row, 1973), pp. 567–88.

Did you find these two differences?

1. Bibliography entry presents publication information in sentence form; footnote, within parentheses.
2. Bibliography entry does not list pages of a book; footnote does.

Here is a sample bibliography with some representative entries that should help you. Our comments appear in parentheses after a few of them. For standard abbreviations used here and in footnotes, see the accompanying table.

Abbreviations Used in Footnotes and Bibliography Entries

c., ca.	approximately; mainly used for dates (c. 1494)
cf.	compare (Cf. Malcolm Ross, *Milton's Royalism,* p. 96.)
diss.	dissertation
ed., eds.	edited by, editor, editors
et al.	and others (used with three or more authors — Murray, James A., *et al.,* eds.)
f., ff.	the page given and the following page (pp. 27 f.) or pages (pp. 27 ff.)
illus.	illustrated
loc. cit.	in the place cited (author and title have been mentioned in text — *loc. cit.,* p. 9)
ms., mss.	manuscript, manuscripts
n.d.	no date of publication given (New York: Harcourt Brace, n.d.)
n.p.	no place of publication given
p., pp.	page, pages
passim	here and there in the pages cited (pp. 23–35 *passim*)
rev.	revised by or reviewed by
rpt.	reprint, reprinted
tr., trans.	translated by
vol., vols.	volume, volumes

BIBLIOGRAPHY

Angell, Roger. "The Sporting Scene (Baseball)." *New Yorker,* 14 April 1975, pp. 90–95.

Cervantes, Miguel de. *Don Quixote.* Trans. J. M. Cohen. Hardmondsworth, Middlesex: Penguin Books, 1950. [Translation]

Dietrich, Daniel. "Annotated Bibliography of Research in the Teaching of English." *Research in the Teaching of English,* 8 (Winter 1974), 396–422. [When volume number is included (8), abbreviation "pp." is omitted.]

Drucker, Peter. "How to Be an Employee." *Fortune,* May 1952, pp. 35–38.

————. *Management: Tasks, Responsibilities, Practices.* New York: Harper & Row, 1973. [The line indicates that this work is by the author just cited.]

Emerson, Ralph Waldo. "Literary Ethics" (1838). *Works.* Ed. James Elliot Cabot. 12 vols. Boston: Houghton Mifflin, 1883–93. [Article appears in collected works.]

Guth, Hans. *Words and Ideas.* 3rd ed. Belmont, Calif.: Wadsworth, 1969. [Edition]

Harris, Zellig S. "Discourse Analysis." *The Structure of Language.* Eds. Jerry A. Fodor and Jerrold J. Katz. Englewood Cliffs, N.J.: Prentice-Hall, 1964. [Article is part of collection in book.]

Jencks, Christopher, and David Riesman. *The Academic Revolution.* New York: Doubleday, 1968. [Two authors; names after first not inverted.]

"Law-School Applications Dip." *The Chronicle of Higher Education,* May 12, 1975, p. 6. [Anonymous article; alphabetize by title.]

Spilka, Mark. "Comic Resolution in Fielding's *Joseph Andrews.*" *College English,* 15 (1953), 11–19. Rpt. in *Essays on the Eighteenth Century Novel.* Ed. Robert Donald Spector. Bloomington: Indiana University Press, 1965. [Reprinted article]

You can realize now why the information on your bibliography cards must be complete and why we suggested that you need not worry about writing the entries in the required form at that time. And what we stated about footnotes applies here also: numerous other types of sources exist than are illustrated here. Consult your instructor, look them up in a style sheet, or, as a last resort, model them after the most similar entry given here.

STEP 10. PROOFREADING

You have sent so much time and effort on your paper that you should proofread it carefully to avoid letting it be spoiled by careless mistakes. Plan to spend at least an hour checking for typing errors, searching for faulty footnotes and bibliographical entries, and trying to find the dozens of other things that can go wrong in a paper of this length. Patience in proofreading is a virtue. Practice it.

FINAL WORDS

We have treated this subject as completely as we think is necessary for most undergraduate research papers that you may write in English, economics, history, sociology, anthropology, political science, nursing, education, and other classes. But, as graduate or professional students, you may be required to follow some practices omitted or presented differently here.

The following student research paper should help you figure out how to deal with numerous matters that we may not have covered specifically in this chapter. Keep it handy as you write your first and final drafts and refer to it frequently. What we particularly like about this paper is that it is relatively free of footnotes, not cluttered with them as so many student papers are. As this statement implies, you should know your subject so well, have digested all the information so thoroughly, and be so filled with the ideas in it that you can write freely without relying constantly on numerous notes.

But when you do use footnotes and write your bibliography, take care. A research paper, like a formal wedding ceremony, is steeped in tradition and protocol that must be followed to the letter. You may not like either, but you should show respect for both. Both are ceremonies of seriousness and dignity that have evolved over the years to reflect the solemnity and significance of the situation. And despite the ordeal imposed on the married couple and the writer, both ceremonies when completed bring great joy, pleasure, and satisfaction.

The task of writing a research paper is formidable; the achievement fulfilling.

TO HELL WITH PORNOGRAPHY CENSORSHIP   Title in capitals

by

Thomas E. Gaston, Jr.

English 102-17

April 27, 1975

TO HELL WITH PORNOGRAPHY CENSORSHIP   Title at top of
                                             outline.

THESIS: Public objection to obscenity and por-   Thesis next.

          nography does not warrant legal censor-

          ship of the constitutional freedom of

          expression.

I.   Recent changes in the sexual morality of

      American society have resulted in much inter-

      social action and reaction.

      A.   A new period of liberalized sexual moral-

           ity has developed in America since the

           1950's.

      B.   This new morality has divided our

           society into factions about the ne-

           cessity of censorship.

II.   Although censorship of obscenity and por-

      nography has always been an area of social

      conflict, only since 1957 has the issue

      come before the nation and divided the

      country.

      A.   The Roth Supreme Court case of 1957 was a

           milestone in the world's long history of

           censorship.

1. The history of formal censorship
    began in ancient Rome and has plagued
    great writers throughout time.

2. The history of censorship in America
    began with the Comstock Act of 1873.

3. The Roth trial marked the first
    effort by a higher court to object-
    ively judge and define obscenity,
    and to consider the constitutionality
    of censorship.

B. Since the Roth trial, considerable fric-
    tion between groups on both sides of the
    issue has perpetuated continuous social
    debate on censorship.

    1. Persons who promote censorship typi-
        cally claim that pornography under-
        mines society by degrading the moral-
        ity of youth and by triggering sex
        crimes.

    2. Persons who denounce government cen-
        sorship assert that pornography is
        protected for adult citizens by the
        First Amendment of the Constitution.

     3.   In search of a mediator between the opposing sides of the issue, the public has turned to its lawmakers, whose decisions on the subject are hindered by ambiguous terms.

III. Those who advocate censorship, and thus bear the burden of proof, have not convincingly argued their case.

    A. The claim that pornography harms the morals of youth can be countered by the fact that because young people have grown up exposed to the promotion of sex, very few of them are particularly interested in or involved with "hard-core" pornography.

    B. The claim that pornography triggers sex crimes is invalid because no conclusive studies on the subject support this contention.

    C. Until substantial proof is submitted to the courts to warrant exception, the First Amendment must stand as is and all forms of censorship must be declared unconstitutional.

568

TO HELL WITH PORNOGRAPHY CENSORSHIP

Title repeated on
first page.

Within recent years American society has
entered a period of new sexual morality. To see
this, one only needs to reflect on recent trends
in fashion, language, and entertainment that have
developed since the 1950's. Ten or fifteen years
ago the very thought of uni-sexual clothing and
long-haired males would have shocked nearly everyone. Even the roughest of those boys dominating
every local soda fountain in the fifties could
hardly ignore some of the words in common usage
today. The public entertainment media have also
changed quite drastically in late years. Those
same movie producers who refused to allow any
actress out of a negligee before the sixties
changed so much that by 1970, not a single part
of the human anatomy remained undisplayed. As a
matter of fact, Judith Crist, the well-known film
critic, has pointed out that "the amount of pubic

hair on show became the industry's standard for deciding whether a teen-ager could see a film under parental escort or not at all."[1]

Just like any major social change, this new sexuality has brought much action and reaction. For example, there are the so-called "conservatives," those shocked at the new morality, who claim that these new trends are sacrilegious and are undermining our society's foundations. In their dismay, these citizens often promote censorship of this new pornography as the road back to the "good old days." Opposing these attempts are those people either reared in or adapted to the new morality. These citizens find themselves pressured to prove that an objection to pornography by only part of society (whether or not it constitutes a majority) does not warrant any legal restriction of the constitutional freedom of expression.

---

[1]From her untitled essay in _Censorship: For and Against_, ed. Harold H. Hart (New York: Hart Publishing Co., 1971), p. 47.

Footnote form for essay in edited collection.

The recent cries for censorship, although unparalleled in degree, are not new either to America or to the world. The history of formal censorship began in ancient Rome, where two public officials, the first censors, were charged with the responsibility for public behavior and morality. Since that time the works of many great writers have been condemned and censored because they shocked or slighted the ideologies and moralities of others. For instance, in 250 B.C. a Chinese monarch had all the writings of Confucius burned because they detracted from his teachings, and later in the 1600's a Catholic Pope had Martin Luther's translation of the Bible burned on charges of immorality and blasphemy.

No footnote: common knowledge.

The history of legal censorship in America, for the most part, began in 1873 when Senator Anthony Comstock convinced Congress to pass the archetype of all American anti-pornography legislation. Even though the Comstock Act was over-wordy, puritanical, and legally imprecise, most states followed soon thereafter in creating their

own version of it.[2] Since at the time of the Comstock Act books were relatively few and expensive,
and most Americans were not literate, the laws
were generally accepted and forgotten until the
approach of the 1950's and the beginning of the
new morality.

Summary of
Rembar's view:
documentation
required.

This period marked the first of a series of
Supreme Court decisions on obscenity, which became
the focal point for the actions of those who promoted censorship. The most important trial of the
series was the Roth case of 1957 because it marked
the first effort in the United States by a higher
court to objectively consider the constitution-
ality of censorship and to decide that obscenity
could be defined to such an extent that it might
be prohibited.[3] When the Court ruled that censor-

Footnote provides
source of statement
that might be
questioned.

---

[2]Charles Rembar, The End of Obscenity (New
York: Random House, 1968), p. 22.

[3]Terrence J. Murphy, Censorship: Government
and Obscenity (Baltimore: Helicon Press, 1963),
p. 3.

ship of pornography and obscenity was constitutional, this case became the launchpad for innumerable "decency" leagues dedicated to the purg-
ing of obscenity and pornography from our society.
These groups have sparked and perpetuated continuous social friction over censorship. While the
"decency" leagues under the banners of social
protection push for the enactment and enforcement
of Comstock-style censorship laws, there are those
on the other side of the issue who assert that
pornography is permitted for adult citizens by
the First Amendment of the Constitution, which
guarantees freedom of expression.

In search for a mediator, these two opposing
factions have turned to our judicial system. As a
result, several complications have arisen which
delay a solution of the issue. The most important
of these hindrances is that the public is asking
our lawmakers to be legally precise and just despite the ambiguous terms. Words such as "obscenity" and "pornography" defy precise definition.
The American Civil Liberties Union has said of
them that "they have no meaning other than in

terms entirely individual and drawing on each
person's religious and moral standards or concepts
of good taste."[4] Words like "prurient," "lasci-
vious," "lewd," and "obscene" have dictionary
meanings, but they cannot be defined with legal
precision nor in such a way that they cannot be
distorted by what McWilliams refers to as "local
bigots and smut hounds."[5]

Furthermore, our judicial system is incom-

Unusual footnote:
refers to secondary
source, not ACLU
reference.

Assimilated
quotation.

---

[4]Quoted by Carey McWilliams in his untitled
essay in Censorship: For and Against, p. 66.

[5]Ibid. Cf. Harry M. Clor, who argues that
obscenity is generally thought to mean "depersonalized sexual desire," although he concedes that
the implications of this definition should be made
more explicit in the law and that the definition
should be extended to include "some obscene por-
trayals of brutality, death, and the human body."
(Obscenity and the Public Morality: Censorship in
a Liberal Society [Chicago: Univ. of Chicago
Press, 1969], pp. 210-14.)

Use of footnote to
provide additional
information for
reader.

574

petent as a mediator on moral issues. Because they
are designed for civil and criminal proceedings,
the courts should be relieved of responsibility
when issues such as obscenity concern the community. The burden of social correction in these
cases belongs to those who feel that the demise of
America is at hand. Let them redirect their strenuous efforts for censorship into other corrective
measures. For example, McWilliams points to another solution for these offended citizens:

> They can peacefully picket bookstores,
> and movies that have given offense.
> . . . If parents are alarmed about the
> danger of obscene materials, let them
> show more interest in their children, in
> what they read, in their leisure-time
> activities, and in the quality of enter-
> tainment available to them. What is
> wrong with relying on parents, teachers,
> and clergymen to express their concern,
> without recourse to criminal law?[6]

Lengthy quotation
is indented, single-
spaced, without
quotation marks.

This non-legal social action can be very effective.
In proof, McWilliams reminds us that public pressure, unaided by legislation, has eliminated ob-

---

[6]Censorship: For and Against, p. 83.

"Ibid." might con-
fuse readers by
appearing to refer
to Clor's book.
"Ibid." should also
not be used because
this citation does
not appear on the
same page as the
first citation.

jectionable racial and ethnic material from the
mass media.[7]

Citizens who oppose what they consider obscene or pornographic have every right to dissent;
however, if they feel that legal action is the
only solution, then they must first prove beyond a
reasonable doubt that the presence of pornography
is detrimental to the community. They must demonstrate to the courts that pornography is significantly damaging. Only that evidence would warrant
some restriction to the First Amendment, which
declares that "Congress shall make no law . . .
abridging the freedom of speech, or of the
press . . . ."

Thus far in Supreme Court obscenity trials,
the constitutional assailants have been unable to
submit convincing evidence to prove their case.
Their arguments before the courts to date in support of censorship have been based on two fundamental contentions. The first of these is concerned

Ellipsis. The First Amendment states in full: "Congress shall make no law respecting an establishment of religion, or prohibiting the free exercise thereof; or abridging the freedom of speech, or of the press; or the right of the people peaceably to assemble, and to petition the Government for a redress of grievances."

---

[7]Ibid., p. 84.

with the influence of pornography on society's youth: that it has a harmful effect on young and tender minds. This emotional argument exaggerates the extent to which young people are absorbed in sex. Children raised in the new sexual morality in America are not nearly so infatuated with SEX as are their parents. Charles Rembar, an author and lawyer who won several famous Supreme Court cases involving the banning of books,[8] vividly makes this point:

> It is the middle-aged who are . . . most adolcescent [sic]. Younger people are less aroused by the new freedom of sexual expression, in both senses; not nearly so alarmed, and not nearly so titillated . . . . The customers at dirty book stores and at peep shows are not young.[9]

Use of *sic* to indicate that this misspelling appeared in the original.

The second basic pro-censorship theme concerns the harmful effects that obscene materials

---

[8]Rembar represented the publishers in the Lady Chatterly case in 1959, the Tropic of Cancer case in 1964, and the Fanny Hill case in 1966.

[9]From his untitled essay in Censorship: For and Against, p. 223.

Footnote for additional information.

may have on the conduct of people. But this charge is purely emotional and without a factual basis. In its extensive study, the Commission on Obscenity and Pornography concluded that there is "no evidence to date that exposure to explicit sexual materials plays a significant role in the causation of delinquent or criminal behavior among youths or adults."[10] In fact, there is no substantive evidence to indicate that such exposure has any adverse effects on individuals or on society as a whole.

Because those who promote censorship have thus far been unable to present any real proof to warrant legal censorship of pornography, the First Amendment must stand as is: no individual, no group, no court has the authority to govern the right of a citizen to free expression, whether or not that expression is considered obscene.

---

[10]Report of the Commission on Obscenity and Pornography (New York: Bantam Books, 1970), p. 32.

Footnote form for report.

BIBLIOGRAPHY

Bender, Paul. "Obscenity Muddle: Supreme Court's Latest Sexual Crisis." Harper's, February 1973, pp. 46-52.

Clor, Harry M. Obscenity and the Public Morality: Censorship in a Liberal Society. Chicago: Univ. of Chicago Press, 1969.

Hart, Harold H., ed. Censorship: For and Against. New York: Hart Publishing Co., 1971.

Kalven, Jr., Paul. "Obscenity." Encyclopaedia Britannica. 1973.   Encyclopedia entry.

McCormick, Kenneth, and W. L. Smith. "Guardians of   Co-authors. Virtue Mount a New Offensive." Saturday Review, 22 July 1972, pp. 24-25.

Murphy, Terrence J. Censorship: Government and Obscenity. Baltimore: Helicon Press, 1963.

Paul, James, and Murray Schwartz. Federal Censorship: Obscenity in the Mail. New York: Free Press of Glencoe, 1961.

Rembar, Charles. The End of Obscenity. New York: Random House, 1968.

Report of the Commission on Obscenity and Pornography. New York: Bantam Books, 1970.

ASSIGNMENTS

For Discussion

(1) What errors can you find in the following footnotes? (Some have more than one error.)

[1] Paul N. Siegel, "The Conclusion of Richard Wright's 'Native Son'", *PMLA*, 89 (May 1974), 517–524

[2] Ibid, p. 522.

[3] Robert Bone, *The Negro Novel in America* (New Haven; Yale University Press, 1966, p. 183.

[4] Robert Bone, *Richard Wright* (Minneapolis: Univ. of Minnesota Press), p. 57.

[5] Dan McCall, *The Example of Richard Wright* (New York: Harcourt, 1969).

[6] Bone, p. 44.

(2) What errors can you find in the following bibliography entries? (Some have more than one error.)

Alter, Robert. *Rogue's Progress: Studies in the Picaresque Novel.* Cambridge: Harvard University Press, 1964, pp. 80–105.

Baker, Sheridan. "Henry Fielding and the Cliché", *Criticism,* 1 (Fall 1959), pp. 354–61.

Baker, Sheridan. "Henry Fielding's Comic Romances." *Papers of the Michigan Academy of Science, Arts, and Letters,* 45 (1960), 411–19.

Braudy, Leo. *Narrative Form in History and Fiction,* Princeton: Princeton University Press, 1970.

Morris Golden, *Fielding's Moral Psychology.* Boston: Univ. of Mass. Press, 1966

Preston, John. *The Reader's Role in Eighteenth-Century Fiction.* London, England: William Heinemann, 1970.

Work, James A. "Henry Fielding, Christian Censor." *The Age of Johnson: Essays Presented to Chauncey Brewster Tinker,* edited by Frederick W. Hilles. New Haven: Yale University Press, 1949.

(3) Which of the following statements should be footnoted?

(a) Since its appearance in print in 1849, *Tom Jones* has been successful.

b Slippery Rock State College is located in Slippery Rock, Pa.

(c) An analysis of 40 prose nonfiction anthologies published between 1956 and 1960 revealed that of 2,529 selections, 10 percent were the same 45 essays, each of which had been published in at least four anthologies.

d Charles Darwin delayed writing *The Origin of Species* for twenty years because he could not explain how evolution was caused.

e Benjamin Franklin was a man of many roles: scientist, diplomat, author, journalist, publisher, inventor, humorist, and philanthropist.

4 Explain the use of brackets in the following:

a In January, 1604, he [King James I] ordered the principal clergymen of the Church of England to come to Hampton Court Palace to settle a dispute between the High Church and the Puritans.

b As a boy, the future English king who would order thousands of men to wage war on the continent, wrote in his diary: "It seems silly for men to fight and be killed in a foreign [*sic*] country, far away from their homes."

For Writing

1 Write footnotes for the following references in a paper about James Joyce's *A Portrait of the Artist as a Young Man.* Assume that three footnotes appear on each page.

a From page 67 of Hugh Kenner's *Dublin's Joyce.* Published in 1956 by the Indiana University Press at Bloomington, Indiana.

b From J. Mitchell Morse's book, *The Sympathetic Alien: Joyce and Catholicism.* Published by the New York University Press in New York, 1959, pages 34–37.

c From page 61 of *Joyce's* Portrait: *Criticisms and Critiques,* a collection of essays edited by Thomas E. Connolly in a book published by Appleton-Century-Crofts in New York, 1962. The reference is from an essay by Dorothy Van Ghent entitled "*On A Portrait of the Artist as a Young Man,*" which comes from her book, *The English Novel: Form and Function,* published by Holt, Rinehart and Winston in New York, 1953.

d From page 91 of the book referred to in footnote 1.

e From page 37 of J. Mitchell Morse's *ELH* article on "Augustine Theodicy and Joyce's Aesthetics," in volume 24, March 1957 issue of this scholarly journal.

f From pages 291–95 of Sidney Feshbach's article, "A Slow and Dark Birth: A Study of the Organization of *A Portrait of the Artist as a Young Man.*" This appeared in volume 4 of the 1967 issue of the *James Joyce Quarterly.*

g From page 82 of the book referred to in footnote 2.

h From page 97 of the same book.

i From page 299 of the article referred to in footnote 6.

2 Write a bibliography based on the following sources for a paper about the modern American novel.

  a *The Fabulators* by Robert Scholes. Published in New York by Oxford University Press in 1967.

  b Leslie Fiedler's *The Return of the Vanishing American,* which was published in 1968 by Stein & Day in New York.

  c *Radical Innocence* by Ihab Hassan, a Princeton University Press book that was published in Princeton, New Jersey, in 1961.

  d Alvin Greenberg's article, "The Novel of Disintegration: Paradoxical Impossibility in Contemporary Fiction." It appeared in volume 8 in the Winter 1967 edition of the scholarly journal *Wisconsin Studies in Contemporary Literature,* pages 1–27.

  e Leslie Fiedler's *Waiting for the End,* a Stein & Day (New York) 1964 book.

  f *Contemporary American Literature 1945–1972: An Introduction* by Ihab Hassan. This book was published by the Frederick Ungar Publishing Co., New York, 1973.

3 In a maximum of three sentences, write summary notes on ~~each~~ one of the following passages:

  a Let's examine the "need" for greatly increased energy supplies for the United States. . . .

According to the United Nations, Sweden's per-capita use of energy in 1972 was 49 per cent that of the United States, West Germany's 46 per cent, the United Kingdom's 46 per cent and Japan's 28 per cent. What about other nations that in the eyes of the world are thought to have a high quality of life? Beautiful, peaceful Denmark uses 48 per cent as much energy per capita as we do, wine-soaked France (complete with its nuclear program) 38 per cent, the notoriously well-off Swiss 31 per cent, and New Zealand—which many people consider to have the highest quality of life on this planet—used only 25 per cent as much energy per person as the United States. Western Europe as a whole uses 34 per cent as much, the whole world 17 per cent.

The case of Sweden is especially instructive. By the measure much beloved by the growthmaniacs, per-capita gross national product, this heavily industrialized nation in a cold climate has a standard of living slightly better than that of the United States. Yet it achieves this superiority while consuming about half as much energy per person as we do. Sweden, by the way, recently postponed 11 of 13 planned nuclear power plants.

Countries like Sweden are simply more clever than the United States in extracting benefit from less energy. Much of the "waste" heat from power plants in Sweden, for instance, is used to heat buildings. Homes and buildings are well insulated, automobiles small, and mass transit systems efficient.

Furthermore, the notion that vastly greater amounts of energy are required to maintain American prosperity has been dealt a lethal blow by the Ford Foundation's massive, detailed study of our energy options. It showed in a "zero energy growth" scenario that the United States could easily forgo nuclear power without serious economic dislocation.[2]

b The drift of younger Americans, avowedly group-minded or not, is toward an ever more openly flaunted individualism. This means that human relationships of all kinds are being redefined on a more temporary basis than ever before. Communes, like ordinary marriages, tend to fold more rapidly than their 19th-century counterparts, as their members keep drifting away. Because of this individualism, the frequently voiced yearning for organic community turns out to be a deceptive illusion. The chances for maintaining such a community, on a sexual basis as on any other basis, were far greater 150 years ago than they are today, despite the earlier intolerance.

The signs are that, outside the marketplace, American culture is generally becoming more individualistic, not less. For self-absorbed Americans, the group is a vehicle to gain insight, liberation, or self-dramatization. It is not truly regarded as its own end.

Yet the self must be reined in, partially renounced in a spirit of sacrifice, if the group is to gain a steadfast life of its own rather than withering away with a sour, morning-after taste. Knowing this, the head nun of the highly successful Vendanta monastic community at La Crescenta, California, years ago said that manifestations of ego must be guarded against "as the zealous cat watches for the mouse." This group, founded by a Hindu swami in 1912, still quietly survives in an atmosphere not unlike the Shakers'.

The paradox that confronts those who would start communes today is that self-love, rather than self-vigilance, remains so much more attractive to most of us. As middle-class Americans, we are taught from birth that our individual destinies are supremely important, and we deal with others throughout our lives on this basis.

On the deepest level, it would seem almost unnatural to abandon such a titillatingly evolutionary conception of the self. Moreover, we now believe that we evolve by "letting it all hang out" in a continual mood of unrestrained self-acceptance.

The historical record of collective sexual ventures seems to teach us that, except in a context of religious or patriarchal authoritarianism, the sacrifices that individuals make will not be great enough to deflect them from the per-

---

[2] Paul R. Ehrlich, "Nuclear Power: Death Trip?" Used with permission of the *Los Angeles Times*.

vasive self-assertion that shows up time after time and tears down the under-
taking. The recent hunger for community may be so great precisely because
we are all being swept farther and farther away from its possible realization.[3]

4 Write a paragraph assimilating the words and ideas of one of the
following selections.

a By the time they reach adolescence, most girls, unconsciously or not,
have learned enough about role definition to qualify for a master's degree.
In general, the lesson has been that no matter what kind of career thoughts
one may entertain, one must, first and foremost, be a wife and mother. A
girl's mother is usually her first teacher. As Dr. Goode says, "A woman is
not only taught by society to have a child; she is taught to have a child who
will have a child." A woman who has hung her life on The Motherhood Myth
will almost always reinforce her young married daughter's early training by
pushing for grandchildren. Prospective grandmothers are not the only ones.
Husbands, too, can be effective sellers. After all, they have The Fatherhood
Myth to cope with. A married man is *supposed* to have children. Often, particularly among Latins, children are a sign of potency. They help him assure
the world—and himself—that he is the big man he is supposed to be. Plus,
children give him both immortality (whatever that means) and possibly the
chance to become "more" in his lifetime through the accomplishments of
his children, particularly his son. (Sometimes it's important, however, for
the son to do better, but not *too* much better.)

Friends, too, can be counted on as myth-pushers. Naturally one wants to
do what one's friends do. One study, by the way, found an absolute correlation between a woman's fertility and that of her three closest friends. The
negative sell comes into play here, too. We have seen what the concept of
non-mother means (cold, selfish, unwomanly, abnormal). In practice, particularly in the suburbs, it can mean, simply, exclusion—both from child-
centered activities (that is, most activities) and child-centered conversations
(that is, most conversations). It can also mean being the butt of a lot of un-
funny jokes. ("Whaddya waiting for? An immaculate conception? Ha ha.")
Worst of all, it can mean being an object of pity.[4]

b It is evident, then, from what has just been said about the complexity
of the writing process and of the task of teaching writing that there can be
no real short cut to writing skill. That is, there can be no quick and painless

[3] Laurence Veysey, "Communal Sex and Communal Survival: Individualism Busts the
Commune Boom," *Psychology Today*, Dec. 1974, p. 78. Copyright © 1974 Ziff-Davis Publishing Company. Reprinted by permission of *Psychology Today* Magazine.

[4] Betty Rollin, "Motherhood: Who Needs It?" *Look*, Sept. 1970, p. 17. Copyright ©
Cowles Communications, Inc. 1970. Reprinted by permission.

way to develop a well-stocked mind, a disciplined intelligence, and a discriminating taste in language and fluency in its use. None of these can be acquired without hard work over a period of years, and it is preposterous to claim or to expect that any single course in either school or college, no matter how well taught or how intensively studied, can assure them. They are to a considerable extent the result of increasing maturity and of the total educational process acting on an intelligent mind. They are of course not absolutes which one either has or does not have; but in their higher manifestations they lie forever beyond the reach of many people, even some of those who attend the most highly selective college.

All teachers of academic subjects can help students to fill their minds, to train and focus their intellectual powers, and to make their use of language more exact; but English teachers and English courses have the opportunity to be especially helpful in moving students toward the second and third of these goals. More than other teachers and courses, they concentrate directly on the *quality* of written expression as well as the thinking embodied in it, on the principles that lie behind it, and on disciplined practice in applying these principles in written composition. But no one should expect a particular device or method or kind of subject matter in the English course to transform what must always be a slow and difficult process into one that is quick, easy, and unfailingly successful. The habit of good writing, like the habit of ethical conduct, is of slow growth; it is an aspect of a person's general intellectual development and cannot be greatly hastened apart from that development.[5]

[5] From *Themes, Theories, and Therapy,* pp. 7–8, by Albert R. Kitzhaber. Copyright © 1963 by McGraw-Hill, Inc. Used with permission of McGraw-Hill Book Company.

Index

B 6
C 7
D 8
E 9
F 0
G 1
H 2
I 3
J 4

Reference Chart